This book is due for return on or before the last date shown below.

SAGE has been part of the global academic community since 1965, supporting high quality research and learning that transforms society and our understanding of individuals, groups, and cultures. SAGE is the independent, innovative, natural home for authors, editors and societies who share our commitment and passion for the social sciences.

Find out more at: **www.sagepublications.com**

Paul Copley

MARKETING COMMUNICATIONS MANAGEMENT

Analysis, Planning, Implementation

SECOND EDITION

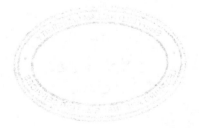

Los Angeles | London | New Delhi
Singapore | Washington DC

Los Angeles | London | New Delhi
Singapore | Washington DC

SAGE Publications Ltd
1 Oliver's Yard
55 City Road
London EC1Y 1SP

SAGE Publications Inc.
2455 Teller Road
Thousand Oaks, California 91320

SAGE Publications India Pvt Ltd
B 1/I 1 Mohan Cooperative Industrial Area
Mathura Road
New Delhi 110 044

SAGE Publications Asia-Pacific Pte Ltd
3 Church Street
#10-04 Samsung Hub
Singapore 049483

Editor: Matthew Waters
Assistant editor: Nina Smith
Development editor: Robin Lupton
Production editor: Sarah Cooke
Copyeditor: Lynda Watson
Proofreader: Audrey Scriven
Indexer: Silvia Benvenuto
Marketing manager: Alison Borg
Design: Francis Kenney
Typeset by: C&M Digitals (P) Ltd, Chennai, India
Printed and bound by Ashford Colour Press Ltd

MIX
Paper from
responsible sources
FSC
www.fsc.org   FSC® C011748

This edition published 2014

First published by Elsevier Butterworth Heinemann 2004

Library of Congress Control Number: 2013956531

British Library Cataloguing in Publication data

A catalogue record for this book is available from the British Library

ISBN 978-0-85702-786-3
ISBN 978-0-85702-787-0 (pbk)

At SAGE we take sustainability seriously. Most of our products are printed in the UK using FSC papers and boards. When we print overseas we ensure sustainable papers are used as measured by the Egmont grading system. We undertake an annual audit to monitor our sustainability.

To my brilliant children Sian and Adam with all my love.

In memory of my much loved parents George Arthur and
Alice Maud Copley.

CONTENTS

About the Author   xii
Preface   xiii
Acknowledgements   xvi

1 Integrated Marketing Communications and its Environment   1

  Chapter Overview   1
  Marketing Communications' Place within Strategic Marketing   2
  Marketing and Exchange – Transactions, Relationships and Change   7
  Integrated Marketing Communications   10
  The Marketing Communications Environment   16
  Assignment   22
  Summary of Key Points   23
  Discussion Questions   24
  Further Reading   24
  References   25

2 Theoretical Underpinnings of Marketing Communications   28

  Chapter Overview   28
  Communication Theory   29
  Kelman's Source Characteristics Model and After   35
  Step Flow or Personal Influence Models   37
  Innovation Theory and Relational Exchange   41
  Assignment   45
  Summary of Key Points   46
  Discussion Questions   46
  Further Reading   47
  References   48

3 Buyer Behaviour and Relationships   50

  Chapter Overview   50
  Communication, Culture and Other Environmental Influences on
  Buyer Behaviour   51
  Culture and Buyer Behaviour   55
  The Complexity of Behaviour and Buyer Learning Theory   58
  Assignment   73
  Summary of Key Points   73
  Discussion Questions   74
  Further Reading   75
  References   76

4 Managing the Marketing Communications Mix   79

  Chapter Overview   79
  The Decision Sequence Model (DSM)   80

The APIC System 84
Assignment 97
Summary of Key Points 98
Discussion Questions 98
Further Reading 99
References 100

5 The Marketing Communications Industry 101

Chapter Overview 101
Practitioners' Views of What Clients Want 102
Roles and Structures in Agencies and other Communications Companies 107
Roles and Structures in Client Organisations 118
Assignment 121
Summary of Key Points 121
Discussion Questions 122
Further Reading 122
References 124

6 Ethics and Corporate Social Responsibility in Marketing Communications 126

Chapter Overview 126
The Impact of Marketing Communications Elements on Society 127
On Being Socially Responsible Marketers 128
Unethical Practice 134
Consumerism and Regulation 142
Assignment 145
Summary of Key Points 146
Discussion Questions 146
Further Reading 147
References 148

7 Advertising and Branding 151

Chapter Overview 151
Advertising Theory 152
Branding and Advertising 157
Advertising Practice 164
Assignment 168
Summary of Key Points 168
Discussion Questions 169
Further Reading 169
References 171

8 Message Creation and Execution 173

Chapter Overview 173
The Importance of Creativity in Marketing Communications 174
Communication Appeals and Execution 177
Message Strategy Design Considerations 182
Assignment 187
Summary of Key Points 187

Discussion Questions 188
Further Reading 188
References 189

9 Traditional Media – Characteristics and Planning 192

Chapter Overview 192
The Characteristics of Traditional Media 193
Media Planning 198
Spend Issues 208
Assignment 216
Summary of Key Points 216
Discussion Questions 216
Further Reading 217
References 218

10 Digital Media: Interaction and Engagement 220

Chapter Overview 220
Technology and Communication 221
Online Design and Management Issues 227
Social Media 236
Privacy, Security and Measurement Issues 241
Assignment 244
Summary of Key Points 244
Discussion Questions 244
Further Reading 245
References 246

11 Sales Promotions 248

Chapter Overview 248
The Nature of Sales Promotion 249
Targeting and Objectives 254
Types of Sales Promotion 256
Assignment 264
Summary of Key Points 264
Discussion Questions 265
Further Reading 266
References 267

12 Direct Marketing 268

Chapter Overview 268
Direct Marketing 269
Database Marketing 275
Managing Privacy Issues 279
Assignment 283
Summary of Key Points 284
Discussion Questions 284
Further Reading 285
References 285

13 Public Relations   287

   Chapter Overview   287
   The Nature and Role of PR   288
   PR and Marketing Theory   296
   Technology, Regulation and Control in PR   307
   Assignment   310
   Summary of Key Points   311
   Discussion Questions   311
   Further Reading   312
   References   313

14 Corporate Communications   316

   Chapter Overview   316
   Background to Corporate Communications   317
   Corporate Identity, Personality and Image   321
   Impression Management and Corporate Image   328
   Assignment   330
   Summary of Key Points   331
   Discussion Questions   331
   Further Reading   332
   References   333

15 Sponsorship   335

   Chapter Overview   335
   The Nature and Role of Sponsorship   336
   How Sponsorship Works   341
   Sponsorship in Practice   345
   Assignment   354
   Summary of Key Points   354
   Discussion Questions   355
   Further Reading   355
   References   356

16 Personal Selling   361

   Chapter Overview   361
   The Nature and Types of Personal Selling   362
   Personal Selling as Part of the Communications Mix   367
   The Selling Process   369
   Making Personal Communication Work for Selling   374
   Assignment   382
   Summary of Key Points   382
   Discussion Questions   383
   Further Reading   383
   References   384

17 Marketing Research and Evaluation   386

   Chapter Overview   386
   Research and Evaluation within a Decision Sequence Framework   387

Application of Research and Evaluation to the Marketing
Communications Mix 394
Assignment 403
Summary of Key Points 404
Discussion Questions 404
Further Reading 405
References 406

18 **International Marketing Communications** 408

Chapter Overview 408
The Nature of International Communications 409
Uniformity or Not – the Standardisation/Adaptation Debate 412
Key Factors Affecting International Marketing Communications 414
Culture, Creativity, Branding and Media 423
Assignment 430
Summary of Key Points 431
Discussion Questions 431
Further Reading 432
References 433

Glossary 436
Index 451

ABOUT THE AUTHOR

Paul Copley, PhD, is Senior Lecturer in Marketing and Programme Leader for the MSc Strategic Marketing Programmes in the Newcastle Business School at Northumbria University, Newcastle, UK.

His career in marketing began after completing the Master's in Marketing at Lancaster University Management School (LUMS). Before entering mainstream higher education he served as an adviser to small firms and before that held management positions in marketing in a number of large firms, in marketing services, publicity and international product management. He has also been involved in consultancy for large and small clients.

He has published articles in journals such as *The Marketing Review, Marketing Intelligence and Planning, Industry and Higher Education* and the *Journal of Travel and Tourism Marketing*, as well as in business magazines such as *The Singapore Marketer* and conference proceedings such as those of the Academy of Marketing (AM) and the Institute for Small Business and Entrepreneurship (ISBE).

He has acted as reviewer for several journals and is on the editorial board of the *Journal of Consumer Behaviour*. He has also been an external examiner at undergraduate and postgraduate level for a number of universities both in the UK and abroad, for example in the Middle East.

PREFACE

INTRODUCTION

Over time there have been a number of definitions of marketing that have involved, for example, the ideas of exchange and transaction. One thing that is ever-present is the notion of change. Changes in the business and marketing environment are clearly important and impact upon how organisations communicate. This has been compounded in recent times as digital and mobile technologies have emerged and led to profound and rapid changes to many forms of communication including those involved with marketing and corporate activity. Economic and social trends too have had an impact on the ways in which organisations and consumers behave. Such developments both challenge and offer opportunities to organisations involved with interaction and engagement that are key to a successful integration of communication activities. Good marketing has always been conducted in an integrated fashion, but it is the quest for truly integrated communication campaigns that started in the late 1980s and came to the fore in the mid-1990s that brought about the interest in the study of integrated marketing communications, or IMC, as it is commonly known.

THE CHANGING NATURE OF MARKETING COMMUNICATIONS

This second edition of *Marketing Communications Management* has been created partly because it was evident that the methods used by organisations to communicate have changed and that the mix of communications elements can be very different from what has gone before. It is still the case that somehow a mutual understanding between buyer and seller has to be achieved. This cannot be realised without effective marketing (and corporate) communications but to be effective communications must be well managed. The increased sophistication of communication elements such as advertising, public relations and sponsorship has been responsible for increased commercial activity and the cluttered environment in which communications have to operate. The managerial orientation of the book is accompanied by an intellectually informed set of theories, concepts and examples that provide the reader with an holistic understanding of the subject.

WHY A TEXT ON MARKETING COMMUNICATIONS MANAGEMENT?

Most organisations need some form of marketing or corporate communications. This text is designed to service both academics and students involved in formal study. It is particularly geared to the needs of those who are on a course that has basic marketing as a pre-requisite. The book has, therefore, been written with the final year undergraduate student, for example BA Marketing or BA Business Studies, and the postgraduate student, for example the Postgraduate Diploma/MA or MSc Marketing, in mind. However the growth of non-business studies students studying marketing and marketing communications is obviously important, as is the number of overseas students studying such subjects in English. Professional marketing and non-marketing courses (where marketing is taught) will also benefit from the book, as will marketing and non-marketing practitioners in the public and the private sector who will find it to be a useful reference source.

THE AIM OF THIS BOOK

The aim of producing this book is to meet the needs of the above students and practitioners by providing a product that addresses strategic and critical issues and reflections which dovetail with the current and continuing interest in marketing communications in management, marketing and society as reflected in the media.

More specifically the aims are to:

- provide a book that balances the theory and practice of marketing communications. The aim is therefore to illustrate to the student how theory can inform decision-making and ultimately improved practice.
- provide a managerial approach to marketing communications by first breaking the various components down and rebuilding them into a managerial whole. The book has a managerial rather than merely descriptive orientation. Some description is used where necessary but ultimately managers need a systematic way to manage in the ever-changing and dynamic marketing environment with its inevitable impact on the organisation.
- provide a usable, accessible book that extends the reader beyond many of the conventional views of the subject. Some less conventional but potentially very useful and more critical ideas are introduced.
- present marketing communications in the widest possible context by using examples from a diverse range of organisations. Marketing and marketing communications situations and contexts have changed dramatically not least because of the growth of the internet and the advent of digital and mobile technologies. Social networking and media especially have changed the ways consumers communicate and how companies communicate their brands.

WHAT THE CHAPTERS OF THE BOOK CONTAIN

The book has 18 chapters that are ordered in such a way as to take the reader from an introduction to the subject of marketing communications management and IMC through to an appreciation of theoretical concepts in communications and behaviour and the provision of a management framework. There is then consideration of the marketing communications industry and ethics and corporate social responsibility. Next, each operational component of the marketing communications mix, along with the media and corporate communications, is examined and this is followed by an exploration of both evaluation and international perspectives.

The author's intention is to present a clear, timely, and engaging exploration and examination of marketing communications management. Each chapter has an introduction and specific, stated learning objectives, and contains key concepts and carefully chosen examples of aspects of contemporary marketing communications in practice. The book therefore draws on as wide a range of materials as possible from small and large firms, consumer and industrial companies, profit and not-for-profit organisations, and the public and private sector. Snapshots of situations, many of which are of actual occurrences, are used frequently in each chapter, and these are followed by Stop Points throughout not only to add flavour but also to encourage the reader to 'stop and think' about key issues. More in-depth case studies can be found on the companion website to help enhance and facilitate application. International aspects run throughout the book and an overall international perspective appears as the last of the 18 chapters. An assignment briefing, summary of key points, discussion questions, suggestions for further reading and a list of references conclude each chapter. The main body of the text is followed by a glossary of marketing communications terms and a comprehensive index.

COMPANION WEBSITE

The aim of creating a companion website is to help make the learning and teaching experience for both students and tutors as effective as possible.

Student resources

Students are provided with a range of resources within the book (as outlined above) and on the companion website. The website provides additional resources to help promote learning, skills and competencies. These include:

- video feeds and other web links. These are provided to direct students (tutors) to additional resources for further research and study which is either directed by the tutor or conducted independently.
- longer case studies, many of which are about real brands, products and services. These are provided to help develop ideas, concepts and issues from each of the chapters of the book. The case studies help develop evaluation and analysis skills in terms a diverse range of organisations from small and large companies to not-for-profit and public sectors contexts.
- Sage journal articles for further reading in the relevant chapters. These are provided via links to the Sage Journals website. These support and expand upon concepts and points made in each chapter and can be used for further research and study which is either directed by the tutor or conducted independently.
- a larger glossary of key terms for each chapter. This helps students reflect on the various chapters and understand the key concepts, ideas and issues in each.

Lecturing and seminar resources

The additional materials available to tutors are provided to help them facilitate learning, skills and competencies. A tutor is able to use materials directly or customise them for particular purposes by including and/or excluding certain materials by adopting and then adapting the materials and approach to the lecture or seminar. This allows them to augment what is in each chapter of the book with additional resources from the companion website or from their own sources and resources. These include:

- a tutor manual. This includes a set of lecture notes that, chapter by chapter, help tutors assemble from the book and the companion website what is needed for a particular lecture or seminar. The manual suggests a number of creative approaches that help the tutor integrate all of the available materials into a dynamic learning experience.
- an outline response to each of the chapter assignment briefings. This is designed to help the tutor promote critical thinking and develop analysis skills around key concepts, ideas and issues in each chapter. These can be set as assignments for a course assessment or adapted for use as examination questions. They can also be used by the tutor in seminars in order to engender discussion or as the basis for presentation work.
- team activities. These are also designed to help the tutor promote critical thinking and develop analysis skills around the key concepts, ideas and issues in each chapter. They are also designed to be used by the tutor in seminars in order to engender discussion or as the basis for presentation work.
- an outline response to each of the chapter discussion questions. This is designed to help the tutor promote critical thinking in seminars and can be adopted and/or adapted to help create examination questions or quizzes.
- PowerPoint presentation slides. These can bring classroom lectures and seminar discussions to life with essential content from the book that can be adjusted to fit with the tutor's own style.

Please visit: study.sagepub.com/copley

ACKNOWLEDGEMENTS

I am grateful to the people in the various organisations, both agency and client, who have given me their time to discuss the many issues that surround the subject of marketing communications management. I am also grateful to students on my advertising and marketing communications courses who took time out to help guide me on the direction of this book and to the editorial people at Sage – Delia Martinez Alfonso, Robin Lupton and Matt Waters – for all of their help.

My thanks to you all.

1 Integrated Marketing Communications and its Environment

CHAPTER OVERVIEW

Introduction

In this chapter the nature of marketing communications is explored and relationships developed with strategic marketing. Marketing communications, seen by many as a mix within itself and firmly as part of the marketing mix, is considered in this chapter in a strategic manner. Marketing communications as an entity is placed within an integrated marketing context surrounded by an ever-present and somewhat turbulent marketing environment. This has had a profound effect on marketing generally but especially the media and the nature of messages within an ever-changing marketing and corporate communications environment. Corporate communications is a mix of activities and tools used to manage internal and external communication with targeted customers and other stakeholders in order to create a favourable marketing environment within which marketing communications can operate more effectively in order to achieve organisational objectives.

Learning objectives

This chapter seeks to explore the nature and role of integrated marketing communications in relation to the rest of the marketing mix. More specifically, after reading this chapter, the student will be able to:

- discuss marketing in the 21st century in terms of exchange, transactions, relationships and change;
- situate marketing communication within strategic marketing;
- appreciate the future of marketing and marketing communications in terms of integration, interaction and engagement;
- outline the major environmental forces that impinge on the marketing communications management function.

MARKETING COMMUNICATIONS' PLACE WITHIN STRATEGIC MARKETING

The basic marketing concept is the managerial philosophy that seeks to identify and satisfy customer needs and wants better than the competition through a series of coordinated marketing activities to achieve organisational objectives. The marketing concept suggests the useful shorthand that is the 'marketing mix' (or '4Ps' that are product, place, price and promotion). This has been and still is the subject of some debate in academic marketing circles. Building on the problem with mnemonics, Kent (1986), for example, underscores the 'seductive sense of simplicity', the point being that to create something that is a memory aid that then becomes an 'article of faith' is dangerous. The 4P 'model' has been interpreted by some as a strategic tool, but for others it is merely a convenient piece of shorthand. Inevitably, issues around product, price, place and promotion will be considered as being at the heart of marketing strategy. However, the 4Ps is a model from the mass marketing era. Given the emphasis now placed on interactivity, engagement and relationships, marketing strategy and hence marketing communications strategy have to be more than a consideration of the 4Ps. It is with this kind of understandable argument in mind that the useful shorthand is adopted here with caution and qualification.

Marketing communications can be described as being every form of communication relevant to marketing. This invites marketing communications managers to question the efficiency of every item of communication as it relates to and affects the whole strategy. The basic promotional mix elements and their derivatives as the requirements for effective communications and customer understanding have been recognised for some time as being 'above-the-line' advertising and 'below-the-line' everything else including the main categories of sales promotion, public relations and personal selling. The line is an artificial construct devised for accounting purposes within the commission system where 15 per cent of billing was the fee in advertising terms for placing the message in the appropriate space and the difference between what the agency paid and what the client paid. There has always been a fee-per-job or service base for much of what agencies did for clients, i.e. fee-based transactions. The percentage rate paid by the media to agencies has never been truly universal. The 15 per cent rate was a US import into the UK for example, as more and more advertising was being conducted by US agencies as advertising evolved during the 20th century (see Chapter 5 of this book for more on the move away from this system). More broadly it is not unusual to see the term 'through-the-line' being used to indicate changes that have taken place in recent times across the marketing communications mix (see Integrated Marketing Communications later in this chapter). Figure 1.1 below shows the relationships between corporate and marketing communication functions and other business functions.

With audiences having become more fragmented, mass communication is rapidly becoming a relic of a former era. It is now recognised in many markets that there is a need for media and media vehicles that match this fragmentation. Mass communication was, traditionally, relatively low cost but had the disadvantages of involving selective perception and poor comprehension of the message. There was also the possibility of a monologue taking place with little or no feedback received and with the added difficulty of measuring

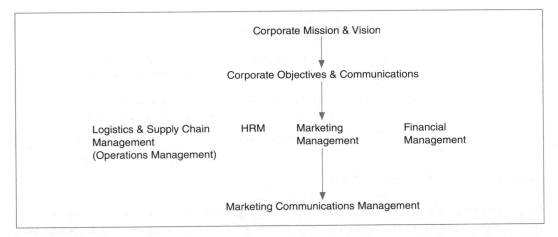

Figure 1.1 Corporate and marketing communications functions and other business functions relationships

effectiveness. Personal communication, on the other hand, has been seen as approximately the opposite of this with high cost per contact at a slower speed but with the opportunity to better get the message across. There is therefore much higher comprehension of the message and the possibility of a dialogue with fast and accurate feedback and consequently a move toward 'narrowcasting', i.e. taking a programme or a message to a narrower but more relevant audience, rather than 'broadcasting' to a wider set of audiences. The promotion 'p' of the traditional marketing mix has become known as marketing communications in part because the term communications better describes the nature of this element of marketing activity. It is not always the goal of the organisation to promote a product, service or the organisation itself. The goal, for example, could very well be to educate or inform. Another issue is that of confusion with the range of marketing tools that are known as 'sales promotions', which have a specific, definable nature (see Chapter 11 of this book on the nature of sales promotion). Added to this is the fact that many things communicate: for example, legible telephone numbers on letterheads; brand name for display on packs; product/ brand/corporate image; price; shape/design of container for recognition on television; shelves and colour of product/pack; and even easy-to-follow instructions. The use of a combination of such devices leads, it is argued, to customer/consumer understanding and better positioning of the company/brand. Jensen (2007) highlights the impact of the Internet and the inevitable inclusion of online activities in the marketing communications mix. Such activities include, for example, email and social networks (see Chapter 10 of this book).

The basic marketing mix, therefore, usually includes communication as a fundamental element (labelled promotion) but the communication itself is a mix of elements. The old promotions mix was usually seen as consisting of the four basic elements of advertising, sales promotion, marketing public relations and personal selling. It is now recognised that this is forever developing and mutating. Corporate public relations might be separated from marketing public relations but both can be seen as elements of the communications mix that might be used in the development of a corporate image and identity. Sponsorship, for a long time seen as part of public relations, is now considered as a marketing and sometimes corporate communications element in its own right. The optimal mix is determined by factors such as the nature of the context, degree of control available, cost, credibility, and size or geographic spread of target audiences. A generalised expression of the communications mix is visualised in Figure 1.2 below.

Figure 1.2   The communications mix

Each element of the mix has characteristics that help the marketer make decisions as to its usefulness or appropriateness in any given context. This can be represented, using just a few examples, in the following way.

Figure 1.3 illustrates that generally speaking advertising is more appropriate to a consumer communications mix than to an organisational/industrial/B-to-B communications mix. The reverse is the case with personal selling. With Public Relations this can be represented with a horizontal line to suggest the recommended constant employment of this element regardless of the context. Exhibitions and trade shows may be more common in organisational contexts, such as the International Materials Handling Exhibition, usually held at the National Exhibition Centre, Birmingham, UK. Of course these do exist in consumer contexts such as the Ideal Home Show, usually held at Earl's Court London, which is both consumer and trade.

The marketing communications elements can be viewed through a control versus spend lens, i.e. some elements such as advertising offer more control over what, when, how, who to, and where communications takes place. If financial resources are abundant then it is up to the organisation how much it will spend on, for example, buying media space or employing celebrity endorsement. On the other hand, public relations, but especially media relations, are much less of a controllable item. Decisions are in the hands of those who control the media (or media vehicles such as a particular magazine, where the controller is usually

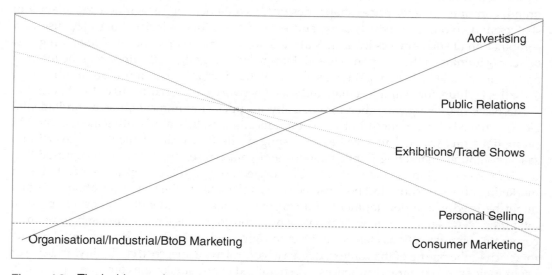

Figure 1.3   The incidence of communication elements in consumer versus organisational marketing contexts

an editor of some denomination, for example the food and drink editor of a newspaper). The marketer can take certain action such as achieving effective media relations but this does not equate to the same level of control as the marketer has with advertising. This matter is expanded upon in Chapter 13 in relation to issues with measuring PR coverage as advertising value equivalence (AVE), which is a constant but problematic measure.

The influx of a relational perspective in marketing has meant that such perspectives must be considered as part of the marketing communications effort. In recent times, and in line with the customer/consumer transition from passivity to interaction, marketing communications has moved to using much more dialogue than monologue, which has re-shaped the marketing communications mix. There is much more potential for shared information, reasoning, dialogue and interaction within relationships between parties that lead to a deeper understanding of customer life cycles and the role of marketing communications (Hougaard and Bjerre, 2009). There is more potential for customer orientation where marketing communications has a role at all stages (Fill, 2009) and to engage with needs whether transactional/remote or relational/close (De Pelsmaker et al., 2010). This approach to understanding the marketing communications mix is still one of 'putting things in boxes' to provide the practitioner with a kind of shorthand, just in the same way as the 4P mnemonic does for the practitioner considering the overall marketing effort.

The aforementioned derivatives of the main communication elements are developing all of the time. For example, a recent development in the UK is in the area of product placement, which for many organisations now has a place within marketing strategy.

The Snapshot below discusses changes to the regulations surrounding product placement on commercial television in the UK as of 28 February 2011, with particular reference both to the ways in which this may change television as a medium and the opportunities for marketers to enhance their marketing communications effort.

Snapshot The Importance of Understanding Context in Television Product (Brand) Placement

Product (or perhaps more accurately brand) placement is a form of impersonal communication that includes brands appearing within films, television programmes and potentially other media contexts such as gaming or books, which have a long history of this activity. For many years in cinema in the UK and around the world we have seen numerous product placements, from James Bond (importantly Sean Connery and others) with, for example, the Aston Martin DB5, to *Top Gun* (Tom Cruise) with Ray-Ban Aviators. In fact there has been product placement in movies from the very start, from when movies were curios through to what we see today in the cinema, online, on television and DVD. In the UK, television watchers, following an EU directive, were given the opportunity at the end of February 2011 to join their US counterparts (where there has been a long history of television product placement) and their counterparts in other countries around the world such as in India. On UK TV there is now a logo at the beginning and end of television shows that contains product placement – mandated by Ofcom, the broadcasting regulator (Hauck, 2011) – and ITV (Independent Television) has created a television spot for an awareness campaign to introduce the new 'P' logo

(Continued)

(Continued)

on behalf of all commercial broadcasters intending to use product placement. It can be noted, however, that when a James Bond movie is shown on television in the UK, the character still drives the Aston Martin, even on the BBC where advertising per se is not possible, and props have been used for many years where no money has changed hands but these are desirable because they add to the realism.

Now, apart from news, children's and religious affairs programmes, real products will be seen (Hauck, 2011). This legalises product placement within films (dramas and documentaries), television series (including soap operas), entertainment shows and sports programmes. This does not apply to the areas of alcohol, tobacco, gambling, baby milk or foods that are high in sugar or salt, escort agencies or weapons. Products cannot be 'unduly prominent' and any references have to be 'editorially justified' to stop the filling of shows with products and services that have 'little or no context in their programmes' (Robinson, 2010).

Ethical considerations include the fear of subliminal messages via product placement that will reduce television's integrity through 'covert advertising'. Potential effects on programme content compound this issue because a commercial product might be at the centre of the programme (Hauck, 2011). With the value of product placement on UK television estimated at 5 per cent of the television advertising market (as it is in the USA) making it worth £150m per annum now (Sweney, 2011) or at least by 2016 (Naish, 2011, using Barclays Corporate figures), there is ethical concern. As Naish (2011) questions, 'will the sight of celebrities munching "unhealthy" foods fuel the child obesity crisis?' This is not a reference to overt celebrity endorsement but to the more subtle, embedded (or as some would have it even subliminal) message. The example of Coke and *American Idol* is used to suggest that 60 per cent of the show's running time is permeated by 'artfully placed cups and Coke-red walls'. Naish quotes the president of the media pressure group Voice of the Listener and Viewer as saying 'It [product placement] makes unhealthy lifestyle habits look normal and healthy. But that is why commercial companies will pay lots of money to place their products.' Naish quotes from a recent Yale University study in the US journal *Annual Review of Public Health* which concluded that product placement in the USA is 'composed almost entirely of messages for nutrient-poor, calorie-dense foods' and claims that the British Heart Foundation wants a complete pre-9 pm watershed ban on placements for products high in fat, salt and sugar, because, according to Katie Chruszcz, a BHF policy researcher 'The laws do not go far enough to protect children from a barrage of junk foods and drinks.'

Stop Point

The evidence suggests that customers and consumers being told what to do by marketers via mass media advertising is now a relic of a former era. Engagement and interaction are essential for success regardless of the form of communication employed. Product (brand) placement has an increasingly important role in this process, particularly on television. Undertake the following: 1. Examine and discuss how and what kind of product placements work in what contexts; 2. Discuss the importance of the creation of a placement that enhances and embeds the brand and the kind of brand damage that might occur if the brand is placed in such a way that exposure to the audience is achieved but without connection to the narrative or the context.

MARKETING AND EXCHANGE – TRANSACTIONS, RELATIONSHIPS AND CHANGE

Marketing is said by many to be in a state of transition, as can be seen from the interest shown in the last decade or so in critical marketing studies (for example Burton, 2001; Tadajewski and Brownlie, 2008). Whatever the changes that it goes through, marketing should always be strategic in nature and is viewed in the business context as a requirement or even a necessity. In other contexts, such as the many that can be described as belonging to social marketing (as in health or social services), this perspective has become the norm ever since Kotler and Zaltman's seminal social marketing article from the 1970s was published (Kotler and Zaltman, 1971). Marketing in this sense has been defined as:

> A social and managerial process by which individuals and groups obtain what they need and want through creating and exchanging products and value with others.
>
> (Kotler et al., 2001: 5)

However, not all writers see marketing in the same way. Some of the key marketing issues of debate today are being expressed in terms of marketing and exchange, not only as transaction but also as exchange occurring through or as part of relationships. Constant change as suggested by increasingly turbulent environments has been a feature in defining marketing for a long time. In the last few decades there has been a lot of activity in the 'what is marketing?' area. Notably Brown (1995: 39), commenting on the marketing concept that he believes is not unassailable, explains that:

> with its tripartite emphasis on customer orientation, overall integration and profit maximisation (the marketing concept) has been the subject of extensive debate and periodic modification.

Since the 1990s' debates on modern (or traditional) and postmodern marketing, much has now been said and ideas expressed on critical marketing perspectives. For example, books such as that of the aforementioned Tadajewski and Brownlie (2008) highlight issues around sustainable marketing, anti-globalisation challenges to marketing, ecofeminism and post-colonialism, among many other critical issues in marketing.

Exchange – market and relational perspectives

Many textbook writers (for example Fill, 2009) agree that exchange involves, in some way or another, something to offer, a 'quid pro quo', in exchange for something else. There are two types of exchange that come in the form of a spectrum between market and relational exchange:

1. *Market exchange* – where dealings are quite straightforward; just a simple exchange of product (or service) for money. This is a market exchange that is short term, self-interest driven and independent.
2. *Relational exchange* – where dealings move to becoming more collaborative, long term in orientation and supportive where relationships are built up between parties. This involves deliberate action on the part of the customer, often via some sort of network activity that is redistributive (i.e. where resources are shared with other parties who work as a collective unit) and even reciprocal (i.e. to do with gift giving and mutuality) as opposed to the self-interest of the market exchange.

Marketing communication in both market and relational exchange situations can take place in the usual way, for example through advertising media, as a *planned process*. However, a fully relational situation that is stronger and much more intense than market exchange needs additional and different marketing communications to help build relationships (for example through loyalty programmes) with a relationship marketing focus. This approach would make far more sense in relation to relatively recent changes to marketing generally in terms of interactivity and engagement. Rather than simply trying to extend the 4P model (the traditional marketing mix mnemonic for product, place, price and promotion) the focus should be on brand values (and therefore feelings) and behaviour (and therefore action) and return on customer investment within exchange networks. However, marketing communication can also take place in a way that is *unplanned* in nature, such as when a news story is released that is out of the control of the marketer. Where positive relationships have been developed, the news story is much more likely to be positive rather than negative or even neutral in nature.

The tasks of marketing communications

Various tasks of marketing communications can be readily discerned and these are:

- to provide information, especially to create awareness;
- to persuade, to create desire or liking;
- to remind;
- to differentiate very similar products;
- to reinforce, reassure and offer comfort;
- to entertain.

These tasks of informing and persuading can be seen quite clearly in the early forms of textbook discussion around tasks, especially of advertising (see Chapter 7 of this book on the nature of advertising and branding). The tasks of *informing* and *persuading* are often followed by the use of *reminders* and the notion of *differentiation* of very similar products often being achieved through the communication employed. Frequently, advertising was seen as the only tool that could differentiate between similar products such as within the carbonated drinks or bottled water product categories. *Reinforcement* can be used to underline for the audience the benefits the product provides and *reassurance* and *comfort* can be offered not only immediately prior to purchase but also in the post-purchase period, which helps retention. These days, however, the idea of *entertainment* is viewed as an essential way to achieve the marketer's tasks through the employment of marketing communication, but in particular communication that uses television, cinema and online advertising. The idea of entertainment of audiences might be part of the *persuasive* task of advertising or added as a task that might include persuasion as a form of public relations (see Chapter 13 of this book on the nature of public relations). Public relations have traditionally been used to *educate* and *prepare* the market so that other communication forms can operate more effectively and efficiently, and in terms of social marketing *education* may be seen as a task rather than mere *information* giving.

Regardless of how the tasks of marketing communications are described and explained, this will involve message content, how the message is presented, and where it is presented, along with timing in order to engage with the audience. Exchange has become much more relational and therefore redistributive and reciprocal. Engagement has become a watchword in the constant quest to find ways to get through the clutter of thousands of planned and unplanned, unintended, controlled and uncontrollable stimuli that appear in front of each of us on a daily basis. Marketing communications uses the traditional promotional mix tools of advertising, sales promotion, public relations and personal selling. Direct marketing and sponsorship have now been included as elements of the mix in their own right. Consideration of these elements in conjunction with media and message can achieve integration. The inclusion of engagement through relationships adds to the potency of the marketing communications effort.

Marketing communications and change

In the face of constant change the marketer is still looking for a customer response, the nature of which will be cognitive, affective or behavioural (see Chapter 3 of this book which discusses behaviour and relationships). A major change in this area is the recognition of the buyer as an interactive rather than passive customer in the age of many forms of interactivity. For example, there is reality television and other media involvement on the part of the 'ordinary' individual. There is permission marketing and permission-based communication where the individual is asked in advance of receiving communication if the marketer can have permission to send the communication. There is also interventionism (following up on people who have shown some interest, especially on website visits, and who 'might buy') or ambush marketing (where a marketer associates itself with a particular marketing activity, say an event like the football World Cup, without being the official sponsor, and hence not paying for it and at the same time getting one over the competition who are paying for the privilege). Hughes and Fill (2007) discuss engagement in relation to communication industry perspectives (and the communications company BBH in particular) and the idea that engagement is the future, with television audiences, for example, no longer being happy to be interrupted by advertising and where communication is done with audiences and not to them. Audiences are smaller because of fragmentation and are more discrete and empowered by interaction. Online activity has gained enormous pace and has overtaken television in terms of total advertising spend. For example, in 2009 the online spend in the UK in the first six months of the year was £1.75bn, which is a 4.6 per cent increase year on year. If this is compared to the 1998 online total of £19.4m, then this change can be seen in perspective (Sweney, 2009). These data from an Internet Advertising Bureau (IAB) report have been looked at more closely by Sweney who reveals that 60 per cent of the £1.75bn is spent on search advertising, up 6.8 per cent year on year. However, as Sweney warns, the use of such figures and comparisons has to be viewed with caution, especially where there have been recessionary effects. While media and spend are central to marketing communications, it can be noted that there has been a shift from spend on advertising to spend on other forms of communications such as sponsorship and product placement but also a move away from mass advertising to specialised/customised advertising to target audiences (see Chapter 9 of this book for a discussion on media characteristics, planning and spend issues).

Change of all sorts is important: changing markets, for example the size of Europe as one market, or the challenge from the Pacific Rim countries to the continued growth of China to the emergence of India or of countries such as Brazil. The ability/inability of the MNCs (multi-national corporations) in the past to communicate internationally or even engage in pan-regional (for example European) advertising has been grappled with both academically and in practice since the 1960s in terms of advertising and communicating with members of the 'Global Village'. This is a reference to the process of globalisation and the influence of technology, associated with Marshall McLuhan in the early 1960s, where the world is seen as being shrunk into a village and where the transmission of information is instantaneous. McLuhan effectively predicted the coming of the World Wide Web (see for example McLuhan, 1962). The adaptation/standardisation debate (whether things can remain as they are across markets with very different variables in operation, as with cultural variables, or whether things have to be adapted) as it applies to communication, but especially advertising, has been around for a number of decades (see for example Elinder,

1961). This debate is still here and now includes, for example, possibilities as regards the use of standardised celebrities, i.e. celebrities who are capable of endorsing a product or brand in more than one country. A key question is 'Should companies think global, act local?', which is a direct reference to strategy development. There has been a move to an era of the globalisation of markets with very different types of companies emerging, underlining a fundamental change to the business ecosystem (see Levitt, 1983). Questions surrounding the relationship between the multinational corporations (MNCs), especially the US companies that dominated much of the 20th century and the development of world regions, impinge on many things but not least of all on the communication process. In particular the 'information explosion' is well under way with the phenomenal growth of Internet accessibility. The worldwide dominance of the USA is waning somewhat. There has been a move chronologically from the US manufacturing and distribution dominance of the 1950s and 1960s through to cost cutting and re-engineering in the 1990s, and the dominance of the media and consumer through ownership of technology and communications in the 21st century (Schultz, 1996).

INTEGRATED MARKETING COMMUNICATIONS

Background

Integrated marketing and integrated marketing communications (IMC) are not new concepts. Integration has been around for years with good practitioners, although it is the case that textbooks began to champion IMC in the early 1990s. Holm (2006) suggests that academics and professionals did not originally consider integration as a realistic approach, with much activity being anchored in little more than the tactical coordination of promotional mix elements. Holm echoes Schultz and Kitchen (2000) and others in suggesting the need for financial consideration and a strategic approach to IMC, which goes beyond the simplistic view of how IMC works; i.e. to concentrate solely on communications elements working together with a 'unified message', where below the line supports above the activity and vice versa. This is the drive toward cost effectiveness and where 'careful planning creates marketing communications synergy which reinforces a consistent message or image in a cost effective manner' (Smith, 1993). This was a good start, but has been taken further. IMC can be described as a process that involves various forms of communications that attempt to achieve tasks such as to persuade, inform, remind, educate or entertain customers and prospects, i.e. affecting and influencing the behaviour of target audiences. The IMC process also includes anything and everything that an organisation, company or its people and brands do with targets and publics, either deliberately or not. To make good use of all forms of relevant communication makes sense. All in all the IMC process, like the more general marketing process, should start and end with the customer or prospect. Like the marketing process the IMC process has been affected greatly by changes in technology whereby cost structures, communication effectiveness and client–agency/communication company relationships have been improved (Hughes and Fill, 2007).

IMC has been defined as being a cohesive mix of promotional and other activities and tools that delivers a co-ordinated and consistent message to target customers and consumers synergistically to achieve organisational objectives (Kitchen and Schultz, 1999). There have been numerous studies during the past decade or so, all of which add to what is a fluid process as the IMC concept mutates. These include studies of the relationship between a specific element of the IMC mix, such as public relations, and those of the relationship between IMC and internal marketing issues. There have been numerous studies concerned with measurement and with media integration. All in all, for Kliatchko (2008), the concern has been to do with the 'definitions, perceptions, understanding and theoretical foundations surrounding the IMC concept'. There is now interest in global perspectives but also those for IMC and branding, media synergy and internal marketing. Many writers have discussed the nature of IMC. A useful summary can be found in Pickton (2010) who pulls together various 'models'.

IMC drivers

The overriding factor that drives IMC is the move away from mass communications. At the same time, ways have to be found to get through the clutter in the most efficient way possible. Cost, accountability and a results-orientation are now seen as being achieved through the coordination of diverse tools targeted at diverse audiences in an increasingly technology-led and global context. Therefore financial factors were important for Schultz et al. (1993) who suggest that in a recession, the trend towards payment by results, restructuring of how agencies are paid in terms of billing/income/profit, pressure to reduce media billing and media fragmentation has contributed towards a consideration of IMC. The sophisticated client for many commentators now is a reality where such clients are more knowledgeable than in the past. The mystique of advertising (especially television advertising) is diminished and a power shift has occurred. Disillusionment with the brand, advertising and agencies in the sense expressed above, i.e. a shift away from the glamorised brands, advertising and agencies of the 1950s and 1960s, is now a reality. Own labels are stronger and advertising less revered. Other elements of communications are deemed important. Communications companies have had to change, and appear to have seen this as a set of opportunities and not threats. The power shift to retailers generally and what they need/expect has meant more scrutiny in the way in which communication is viewed.

Since the early 1990s the factors that Schultz and colleagues (1993) and others highlighted have gained in strength, especially since the growth and development of the Internet, which for the first time in 2010 saw greater advertising revenue in the UK than that generated from television advertising. In the run-up to the new millennium it was clear that the drive for IMC was a reaction to such factors, with 'new forms of information technology including the development and usage of databases, media fragmentation, client desires for interaction/synergy, and global and regional coordination' being the order of the day (Kitchen and Schultz, 1999: 21). With such changes, however, came problems associated with how to measure and evaluate IMC programmes. Now that IMC as a formal concept is over two decades old it can be seen to have surpassed the notion that it was just a management fad. The concern expressed by Kitchen and Schultz (1999: 23) that specialists (for example in advertising) 'may not want to see the whole' may still be a reality, but this has not dented the progress of IMC and the move to what Kitchen and Schultz called an 'outside in' (i.e. consumer-driven) approach rather than an 'inside-out' (i.e. company-driven) perspective. This continues to develop, in terms of both the 'academic and professional', but change is 'never easy' (Kitchen et al., 2008). Since the late 1990s, the last stage in the development of IMC – what Kitchen and Schultz (1999) called 'Financial and Strategic Integration' – has been a difficult one to achieve, but it is desirable because of its emphasis on return on investment where information and knowledge are linked to continuous evaluation. ROCI, or return on customer investment (Schultz and Kitchen, 2000; Kliatchko, 2008), is part of the growing concern over the financial measurement and effectiveness of IMC programmes. This has been applied to other programmes such as brand development with ROBI, or return on brand investment, which is part of the attempt to measure the less tangible aspects of assets such as brands (Kliatchko, 2008).

The benefits and beneficiaries of IMC

The benefits of IMC to organisations have been documented since the early 1990s. These include creative integrity, where theme and style are consistent throughout and therefore a positive impact is achieved as opposed to confusion. This can aid campaign build-up and provide materials for other uses with consistency of messages. Straplines and other parts of the message can provide the basis for reinforcement and reminder leading to, for Linton and Morley (1995):

- the development of the key message;
- visual standards;
- consistent use of company colours;
- unbiased recommendations (usually through one agency and 'through the line' with no worries about earning commission from advertising billing only);
- better use of all media;
- greater marketing precision (databases and information processing generally);
- operational efficiency (takes fewer people, can be a single interface and so less conflict, which is simple compared to the potentially messy multi-agency situation);
- cost savings (in administration, rationalisation of materials, artwork);
- a high calibre service (IMC means professionalism for below the line as well as above where, overall, service is improved 'through the line');
- easier working relationships (one agency means no new learning curves because of knowledge of the client's business, simplified administration, and no re-learning but ongoing and consistent);
- accountability (this has to be true if only one agency is used and value for money should result).

The creation of competitive advantage in this way can boost sales/profits and save time/money on workload/artwork. This can then increase effectiveness and consolidate image and relationships. IMC can help ensure a successful buying process by being wrapped around it, moving some way towards if not loyalty then trust, commitment and repeat purchase in relation to the competition, dialogue with customers, a decrease in risk, help with choice and reassurance. All of this shortens the search process and reduces choice in a positive way for the busy consumer whilst providing consistency, which in turn means credibility and a sense of order. Time and money are also saved on, for example, artwork, a reduced workload or fewer meetings. Communications companies, clients and consumers benefit from IMC. Communications companies, if they meet the needs of clients, will gain from the opportunities that are presented, including in media developments. Clients, who are constantly trying to make their budgets work harder for them, will benefit in this way but there is a recognised need for client leadership from the top of organisations (Kitchen and Schultz, 1999; Swain, 2004). If consumers do not benefit then the full benefit of IMC has not been passed on. There is no real evidence as yet as to whether the consumer is benefiting, but it is certainly looking this way (see Chapter 10 of this book with particular reference to the Internet as an interactive, integrating tool).

The barriers that inhibit IMC and its future

In the past the lack of a clear definition of IMC has inhibited its development and there has been some debate as to just what IMC really is. This is now close to being resolved but practical difficulties, for example the complexity of different objectives being achieved by different strategy and tactics, remain a reality. Implementation can be very difficult to achieve. Cultural factors inhibit the development of IMC, especially in international campaigns, but the main factor is change, or resistance to it. For example, the culture of the organisation may dictate that advertising is on television or it may be that sales promotions have been the norm, linked to bonuses. Any change would be accompanied by conflict. A deeper dimension is provided by Cornelissen (2000) who points to the failure of academia to provide an adequate managerial approach to IMC and suggests the notion of integration should be rephrased into 'the more operational constructs of interaction and co-ordination between areas'. The provision of useful and memorable constructs as performance indicators, for example the degree of interaction being positively related to the degree of coordination between departments, is desirable. In functional terms managers will want to, for example, protect territories or create a power base through control of budgets (or 'turf battles' as Sheenan and Doherty, 2001, would have it). There may be restricted creativity because of a need to operate within the tighter integrated creative brief. Timescales may be shorter, which conflicts with longer-term realities so that there is a need for careful planning to cater for objectives within time frames. There are single-discipline agencies where coordination experience, a lack of management know-how in achieving integration and/or a lack of commitment to do so may exist.

It has been recognised that an organisation's communication function should be consolidated rather than divided up where 'managers can install co-ordination mechanisms to achieve required levels of interaction between functional areas or departments of communication' (Cornelissen, 2000: 599). Whiting (2010) suggests that there may now be an over-emphasis on communications in marketing while conceding that marketing communications is part of successful brand building, playing a vital role both strategically and tactically, and that social media offer a 'game-changing challenge' that engages with and empowers consumers. Whiting still worries that marketing is seen as a function that is charged with 'building sales tactically via communications platforms' – in other words, marketing is seen as selling. However, in practice, many communications companies have seized the opportunity and now add value beyond media buying and creativity. New structures have emerged and continue to do so. Many clients also understand the importance of continuity and the depth of the relationship will remain strong or become even stronger as relationships develop. This has implications for the role of senior management since integration is desirable at all levels where the goal is consistency across the organisation. IMC is wrapped around the buying process and is tailored for each stage of a campaign while building relationships and brand values.

Kliatchko (2008) suggests the transition from IMC as a process that is a limited view of communication tools being coordinated towards a strategic process. Kliatchko purposively revisits 'the IMC construct' and discusses the 'four pillars of IMC', which are:

1. Stakeholders – all the relevant publics/markets/audiences with which the organisation interacts, whether internal or external, ethically.

2. Content – development from a deeper knowledge and understanding of markets beyond traditional demographic and psychographic data in an era of digital technologies and participatory media where the empowered customer is part of the process as a whole and is more than a mere receiver of a message (whether controlled or uncontrolled by a marketer). The dawn of user-generated content has arrived in the form of tools such as blogs, forums, wikis, podcasts and not least social media platforms such as www.wikispaces.com. The marketer's job is to discover how best to use such spaces given the difficulties that are inherent in user-generated content, not least in the areas of propriety, decency and good taste, especially where brand values and vision are involved.

3. Channel – the notion of a channel being beyond the traditional view of what a channel of communication is to include other contact points where customers and prospects can experience the brand on their own terms. Media channels may be in the foreground (main media used) and background (secondary media channel) but usage is controlled by audiences, not marketers, thus rendering the traditional media planning concepts of reach, frequency (weight) and duplication at the very least questionable (see Chapter 9 of this book on media and media planning).

4. Results – the drive for the measurement of effectiveness has become an essential part of today's marketing communications landscape. The aforementioned ROCI and ROBI systems that predict performance in terms of customers and brands are financial approaches to measuring effectiveness rather than the traditional measures of communications effects. While the latter are still important, the former are seen as essential measures of investment in marketing communications (see Chapter 9 of this book on spend issues).

Kliatchko builds upon these pillars to provide the interplay between them and the four levels of IMC development as provided by Schultz and Schultz (1998) and Kitchen and Schultz (1999) in the following way:

1. Tactical coordination – to achieve synergy, consistency and integration – (focuses on pillar 2, content).
2. Redefining the scope of marketing communications, which is concerned with the nature and relevancy of channels (pillar 3, channels).
3. Application of IT for database building and as deeper knowledge of audiences gives prominence to stakeholders (pillar 1).
4. Financial and strategic integration is concerned with return on investment (pillar 4, results).

As Kliatchko (2008) points out there has yet to be any agreement among scholars about a formal definition of IMC. Perhaps this is because of the fluidity of the process which is constantly mutating, especially in terms of the impact of digital developments. Kliatchko (2008: 140) defines IMC as 'an audience-driven business process of strategically managing stakeholders, content, channels, and results of brand communication programs'.

The final pillar and level are the latest and most discussed among academics and practitioners alike. Swain (2004), for example, links measurement to the basis upon which agencies might be compensated for IMC services but points out that there is a difference between activities being conducted and actual achievement. The old goal of achieving exposure is being replaced by measuring actual results (see Chapter 5 of this book on payment systems in the marketing communications industry). Kliatchko (2008) recognises that 'business process' is important because it suggests integration not just among functional areas of marketing but also across the whole business (after Schultz and Schultz, 1998).

From the standpoint taken in this book, the term organisation is preferred to business since it is intended to include not-for-profit and other organisations that might not be best described as a business. The IMC plan from this standpoint (see Chapter 4) is a cohesive and comprehensive blueprint or framework that facilitates the coordination of a mix of communications activities and tools and delivers a coordinated and consistent message to target customers and consumers synergistically to achieve organisational objectives. The Snapshot below illustrates how relationships, integration and engagement can work within the IMC efforts of large companies and SMEs alike. The emphasis is on what smaller firms can learn from the efforts of larger companies about IMC but also it is about what larger companies can learn from the creativity and innovativeness of smaller firms that are born out of necessity.

In practical marketing communications terms, the future was thought to lie not with outdated constructs that relate to mass communication, but with the increasingly fragmented mass into one-to-one situations involving digital technologies (Kliatchko, 2008). Client–agency relationship difficulties were potentially the biggest area of concern. Agencies, or communications companies, needed to understand and serve clients' needs better in this fragmented rather than mass world and, of course, the marketing communications industry has responded massively (see Chapter 5).

The Snapshot below suggests ways in which SMEs can use IMC effectively to create marketing communications strategy.

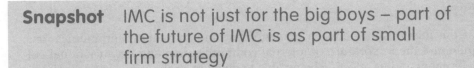

Snapshot   IMC is not just for the big boys – part of the future of IMC is as part of small firm strategy

Smaller firms can ill-afford to waste money on marketing generally and more specifically in the communications arena. As Hills (2006) suggests, a small business owner might be tempted to focus on only one aspect of marketing, but if this fails then marketing as a whole fails. Hills provides practical tips such as making sure the web has the same key words as (say) radio advertising or making sure the frequency of impacts of three hits the target with the same message rather than three different messages. This is in line with an IMC plan that delivers a consistent message through all media used, both on and offline and indeed through other forms of communication that are interpersonal. Hills suggests that the small business 'integrate all aspects of the company into a single, cohesive plan', just as a larger business would. This means the SME has to have the ability to understand the situation or context before setting goals and devising strategy in order to achieve those goals.

The firm has to have the means to be able to put an IMC plan into action. Research conducted by Gabrielli and Balboni (2009) with Italian SMEs suggests that while SMEs have the intent they do not necessarily manage the internal processes required for marketing communications planning. There are gaps in a range of activities and of message and goal definition so that structural characteristics are important as is internal dynamism. Gabrielli and Balboni (2009) call this a gap between theory and practice in IMC. Despite there being 'a virtuous marketing communication behavioural profile in firms we name as active firms' that have 'an articulated communications mix' aspects of marketing communications could be improved, for example public relations. Outside of these virtuous firms there were others in this study that focused on one activity, often one of the interactive activities or trade shows, and opportunities were not being adequately exploited. There is 'scant communication awareness and a short-sighted outlook' that is 'evident in content and goal definition'. Nor do such firms go beyond the behavioural, i.e. actual buying response. Rather, they have concentrated on transferring technical information about products, whereas those firms that use a wide range of activities look at attitudes, self-identification with the brand and diffusion of brand elements. These latter firms are able to integrate and therefore there is the possibility of a 'strategic approach aimed at increasing the relationship value for the customer' rather than a simple 'operational focus on products'. However, even these firms in Gabrielli and Balboni's study have gaps in the process. In particular, content formulation, goal definition and budgets being determined '*ex post*, after having fixed which kind of activities the firm intends to implement, or when it is fixed in advance it is calculated as a percentage of the total turnover' are identified as gaps in the strategic process, which is retrospective rather than goal driven.

There is a lack of consistency in internal communications and decision-making yet there is internal dynamism in SMEs where owner-managers may only feel the need to communicate during critical incidents, such as managing relationships with different kinds of customers or when attempting to penetrate new or unfamiliar markets (Gabrielli and Balboni, 2009). Gheorghe et al.'s (2009) study of Romanian SMEs

(Continued)

(Continued)

looked at the relationship between management and marketing communications. This highlighted the importance of internal communication and organisational culture development and its effect on being able to develop strategic marketing communications. This study recognised the importance of the owner-manager's managerial communications skills, communication style and personality and the need for a good (internal) communications infrastructure 'at every level of the organisation' and also 'to get the group of subordinates to work for a common goal' in order to 'develop a good managerial culture'.

Stop Point

There are many examples of successful IMC campaigns in the literature as well as clear evidence that IMC is desirable but difficult to achieve in practice. The problem is compounded for smaller firms because of the additional barriers that exist due to the very nature of smaller firms and not least the nature and personalities of their owner-managers and principals. Undertake the following: 1. Discuss the benefits of IMC to SMEs and examine the barriers that exist to implementation of an IMC approach to communications; 2. Examine the changes that have taken and are taking place with the Internet and other technologies and discuss how the results of such change might be the way forward in breaking down such barriers.

THE MARKETING COMMUNICATIONS ENVIRONMENT

Environmental factors as an integral part of the planning and managing process are dealt with in Chapter 4 of this book and, where appropriate, will be referred to throughout the rest of the book. The general aim in this first chapter is to sketch the environment in which organisations/marketers and communicators work. The reader may already be familiar with the PEST/STEP/SLEPT-type models (acronyms for political, economic, social, technological and legal forces) of the business or marketing macro environment and therefore of a model or framework approach that is considered essential for marketing analysis. These also apply in the communications context, since they represent many of the factors that impact on corporate and marketing communications elements. For example cultural factors have a direct impact on what is acceptable in advertising messages for lingerie; legal factors might dictate what must go on the packaging of particular products such as cigarettes. The term 'Marketing Environment' therefore, refers to forces that impact on the organisation, affecting management's ability to deliver the marketing concept successfully to target customers. Such forces are either micro, such as suppliers, distributors and competitors, or macro, such as political, technological or economic.

Approaches to the marketing communications environment may vary in language and structure. Some writers have referred to the 'near' and 'far' environment (for example Smith et al., 1997, 2002). This is a useful reference to external factors that can be considered in these two ways: the near or competitive environment, which includes structure of the market, trends in the market, microeconomics and power forces; and the far or wider environment, which involves sociological, technological, macroeconomic and political factors. In this chapter the marketing communications environment is discussed in three ways: characteristics of the micro (suppliers, the company itself, competitors, marketing intermediaries and customers) and macro (demographic, economic, natural, technological, political and cultural) environment; strategic environmental issue management; and critical components of the micro and macro environment.

Characteristics of the micro and macro environment

Modernist marketing authors like Kotler (for example 1984 or 1988, or more latterly Kotler and Keller, 2009) for many years have philosophised in this area. Kotler has used at least two anonymous sayings that mean something in this area. These are: 'it is useless to tell a river to stop running; the best thing is to learn how to swim in the direction it is flowing' and 'there are three types of companies. Those who make things happen. Those who watch things happen. Those who wondered what happened.' These allude to the company purpose. This position holds that the purpose should be specific as to the business domain where products and technologies are transient while basic market needs generally remain. The company should shift its business domain definition from a product to market focus. The modernist position sees the marketing environment (ME) as an important concept for the practice of good marketing management. The ME consists of all those factors that affect the organisation and its markets and any factors that affect the relationship between an organisation and its markets. Matching takes place in the ME, i.e. the matching of the organisation's capabilities to customer needs and wants. There is therefore a requirement of management to monitor the ME and adapt product and marketing strategies to meet changing needs. Markets are dynamic and needs fast-changing and there is, therefore, the need for some form of marketing information system which would necessarily include marketing research and intelligence that should be built into the organisation's decision-making process. With many of the aforementioned factors, the organisation usually has little or no control over them but can influence them. These factors or components are discussed below.

Strategic environmental issue management

Most managers involved in companies are aware of the importance of environmental analysis. More experienced ones are perhaps also aware of the difficulties of monitoring the environment that is both within and surrounding their organization. In order to implement environmental issue management four stages of such a process need to be considered. First, environmental scanning must take place in order that key environmental issues can be identified and impact the evaluation allowed before the formulation of a response strategy occurs. This applies across the business (including marketing) board but, of course, part of this response is marketing and corporate communications.

Critical components of the micro and macro environment

The micro and macro environment are well-known constructs in general marketing terms and their respective components as alluded to above are depicted in Figure 1.4 below.

From this general model of the marketing environment the components or elements of each of the micro and macro environments can be seen in relation to what they might mean to marketing communicators.

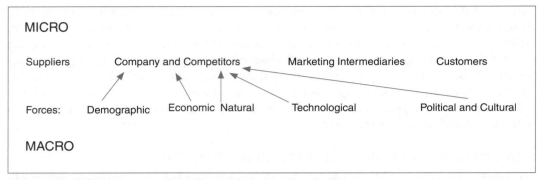

Figure 1.4   Critical components of the marketing environment

The micro environment (MIE)

The micro environment (MIE) consists of a number of elements. Taking the elements of the MIE in turn:

- The *organization* itself – there obviously exists an *internal* environment with all organizations and this is concerned with *strengths and weaknesses*. Management structures vary vastly but whatever the structure of the organization marketing management has the task of making marketing decisions within this context and in the context of corporate mission, objectives, strategies and policies. It is especially important to note the notion of conflict within organizations. There are very many possible sources of conflict that could occur in organizations. For example how marketing, production and finance interact, or how sales and marketing interact (see Chapter 13 of this book for further reference to internal publics).

- *Suppliers* – in the *external* environment, every company needs resources of some sort in order to function, for example material and fuel. There is therefore a need to monitor *suppliers'* prices, shortages and alternatives. There may also be a need to consider more than one supplier to avoid total cut-off while not getting the benefits of economies of scale.

- *Marketing* Intermediaries include middlemen – agents, manufacturers' reps, wholesalers, and retailers – who have a place/time/possession utility. The notion is that such players can act more efficiently and hence more cheaply than a manufacturer. There are also physical distribution firms – warehousing, transportation – who can increase the cost effectiveness of operations in terms of speed, safety and so on. Marketing Services – advertising, PR, marketing research agencies, marketing analysts – can also be classed as marketing intermediaries, as can financial services – banks, credit brokers and so on.

- *Customers* can be: consumers or buying for someone else; they might be organizational buyers or resellers; they might be national or local government; they might be at home or abroad. Each type of customer has particular characteristics that call for careful study and consequently differing approaches. There are four basic considerations from a customer viewpoint: desire (where one type is satisfied but not another, for example a new car as opposed to a holiday); generic (one problem-solver versus another, for example a car or bike); product form (one product rather than another, for example a saloon or sports car); and branding (one brand rather than another, for example Own Label, Oxo or Bovril stock cubes). The *Internet* has had a profound effect on the marketer's ability to *sell direct* to the consumer.

- *Competitors* lie somewhere on a spectrum between cooperation and open warfare. Competition can come in many forms.

- *Publics/stakeholders* – the term publics alludes to the organization seeking goodwill, usually via Public Relations activities, on a continual basis. There are a number of established publics; financial (for example the banks), media (press, TV, radio), and government (national, pressure groups and local). A related concept, that of the *stakeholder*, has been used relatively latterly to describe the actors in such a system as suggested above, which is associated with strengths and weaknesses of organizations and is returned to from a communications management perspective in Chapter 4 of this book.

The macro environment (MAE)

The macro environment (MAE) also consists of a number of *external* elements that are listed below. All micro elements operate under a larger macro environment (MAE) consisting of forces that have been traditionally thought of as uncontrollable (as opposed to the elements of the marketing mix). The forces of the MAE therefore influence *opportunities and threats*. The organization should be aware of any trends or changes in the MAE.

The *technological* environment – products developed in the technological environment range from wonder drugs to hydrogen bombs to soft as floss white bread full of vitamins and mobile phone apps. It has been argued that new technologies have a creative destruction, especially where real innovation is present and not just gimmicks or compromises such as freeze-dried coffee rather than fresh-ground coffee. The accelerating pace of change perhaps underscores the importance of research and development being conducted hand-in-hand with marketing research. Innovation opportunities/threats should be delineated from minor improvements and the need for regulation, e.g. for food and drugs, recognised. Technology is constantly changing. It can no longer be assumed that current ranges of products will continue to satisfy customer demands. In an early volume of marketing management, Kotler uses the example of non-drip paint as a product that had a profound effect on what had been a stable market. We could extend this now with the recent developments in 'one coat' paints.

The *political/legal/ethical* environment involves increasing and changing amounts of legislation. This includes the protection of companies from each other; for example Antitrust Laws (USA) and the Monopoly and Mergers Commission (UK) (now the Competition Commission) prevent unfair competition. It also includes the protection of consumers from unfair business practices, for example advertising and packaging and protection of the larger interests of society against unbridled business behaviour. Acts of Parliament, changing government agencies and changes in their roles (whether this is, for example, leanings towards deregulation or the opposite), the growth of public interest/pressure groups and the notion of consumerism as major social force all have a potential impact.

The *demographic* environment involves age, for example an aging population and therefore new and different markets. Children, youth, young adults, early middle aged, later middle aged, retirees – all could form the segments of a market based on age that would change quite radically percentage-wise over the course of time. Increased life expectancy, a slowdown of the birth rate, fewer young people, family size/number of children, later marriage, fewer children, a higher divorce rate, more women/mothers working, or men as the target for food manufacturers. The rise of non-family households, the single adult, and two person cohabiters – groups all with special needs. There are also better education standards, less indiscriminate TV viewing, vast increases in the use of the Internet, increases in magazine reading and travel. The *geo-demographic* perspective sees geographic shifts, rural to urban, urban to rural, city to suburbs, suburbs to city (very important if such shifts mean suburban facilities) and regional, for example from the north east to the south east of the UK. The *economic* environment is closely linked to demography and markets that require purchasing power that is a function of real income and any changes in disposable and discretionary income that are affected by inflation, unemployment and taxation. Savings are clearly pitted against expenditure but this also involves things like credit facilities, lending and mortgages. Changing expenditure patterns – as, for example, when income rises the percentage of income spent on food might very well decrease while that on leisure and recreation increases – need to be recognised.

The *socio-cultural* environment involves beliefs, norms and values. Primary concerns are things like 'the institution of marriage' while secondary concerns would follow sentiments such as 'you ought to marry early'. It is said that primary values are more difficult to change than secondary ones – although this is clearly not impossible. Core values are things like 'the American way' and 'Englishness' in terms of culture. Sub-cultural values belong to groups such as 'teenagers'. Secondary cultural values may involve shifts over time. In one era 'teenagers' may have a particular set of values. These can change quite radically. 'Tweenies' are a relatively new group to emerge that are post young child and pre-teen, i.e. aged about 5–12 years but who have spending power and are therefore of interest to some marketers. The socio-cultural environment is hence to do with people's relations with themselves, for example a 'me society' seeking self-fulfilment, reflected in the use of and expenditure on leisure, recreation and fun. People's relations to others (a 'me' to 'we' shift involving others) are reflected in the use of, for example, 'honesty' in advertising. In terms of ethnicity, Hispanics are seen in the USA as an important sub-cultural group but this may not be refined enough, i.e. Hispanic would include Cubans, Puerto Ricans and others. In the British context it may make more marketing sense to look at British South Asians as a target group rather than 'the Asian community in Britain', which clearly has a wider and more complex make-up. People's relations to institutions, including shifts in loyalty to marriage or the work ethic, can be readily seen. People's relations to society, again including shifts in loyalty, for example, the erosion of patriotism, are also visible, as are people's relations to nature and the universe, again including shifts such as a move from a specific religion to (say) worldliness or some other form of spiritualism.

The *natural/environmental/green* environment has particular resonance with the recent rise of environmentalism and 'green' issues that show clearly the interaction that can occur between the various elements of the MAE and MIE. The natural/political/public pressure groups involving 'limits to growth' debate that came to the fore in the 1970s centred on the environment, finite oil resources, the role of nuclear power and other such issues. These can be clearly seen today. The natural environment therefore involves shortages of raw materials, divided into the following: *infinite resources* such as the air we breathe and long-term dangers or shorter term ones such as the use of CFCs; *finite, renewable resources* such as forests but with similar long- and short-term dangers; *finite, non-renewable resources* such as coal, oil and gas. Increased cost of energy, levels of pollution and government intervention in natural resource management are all items for consideration. Each of these issues begs the question 'what opportunities are there for the development of new sources and new materials?' Clearly there are opportunities for marketers to communicate benefits or use particular imagery in this area while at the same time there is the danger of the 'band wagon effect', i.e. simply milking an environmental issue by jumping on a current wave of favourable opinion without any real justification for so doing. Environmentalists are perhaps more critical of marketing than the original consumerists (consumer activists in favour of consumer rights) were as developments have occurred. For example environmentalists complain more vigorously about (wasteful) packaging whereas consumerists like the idea of convenience packaging. Consumerists worry about deception in advertising whereas environmentalists do not like the idea that advertising leads to greater (than necessary) consumption. The cost of including environmental issues and criteria in marketing decision making is in many cases not insignificant but at the same time managers have realised that, at the very least, respecting the environment is in itself worthwhile.

A communications management perspective on MAE elements will be dealt with in Chapter 4 of this book.

The Snapshot below looks at the ways in which one of the world's most famous companies, Levi Strauss & Co., has tried to navigate the ever-changing and often turbulent marketing environment.

Snapshot   Levi revival – how an iconic brand managed to stay connected

Brands need to be 'so disruptive that they can make a powerful connection with their core audiences'. According to Precourt (2010) this is the view of Jamie Cohen Szulc, Chief Marketing Officer of Levi Strauss & Co. Apparently Levi are now acknowledging that change happens and there is a need to connect with core human values. At this core there is a need to feel more productive. Precourt lists Szulc's four trends that are driving the 21st century, which are faster production cycles, message distribution change in the face of fragmentation and consumer control, the loss of control to gain other advantages and more complex marketing mixes. Hence the need to be disruptive because with so much going on the consumer needs to know who is authentic and who is not. These sentiments fit well with the Levi's brand core values, so the question is, is this simply a return to core values after many years of trying new and different approaches? This is, apparently, not the case. Rather, it seems to be a sea change away from an attitude of selling products to engagement with consumers and seeing through a different lens. Yet Levi Strauss & Co. seems to have the notion that jeans will never go out of fashion firmly fixed. As Precourt (2010) suggests, this is a 'flashback to the Levi's legacy of craftsmanship' where the 're-launch of the brand's London flagship store in 2010 on Regent Street' was driven by this notion. Precourt quotes a news commentator as describing it as 'part store, part art exhibit'. The idea was to present Levi's as authentic, associated with crafts and artisans, where shoppers could buy into this.

The 'Levi's Story' is one of the best-known stories about companies and brands. Its history from tent-making to blue jeans is well known and documented. Fashion changes are of course important to companies like Levi Strauss & Co. and yet by the mid 1980s denim was out of fashion. It is not surprising that the basic positioning of Levi's advertising was virtually the same all over the world. Originally Levi's products were seen as being straightforward, honest, independent, adventurous and rebellious by both men and women, 15–25 years of age, who cared for what is genuine, enjoyed the company of other, similar, people, felt attracted to the opposite sex and expressed their sense of freedom and enjoyment – in an acceptable manner. New advertising began in the mid 1980s, which was a move away from the 'western' towards music. The Levi image was revitalised while the product remained the same. 'Real' people were used to target and position an international brand. 501s became the authentic blue jean. For Levi's European agency, Bartle, Bogle and Hegarty, or at least its creative source, John Hegarty, the secret to branding is to take a head and heart approach – namely be rational and creative (BBC, 1999). Moving pictures and music combined to produce the desired image and at the time television and cinema were seen as the ideal media vehicles. The actual commercials were familiar to most across Europe and there were no worries about language or complicated (and potentially disastrous) dubbing or the need for any icons

(Continued)

(Continued)

other than those with universal appeal to the target audience – especially in the age of satellites. Hoardings, trade magazines and merchandising were also used but the all-important form of communication was the film, which was expensive but clearly effective in its time. Music was the key to Levi's advertising during this period. 'Launderette' was the first and most iconic with its Marvin Gaye *I Heard it Through the Grapevine* track. Another example out of many was Muddy Waters' *Mannish Boy*.

Since this time Levi Strauss & Co. have been striving (and struggling) to address its problems and after a number of new product launches have not only moved towards the Levi's image rather than a focus on product but have also recognised the importance of authenticity. The Levi Strauss & Co. President and CEO, John Anderson, now talks about inspiring a new generation with 'our pioneering spirit' having 'always embodied the energy and events of our times. People have worn our products during the seminal moments of social change over the past 155 years.' The talk is about products, profits and principles – about being 'active on behalf of issues such as equality, HIV/Aids and environmental sustainability' yet still be 'a dynamic, competitive force in the marketplace ... and surprise and delight our consumers at every touch point – this strong bond has always defined us. It will continue to define us as we create a sustainable, profitable future' (Anderson, 2011).

Stop Point

The evidence suggests that the Levi's brand is apparently being viewed in a different way by younger consumers. Undertake the following: 1. Examine the ways in which older consumers see the brand differently from a younger audience and discuss how they might feel toward the Levi's brand, and then outline what you think Levi Strauss & Co. can do to ensure the brand's survival; 2. Look at the Levi Strauss & Co. website and consider the company's commitment to corporate social responsibility (CSR). In the light of this, discuss the company's assumption that there still exists a strong bond between Levi Strauss & Co. and consumers.

Assignment

The macro environment (MAE) – organisational response to environmental change

It has been said that the organisation has little or no control over the forces of the MAE but can influence them. Organisations need to address environmental change by predicting change and developing responses based on, among other things, impact evaluation.

Your task

For an organisation of your choice, write a 2,000-word report on the key elements of the macro marketing environment. Include in your report a list of macro environmental factors that such an organisation might take into account when analysing its markets. Include also your evaluation of the likely relative impact for each factor. You are encouraged to discuss your ideas with other students on the module in the designated seminars.

Typical organisations that you might choose from are:

- a domestic central heating equipment manufacturer;
- an Internet-based holiday company;
- a political party;
- a small country crafts business;
- a surface coatings (e.g. paint, varnish) manufacturer;
- a construction, plant and equipment manufacturer;
- a charitable trust;
- a police force.

Summary of Key Points

- Marketing and corporate communications are built from elements and together form an organisation's communications mix that will vary depending upon the context.
- Marketing communications is either planned or unplanned, the latter being positive or negative towards the organisation.
- Exchange is either market or relational. Exchange has to operate in a climate of constant and often turbulent change.
- This is now an era of increased consumer control where organisations have to forfeit control to achieve profitable engagement. There is also media and consumer dominance, with a greater relational emphasis on marketing communications practice and one that is increasingly global.
- Marketing and corporate communications' role is mutating continually. The old communications mix within the original marketing mix mnemonic has changed to reveal new strategic tools such as sponsorship as well as relational and critical marketing practice.
- The notion of IMC is no longer acceptable when expressed in very simple terms such as synergy. The IMC concept is still developing but has reached the stage with many organisations of being an outside-in rather than inside-out approach.
- IMC needs to be contextualised both within and outside of the organisation and will have to become a more functionally endemic part of what an organisation is and does.
- The marketing environment is constantly changing. The biggest challenge for marketing and corporate communications management is meeting this change. This is not simply coping with 'shifting sands' but more to do with anthropomorphic, organic, living, growing and mutating organisations leading rather than following.

Discussion Questions

1. Outline the different kinds of exchange that might exist in marketing. In particular, expand upon relational exchange, illustrating with examples.

2. Choose two contrasting product categories, such as confectionery and construction plant and equipment, and highlight the likely communications' mix differences when launching a new product within each category.

3. Discuss the notion that communications can be planned or unplanned. If communications are unplanned, explain how an organisation can capitalise on any positive effects and mitigate any negative effects of unplanned communications, illustrating your discussion with examples.

4. 'Consumers are now in control of all transactions. Companies have to be flexible and forfeit some control for success in the marketplace.' Discuss this sentiment, relating your discussion to examples of your choice.

5. 'The absence of IMC now is the equivalent of having marketing myopia in the 1960s.' Explain why you either agree or disagree with this sentiment using examples to illustrate.

6. 'Organisations need to take an outside-in rather than inside-out approach to marketing and marketing communications.' Explain, using examples of different kinds of organisation, why you agree or disagree with this statement.

7. Explain the relationship between the micro and macro environments. Discuss the effect of this on marketing communications outputs. Provide examples to illustrate.

8. 'The natural or green environment is the most important element in any environmental scanning exercise for any organisation these days.' Explain why you agree or disagree with this statement.

9. Choose any element of the macro environment and put it in the context of a brand of your choice. Discuss the likely communications issues that would have to be dealt with by a brand or category manager.

10. 'Organisations now have to be more human, more organic and less mechanistic than in the past, the "organism metaphor" rather than that of the machine.' Explain and illustrate why you agree or disagree with this assertion.

Further Reading

McCartney, G., Butler, R. and Bennett, M. (2012) 'A Strategic Use of the Communications Mix in the Destination Image-formation Process', *Journal of Travel Research*, 47 (2):183–96. http://jtr.sagepub.com/content/47/2/183.full.pdf+html

This article reports on a study on destination brand image perceptions of outbound travellers from four major cities regarding Macao. The study sought to address a gap in the literature on how to convince tourists to travel to a particular destination. The authors suggest that the answer lies in developing a persuasive communications mix strategy that would manage tourist destination image perceptions. The article presents a communication effectiveness grid to indicate marketing resource effectiveness.

Pope-Ruark, R. (2008) 'Challenging the Necessity of Organisational Community for Rhetorical Genre Use: community and genre in the work of integrated marketing communication agency writers', *Business Communication Quarterly*, 71 (2): 185–94. http://bcq.sagepub.com/content/71/2/185.full.pdf+html

This article looks at writing in the workplace and community through the vehicle of IMC agency writers. The study is involved with the ways in which IMC writers create complex internal and external messages where writing is shaped not only by their organisational community but also by their outsider status with clients, their occupational writing and their genre expertise. The author claims to add a new layer of understanding to community theory and genre practices.

Sarkar, A.N. (2012) 'Green Supply Chain Management: a potent tool for sustainable green marketing', *Asia-Pacific Journal of Management Research and Innovation*, 8 (4): 491–507. http://abr.sagepub.com/content/8/4/491.full.pdf+html

This article looks at green supply chain management (GSCM) in the context of the Kyoto Protocol and in terms of the development of GSCM within the notion of 'going green' and what this means to an increasing number of consumers who prefer products that are toxin-free, lacking in contaminants and present minimal environmental or ecological hazards. The author argues for developments in GSCM that can be utilised for both corporate and product brand building. This has implications for marketing communication practice.

Sundstrom, B. (2012) 'Integrating Public Relations and Social Marketing: a case study of planned parenthood', *Social Marketing Quarterly*, 18 (2): 135–51. http://smq.sagepub.com/content/18/2/135.full.pdf+html

This article reports on a case study of the relationship between PR and social marketing in the context of a not-for-profit health organisation. The study revealed an integrated communications function. Publicity and other forms of promotion were being used in a tactical way but underlying this was the organisation's relational approach to a two-way dialogue within social marketing initiatives.

Thackeray, R., Neiger, B.L. and Keller, H. (2012) 'Integrating Social Media and Social Marketing: a four step process', *Health Promotion Practice*, 13 (2): 165–8. http://hpp.sagepub.com/content/13/2/165.full.pdf+html

This article argues that practitioners can realise social media's potential by using it as part of social marketing strategy. The authors claim that social media can put the consumer at the centre of the social marketing process and offer a four-step process that is a template for others to adopt for consumer-oriented health promotion programmes that utilise social media for real time, two-way communication.

REFERENCES

Anderson, J. (2011) A message from the CEO, Levi Strauss & Co., available at: www.levistrauss.com/about/leadership/message-ceo

BBC (1999) *Branded, Levi Strauss & Co. – Blue Dreams – exploring the success of the Levi jeans company*, BBC/Elgin Productions.

Brown, S. (1995) *Postmodern Marketing*. London: Routledge.

Burton, D. (2001) 'Critical marketing theory: the blueprint', *European Journal of Marketing*, 35 (5/6): 722–43.

Cornelissen, J. (2000) '"Integration" in communication management: conceptual and methodological considerations', *Journal of Marketing Management*, 16: 597–606.

De Pelsmaker, P., Geuens, M. and Van den Bergh, J. (2010) *Marketing Communications – a European perspective*, 4th edn. Harlow: Pearson Education Limited.

Elinder, E. (1961) 'How international can advertising be?', *International Adviser*, December: 12–16.

Fill, C. (2009) *Marketing Communications*, 5th edn. Harlow: Pearson Education Limited.

Gabrielli, V. and Balboni, B. (2009) 'SME practice towards integrated marketing communications', *Marketing Intelligence and Planning*, 28 (3): 275–90, available at: www.emeraldinsight.com/journals.htm?articleid=1863340

Gheorghe, P., Gardan, D. and Geangu, P. (2009) 'The importance of managerial communication in establishing the company marketing communication', The International Conference on Administration and Business, University of Bucharest, 14–15 November, pp. 316–22.

Hauck, B. (2011) 'Will product placement change TV?', *BBC News Magazine*, 17 February, available at: www.bbc.co.uk/news/magazine-12449502

Hills, J. (2006) 'Why integrated marketing communications is essential for small businesses', Ezinearticles, available at: www.ezinearticles.com/?Why-Integrated-Marketing-Communications-is-Essential-for-Small-Businesses&id=373353

Holm, O. (2006) 'Integrated marketing communication: from tactics to strategy', *Corporate Communications: An International Journal*, 11 (1): 23–33.

Homer, P.M. (2009) 'Product placements – the impact of placement type and repetition on attitude', *Journal of Advertising*, Fall, 38 (3): 21–31.

Hougaard, S. and Bjerre, M. (2009) *The Relationship Marketer: rethinking strategic relationship marketing*, 2nd edn. Heidelberg: Springer.

Hughes, G. and Fill, C.F. (2007) 'Redefining the nature and format of the marketing communications mix', *The Marketing Review*, 7 (1): 45–57.

Jensen, M.B. (2007) 'Online marketing communication potential – priorities in Danish firms and advertising agencies', *European Journal of Marketing*, 42 (3/4): 502–25.

Kent, R.A. (1986) 'Faith in Four Ps: an alternative', *Journal of Marketing Management*, 2 (2): 115–53.

Kitchen P.J., Kim, I. and Schultz, D.E. (2008) 'Integrated marketing communications: practice leads theory', *Journal of Advertising Research*, 48 (4): 531–46.

Kitchen P.J. and Schultz, D.E. (1999) 'A multi-country comparison of the drive for IMC', *Journal of Advertising Research*, 39 (1): 21–38.

Kliatchto, J. (2008) 'Revisiting the IMC construct – a revised definition and four pillars', *International Journal of Advertising*, 27 (1): 133–60.

Kotler, P. (1984) *Marketing Management – analysis, planning, implementation and control*, 5th edn. New Jersey: Prentice Hall.

Kotler, P. (1988) *Marketing Management – analysis, planning, implementation and control*, 6th edn. New Jersey: Prentice Hall.

Kotler, P., Armstrong, G., Saunders, J. and Wong, V. (2001) *Principles of Marketing*, 3rd European edn. Harlow: FT Prentice Hall.

Kotler, P. and Keller, K. (2009) *Marketing Management*, 13th edn. New Jersey: Prentice Hall.

Kotler, P. and Zaltman, G. (1971) 'Social marketing: an approach to planned social change', *Journal of Marketing*, 35, July: 3–12.

Kydd, J.M. (2009) 'Product placement's rise can be good for brand and viewer', *Admap*, 504, April: 44–5.

Levitt, T. (1983) 'The globalization of markets', *Harvard Business Review*, 61 (3) May–June: 92–102.

Linton, I. and Morley, K. (1995) *Integrated Marketing Communications*. Oxford: Butterworth-Heinemann.

McCartney, G., Butler, R. and Bennett, M. (2012) 'A strategic use of the communications mix in the destination image-formation process', *Journal of Travel Research*, 47 (2): 183–96.

McLuhan, M. (1962) *The Gutenberg Galaxy*. London: Routledge and Kegan Paul.

Naish, J. (2011) 'Not now Mum, we're watching junk food TV', *The Times*, 8 February: 48–9.

Percy, L. (2006) 'Are product placements effective?', *International Journal of Advertising*, 25 (1): 112–14.

Pickton, D. (2010) 'Integrating integrated marketing communications; 3 models, 4 Cs, 4 Es, 4 Ss and a profile'. Academy of Marketing Conference, Coventry University, July.

Pope-Ruark, R. (2008) 'Challenging the necessity of organisational community for rhetorical genre use: community and genre in the work of integrated marketing communication agency writers', *Business Communication Quarterly*, 71 (2): 185–94.

Precourt, G. (2010) 'Revival through disruption: how Levi's reconnected with its core audience', Warc Exclusive, April, available at: www.warc.com

Robinson, J. (2010) 'Ofcom confirms product placement on UK TV', available at: www.guardian.co.uk/media/2010/dec/20/ofcom-product-placement-uk-tv

Sarkar, A.N. (2012) 'Green supply chain management: a potent tool for sustainable green marketing', *Asia-Pacific Journal of Management Research and Innovation*, 8 (4): 491–507.

Schultz, D.E. (1996) 'New trends in communication and advertising', lecture to the University of Strathclyde Business School, 16 October.

Schultz, D.E. and Kitchen, P.J. (2000) *Communicating Globally: an integrated marketing approach.* London: Macmillan Press.

Schultz, D.E. and Schultz, H.F. (1998) 'Transitioning marketing communication into the twenty-first century', *Journal of Marketing Communications*, 4 (1): 9–26.

Schultz, D.E., Tannenbaum S.I. and Lauterborn R.F. (1993) *Integrated Marketing Communications – pulling it together and making it work.* Chicago: NTC Business Books.

Sheenan, K.B. and Doherty, C. (2001) 'Re-weaving the web: integrating print and online communications', *Journal of Interactive Marketing*, 15 (2): 47–59.

Smith, M. (1999) 'Levi Sta-Prest Denim', IPA Advertising for Education Seminar, London.

Smith, P., Berry, C. and Pulford, A. (1997, 2002) *Strategic Marketing Communications.* London: Kogan Page.

Smith, P.R. (1993) *Marketing Communications.* London: Kogan Page.

Sundstrom, B. (2012) 'Integrating public relations and social marketing: a case study of planned parenthood', *Social Marketing Quarterly*, 18 (2): 135–51.

Swain, W.N. (2004) 'Perceptions of IMC after a decade of development: who's at the wheel, and how can we measure success?', *Journal of Advertising Research*, 44 (1): 46–65.

Sweney, M. (2009) 'Internet overtakes television to become biggest advertising sector in the UK', *The Guardian*, 30 September, available at: www.guardian.co.uk/media/2009/sep/30/internet-biggest-uk-advertising-sector

Sweney, M. (2011) 'What future for product placement?' *The Guardian*, 28 February.

Tadajewski, M. and Brownlie, D. (eds) (2008) *Critical Marketing: Issues in Contemporary Marketing.* Chichester: John Wiley and Sons.

Van Reijmersdal, E., Neijens, P. and Smit, E.G. (2009) 'A new branch of advertising: reviewing factors that influence reactions to product placements', *Journal of Advertising Research*, December, 49 (4): 429–49.

Whiting, D. (2010) 'Is marketing playing with just one club?', *Market Leader*, Quarter 3: 51.

2 Theoretical Underpinnings of Marketing Communications

CHAPTER OVERVIEW

Introduction

In this chapter the nature of communication theory is explored in terms of what this means for both marketing and corporate contexts. Many of the theoretical models available were established during the 1960s but some of the key ideas have been around for much longer. Other, more recent, developments have tried to bring buyer behaviour theory closer to that of communications. In particular the traditional view of the communications process has been fused with the 'hierarchy of effects' model to offer further insight into the workings of marketers' communications and the likely effects of such communications on recipients, and this is looked at in Chapter 3 of this book. This chapter concentrates on the ways in which senders of a message can get meaning across to a recipient. Clearly the idea is to have fidelity or truth, i.e. the marketer as transmitter of a message wants that message to be received without ambiguity so that there is purity about the shared meaning of the message between transmitter and receiver. This is a difficult task, there being degrees of complexity in the transmission process. There are many and varied ways of putting a message across but not all are 100 per cent accurate by any means. It is recognised that the context in which communications takes place is important and that the interaction, engagement and co-creation of messages and brands are now firmly established as essential ingredients in the communications process. The role of personal influence, the power of word-of-mouth and the usefulness of adoption/diffusion models are explored. Traditional, relational and critical approaches to marketing and marketing communication in such contexts offer alternative views of communications working in practice.

Learning objectives

The chapter seeks to explore and explain the theoretical underpinnings of communication and to underscore the usefulness and limitations of theory to practice. More specifically, after reading this chapter the student will be able to:

- understand marketing communications theory in terms of the needs of communications practitioners and their clients;
- appreciate the basic model of communication within an historical context;
- assess the impact personal influence has on the communications process;
- assess the usefulness of the adoption and diffusion process as an aid to the marketing communicator;
- appreciate other communications models and theories that can help inform practitioner decision-making.

COMMUNICATION THEORY

A model of mass communication

Marketing communicators tell marketing stories about organisations and brands and as Fletcher (2003) points out, marketing stories can be 'expressed in terms of words, music, images, staff behaviour, attitudes and dress' and can involve 'POS materials, packaging design and interior design of the retail space'. Stories 'range from highly aspirational and/or symbolic to the profoundly functional; from the knowingly ironic to the bluntly straightforward; from the apparently rational to the unashamedly emotive; from the humorous to the heavy; the sexy to the sage'. These can be embodied in many forms, from complex mini films to simple straplines or statements of product benefits.

The communications process is about meaning transfer. Numerous models have been developed in this area that help further develop this general framework for understanding, there being a number of views on how communication conveys meaning and whether this is mediated or unmediated communication. The commonest framework presented in the literature and in textbooks deals with the problems of one-way mass communication, although it does have a feedback loop that indicates the source is likely to search for, or expect some form of, recipient feedback. The source is usually the marketing organization and the receiver the consumer, though not always. To complete this process accurately is a very difficult task to achieve. The process looks simple but in practice is far from this. The basic model is shown below:

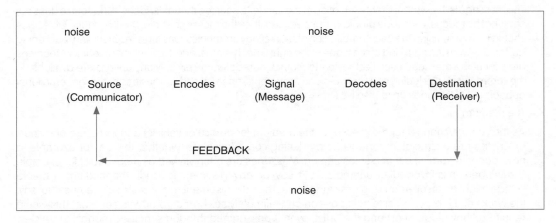

Figure 2.1   A basic model of the communications process

For this to be of any practical use in the real world it has, of course, to aid the marketer in terms of effective and efficient communications. Fundamentally, the idea is for the communicator to be in a position to understand the (target) recipient well enough to be able to encode desired messages with a high degree of certainty that there will be no 'noise' in the system that may distort the message. The task is to understand how decoding will occur and allow for the subsequent transfer of pure, unadulterated meaning free from distortion.

A frequently adopted model of the communications process in marketing terms is that of Schramm (1971), revised from Schramm's 1955 model and in itself derived from Lasswell's (1948) semantic description, and the original model by Shannon (1948) and Shannon and Weaver (1949, revised 1962) of the communication process. Many textbook and journal article writers have adopted this model to help explain the basic communications process and use this as a fundamental building block. It has long been recognised that there are linkages between each of the elements or stages and that these are important to how communication works. The elements of the process are here explained and broken down into their own constituents in order that the model can be better understood.

Taking these in turn:

- Sender/Source

   A person, group of people, company or some other organisation may wish to transmit/relay an idea, set of ideas or a proposition in order to share something with another party. This, out of necessity, includes the encoding of a message in some shape or form with the intention of achieving one or more of the communications objectives and necessarily involves the sender/source itself as part of that message. The source characteristics outlined in the Kelman (1958, 1961) model later in this chapter (including the use of celebrities) apply here so that sales people, advertising and so on should have elements of trust, likeability, attractiveness, power or other characteristics in order to, for example, influence or persuade.

- Encoding

   If the problem is perceived incorrectly by the source then the wrong concept might be developed and encoded making the communication faulty. Some form of situation or context analysis is useful here, which should be based on sound research. There is concern for actuality and perception, where any mismatch is the perception itself in the mind of the transmitter. This makes a lot of sense in the real world of everyday experience where thoughts/ideas have been translated into symbolic form. The problem lies in the task of getting the right sentences, words and symbols and so on from a vast array of verbal and non-verbal elements that will communicate effectively.

- The message

   The message is the symbolic representation of the sender's/source's thoughts/ideas. If the source does not say what he means, even if the problem is understood, then the message strategy will be faulty. Objectives should be met by using the best combination of marketing communications tools – advertising, packaging and so on – with the right kind of message at the right time. The message itself has no meaning. Meanings are part of the message user, i.e. the sender/source or recipient/receiver. Many options are available to the communicator including one- or two-sided arguments, open/closed conclusions or rational/emotional appeals. All of this adds up to creative strategy.

- The medium

   As the conduit/channel for the message, the medium (or particular vehicle) and its nature and characteristics are of crucial importance to marketing communicators, whether this be, for example, a newspaper, a trade show or a sales person. Messages are often viewed as mediated (if for example a sales person is involved) or unmediated (if, say, an advertisement is used). The medium or media vehicle might be an up-market, glossy magazine. The advertisement might well use references to, say, the works of a famous artist to help position and ultimately sell brands/products/services. This would require a knowledge of art and the artist, even if only gained through simplistic magazine articles, which would be enough to allow the advertisement to work on the reader. In other words, as Marshall McLuhan famously remarked, 'the medium is the message', i.e. the medium is seen as all important. In this sense it is not only what the marketer says or even how the marketer says it, but also the means by which it is said that are important.

- Decoding

  This involves deriving meaning from the received message that is a composite of the actual message sent and any influences the medium may have had upon it. If the receiver does not understand the message or does not interpret it in the way it was meant then communication is faulty. Many feel that in marketing communications terms there is a need for clarity and simplicity where, for example, key selling points are understood. Others advocate much more complex approaches involving devices such as metaphors or metonyms, which have meaning not only for the sender but also for the receiver of the message. It is from this perspective that it can be seen how even the largest of corporations will make faux pas, often through misreading cultural values, customs or practice.

- Recipient/Receiver

  The receiver is normally the person or people, or organization (hence the reason why some writers prefer to use the catch-all DMU – decision making unit), that the sender wishes to share thoughts, ideas and so on, with. This of course will not always be the case since, clearly, others will receive the message that is not intended for them. The receiver might understand the message but might ignore or forget it. In marketing communications circumstances some believe that repetition can 'educate' the customer/ consumer over a period of time.

- Feedback

  This loop of the process provides the sender/source with a channel of evaluation of the message encoded and sent. This can be viewed in two ways. First in terms of how accurately the message has hit the target and second in terms of the degree of correctness of interpretation on the part of the recipient/receiver from that intended. This then allows the sender/source to correct any ineffectual or misdirected messages. Typically viewed in marketing terms as a marketing research opportunity, this involves straightforward activities such as coupon redemption in sales promotions as well as things such as awareness scores, attitudinal change, image studies and tracking studies. It could also be instantaneous as in the personal selling situation where questions can be asked directly to obtain feedback or through observation of, say, non-verbal behaviour or body language. Some of this may be continuous rather than ad hoc.

- Noise

  The notion of noise can be misconstrued. It is not a question of making enough noise in order to be heard, like a shelf screamer in a supermarket that is designed to attract attention. Rather, the term noise was used originally to denote interference or impedance, for example of a radio signal. These are terms often used interchangeably to describe the blocking or distortion of the message at any stage in the marketing communications process. This can take many forms, from the poor signal on radio or television resulting in poor sound and/or vision to the lack of knowledge or information that causes a consumer to be unable to fully understand. Noise can therefore be physical or cognitive and can be anything from interruption by a secretary to the sheer amount of clutter in a newspaper or magazine. The communicator's task is to minimise noise. This becomes more complex at the international level, but the communicator must seek 'high fidelity', otherwise there will be decoding problems.

Critique of the original process

There are 'strategic consequences of miscommunication' according to Anand and Shachar (2007), who refer to 'the uncertainty over receivers' perception as "noisy communication"' where senders do not have full control over this perception but where senders can improve their communication, for example by providing more information to consumers. These authors are interested in how 'much the sender invests in improving the precision of his message' rather than what the sender says or does not say and they argue that using 'multiple ads' can be a costly way to improve the precision of the message. It is of course recognised that the marketer is not the only player in this game. The target is another player but other influences are part of the process – the bullet theory (Schramm, 1971) or hypodermic effect (Klapper, 1960) having been rejected for some time with an emerging preference for interaction, engagement and integration rather than linear thought. At the heart of this are technological (especially media) changes and the ways in which the consumer has changed, as discussed in the first chapter of this book where creating a dialogue rather than mono-logue was emphasised. Buttle (1995) provides a clear analysis of commonalties within the various representations of the communication process, identifying four such commonalties and concluding that marketing communications theory fails to draw on the very disciplines it should. Four common themes emerge in what Buttle calls 'normal marketing communica-tions'. These are:

- A focus on the individual, where family/household, institutional and cultural levels are left out. For example the age-old 'what we do during the commercial break' question or the social context of advertising reception would apply to family or household contexts. Institutional effects include the message production and delivery systems involving companies, agencies and so on that are an interlocking network of institutions like voluntary codes and lobby groups. Cultural effects are both cognitive and critical. Cognitive involves for example cultural values, mores and so on whereas critical involves Marxist and feminist views, dealing with institutional structures and the way society is organised.
- A focus on individual messages is clearly a problem if estimates such as 3,000 marketing-controlled messages bombard individuals each day are accurate. Cumulative impact should be taken into account. Added to the effect of marketing communication stimuli, other stimuli exist outside of the marketing communications area that have impact.
- A focus on the source's intent where cumulative impact, shared meaning, derived symbolic meaning and, not least, meaning derived from non-promotional marketing and other variables are bound to have some sort of effect. Belief in the notion of the passive audience is long gone. The view that 'people do something to the content' has superseded the view that the communications content 'does something to people', at least in the minds of those who favour the interactive approach. The notion of source intent is clearly not without problems. The relationship (between content and audience) to message content whereby the 'exposure tradition' holds that power is in the content whereas the 'gratification tradition' holds that power is in the hands of the audience. The 'interactive tradition' has power with both.
- A focus on co-orientation, whereby to avoid problems with fidelity the communicator can opt for a closed text to avoid misreading, misunderstanding and so on. This, of course, ignores the social and other contexts people necessarily operate in and that might produce multiple meanings because messages get 'contextualised'.

Buttle therefore condemns the usual marketing communications theory as ill-informed and narrowly focused. The danger in educational/learning terms is that lecturers think that this is what students need to be practitioners. Much of this is steeped in 1940s and 50s thought with many important parameters unaccounted for and ignored. In a sense one can argue that such parameters are accounted for within the notion of 'realm of understand-ing/field of experience/frame of reference' as depicted in Figure 2.2 below.

Realm of understanding/field of experience/frame of reference

This is often included in representations of the marketing communications process to indi-cate the possibilities of overlap between sender and receiver so that 100 per cent common-ness of field of experience or 'perceptual field' (Shimp, 2010) is a possibility. This is referred to by Dahlen et al. (2010) as 'frame of reference'. It is in this light that one cannot escape the feeling of opportunities being lost through not pursuing a greater understanding of such effects. The marketing communicator, it has been argued, has a lot to gain from the partici-pation of a broader spectrum of professionals such as sociologists, anthropologists, semio-ticians, cognitive scientists or psychoanalysts. This was a qualitative shift that suggested at

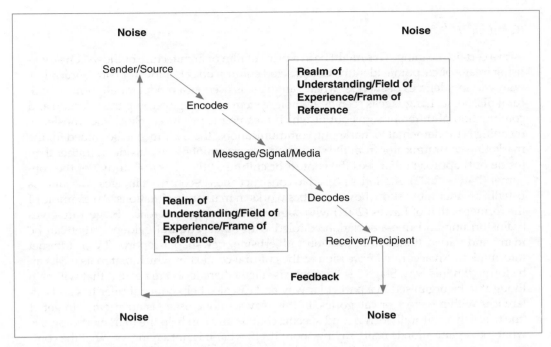

Figure 2.2   The marketing communications process

Sources: Fill (2009), Shimp (2010) Danlen et al. (2010))

the time a new phase 'in the attempts to penetrate the secrets of the black box' (Mattelart and Chanan, 1991). This was one attempt to better understand the 'encode–decode' process, which continues to this day.

The Snapshot below illustrates the attempts at 'black box penetration' through the application of semiotic research where manufacturers and consumers create and extract meanings in the marketplace. Often intricate theory has to become a practical reality and help real companies with real challenges, whether such challenges are in creative advertising, with the brand or with design.

Snapshot   What is a butler? An argument for the use of semiotic approaches in everyday marketing communication practice across cultures

Semiotics (applied semiology, the science of signs and symbols) can be seen in many fields of endeavour, not least marketing and (consumer) marketing research. Hetzel and Marion used Fouquier's 1984 work to depict the communication process in terms of the 'field of semiotic description' (Hetzel and Marion,1995). The way in which the semiotician tackles the real world is by seeking to describe not what is real but that which is constructed in and by a particular discourse. Self-images of senders and receivers and the constructed world must be taken into account. Semiotic reality is the reality of language (used in the widest sense of the word) and its goal is to build models that are constructed

(Continued)

(Continued)

with a certain meaning. This might be in a piece of film or architecture or indeed an advertising image or corporate identity. Constructed cultural objects allow for communication, with varying degrees of success, where language is used as a model for all forms of cultural discourse. Language is seen as a whole system of rules governing the selection and combination of different signs out of which meaning is produced. Since the transfer of meaning is fundamental to marketing communications, there is much to be gained for the marketing communicator from the study and use of semiotics, an outside-in (rather than inside-out) approach that sees the context or culture as the object of study not the consumer (Lawes, 2002). Semiotics is used to construct and de-construct images. The latter is usually an attempt to show how semiotics works in marketing situations. An example of the former is that of Lawes (2002) who suggests a two-stage approach. Stage 1 involves brainstorming and free association coupled with other 'cultural evidence' that can be many and varied things from previous advertising, newspaper reports, TV or Internet information. An accurate impression of the cultural context in which materials exist can be formed in this way. Stage 2 is the analysis stage where tools are needed that will help thought to be organised in a particular way and can also help notice similarities and differences within sectors or categories. In this way semiotic usage is an attempt to get at 'the truth' in a culturally driven and specific context and can help the marketer recognise what the organisation is really saying about itself, what it is not saying, or what the competition is saying about itself. It is capable of providing firstly codes that are the organisation's own and those of others. It can also highlight subtle differences in behaviour that can aid more effective communication. Through semiotic study, consumer culture can be monitored and changes detected as with, for example, emergent and discontinued codes, personal expression through taste, or how consumption interacts with lifestyle.

In a semiotic world the receiver is no longer a passive receiver of messages but brings in their own experiences and culture, even if their response is a silent one. The advertising industry has for some time used the work of sociologists, anthropologists, semioticians and other professionals who are expert in particular aspects of qualitative research (Mattelart and Chanan, 1991). Language is seen as a whole system of rules governing the selection and combination of different signs out of which meaning is produced. A semiotic study is an applied study of the system of signs where a sign is something that has significance within a system of meaning.

Semiotic analysis has been applied across many areas of life. For example Pang's (2008) study looks at the semiotics of the counterfeit in relation to China being 'understood by the world as a pirate nation' rather than counterfeiting being an outcome of global capitalism and not the character of a particular people. Pang is interested in the negative meanings associated with copying and the myth of creativity that the economic system needs to hold it together.

Stop Point

Try asking people from different cultures whether they understand the concept of a butler. This can be very difficult if they have not (culturally) experienced this phenomenon. Undertaken the following: 1. This kind of dilemma arose for Nestlé with the Rowntree chocolate brand Kit Kat whereby the brand's strapline had been 'have a break, have a Kit Kat', based on the British (or even English) notion of a tea break. Write a 300-word explanation that would enlighten brand mangers as to how thinking semiotically might help; 2. Discuss the notion of negative meaning that can be generated by culture-specific symbols or practices in the context of how semiotic approaches can enhance our understanding of such meaning.

KELMAN'S SOURCE CHARACTERISTICS MODEL AND AFTER

Social influence processes of, in particular, identification and internalisation but also of compliance (Kelman having identified a conflict between external compliance and internal agreement) have for some decades provided a framework that helps explain the persuasive (marketing) influences on consumers and customers. Kelman (1958) had proposed three processes of attitude change. These are:

- *Compliance* – where a person acts on a request while apparently agreeing to it but they in fact may not and may very well feel tension and even dissonance if the action is at odds with their beliefs. In marketing and marketing communications terms this has been to do with stimulus and response, with reward and punishment. For example, for a consumer not to respond to a sales promotion is an opportunity lost. Similarly a sales person can be incentivised by a bonus system to behave in a certain way, to try to achieve sales targets set where the reward is in the bonus system and the punishment is losing out while other, similar, colleagues gain. A manufacturer used to be able to use trade promotions in the same way with retailers in terms of trade incentives as a way of achieving compliance in stocking products but this has changed somewhat in recent years with the transference of some channel power to retailers, as discussed in Chapter 1 of this book. The power of some 'super brands' or 'power brands' is also in a state of flux with, for example, the UK retailer Tesco deciding to have a cull on suppliers and 'replace their products with its own brand and "power brands" produced by its key strategic partners in its Central European stores', meaning much less shelf space for tertiary brands and more for own label and the likes of Procter and Gamble (Quinn, 2011).
- *Identification* – where the person identifies with the speaker and accepts/believes the point of view put forward. This may involve some sort of leadership role for the originator. In marketing and marketing communications terms consumers or customers may identify and even bond with the speaker (often a company or company spokesperson) where values are accepted and trust, commitment and potentially loyalty to the company and its brand may follow.
- *Internalisation* – where the person accepts and adopts the proposition, idea or belief without coercion or need to conform or be associated with others. This takes considerable thought in order to accept or modify ideas into a consumer's or customer's belief system. This is allied to the elaboration likelihood model and the 'central route' (as opposed to the peripheral route) of conscious persuasion that requires rational argument and to high and low involvement products, as discussed in Chapter 3 of this book. Kelman's (1961) model is depicted in Figure 2.3 below.

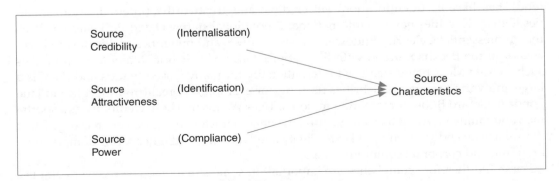

Figure 2.3   Kelman's (1961) Source Characteristics Model

The source of persuasive influence in marketing and marketing communications' terms might be a commercial company but equally it might be some other organisation such as a charity or a government department. A spokesperson might be used to represent the organisation. Endorsers such as Sir Robert Mark, an ex-top UK police chief, were thought to be very *credible* with issues such as road safety and hence good, credible, endorsers of, say, quality car tyres (the Goodyear brand) that will stop well in difficult conditions. For many decades sports men and women have been persuaded (often by lucrative fees) to become the spokesperson for the brand. Part of this arrangement is the credibility for example in terms of achievement in the sport, leadership/captaincy of others or knowledge of the game.

As might be expected, a high credibility source is not necessarily the most effective tool in certain situations. The use of a high credibility source is of less importance when receivers have a neutral position. This is clearly plausible with regard to low and high involvement products and where risk is or is not involved. This is dependent upon product type whereby everyday, low-involvement products can be promoted in such a way that the source does not need credibility, but promotion with the aid of a celebrity endorser could be effective through attractiveness. Credibility can also come through association with another organisation. Attempts have been made to associate a manufacturer's products with the bravery of fire crews, as often seen on news bulletins and other media coverage. However, care must be taken when attempting to associate products or services with organisations like those of the rescue services, such as that of the Automobile Association (AA) in the UK with the relatively recent and somewhat controversial 'The 4th Emergency Service' campaign. Another long-running campaign of association is that of Cadbury's Milk Tray brand of chocolates that lasted 35 years until 2003. This campaign had a James Bond-like 'action hero' figure as the main protagonist who would go to any lengths to bring home the chocolate 'all because the lady loves Milk Tray'.

That is not to say that all credible sources have to be celebrities. Sales staff can have credibility through the way they dress or acquire credibility through knowledge acquisition. Industry specialists such as civil engineers who are known in a particular context to have expertise can have a high level of credibility in terms of, say, bridge building and therefore can be extremely good endorsers of products such as construction, plant and equipment; for example a rough terrain handler forklift used to help build bridges.

Empathy or correlation between source and recipient means that the receiver will find the source *attractive* and a relationship can then develop where the latter sees themself in the situation depicted – say, through slice of life advertising – i.e. relates to it, identifies with it and the problems it solves. Actors are often put in situations intended to reflect the lives of the recipient of the message. Celebrity endorsers such as TV chef Jamie Oliver, 'The Naked Chef' (who was the endorser of the UK retailer Sainsbury's – especially Sainsbury's food), has likeable (identification) yet credible and trustworthy (internalisation) qualities. Other celebrities have an international if not global status. David Beckham has been the quintessential Celebrity Endorser across the 1990s and noughties and is of course co-creator of the Beckham brand with his ex-Spice Girl wife Victoria. Many fashion models such as Kate Moss have been used internationally for many varied brands and there is a large and varied range of celebrities used by, for example, L'Oreal (from Beyonce to Jane Fonda to Gerard Butler for targeting reasons). Tiger Woods had both credibility as a sportsman and family man and likeability/attractiveness characteristics until very recently. These days celebrity endorsers are used extensively in advertising and other forms of marketing, branding and corporate communications).

Power and therefore compliance are important in some situations. The receiver complies in order to either obtain a reward or avoid punishment. The portrayal of a police officer as the source in an anti-drink driving or speed message is an example of the use of power. Power is more easily seen in a personal communications situation where both the stick and carrot are in evidence. Expense accounts, type of car allowance, bonus rewards and penalties and so on are commonplace. Sales people may have the power to give discounts and sales managers to give incentives, for example. A relatively recent trend (started in the USA) in advertising has been to use CEOs who might be said to have all three types of characteristic. CEOs such as Victor Kiam (USA and globally, Remington shavers) who famously said that he liked the product so much that he bought the company. Kiam was the spokesperson for the company and he inspired people through his enthusiasm and likeability as part of source characteristics. He also did all of his own television advertising voice-overs in the language of the market the advertising appeared in, making him quite an impressive source. Other famous CEOs are Richard Branson (UK and global, Virgin) whereby the promotion of the person has been used to promote both the Virgin brand and the company. There are many other examples from Bill Gates (USA and globally, Microsoft) to Ratan Tata (India and globally, Tata Group).

Research by Newell and Shemwell (1995) supports the importance of credibility for CEO endorsers where source credibility has a strong and direct impact on purchase intentions. This research underlines the importance of testing with the target market the believability of the executive concerned. These researchers suggest that, for example, for radio and television, warmth meter tests might be appropriate in establishing a sounder theoretical base in the area and in particular measuring believability. Also, the findings from this research support a model in which beliefs about product/brand attributes mediate the effect of source credibility on behavioural intentions, leading to the assertion that CEO endorsers may be better suited to informational advertising rather than advertising that emphasises affective associations and brand recognition. If a product needs supporting at the introductory or growth stage of the product lifecycle the CEO endorser might be used to communicate significant product improvements (Newell and Shemwell, 1995). These writers note that the research finding should be viewed as being context-specific and that much more work would be needed before any generalisations could be made.

STEP FLOW OR PERSONAL INFLUENCE MODELS

These are very simplistic and usually involve one, two or multi step flows, *opinion leaders/formers/followers*. Opinion leaders and formers are described and illustrated later in this chapter. Opinion followers are those people in a particular context who simply follow the leader/former. Opinion leaders/formers/followers can have relevance to the theory of adoption and diffusion of innovations (discussed below) and to the strength of word-of-mouth (also dealt with in Chapter 3 of this book from a behaviour point of view). Numerous models have been developed in this area that are said to provide general frameworks for understanding. Step Flow or Personal Influence 'models' were established by the 1960s. Here the message is encoded, transmitted and decoded by the receiver but this then includes the role of the opinion leader and word-of-mouth with others to move from one to two to multi step flows of the message, which necessarily mutates, and where the meaning intended by the sender can be either enriched or changed in some other way. This is illustrated in Figure 2.4.

People are affected by family and friends (homophilous groups) and by those outside an individual's personal network (heterphilous groups) rather than the mass media (Dahlen et al., 2010). This is social mediation that produces opinion leaders and opinion formers. The bullet theory mentioned earlier would have us believe that a message can be shot like a bullet

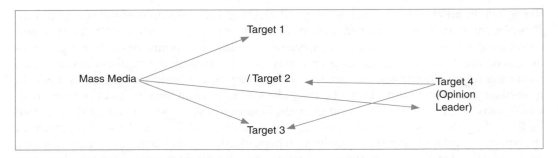

Figure 2.4 Step flow personal influence model

at a target. However, the simplest of situations can become very complex. Each target can either be passive or reactive, depending upon the effect of the message. Figure 2.4 above illustrates the situation where target 1 is passive (illustrating a one-step flow) while target 2 is blocked from the message by some sort of noise. Target 2 is informed of the message by target 4 who is also an opinion leader. Target 3 receives the message directly but is also informed by the opinion leader, target 4, who in this case has received the message but in other cases may not have done but might still have influenced other targets. In other words the mass media is not the only influence and may not be an influence at all. Some form of multi-step flow of information is much more likely in reality. This is illustrated in Figure 2.5 below.

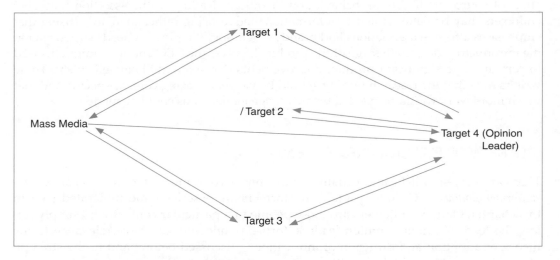

Figure 2.5 Multi-step flow personal influence model

Opinion leaders, formers and followers are important links in the communications chain. From the above it can be clearly seen that interaction takes place. Closely related to this is the power of word-of-mouth, whereby personal recommendations can enrich the communication process.

The literature has supported and continues to support the idea of the potency of word-of-mouth (the phrase word-of-mouse has now been coined to reflect the impact of online marketing) that can give a depth of credibility other forms of communication cannot. There are long-established characteristics of opinion leadership (after Dichter, 1966), which are:

- *product involvement* (people have a high propensity to discuss matters that are distinctly pleasurable or unpleasurable);
- *self-involvement* (people might wish to show ownership for prestige reasons or may wish to seek reassurance to reduce dissonance);
- *other involvement* (expressions of love, friendship and caring are aspects of the motivation to help others whereby product benefits can be passed on or shared); and
- *message involvement* (the motivation to discuss products comes from the marketing stimuli that surround them, in particular advertising, provoking conversation and to stimulate word-of-mouth recommendation).

Getting people talking about a brand is clearly important. One of the ways to achieve this is through advertising in various media (including the actual wearing of branded clothes). The marketer's objective should be advocacy of the brand. This means getting the brand, advertising and other communication talked about in a positive manner and many organisations have been successful at this for their brands in multiple, international markets; for example Guinness.

Targeting those who will carry the message on is therefore clearly important. Opinion leaders can thus be ordinary people but who will be predisposed to having an effect on others. Not just in brand/marketing terms but also in many other walks of life that may or may not interface with marketing activities. They are normally the same social class but have a higher status within a particular context. For example an opinion leader may be a colleague who just happens to be the biggest influence when it comes to a particular activity. Within this context they may have the highest level of confidence because of their knowledge base (of products and brands, the activity itself, or the media, for example specialist magazines), are more outgoing. Opinion leaders can be used in advertising of any sort. They are used to promote washing powders, for example, in the consumer packaged goods context but also to promote in more specialist contexts such as upmarket outdoor clothing.

Closely allied to the opinion leader is the opinion former who is normally some form of professional rather than an ordinary person who for whatever reason has some form of authority or status. Celebrity endorsers can be seen as opinion formers, especially on the consumer side where many examples exist from breakfast cereal to packets of crisps. On the organisational side, an example might be a civil engineering project manager who could be used to sway an entire industry's buyers into at least considering a particular brand of rough terrain dump truck. The term 'brand ambassador' has also been used by the likes of the ice-cream brand Haagen Dazs to describe someone in the media spotlight who is prepared to become an advocate of the brand in a PR manner, as opposed to celebrity endorsers who are allied to advertising. It need not be actual people who form opinions. In any market, perceived experts can be used to help form opinions, especially through devices such as columns in national newspapers or magazines. It can be whole TV shows and other media items that become formers of others' opinions on anything from forklift trucks to cars, wine to restaurants. It is not always the case that an opinion former is a deliberate ploy to shape things, as the example of Jack Daniel's illustrates, since this brand was fortunate enough to acquire unofficial but famous spokespeople willingly singing the brand's praises.

Opinion followers, often referred to as the 'admass' in mass media terms, are usually the majority of people in a given context who by definition do not lead or form but follow opinion and are influenced by both personal and non-personal communications. Opinion followers are referred to again below in terms of the adoption and diffusion of innovations.

The Snapshot below discusses the employment of celebrity endorsers for use in marketing communications but especially within advertising. The use of such sources is clearly linked to some of the theoretical models discussed in this chapter. The opportunities for the use of celebrity endorsers and some of the problems that might accompany such use are explained.

Snapshot   Celebrity endorsement – lost in translation?

Celebrity endorsement is now a common feature in advertising of all types, from television to magazines, cinema to online. There is a relatively high percentage share of celebrity endorsement used in advertising. Estimates suggest that a quarter of all US commercials contain some form of celebrity endorsement (for example Silvera and Austad, 2004; White et al., 2009). Another source suggests that by the mid-noughties the endorsement value of the world's 75 top athletes was more than half a billion pounds (Shank, 2005). An endorser can be 'broadly defined as any individual who appears in an advertisement as a spokesperson' (Lafferty, 2008) for a product or more likely a brand. If the endorser is well known and has celebrity status then this practice is usually known as 'celebrity endorsement'. Typically a celebrity endorser is therefore a famous person who uses public recognition to recommend or to co-present a product or brand in an advertisement. It is not just in the consumer products arena where endorsement takes place. Canning and West (2006) discuss celebrity endorsement in business markets, highlighting prominent individuals but also 'celebrity organisations' who might be customers or associated with the organisation in some way. An example of a prominent individual who fits the 'cultural milieu' of customers in the business environment is Virgin boss Richard Branson who is associated with a relaxed management style, competitive spirit and fun. An example of 'celebrity organisation' is Lufthansa Cargo as used with the Windows Server System, i.e. an organisation with a compatible image is used to endorse another through the use of congruence (Canning and West, 2006). The effects of celebrity endorsement can be felt beyond those who identify with an actual celebrity. Celebrities can activate bundles of social norms and influence the behaviour of other people (Lindenberg et al., 2011).

The characteristics of the celebrity, whether an actor, singer, sports personality or CEO, are usually centred on either credibility and/or attractiveness. The former requires expertise for validity. The latter needs trustworthiness and willingness for validity, but there are other characteristics such as likeability. A study by Magnini et al. (2008) suggested that celebrities need to be perceived to have trustworthiness and expertise but also that they genuinely support the endorsed item. The study also found that the endorsement will work better if the celebrity is perceived to be part of the consumer's reference group. The endorser might not be famous but might have high credibility as an opinion former, such as a dentist or wine expert. The objectives behind the use of endorsement are to gain attention, enhance the persuasiveness of the message, increase recall and differentiate the brand from the competition (Lafferty, 2008). Gaining attention to get through the clutter is a key objective and the use of celebrity endorsement can help in the process of getting consumers to listen in the first place and then remember the message and the brand name (White et al., 2009). Magnini et al. (2008) underscore the use of the 'proper celebrity' to get through the clutter and to bolster brand image and actual sales, but when 'an inappropriate celebrity' is selected this can 'severely reduce sales and brand reputation'; there has to be a match between 'the celebrity's and company's image and values'. Fionda and Moore (2008), on luxury fashion brands, suggest the importance of celebrity endorsement in advertising that can establish brand image and assist with identity and attraction. The employment of celebrity endorsement is an attempt to build a congruent image for the brand as perceived by the consumer, as was the case with the successful use of the source characteristics of Jamie Oliver (*The Naked Chef* in the UK television series) for Sainsbury's in the UK and for Foodstuffs in New Zealand (Byrne et al., 2003).

Stop Point

The source characteristics-type models of Kelman and others can be seen in the use of celebrity endorsement, which is clearly visible but its value is being questioned, largely because of the costs involved but also because of the problematic nature of some celebrity endorsements. Undertake the following: 1. Outline the issues that surround the use of celebrity in terms of cost and problems; 2. Examine the international context in terms of crossing borders, an action that brings with it another dimension and layer of issues.

INNOVATION THEORY AND RELATIONAL EXCHANGE

The adoption and diffusion of innovations

The work on the adoption and diffusion of innovations and more specifically the innovation curve as provided by Rogers (1962) is much referred to in marketing theory and may be known to the reader already. Innovation Theory links to the previous section in that innovators and early adopters of products/brands and ideas generally have opinion leading and forming characteristics. This deals with prior conditions of previous practice, felt needs/problems, innovativeness and norms of the social systems that feed in to communications channels as illustrated in Figure 2.6.

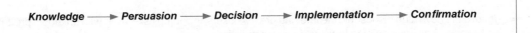
Knowledge ⟶ *Persuasion* ⟶ *Decision* ⟶ *Implementation* ⟶ *Confirmation*

Figure 2.6 The innovation-decision process

This is influenced by the characteristics of the decision-making unit (DMU) that are based on sociometrics, personality and behaviour and the perceived characteristics of innovation (relative advantage, compatibility, complexity, trialability and observability) leading to either continued or later adoption or rejection by discontinuance or continued rejection.

As with all stage models each stage is sequential, hierarchical and in this sense is open to the usual criticism of stages being left out, or stages being out of sequence. This model is, however, useful from the marketing communications perspective with regard to objectives and strategy (for example providing persuasive information through a particular media vehicle). Roger's five stages are:

- *Knowledge* – the DMU becomes aware of the innovation but has nothing to go on. The opportunity is there to provide (persuasive) information through channels such as the media.
- *Persuasion* – the perceived characteristics of the innovation become important, as do the messages from the media, opinion leaders and other sources.
- *Decision* – attitudes are formed and a decision to adopt or reject the innovation made. Communication is clearly important in this.
- *Implementation* – the DMU needs to know how to access the innovation for trial if not rejected and communication has its role to play in this.
- *Confirmation* – post-trial the innovation will either continue or be delayed or be rejected. It may well be re-adopted or rejected continuously. The DMU can be assisted in this process by persuasive communication, helping dispel worries or negativity and a reaffirmation of the original decision with post-behavioural consolidation.

Generally these five stages can be linked to objectives. The earlier stages are usually linked to impersonal communications and the later stages to personal communication.

The process of adoption and diffusion of innovations is theoretical and the curve need not be normal as depicted, but can be skewed depending upon the make-up of the population or sample. It can also have a shorter time span to indicate the rate of diffusion. The importance of innovators and early adopters in terms of word-of-mouth communications should not be underestimated. The normal diffusion process can be visualised as in Figure 2.7.

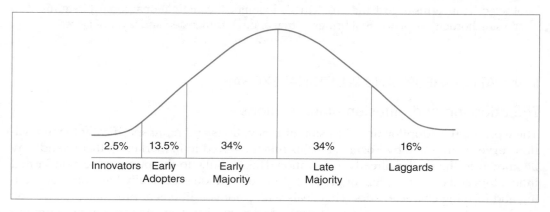

Figure 2.7   The adoption and diffusion of innovations process

Taking each of these types in turn:

- *Innovators* have high disposable income and are risk-takers, including risk-taking with unknown products or brands. They have opinion leadership characteristics.
- *Early Adopters* too are opinion leaders and they are the biggest influence on the speed of adoption and diffusion. They tend to be younger and have an above the norm education.
- *Early and Late Majorities* are the aforementioned 'admass' of opinion followers who watch more TV and read and take publications less than the previous two groups. Respectively they will be slightly above and slightly below the norm on characteristics such as income, education.
- *Laggards* as the tag suggests are very slow to take up innovations and generally would be attracted by sales promotions on the pricing of products, which might be 'last year's model'. Generally they are low on characteristics such as income, education, reading specialist publications and status.

Clearly there are other ramifications for communicators in this scenario. Targeting parameters such as age, income and education is clearly in need of addressing as is the communications mix in relation to the speed of diffusion and other factors that might cause a skewed distribution curve such as nature of the product and the market in question i.e. a company dealing in specialist products might have a highly specialised market to cater to, which is populated by very innovative people. Similarly the other extreme may be the case with little or no innovation taking place.

The continuing importance of word-of-mouth

Word-of–mouth is becoming more and more powerful as Internet access increases and becomes faster with broadband readily available. Ordinary people can make a good, spoken endorsement with peer credibility. Add this to social networking expansion, the popularity of blogging and the many forums that are now easily accessible. Viral marketing where messages are passed on electronically and the aforementioned 'word-of-mouse' have important parts to play in online marketing communications.

Non-linear, relational perspectives

Rather than the linear approaches discussed above, it is much more likely that communication occurs in a particular context within which there are a great many variables. Non-linear communications are shaping the brand narrative in an interactive way (Dahlen et al., 2010) within such contexts where meaning is socially constructed and communication is based less on formal and more on informal approaches. The disclosure of increasing amounts of personal and organisational information develops levels of intimacy that serve to build interpersonal, inter-organisational relationships. This may mean an exchange of information that is in the public domain but then the building of closer relationships with greater sharing of information and a move towards shared values and beliefs. A wider array of participants might be inevitable where a communications network can be seen. Organisational boundaries in this scenario would be transcended to form an intra-organisational network. This again may be formal or may have developed towards the informal. This could very well involve a co-branding approach.

Brand image and trust

The components of brand image are seen as being potentially both rational and emotional and this is fundamental to the notion of what a brand really is in any given situation. A mix of brand facets can be found in any brand's make-up that provide a brand's emotional and rational character that can be projected to the consumer. Whatever facets there are to a particular brand, it seems likely that trust plays a vital part in the process that leads from consumers' perceptions and experiences of a brand-to-brand loyalty. Trust, pragmatically, is seen as a powerful marketing weapon in the armoury and is something that can be lost and won (Bainbridge, 1997). Trust in this light becomes an important brand attribute making major fmcg brands more powerful than the Church (according to the Henley Centre's 'Planning for Social Change 1998' report). Marks and Spencer have trust and this enables them and others, such as Virgin, to extend into hitherto unknown (to them) areas but where consumers welcome brand extension under certain conditions. Marks and Spencer and Tesco in this sense have become choice editors, manufacturers in their own right (own label) and service providers. These organisations know that trust can be just as easily lost as won and is best kept by a philosophy that runs across the whole organisation, not just the marketing department. This raises questions of just who should be the guardian of the brand image and just how far is it credible and fair to stretch brands and still maintain a long-term, mutually beneficial consumer/brand relationship.

Trust, commitment and loyalty in the brand/consumer relationship

There is interest in relationship quality that stems from trust and the high degree of certainty of predictable and obligatory behaviour that leads to sales, giving the seller integrity and the process a high degree of certainty (Crosby et al., 1990). The process proposed by Morgan and Hunt (1994) is central here, i.e. that trust leads to commitment which leads to loyalty and that this is essential for successful relationship marketing. What is proposed is that this process is transposed to the consumer/brand relationship, thus the brand inspires the same degree of relationship quality that is usual in human relationships. This trust in brands requires investment that carries with it some degree of risk that consumers will cease to cooperate and cease resisting attractive alternatives. Trust within the consumer/brand context has not been adequately explored and lacks suitable definitions and measurement. McDonald's (1981) analogy of marriage – mutual social trust leading to commitment and the establishment and maintenance of exchange relationships – is helpful in conceptualising how consumers might choose brands, as are the ways in which people choose friends based on personality. The resultant loyalty to brands is rather more than the simplistic notion of repeat purchase over time (see Chapter 7 of this book for more on branding and communications).

The Snapshot below discusses some of the pros and cons of the use of WOM and e-WOM by charitable causes and other not-for-profit organisations when considering the make-up of marketing and marketing communications approaches.

Snapshot   Is word-of-mouth (WOM) best for charitable causes and similar not-for-profit organisations?

WOM generally has been around for many years. On *Bloomberg Businessweek* (2012) there is a debate on WOM generally, which discusses the pros and cons of this tool. For those in favour, consumers trust friends and this is valuable when passing messages on to them whether this be for recommendations for choosing a restaurant or a new smartphone. The argument is that WOM is still the most effective way to win customers. Traditional advertising was always used for awareness but this situation has changed in recent times. There is now a recognition that paid for advertising (and other marketing communications) is viewed with some suspicion or impacts less than it used to on target audiences, especially those who are younger and who are particularly savvy when it comes to things online and on mobile. Reviews in particular will not necessarily cut it with a younger demographic. WOM referrals, however, can be a very different, naturally occurring experience that involves product and brand involvement, social involvement and often identification with certain brands. The pro argument suggests that the multitude of media platforms available aside, some positive form of buzz about an organisation or a brand will help build that business or brand as long as there is trust and reliability involved.

On the con side of this argument there is the general suggestion that a multi-platform will work best. It is argued from this position that WOM is insufficient in itself and there is a need for a marketing communications mix that involves a number of tools executed in an integrated fashion. In other words there is not a single way of marketing an organisation or a brand, the organisation needing to market brands across multiple channels. This is, of course, more difficult to put into practice than to say, but put it into practice a marketer must; however, there are tools evolving all of the time to help in this quest. For example, early in 2013 Twitter introduced the Vine video service that allows the sharing of short videos (up to six seconds) from mobiles. Charities can and are using Vine, which has great potential to use video embedded in Tweets, but this potential will always be constrained by the limited space available as with Tweets. Despite the constraints the potential is enormous for things like job announcements or simply sending a different kind of and maybe more speedy, spontaneous and personal thank you to supporters. Vine could be big, if a slow burner, in social media e-WOM.

These suggestions underscore what WOM or e-WOM can be used for in not-for-profit, charities, causes and the 3rd sector generally. Of course, one of the advantages of WOM to such organisations is the practical reason of a lack of resources, especially in the area of marketing communication, including advertising and other promotional forms. In addition, the idea of charities in particular spending money on paid forms of promotion is problematic if it is perceived by various stakeholders that the organisation is spending donations or sponsorship money on such activities.

WOM (or e-WOM) provides an element of trust that advertising may no longer be able to deliver. There is likely to be greater credibility in the organisation and its brands, whereby people will respond in a much more positive way when making a donation or buying a product from a charity shop if the recommendation comes from a credible source regardless as to the means of communication – whether face-to-face, online or down a telephone line – as long as that source is trustworthy. Many recommendations start in simple conversations but may be prompted by other forms of marketing communication such as a press article or something that manifests itself in a social network, is forwarded in an email, or is posted on social media where closer bonds exist between people who are friends, colleagues or associates.

Stop Point

The rewards people seek when engaging in WOM or e-WOM are rarely monetary. Undertake the following: 1. Discuss how a charitable cause can use a website to martial people into action in terms of getting involved through engaging in WOM and e-WOM; 2. Outline how a charitable cause can use WOM in order to ensure that a local fund-raising event is effective and successful.

Assignment

Write a 2,000-word paper that illustrates how management might benefit from the consideration of communications theory. Include in your response ideas around:

- the basic communications process;
- source characteristics;
- step-flow models;
- innovation theory and the adoption and diffusion of innovations;
- brand and customer/consumer relationships including trust, commitment and loyalty.

Include in your assignment examples from both consumer and organisational marketing contexts.

Summary of Key Points

- The communications process can be modelled with source of message the encoder and the recipient the decoder. The message may be distorted by 'noise' in the system.
- The original process has been criticised for its overly simplistic view of communication and that much more has to be considered in the process to make sense of reality. Considering the realm of understanding and field of experience of both sender and receiver caters for some of this.
- The basic model of the communications process should be considered in the light of problems that occur if there is a focus on the individual, on individual messages, on source intent and cumulative impact, and on co-orientation which might lead to closed texts being used in communication.
- Source characteristics can be broken down into credibility, attractiveness and power to include trustworthiness, identification, likeability, compliance and reward and punishment.
- There are three established processes of attitude change, which are internalisation, identification and compliance.
- Step flow and personal influence models can be useful in the understanding of flows of information and the role of the opinion leader, former and follower.
- The strength of word-of-mouth is clearly important historically within innovation theory but also now and for the future with the influence of technology seemingly increasing its importance.
- Non-linear relational perspectives add to communications theory by shedding more light on the communicator's task in terms of organisational and consumer markets. Networking is increasingly important with the former and with the latter trust, commitment and loyalty need to be understood in a more holistic manner.

Discussion Questions

1. Explain the basic model of communication. Illustrate how this can help marketers in their communications decision-making.
2. Discuss the kinds of problem the marketer has when attempting to encode particular ideas. Give examples of the kinds of tool and choice at the marketer's disposal.
3. Explain what a message is in terms of its social context and its elements. Illustrate the kinds of signal that can be transmitted to different targets by the same marketer.
4. Elaborate, using examples, on the use of semiotics in the communication process generally and in terms of encoding and decoding in particular.
5. Explain the role of feedback in the communication process. Illustrate why the situation is more complex than the simple feedback loop looks on communications diagrams.
6. Discuss 'noise' as an integral part of the communications process. Use a key source of 'noise' to illustrate your discussion.

7. Explain and expand upon the 'source characteristics' model using examples from both consumer and organisational marketing fields.

8. List the key management benefits to using communications theory illustrating the kinds of theory that could be useful at different stages of the management process.

9. Explain the basic idea behind 'step flow' models. Illustrate the importance of 'word-of-mouth' and opinion leadership.

10. Critically examine the usefulness or not to marketers of the theory of adoption and diffusion of innovations.

Further Reading

Buttle, F.A. (1995) 'Marketing Communications Theory: what do the texts teach our students?', *International Journal of Advertising*, 14: 297–313.
This is now a classic article on marketing communications theory. Buttle provides two things: first, a history and ethos of how communications works; second, an incisive critique where he points to a lack of explicitness. Buttle's argument is that theory should inform practice otherwise it is pointless, but practice needs some theoretical underpinnings to provide stability. This argument is central to this book.

Carl, W. J. (2006) 'What's all the Buzz About? Everyday communication and the relational basis of word-of-mouth and buzz marketing practices', *Management Communication Quarterly*, 19 (6): 601–34. http://mcq.sagepub.com/content/19/4/601.full.pdf+html
This article is about the influential role of word-of-mouth but also about the more recent emergence of 'buzz' marketing as a marketing tool to stimulate talk about the brand, product or service. As such the article is about the effectiveness and ethics of buzz marketing.

Hirschman, E. (2007) 'Metaphor in the Marketplace', *Marketing Theory*, 7 (3): 227–48. http://mtq.sagepub.com/content/7/3/227.full.pdf+html
This is an account of the existence of the multi-vocal presence of symbolic meanings in the marketplace. The article argues that essentially metaphors are immortal whereas brands fade over time despite attempts to attach brands to particular meanings, persons, companies and other social institutions.

Lindenberg, S., Joly, J.F. and Stapel, D.A. (2011) 'The Norm-activating Power of Celebrity: the dynamics of success and influence', *Social Psychology Quarterly*, 74 (1): 98–120. http://spq.sagepub.com/content/74/1/98.full.pdf+html
This article looks at celebrity endorsement from the standpoint of people being influenced by celebrity endorsers, even when they do not identify with a particular celebrity, through the activation of bundles of social norms that become relevant for behaviour. The authors argue that the celebrity has to have prestige to activate norms but when tarnished by waning success fails to activate norms entirely. The article also discusses the impact of the person's environment on norm conformity and as such provides a robust discussion on the micro processes and macro conditions of norm activation.

Martin, I.M., Stewart, D.W. and Matta, S. (2005) 'Branding Strategies, Marketing Communication and Perceived Brand Meaning: the transfer of purposive, goal-oriented brand meaning to brand extensions', *Journal of the Academy of Marketing Science*, 33 (3): 275–94. http://jam.sagepub.com/content/33/3/275.full.pdf+html
This article looks at the transfer process (in terms of brand meaning) between parent brand and extension brand and how marketing communications can be used to facilitate the transfer process.

REFERENCES

Anand, B.N. and Shachar, R. (2007) 'Noisy communication', *Journal of Quantitative Marketing and Economics*, 5 (3): 211–37.

Bainbridge, J. (1997) 'Who wins the national trust?', *Marketing*, 23 October: 22–3.

Bloomberg Businessweek (2012) 'Word of mouth is the best ad', *Bloomberg Businessweek*, January, available at: www.businessweek.com/debateroom/archives/2011/12/word_of_mouth_is_the_best_ad.html

Buttle, F.A. (1995) 'Marketing communications theory: what do the texts teach our students?', *International Journal of Advertising*, 14 (4): 297–313.

Byrne, A., Whitehead, M. and Breen, S. (2003) 'The naked truth of celebrity endorsement', *British Food Journal*, 105 (4/5): 288–96.

Canning, L. and West, D. (2006) 'Celebrity endorsement in business markets', Proceedings of the Industrial Marketing and Purchasing (IMP) Group 22nd Conference, Milan, Italy, available at: www.impgroup.org/uploads/papers/5651.pdf.

Carroll, A. (2008) 'Brand communication in fashion categories using celebrity endorsement', *Journal of Brand Management*, 17 (2): 146–58.

Charbonneau, J. and Garland, R. (2005) 'Talent, looks, brains: New Zealand Advertising Practitioners' views on celebrity and athlete endorsers', *Marketing Bulletin*, 16, June, Article 3.

Charbonneau, J. and Garland, R. (2010) 'Product effects on endorser image: the potential for reverse image transfer', *Asia-Pacific Journal of Marketing and Logistics*, 22 (1): 101–10.

Crosby, L.A., Evans, K.R. and Cowles, D. (1990) 'Relationship quality in services selling: an interpersonal influence perspective', *Journal of Marketing*, 54 (July): 68–81.

Dahlen, M., Lange, F. and Smith, T. (2010) *Marketing Communications – A Brand Narrative Approach*. Chichester: Wiley.

Dichter, E. (1966) 'How word-of-mouth advertising works', *Harvard Business Review*, 44, November/December: 147–66.

Fill, C. (2009) *Marketing Communications*, 5th edn. London: Prentice Hall.

Fionda, A.M. and Moore, C.M. (2008) 'The anatomy of the luxury fashion brand', *Journal of Brand Management*, 16 (5/6): 347–63.

Fletcher, J. (2003) 'A data factory in the middle of Storyville', The Market Research Society Annual Conference, available at: http://www.warc.com/Content/ContentViewer.aspx?ID=aff11a78-7b41-428c-9f81-ebab72ebb45c&q=AID%3a77540&CID=A77540&PUB=MRS&MasterContentRef=aff11a78-7b41-428c-9f81-ebab72ebb45c.

Harris, F. (2006) 'Bad boys, good business?', The Open University, available at: www.open.ac.uk/openlearn/money-management/management/business-studies/bad-boys-good-business.

Hetzel, P. and Marion, G (1995) 'Contributions of French semiotics to marketing research knowledge', *Marketing and Research Today*, Parts 1 & 2, February & May: 35–40 and 75–85.

Jensen, M.B. (2007) 'Online marketing communication potential – priorities in Danish firms and advertising agencies', *European Journal of Marketing*, 42 (3/4): 502–25.

Kamins, M.A. and Gupta, K. (1994) 'Congruence between spokesperson and product type: a matchup hypothesis perspective', *Psychology and Marketing*, 11 (6): 569–86.

Kapitan, S. and Silvera, D.H. (2010) 'Consumers under the influence: endorser effectiveness through source characteristics and attribution of authenticity', The University of Texas at San Antonio, College of Business Working Paper Series.

Kelman, H. (1958) 'Compliance, identification and internationalisation: the three processes of attitude change', *Journal of Conflict Resolution*, 2 (1): 51–60.

Kelman, H. (1961) 'Processes of opinion change', *Public Opinion Quarterly*, 25: 57–78.

Klapper J.T. (1960) *The Effects of Mass Communication*. New York: New York Press.

Lafferty, Barbara A. (2008) 'Advertising, endorsements', in Wolfgang Donsbach (ed.), *International Encyclopedia of Communication*. Oxford: Blackwell Publishing.

Lasswell, H. (1948) 'The structure and function of communication in society', in L. Bryson (ed.), *The Communication of Ideas*. New York: Institute for Religious and Social Studies. pp. 37–51.

Lawes, R. (2002) 'Demystifying semiotics: some key questions answered', *International Journal of Market Research*, 44 (3): 251–64.

Lindenberg, S., Joly, J.F. and Stapel, D.A. (2011) 'The norm-activating power of celebrity: the dynamics of success and influence', *Social Psychology Quarterly*, 74 (1): 98–120.

McCracken, G. (1989) 'Who is the celebrity endorser? Cultural foundation of the endorsement process', *Journal of Consumer Research*, 16 (3): 310–21.

McDonald, G.W. (1981) 'Structural exchange and marital interaction', *Journal of Marriage and the Family*, November: 825–39.

Magnini, V.P., Garcia, C. and Honeycutt, E.D. (2010) 'Identifying the attributes of an effective restaurant chain endorser', *Cornell Hospitality Quarterly*, 51 (2): 238–50.

Magnini, V.P., Honeycutt, E.D. and Cross, A.M. (2008) 'Understanding the use of celebrity endorsers for hospitality firms', *Journal of Vacation Marketing*, 14 (1): 57–69.

Mattelart, A. and Chanan, M. (1991) *Advertising International*. London: Routledge.

Morgan, R. and Hunt, S. (1994) 'The commitment-trust theory of relationship marketing', *Journal of Marketing*, 58 (3), July: 20–38.

Newell, S.J. and Shemwell, D.J. (1995) 'The CEO endorser and message source credibility: an empirical investigation of antecedents and consequences', *Journal of Marketing Communications*, 1 (1): 13–23.

Pang, L. (2008) 'China who makes and fakes: a semiotics of the counterfeit', *Theory, Culture and Society*, 25 (6): 117–40.

Quinn, Ian (2011) 'Tesco: supplier cull to benefit "power brands"', *The Grocer*, 1 July.

Rogers, E.M. (1962) *The Diffusion of Innovations*. New York: Free Press.

Schramm, W. (1955) 'How communication works', in W. Schramm (ed.), *The Process and Effects of Mass Communication*. Urbana: University of Illinois Press. pp. 3–26.

Schramm W. (1971) 'How communication works', in J. De Vito (ed.), *Communication: concepts and processes*. Englewood Cliffs, NJ: Prentice Hall, pp. 13–20.

Shank, M.D. (2005) *Sports Marketing: a strategic perspective*, 3rd edn. Upper Saddle River, NJ: Prentice Hall.

Shannon, C. (1948) 'A mathematical theory of communication', *Bell System Technical Journal*, 27 (July): 379–423; and (October): 623–56.

Shannon, C. and Weaver, W. (1949) *A Mathematical Theory of Communication*. Urbana: University of Illinois Press.

Shimp, T.A. (2010) *Integrated Marketing Communication in Advertising and Promotion* (8th international edn). Mason, OH: South Western CENGAGE Learning.

Silvera, D. and Austad, B. (2004) 'Factors affecting the effectiveness of celebrity endorsement', *European Journal of Marketing*, 38 (11/12): 1509–26.

White, D., Goddard, L. and Wilbur, N. (2009) 'The effects of negative information transference in the celebrity endorsement relationship', *International Journal of Retail and Distribution Management*, 37 (4): 322–35.

3 Buyer Behaviour and Relationships

CHAPTER OVERVIEW

Introduction

The nature of behavioural theory in relation to marketing communications is explored and relationships examined and developed within the context of the marketing communications mix. Target market behaviour has to be understood by the marketer. The theoretical focus of this understanding has become, over the last four decades, the cognitive, affective and behaviour stage models that are of the hierarchy of effects (or response) type. However, the buying process has also been modelled and applied in practice. The marketer needs to know the 'who, why, what, how, when and where' about buying. This can be made memorable by thinking of Rudyard Kipling's 'Six wise serving men' who taught him all he knew, 'Their names are What and Why and When, and How and Where and Who' (*Oxford Dictionary of Quotations*, 1979: 300). It is the 'why' that is the most mystifying and problematic but it is clear that what is bought is an important consideration, especially in relation to the amount and kind of information sought.

Learning objectives

The chapter seeks to explore and explain behaviour theory in relation to the communication process. More specifically, after reading this chapter the student will be able to:

- place communication within a cultural context and discuss other environmental trends and influences on buyer behaviour;
- outline the major inputs of buyer learning theory and show the complexity of buyer behaviour;
- facilitate understanding and use of the buyer decision-making process.

COMMUNICATION, CULTURE AND OTHER ENVIRONMENTAL INFLUENCES ON BUYER BEHAVIOUR

Culture defined

Communication and culture are looked at more closely in the international context in Chapter 17 of this book but generally speaking culture is crucial to the workings of both marketing communications and buyer behaviour. Culture has many definitions. Many studies rely heavily on the work of Geert Hofstede (for example 1980, 1989, 1990, 1993, 2001) who refers to culture as 'the collective mental programming of the people in an environment', where 'culture is not a characteristic of individuals'. Rather, culture 'encompasses a number of people who are conditioned by the same education and life experience' (de Mooij, 2010: 48, after Hofstede and Hofstede, 2005: 3). Culture has also been defined as 'the sum total of learned beliefs, values and customs that serve to direct the consumer behaviour of members of a particular society' (Schiffman et al., 2008: 368).

Hofstede's large and diverse study, which resulted ultimately in the 4- (then 5-, now 6-) dimension model of culture, is discussed later in this chapter and in Chapter 18 of this book in the international context. This was a study of IBM employees around the globe and is used by many writers across the business spectrum, for example Hunt (2002) on management and leadership competencies across cultures or in marketing, for example Blodgett et al. (2008) who test the model in a particular consumer marketing context. In marketing and communications' terms Hofstede's work has been used extensively, for example by Marieke de Mooij (1994, 1998, 2001, 2003a, 2005, 2010, 2011a; de Mooij and Hofstede, 2010, 2011). Culture encompasses a number of people who are conditioned by the same kinds of experience, for example in terms of life experience or education. Marketers should, of course, be concerned with the size of markets and demography but also other factors that give rise to trends within markets or segments. For example time pressures have given rise to convenience foods. The home environment has become somewhat of a cocoon leading to many changes in the products and services on offer. Home entertainment, take-away food delivery and 'do-it-yourself' (DIY) products are examples. Indulgences such as weekend breaks and excitement, fantasy, health and many leisure pursuits are other examples.

Expressions of culture

The ability to measure the size of such markets is of little use if the product and communications do not fit in with the culture. People worldwide share certain needs but needs may be met differently in different cultures. Language as a cultural variable is important but there is more to culture than this, such as customs and religion. There are believed to be four factors that describe the concept of culture (Hofstede, 1990). These are symbols, heroes, rituals and values; customs and practices result. This is often presented in the literature rather like the layers making up an onion, as depicted in Figure 3.1 below.

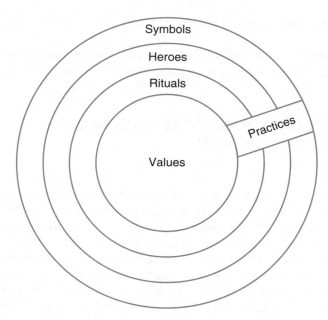

Figure 3.1   Hofstede's (1990) expressions of culture 'onion' model

- *Values* – At the core are values of a particular culture. Such values do change but not very often and when they do this can be a slow process. Values are therefore durable and influential, even subconsciously, on the way in which a society behaves. Beliefs are related to values. Beliefs are the feelings we have about things, expressed through non-verbal communication or verbal statements. Values that are learnt can influence beliefs because they are seen as guidance by many in a society. The images used in marketing and advertising can affect how a person will respond to an advertisement or brand and whether the effect will be desirable where the whole brand offering is evaluated according to their values and beliefs. People tend to have values about what is good or evil, rational or irrational, natural or unnatural, beautiful or ugly, dirty or clean, normal or abnormal or what is logical or paradoxical.

- *Rituals* – These surround the core values of a culture or society. Rituals also change, most often slowly over time. This involves things like handshakes or personal hygiene. Such rituals can be considered essential within a society.

- *Heroes* – These can take many forms and can be real people, fictitious characters or cartoon characters. A hero can be a person who has characteristics that are valued by society. The person may be living, dead or imagined. Therefore Superman, Donald Duck, King Arthur, or actors such as Steve McQueen, James Dean or Marilyn Monroe are all potentially useful in establishing cultural values and links in advertising or endorsing a product or brand. The links with product merchandising are obvious as can be seen in the advertising of many brands.

- *Symbols* – These can be brand symbols such as those of Apple, Virgin, Nike or Emirates. Symbols carry meaning that is interpreted differently according to the culture. These symbols include objects, pictures, gestures or words. Language is not just the words that are used but also their individual meanings in different cultures and societies. Gestures are important forms of non-verbal communication and can cause unintentional confusion or even offence. There are lots of faux pas around because of this and, for example, because of poor translation, or meaning being lost or distorted in translation. A lack of understanding of the symbolic importance to meaning of colour can be disastrous for marketers.

All of these elements result in different *practices* in different cultures. Certain behaviour is seen as correct in certain societies and situations. For example an advertisement in the UK dealt with a divorcing couple. This would not be seen as an appropriate story line in another country where the divorce rate is very low. Consider how the following might vary between different contexts, for example with a group of colleagues in a restaurant and being at home alone:

- Eating habits.
- Dress habits.
- Sunday dress habits.
- Gender roles.
- Social class roles.

Culture is therefore important in marketing communications because it differs within a society and between societies. What may be very acceptable in one context or country will not be in another. Cultural aspects are fundamental to the shaping of the buyer behaviour of people in a particular societal context. Marshall McLuhan, writing in the 1960s, comments upon early manifestations of globalisation (for example, McLuhan, 1964) and the idea that we are said to be all citizens of the global village. This is a reference in particular to the apparent convergence of the media but in general to culture. It is because of increasing world business and communication that some believe that certain global cultures exist. There exists what many would accept as global marketing with, for example, Pepsi or Coca-Cola advertising and other corporate and marketing activities. The corporate cultures of multinational companies tend to reflect the cultures of the companies involved. There is much discussion as to the extent to which advertising can influence culture worldwide. Undeniably, global companies such as Benetton and McDonald's have influence in many countries. However, the success of the company will still depend on customers' willingness to buy. Brand consumption will inevitably lead to a change in behaviour. The international context is discussed at length in Chapter 18 of this book.

Sub-culture, social class and reference groups

When considering the importance of buyer behaviour in the development of an effective marketing communications strategy, the marketer must also take notice of the fact that very few consumers live, work or make decisions in social isolation. Individuals are influenced by culture, as discussed above, in terms of for example traditions or lifestyles associated with a particular country. Culture can affect the ways that consumers seek to satisfy needs, the weighting given to choice criteria or a preference for certain brands. The study of culture is also helpful in understanding the use of cultural stereotypes in advertising. For example, to make a product look chic it might be placed in a French, or more specifically, a Parisian setting. In other words the context in which the consumer receives the communication plays a very important part in the process, so that if a consumer listens to a radio advertisement in the workplace, he or she may well do so surrounded by work friends and colleagues. More broadly, most people live as part of a community and as such are subject to the norms, values and influences of those around them.

Sub-cultures

Groups are very influential on individual consumers. Sub-cultures are smaller groups where beliefs and values are different from those of the mainstream. Like any segment, sub-cultures are based upon parameters such as age, religion and ethnicity. Sub-cultures will only be important to marketers if they conform to the rationale behind segmentation, i.e. whether they are, for example, substantive or accessible. A sub-culture therefore consists of a set of people with behaviour that results from values and beliefs that are different from those of the larger culture of which they are a part. People who belong to a sub-culture are therefore different from the majority of people in a society who are usually opposed to the values and beliefs of the dominant culture. If such values and beliefs are diametrically opposed then this might be described as 'counterculture'. There are many examples of sub-cultures across time, such as 'Punks', 'Goths' or 'Skinheads'. Such groups variously decay and disappear, survive but in smaller and less visible numbers, or are subsumed into the larger culture. Other sub-cultures that are resilient and persistent are often based on religious beliefs and manage to co-exist within the larger culture alongside other groups. An example of a charitable trust that operates in Great Britain is the British Asian Trust, whose President is HRH The Prince of Wales. More specifically this endeavour tackles poverty in South Asia (visit http://www.britishasiantrust.org/).

Social class and social grades

It may be that the social class a person is in, or aspires to be in, is a key factor for the marketer. Most societies are stratified into some form of class system where relatively homogeneous groupings exist based largely in the past on, for example, income, educational platform and occupation. This notion does differ from country to country but in many countries the stratification is very similar, based as it is on a grading system originally designed by soci-ologists. In the UK the social grades of A, B, C1, C2, D and E have been used for some time as a way of describing socio-economic types in the population. These are now based on occupation and in particular the occupation of the CIE (Chief Income Earner). According to Ipsos MediaCT (2009), part of www.ipsos-mori.com and the Ipsos Group, a leading global research company, social grades can be used as a powerful discriminator. Examples of this are media such as newspapers and holidays abroad. Differences can be seen by using indi-ces. For popular daily newspapers the score is only 52 for ABs while for C2s it is 137 and for Ds it is 147. Conversely, for at least one holiday abroad of two nights or more in the last 12 months the score for ABs is 123 but only 66 for Ds (Ipsos MediaCT, 2009).

The social grade in the UK has been part of the NRS (National Readership Survey) for more than 50 years. These social grades are:

A – Higher managerial, administrative or professional (4% of the UK population);

B – Intermediate managerial, administrative or professional (23% of the UK population);

C1 – Supervisory, clerical and junior managerial, administrative or professional (29% of the UK population);

C2 – Skilled manual workers (21% of the UK population);

D – Semi and unskilled manual workers (15% of the UK population);

E – State pensioners, casual or lowest grade workers, unemployed with state benefits only (8% of the UK population).

This is based on households and information extending to all members of the household. Social class (as opposed to social grade) is based on the occupation of the individual, i.e. professional status not purchasing power. Social class as a system can be the basis of a classification of the working population, but since the 2001 census the NS-SEC (National Statistics Socio-Economic Classification) groups occupations by employment conditions rather than skills and so applies to all and not just those in work (Ipsos MediaCT, 2009).

Reference groups

The marketer has to recognise the influence of others in the various groups to which an individual might belong, such as family. Family and home life are a constantly changing part of the environment. Learned behaviours are not uncommon. Not spending enough time with children has resulted in behaviours on the part of working parents that are far removed from previous generations. Family life cycles have also changed. The traditional move from being single to being a newlywed, to having young children then growing children (full nest), to an empty nest (children move out) and being on one's own (remaining partner, spouse having died), is no longer a certainty (not that it ever was for some people anyway). Changes such as both partners working have meant, for example, dual incomes and there are more single person and gay households. Communicators have consequently had to use different media and media spots to be able to cater for these changes.

Returning to work has meant that for many mothers work colleagues are as important as daytime television or radio spots. Of course a reality these days are things like divorce and remarriage. This has given rise to the so-called 'second chancer', a target market that has different characteristics from those of other targets that may exist even within the same segment of a marketplace. For example, 'second chancers' tend to be older than 'normal' married people and have a higher household income, are more content with life, and spend time seeking to enrich their lives rather than please others.

Reference groups are those groups with members whose presumed perspectives or values are used by an individual as the basis for his/her judgements, opinions or actions. Marketing communications often seeks to replicate the communication and interaction between individuals in groups where one member offers a solution to other members' problem. Sales promotional strategies will often encourage the group interaction. For example a wine club may offer a discount or some other incentive for a member to introduce a friend. The same wine club (in this case Naked Wines) might also offer incentives for people to become 'wine angels', i.e. a scheme that involves people willing to put money in up-front that is then invested in small wine-makers and spent on the wine later with discounts and other incentives for members (visit www.naked-wines.com/angels).

Marketers have long used reference groups for aspirational advertising and have also long been aware of disassociate groups, i.e. groups to which consumers do not belong (or do not wish to belong) but which can be used in advertising.

CULTURE AND BUYER BEHAVIOUR

Buyer behaviour can be thought of by marketers as being the things buyers do while satisfying wants, needs and desires. This is done through searching for and selecting purchases, using these products and services, and then re-evaluating their usefulness and either going on to re-purchase the same products and services or rejecting them. This process may be almost involuntary or impulsive but other times more detailed and exhaustive. For more on buyer behaviour, including the buyer decision-making process, the reader should consult texts such as Blackwell et al. (2006).

Values and lifestyles

Care must be taken when applying generalised models of culture. Generalisations of culture can often be more harmful than useful. For many years now values and lifestyles have been of interest to marketers whether this is in a particular market or multiple markets in which a marketer might operate. The interest in combing 'life style patterns' and market segmentation was established by Plummer (1974) in the 1970s with the former being based on activities, interests and opinions. Plummer listed four types of activities: how people spend their time; what they are interested in ranked in terms of importance; opinions and people's view of the world; and basic characteristics such as income or life cycle stage. Since that time many marketing-related studies have engaged with values and lifestyles. For example Fraj and Martinez (2006), with an interest in psychographic variables, looked at which 'values and lifestyles best explain environmentally friendly behaviours' in a study that explored the relationships between lifestyles and values. These authors argue that a growth in ecological awareness has occurred alongside a willingness to contribute to environmental issues. This study reinforced the idea that it is difficult to draw an accurate profile of those consumers who are most worried about the environment, but that certain environmental types of consumer profiles exist and that marketers should take positive environmental steps such as a demonstration of their commitment to environmental care. Another example of psychographic study is that of Valentine and Powers (2013) who looked at values and lifestyle segments within 'Generation Y'. This study is said to provide 'marketers with insights' into Generation Y's 'values, attitudes and media habits'.

The context of culture

The context of culture work of various writers, for example Mueller (1987, 1996) after Hall (1976), is discussed more fully in the international context in Chapter 18 of this book. Mueller distinguishes between high- and low-context culture, citing Japan as collectivist and the USA as individualist, and illustrate the importance to marketers of such differences. Although the concept of context is a useful construct when looking at different cultures, this approach has to be used with caution. For example, high-low-medium product involvement may be more important in some contexts than in others. Appeals and associations might therefore work differently in different cultures.

Hofstede's five (now six) dimensions

The study of culture from a marketing perspective involves behaviour patterns, societal norms, attitudes and personality variables. Hofstede's 'five dimensions of national culture' model that deals in essence with value differences in differing societies is used by many writers generally and extensively in marketing by de Mooij (for example 1998, 2005, 2010). The model represents a typological system of classifying people by cultural parameters.

The Snapshot below illustrates Hofstede's 'dimensions of national culture' model in the context of behaviour, or more specifically making decisions and choosing one brand above another and how people react to stimuli such as those within the marketing communications tool box.

Snapshot   Hofstede's Six Dimension Model – the influence of culture on how people behave and react to marketing communication stimuli

The five (now six) dimension model of national culture was created by Geert Hofstede (http://geert-hofstede.com/). These dimensions have been used by many writers, academics and practitioners in many fields. Here of course the concern is for the marketing context. De Mooij (2010) has taken each of the first five dimensions and discussed these in a behavioural context. They are summarised below.

The *Power Distance* (PD) dimension is to do with everything having a place in an order. This is therefore to do with social distance and social hierarchy; acceptance of given authority in a natural order of things. It therefore influences, for example, social greeting. If PD is large, people in such a society will appear well groomed, especially in public. Clothes, make-up and posture are used to differentiate position or the appearance of position. If PD in a society is small, people do not differentiate position generally and will wear in public what they might in private such as training shoes, t-shirts or jogging bottoms.

The *Individualism/Collectivism* dimension involves people who are 'I' oriented rather than 'WE'. With individualism people look after themselves and choose to join groups for some benefit or other but individual identity is important. Expression of personal opinion, of individual opinion, is valued and self-actualisation is important. Aspects of the individual, for example making decisions, are more important than things emanating from group situations. In collectivist societies and cultures people are 'we-conscious'.

The *Masculinity/Femininity* dimension deals with performance, achievement and success with the former and caring for others and quality of life with the latter. In masculine cultures status and winning are important and big (and fast) is beautiful, whereas with feminine cultures that are more people-oriented small is beautiful and modesty, togetherness, cosiness, sympathy for others and not showing off matter more. In marketing terms these aspects feature, in particular with advertising, which generally reflects societal norms and values (and which of course follows the marketing concept of meeting and satisfying needs).

The *Uncertainty Avoidance* dimension looks at the degree to which people feel threatened by uncertainty and ambiguity and how they avoid situations or not. This dimension is about rules and prescriptive behaviour. Where uncertainty avoidance is strong there is a need for such rules and prescribed ways of living. This makes things more formal, including the search for the truth and lines of communication, where experts are sought after. Conflict and competition are threats where anxiety and tension need release through showing emotion in various ways, which can be verbal or non-verbal. In weak uncertainty avoidance situations the (almost) opposite is the case with fewer rules and less formality. Common sense prevails over ritualistic behaviour and conflict and competition are not a threat and even welcomed. From a marketing perspective this dimension is said to have an effect on resistance to change and therefore to the acceptance of innovation where there is high uncertainty. It is also the case where there is low uncertainty avoidance that creativity is more likely to be high.

The *Long Term Orientation (LTO)* dimension is about the future in terms of pragmatism. This means that what works is preferred to what might be true or right. Perseverance, ordering relationships by status, thrift and a sense of shame are characteristics that are the opposite of those found in the short-term orientation of some societies. The latter has respect for tradition, personal steadiness and stability, and the reciprocation of favours, greetings and gifts.

The sixth dimension, added in 2010 by using the work of Minkov, is the *Indulgence/Restraint* dimension. Indulgence can be described as the 'tendency to allow relatively free gratification of basic and natural human desires related to enjoying life and having fun'. Restraint can be described as 'a conviction that such gratification needs to be curbed or regulated by strict social norms' (Hofstede et al., 2010: 232). Of the 93 countries included in Minkov's study most English-speaking countries scored relatively highly, which suggests they are relatively permissive and lacking in restraint.

> ## Stop Point ⚠
>
> Each of the six dimensions can be considered in terms of influence and meaning to marketing communication stimuli. Undertake the following: 1. Outline the kinds of corporate and marketing communication approaches that might be taken in differing marketplaces based on each of the dimensions listed; 2. Consider the relationships between the dimensions and discuss how they might interface in different contexts, and how each context might vary because of its make-up in terms of subcultures within a particular culture or having more than one culture within a particular society.

THE COMPLEXITY OF BEHAVIOUR AND BUYER LEARNING THEORY

The basic buying impulses of incentive, purchasing power and availability are fairly simple and straightforward in nature. Satisfying needs, whether physical, social or emotional can be seen to be easily achieved through situational factors such as living in a particular environment that pre-determines, for example, what one eats. For example the weather, utilities or services available may be determining factors in buying behaviour. Motorway services might not be the preferred place to refuel one's car and body but might, in some circumstances, be highly convenient or the only option. Getting cash from a machine in a wall might be the only means of obtaining spending money on a holiday island using a particular credit or debit card but with a significant charge for each transaction.

Involvement

More complex theories of consumer and organisational buyer behaviour and of consumer and organisational buyer decision-making abound in the literature, as do models of buyer behaviour. There is also a need to reflect on the practical analysis of buyer behaviour in relation to marketing communications. The intimate relationship between the two processes of buyer behaviour and marketing communications is well recognised in the traditional marketing literature. The notion of involvement is fundamental to this since this represents the degree to which a stimulus of some sort, marketing or corporate communications-originated included, is relevant to an individual's need or want. The greater the relevancy, the more extensive the search is likely to be. The degree of involvement can depend upon many things including low or high cost of the item and whether the purchase situation is an on-going one or a one-off or even on impulse. It is not simply the case that because an item is low in cost that it is low in involvement. For this reason alone the notion of involvement has become a key concept in the way consumer behaviour in particular is seen.

Involvement as a concept takes into consideration all three of the established domains of buying decision-making:

- Cognitive (think).
- Affective (feel).
- Behavioural (do).

This means that personality components such as ego or perception elements such as perceived risk form the basis of a cognitive perspective. This perspective might be influenced through marketing communication activities that, for example, capture attention. In the affective domain interest and liking are important and marketing communications activities are vital influences in this area. The behavioural domain involves moving towards purchase and therefore intentions are important. The need to search for and evaluate information can be critical, depending upon the level of involvement. Generally, within the decision-making process, there will be varying levels of uncertainty experienced by consumers and professional buyers. This important process is discussed later in this chapter. It is rare to have a situation where there is no discernible involvement with the choice of products or services. There are usually two distinct levels of involvement: high involvement and low involvement.

High involvement

A high level of perceived risk is associated with 'big ticket prices' but also when the potential purchase has high perceived risk in terms of personal or psychological relevance. It may be easy to see the risk associated with the purchase of a new car or even household goods such as washing machines. What is less visible are the psychological risks associated with relatively low-priced products but ones which involve, for example, social settings with peer or reference groups where a particular way of dressing or a particular 'badge' is required. A great deal of time and resources is devoted to researching, gathering information and building knowledge in order to reduce risk. In such situations, consumer activity behaviour moves towards that of the professional buyer who runs the high risk of a professional failure in product purchase as part of the job for the organisation.

Low involvement

If a consumer has little involvement regarding the purchase of a product or service then there is little or no threat or risk associated with that purchase. Many products such as milk, pasta or baked beans are bought frequently and routinely. This is also the case with the organisational buyer who, for example, with certain component parts, may have a routinised, computerised response to regular re-order purchase. Past experience of the product class and of course brands can result in little or no information search. In such cases purchases might be routinised or habitual and marketing communications used to perpetuate the situation. From a competitor perspective marketing communications will be used to try to break routines and habits in order to gain market share.

Motivation

Motives, or why we feel compelled to take particular actions, can be viewed from a number of different standpoints. The commonest approach over decades has been to look at Maslow's 'Hierarchy of needs' (Maslow, 1943, 1954 for example). This model suggests that human needs are built on a pyramid structure with the most basic (physiological needs, for example hunger or thirst) at the base of the pyramid, whereby humans need things like food, shelter and sex in order to sustain life. Next up the hierarchy are safety needs (for example security and protection from physical harm), followed by social needs (for example love, affection, belonging and acceptance). Esteem needs are next in the pyramid, where a sense of accomplishment, status and respect from others is sought. At the top of the pyramid are the needs for self-fulfilment and the realisation of one's own potential, which Maslow called self-actualisation.

The simple premise here is that the lower level must be satisfied before other levels can be. Once basic needs are met the human can move up the pyramid to higher-order needs such as those at the top. The marketing reality is far more complex than this simple concept. Many products are sold on different levels. A product that nourishes might well be sold on parental love (social). A person wishing to achieve the ultimate in self-actualisation by climbing a mountain or shooting some rapids might well ignore safety needs from the start. On the other hand, in simpler situations, it is easy to see how needs can be different within a product category. For example Volvo some time ago was emphasising safety and love for children in its advertising. Other car manufacturers might emphasise speed, practicality, the environment or style and use, for example, celebrity endorsement in the process. The French car company Renault used the French footballer Thierry Henry to help epitomise style in the Renault Clio car with a 'va va voom' strapline.

Human motives can be understood further by studying personality. The psychoanalytic theory of Freud explains much about motivation and personality and this has been applied to consumer behaviour situations. This is a probe for deeper-seated motives that are the basis for buying behaviour and purchase decisions but that are unclear even to the consumer. Probing the unconscious appeared to provide the answer. Motivational research, pioneered by Ernest Dichter, saw the development of new (for the time) methodologies and tools including projective techniques and association tests. Motivational research has since been seen as both interesting and problematic. Dichter founded the Institute for Motivational Research near New York in 1946 and took Freudian psychoanalysis and applied it to consumer behaviour in real situations. Through this the focus group and to some extent the depth interview did grow and flourish but some of the stranger tools were discredited, although certain tools and techniques are still used today (see Chapter 17 of this book). At best it might be said that interesting insights can be had from such research, although some large companies such as Guinness and Heinz continue to support and use these kinds of techniques.

It is easy to be sceptical of motivational research when the outcomes suggest, for example, that women bake cakes because this is the symbolic act of giving birth, or that men smoke cigars as a substitute for thumb-sucking. These and other motivational research outcomes, such as the notion that men associate convertible cars with freedom and having a mistress, and therefore convertibles should be used in advertising to help sell the sedan version of the same model, appear rather fanciful. However, Dichter was dealing with unspoken desires (for example Dichter, 1947). Dichter used in-depth consumer interviews and learned how consumers arrived at a chosen brand of soap through perceptions of the brand's personality. The brand was being bought for more than its functional properties. Dichter's idea was that if the marketer could understand the personality of a product then that marketer would understand how to market it.

The kind of research employed to explore motivation necessarily involves the use of small samples, which is a perennial problem in any research field particularly in terms of not being able to generalise to a wider group of people. The research will most likely lead to insights but might be charged with only discovering the idiosyncrasies of a few individuals. Interpretation of results is another problematic area. If the researcher is using projective techniques to facilitate an outcome through providing a means of expression such as cutting and pasting magazine images or psychodrawings (where participants are asked to draw experiences, such as having a headache) there is still the problem of the interpretation (including the participants' own interpretation) as to what the image might mean. Still, these techniques are believed to enrich and enhance qualitative research. The usual advice is that such techniques should be used with caution and in the end it might be worth remembering that sometimes 'a cigar is just a cigar', something Freud is alleged to have said but may not have done. However, the meaning is clear – that sometimes there is no hidden or underlying desire in a particular context. As Pychyl (2009) suggests, and referring in his case to procrastination and delaying things, the message is valid in any case and sometimes a delay is just a delay, nothing more.

The Snapshot below illustrates how BMW moved back to its successful strapline – ultimate driving machine – after a brief dalliance with its 'joy' campaign, although BMW maintain that 'joy' was part of the ultimate driving machine and experience anyway.

Snapshot High involvement with BMW – the Ultimate Driving Machine again

The strapline

BMW has returned, in North America at least, to its long-running strapline – the Ultimate Driving Machine, which is nearly 40 years old – as it gears up to dominate the North American automobile market at the high end. In terms of the marketing communications tools required to achieve this, television advertising has been, once again, a key ingredient. Henry (2012) suggests that BMW is still indeed 'The Ultimate Driving Machine' and that in fact it always has been. A recent TV ad says, 'We don't make sports cars. We don't make SUVs. We don't make hybrids. We don't make luxury sedans. We only make one thing: The Ultimate Driving Machine.' For Henry this is a statement of the obvious: 'Yet the tagline is a touchy subject inside BMW. BMW came up with what eventually became a worldwide ad campaign called "Joy" in time for its sponsorship of the 2010 Winter Olympic Games in Vancouver, Canada. The idea was to reinforce the user benefit of owning The Ultimate Driving Machine. BMW never entirely abandoned "Ultimate Driving Machine" but the "Joy" campaign started a public uproar that BMW was turning its back on one of the best taglines ever' (Henry, 2012).

The Target

BMW models have been targeted at customers who want luxury, the latest technology and the latest in design. These are customers who are willing to pay a premium price for a very desirable brand. There is, however, a range of target customers including independent, private buyers but also those who are corporate customers who influence the purchase of executive, luxury cars. The latter consist of top executives and business leaders and decision makers from many companies around the world. The target market can be said to be made up of particular types who have certain characteristics; for example who read business magazines and broadsheet newspapers and who watch television news programmes for insights and ideas on trends in relevant sectors and markets including financial and product issues, encompassing high-end products and services such as a BMW. These are:

- top/senior executives;
- middle management and sales executives who are decision makers and who would influence car purchase within their companies;
- other expert decision makers who work with management who are also influencers on the purchase process;

(Continued)

(Continued)

- affluent individuals with high disposable incomes;
- other professionals and investors;
- SME (small to medium sized enterprise) owner-managers and directors.

These types of potential customer are likely to be highly involved with the BMW brand. They expect quality, luxury and performance from such a high-end brand.

The Dilemma

The dilemma that BMW face lies in the notion that high performance vehicles might not be seen as fuel efficient or vice-versa, i.e. if a car is seen as fuel efficient and therefore good for the environment (some might say better for the environment at best), then it will not be seen as dynamic. Certainly the way BMW see it, it does not matter which model of BMW that is in focus since all BMWs are ultimate driving machines, so that in other segments of the marketplace, say small cars, the BMW positioned there will be an ultimate driving machine, as a premium brand and a great product with high credibility and authenticity. The 'Joy' campaign was merely part of the BMW experience, especially for women, and part of the ultimate driving machine experience. Vijayenthiran (2012) comments that 'all we've seen from the automaker in the past three years or so have been ads centering on the joy of driving one of its cars ... now BMW of North America has revived those famous four words for its newest series of ads, the first of which aired over the weekend ... there's no denying that the tagline has been a roaring success over the years and it looks like it will continue to do so into the future as well.'

Stop Point

BMW appear confident that all BMW models are seen as being ultimate driving machines no matter which segment of the market a model is in. Undertake the following: 1. Explain the importance of the strapline that embodies the essence of the brand; 2. Discuss the importance of clear positioning in the marketplace and also as regards the changing nature of the communications mix for a brand like BMW, as well as the potential limitations of online activity such as social media.

Perception

External information exists in many forms. How we perceive stimuli whether marketing-controlled or otherwise will depend upon how we receive and select information and organise it for our own devices. An understanding of this can help inform marketing communications strategy. Perception involves the processing of information that is received, selected, and interpreted by the individual to create meaning for that individual with his or her own beliefs, attitudes and many other idiosyncratic characteristics. Belch and Belch (2009) divide perception into three areas:

1. First, how consumers sense and attend to various information. Here consumers use the senses to create a representation of the stimulus but the marketer can manipulate this situation by using the senses in a particular way. For example, with perfume the marketer can not only use eye-catching visuals in a

magazine advertisement but can also allow the consumer to sample the product and take advantage of the sense of smell by using a strip or scratch mechanism to release a small quantity of the perfume.

2. Second, the selection of information where the consumer's personality, needs, motives expectations and experiences are the psychological factors that explain why the consumer focuses on one thing but ignores another. The consumer will attend to a stimulus that is perceived to be a problem solver.

3. Third, the consumer then interprets the stimulus depending upon the internal psychological factors at play but will be selective with regard to exposure, attention, comprehension and retention.

The consumer therefore might either choose (or not) to be exposed to stimuli by, for example, channel flicking while watching television or responding to online pop-up advertisements. Consumers are also very capable of screening out many of the stimuli that they are exposed to every day. In other words they will choose to focus on some but not on others. The marketer's job is to get through this clutter and gain attention but even if this is successful the consumer may still selectively comprehend only certain ones depending upon their own disposition where information may be interpreted in a way that supports a particular position. The final, retention, stage of this selection process is perhaps the trickiest for the marketer since the consumer will only see/hear what he or she wants to see/hear and will disregard the rest of the information. The marketer, however, has quite an armoury at their disposal in order to induce in the consumer retention of the message rather than not. Images, rhymes, symbols, associations, jingles, pop songs or memorable tunes and many other devices can be used as emotional triggers to aid memory and help consumers learn about brands. Belch and Belch (2009: 122) note that subliminal perception is a possibility whereby consumers perceive a message subconsciously. The possibility of using such triggers or cues is intriguing but problematic in an ethical sense (see Chapter 6 of this book). Also, the use of such 'hidden persuaders' could pave the way for a consumer backlash if the company concerned were 'found out'.

Cognition

Consideration of cognition in terms of buyers involves intellect and processing of information. This is viewed by many writers as a rational process whereby information is sought, stored, evaluated and used in an intra-personal manner (for example Pickton and Broderick, 2005). The consumer and buyer decision-making processes, which form the central plank of most models of buying behaviour, are dealt with in a separate section later on in this chapter. Marketers should be aware of the major influences on their customers or potential customers and consideration of the more general model can help with this. Other more specific models are discussed below.

Information processing model

Messages may fail at any one of the stages prior to their retention. A message might not be understood, or remembered, or acted upon. The consumer and the type of purchase situation will affect this process. If the consumer is inexperienced and the purchase situation is a high involvement or risky one, then the consumer is more likely to pay attention to a message than for routine low involving situations. Television advertising with simple messages and involving devices such as jingles, music, celebrities or humour is ideally suited to this type of situation since the consumer is not really interested in what is said. Conversely, printed advertisements or brochures are more suitable for high-risk purchase situations where the prospective or actual customer or consumer is motivated to gather information in order to make the important decision. This would apply equally to other situations, for example, online on websites, blogs, customer reviews or within social media, where information is provided that is perceived as credible.

As already discussed in Chapter 2 of this book, marketing communicators should be aware that a huge difference can exist between the meaning intended by the sender and the meaning as interpreted by the receiver of messages. As suggested in the section above on perception, people see and hear what they want to see and hear and disregard other things. The communicator should endeavour to understand what happens in a consumer's mind from the first exposure to a message to the ultimate response, whether this be to ignore, take notice but quickly forget, or forget after a period of time, store in the memory and act later, or act immediately. The literature suggests a five-stage model that a marketing communications message needs to pass through for it to be effective, i.e. retained in the memory. The stages are:

- Exposure – information processing begins when a message reaches at least one of the senses among target audience members. There are many estimates as to how many stimuli a person on average is exposed to in a day. Some say 3,000 while others see it less than this at 1,800. Not all of these would be noticed by any means and the ability to zap or zip allows the receiver to terminate the potential exposure before it begins, making it increasingly difficult for marketers to communicate.

- Attention – is the allocation of processing capacity to an incoming message. Since capacity is limited some messages will receive attention and others will be ignored. An affective (feeling or emotion) reaction might precede a cognitive reaction, which is then followed by a more elaborate affective reaction. In this case there is a primary emotional response to a stimulus that determines whether a consumer is going to pay attention to it, produced by, for example, needs or attitudes (see attitudes below).

- Comprehension – the desired meaning being attributed to a message depends on how a consumer categorises and elaborates a stimulus through the use of existing knowledge and beliefs. This has been called field of experience and realm of understanding (refer back to Chapter 2 of this book and references to Schramm and others). Categorisation occurs when the incoming stimulus is compared with the memory content (something else in the memory bank such as the use of a particular technique in the past) to be classified and assigned meaning. The categorisation will therefore involve the consumer associating this new information with something already existing. The consumer therefore engages in elaboration, the integration between new information and existing knowledge.

- Acceptance – the consumer's comprehension of a message does not automatically lead to its acceptance. He or she may understand a message but not alter their buying intentions or behaviour. In this case acceptance probably means having to change consumer attitudes.

- Retention – is the stage where the stimulus finally is transferred into the memory, i.e. the message is noted and stored for use on a future occasion; the next relevant purchase occasion for example.

Simulated consumer decision-making process models

Two tools have been developed in this area to simulate decision-making processes:

- The 'rational consumer'-based elaboration likelihood model (ELM) advocates that consumers take time to consider messages designed to change attitudes. Information is processed via a central and also a peripheral route. If the key message from a piece of communication is believed then it will come in through the central route, making the message more likely to be firmly held, last longer and resistant to change. This makes repetition of the message important since the more the consumer sees the communication, the more likely he or she will attend to the core message and take it through the central route. It is the less than key messages that come in through the peripheral route. The result here is a lessening of the grip held, held for less time and less resistant to change. BMW's 'The Ultimate Driving Machine' strap/tagline created in 1975 but dropped in 2006 only to be resurrected in 2012 in the USA (revisit the Snapshot above) might come in through the central route while the voiceover tone of voice might come in peripherally. However, two intervening variables have been established here. First, motivation plays a key role. The more motivated a person is to search for information the more likely he or she is to process information via the central route. Second, the consumer's ability and desire to use cognitive skills will determine whether or not the information will be used via the central or peripheral route. Someone who likes to engage in thought and can do so will be in the former mode.

- The less than rational consumer, the person who impulse buys or buys for fun, fits in with the hedonic experiential model (HEM). The HEM tends not to follow a rational cognitive, systematic and reasoned consumer processing approach. The fun, fantasies and feelings of the HEM were introduced by Hirschman and Holbrook (1982) who were some of the first to challenge the traditional view of consumption, particularly from the (marketing) research methodological standpoint. In their seminal article, Hirschman and Holbrook dispel the myth of the traditional view of the consumption of products with their belief that consumers behave in a far more sensorily complex, imaginative and emotion-laden way, which is why they are interested in multiple facets consumption. They are therefore interested in things like the way the scent of a perfume involves the recall of an event that actually occurred (past episode in a romance) and indeed in fantasy imagery whereby the consumer constructs an imaginary sequence rather than an experienced, historic one. HEM assumes the tendency exists to maximise pleasure and minimise pain. Following such impulses ignores the longer-term consequences of action in favour of short-term pleasure. Here the consumer will relate to emotions and feelings. Fun and new or unusual experiences might be being sought in certain situations where more rational considerations such as price do not matter as much as the experience. Things on the outside of the ELM model become central in the HEM model.

Cognitive maps can help to explain the links between various ideas and assess and evaluate information. Logman (2008: 69) suggests that 'companies should be aware of the real signals and cues that are being used by their customers'. These might also be called 'buying signals' in the context of complimentary and competitive products in an environment full of trends and forces that impinge on all concerned. For Logman, 'consumers' knowledge structures and cognitive maps may be totally different from the company's initial point of view'. Marketers should not forget that the consumer does not see the marketing mix in the way the company does when it constructs its market offering. This is the rationale behind having an integrated effort and 'one marketing concept' that includes 'authenticity, consistency and simplicity', the lack of which becomes 'three important drivers of cognitive discrepancies between the company and the consumer' (Logman, 2008: 69). This fits in with the IMC concept.

Cognitive maps are described by Clow and Baack (2011) as simulations of the brain's knowledge structures containing, for example, assumptions, beliefs, attitudes and interpretations about the world. For new situations these structures help the individual produce an appropriate response. Linkages are made between competing brands in terms of attributes and this helps the consumer make decisions. For example, if the decision is about which fast food restaurant to visit, the consumer might think of McDonald's and the choice of food (say a vegetarian option), the service (going on past experience it was really fast) and the décor (last time it was nice and clean). The consumer might think about these factors in relation to Pizza Hut, KFC, Burger King and a few others. Clow and Baack (2011) also discuss levels and layers (beyond the actual message to include other things that might matter such as parking availability, ambience and so on) in terms of linkages. They also discuss linkages that already exist and messages that have no linkages at all to demonstrate the complexity of what on the surface is a simple situation. Obviously, different reactions will take place depending upon the levels and layers of linkage that exist and whether or not the message already has linkage with the brand or company. Repetition is important for transference from short- to long-term memory and the message is processed and fitted into previously constructed cognitive maps. Added to this is the idea that the marketer could link the message to a new concept that the consumer may not even have tried. Since, from a marketing perspective, it is easier to strengthen linkages that already exist, it would be worthwhile setting up links, even if tenuous, to build upon later. Marketers should continuously look for linkages that will have allure for consumers and help gain trust, commitment and maybe even loyalty.

Learning and the consumer learning process

Clearly, the amount of experience and information that a buyer has will affect the type of decision-making process they are likely to go through. The ways in which consumers learn about things have an influence on the marketing communications strategy.

Learning theories

Learning has been described as 'the process by which individuals acquire the purchase and consumption knowledge and experience they apply to future related behaviour' (Belch and Belch, 2009). The two basic approaches of behavioural and cognitive learning are well established in the marketing literature. Behavioural learning emphasises the role of external, environmental stimuli in terms of the behaviourist stimulus-response (S-R) 'school of thought'. Learning through classical conditioning can play an important part in marketing. Pavlov, the Russian physiologist, had sorted out the unconditioned stimulus and response from the conditioned stimulus and response in terms of food, dogs and the ringing of a bell. In other words the dogs originally salivated (unconditioned response) when they saw the food (unconditioned stimulus), but a conditioned response of salivation to a conditioned stimulus (not food but the ringing of a bell) was to be had. The contiguous presentation of the two stimuli is essential for the association to work and the more this happens the stronger the association. It was surmised that the consumer could also be conditioned to form favourable impressions and images of various brands through an associative process. Marketers strive to associate their products and services with perceptions, images and emotions known to evoke positive reactions from consumers. This has interesting implications for the use of many tools and techniques such as celebrity endorsements or music in advertising. What is hoped for is a more favourable attitude towards a brand when it is placed in certain situations with emotional triggers, such as likeable music, that are well received. Of course the opposite would be the case so that rather than the arousal of positive feelings, negative ones ensue.

The principles of operant or instrumental conditioning have been used by marketers through the use of the concept of reinforcement, i.e. reward or punishment as a consequence of action or indeed inaction. Behaviourists such as Skinner, using pigeons, had shown that reinforcement of behaviour strengthens the S-R bond. Positive experiences will reinforce while negative ones will have the opposite effect. Marketing communications can emphasise the benefits of purchase of a particular brand. Advertising can instruct the consumer to use a product to solve a problem (say deodorant). Sales promotions can reward a purchase with an additional benefit such as an offer the next time round. Belch and Belch (2009) point out that schedules of reinforcement can have an effect on the speed of learning. Continuous reinforcement can mean loyalty but if the reinforcement stops the consumer is likely to switch brands. Learning might be slower with intermittent or partial reinforcement but lasts longer. Therefore if appropriate, the cost of using the latter rather than the former would suggest there are instances when intermittent reinforcement could be employed.

Shaping is another option whereby the reinforcement of successive acts leads to the concept of the diminishing reward. The marketer might begin with free samples to achieve trial, followed by coupons to induce purchase for a small financial outlay, and then a larger one until finally the consumer purchases without inducement. The use of such techniques is the foundation of sales promotion strategy for new brands but the over use of them can have a disastrous effect on brand image.

Cognitive learning theory advocates much of what is discussed below in terms of the buyer decision process. Problem solving, information gathering, choices and decision making, mean that marketers need to respond to this type of learning by providing information in the right sort of detail and format. For example, sales people and brochures might be enough to do this. On the other hand detailed infomercials that perhaps use two-sided arguments that replicate the problem-solving process – that is, make it easier for the consumer to weigh up the pros and cons of different brands by presenting them with a carefully edited version – might be required. The avoidance/reduction of cognitive dissonance by not overstating brand strengths in the first place, or follow-up communication in post-purchase situations, are examples of tools that can contribute to this end. Of course, as indicated earlier in this chapter, environmental influences on buyer behaviour are expected and do exist, so that learning would not simply occur cognitively, in a vacuum.

The evoked set

The 'evoked set' is an idea developed by Howard and Sheth in the 1960s (for example, Howard and Sheth, 1969) as part of the evaluation of the alternative evaluation step of the consumer decision-making process. As part of this process (see the consumer decision-making process below), the 'evoked set' has become a useful construct. The evoked set is basically a list of those preferences or options that a consumer places in a sort of shortlist. In brand terms, the evoked set consists of those brands within a product category that the consumer creates a menu from, excluding all other potential menu members in the process. This helps make brand choice manageable and it saves time and energy in making decisions. The marketer's job then is to make sure that his brand is in the evoked set or on the menu. Salience or 'top of the mind awareness' is important here to gain entry onto the consumer shortlist and this can be achieved through the use of other marketing communication devices such as in-store sales promotions and certainly such devices can be used to help the consumer make the final choice of a brand from the evoked set. Typically a consumer might have four or five alternatives on the menu, including a particular own label. These brands will have arrived there by some means such as advertising. Belch and Belch (2009) point out that evaluation criteria will be much broader than simply this since products or services come with 'bundles of attributes'. They use Peters and Olson's distinction between functional and psychological consequences to highlight the difference between more concrete and tangible consequences of a particular brand choice (say taste) and the more abstract and intangible ones such as how a brand makes the consumer feel. However, it is not until the consumer is in-store that the final decision to purchase will be made. The consumer may choose one particular brand from the menu simply because of an attractive sales promotion or an end of aisle display.

Clow and Baack (2011) distinguish between the inept and the inert set. The inept set consists of brands not considered even though they are in the person's mind because they elicit negative feelings through a bad experience or an influential negative comment. The inert set consists of brands that again the consumer is aware of but has negative feelings about. Thus neither of these sets becomes part of the final evoked set, unless something happens whereby the linkages become stronger rather than weaker and the consumer feels more positive than negative about a particular brand.

The Ehrenberg and Goodhart (1979) ATR (awareness, trial, and reinforcement) model suggests that it is the big brands that benefit from consumer behaviour regarding brand switching. As long as the brand is the most frequently purchased (but not the only one purchased) then brand management is doing its job. This suggests that consumers shop around to check that consumption patterns bring the best results (Pickton and Broderick, 2005). The consumer may very well take a multi-attribute approach and actually rate these attributes across brands. The consumer may partake in 'affect referral' whereby they will buy a particular brand from a product category even though the consumer has no experience of the brand in that context simply because there is trust in the brand already from experience elsewhere (Clow and Baack, 2011). Latterly this has been proven to be the case with rather diverse product categories involved and not just the obvious such as Nestlé or Cadbury chocolate and other confectionery and cakes. Virgin for example has been successful in music, soft drinks, airlines, financial services and trains. Tata (over 100 years old) has been successful with steel, tea, auto-mobiles and coffee, among many other things, and is now fast becoming recognised as a global brand.

Attitudes

Attitudes are learned predispositions towards things that will influence the person's per-ceptions, feelings and ultimately perhaps behaviour toward those things. The thing might be, for example, an object, a person or an idea, and the attitude might be trivial or more strongly held. The literature suggests that attitudes have three components:

Cognitive – mental images, interpretation and understanding of the thing.
Affective – feelings and emotions towards the thing.
Conative – intentions, actions and behaviour with regard to the thing.

This sequence might change but in this example, from a marketing standpoint, the con-sumer has first to get some idea mentally about the thing (say an advertisement for a par-ticular brand) that might involve humour. Then they are in a position to feel about both the commercial and its content, including the brand, and feel good about the experience. The consumer is now in a position to act (or not) in one way or another and that action might be to try the brand because of the positive feelings towards it. The consumer may be made to feel first, then take action (try the brand) and then understand it so that the sequence might be different (see hierarchy of effects below). Therefore in marketing terms it is much more relevant to talk about, for example, attitudes towards brands, advertise-ments or the celebrity endorser used within the advertisement. Attitudes are important to marketers and marketing because they hold the key to positive or negative leanings consumers may have towards a company or brand. Having a favourable attitude towards a brand may not necessarily lead directly to purchase since some other, intervening vari-able such as price may get in the way, but clearly attitudes and the verbal expression of those attitudes – opinions – are highly sought after by marketers in their pursuit of creat-ing more and more effective communications.

Multi-attribute attitude models are particularly useful to marketers as they view an attitude object, such as a brand, as possessing a number of attributes that provide the basis on which consumers evaluate and form attitudes (Belch and Belch, 2009). Thus consumers have values that become beliefs about specific brand attributes and attach different levels of importance to these attributes. By appealing to basic values, the mar-keter can influence consumers that a particular brand can help them achieve a desir-able outcome. For example toothpaste may have the attributes of cleans teeth, freshens breath, reduces tartar, reduces the risk of gum disease, tastes nice, looks nice, pump dis-penser, or a certain price level. Having clean, white teeth might reflect the basic personal value of self-respect (but not necessarily in all cultures). Marketers, through product positioning, can associate brands with one, some or all of these attributes. The brand that is associated with those attributes that are important to a particular consumer will most likely go into the evoked set, and may perhaps be purchased. In fact, many brands may offer the same level of performance, but it is the brand that is associated with those attributes by the consumer that will be preferred. Belch and Belch (2009) point out that it is salient beliefs, i.e. beliefs concerning specific attributes or consequences, that are activated and form the basis of the attitude and that such beliefs will vary across market segments, over time and across different consumption situations. Belch and Belch (2009) suggest that attitude change can be brought about through understanding such beliefs in four ways:

- By increasing or changing the strength or belief rating of a brand on an important attribute. Reinforcing a brand attribute is an example of this where a Toyota is 'the car in front' and a BMW is 'the ultimate driving machine'.
- Changing consumers' perceptions of the importance or value of an attribute. Tapping into current trends or fashions can help achieve this. The Co-operative Bank in the UK made a big play for the moral high ground on not investing in oppressive regimes, as part of the values of their own heritage and raison d'être.
- Adding a new attribute to the attitude formation process, in a similar vein to point two above, only with something new added. Belch and Belch use the example of product improvement by the brand Ragu with organically grown tomato in the sauce.
- Changing perceptions of belief ratings for a competing brand. More prevalent in the USA than anywhere else, this leads directly to comparative advertising and the use of knocking copy where the marketer compares the brand, in a more favourable light of course, to the competition. For example, in the UK in 2012 the German-owned discount supermarket chain Aldi started a long-running campaign against manufacturers' brands on price and quality.

Hierarchy of effects

When a message is sent to an audience it is assumed that the audience responds in some way. There are many possible responses that can be grouped into three distinct categories: cognitive; affective; and conative. All messages attempt to influence at least one of these responses. The hierarchy of effects therefore states that a consumer must pass through a series of stages from unawareness to purchase and brand loyalty. A number of 'models' have been developed over the years and a précis is shown below in Table 3.1.

Table 3.1 Various 'hierarchy of effects' models

Model	Cognitive	Affective	Conative
AIDA (St Elmo Lewis, 1900)	Attention	Interest, Desire	Action
AIDAS (Sheldon, 1911)	Attention Satisfaction	Interest, Desire	Action
AIDCA (Kitson, 1921)	Attention Conviction	Interest, Desire,	Action
AIDA (Strong, 1925)	Attention	Interest, Desire	Action
DAGMAR (Colley, 1961)	Awareness, Comprehension	Conviction	Action
AIETA (Rogers, 1962)	Awareness	Interest, Evaluation	Trial, Adoption
AKLPPC (Lavidge and Steiner, 1961)	Awareness, Knowledge	Liking, Preference, Conviction	Purchase
AIIETA (Howard and Sheth, 1969)	Adoption	Attitude, Intention	Purchase
EAYACPR/Online Information (Hofhacker, 2000)	Exposure, Attention	Yielding, Acceptance Comprehension, Perception	Retention

It was, apparently, the teachings of E. St. Elmo Lewis that first raised the idea of AID (Awareness, Interest, Desire) in 1898, adding action to form an extended model in 1900. It would be Strong (1925) who would cite Lewis as author of AID then AIDA. This was not in print but most likely as part of Lewis's talks to Rotary Clubs, Chambers of Commerce and other such organisations.

These models or frameworks deal then with the think-feel-do sequence of events regarding the cognitive (awareness, knowledge), the affective (interest/liking, desire/preference/conviction) and the conative or behavioural (action/purchase). They are subjected to the usual criticism that is applied to stage models but also that knowing the level of communication input in order to facilitate change is difficult to measure. Until this is known an optimal communications mix cannot be devised and implemented. The state of mind of the customer and changes to the usual think-feel-do sequence are important in terms of levels of involvement. This was recognised by Vaughn (1980, 1986), for Foot, Cone and Belding. This agency was concerned with the importance attached to products. High-involvement products that tend to follow the think-feel-do sequence are things like cars, furniture, loans and appliances (classical hierarchy of effects). Those that follow the feel-think-do sequence tend to be jewellery, perfume and fashion because the consumer wants to be emotionally attracted by the brand image. Low-involvement products that follow a do-think-feel sequence tend to be things like detergents, food and toilet paper – products that are bought without too much cognitive effort. Low-involvement items like sweets, soft drinks and ice cream follow a do-feel-think sequence and are thought of as 'life's little pleasures' (De Pelsmaker et al., 2004).

Here, then, involvement – the importance of the product to people as expressed by the buying decision – is recognised. Risk comes into play with regard to performance and psychological aspects. However, this can be challenged in the sense that some seemingly simple products are no longer low involvement products. Some three decades ago the Ogilvy Centre for Research & Development (1984) distinguished between performance risk such as the product not coming up to scratch or living up to what is expected and psychological risk. This latter type of risk exists where the choice of a particular brand reflects badly on the purchaser in the eyes of others. Within this there are badge categories where the brand name remains prominent while the product is used, such as beer or blue jeans. There are also closet categories where only the purchaser knows the brand name. A particular brand of petrol would be an example of a closet brand. Both of these categories can be linked to the consumer's self-image. This can perhaps be more clearly seen with the badge-type brand whereby use of the brand makes the consumer feel better about themself as a person. Motives for buying a particular brand of an otherwise banal product like toilet paper or cleaner can therefore be complex. Advertisers have understood this for some time, finding very clever ways, for example, to get around the anxieties attached to many aspects of the toilet.

The Ogilvy Centre also makes the distinction between new and established brands in terms of how communication works. For an established brand, salience (top of the mind), reinforcement and repurchase are the expected sequence. For new brands the picture is rather more complex. Four models are suggested:

1. For new brands that are distinctive and high risk, awareness should be followed by comprehension, then attitude formation and purchase.
2. For new brands that are distinctive and low risk, awareness should be followed by purchase then comprehension, and attitude formation.
3. For new brands that are similar to competitors and high risk, awareness should be followed by attitude formation, comprehension and purchase.
4. For new brands that are similar to the competition and low risk, awareness should be followed by purchase then attitude formation and comprehension.

Types of customer

The development of successful marketing communication programmes begins with understanding why consumers – or customers – behave as they do. Consumer behaviour has long been seen as a process that has consumers searching for products and services (or particular brands) in order to meet needs, wants and desires. Therefore, marketing communicators need to recognise that while much of promotional activity has the goal of influencing consumers' purchase behaviour, the purchase is only a part of what can be a long and detailed process of information search, brand and retailer comparisons and evaluation. Armed with customer knowledge, marketing communicators can begin the task of developing an effective message strategy, choosing appropriate media, deciding the promotional mix weighting and setting objectives, i.e. designing, developing, planning and executing a communications campaign.

Think-feel-do

A customer who learns before anything else and is highly involved in a buying decision, looking at a large range of alternatives, comparing features, prices and so on, expresses a high-risk position. The marketer will need to provide technical detail using print media, and sales staff and friends/family might also be consulted so communications should be designed with the multi-step flow of communication in mind. Such a customer will therefore go through a think-feel-do sequence to resolve a problem.

Do-feel-think

A customer who buys quickly with little thought or evaluation, and then evaluates post-purchase, usually does so because there is little difference between the products on offer and little risk involved. The marketer will need to help the consumer justify their purchase, thus avoiding dissonance cognitive. Such a customer will go through a do-feel-think sequence.

Think-do-feel

Many products purchased in a routine fashion are associated with low risk, where there is little between brands and the consumer has experience of purchasing the product. The marketer needs to remind the consumer that the brand is still there and provide reasons why it should remain as part of the consumer's repertoire and try to avoid switching since this customer will think-do-feel in sequence.

Do-think-feel or think-feel-do

Trained, professional buyers will tend to be methodical and follow set practice for risk-reduction. Much of this is routinised but on occasion there will be more highly involved purchase. This customer then is either do-think-feel (routinised) or think-feel-do (new task).

The Snapshot below challenges the notion that the over 50s as a consumer group is a false one. Ultimately, from a marketing perspective, older people have to be treated in the usual marketing way that involves segmentation, targeting and communication with particular targets with particular characteristics.

Snapshot   The over 50s – a sub-cultural phenomenon or a Peter Pan, Harley Davidson-riding generation?

'They used to be called Senior Citizens. Then the "Wrinklies". That changed to the "Crinklies", soon after. For a long time, they were known as the "Grey Market". The insurance market calls them Grey Eagles. Contemporary marketing speak now calls them Third-Agers' (Owen, 2012).

The marketing practitioner perspective suggests that growing older is getting cooler (Benady, 2008). Benady is of course commenting on the trend in the 1990s for the purchase of, for example Harley Davidson motorcycles by 50-somethings who's children had left home and who had become 'empty nesters' with the time and money 'to live out their fantasies'. These are people who grew up in the late 1970s as opposed to those who did so in the 1960s but are, in a similar fashion, in a position to spend money on themselves as opposed to buying things for the children and the home. Owen (2012) suggests that this sector is the most affluent in countries like the UK, 'with 36% of over 50's having a gross income in excess of £20.000' and '80% of the country's wealth is held by people aged 50 or over'. Owen adds 'if your products or services are relevant to this group I'd review your plans and fast!'

It is not, however, just about the money, although that of course is always a consideration. It is about changing lifestyles and generally being fitter and living longer. The forum and website silverhairs.com (Silverhairs, 2012) suggests that according to a BBC survey middle age now begins much later than was previously thought, with older British people not seeing themselves as elderly until they get closer to 70 years old. This can be compared to the age of 36 being the belief of people in earlier times as the start at least of middle age. Further, a lot of people apparently believe that middle age is a state of mind and not a specific age (19 per cent of those surveyed) and that 55–69 is the span of middle age. The Silverhairs forum (2012) also cites research from the charity Age UK that looked at how Europeans categorise themselves, suggesting that old age is perceived to start at 62. The research also found that there was less of a consensus among European countries on when youth ended. This apparently ranged from 34 years old in Sweden to 52 years old in Greece. The average age of the end of youth was 40 years old, which perhaps ties in with the old adage 'life begins at 40'.

Does this mean then that Harley Davidson motorcycles are just for men in the 50+ bracket? Not at all, but the product range will vary depending on where in the world you are. The archetypal 50+ male 'empty nester' might well be a key customer in North America or parts of Europe but in other countries the market is different. For example Anabtawi (2012) looks at Harley Davidson in the Middle East and North Africa region (MENA) through the eyes of one of its country managers who suggests that buying a Harley is in effect joining a club and gaining a large group of friends where there is 'a culture of brotherhood and camaraderie'. In the UAE the Harley Davidson business had initially been grown on a Western, male expat basis but the market has developed to include Arab expats, local people and women. The product is not the same for all users. Harley Davidson found that women would ride a motorcycle that was not too heavy or high for them and that they would do so because their husbands did (Arabian Business, 2012). There is, therefore, in markets such as Lebanon and Jordan, a much younger customer profile, including women who now want to ride independently, with 70 per cent of Harley sales in North America but the remaining 30 per cent largely in Europe, the Middle East and Africa (Arabian Business, 2012).

Stop Point

It is essential that marketers do not make assumptions about older consumers and take note of the many misconceptions that are bandied around that can cause myriad problems. Undertake the following: 1. Explain the marketer's continued need for segmentation studies and accurate target market data; 2. Consider and discuss the likely communication tools and mix required in different, older consumer contexts.

Assignment

Review consumer and trade/business and management magazine advertisements and identify and provide an analysis of one advertisement that you feel is aimed at each of the types of consumer or buyer from the following list:

- Think-feel-do (consumer);
- Do-feel-think (consumer);
- Think-do-feel (consumer);
- Do-think-feel (professional buyer);
- Think-feel-do (professional buyer).

Comment on anything you perceive might be to do with the buying decision process outlined in this chapter.

Summary of Key Points

- The size of markets is important but the ability to measure this is of little use if your product and communications do not fit in with the culture.
- People worldwide share certain needs but needs may be met differently in different cultures.
- Language is a cultural variable but culture is much more than this. It includes things like religion, customs and practices and involves values, symbols, heroes and rituals as expressions of culture.
- There is a case to be made for the notion of 'global culture'.
- There is often discussion of global culture but it is more realistic for marketers to look at models such as the high/low context of culture as well as the characteristics of culture and aspects of consumer behaviour.
- Models of consumer behaviour deal with cultural (and sub-cultural) elements as do lifestyle and value approaches.

(Continued)

(Continued)

- Cross-cultural comparisons of advertising can be made. Models of culture such as the dimensions model of Hofstede have also been a big influence on thinking about culture.

- Buyer behaviour theory is quite complex but can be broken down into component parts such as motivation, perception and cognition.

- Involvement is a key concept in terms of the way buying is conducted and the activities that are engaged with.

- The same can be said of buyer learning theory in terms of classical and operant behavioural theory and cognitive learning theory. The evoked set, attitudes and the hierarchy of effects are also key to understanding behaviour.

- The buying decision-making process can be modelled but should be used with caution in either the consumer or organisational buyer context. There are variations to the conventional models and also communication implications of such variations.

Discussion Questions

1. Distinguish between beliefs, attitudes, opinions and interests. Explain the elements of culture that are likely to be important in any given situation using examples to illustrate.

2. Using an example of a values and lifestyle model explain why understanding of cultural elements alone is not enough for effective marketing and marketing communications practice.

3. Illustrate the importance of 'word-of-mouth' and opinion leadership in terms of buyer behaviour. Explain how peer group pressure might be made to work in magazine advertising.

4. Critically examine the usefulness or not to marketers of Holbrook and Hirschman's Hedonic and Experiential theory of buyer behaviour. Contrast this with the more traditional ELM.

5. Explain the role that family members might have within the consumer buying decision making process.

6. Explain selective perception and retention in terms of a communicator's effort to 'get through the clutter'.

7. Differentiate between ordinary and subliminal advertising using examples to illustrate.

8. Compare and contrast the consumer and organisational buyer in terms of the hierarchy of effects sequence.

9. Explain the five stages of the conventional consumer decision-making process. Contrast this with the organisational buyer decision-making process.

10. Discuss the likely variations in consumer and buyer decision making and illustrate with examples of communications implications.

Further Reading

Bradfield, O.M., Parker, C. and Goodwin, L. (2009) 'Sustaining Performance: learning from buyers' experience of Viagra', *Journal of Medical Marketing*, 9 (4): 343–53. http://mmj.sagepub.com/content/9/4/343.full.pdf+html

This is an account of Pfizer's reflections on past experiences of Viagra users in order to re-assess a future marketing strategy. The first part of the article examines the buyer (the end-user, not doctors or pharmacists) behaviour literature for these kinds of product that deal with erectile dysfunction. The second part assesses Pfizer's current marketing and promotional strategy and materials, and the third part draws on the literature to examine the ways in which the company can invigorate their marketing effort.

Kim, H., Lee, E-J and Hur, W-M. (2012) 'The Normative Social Influence on Eco-friendly Consumer Behaviour: the moderating effect of environmental marketing claims', *Clothing and Textiles Research Journal*, 30 (1): 4–18. http://ctr.sagepub.com/content/30/1/4.full.pdf+html

This study uses normative conduct theory and the literature on environmental marketing to explore whether eco-friendly behaviour in the apparel market is influenced by variations in social norms and environmental concerns. The results confirm the significant effects of social norms but go further to suggest that the types of environmental marketing claim moderate positive influences of injunctive norms on purchase intention.

Schatzel, K. and Calatone, R. (2006) 'Creating Market Anticipation: an exploratory examination of the effect of preannouncement behaviour on a new product launch', *Journal of the Academy of Marketing Science*, 34 (3): 357–66. http://jam.sagepub.com/content/34/3/357.full.pdf+html

This article looks at preannouncements as strategic marketing communications directed at market participants such as distributors and buyers. The authors suggest that this study is different from studies that focus on the antecedents influencing a firm's preannouncement behaviour in that it looks at preannouncement behaviour as a deliberate marketing communications process. A test model is developed that includes the effects of preannouncement behaviour on the successful launch of a new product through market anticipation, competitive equity and NPD resources. The authors report on the positive effect on market anticipation by preannouncements as B-to-B marketing communications that influence prospective partners in the supply chain.

Walsh, G. and Gwimmer, K.P. (2009) 'Purchasing Vacation Packages through Shop-at-home Television Programmes: an analysis of consumers' consumption motives', *Journal of Vacation Marketing*, 15 (2): 111–28. http://jvm.sagepub.com/content/15/2/111.full.pdf+html

This article discusses non-store retailing but more particularly buying through shop-at-home television programming. Consumer behaviour in the complex, high-involvement arena is investigated through looking at vacation travel services. The authors adopt a choice motivation typology as a framework to investigate booking motives. They use a form of factor then cluster analysis to identify four significant and distinct buyer groups. The article provides implications for travel-marketing practice and research.

Wells, V.K. (2012) 'Foraging: an ecology model of consumer behaviour?', *Marketing Theory*, 12 (2): 117–36. http://mtq.sagepub.com/content/12/2/117.full.pdf+html

The author introduces the uninitiated business and marketing reader to foraging ideas and terminology in terms of consumption and behaviour. There are a number of suggestions made for the use of the foraging model in both academia and practice. The article goes further with the idea of a foraging ecology model of consumer behaviour and implications for both on- and off-line marketing and retailing practice.

REFERENCES

Age UK (2010) 'The golden economy: the consumer marketplace in an ageing society', available at: www.ilcuk.org.uk/files/pdf_pdf_155.pdf

Anabtawi, S. (2012) 'Easy rider', *Arabian Business*, 23 September.

Arabian Business (2012) 'Harley Davidson tells Arab women to get on their bikes', *Arabian Business*, 27 September.

Belch, G. and Belch, M. (2009) *Advertising and Promotion* (8th edn). New York: The McGraw-Hill Companies Limited.

Benady, D. (2008) 'Marketing to the over-50s', *Marketing Week*, 30 April, available at: www.marketingweek.co.uk/marketing-to-the-over-50s/2060579.article

Blackwell, R.D., Miniard, P.W. and Engel, J.F. (2006) *Consumer Behavior* (10th edn). Mason, OH: Thomson/South Western.

Blodgett, J.G., Bakir, A. and Rose, G.M. (2008) 'A test of the validity of Hofstede's cultural framework', *Journal of Consumer Marketing*, 25 (6): 339–49.

Bradfield, O.M., Parker, C. and Goodwin, L. (2009) 'Sustaining performance: learning from buyers' experience of Viagra', *Journal of Medical Marketing*, 9 (4): 343–53.

Clow, K.E. and Baack, D. (2011) *Integrated Adverting, Promotion and Marketing Communications* (5th edn). New Jersey: Pearson Education.

Colley, R.H. (1961) *Defining Advertising Goals for Measured Advertising Results*. New York: Association of National Advertisers.

de Mooij, M. (1994) *Advertising Worldwide* (2nd edn). Hertfordshire UK: Prentice Hall International (UK) Ltd.

de Mooij, M. (1998) *Global Marketing and Advertising – Understanding Cultural Paradoxes*. Thousand Oaks, CA: Sage Publishing Inc.

de Mooij, M. (2000) 'The future is predictable for international marketers – converging incomes lead to diverging consumer behaviour', *International Marketing Review*, 17 (2): 103–13.

de Mooij, M. (2001) 'Convergence and divergence in consumer behaviour – consequences for global marketing and advertising', Doctoral Dissertation, University de Navarra, Navarra, Spain.

de Mooij, M. (2003a) *Convergence and Divergence in Consumer Behaviour – Consequences for Global Marketing and Advertising*. Thousand Oaks, CA: Sage Publishing Inc.

de Mooij, M. (2003b) 'Convergence and divergence in consumer behaviour – implications for global advertising', *International Journal of Advertising*, 22 (2): 183–202.

de Mooij, M. (2004) 'Translating advertising – painting the tip of an iceberg', *The Translator*, 10 (2): 179–98.

de Mooij, M. (2005) *Global Marketing and Advertising – Understanding Cultural Paradoxes* (2nd edn). Thousand Oaks, CA: Sage Publishing Inc.

de Mooij, M. (2010) *Global Marketing and Advertising – Understanding Cultural Paradoxes*, (3rd edn). Thousand Oaks, CA: Sage Publishing Inc.

de Mooij, M. (2011a) *Convergence and Divergence in Consumer Behaviour – Consequences for Global Marketing and Advertising* (2nd edn). Thousand Oaks, CA: Sage Publishing Inc.

de Mooij, M. (2011b) 'Convergence and divergence in consumer behaviour', *Admap*, October: 30–3.

de Mooij, M. and Goodrich, K. (2011) 'New technology mirrors old habits: online buying mirrors cross-national variance of conventional buying', *Journal of International Consumer Marketing*, 23 (3-4): 246–259.

de Mooij, M. and Hofstede, G. (2002) 'Convergence and divergence in consumer behaviour: implications for international retailing', *Journal of Retailing*, 78 (1): 61–9.

de Mooij, M. and Hofstede, G. (2010) 'The Hofstede model – applications to global branding and advertising strategy and research', *International Journal of Advertising*, 29 (1): 85–110.

de Mooij, M. and Hofstede, G. (2011) 'Cross-cultural consumer behaviour: a review of research findings', *Journal of International Consumer Marketing*, 23 (3-4): 181–92.

de Mooij, M. and Keegan, W. (1991) *Advertising Worldwide*. Hertfordshire, UK: Prentice Hall International (UK) Ltd.

De Pelsmaker, P., Geuens, M. and Van den Bergh, J. (2004) *Marketing Communications: a European perspective* (2nd edn). Harlow, Essex: FT Prentice Hall/Pearson Education Limited.

Dichter, E. (1947) *The Psychology of Everyday Living*. USA: Barnes and Noble Inc.

Ehrenberg, A. and Goodhart, G. (1979) *Essays on Understanding Buyer Behaviour*. New York, NY: J. Walter Thompson Co. and Market Research Corporation of America.

Fraj, E. and Martinez, E. (2006) 'Environmental values and lifestyles as determining factors of ecological consumer behaviour: an empirical analysis', *Journal of Consumer Marketing*, 23 (3): 133–44.

Hall, E.T. (1976) *Beyond Culture*. New York: Anchor Press.

The Henley Centre (1998) *Planning for Social Change*. London: The Henley Centre.

Henry, J. (2012) 'BMW: still The Ultimate Driving Machine, not that it ever wasn't', *Forbes*, 31 May.

Hirschman, E.C. and Holbrook, M.B. (1982) 'Hedonic consumption: emerging concepts, methods and propositions', *Journal of Marketing*, 46 (Summer): 92–101.

Hofhaker, C.F. (2001) *Internet Marketing*, 3rd edn. New York: John Wiley and Sons.

Hofstede, G. (1980) *Culture's Consequences: International Differences in Work Related Values*. Thousand Oaks, CA: Sage Publications.

Hofstede, G. (1989) 'Organizing for cultural diversity', *European Management Journal*, 7 (4): 389–96.

Hofstede, G. (1990) 'Marketing and culture', Working Paper, Maastricht: University of Limburg.

Hofstede, G. (1991) *Cultures and Organisations: software of the mind*. Berkshire, UK: McGraw-Hill Education.

Hofstede, G. (1993) 'Cultural constraints in management theories', *The Executive Management Journal*, 7 (1): 81–94.

Hofstede, G. (2001) *Culture's Consequences: comparing values, behaviors, institutions, and organizations across nations* (2nd edn). Thousand Oaks, CA: Sage Publications.

Hofstede, G. and Hofstede, G.J. (2005) *Cultures and Organisations: software of the mind* (2nd edn). UK: McGraw-Hill International.

Hofstede, G., Hofstede, G.J. and Minkov, M. (2010) *Cultures and Organisations: software of the mind* (3rd edn). UK: McGraw-Hill International.

Howard, J.A. and Sheth, J.N. (1969) *The Theory of Buyer Behaviour*. New York: John Wiley and Sons.

Hunt, J.B. (2002) 'A comparative analysis of the management and leadership competency profiles reported by German, US and Australian managers', *International Journal of Organisational Behaviour*, 5 (9): 263–81.

Ipsos MediaCT (2009) 'Social grade – a classification tool', available at: www.ipsos-mori.com/DownloadPublication/1285_MediaCT_thoughtpiece_Social_Grade_July09_V3_WEB.pdf

Kim, H., Lee, E-J and Hur, W-M. (2012) 'The normative social influence on eco-friendly consumer behaviour: the moderating effect of environmental marketing claims', *Clothing and Textiles Research Journal*, 30 (1): 4–18.

Kitson, H.D. (1921) *The Mind of the Buyer: a psychology of selling*. New York: The Macmillan Company.

Lavidge, R.C. and Steiner, G.A. (1961) 'A model for predictive measurements of advertising effectiveness', *Journal of Marketing*, 25: 59–62.

Logman, M. (2008) 'Understanding consumers' cognitive maps in today's complex marketing environments', *Innovative Marketing*, 4 (3): 69–73.

McLuhan, M. (1964) *Understanding Media*. New York: Mentor.

Maslow, A.H. (1943) 'A theory of human motivation', *Psychological Review*, 50 (4): 370–96.

Maslow, A.H. (1954) *Motivation and Personality*. New York: Harper and Row.

Mueller, B. (1987) 'Reflections of culture: Japan versus USA', *Journal of Advertising Research*, June/July: 51–9.

Mueller, B. (1996) *International Advertising – Communicating Across Cultures*. Belmont, CA: Wadsworth Publishing Company.

Ogilvy Centre for Research & Development (1984) *How Advertising Works: an up-to-date view*. Ogilvy Centre for Research & Development. San Francisco, CA: Ogilvy and Mather.

Owen, A. (2012) 'Marketing to the over-50s', Andy Owen & Associates Ltd, available at: www.andyowen.co.uk/art5.html

Oxford University Press (1979) *Oxford Dictionary of Quotations* (3rd edn). Oxford: Guild Publications.

Pickton, D. and Broderick, A. (2005) *Integrated Marketing Communications*, 2nd edn. Harlow, UK: FT Prentice Hall/Pearson Education Limited.

Plummer, J.T. (1974) 'The concept and application of life style segmentation', *Journal of Marketing*, January, 38 (1): 33–37.

Pychyl, T.A. (2009) 'Don't delay – sometimes a cigar is just a cigar', *Psychology Today*, 21 March. Available at: http://www.psychologytoday.com/blog/dont-delay/200903/parenting-style-and-procrastination.

Rogers, E.M. (1962) *Diffusion of Innovation*. New York: Free Press.

Schatzel, K. and Calatone, R. (2006) 'Creating market anticipation: an exploratory examination of the effect of preannouncement behaviour on a new product launch', *Journal of the Academy of Marketing Science*, 34 (3): 357–66.

Schiffman, L., Hansen, H. and Kanuk, L.L. (2008) *Consumer Behaviour: a European outlook*. Harlow, UK: Pearson Education.

Sheldon, A.F. (1911) *The Art of Selling*. Chicago: The Sheldon School.

Silverhairs (2012) 'Some say middle age is a state of mind', 18 September, available at: www.silverhairs.com/forum/are-you-middle-aged/some-say-middle-aged-is-a-state-of-mind/

Strategic Business Insights (2012) 'US framework and VALS types', available at: www.strategic-businessinsights.com/vals/ustypes.shtml

Strong, Jr., E.K. (1925) *The Psychology of Selling and Advertising*. New York: McGraw-Hill.

Valentine, D.B. and Powers, T.L. (2013) 'Generation Y values and lifestyle segments', *Journal of Consumer Marketing*, 30 (7): 597–606.

Vaughn, R. (1980) 'How advertising works: a planning model', *Journal of Advertising Research*, 20 (5): 27–33.

Vaughn, R. (1986) 'How advertising works: a planning model revisited', *Journal of Advertising Research*, 27 (February/March): 57–66.

Vijayenthiran, V. (2012) 'BMW is once again "The Ultimate Driving Machine"', 12 January, available at: www.motorauthority.com/news/1071633_bmw-is-once-again-the-ultimate-driving-machine

Walsh, G. and Gwimmer, K.P. (2009) 'Purchasing vacation packages through shop-at-home television programmes: an analysis of consumers' consumption motives', *Journal of Vacation Marketing*, 15 (2): 111–28.

Wells, V.K. (2012) 'Foraging: an ecology model of consumer behaviour?', *Marketing Theory*, 12 (2): 117–36.

Managing the Marketing Communications Mix

Introduction

The concept of marketing communications management that utilises different models/theories within a process is well developed in the literature. The process usually begins with some form of analysis as a first 'where are we now' stage. This can involve considerable detail. The communications mix needs to be part of a carefully planned strategy in order to maximise effectiveness and obtain a unified message. The key purpose of this chapter is to provide a decision sequence model (DSM – a framework and template) that can be easily adapted by the manager of communications of one sort or another in different contexts. This, broadly, is the APIC (Analysis, Planning, Implementation, Control) system for managing communications. Although this approach is used here, not unlike many other authors in the marketing communications area, it is acknowledged that other writers are somewhat critical of this kind of approach to managing marketing, notably Brown (2001). It is recommended that practitioners develop a decision sequence model/framework that includes marketing communications theory, the communications environment, and key issues in understanding consumer behaviour such as information processing and decision making. There is therefore a need to deal with the development of communications strategy and then with the implementation and execution of such a strategy. It is at this point that marketers can begin to develop and manage marketing communications.

Learning objectives

The chapter seeks to propose a management framework for use across the remainder of the book and individual communications elements such as advertising and public relations. More specifically, after reading this chapter the student will be able to:

- appreciate what the DSM is and what it offers to marketing communicators;
- place the elements of the APIC system in broad DSM terms;
- understand the framework for the management of the marketing communications function;
- assess and critique the adoption of such an approach to marketing communications management.

THE DECISION SEQUENCE MODEL (DSM)

The DSM is a commonly used model that deals with both the 'art' and 'science' aspects of communication. A decision sequence framework holds a logical sequence of decisions that managers make when preparing, implementing and evaluating marketing communications strategies and plans. The decision sequence imposes a managerial framework on a process that is often otherwise conducted in a 'seat of the pants' way. In this book a vertical representation is used (which is the commonest form). It is acknowledged that other authors offer an approach that is represented horizontally, and even in what appears to be a non-linear way, but deal essentially with the same kinds of issue of, for example, market structure, environmental monitoring and management, setting objectives, developing strategy and tactical approaches, implementation issues and evaluation, monitoring and control.

The rationale for segmentation and targeting

Descriptors of the target market must be derived so that the most appropriate segment of consumers can be reached. This classification process needs to identify customers/consumers on a number of criteria such as demographics, usage levels or knowledge. In order to communicate with targets, it is advantageous to assess their perceptions of the product/brand, its competition, and the relationships between the consumer and the product class. Understanding how customers/consumers make decisions on where the brand can be bought and how they process information is important. How involved customers/consumers are in decisions and how product/brand decisions are made in the home or in the store is also useful information.

Mass marketing is a thing of the past – the 1970s saw segmentation and line extension. Niche marketing followed into the 1980s and the forecast is for atomisation. Everyone is capable of being a target and a segment since every person is unique. This does not help most marketers simply because it is not economical or efficient to approach each customer or potential customer in the vast majority of situations, although in some industrial, business-to-business or bespoke contexts there may be very few players and each target might indeed be approached individually but, generally, aggregated or mass marketing is a very rare occurrence. Not even the classic examples of mass marketing of commodities such as sugar and coffee can be used any more to explain mass marketing. Goods are no longer standardised. For this to work all people must have the same basic needs and wants, which is highly unlikely even though economies of scale are attractive with lower costs, including those of advertising and other forms of communication. Glimmers of this can be seen through environmental pressure, for example, to reduce packaging, but generally needs and wants are different. Homogeneous groupings became a reality with the marketer dealing with smaller groups where, although not perhaps a perfect fit for their needs, customers are able and willing to compromise, to trade off, and accept something that is nearly what they want, for example at a much lower price than they would otherwise have to pay. Segmentation is at the heart of modern marketing. Markets can be broken up into segments, populated by homogeneous groups whose needs should be known to the marketer through the use of marketing research, intelligence and experience. There are market segmentation variables or bases for segmentation. Profiling with likely buying behaviour through further research can then be developed before market targeting begins.

Once a target is established, if it is substantive enough and accessible, then marketing, including marketing communications, can be implemented to approach the target. This is a way to cover the market by identifying attractive segments in a market and developing a market and product positioning strategy in that market. Companies such as Procter and Gamble have done this successfully for many years whereby, for example, different soap brands are placed in different parts of the market to cover the whole of the needs and wants (softness, smell and so on) of that market. Databases via research and technology have developed at an incredible pace and are of ever-increasing importance. Parameters such as demographics, psychographics, behaviour/usage and geography can be used to build databases. Only by understanding how customers like to be contacted will the company be able to truly interact with them. The company must start with segmentation and identify target groups from the outset and follow on towards objectives and where the company/product/brand should be positioned. This can be helped by applying a number of concepts.

Product differentiation and branding

Product differentiation should be based on customer perceptions, for example association of the product with something that is valued. For this to work there are three requirements: the customer must be able to distinguish between products; the differences between competing products should not be small/trivial; and the customer must care about the product. This supports the idea of branding, since it is brands that help distinguish products, a brand is unique and differences between it and the competition not trivial, and brands are (hopefully) liked and desired.

Bases for segmentation

Many things qualify as a base for segmenting a whole into constituent parts. Clearly, segments must be attractive enough for the company to be interested. A segment has to be large enough to be worthwhile, and substantive enough not just in volume but also in value. Segments need to be identifiable and reachable. Where there is a media vehicle available there is the means to reach the segment, i.e. the segment is accessible. Segments also need to be responsive and targets want the offering. Stability, without the problems of volatility or fickleness, is also desirable. Bases are at the centre of targeting. For *consumer* marketing many have been developed including demographics, psychographics and systems based on geodemographics. There are others, such as benefit segmentation, and rather different approaches for *organisational* market bases such as customer size, location, industry classification, usage rate and nature of operations are commonly used.

Consumer bases

Most writers would agree that for the *consumer* there are basically two types of base – descriptive and behavioural:

Descriptive variables can be grouped into:

- *Geographic*, i.e. local/regional/country-wide using, for example, government statistics to help measure size of population in a given area. Examples involve products such as beer, soft drinks, refreshing drinks (perhaps for climatic reasons) or cider as opposed to wine (in northern France this is important because cider is traditionally consumed in the north). Internationally it may be attractive to group countries into (say) the Middle East, but this can cause problems because they have differences. Therefore, care should be taken.

- *Demographic* variables are parameters such as age, sex, and socio/economic class; they are easy to measure and can prove to be good indicators of needs and wants but rarely stand alone.

- *Geodemographic* systems are systems based on geography and demography that have also been around since the 1970s – since in fact the ability to use IT to process information (particularly census and electoral roll data) into a usable form. Acorn (a classification of residential neighbourhoods) was the first such system in the UK: visit CACI at www.caci.co.uk/acorn-classification.aspx. This was followed swiftly by another system called, aptly, Mosaic, now Lifestyle Mosaic: visit Experian at www.experian.com/small-business/geodemographic-segmentation-mailing-lists.jsp. Such systems are used in direct marketing campaigns and by companies wishing to locate to an appropriate area with particular housing or other characteristics. In short they are mapping systems, geographically, but with a demographic breakdown thrown in. Different countries have different approaches but are based on the same principles.

Behavioural variables can give the marketer an insight into motivation. People may qualify to be a 'member' of a target market but may take no part in it, nor wish to. Behavioural variables include:

- *User status*, i.e. some members of the market may never have been users, and will have to be persuaded otherwise. Some will have been users and lapsed, while others remain users (loyal to the brand or loyal to a menu of brands for the same type of product). Each group needs to be assessed and approached accordingly.

- *Usage* involves distinguishing non-users from light and from heavy users. Here the 'Pareto Principle' may be assumed, that is, 20% of the market will account for 80% of sales. This indicates the importance of small groups of consumers.

- *Benefit* segmentation assumes that the difference in benefits sought is the basic reason for the existence of different market segments. This is very plausible and is at the heart of the modernist marketing philosophy – the old dictum that 'people do not buy drill bits, they buy holes' exemplifies this.

- *Personality* attached to brands deliberately for the purpose of matching product to target can be a segmentation base. Attributes such as dominance, thoughtfulness and impulsiveness are very plausible but rely on an understanding of buying behaviour. Where there are so many other variables in operation it is difficult to have one personality trait win the day.

- *Social class* is, in the UK, classified by the Office of National Statistics' NS-SEC (National Statistics – Socio-Economic Classification) system, which has moved away from the skills-based system to produce a classification system based on occupation. There are now eight categories plus a non-classified category for those excluded from any of the eight, including full-time students. This is an improvement, somewhat, from the marketer's perspective, since income had always been problematic and the basis of the old system. Many countries have similar systems that are useful to marketing and marketing research, for example the USA.

- *Occasions* can be used as segmentation where products and services are appropriate to a particular situation or occasion. For example chocolate and flowers are appropriate to certain situations. Not so obvious is the marketer's ability to create new uses for a product or service through this approach to segmentation. For example orange juice has been moved from being just a breakfast drink to one that can be used for different occasions such as an alcohol-free accompaniment to lunch or dinner. It can also be a healthy alternative for children yet at the same time an essential part of cocktails like a 'screwdriver' (vodka and orange juice) or 'Bucks Fizz' (Champagne and orange juice) that are associated with occasions, the former with evening drinks and the latter with wedding and other receptions.

- *Stage of buyer readiness* (how much they know about a product/brand and how aware) may be applicable and can also be used as bases for segmentation, but are often part of a combination of tools.

- *Psychographic* variables are the basis for *Lifestyle systems. Lifestyle* is a 1970s phenomenon that has developed and continues to be used in commercial systems. Its basis can be found in AOI studies (activities, interests and opinions) whereby the marketer is not reliant solely upon some sort of social class/socio-economic classification system, as above. Shared need based on what consumers like – not what they earn – is the rationale for employing such studies. Plummer's (1974) 'Lifestyle Dimensions' list of AIO has been replicated many times and this includes, for example, work and social events (activities), family and community (interests) and social issues and politics (opinions). Following the AIO idea, typographic studies took hold in marketing.

The original work on values, attitudes and lifestyles as devised at the Stanford Research Institute in the 1970s, blended demography with lifestyle variables to arrive at lifestyle typographies, with people being classified as one of eight types, for example strivers, achievers or actualisers. The use of survey research of some sort is, of course, a requirement in order to arrive at a typology for a particular market. Leaving aside any marketing research-type problem, the marketer needs to be careful with this kind of approach. It is very plausible from the communications viewpoint but putting such an approach into practice can be difficult without expert help.

Organisational bases

With *organisational* marketing bases may come in a number of forms such as *customer size, location*, or *product end-use*. There is therefore a need to understand the organisational decision-making unit DMU, as opposed to the consumer, where purchase motivations need to be appreciated (see Chapter 3 of this book). Also, perhaps even more so than with consumer systems, within organisational marketing there is a need for very specific, tailored approaches. Miles and Snow (1978) provided a typology of organisations having four general strategic types (defenders, prospectors, analysers and reactors) that can be applied to a given market context. This typology has been, and still is being, applied across a wide range of organisational contexts, including those of marketing, sales and marketing communications. These types can be said to be mutually exclusive, internally homogeneous, and collectively exhaustive, i.e. making up the whole of the sector that is being explored and analysed. Within such applications:

Defenders, for example, have a narrow product focus and do not tend to search outside of their domains, rarely change their service requirements such as banking, penetrate deeper into current markets and compete on price, delivery and quality. They invest in processes, and have mechanistic structures and centralised control.

Prospectors continually search for market opportunities, readily change things such as banking requirements, and regularly experiment with and respond to the environment. They are opposites of defenders in that they seek and create change in their industries.

Analysers are those who operate in a stable domain but ponder about all aspects and in turbulent areas they watch the competition closely, can rapidly adopt ideas, and their planning is intensive and comprehensive. Service requirements such as banking are routinised, as are ways of doing business.

Reactors are inconsistent as the label suggests. They respond only when forced to react to environmental pressures. Their service requirements are not linked to a strategic approach.

The Miles and Snow (1978) typography continues to be applied, for example, to electronic commerce. The four strategies are shown to be extended to the context of online businesses and the concept of co-alignment is validated (Auger, 2003). Another example is that of Jennings et al. (2003) where the typography is applied to service firms and test for equifinity (or functional equivalence) in the firms' strategies. Slater et al. (2010) take a modified version of the typography into the area of marketing performance in terms of actions and policies (see Chapter 16 of this book and in particular the section on selling styles).

THE APIC SYSTEM

APIC is a memorable piece of shorthand for the following:

Analysis – where are we now?

Analysis is necessary to guide the assessment of the problem, the 'current state of the world', the 'where are we now' review. This requires:

- an assessment of actual and/or potential targets – the customers or prospective customers;
- an assessment of product class;
- an (internal) assessment of the company/organisation;
- an (external) assessment of the micro environment (for example competitors) and macro environment (usually found in PEST/STEP/PESTEL form).

An assessment of actual and/or potential targets – the customers or prospective customers

Targets should have been arrived at by the analysis stage of the DSM and certain tools and approaches used where appropriate, such as those mentioned above. The rationale for this is simple; marketing communications approaches should be made to target markets and not markets as a whole. Such approaches will be different for each of the identified targets. The company may have only one target but it is likely that more than one target will exist for most companies at any given time.

An assessment of product class

This requires knowledge of customer/consumer perceptions, attributes and benefits of the brand, performance of the brand, the uniqueness offered by the brand, how well each of the relevant brands performs in these areas, and what unique features/benefits are offered. Additionally, this analysis should consider past strategies and market shares for the brands in question.

An (internal) assessment of the company/organisation

This involves assessing the strengths and weaknesses and the understanding of corporate goals and philosophy, financial and production capabilities, and marketing support (distribution, sales).

Analysis of the present situation (regarding the company, the product, the market, the target customer – where we are now) followed by

Planning including objectives and positioning (direction and mapping, where we want to go) and strategy and tactics (communications mix choice within creative and media boundaries – how we get there) then

Implementation (costing, budgeting, production, scheduling – how we put it into practice) and finally

Control (research, monitoring and evaluation – did we get there?).

Figure 4.1   The APIC system

*An (external) assessment of the micro environment
(for example competitors) and macro environment (usually
found in PEST/STEP/PESTEL form)*

This involves an assessment of opportunities and threats being made. Analysis, therefore, necessarily includes information on previous marketing strategy, buyer information processing, buyer decision-making processes, stakeholders, any intra-organisational issues, and any research and evaluation that may have been conducted, usually on aspects of the environment. Most of the marketing communications planning models alluded to above share this common initial stage of analysis.

Planning – where do we want to go and how shall we get there?

Planning is a necessary requirement for direction, and determining what is needed for the journey, the 'where do we want to go' (objectives and positioning) and 'how shall we get there' (strategy and tactics) review. This requires:

- objectives;
- positioning;
- creative strategy and tactics;
- media strategy and tactics.

Objectives

Objectives are involved with direction, are a means to performance measurement that are consistent with time management. There is a need for a clear statement of the 3Ts; i.e. *Target* market, *Time* deadline and *Task* of message. Objectives can be viewed in a hierarchical way from the mission down to the marketing communications level, as shown in Figure 4.2.

Objectives should also be SMART, i.e. specific, measurable, achievable, relevant and timed. The role of objective setting is to constrain strategy and help eliminate the large number of strategy options. In marketing communications terms, the DAGMAR model as discussed in Chapter 3 of this book is perhaps the best known of the hierarchical models. This stands for designing advertising goals for measured advertising results and looks to measure the result of a specific communication task in terms of the think-feel-do/cognitive-affective-behavioural hierarchy of effects on a defined audience, as well as an attempt to measure the degree of change in a given time period as one moves through the hierarchy. An example might be to make 70 per cent of the target audience aware of the new product and to achieve a 50 per cent understanding of the proposition

Business *mission* includes overall vision and involves corporate values and leadership

Business *level objectives* include survival, growth, and expansion

Marketing level objectives include market share achievement, sales by volume, value or profit

Marketing communications objectives include creation of awareness of and interest in the brand

Figure 4.2   The differing levels of objective

with 40 per cent convinced but with the expectation that when it comes to it 20 per cent will purchase in the first period.

The distinction between marketing and marketing communications objectives should be clear. In the above simple example the marketing objective is to achieve a 20 per cent market share in the first trading period, say, one year. The marketing communications objectives to help achieve this could be many and varied with the first being the creation of 70 per cent awareness through, say, advertising but for conviction a combination of advertising and public relations may be used. Towards purchase sales promotion could very well have a role.

Positioning

Positioning describes how the target should perceive the product relative to the competition. This means seeing things from the customer's perspective (and sometimes vis-à-vis the competition). It consists of all actions taken to make sure that the marketplace's perception is managed. Strategic positioning is a result of communicated perceptions about a product or brand (whereas image is a more global impression). Position is a reference point, especially against the competition, and involves product attributes/features with related (perceived or otherwise) benefits that can be seen in the statements made about the product/brand in marketing communications whether these be verbal or nonverbal (or both). There are many ways to achieve positioning; through actual attributes, through benefits/solutions to problems or through price/quality. In terms of developing a positioning strategy the marketer has first to determine which market (or markets) and targets are relevant and how such targets evaluate options and reach decisions. The kind of competition that exists (if any) in primary and secondary form, and how it is perceived, should be evaluated and any gaps in the market identified, paving the way for a strategy to be developed, which might include the domination of one segment rather than spreading resources too thinly across a number of segments. On the other hand, the company may be large enough to cover the whole of the market with a balanced product portfolio of brands against the competition. Consider the classic competitive situation of P&G and Lever, whereby these two corporations have many brands that compete, often head on, and between them take the lion's share of the market. This has been tempered somewhat by own label, but by and large remains a truism.

Perceptual maps can be constructed from customer/consumer responses in research, where relevant parameters such as pricing and quality can be established. A simple representation, illustrated in Figure 4.3, might apply to the airline industry currently.

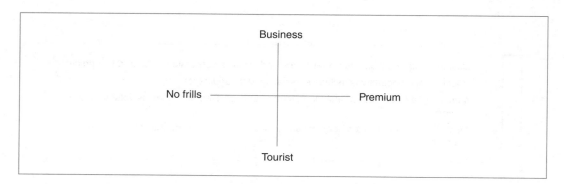

Figure 4.3   A simple perceptual map of the airline industry

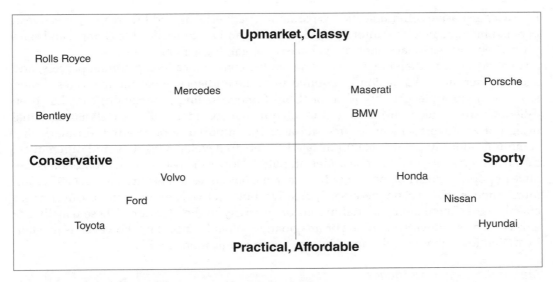

Figure 4.4 A simple perceptual map of the UK car market

A generalised form of perceptual mapping can be constructed for any market. The car market has been 'mapped' many times. Mapping of this sort is, of course, only a snapshot at a given time since markets change and mutate and new entrants will upset the status quo. A simple map of the UK car market, based on just two of a number of parameters, is illustrated above in Figure 4.4.

Clearly this is general to the marque and certain models may defy the general perception.

Strategy and tactics

The communications mix can be considered in many forms and in an integrated fashion (see Chapter 1 of this book). If *objectives* are to do with direction then *strategy* involves choosing the best means, in terms of both creative and media, of achieving them. Strategy involves the '3Ps', i.e. *'push'* through the trade, and *'pull'* to persuade end-users to demand. These can be combined with a *'profile'* strategy to build goodwill (public relations, or PR). This suggests that strategy itself is a pluralistic concept of attack.

Creative strategy and tactics

Creative strategy (refer to Chapter 8 of this book) is one of the most important elements of an integrated marketing communications programme, especially message development. Traditionally, advertising has been used to communicate information about a product or a service. Within an IMC framework the message is transmitted through packaging and other promotions, as well as through advertising and all other communications forms. Information is still an important component but creative strategy also has to:

- create and support brand images/positioning;
- demonstrate how a product/service can solve a problem or satisfy consumer needs;
- persuade;
- shape consumer decision-making and brand choice;
- remind consumers why they purchased a brand in the first place;
- reassure consumers (reduce dissonance) that they have made the right decision.

In IMC, persuasive communication is paramount, advertising and PR are most effective in persuading audiences that information is accurate and attitudes need to change, and sales promotion and personal selling are persuasive in gaining action.

Creative strategy therefore is a key stage in the communications planning process, and should determine what action is required from the audience, what the messages should say or communicate; the 'big idea' or 'USP' (unique selling proposition) as it has been called. Creative tactics are used and involve media considerations as well as the actual design of an advertisement or press release. The importance of creativity in marketing communications in an over-communicated society to develop a position and differentiate products/services should not be underestimated. However, just because promotion is creative or popular does not mean it will achieve the objectives it sets out so to do. Good communication is effective, not necessarily creative, but creative communications can enhance effectiveness. There are many definitions of creativity in the literature. These usually use words such as innovative, unique or imaginative. What is important, however, is the ability to find ideas that are relevant solutions to communications problems.

Media strategy and tactics

The marketer first has to understand relevant media before being able to plan the media. The media can, therefore, be looked at in two ways: first, the nature, pros and cons and characteristics of the media should be appreciated; and then, second, media planning can be considered (looked at in more detail in Chapter 9 of this book). The various media at our disposal quite obviously have certain characteristics. Some of the pros and cons are that: magazines have a long life but also long lead times and this requires more forward planning than some other media types, but then less than others; newspapers have a short lead time but a short life in comparison to other forms; television has animation but is expensive; radio has sound but is largely a spoken message only, although it can be high in the imagination stakes; posters and other ambient media can be dramatic but have short messages; and transport and signage have a low cost but effectiveness is questionable. The real task is choosing media categories and vehicles. The marketer should know the relevant media and the various characteristics of the media, who works in them and on various media vehicles; such as editors and sub-editors on a particular magazine. This is not just for advertising but also for PR purposes. The inclusion of those media at the cutting edge of technology is much the same as the way previous generations viewed television as essential. Whether the Internet is the ultimate narrowcasting medium and whether a truly in-home multimedia environment will exist are questions that are not yet answered.

The various media are often selected for their geographical reach, the ability to dramatise, frequency of exposure and so on. This understood, the practitioner can then move on to the more difficult area of planning and associated costs and budgeting. The media planner has to decide which media are feasible and pick the main medium and how it should be used, then make decisions on support media based on, for example, creative suitability in terms of the ability to dramatise, and experience of effectiveness, availability and lead time (long/copy deadlines), regional availability, competition, effect on trade and sales force, coverage and cost per thousand. Media planning is therefore about matching the media to the target audience after careful consideration of many things but especially audience characteristics. International campaigns are shaped by strategy, i.e. whether the multi-local or global (or something in between) approach is taken. For a number of years international media vehicles such as *International Herald Tribune, Wall Street Journal, Time, Fortune, Newsweek, Readers Digest, Cosmopolitan* – to name but a few – have been available to marketers, even if some have been English only. In short the media planner has to understand the media planning process through to evaluation and within this must intertwine creative and media work. There is concern here therefore with things such as changes in media technology, the development of mass markets, the standardisation of brands, and changing lifestyles of consumers. This adds up to the central question of *narrowcasting*, i.e. using highly selective media for special target groups. This is by no means new. MTV is an advert channel that is now over 30 years old. When it was launched in 1981 it had a target audience of 14- to 34-year-olds and was even then, to some extent, an opportunity for global narrowcasting. Now the opportunities are even greater. MTV's success with the reality TV show *Jersey Shore* has been renamed *Geordie Shore* in the UK, set in the North East of England in Newcastle, and first aired in May 2011 with the Spanish 'Costa' resort of Magaluf for the 'special' episodes, choosing young Newcastle inhabitants (Geordies) for the city's sense of fun, partying – and miniskirts. As in the USA with *Jersey Shore*, controversy has already surrounded *Geordie Shore* for its brashness and bawdiness, but that was its intent. As a local newspaper suggested, being shocked by *Geordie Shore* because of its lasciviousness is the equivalent of being shocked by the lack of nutrition in a Pot Noodle.

Media costs can be extremely high. Buyers must be aware of how to reach target audiences via the best and most advantageous media, negotiations for favourable rates, size, length and frequency. Traffic and production (artwork, scripts and associated deadlines, timings and so on) have to be controlled. Supporting publications for wider coverage and experience of such media are also important considerations. In short they should be able to choose the channel(s) of communication that can give the message the best chance of being clearly expressed, be able to communicate to as many of the selected audience as possible at the lowest cost, and eliminate the problems of judgement via facts/figures that will support. Buyers therefore must have information, authority, respect and persistence. Choosing appropriate media is of crucial importance. The notion that the 'medium is the message' is not without foundation but has been challenged to some extent in the newer digital media. There is a link between marketing and media planning, i.e. from a marketing plan down a hierarchy to the media and creative plan. This implies that a consideration of marketing objectives, product, profit, channels, resource constraints, IMC strategy and the target audience is necessary as part of the planning and managing process.

Implementation (and spend issues)

Implementation should be considered in a test market fashion before full-scale commercialisation, but not every company will do this automatically. Budgets need to be realistic and within resources (see Chapter 9 of this book). As strategies are developed, budget constraints need to be considered and objectives perhaps reviewed since there may be a need to change objectives/strategies because of overly ambitious campaign development. This requires consideration of:

- funding;
- appropriation;
- budgets.

Funding

Lack of certainty as to what the money actually does has not helped the spend situation but it is notoriously difficult to set budgets. The old adage 'half the money I spend is a waste, the trouble is I don't know which half' – often attributed to John Wanamaker, the retailer, and Lord Leverhulme, the soap-maker whose company became Unilever, but to others also – is a reference to this difficulty. Measurement is the key to understanding this but it is clear that some in senior management, while recognising the need for communications, have, in the past, treated the function with a certain amount of derision and suspicion.

Appropriation

The tried and tested methods of arriving at how money should be spent are relatively well established in the literature (see Chapter 9 of this book for a summary). The conclusion drawn by most if not all writers in this area is that no one method prevails or is best at any given time. It is argued that spending on promotion is an investment and should be viewed as such, and not as a cost or expense as accountants would have it. Personal communication is often but not always associated with fixed costs and the rest of the mix with variable costs. The former applies to sales management and the latter to brand or product management. An often-quoted statistic is that 80 per cent of new products fail. If so, then it is necessary to spend on the other 20 per cent to ensure success, but also to bring the failure rate down. This is allied to brand building in the longer term. Generally speaking, personal communication dominates appropriation in organisational markets and advertising in consumer markets, but this is a fluid and changing dynamic.

Budgets

Budgets are to do with the timing of the spread of financial resources. Media scheduling has to be considered. Appropriation is the total sum allocated while a budget is specific to the media or a market. These are the two broad tasks the organisation faces. The size of budgets in the end depends on objectives that of course may have to be revised in the light of the amount of money available. It also depends on the stage in the Product Life Cycle (PLC) and the competitive environment. Costs will depend on which media slots are bought and how much is spent on production, administration and research. A reserve of some sort should be considered.

Control

Control (considered in detail in Chapter 17 of this book) needs to be considered before full-scale commercialisation, but not every company will do this automatically. Budgets need to be realistic and within resources. As strategies are developed, budget constraints need to be considered and objectives perhaps reviewed since there may be a need to change objectives/strategies because of overly ambitious campaign development. Control involves:

- evaluation;
- monitoring;
- research.

Evaluation

Evaluation is necessary in order to find out if objectives are being achieved. This then merges with a new situation analysis. There is a need, however, to consider research at each stage of the model and what research and evaluation means for different kinds of communications mix elements. Evaluation of the marketing communications effort can involve the obvious – sales increases for example – but to be 100 per cent sure is an impossible dream. This kind of evaluation is very tempting, especially in today's climate of pressurised performance. Cause and effect, especially with advertising, is not as concrete as it is with, for example, sales promotion coupon redemptions.

Monitoring

The ideal of putting in place a process of continual effectiveness monitoring that would lead to the achievement of the desirable goals would need a set of perfect return on investment (ROI) metrics. The acronym ROCI, which has been coined by Schultz and Kitchen (2000), stands for 'return on customer investment' but could also stand for 'return on communications investment' (Copley, 2011), just as the acronym ROBI has been used for 'return on brand investment' (Kliatchto, 2008). This would help ascertain current situations, trends and any relevant change, such as adjustments to objectives or, as is often the case, tactical changes with the message, for example an alteration to the strapline of an advertisement.

Research

Research has become one of the cornerstones of communications management and is vital in giving direction to a campaign. Research should be regularly used to both create and assess the creative effort. Most authors consider communications research in terms of pre, during and post testing, i.e. diagnostic testing of messages for the development of effective communication as well as an assessment of how well objectives have been achieved in terms of sales or market share indicators or attitude changes. This might involve campaign tracking and evaluation. Some typical research activity within the APIC communications decision sequence model is outlined below in Figure 4.5.

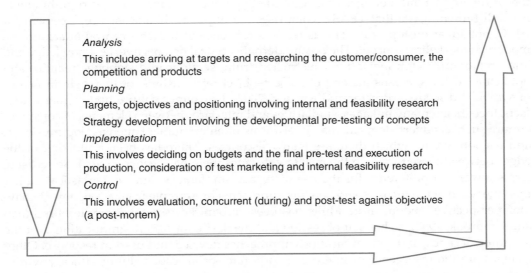

Analysis

This includes arriving at targets and researching the customer/consumer, the competition and products

Planning

Targets, objectives and positioning involving internal and feasibility research

Strategy development involving the developmental pre-testing of concepts

Implementation

This involves deciding on budgets and the final pre-test and execution of production, consideration of test marketing and internal feasibility research

Control

This involves evaluation, concurrent (during) and post-test against objectives (a post-mortem)

Figure 4.5 Typical research activities within the APIC communications decision sequence model

This process is cyclical. When a cycle ends a new one begins with a new analysis as the cycle begins again.

Clearly there are good reasons for wishing to measure the effectiveness of a communications campaign, such as avoiding costly mistakes, discovering other ideas and increasing efficiency, but all of this comes at a cost, not just in money but in time, where a delay might mean lost opportunities.

A brief critique of the APIC DSM approach

Corporate and marketing communications now leads and does not simply support the marketing effort and should be seen as an investment rather than a cost. Management of the corporate and marketing communications functions has traditionally been under command and control management. There are basically two areas of concern with the use of a DSM approach generally and more specifically APIC as a version of a DSM. First, return on customer investment (ROCI) as mentioned earlier in the chapter is seen as mandatory by Schultz and Kitchen (2000) who consider much that is done in terms of evaluation, monitoring and research 'too soft', dealing as it has done with trying to measure communication effects using the hierarchy of effects-type models. Schultz and Kitchen advocate the importance of measurement time frames, both short and long term, as a basis of communications planning and completing the communication planning matrix. This is an outside-in rather than inside-out approach to budgeting, i.e. that money spent on communication should be driven by the amount spent by the customer. This will drive spend down and profits up. Spend issues are examined more closely in Chapter 9 of this book.

Second, Brown (2001) is perhaps the UK's greatest APIC critic. For Brown, APIC is a modernist marketing ideal. As a postmodernist, Brown prefers to see TEASE as the acronym to entice us in. This stands for marketing as a *Trickster*, *Excessive*, *Adolescent*, *Spirited* and *Entertaining*. The problem for many brought up on the modernist approach to marketing management is that even Brown's 'retro-orientation' can fit into the APIC system. Brown recognises this and acknowledges that it might appear that it is just another version of the argument that 'marketing is artistic, marketing is creative, marketing is right-brained'. But still Brown insists that TEASE 'comprises the Big Crunch' and is 'a replacement for APIC, not sugar on top of it'. This is really a reference to Brown's central attack on the modernist marketing concept. The postmodern theoretical perspective, i.e. knowledge and interpretation through metaphor, constructed truth, semiotic and symbolic realities and not actual realities, means the end of subject–object relationships, of literalism in favour of symbolic discourse (Proctor and Kitchen, 2002). Consumer culture houses many artefacts, there being many linkages, similarities and interfaces between elements of consumer culture such as advertising, cinema, other forms of entertainment such as pop music, art and fashion, within which there are many discourses. There has been a blurring of the edges between these forms. In the past few decades there has been a move in advertising terms towards a preference for the use of surrealism, fantasy and the fantastical, rather than the norm of the features and benefits approach. For example from a consumer behaviour perspective, hedonism in adults has been recognised (see for example Hirschman and Holbrook, 1982), as has self-obsession and the desire for instant gratification over the last three decades, and communications approaches devised and used in response. Other changes are the resurgence of interest in corporate social responsibility, ethics, environmentalism and concern with the authenticity of brands, which have had an influence on consumer and corporate behaviour and require an appropriate response in corporate and marketing communications' terms (see Chapter 6 of this book).

There is, however, continued use of the APIC approach to managing generally and to corporate and marketing communications in particular, even though there may very well be problems with actually making such a model work in practice. The apparent linear, inflexible, hierarchical model does pose problems, but in the absence of anything tangible to replace it the APIC system, model or framework is still prevalent in the marketing and management literature and also used by marketing and management consultancies. Most would agree, however, that the framework has to be used in an organic rather than a mechanistic way.

The APIC framework for managing marketing communications

The following is a summary of the management framework that has been discussed above and will be used throughout the rest of this book.

ANALYSIS

Targets/potential targets (customer or prospect)	TARGET 1	TARGET 2	TARGET 3
Customer database (size, profitability, %share)			
Bases for segmentation and targeting:			
Descriptive			
Behavioural			
Opinion leader			
DMU			

Product	TARGET I	TARGET 2	TARGET 3
Perceptions			
Attributes			
Benefits			
Performance			
(Sales, profits, against			
previous, average, best)			

Company/Organisation	STRENGTHS	WEAKNESSES
Corporate goals and philosophy		
(Mission, vision, policies)		
Capabilities and competencies		
(Resources, financial, technological,		
managerial)		
Marketing mix/strategy		
Trends in buyer information process		
Trends in buyer decision-making process		

Micro Environment	OPPORTUNITIES	THREATS
Stakeholders		
Competition		
Suppliers		

Macro Environment	OPPORTUNITIES	THREATS
Socio-cultural		
Technological/scientific		
Economic		
Political/legal		

PLANNING

Targets	TARGET I	TARGET 2	TARGET 3
Targets			
Time			
Tasks			

(Continued)

(Continued)

Objectives (SMART)	TARGET I	TARGET 2	TARGET 3
Business mission			
Business objectives			
Marketing objectives (Penetration, development, diversification, actual sales/profit))			
Marketing communications objectives (Awareness, develop interest)			

Position	TARGET I	TARGET 2	TARGET 3
Perceptual map parameter 1			
Perceptual map parameter 2			
Perceptual map parameter 3			
Perceptual map parameter 4			

Strategy	TARGET I	TARGET 2	TARGET 3
Communications mix			
Creative strategy & tactics			
Rational message			
Emotional message			
Media strategy & tactics			
Media type			
Media vehicles			

IMPLEMENTATION

Funding	TARGET I	TARGET 2	TARGET 3
Appropriation & Budgets			

Scheduling	TARGET I	TARGET 2	TARGET 3
People			
Media			
Traffic & production			

CONTROL

Research	TARGET I	TARGET 2	TARGET 3

Pre
(Concept testing, product testing,
    test marketing etc.)
During (monitoring)
(Aided, unaided recall, recognition,
objectives being achieved e.g. sales)

Post (evaluation)
(Aided, unaided recall, recognition,
objectives achieved e.g. sales)

Figure 4.6 A summary of the APIC framework for managing marketing communications

The Snapshot below illustrates how this framework can translate into any marketing communications management scenario.

Snapshot Managing the Marketing Communications effort – building a marketing communications management model in a small firm

Many small firms are constantly looking for new ideas for niche products. It was suggested to one small firm by a local enterprise agency that there might be an opportunity aimed at gardeners with a product that would help lift off ingrained dirt after working with soil. At the same time the company was working with another support agency regarding the general marketing of products and mentioned this new idea to the marketing advisor. After some research the advisor felt that there was definitely a niche market for a product of this nature, which should be much better than a simple barrier cream, and suggested the company form a separate marketing company to develop and market it. With his marketing expertise it was felt that he would be a perfect third partner and he agreed to join as a director and investor.

The new company was formed and the first version of the product was formulated. A professional gardener was persuaded to test it out, and he very quickly came back with the comment that one of his main problems in gardening was infection in the small cuts and grazes caused by thorns and sharp stones. He added it was not always desirable to wear gloves, and even then dirt could get trapped inside them. The antiseptics and bactericides were researched until the company found what was felt to be the best on the market, and this was added to the product in the recommended quantities for maximum effect. The professional gardener and other testers were delighted with the results and by the end of the year all the packaging was designed and the first production batch of product made.

The company then carried out a press release mailing to over 1,000 newspapers and magazines and from the resulting publicity sold over 150 bottles by mail order all over the UK. Many of these customers then placed repeat orders, which suggested to the company significant proof that the product, now a brand, was doing the job for which it

(Continued)

(Continued)

was designed. Mail-order sales quickly totalled over 500 bottles. A leading PR company in the area was engaged to provide press releases and promotional activity, a website designer was employed, an employee with social media skills was assigned to work on Facebook, Twitter, LinkedIn and other social media opportunities, and the company also worked closely with a brokerage that bought media space and advised on advertising. Accordingly the company produced a commercial that was first shown on regional television in May the following year.

The retail launch was scheduled for just before Easter, through garden centres. The company was well supported by local garden centres that ordered as soon as they saw the bottle. A top horticultural agent began acting for the company in the north and he gradually increased the number of outlets that stocked the product. A stand was booked at a gardening and leisure exhibition in the September where the prototypes of two new and complementary products to build the brand into a range were shown. A significant number of serious enquiries, including from some overseas companies, were received. Although the major wholesaling chains were not enthusiastic about stocking and selling the brand the company went ahead and appointed a national selling group to take the brand to the independent chemist trade, as the range has many other applications outside the gardening sector. Once again, although they felt the product had good potential, the company had problems persuading the major chemists' wholesalers to stock the line to deal with referred orders. The company realised that the brand could not really start selling until this started to happen. An arrangement was agreed for the brand to sponsor a national not-for-profit gardening competition to the tune of 10p for every bottle sold in the UK in return for the use of their publicity machine and other PR opportunities. To pay for communication the company set a sales target of at least 250,000 bottles in the next year of trading to allow an annual marketing communications spend of 30p per bottle, including the 10p to the not-for-profit competition, the beginning of a serious attempt to engage with corporate social responsibility (CSR).

A preliminary report on the results of a questionnaire (to be administered to the general public) was expected to give the company some ideas about the following:

1   How the public would react to the existing packaging and the kinds of devices/ on-pack messages, on-counter displays, leaflets, etc., that would help sell it. Also opinions about the appeal the product might have in terms of age, class, sex and so on in its present form.

2   Both creative and media ideas, an integral part of the marketing effort, needed to be informed by opinions and perceptions relating to design, messages and so on and the kinds of media and media vehicles that might work most effectively, and these were sought using the questionnaire.

The company decided to conduct more research in order to get a clearer message across to general public end-users about what the product could do. This included more on the above, any PR possibilities, any future developments in packaging such as tubes, any export considerations such as labelling requirements for the EC, and any other marketing communications opportunities.

Task

The scenario above was deliberately not structured with the use of heading and sub-headings from a Decision Sequence Model. However, these should be easy to see.

This task involves extracting details from the Snapshot and organising them into the various stages of the APIC model, and then developing the model with the aid of additional research. The analysis (or situation analysis or context if readers prefer) stage should by now be familiar. In order to facilitate analysis some prefer the use of tools such as mind maps in order to thoroughly explore and analyse the situation or context. Current and potential targets are identified. However, the use of tools such as SWOT or PEST(EL) is not explicit but there is evidence of the company's strengths and weaknesses and of relevant environmental forces. Planning can be seen with the establishing of direction, objectives and the beginnings of positioning of the new brand in the marketplace. The strategic and tactical ideas can be readily seen. Implementation ideas are mentioned in terms of, for example, the timings for certain activities, and control issues should be developed.

Questions

Consider the prospects and problems for this brand and its owners. Undertake the following: 1. Consider the financial limitations that are common to all SMEs, especially when it comes to advertising costs. Outline other, less costly, tools that are available to companies like this one and discuss their likely effectiveness; 2. The company should be applauded for its attitudes towards marketing communications and research but should it attempt a more integrative approach?

Assignment

Choose an organisation – a business, a charity, a local authority function – and apply the APIC management framework to part of its communications activity. For example, problems or opportunities may exist now or arise in the future in the environmental/'green' part of the marketing environment for such organisations. Follow this through with basic ideas on the rest of the marketing communications management APIC framework.

In particular create simple Gantt charts to illustrate the scheduling for (a) communications tools; (b) advertising media and media vehicles; (c) production of materials and other traffic issues. A Gantt chart is a type of forward planner, a simple but effective device that can easily be constructed, and is designed to provide a snapshot of activities over time periods. Consider the illustration below in Table 4.1:

Table 4.1 A simple example of a GANTT chart

	TIME PERIOD							
ACTIVITY	Jan	Feb	March	April	May	June	July	August
Advertising medium (1)	x	x	x	x	x	x	x	x
Advertising medium (2)	x		x		x			x
Public Relations (1)	x							x

(Continued)

(Continued)

Public Relations (2)		x	x	x		
Public Relations (3)				x	x	x
Sales Promotion (1)	x					
Sales Promotion (2)						x
Exhibition (1)	x					
Exhibition (2)			x			
Exhibition (3)					x	

Summary of Key Points

- Analysis deals with assessments of customers, products, the organisation and its environment. This is the 'Where are we now?' question.

- Planning deals with targets, objectives and positioning. This is the 'Where do we want to go?' question and is followed by consideration of creative and media strategy. This is the 'How do we get there?' question.

- Implementation is a consideration of 'How do we put this into practice?' and involves the allocation of spend to the campaign.

- Control involves evaluation, monitoring and research and is the 'Did we get there?' question. This is not only a check on whether objectives have been achieved but also a consideration of the place of research in the entire framework.

- Most writers would subscribe to a form of decision sequence model when attempting to manage marketing communications. There are, however, challenges to the APIC type of system, but such challenges are not accompanied by tangible alternatives.

Discussion Questions

1. Explain why you agree or disagree with the contention that the APIC-type model is useful as a framework for communicators to operate within.

2. Outline what you consider to be the important elements of the analysis stage of a marketing communications' decision sequence model.

3. The planning stage of a DSM involves consideration of 'Where do we want to go?' and targets. Discuss the importance of establishing targets early on in campaign planning and managing.

4. Explain the usefulness (or not) of perceptual mapping using illustrations of your choice to aid the explanation.

5. Creative strategy is part of 'How do we get there?'. Discuss, broadly, the difference between rational and emotional appeals.

6. Discuss the importance of involvement with particular reference to creative appeals.

7. Media strategy is also part of 'How do we get there?'. Explain why you agree or disagree that a firm understanding of media characteristics should be the first step in this part of the framework.

8. There are a number of practical issues when considering how to put a campaign into practice. Discuss at least one method of arriving at expenditure levels for a product of your choice.

9. Discuss the logic behind pre, concurrent and post testing within the marketing communications arena using examples to illustrate.

10. Comment on the idea that the battle to view marketing communication as an investment not a cost has been won. Explain what you understand the acronyms ROCI and ROBI to mean.

Further Reading

Ashcroft, L. (2010) 'Marketing Strategies for Visibility', *Journal of Librarianship and Information Science*, 42 (2): 89–96. http://lis.sagepub.com/content/42/2/89.full. pdf+html

Building on reputation and image as a basis for relevance and being indispensable, according to Ashcroft, should be a goal of any organisation in order to promote themselves favourably across a wide range of audiences. This article discusses getting the timing right, with the right resources and the right communication, regardless of the type of organisation, but focuses on libraries and the use of sponsorship and getting favourable media coverage. The article also advocates ongoing evaluation to inform the use of marketing techniques to build on success and maximise publicity.

Fall, L.T. (2004) 'The Increasing Role of Public Relations as a Crisis Management Function: an empirical examination of communication re-strategising efforts among destination organisation managers in the wake of 11th September, 2001', *Journal of Vacation Marketing*, 10 (3): 238–52. http://jvm.sagepub.com/content/10/3/238.full. pdf+html

The article discusses the increasing role of public relations as a crisis management function. Fall's study looks at the relationship between advertising and PR in the tourism context post-9/11. This is examined within a crisis communications framework and the study examines how messages are being restructured, how primary publics are being re-focused, and how communication tactics are being retooled. The study shows that after this watershed, a sizable proportion of tourism professionals have re-focused efforts and re-adjusted objectives, and that adverting has decreased while PR has increased in marketing communications mixes.

Huang, L., Yung, C. and Yang, E. (2011) 'How do Travel Agencies Obtain a Competitive Advantage? Through a travel blog marketing channel', *Journal of Vacation Marketing*, 17 (2): 139–49. http://jvm.sagepub.com/content/17/2/139.full.pdf+html

This article looks at the external environmental forces in a travel agency context, with particular reference to the adoption of a travel blog marketing channel, and consequently looks at strategy development and performance measurement indicators. At the heart of this is the use of blogs as part of a business strategy impacting on distribution and communications.

Miller, R. (2002) 'A Prototype Audit for Marketing Communications Professionals', *Marketing Theory*, 2 (4): 419–28. http://mtq.sagepub.com/content/2/4/419.full.pdf+html

Identifying and measuring the functional marketing skills that organisations need in the marketing communications area is advocated in this article that is concerned with job design, recruitment, training and outsourcing. The author provides a framework for skills definition and measurement in planning their careers in the knowledge that a better understanding of the marketing communications expertise required enables educators to offer courses in relevant applied marketing communications.

Payne et al. (2011) 'Placing a Hand in the Fire: assessing the impact of a YouTube experiential learning project on viral marketing knowledge acquisition', *Journal of Marketing Education*, 33 (2): 204–16. http://jmd.sagepub.com/content/33/2/204. full.pdf+html

The authors' goal in this article is to evaluate the effectiveness of an experiential learning social media project that was integrated into the curriculum. The article shows how this project had an effect on student engagement, motivation, team management and communication skills while at the same time showing how the project promoted learning in the area of consumer-generated advertisements and viral marketing.

REFERENCES

Ashcroft, L. (2010) 'Marketing strategies for visibility', *Journal of Librarianship and Information Science*, 42 (2): 89–96.

Auger, P. (2003) 'An empirical investigation of the Miles and Snow typography for small online businesses', *International Journal of Internet and Enterprise Management*, 1 (3): 245–64.

Brown, S. (2001) *Marketing – the Retro Revolution*. London: Sage.

Copley, P. (2011) 'Integrated marketing communications (IMC) is not just for the big boys – part of the future of IMC lies in SME marketing strategy'. Proceedings of the 34th Institute of Small Business and Entrepreneurship (ISBE) Conference, November, Sheffield: ISBE, CD.

Fall, L.T. (2004) 'The increasing role of public relations as a crisis management function: an empirical examination of communication re-strategising efforts among destination organisation managers in the wake of 11th September, 2001', *Journal of Vacation Marketing*, 10 (3): 238–52.

Hirschman, E.C. and Holbrook, M.B. (1982) 'Hedonic consumption: emerging concepts, methods and propositions', *Journal of Marketing*, 46 (3) Sumer: 92–101.

Huang, L., Yung, C. and Yang, E. (2011) 'How do travel agencies obtain a competitive advantage? Through a travel blog marketing channel', *Journal of Vacation Marketing*, 17 (2): 139–49.

Jennings, D.F., Rajaratnam, D. and Lawrence, F.B. (2003) 'Strategy-performance relationships in service firms: a test for equifinality', *Journal of Managerial Issues*, 15 (2) June: 208–20.

Kliatchto, J. (2008) 'Revisiting the IMC construct – a revised definition and four pillars', *International Journal of Advertising*, 27 (1): 133–60.

Miles, R.E. and Snow, C.C. (1978) *Organisational Strategy, Structure and Process*. New York: McGraw-Hill.

Miller, R. (2002) 'A prototype audit for marketing communications professionals', *Marketing Theory*, 2 (4): 419–28.

Payne, N.J., Campbell, C., Bal, A.S. and Piercy, N. (2011) 'Placing a hand in the fire: assessing the impact of a YouTube experiential learning project on viral marketing knowledge acquisition', *Journal of Marketing Education*, 33 (2): 204–16.

Plummer, J.T. (1974) 'The concept and application of lifestyle segmentation', *Journal of Marketing*, 38, January: 33–7.

Proctor, T. and Kitchen, P. (2002) 'Communication in postmodern, integrated marketing', *Corporate Communications: An International Journal*, 7 (3): 144–54.

Schultz, D. and Kitchen, P. (2000) *Communicating Globally*. London: McMillan Business.

Slater, S.F., Olson, E.M. and Hult, G.T.M. (2010) 'Worried about strategy implementation? Don't overlook marketing's role', *Business Horizons*, 53 (5) September–October: 469–79.

5 The Marketing Communications Industry

CHAPTER OVERVIEW

Introduction

In this chapter the nature and workings of the marketing communications industry are explored. Practitioners' views of what clients want and client-driven change are discussed in relation to what theory offers practice. The management of an organisation's marketing communications programmes (as discussed in Chapter 4 of this book) normally requires the efforts and inputs of a number of individuals both internally and externally so that there are players in agencies or marketing communications companies as well as client organisations. The nature of such players and type of system, whether decentralised or centralised, is discussed in terms of the degree to which agencies are involved with an organisation's strategy and the degree of responsibility for the development of an integrated campaign. The adoption of an in-house function is considered in relation to the advantages of cost savings and control but also the potential lack of experience and objectivity. Agencies are discussed in terms of the various types and structure including full service (one-stop shop), creative boutique, media specialist or 'à la carte'. Agency selection issues, agency operational relationships and remuneration and evaluation of performance are also considered. Other, more specialised agencies and marketing communications companies are discussed so that direct marketing, sales promotion, public relations and interactive communications firms as well as those specialising in elements such as sponsorship or product placement are considered against the backdrop of integration (as discussed in Chapter 1 of this book).

Learning objectives

The chapter seeks to explore and explain the nature and structure of the marketing communications industry. More specifically, after reading this chapter the student will be able to:

- appreciate what clients want from the communication practitioner perspective;
- critically assess client-driven change;
- identify the players involved in marketing communication from both the demand and supply sides;
- evaluate the ways in which client organisations deal with agencies and communications companies and the advantages and disadvantages of varying levels of involvement;
- assess the advantages and disadvantages of an in-house marketing communications function;
- understand the role of advertising agencies and the services they offer as well as key issues such as agency selection and remuneration;
- understand the role of other types of agencies or communication companies and the services they offer as well as key issues such as selection and remuneration;
- examine the use of integrated services and the nature and responsibilities of transnational agencies and communications companies.

PRACTITIONERS' VIEWS OF WHAT CLIENTS WANT

Theory to practice

The theoretical models and frameworks as expressed in Chapter 2 of this book have been used by writers to help students and practitioners understand and manage the various forms of communication – whether mediated or interpersonal – that they are or will be involved with. The simple argument is that theory should inform practice otherwise it is pointless but practice needs some theoretical underpinnings to provide stability. This argument is central to this book since there is concern with practitioners and what they can gain from the theoretical stances taken by writers – whether practitioners themselves or academicians – in order to provide a basis from which to build the desired communications. However, many in the industry feel that marketing communications professionals need to evolve to stay relevant (Farnworth, 2010), but it is how this can and will occur that is crucial. Rethinking ideas and reimagining strategies may be the way forward, in order to avoid stagnation and 'constantly … meet the quickly changing digital landscape' which has 'been underway for more than a decade', and there is a need to keep skills relevant for all in the company who have a 'public-facing role' (Farnworth, 2010), which now requires social media capabilities. This attitude is new in the sense of dealing with relevant media but not so new when the 'what clients want and need' question is looked at more closely across time.

Outsourcing and specialisation

More than two decades ago Sommers (1990) suggested that clients 'pay outside people for things they can't do as well themselves' and that, at the time, the recession and the 'disaggregation of future media patterns suggests that agencies need to become communications consultants, maybe unbundling creative as well as media functions – and earn on a non-billing basis'. This has, of course, come to pass. Sommers highlights the difficulties with longer-term forecasting but maintains that one thing that is predictable is that clients will continue to pay for things that others can do for them better than they can themselves, so that the buying in of relevant consultancy would continue, and this consultancy might be bought in a hierarchical fashion, i.e. from business strategy and its elements such as 'the building of new factories or new work procedures' through to marketing strategy and its elements such as advertising. For Sommers (1990) the latter was perhaps not best handled by management consultants but by specialists in the field and highlights the problem of not being clear about what is involved, with confusion arising over what communications strategy or advertising strategy is or should be. Here Sommers argues that 'we tend to hobble all the other means of communication ... and relegate them to a tactical role'. This fits in with the ethos of IMC in the early 1990s as discussed in Chapter 1 of this book.

The quest for IMC

As Duncan and Everett (1993) suggested, there were numerous pressures at that time to integrate marketing communications. From a client perspective this appeared to be one of the easiest ways an organisation could maximise its return on investment. Yet by the late 1990s some were declaring IMC to be 'dead' and that it had died because of indecision over the selling of advertising and public relations agency services and what 'integrated' actually means, one problem being the existence of separate departments 'arranged in silos' (Drobis, 1997). However, it was not really a case of IMC being 'dead'. Rather, at this point in time (one of increasing globalisation and turbulent environments) organisations had simply not been able to make the concept work. By the late 1990s there was the opportunity to elevate integrative communications to a new status. This would give the function a new meaning (Drobis, 1997).

Clients clearly wanted to make integrated communications work, which meant being able to achieve objectives by identifying targets and developing strategy that provided consistent messages in an efficient and effective manner. However, the technological and media changes (discussed in Chapter 1 of this book) meant that control of such messages had been passed from sender to receiver, and clearly much has changed. It was fairly clear over a decade ago that clients wanted IMC, and indeed integrated communications to include activities at the corporate level. It was also clear that it is easier to say IMC than to achieve IMC, and the IMC concept was not being embraced by marketing communications specialists (Padsetti et al., 1999). It was thought that the effort would be worthwhile since it was 'perceived as having a direct, positive impact on market share – largely by the support it provides for the brand', even though by the end of the 1990s the evidence was still anecdotal (Jeans, 1998).

Rethinking IMC

The drive towards IMC and paying more attention to consumer needs has meant the realisation that linear models of marketing communications and the ways in which communication is received have had to be rethought. Part of this was the need to turn certain things on their heads. For example there was a need to think not what advertising does to consumers but what consumers do to (or with) advertising and other communication elements. There was also recognition of the need to evaluate marketing communications' effects in the best way possible. This meant measurement also of the return on communications investment and measurement of how effective integration had been. Two key reasons are highlighted by Binet (2005) as being: marketing accountability moving up the management agenda, leading to performance measures affecting remuneration; and 'what you measure affects what you do (especially if your bonus is at stake)'. Of course this has to be done in the right way. What clients need, in Binet's view, are things like a good brief, time and money for analysis and evaluation, and the ability to look for effects beyond profit.

Client-driven change in marketing communications

Beyond quantitative data collection

In terms of client-driven change and the client perspective on marketing research generally, Chadwick (2006) suggested that there are different and distinct categories or levels of research need and demand. These, in ascending order, are: knowledge management and business decision support; integration of information and insight generation across multiple data sources; design, analysis, reporting and generation of insights across multiple studies (or a single source); project management, data processing and quality control; and finally primary data collection. Clients, it seems, are increasingly wanting more than mere data collection. There have been calls before now for 'more qualitative, interpretative approaches' (Fletcher, 2003). Chadwick (2006) suggests that some clients are re-arranging their own departments to make room for more involved inputs from research companies as outside consultants in decision making and not just data collection.

Changing media landscape

As has been suggested in Chapter 1 of this book, some of the key drivers of change generally but for marketing communicators particularly lie in the digital arena. The media landscape is clearly radically different at the start of the second decade of the 21st century from what it was at the start of the first. Mass audiences are increasingly a thing of the past but not only that; consumers of all sorts are involved much more and 'user generated content' is now common. 'The current changes in marketing communications are apocalyptic stuff' wrote Saunders (2006) while questioning whether or not the big brands were really changing. Saunders' interviews with senior marketers, agency people, trainers and academics revealed three majors trends that are causing companies to change: *the drivers*. First, the service business driver with quicker, better service that is more flexible, where prices are keen and brand promises are joined up to service delivery through marketing activities. Second, the customer satisfaction driver and the goal of keeping customers happy, where word of mouth and referrals are often part of decision-making and customer problem-solving. This is especially the case in a digital and social networking age where frequency and coverage are part of the old and relationships and customer engagement part of the now; *the enablers*. Interactivity in terms of both traditional and the newer digital forms is being used to enable people, and for co-creation and data capture; *the big ideas*. These are problem solvers and come from brand vision, are part of any communications plan, and are the creative glue in the branding and communications process. There are big ideas essential for organising communications, identifying values, and making execution easier. According to Saunders (2006) research to help marketers reduce risk is changing in line with changing times, with much more innovative observational research being used.

Proven effectiveness

Clients are looking for agencies with 'effectiveness credentials' and as such agencies have to 'live, breathe and practice an "effectiveness culture"'. However, it is 'very difficult for a client to understand what an agency is really effective at' (Thompson, 2008). What the agency is good at could be any number of things or just a few – or even one specialist service. Clients claim they are more interested in results than agencies that win awards. They also want to have people around them that understand the business and who can think beyond today, immerse themselves in the brand and have an external, objective perspective. Agencies need to have energy, provide inspiration, and show rigour have logical and analytical ability (Thompson, 2008). These are qualities and characteristics that have not changed over the years but there is a bigger emphasis on trust than ever before in an increasingly challenging environment. In Thompson's view this requires creative excellence while at the same time balancing creativity with relevance. A not unreasonable plea for a clear and stimulating brief comes from Baskin (2010) who suggests that clients expect 'agencies to put a lot of time, effort and money into fulfilling the task … so it is only fair and professional'. Others in the advertising industry are more cautious with the client–agency relationship in recessionary times.

Perceptions of competence and other reasons for relationship severance

A perceived lack of competence, a lack of trust about the financial leadership an agency has with its suppliers, and a failure by agencies to articulate the added value to a client through agency involvement, are three reasons given by Baker and Handyside (2010) for why decoupling might happen. The answer might lie in clients working with multi specialists (post the decline of the traditional everything for everybody model) but this is not necessarily what clients want. Although they have been forced to take this route in the long term it could cost them more according to Baker and Handyside, who argue that clients could actually 'reduce overall transaction costs (and potentially improve quality) by working with fewer providers … there is the basis for a strong and proactive value proposition here'. There are some established reasons why agencies lose clients. For example size can be a factor on both sides. If an agency or the client outgrows the other then there may be a natural parting of the ways. There may also be changes to the client's approach that the agency is not equipped to handle, whether this is a move to digital, different media, a more integrated approach, or new business where the agency lacks the necessary creative expertise or knowledge. A fresh creative approach may be sought if sales stagnate and decline. Disagreement over remuneration may arise in relation to performance and a conflict of interest may arise because of acquisitions or changes in the agency client base.

The Snapshot below illustrates the notions of change, globalisation, interactivity, engagement and impact on the communications process. The late 1990s saw technological influence in terms of, for example, digital and mobile technology and the power of retailers such as Wal-Mart and Tesco was clearly visible. The future appears to be in the realms of interactivity but also in the reality of a 24/7/365 world.

Snapshot Marketing and corporate communications professionals' views of the nature of marketing communications

Agencies and communications companies have had to change to meet the needs of clients, who in turn have been driven to an extent by changes in customer and consumer behaviour. The latter has changed and continues to do so not least because of the technological and communications landscape that has provided both opportunities and threats to marketers. Engagement and interaction are achievable 'in a timely and cost-effective manner', according to Rooseboom (2010) who has identified a number of trends and tested these out on professionals such as PR, marketing and communications experts, journalists, media people and customers. Companies have become their own media, especially with the advent of social media and networks that allow them to communicate directly with consumers. Control of media, however, is gone

(Continued)

(Continued)

and flexibility and adaptability count. There has been the rise of the fearless communicator to meet these media changes. When control is relinquished, companies have to meet the challenge of dealing with consumers with more power, especially over brand messages. Internal becomes external when employees are utilised to deliver the brand promise through the whole organisation for a consistent consumer experience. There has been a move to 'B-to-P', i.e. business-to-people rather than the old assumption that a company is B-to-B or B-to-C where lines have blurred, and eventually the model will be people-to-people. Other trends to look out for are digital media, especially mobile phones, which means marketers will need to repackage messages, pay walls and online news provision and unsurprisingly social media and networks.

A study by Swain (2005), on what marketing communications professionals think about interactivity and consumer perception and consumer control, although exploratory using a purposive sample of professionals, recognised the usefulness of measuring impacts but wished to go further and sought insights from such participants. The results suggested that there was an awareness of interactivity and the need to plan for it as well as a necessity to include the Internet. The importance of special events 'when consumer-controlled interactivity dominates' was recognised. However, the participants did not 'envision an impact on traditional media when consumers can control reception of messages, including the advertising that supports those media'. It was anticipated that advertising and advertising agencies would experience a decline but that public relations and other promotional activities would increase in importance as consumer control grew. It was expected that clients should be prepared to communicate interactively at the consumer's convenience, with reputation and 'fit' increasing in importance. This follows the idea of the increasing significance of the relationship between consumer and brand. The marketing communications mix was expected to change accordingly. However, payment between client and agency (compensation) was still being viewed in the traditional way and not as measures of interactive communications' success, which is clearly an important issue. In a study of Danish firms and advertising agencies, Jensen (2007) looked at the state of play for online marketing communications and where resources might be directed, concluding that 'usage of offline MARCOM is negatively related to the priority of online … and offline and online communications are therefore compensatory'. This agreed with Swain (2005), i.e. as online grows, offline will decline. Jensen argued that this was potentially disintegrative and therefore companies would have to take greater control. There is agreement too that online interactivity will affect the nature of the communications mix with elements such as online games, coupons or competitions needing to be prioritised, and room for improvement in online relationship communication. Fragmentation and other changes are a challenge to companies who have begun to realise that increased interactivity has to be harnessed and managed.

Stop Point

The move towards Integrated Marketing Communications and measurement of return on customer investment has been in place for at least the last two decades but it is the areas of interaction and engagement, brought about through changes in technology and communications, that are the focus of the marketer's attention. Part of this is the handover of control to the consumer. Undertake the following: 1. Discuss the notion that control has been handed to the consumer and the need for companies to manage this process; 2. Examine the importance of flexibility and the skills required by companies and agencies if they are to equip themselves to get the most out of digital changes and changes in the media, especially the use of the social media and networks but also the many other aspects of the digital frontier.

ROLES AND STRUCTURES IN AGENCIES AND OTHER COMMUNICATIONS COMPANIES

Changing roles and structures

The marketing communications industry is unsurprisingly sensitive to changes in the economic climate. Any downturn is likely to see spend by clients reduced, as has been the case since 2008. However, research on, for example the Australian economy, from IBISWorld forecasts the advertising industry to 'generate revenue of $1.3 billion in 2013–14, which is an increase of 1.9% from the previous year'. This of course is dependent upon a recovering and improving economy and increased consumer confidence: 'During previous years, clients cut advertising budgets amid weaker consumer spending, particularly on highly discretionary and big-ticket items' (PRWeb, 2013). This is coupled with three other key factors; the effects of globalisation, the fragmentation of the media and the advent of digital media, including social media. Globally there has been a consolidation of marketing communications businesses 'as increasing globalisation of clients necessitates the provision of services on a global basis. Further consolidation is expected over the next five years, as the major players acquire emerging digital agencies' (PRWeb, 2013).

Changes to the ways in which consumers view marketing communications and particular advertising messages fuelled by a more interactive environment have meant a fundamental change in audience media consumption habits, the continued development of web-enabled devices, and a shift towards other marketing communications tools (as discussed in more detail in Chapter 10 of this book). This has had a profound effect on the structure of the industry. Even before the development of the Internet during the 1990s the industry had changed with some firms becoming marketing communications companies rather than advertising agencies and, for example, media departments breaking off and becoming independent media brokers and specialists with others becoming digital advertising firms or web development entities: 'Over time, the mid-size independent agency is expected to become rarer, with most firms operating at the extremes of the spectrum. There will be large firms operating under the holding company model, and small firms serving niche and emerging markets' (PRWeb, 2013).

There is a perception that working in marketing and especially advertising is primarily a creative role. In many ways this is not far off the mark, depending upon how creativity is defined, but there are many other roles in advertising and other communications firms that are less creative in the 'creative ideas' sense. Creativity in this sense has recently been re-defined by Andjelic (2010), writing in *Advertising Age* (AdAge Digital), because of the changes that have occurred since digital media began to take hold. According to Andjelic it is the creatives (the 'people who make stuff') who hold sway over strategists (the 'people who talk about stuff') when it comes to 'creative matters'. However, digital is different from analogue. In the latter world 'creative is typically a static commercial art piece (or a "portfolio" of these). Creativity represented by great copy, an idea that makes a twist on popular culture or "captures the zeitgeist", or as a piece-of-art logo and print ad, may indeed belong to the same era as those media that defined it.' In the digital world, for Andjelic, 'The best creative is the creation of relationships, connections and interactions. It connects tools with behaviors, locations, and objects. It creates networks or systems.' Andjelic argues for strategic creativity now that digital is here and connectivity and networks are all important. There is a need to 'plan for a chain reaction' and for advertising people to go beyond the conventional creative team, but 'advertising's creative class needs strategists in order to find their way in the digital world'.

Advertising agencies

Roles and responsibilities

There are many people who work within or with the marketing communications industry in many countries throughout the world. Some sell advertising space in publications such as newspapers or magazines and others, for example, work in broadcast media or with online media. All in all there are many roles that are fulfilled. Below are just some of the key roles that can be found in advertising agencies.

Creative roles

In advertising agencies there have traditionally been a number of directly creative roles such as designer or copywriter. Creative roles require high-level skills and competencies. For some time this has included computer literacy as well as paper-based skills and competencies, but more specialist areas are in writing copy or making films.

Graphic designer or creative designer   The difference between creative design and graphic design is that the former is part of the creative process that involves being original, fresh, imaginative and inventive, and that leads to problem solving. The latter involves a specific, functional skill set that facilitates the solution. A person could be both but graphic designers are not always creative and creatives do not always have a graphic designer's skills.

Illustrator   An illustrator has artistic and design creative skills and is essentially a visual storyteller with a message that fulfils the client brief in terms of mood and style. Illustrators may work in a number of areas but from a marketing communications perspective this will include advertising, merchandising (for example calendars or t-shirts), brochures, catalogues and animation. Illustrators will often specialise, as with for example medical illustrations, and many prefer to work as freelancers, working for a variety of clients and not only in advertising or another aspect of marketing communications.

Art director   An art director is responsible for the 'look' of a campaign and works with others, such as copywriters or photographers, so as to meet the client's brief. An art director should therefore understand how, for example, photography or typography works.

Producer   A producer develops commercials and other forms of marketing for clients in a wide variety of sectors and media such as television, print, radio or online. A producer might get involved with other marketing communication elements such as public relations, perhaps press work such as press releases, or press receptions or conferences. Producers need to be innovative and able to develop strategy for clients, working with a team of people such as graphic designers or photographers.

Director of photography   A director of photography, in advertising as in film, has to collaborate with others, for example a camera crew, costume, hair and make-up and lighting, in order to capture the desired 'look' of a film, and must understand what is required to get to the photographic 'heart' of the piece that is being produced.

Copywriters   Copywriters are responsible for word generation such a straplines, slogans or scripts, some of which accompany visuals. Copywriters need to be able to work with others in a creative team, with clients, and in particular with art directors, to make sure all aspects of a campaign are in place.

Artworker   An artworker produces a print-ready product and needs to understand the printing process and graphic applications. An artworker takes creative design concepts from a designer and finishes the job by fixing whatever needs fixing in terms of, for example, colours or typography. An eye for detail is essential and for design usual. Technical knowledge of hard- and software is essential for consistency across platforms, from advertising materials to brochures and other literature, exhibition stand work to direct marketing and online materials. A creative artworker may also be involved with the mock-up stage of the process as well as other materials.

Management roles

Account director   An account director has full responsibility for a portfolio of clients with the help of a team of people consisting of account managers or executives. Therefore revenue from the portfolio and the performance of the team falls within this responsibility. The account director usually has a small number of clients and therefore has relationships with brand managers or other, more senior managers depending upon the structure of the client organisation. The account director also has relationships with other agencies and specialists who might be brought in because of their expertise in particular areas.

Account executive   The account executive (or account manager or representative) has a key liaison role where the 'account exec' has to be able to translate ideas from client to creative teams and vice versa in an effective way. The role requires a certain skill set, including sales and negotiation (and therefore listening skills), presentation skills and organising and coordinating skills. Traditionally a 'go-between', the account executive has to get to know clients' business and be able to take ideas and issues back to the appropriate people in the agency and vice versa.

Account planner   Account planners gather and use research and information that (insightfully) feed into a client's marketing communications campaign. Account planning therefore helps both the creative and media effort in relation to the creative and media brief and is also part of the feedback when looking at performance.

Media buyer and media planner   Depending upon the size and type of agency those two roles might be separate or combined and rolled into one. The media buyer is essentially involved in obtaining the best media rates and managing the budget whereas the media planner is involved with adjusting media schedules, often in response to changes in a campaign, and therefore also responsible for monitoring the effectiveness of chosen media. The planner needs research skills and ability, and also needs to know the nature of the target audience and the best media that can access that target. The buyer needs negotiating skills and ability and both require interpersonal skills, especially in order to interface with clients and creatives.

The full service agency

As the name suggests a full service agency can provide clients with a full range of services necessary to marketing communications campaigns, and may even offer services that go beyond the usual elements of creative inputs or media selection such as a requirement for help with marketing strategy formulation and execution. Certainly marketing research is a necessary offering from the full service agency. Marketing research (for example copy testing or the pre-testing of packaging) is a necessary part of the marketing communications planning process (as discussed in Chapter 4 of this book) and features strongly in each of the marketing communications elements (as discussed in Chapter 17 of this book). Freeland (2010) discusses why clients need a full service agency, suggesting that they do so because such agencies have become trusted strategic partners and not merely suppliers. The full service agency may then work with other specialist agencies such as the direct marketing, sales promotion, digital or PR agency, with strict demarcation lines. Freeland cites Unilever having worked this way successfully in the past. However, Freeland goes on to argue that such working in a silo-type way has become increasingly difficult to manage in leaner times and 'It's also potentially blinkering clients by pushing them to decide up front which route to take and therefore which specialist agencies they need to employ'. The answer lies in the advent of the full service communications agency that can embrace 'the opportunities offered by both long-established and new media channels' and achieve 'joined up thinking' and 'a true culture of continuous learning and improvement and ultimately maximise your return on investment'.

Agency remuneration   Agency remuneration has seen varying trends over time but it is the advent and rise of digital communications that have shaped the latest changes. Marketing communications campaigns are more sophisticated than in the past because of digital impact with more and different types of media available that provide opportunities to help break through the clutter that exists in an ever-changing business and marketing environment. Media choice can be quickly reviewed and changed, much more so than in the past, which underlines the need for clarity in the client–agency relationship.

In the best practice guide on how to pay agencies, the Institute of Practitioners in Advertising (IPA) guide (IPA, 2012) suggests the first edition guide of 2005 'reflected the trend from commission to fee-based remuneration with some development of payment by results'. There are now, however, 'more complex and sophisticated remuneration models as agencies and clients seek to provide for more value-based efficient relationships'. The IPA document argues that such trends are a result of slimmer budgets and that remuneration models will continue to evolve, and offers a ten-point checklist of best practice remuneration agreements and eight principal payment systems. The checklist consists of the following:

1. Simple to understand and easy to administer and execute.
2. Fair to both client and agency with equitable remuneration, including fair and transparent profit.
3. Aligning client and agency interests, priorities and needs.
4. Finalised before agency resources are committed.
5. Recorded in a ratified client–agency written contract that provides reassurance and clarity over time and a basis for dispute resolution.
6. Flexible enough to accommodate possible changes to many things, for example, services, new products or corporate objectives.
7. The involvement of senior management stewardship whereby principles are clearly communicated to both parties so that understanding of the mechanics is established and conflict is avoided.
8. Capable of enduring over time and robust enough to survive change.

9. Based on agreed and understood terms and definitions whereby everyone is talking the same language.

10. Specified tracking and review dates should be part of a formal review and evaluation process and ideally every six months, but for a newly formed relationship a review should be completed after the first quarter.

The IPA (2012) guide suggests that fees of various types account for 90 per cent of all creative agencies agreements with the rest being hybrid agreements that might include a commission element. The eight IPA principal payment systems are listed below.

Retainer fees were introduced when media and planning functions were split so as to remunerate creative agencies. Such fees are agreed in advance for a period of time and are based on estimates of staff costs, overheads and an appropriate level of profit, having followed a detailed plan that includes a work schedule for those involved. This is usually billed on a monthly basis but can be reviewed over time and there is usually a guaranteed minimum and an element of pay by results (PBR). The advantages for both client and agency are numerous according to the IPA guide. The agency has knowledge of its income and can therefore plan for costs and cash flow. The client can budget for the advertising and agency cost and any other third party (net) costs including production. There are no ties to specific media or commission making it media-neutral. On the down side the scope of the assignment has to be accurate otherwise it will not work, it is less accountable because it is input- rather than output-based, and it is not based on performance so might then not encourage the agency to be proactive. It is also time-consuming to negotiate and administer and increases overhead costs.

Project fees are often used in conjunction with retainer fees and usually applied as a one-off or ad-hoc cost for a particular project, as the name suggests, and are also often used to pay for supplementary services such as direct marketing, PR or sales promotion. There is no notice period, money up-front or financial security as there is with retainers so that this attracts a premium and thus is ideal as a top-up. There is ease of control and flexibility when dealing with client needs and it can fit in with integrated or niche approaches. On the down side it is a short-term rather than long-term relationship in nature and not for brand building, there is less confidence than with longer-term approaches, and performance incentives are difficult to build in to the agency's output.

Variable fees are based on actual time spent and is used in marketing communications services such as sales promotions rather than in creative advertising. This is a charge-out, cost-plus rate for staff services and is based on staff salary, overheads and profit and not estimated cost as with retainers: it is paid after the event. Although this is easy to administer, is flexible, reflects client need and is a clearly defined process of delivery and payment, there is no way of knowing or predicting the cost in advance. The client cannot budget and the agency staff cannot act with confidence, and according to the IPA guide there is a perception of an accountability problem and no direct incentive for efficiency. If the agency spends more time on a task they will be paid more unless an agreement is reached or a cap set.

Scale fees and bonuses are likened by the IPA to a 'salary' that is a fixed percentage of either sales or the annual marketing budget. With the case of a scale fee based on sales the bonus is built in. This can be either a matched percentage of sales increase or a scale fee pegged on the marketing budget. This is a bonus based on results, calculated on a mix of subjective and objective elements. The advantages are that it is good for companies seeking sales as a key performance indicator, as with fmcg companies. It is linked to client success rather than man hours whereby if the clients sales increase so does the agency's pay, and if based on the marketing budget the agency benefits according to increases in the volume of activity but is media neutral. On the down side this system does not appeal where sales are not the main determinant of success, it is less accountable, not being based on scope of work and spend level, and it is potentially unfair on the agency since sales are affected by many other things such as the economy and change and the fact that some marketing communications services are not related directly to sales.

Consultancy and concept fees are agreed one-off fees that cover the cost of developing the creative concept of a campaign, based on the estimated value of an idea to the client's business. This system will work when work is needed beyond the existing remit and is usually priced at a premium due to the short-term nature of the assignment. The concept is retained by its creator who is either paid some form of royalty, licence fee if used again or outright purchase. This system has the advantage of a client being able to buy into a first-class concept that will enhance the brand but there are problems with this system. The value of the idea can be the only determinant of the fee and this can become contentious because it is outside of the agreement.

Licensing fees are different to the concept fee in that there is a lower rate but no client ownership of the concept since a licence fee is paid, and this system is useful with online advertising. Agencies are incentivised to produce ideas that are big, flexible and long term to build the brand, the up-front costs are minimised, and the concept can be retained by the agency yet work well for clients in other markets, which can be negotiated when needed, and this avoids a dispute over extended rights. On the down side copyright does not apply to idea-only and straplines cannot be protected by copyright and must be registered as trademarks.

Output or off-the-shelf rate fees are a fixed price per unit, like pay per click, for commoditised output. It is simple and reflects what the client is buying in terms of a standardised purchase but clearly is not suitable if the desired output is not standardised or commoditised but is in fact tailored to client need.

Commission fees come from media owners and are still in place. This system of basing the agency's remuneration on the commission earned from the media owner (15 per cent gross of media spend) is still the basis for many media agreements despite much speculation about its demise over the last 10 years or so. The IPA guide, however, suggests that it is almost extinct as the sole means to agency remuneration because of the changes to the industry and especially the split between media and creative functions. The IPA guide also suggests that 84 per cent of media agreements are with independent media agencies. It is simple and easy to administer in mainstream advertising cases, the rate can be negotiated depending upon level of service and both parties can forget price and concentrate on service quality. It is, however, a system that does not take output into account as it relies purely on media spend and because of the dependency on volume it is not suitable for digital contexts and it is not media neutral. This can lead to a situation whereby agencies are suspected of promoting media expenditure rather than finding solutions to marketing communications problems. On the other hand spend cancellations can affect agency revenue.

The IPA (2012) guide suggests that a mixture of remuneration types might be fairest. For example, retainers can be used with a project fee but such hybrid systems still need to be guided and mutually agreed.

Payment by results (PBR) schemes

Such schemes are incentive-based and involve key performance indicators (KPIs) that are used by nearly 70 per cent of agencies in the UK (IPA, 2012). PBR schemes are structured to wrap around a particular remuneration scheme with the intention to be mutually beneficial and win-win by providing the client with measurable outcomes while the agency potentially gets a higher return. Stable, long-term relationships work best and enable measurement of goals whether based on subjective (relationship) or objective (actual results such as sales or market share) criteria. The PBR scheme has the advantage as accountability in terms of performance and delivery and the long-term nature of such schemes allow agencies to demonstrate their contribution. On the other hand it may be difficult to calculate one agency's contribution when other factors are at play in a complex and complicated situation. This can lead to relationship damage so that care needs to be taken over the budgeting and finance and that the scheme is properly set up.

Value-based remuneration

This system works by putting a valuation on agency results whereby a client sets a base fee to cover the cost of producing outputs and then a mark-up is added (rather than a discretionary bonus) based on actual performance. This fee is based on mutually agreed criteria so that reward is based on agreed performance and delivery and has the advantage of clarity and accountability, but may not work as well for the agency if the mark-up affects profit adversely. It is complex and resource-heavy to manage and performance criteria are a significant qualitative element.

Evaluation of agency performance

Monitoring and evaluation in general are a good idea. As suggested in Chapter 4 of this book, this is a fundamental part of the marketing communications management process. It is a different kind of evaluation that sees clients evaluating the actual performance of their advertising agency. For example, Leggatt (2009) reports on a survey by the American Association of National Advertisers (ANA) which suggests that 'the majority of marketers regularly conduct formal agency performance evaluations'. In fact from the sample of 117 marketers, 82 per cent said they did just this as part of an emphasis on accountability. The aim is to improve relationships rather than simply find under-performing elements whereby the evaluation can lead to constructive dialogue and the support of collaborations within integrated marketing communications and brand-building activities. The kinds of criteria looked at are innovation, strategy, implementation and follow through, fiscal stewardship and ideas.

Specialist agencies or communication companies

Direct marketing companies

Direct marketing, discussed more fully in Chapter 12 of this book, is a method of selling products or services direct to customers rather than through an intermediary, there being direct communication between the two parties. The original direct marketing effort may be created in-house by the manufacturer or service provider or this organisation may become a client of a direct marketing company. In many cases the direct marketing company may have been subcontracted to do the work by another communications company or agency. Direct marketing relies heavily on measurement of response rates, whether this be in a direct mail or other direct sales method such as telemarketing, newspaper inserts or online. Direct marketing also relies heavily on customer lists and databases. The direct marketing company therefore has to have this kind of expertise but may also specialise, for example on direct mail services.

Many direct marketing companies offer outsource fulfilment services, integrated digital campaign management, database management, or some form of testing such as A/B (a simple comparison) or multivariate (a more complex) testing. For example A/B testing can be used very simply online by producing two versions of a web page and is therefore a method of validating a new design over an older version. It is a form of measurement rather than guesswork as to which design will produce the best results but regular testing will ensure the best design is in place to optimise results. Multivariate testing in the same example would compare many more design variables of the web page. These tests can be used in all forms of media to compare, for example, copy, images, or even the method of delivery. The UK Direct Marketing Association (DMA, www.dma.org.uk/) and the Institute of Direct Marketing (IDM, www.theidm.com/) are two bodies that compete for attention in the direct marketing arena in the UK. The DMA in the UK is part of the US parent DMA (http://thedma.org/) whereas the IDM is a UK home-grown industry body.

Sales promotion agencies

Sales promotion, discussed at length in Chapter 11 of this book, is the marketing communications element that adds value to a brand and actively promotes sales increases, product usage or trial. There are a wide number of techniques that can be employed to achieve these objectives, the commonest still being coupons of one sort or another. Sales promotion agencies exist to help clients create tools that will successfully impact directly on sales with better conversion of intent to actual purchase and higher returns. The dilemma for brand owners when employing sales promotions is the warnings often received about brand damage caused by the over-use of sales promotions that are perceived as short-term solutions, while at the same time the results of sales promotions are much easier to quantify than other forms of marketing communication as the results are usually much more tangible and attributable to the sales promotion variable. Sales promotions can produce quick results, which makes these techniques attractive for short-term sales objective achievement. However, longer-term brand strategy will dictate that brand image is an important commodity and brand damage needs to be avoided whereby too many and frequent sales promotion offers can cheapen the brand.

The range of people involved in sales promotion agencies is not dissimilar to those in advertising agencies. There is usually an account management function that includes, for example, a sales promotion account executive who is involved in all of the stages of the process but who reports to an account manager or director. A sales promotion campaign involves devising, developing and implementing sales promotion ideas that may be new to a particular context but not new as a sales promotion technique since, after all, a competition is a competition and a free sample is a free sample. The account executive classically acts as a liaison between the client and the rest of the agency and external suppliers of goods and services. Briefing other agency staff, such as the creative team, the production department or administrative staff, is part of this role. The Institute of Promotional Marketers (IPM) (www.theipm.org.uk/Home.aspx), formerly the Institute of Sales Promotion, is a key UK professional body in the sales promotion area.

Public relations firms

Public relations (PR) as an element of marketing communications is discussed more fully in Chapter 13 of this book where the differences between advertising and PR are explained. These differences are reflected in the nature of the PR sector of the marketing communications industry. The overall job of PR agencies or firms is to create positive relations between an organisation and its publics, including of course its customers where customers are considered to be a key public.

Typical jobs in PR firms include working on media, community and employee relations, and special events, or helping a charity client with fundraising activities. The PR executive will act on behalf of a client and gather facts and figures and other relevant data that will help track public concerns and relevant trends in the client's sphere of operations and relevant publics. The work involves creating PR events to gain awareness or achieve other client goals by the employment of tools such as press releases or press receptions. The PR account executive needs skills such as imagination, communication and writing and must be able to have the confidence to deal not only with clients, the media and journalists but also other staff including the account manager or director. A degree of diplomacy is required but so also are organising, planning and managing skills. Many people who start or work in PR firms do so after experience in journalism. The professional body in the UK for PR is the Chartered Institute of Public Relations (CIPR, www.cipr.co.uk/), formerly the Institute of Public Relations.

Digital/interactive agencies

The trend towards interactivity, enabled not least through digital technology developments, is said to enhance the ability of companies to get brands closer to customers. Digital experiences help to build online audiences and communities and often it is design that is at the heart of the online experience. Online promotional materials include tools such as brochures and display materials. These days in the wired yet wireless 24/7/365 world, a client's website as well as other interactive services such as mobile applications, e-mail or search engine marketing often drive e-commerce because of the ability to target digital audiences. Many agencies claim to offer website designs that are search engine friendly. They do so because search engine marketing is such an important part of marketing for many organisations. Many digital agencies offer a full service across marketing communications functions. For example PR involves blogs and social networks that cannot be ignored. The rationale is that it is better to be involved than to ignore what is going on with social media and online in forums so that activities include proactive brand monitoring and listening to what customers are talking about.

Digital media planning and buying is often offered by digital agencies. Clearly the days of a limited, simple choice of television and radio stations that could be put together with outdoor or press are over. There are many variations of online display, pay per click (PPC) advertising words such as Google AdWords, pay-per-post blogs, iAds from Apple, and many other online forms of conventional marketing communications elements such as product placement or sponsorship. The kinds of jobs to be found in digital agencies are similar and often the same as traditional advertising agencies and in practice an agency may deal with both traditional and digital work. For example in the digital agency or that part of an agency that deals with digital work, an account director will need experience of leading, managing and of integrated marketing communications thinking across traditional and digital communications. This role requires account handling experience and the ability to have strong relationships with clients. An example of more specific digital roles is that of the digital designer of rich media advertising solutions for clients. This could involve a range of digital advertising from banners to mobile advertisements using desktop, mobile phones or tablets, and requiring experience of, for example, Flash design. If this role is senior in nature then the usual qualities of leadership and maturity would also be required. Other specialist digital roles are in the areas of, for example, search engine optimisation (SEO), mobile advertising or social media.

In-house communications function

The main motivations of cost and control drive some organisations to set up an in-house communications function. The scale, however, is an important consideration and the difference between having a communications or advertising manager or even a department rather than an independent entity within the organisation. One organisation that has achieved this latter position is Benetton with its in-house Fabrica agency (see the Snapshot immediately below). This is not to say that everything will be done in-house but certainly control and co-ordination will, though with liaison and effective communication critical to success. Outsourcing of services generally is not an uncommon occurrence so it should come as no surprise that this would happen with an in-house communications function. As discussed earlier in this chapter, the marketing communications industry has changed radically, especially since the development of digital communications. Media specialists in particular are sought after by companies who are happy to outsource media and to an extent creative services.

The control advantage of an in-house function is created from a number of sources, for example the greater stability of personnel that comes from continuity in staff, time controls, knowledge of products/services and markets or better access to top management and decision makers. It may also help with consistency of brand image, especially internationally where the number of partnerships with outside bodies is reduced. On the down side of having an in-house facility are issues such as internal conflict, the danger of an inward-looking focus, or less access to creative talent than on the open market where a fresh set of ideas may lie. A key issue is a lack of objectivity, with the in-house facility being perhaps too familiar or too close to the company's offerings. There is also the issue of the skilled specialists who may be required, but these can be bought and used in conjunction with in-house and there is greater flexibility when there is an ability to hire and fire if not satisfied.

The Snapshot below discusses fashion brand Benetton's 'unhate' campaign that was created by its in-house agency Fabrica, and the fast-rising Amsterdam and Los Angeles-based agency 72andSunny, with a theme of peace and tolerance that has ignited the 'cultural conversation' for Benetton yet again.

Snapshot   In-house and the external agency – Benetton's 'unhate' campaign by in-house agency Fabrica and external agency 72andSunny

In 2011 Benetton's 'unhate' campaign saw the withdrawal of an advertisement that showed a fake picture of Pope Benedict XVI kissing Muslim Grand Sheik and Egyptian Imam Mohammad Ahmed el-Tayeb. The Vatican called the touched-up Photoshop image unacceptable. It was part of a global campaign that used similarly faked images of world leaders in a similar embrace. So presidents Barack Obama of the USA and Hugo Chavez of Venezuela, Mahmoud Abbas of Palestine and Benjamin Netanyahu of Israel, Angela Merkel of Germany and Nicolas Sarkozy of France, were all portrayed in similar fake poses. The advertising according to United Colors of Benetton Executive Deputy Chairman Alessandro Benetton was created to promote the concept of 'unhate'. The 'unhate' campaign could be construed as a 'peace and love one world harmony' campaign, making it not so much a new concept but a continuation of Benetton's long-running creative concept. Benetton was reported in the press as saying that these are very strong images in order to send a strong message, without being disrespectful of the various world leaders. It would seem the images are seen by Benetton as 'conception figures' that represent 'brotherhood' sealed with a kiss. According to *The Huffington Post* (2011) reactions to the images were fierce with, for example, Whitehouse spokesman Eric Schultz telling *The Huffington Post* that 'The White House has a longstanding policy disapproving of the use of the president's name and likeness for commercial purposes.'

However, according to Cassidy (2012), while UK agencies 'put in a stronger show-ing in the Press category this year … the Grand Prix went to a controversial Benetton ad from Italy featuring world leaders kissing'. The Benetton campaign was created by in-house agency Fabrica and it was 'roundly praised by the jury for prompting a global debate as well as instigating a comeback for Benetton, which has a history of controversial advertising'. Cassidy quotes, according to Tham Khai Meng, Ogilvy & Mather Worldwide chief creative officer and president of the Press jury, that the advertising campaign was 'above the others by a million miles'. However, Fabrica was aided and abetted by 72andSunny, which describes itself as a modern full-service design and advertising company with offices in Los Angeles and Amsterdam. This agency was founded in 2004, born out of 'Frustration that our industry was slow to adapt to the changing technology landscape and excitement for all the new ways we can connect with people and a desire to explore that power'"(72andSunny, 2013). The agency's clients have included Samsung and Nike.

It was the Amsterdam arm of 72andSunny that worked on the Grand Prix win-ning campaign. However, the credit for the top prize went to Fabrica at the client's request. The Press Lions competition honoured three executions in particular – US president Barack Obama and Venezuelan president Hugo Chavez, Palestinian president Mahmoud Abbas and Israeli prime minister Benjamin Netanyahu, and German chancellor Angela Merkel and former French president Nicolas Sarkozy: 'Notably absent was the campaign's most incendiary image – a photo of Pope Benedict XVI kissing a senior Egyptian imam. Benetton pulled that particular ad almost immediately after the campaign broke last November' (Nudd, 2012). It is argued by Parekh (2012) that 72andSunny, as intended for the client, sparked debate, and even outrage, among world leaders in Washington and Rome and beyond. More importantly they 'also reversed a trend of dwindling relevance for Benetton, which has built its brand on espousing ideals like peace and tolerance, and got people talking about the Italian retailer again'. Quoting Matt Jarvis, part-ner and chief strategy officer at Los Angeles-based 72andSunny, Parekh highlights that 'The most valuable thing you can do in marketing is get your clients and brands into a cultural conversation' and 'We're not the only people doing it, but I think we're particularly good at it.' Other clients, according to Parekh, agree. For example the work they do is 'unignorable' (Eric Hirshberg, CEO of video-game giant Activision) and 'The guiding principles for the brand they devel-oped years ago are so relevant, and we still use them … They really built our global brand with us' (Madeleen Klaasen, chief marketing officer at Bugaboo, the Dutch mobility company).

Stop Point

Benetton has a long history of controversy in its advertising. The 2011 'unhate' cam-paign is clearly in that same vein. The role of an outside company like 72andSunny is an interesting move on Benetton's part. Undertake the following: 1. Discuss the rea-sons why Benetton would wish to buy-in the help of 72andSunny when they already have Fabrica; 2. Consider and explain what Benetton might look out for in terms of Fabrica personnel's morale.

ROLES AND STRUCTURES IN CLIENT ORGANISATIONS

Structures

A client can have a centralised or decentralised structure. A centralised structure is one that offers greater authority on making decisions and there is consequently less internal conflict. Within marketing communications, the functional activities such as budgeting, creation and production of promotional materials, media planning and scheduling or marketing research, might all be controlled by one function (and even one person) that coordinates all such activities, including liaison with outside agencies and services.

Generally speaking, as an organisation grows larger it becomes more difficult to maintain a centralised structure, mainly because decision making becomes difficult. A decentralised structure offers the advantages of flexibility and faster problem solving where attention can be focused on matters at hand. The 'brand man' that became the brand manager position came from such growth in Procter and Gamble (P&G) in the early 1930s and heralded a decentralised structure for corporations such as P&G and Unilever. Brand (or product) mangers became responsible for all aspects of the brand or product range in their charge.

Brand manager

Brand management, which began in the 1930s (with Proctor and Gamble, P&G), persists today, with the role involving the usual elements of a planning and managing system as discussed in Chapter 4 of this book, such as dealing with targets or budgeting. The brand manager has to work closely with whoever is dealing with marketing communications whether internal or external. The brand manager role, however, has had to evolve to survive, principally because of the shift towards the more interactive consumer as digital platforms were developed in the wake of media fragmentation. A common argument is that brand managers may spend too much time on internally focused skill sets such as setting and revising budgets and are too focused on short-term planning and administrative tasks, which results in their neglecting the development of long-term plans, often because they must compete for the attention of senior management in order to access resources, but also for career development, perhaps reflecting a lack of authority over brand development. These were the kinds of reason why P&G decided to abandon brand management for category management in the 1980s and then adopt a cohort strategy in 2000.

Category manager

Category management is an additional layer of management above that of the brand manager that enables the coordination of brand manager efforts so that brand and other managers, such as advertising managers, come under a category manager for a whole product category. It is a strategic role devised to help build brands and profit and market share. During the initial years of the new millennium, P&G introduced its new brand management strategy that grouped brands together to appeal to consumers with similar attitudes and needs. This was labelled cohort management but it is in effect a system of bundling brands together that are aimed at similar consumer groups. This was contrary to P&G's previous practice of category management, which is the grouping of brands according to similar product categories.

Marketing services manager

Some organisations group marketing services together under a marketing services manager who oversees all aspects of marketing communications management, but also marketing research and any other marketing activity that does not fall into these two broad functions. In this way the former's support services would include PR, sales promotions, packaging design, merchandising or sponsorship, and with the latter all aspects of secondary and primary marketing research, including a marketing information system, would come under the marketing services manager's remit.

Advertising, promotions or marketing communications manager

Many organisations have a management function where the advertising, promotions or marketing communications manager would liaise with brand managers. These managers would most likely operate under the overall leadership of a marketing director. The duties of these managers will depend upon the size of the organisation but usually a marketing communications manager is responsible for all communications activities except sales, which may operate separately under a sales director. The advertising, promotions or marketing communications manager would therefore coordinate the work of the various agencies employed.

Public relations officer or manager

The PR professional working for an organisation that is not-for-profit usually has the title PRO (public relations officer) but in other organisations may have the title PR manager. The job entails managing the organisation's image and reputation. The PRO or manager needs to have excellent communication skills. Good time management is essential as is the desire and ability to work with lots of different kinds of people. The job might be in-house within a PR department or stand-alone but with agency connections. It involves planning and managing PR campaigns and therefore building strategies, monitoring public and media opinion and, depending upon the size of the organisation, writing and editing brochures, press releases, newsletters, websites or social media activities. It might also involve arranging press receptions or conferences, organising exhibitions or open days, and being involved with sponsored events. Other stakeholders might involve professionals at conferences, charities or community leaders. The job title might be communications, media relations or press officer.

The Snapshot below discusses the client–agency relationship and some of the differing perspectives from both sides of this particular coin.

Snapshot   Rethinking the client–agency relationship – differing perspectives from either side

Liu (2013) comments from client advertising experience that whether it is 'briefing the agency, running a pitch process, or managing a creative project, client-side marketers all have their own styles when it comes to managing the client/agency relationship'. As Liu suggests and has been common knowledge for some time,

(Continued)

(Continued)

the client–agency relationship is central to what marketers do. This relationship is critical to the success of marketing communication campaigns. As Liu says, such a partnership needs 'thoughtful management, transparency, and effective ways of working that all parties respect'. The corollary to this is that there are ways of working that are not effective and these, of course, have to be avoided otherwise damage to this critical relationship will ensue. This, for Liu, would affect creative output since there is a need for innovative solutions to creative challenges. Liu admits that as a client he is 'sometimes guilty of thinking quite linearly', the danger being a presumption of having the answers. The advice is not to 'draw a solid line between the client team and the agency team' but rather, as a client/agency team, the work should be jointly owned, presented and the accountability for outcomes jointly held. Liu reckons that it is sheer folly for the client to try to 'squeeze as much work as you can out of them, to dictate exactly what you want', but rather that the view should be that 'you can disagree without being disagreeable' and that 'you can be clear about your expectations while also being collaborative' with '100 per cent candour in both directions'.

Benady (2013), recognising the subjective nature of the client–agency issue within a PR context, asked senior agency and client-side people for views on agency–client relationships because agencies 'fret constantly about the quality of their association. They pick it over and seem to want to talk about it all the time. Like an insecure lover, they live in constant fear of being dumped.' Benady suggests that there is a 'serious gulf between agencies and clients in what they feel matters most in their relationships', and reports that as part of its 2013 In-House Benchmarking report, the PRCA (Public Relations Consultants Association) asked both agencies and clients to list ingredients for a successful relationship. The response included:

Personal chemistry – only half of the agency respondents held this to be a key ingredient and only about one fifth of client respondents thought this.

Regularity of communication – less than a fifth of agency respondents thought this mattered and only 6 per cent of client respondents did. Apparently there is a fundamental difference in that 'agencies think they are having a relationship, while clients think they are having a transaction'.

Effectiveness – almost half of those from agencies believed that demonstrating ROI was key but in contrast only about one third of clients thought this.

Value for money – less than one third of agencies thought value for money was key while more than one third of clients thought this.

Overall, Benady says that the report suggests that 'there was surprisingly little consensus on the issues that really matter in client–agency relationships'.

Stop Point

The client–agency relationship has been talked about for decades and yet there still appear to be some differences between the perspectives of clients and agencies.

Undertake the following: 1. Compare and contrast the views of Liu and Benady as expressed above; 2. Discuss the similarities and differences that might be found in the client–agency relationship in advertising agencies and PR consultancies.

Assignment

Write a 2,000-word report that illustrates how management might benefit from the installation of an in-house communication function for both internal and external communication purposes. Take into consideration the fact that such a function does not preclude the use of external agencies, experts and specialists.

Summary of Key Points

- The nature and workings of the marketing communications industry involve what clients want and client-driven change.
- Marketing communications professionals know they need to continually evolve to stay relevant.
- Marketing communications professionals need to rethink ideas and reimagine strategies in the knowledge that clients will pay for things they cannot do as well themselves.
- Management of an organisation's marketing communications programmes normally requires the efforts and inputs of a number of individuals both internally and externally. There are, therefore, players in agencies or marketing communications companies as well as client organisations.
- Agencies now need, more than ever before, effectiveness credentials.
- The nature of such players and type of system, whether decentralised or centralised, involves the agencies in an organisation's strategy with varying degrees of responsibility when developing an integrated campaign.
- The adoption of an in-house function is a consideration in relation to the advantages of cost savings and control against the potential lack of experience and loss of objectivity.
- Agencies are structured in varying ways including full service (one-stop shop), creative boutique, media specialist or 'à la carte'.
- Agency selection issues, agency operational relationships and remuneration and evaluation of performance are important issues that need to be considered.
- There is a need to rethink the notion of communications doing things to consumers and to think about what consumers do in terms of interactivity.
- Specialised agencies and marketing communications companies exist to service client need, such as direct marketing, sales promotion, public relations and interactive communications firms as well as those specialising in elements such as sponsorship or product placement.

Discussion Questions

1. Players in the marketing communications industry's agencies and firms need to address what clients want and client-driven change. Discuss this notion using examples to illustrate.

2. Marketing communications professionals know they need to continually evolve to stay relevant. They also need to rethink ideas and reimagine strategies in the knowledge that clients will pay for things they cannot do as well themselves. Discuss the challenges agencies face in negotiating compensation.

3. The management of an organisation's marketing communications programmes normally requires the efforts and inputs of a number of individuals both internally and externally. Discuss the changing role of the account executive in advertising or other agencies. Include in your discussion a reference to the idea that this role might become obsolete.

4. Explain why agencies now need, more than ever before, effectiveness credentials. Include in your discussion examples where agencies have lost accounts and the reasons why.

5. Discuss the brand management and its relationship with marketing communication campaigns using examples to illustrate.

6. Discuss why the adoption of an in-house function is a consideration in choosing and using communications agencies or companies.

7. Explain the role of the media specialist company and suggest reasons why a client might choose such a company to handle media buying and planning.

8. Agency selection issues include relationships, remuneration and the evaluation of performance. Discuss agency selection criteria in the context of an industry or sector of your choice using examples to illustrate.

9. Explain why there is a need to rethink the notion of communications doing things to consumers and to think about what consumers do in terms of interactivity.

10. Specialised agencies and marketing communications companies exist to service client need yet there is a desire to have a campaign that is fully integrated. Discuss the use of specialists in the marketing communications industry in the light of integrated marketing communication.

Further Reading

Chalaby, J.K. (2008) 'Advertising in the Golden Age: transnational campaigns and pan-European television channels', *Global Media and Communication*, 4 (2): 139–56. http://gmc.sagepub.com/content/4/2/139
The change that has taken place with regard to pan-regional advertising campaigns by companies operating in Europe is discussed in the article, which suggests that there

were too few companies wanting to go pan-European leading the stations concerned into financial difficulties. As the number of companies with an interest in meeting the globalisation challenge grew, the advertising industry was restructured. The article discusses the role of media buying agencies with the knowledge to facilitate such campaigns, essentially 'glocal', i.e. as the authors put it, a mix of local and global objectives met by 'flexible local advertising' and 'integrated communication solutions involving cross-format and cross-platform opportunities'.

Deuze, M. (2007) 'Converging Culture in the Creative Industries', *International Journal of Cultural Studies*, 10 (2): 243–63. http://ics.sagepub.com/content/10/2/243.full. pdf+html

This article looks at emerging practices in the media professions, including advertising and public relations as part of marketing communications, in response to the changing global environment that is now technology-led where interactivity is at the centre. The article looks at the key trends such as upstream marketing and citizen journalism that are part of culture convergence and media production and consumption. Deuze looks through a lens of a combination of individual creativity and mass production, known as 'creative industries'.

Johnson, M. and Tennens, M. (2005) 'The Challenges of Implementing a Marketing Strategy: a practitioner's view', *Journal of Medical Marketing*, 5 (1): 44–56. http://mmj. sagepub.com/content/5/1/44.full.pdf+html

This article is concerned with marketing campaigns that are linked to bottom line results and driven by strategic objectives, and as such is a case study of a pharmacy business that for many years did not consciously use marketing tools and techniques. Written by the Chief Operating Officer of the business and the MD of the marketing agency specialising in the design and implementation of marketing communications programmes, the article discusses the implementation of a programme that includes research, telemarketing, brand image, collateral development, public relations and customer relations management. The resultant marketing strategy, integrated with sales strategy and the development of the people in the business, is explained.

Miller, R. (2002) 'A Prototype Audit for Marketing Communications Professionals', *Marketing Theory*, 2 (4): 41928. http://mtq.sagepub.com/content/2/4/419.full. pdf+html

Identifying and measuring the functional marketing skills organisations need in the marketing communications area is advocated in this article, which is concerned with job design, recruitment, training and outsourcing. The author provides a framework for skills definition and measurement in planning their careers in the knowledge that a better understanding of the marketing communications expertise required enables educators to offer courses in relevant applied marketing communications.

Sinclair, J. (2009) 'The Advertising Industry in Latin America: a comparative study', *The International Communication Gazette*, 71 (8): 713–33. http://gaz.sagepub.com/ content/71/8/713

The author collaborates with several others from four Latin American locations (Brazil, Mexico, Argentina and Chile) and discusses economic and cultural globalisation. Beginning with the great debate about the cultural imperialism of earlier decades whereby the rich countries of North America and Europe tended to dominate 'third world' countries and moving on to the neglected area of the advertising industry, Sinclair suggests that the article presents a 'detailed empirical account' of the modes in which the advertising industry now binds the four countries of the study economically and culturally.

REFERENCES

72andsunny (2013) 72andSunny website, available at: www.72andsunny.com/

Andjelic, A. (2010) 'Do we need a new definition of creativity? In today's digital world, the answer is yes', *AdAge Digital*, 20 August, available at: http://adage.com/article/digitalnext/a-definition-creativity/145448/

Baker, C. and Handyside, M. (2010) 'The agency model is broken – but you can fix it', *Market Leader*, Quarter 1, available at: www.warc.com

Baskin, M. (2010) 'Briefing your agency', *Warc Best Practice*, February, available at: www.warc.com

Benady, A. (2013) 'What makes a successful client-agency relationship?', *PR Week*, 22 August, available at: www.prweek.com/article/1208278/makes-successful-client-agency-relationship

Binet, L. (2005) 'Evaluating marketing communications: a guide to best practice', *Market Leader*, Issue 29, Summer, available at: www.warc.com

Cassidy, A. (2012) 'Cannes 2012: Italy's controversial Benetton ad takes Grand Prix for press', 20 June, available at: www.campaignlive.co.uk/news/1137354/

Chadwick, S. (2006) 'Client-driven change – the impact of change in client needs on the research industry', *International Journal of Marketing Research*, 48 (4): 391–414.

Chalaby, J.K. (2008) 'Advertising in the global age', *Global Media and Communication*, 4 (2): 139–56.

Deuze, M. (2007) 'Converging culture in the creative industries', *International Journal of Cultural Studies*, 10 (2): 243–63.

Drobis, D. R. (1997) 'Integrated marketing communications redefined', *Journal of Integrated Communications*, 8: 6–10.

Duncan, T.R. and Everett, S.E. (1993) 'Client perceptions of integrated marketing communications', *Journal of Advertising Research*, 33 (3): 30–9.

Farnworth, S. (2010) 'To stay relevant how do communications professionals need to evolve?', *Jolt Social Media*, available at: http://stevefarnsworth.wordpress.com/2010/09/15/to-stay-relevant-how-do-communications-professionals-need-to-evolve/

Fletcher, J. (2003) 'A data factory in the middle of storyville? Preparing the market research industry for the dream economy', the Market Research Society Annual Conference, MRS on WARC.com, available at www.warc.com

Freeland, C. (2010) 'Why clients need a full-service agency', *Marketing Week*, 12 July, available at: www.marketingweek.co.uk/why-clients-need-a-full-service-agency/3015695.article

The Huffington Post (2011) 'Benetton "unhate" campaign shows world leaders kissing', 17 November, available at: www.huffingtonpost.com/2011/11/16/benetton-unhate-campaign-world-leaders-kissing_n_1097333.html

IPA (2012) 'Agency Remuneration: A best practice guide on how to pay agencies', *Joint industry guidelines for marketing professionals in working effectively with agencies*, 2nd edition, London: IPA. Available at: www.ipa.co.uk/document/agency-remuneration-best-practice-guide

Jeans, R. (1998) 'Integrating marketing communications', *Admap*, December. Available at: www.warc.com/Content/ContentViewer.aspx?ID=7d532321-177b-4739-9134-ded1cf4d9648&q=integrated+marketing+communications&CID=A7299&PUB=ADMAP&MasterContentRef=7d532321-177b-4739-9134-ded1cf4d9648

Jensen, M.B. (2007) 'Online marketing communication potential – priorities in Danish firms and advertising agencies', *European Journal of Marketing*, 42 (3/4): 502–25.

Johnson, M. and Tennens, M. (2005) 'The challenges of implementing a marketing strategy: a practitioner's view', *Journal of Medical Marketing*, 5 (1): 44–56.

Leggatt, H. (2009) 'Are you evaluating your agency's performance?', *BizReport Research*, 16 September, available at: www.bizreport.com/2009/09/are_you_evaluating_your_agencys_performance.html

Liu, J. (2013) 'Rethinking the client-agency relationship', *The Drum*, 17 July, available at: www.thedrum.com/opinion/2013/07/17/rethinking-client-agency-relationship

Miller, R. (2002) 'A prototype audit for marketing communications professionals', *Marketing Theory*, 2 (4): 419–28.

Nudd, T. (2012) 'Press grand prix goes to Benetton's kissing ads from Fabrica, 72andSunny', *Adweek*, available at: www.adweek.com/news/advertising-branding/press-grand-prix-goes-benettons-kissing-ads-fabrica-72andsunny-141244

Padsetti, M., Fourie, W., Hyde, K., Kitchen, P. And Eagle, L. (1999) 'Perceptions of integrated marketing communications among marketers and advertising agency executives in New Zealand', *International Journal of Advertising*, 18 (1): 89–119.

Parekh, R. (2012) '72andSunny is no. 5 on the Ad Age Agency A-list', *AdAge*, available at: http://adage.com/article/special-report-agency-alist/72andsunny-5-ad-age-agency-a-list/232187/

PRWeb (2013) 'Advertising agencies in Australia industry market research report now updated by IBISWorld', PRWeb, 31 August, available at: www.prweb.com/releases/2013/8/prweb11060136.htm

Rooseboom, M. (2010) 'PR, communication, and marketing trends 2011 parts 1 & 2', available at: www.mynewsdesk.com/uk/mynewsdesk/blog_posts

Saunders, J. (2006) 'Growing up digitally: change drivers in marketing', *Market Leader*, 33, pp. 31–9, Summer.

Sinclair, J. (2009) 'The advertising industry in Latin America: a comparative study', *The International Communication Gazette*, 71 (8): 713–33.

Sommers, M. (1990) 'Agencies: what changes are clients looking for?', *Admap*, July, available at www.warc.com

Swain, W.N. (2005) 'Perceptions of interactivity and consumer control in marketing communications: an exploratory survey of marketing communications professionals', *Journal of Interactive Advertising*, 6 (1): 109–24, Fall.

Thompson, S. (2008) 'The importance of an agency effectiveness culture to clients', The Institute of Practitioners in Advertising, available at: www.warc.com

WordPress.com (2012) 'United Colors of Benetton – unemployee of the year', WordPress.com, 18 September, available at: http://thisisnotadvertising.wordpress.com/tag/72andsunny/

 # Ethics and Corporate Social Responsibility in Marketing Communications

CHAPTER OVERVIEW

Introduction

This chapter deals with the nature of marketing communications' relationships and influence on society. Marketing communications as a function is placed within an ethical context. Corporate social responsibility is presented as a positive step forward for both society and all organisations whether large or small, profit-making or not-for-profit, governmental or non-governmental. Business, especially big business, is often perceived and portrayed as being unethical, greedy, seedy, or downright unfair. Although for the most part business is none of these, there are instances of unethical, poor practice that fuel the flames. Such practice includes aspects of marketing communications, particularly advertising, that are seen at times as misleading, dishonest, and even illegal. Companies and other organisations such as charities and governments have been accused of deception and of other activities, including targeting vulnerable groups such as the very young or the elderly, using shock tactics that are too shocking, stereotyping, using subliminal images that are covert, or using brand placement in a deliberate attempt to get around bans on other forms of communication. None of the tools of marketing and corporate communications escapes such potential criticism. However, in most cases organisations are honest, truthful, legal and decent but need to have frameworks that enable them not to fall foul of the laws and codes of conduct that exist in most countries (see Chapter 18 of this book for international perspectives).

This chapter looks at these issues within a context where self-regulation, a concept not entirely trusted by all players, is at the centre of ethical standards and practice.

Learning objectives

The chapter seeks to explore marketing communications' role and place in society and explain the nature of social responsibility and ethics. More specifically, after reading this chapter the student will be able to:

- discuss sustainable development, including what being socially responsible is;
- define and discuss cause-related marketing, fair trade and environmental marketing;
- discuss criticism of marketing and marketing communications and unethical practice;
- appreciate unethical practices that can lead to brand damage or loss of reputation;
- consider the marketing communications mix elements and their impact on society;
- define consumerism and the role of pressure groups;
- appreciate the regulatory environment and the role that self-regulation plays in marketing communications practice.

THE IMPACT OF MARKETING COMMUNICATIONS ELEMENTS ON SOCIETY

As discussed in more detail in this chapter, the various elements impact in both similar and different ways to each other on society. Each of the key elements is discussed in this section in order to put this in perspective.

Advertising

Advertising has traditionally been singled out for criticism when considering not only marketing's relationship with society and the self-regulation concept but also what advertising can and cannot do in terms of reflecting societal norms or shaping them. For many years marketing academics have proudly stated that marketing is the function of business that sells people things they never knew they wanted, so it is not surprising that arguably marketing's most visible element, advertising, is seen by some as an instrument of manipulation. Others, of course, champion advertising and often use social marketing examples as a counter to criticisms. The real issues, however, are things such as message construction that raise fear or anxiety, vulnerable target groups, the use of covert techniques like subliminal advertising that can appear clever yet devious, or the use of exaggeration or even false claims (puffery).

Sales promotion

Much of the criticism levelled at advertising is also levelled at sales promotion especially in terms of deceptive or dishonest practice. Issues arise around different types of promotion. For example, consumers may complain that they have no real chance of winning a prize if the offer is only limited to the first (small) percentage of customers or if the submission date has passed, especially where this is only detailed in the small print. Not having enough of a special offer in stock yet still drawing the customer into a store can be problematic, as can advertising the promotion price as being much less than 'normal' for a limited period only whereupon the price will revert to the higher one, which is not ethical if the higher price is inflated in the first place. More broadly there are promotions aimed at children from the likes of McDonald's where Happy Meals come with a toy (usually a children's movie tie-in such as *Toy Story* or *The Smurfs*) and have done since 1979. However, in July 2013 Taco Bell announced it would stop selling kids' meals. McDonald's in particular have been fending off criticism that both advertising and the use of sales promotions aimed at children are simply wrong and McDonald's were fined in $1.6 million in Brazil for including toys in Happy Meals to aggressively target children. There are also problems with giveaways and the overuse of sales promotions that can cheapen the organisation's image and cause brand damage.

Direct marketing

With direct marketing there are similar issues with the actual message sent as with advertising with regard to the potential for misleading and dishonest content. With the advent of telesales came the problem of nuisance calls and unsolicited mail (conventional or email) and issues with privacy and unwanted sales approaches. However, the biggest concern is over data collection and storage and the building of databases.

Packaging

Packaging performs a functional role but is also a medium for communications. Both aspects pose differing kinds of problems for marketers. The use of non-biodegradable materials has been an issue for some time and continues to be so, with concern over land-fill disposal and recycling availability. The communication issues are many and varied, from legal labelling requirements to the use of images that may be deceptive in terms of size of the actual product inside or misleading in terms of what is actually being bought. For example, if an image on the packaging shows accessories alongside the main product but it is only the main product such as a child's doll that is in the pack then this could be deemed to be misleading.

Public Relations

The idea of the 'PR stunt' has been around a long time in business but also in other areas such as politics. The role of PR should be to create a more favourable environment for the rest of marketing to operate in but it is sometimes seen to be used to cover up or hide issues. The danger is that the various publics may see this as an attempt to deceive, to not tell the whole truth, and even to lie or at best mislead. The idea of using PR in this way will undermine any good work on image or reputation that the organisation has done. Organisations should also be cautious about the amount spent on or the overuse of corporate hospitality as this can send the wrong message to the various publics, including the media that the organisation has to deal and engage with.

ON BEING SOCIALLY RESPONSIBLE MARKETERS

Sustainable development and Corporate Social Responsibility (CSR)

Sustainable development (of a business) is about how the company operates, how it consumes, directly or indirectly, natural resources, and how the company can be profitable while not compromising the needs of future generations and at the same time building a long-term future for itself. This is, of course, an ethical stance that not all companies take. It is based on a belief in give and take, in a commitment to protecting the environment, reducing the company's carbon (ecological) footprint, and gaining acceptance of its corporate behaviour by society.

CSR is a strand of the sustainable development concept, which is a stakeholder approach that requires the company to meet its responsibilities as a member of society. It is therefore a social strand that is affected by the external (or macro) elements of the marketing environment. For some, engagement with CSR is primarily an ethical and moral stance that should be taken in isolation 'from strategic communication including public relations and reputation management' (Nielsen and Thomsen, 2009b: 176). From this position, the personal beliefs and values of those running companies should override the connection with the external world. The primary concern should be 'internal and local stakeholders'. Nielsen and Thomsen (2009a: 83) suggest an 'inside-out approach to CSR, with a strong emphasis on the internal (corporate culture) dimension'. The evidence from this study of Danish SMEs suggests that 'SMEs have no interest in turning their local and authentic practice into a forced marketing and branding exercise, leaving them with an artificial picture of who they are and strive to be in the future'. These authors do argue more generally that this is then a 'fruitful platform for adopting strategic CSR communication' (2009b: 176), the problem being one of 'how they should communicate CSR to their external stakeholders'. These authors conclude in their (2009a) study that SMEs 'should keep on acting locally but force themselves to think globally' in the face of the challenges posed by the global economy. In a CSR comparative study of Italian firms, both large and small firms were considered (Perrini et al., 2007: 285). For these authors, SMEs are increasingly being considered as important but that 'large firms are more likely to identify relevant stakeholders and meet their requirements through specific and formal CSR strategies'.

Another view is that CSR has arisen out of the old public relations idea of the good corporate citizen. CSR is a tool that can be used to build and develop the image and reputation of the corporate and brand levels that can also counter negative publicity. Consumers can feel good about buying products and brands that in turn support some kind of social issue. Employees can feel good about the activities of their company and pass a feel-good message on in their own wider context. There are a number of approaches to CSR available to marketers, some of which are discussed later in this section of the book individually – fair trade, environmental (green) marketing and cause-related marketing. In a study of Spanish SMEs that looked at developing influence on image and positioning, Fraj-Andres et al. (2012: 266) suggest 'proactive and consistent SMEs may build up a good image and strong positioning' but that 'reactive and opportunistic firms may be penalised by stakeholders'. In other words if a company is perceived to be merely opportunistic by, for example, customers, then they will not be taken in by this and damage will occur.

Much more is now known about the effects of engaging with CSR and much more is also known about how smaller firms can engage with the concept (Copley et al., 2012). The values of the founders of firms that might grow into large companies (for example as Body Shop International did under the stewardship of Anita Roddick) can play a crucial role in the implementation of CSR but, according to Murillo and Lozano (2006: 227), SMEs 'have a long way to go towards learning how to inform both internal and external stakeholders of their best practices', and that it is up to public organisations to create a 'favourable framework for responsible competitiveness, as a way to deal with CSR when addressing SMEs'.

Cause-related marketing

Cause-related marketing has been in existence for many years and there are numerous benefits for the sponsor organisation. However, over time, sponsee organisations have become increasingly professional, with different expectations from those their predecessors had of strategic alliances or partnerships. Balabanis et al. (1997) suggest that although it does appear that causes are becoming more marketing oriented, if compared to commercial organisations this is still a comparatively low occurrence that in the past might have had a link with the size of the organisation, the ideological or attitudinal barriers posed by management, but also an identified time lag which affected performance.

The ideas of 'strategic fit' and symbiosis are not without practical meaning within cause-related marketing contexts, there being a need to take such an approach whereby integration in marketing communications can be achieved. Accountability is at the heart of relationships and for some this has been a preoccupation of big business. There are differing levels to involvement with causes. For example, Kolk and van Tulder (2009: 119) look to sustainable development for the multinationals involving NGOs (non-governmental organisations). This involves 'global problems such as climate change and poverty'. There are many other examples of large corporations becoming involved with causes, such as Rio Tinto-Earthwatch and Royal Bank of Scotland-Prince's Trust. As Seitanidi and Crane (2009: 413) suggest 'partnerships between businesses and non-profit organisations are an increasingly prominent element of corporate social respon-sibility implementation'. Regardless of size of organisation the principles remain the same where there are 'management issues within partnership implementation' regard-ing 'accountability and level of institutionalisation of the relationship to address any possible skills gaps'. Seitanidi (2009: 90) suggests that accountability is 'prominent in safeguarding that the voices of the internal and external stakeholders are being heard' and it is the role of the not-for-profit organisation to 'safeguard social standards and high quality program implementation'.

The other end of this scale is much more localised and involving of small organisations rather than very large ones where there are initiatives of various sorts. Copley et al. (2012) report on the move towards legitimacy of SMEs supporting causes – for example *The Guardian* newspaper's 2001 'Investment Challenge', which was a scheme to help inves-tors put money into the children's UK charity Barnardo's and more recently the National Endowment for Science, Technology and the Arts (NESTA), a public body formed by the government by Act of Parliament in 1998 and now a charitable body (since 14 October 2010). According to *The Guardian* (2012) this is a charity funded by interest accrued from an original £250m UK National Lottery endowment that created the Neighbourhood Challenge programme which 'has invested in 17 communities that test out innovative ways of involving new people in locally led action', whereby local groups have taken advantage of pre-existing local assets in the form of 'unused buildings or equipment to new ideas, or people with skills, talents or time to support locally led change'. The idea is to use such unused assets plus supportive, catalytic investment to develop causes such as the YES ini-tiative in Brixham (Devon) which saw an unused building refurbished with local volunteer skills that helped turn it into a creative café and social centre. This 'enables communities to draw more effectively on their own strengths and develop more resilient networks for themselves' and not be reliant on 'expensive, top-down delivery from external agencies', but rather become 'dependent on local facilitation and active collaboration with and lead-ership from local people' (*The Guardian*, 2012).

The commodification of CSR is discussed by Nijhof and Jeurissen (2010: 618) who suggest that there are limits to which the concept can be taken and talk of a kind of glass ceiling to opportunities in dealing with 'ecological and social problems'. These researchers conclude that social values are key and should be defended in 'good and bad times'. In other words sponsors should be doing it for the right reasons and cer-tainly should avoid being seen as merely opportunistic. From the cause perspective the objectives for marketing communications go beyond simply soliciting donations. In order to achieve this creating awareness of the problems that the cause is confronting is needed. There is a kind of irony in that the restrictions on funding through government and ever-increasing competition for donations mean that causes need to use and spend money on marketing communications in order to raise money, which may also attract criticism. There is a need to secure future funding through, for example, covenants, legacies and trusts. However, a lot of communication activity has been, and is expected to continue to be, advertising through local and national press and television, as well as newer digital forms such as social media. There is a need for causes to keep a strategic focus in integrated marketing terms, which includes, in many cases, activities in retailing and distribution, and to remain cautious of mere tactical approaches in order to raise funds in the short term.

Fair trade

The concept of fair trade and Fairtrade the organisation are both about 'better prices, decent working conditions, local sustainability, and fair terms of trade for farmers and workers in the developing world' (Fairtrade Foundation, 2013). Although there are a number of ethical labels The Fairtrade Foundation claims that Fairtrade is unique in that 'Fairtrade's focus is on helping farmers and workers improve the quality of their lives and take more control over their futures. Fairtrade is the only certification scheme whose purpose is to tackle poverty and empower producers in developing countries' (Fairtrade Foundation, 2013).

Fair trade is about trading partnerships that include empowerment and sustainable development for farmers and other artisans formerly excluded, marginalised and disadvantaged. One of the key roles of marketing and corporate communications is raising awareness; another is campaigning. The objective is better trading conditions and it is not only about economics but also social and environmental issues, such as a living wage and health and safety. Fair trade is not, therefore, merely about fair prices for commodities or products. This would be a narrow view of practices that have gone beyond commercialism both in terms of buying commodities and products and selling into developing markets on an ethically-driven basis. However, such arrangements are partnerships with producers and agencies and a key issue is the use of an agency label such as Fairtrade for marketing purposes.

There is much research in this area, a key issue being consumer reaction to the concept of fair trade. For example, Hainmueller et al. (2011) looked at demand for the fair trade label in a study in a major US grocery store chain. These researchers suggest that previous research has shown that most respondents claimed to prefer ethically certified products and to be willing to pay more for that privilege, but also that there was no evidence of respondents actually seeking out such products. The Hainmueller et al. research (experiments within the stores) found that the Fair Trade label did have a substantial positive effect on sales and therefore on consumer behaviour: 'Sales of the two most popular bulk coffees sold in the stores rose by almost 10% when the coffees were labelled as Fair Trade.' The experiment found a certain degree of inelasticity in the pricing of the coffee where demand remained stable when prices were increased until the increase went to 9 per cent, which then saw a 30 per cent decline in sales. In another study the communications challenge of fair trade marketing is discussed by Golding (2009) in terms of achieving sustainable consumption. This is about communications strategies in the context of whether sustainable consumption can be achieved within the existing social paradigm or whether a new paradigm is needed. The article involves the Divine Chocolate Company. The radical and pragmatic visions of fair trade represent a polarisation of positions but in this campaign a level of synergism was achieved. This was done through 'rendering social and environmental externalities visible' (Golding, 2009: 169) which penetrated the lifestyle of consumers. There are many other studies as fair trade has moved from being a niche concept to one of the mainstream, including those which suggest that fair trade labelling does not by any means always come at the top of the consumer's list of what to look for while shopping. Brand influences and quality are bound to feature, as might age and idealism.

Environmental (green) marketing

Environmental marketing, often referred to as green marketing, has developed into an attitude and performance commitment that places corporate environmental stewardship fully in perspective. It is a response to the relatively recent rise of environmentalism and 'green' issues highlighted by the growing number of pressure groups around the world. By the 1970s the 'limits to growth' debate had raised many issues not only to do with population growth and economics but also the natural environment, which involved shortages of raw materials and consideration of infinite resources, such as the air we breathe, and long-term dangers or shorter-term ones, such as the use of CFCs, as well as finite, renewable resources such as forests but with similar long- and short-term dangers. There are also finite, non-renewable resources such as coal, oil and gas and issues such as the increased cost of energy and levels of pollution. Although much of the initial pessimism was rejected, this gave rise to discussions around levels of government intervention in natural resource management and the question of what opportunities for the development of new sources and new materials there might be. This, inevitably, had to involve private corporations and clearly there are opportunities for marketers to communicate benefits or use particular imagery in this area.

Latterly the debate has shifted and focused on global warming and sustainable development and there are real concerns about, for example, energy use, carbon 'footprints' and emissions, and widespread consumption of all manner of goods and services that go with higher and rising living standards where there is a debate as to whether these can be sustained as countries like China and India add to increased consumption. Environmentalists are more critical of marketing than the consumerist or the Consumer Movement. For example, environmentalists complain more vigorously about (wasteful) packaging, whereas consumerists like the idea of convenience packaging. The consumer movement worries about deception in advertising but consumerists promote consumption, whereas environmentalists do not like the idea that advertising leads to greater (than necessary) consumption. The rise of environmentalism has made the marketer's life more complicated, probably much more so than the consumer movement ever did. The cost of including environmental issues and criteria in marketing decision making is in many cases not insignificant but at the same time managers have realised that, at the very least, respecting the environment is in itself worthwhile while concurrently it is probably the richest area for marketing opportunities.

It has been understood in business circles for decades that more than mere reactions to the environmental events is a requirement in order to convince environmentalists and indeed the public that the company way is best. Many businesses now embrace environmentalism and this has led to a range of marketing communications strategy and tactics, especially with regard to message strategy. Companies have learnt to be more proactive through engagement but at the same time the environmental lobby has grown and many organisations are watching the activities of many companies.

The Snapshot below discusses the partnership between the Baggers Originals brand of children's wear and Tyne Gateway, an award-winning charity engaged with families in poverty. The partnership illuminates the concept of symbiosis in a win-win-win context.

Snapshot Small firms can engage with CSR too – the Baggers Originals brand and Tyne Gateway cause achieve win-win-win

The small business-owned children's wear brand Baggers was launched in the UK over 20 years ago by Angela McLean, then a mother of young children and a business woman. Angela set the company up with little more than £10, a kitchen table and a sewing machine. The company experienced rapid growth, achieving sales of over 10,000 units a month of an innovative rainwear product to achieve a turnover of over £2,000,000 in three years. Despite a number of successes with involvement from The Body Shop and Anita Roddick (who said Baggers was the best new product she had seen on the market in years), Heinz with a large order of Baggers' rainwear to use as an on-pack promotion, interest from Disney World USA and winning a number of awards, the rapid growth brought a plethora of challenges and the company became a victim of its own success. The then lack of management skills, plus being under-capitalised from the start, and compounded by the move of manufacturing from the UK to China/Malta and late payment by retailers, contributed to the business running out of cash.

Over the last 20 or so years, the concept of Baggers has been kept alive through the work of Angela's company Fast Forward Now Ltd (an enterprise development and business and management consultancy). Angela has told the Baggers' story to audiences up and down the UK and has reached over 4,000 learners internationally. Baggers have now been re-launched as Baggers Originals (www.baggersoriginals. com) with Angela's daughter Jessica, one of the young Baggers models 20 years ago. Baggers Originals offer fun, fashionable and practical clothing. The primary unique selling point of Baggers Originals, as the name suggests, is that the articles of clothing push into an attached pocket and form a bag for children to carry the clothing. The swimwear, which is design copyrighted, has a small zipped waterproof inside pocket that can be used to store locker keys/money when the swimwear is worn. When the swimwear is wet it can be contained in the waterproof pocket. Shorts and swimming costumes are available in this range, and are aimed at boys and girls aged 1–8 years old. The rainwear comprises of shower-proof trousers and jackets and follows the same concept, again aiming at boys and girls aged 1–8 years old.

Before the re-launch Angela was already involved with Tyne Gateway, a charity working with children and families who experience poverty. Angela's involvement with Tyne Gateway came when working with her company Fast Forward Now when she was invited to write and deliver the Enterprise and Entrepreneurship module for the Foundation Degree, which would form an intrinsic part of the training for the Community Entrepreneurs. Angela's passion is to inspire and teach enterprising skills to nascent entrepreneurs so they can learn from her business mistakes of the past and take the lessons forward into their own organisations. As it turned out, She drew inspiration from the Community Entrepreneurs. She was intrinsic to the formation of Tyne Gateway as an established independent company and has become a director of the new organisation. Funding is clearly an issue for Tyne Gateway although many of the projects are working towards becoming self-sufficient; like any new business they need time to become profitable and 'find their feet'.

(Continued)

(Continued)

Angela decided that the success of Baggers Originals should be tied in with making a difference to lives – a major driver for Angela, especially when the going gets tough in the business and the hurdles seem massive. She commented: 'The ethos of Tyne Gateway is proven to be a success and by giving we can employ more and more Community Entrepreneurs who have the knowledge and understanding to help the communities they come from. My motive for re-launching Baggers Originals is to show others that failure is OK and that with determination, support and self-belief you can change your life to succeed and that there is always a way. I suppose the message is don't give up.'

Stop Point

As well as engaging with traditional marketing communications and newer digital forms such as social media like Facebook and Twitter, the brand has engaged successfully with CSR with its partner Tyne Gateway. Undertake the following: 1. Discuss the kind of CSR exhibited between Baggers Originals and Tyne Gateway in terms of how the three parties involved – Baggers Originals, Tyne Gateway and the charity's clients – all gain from the venture; 2. Discuss the ways in which the two corporate parties – Baggers Originals and Tyne Gateway – can use what they have created to help market their organisation.

UNETHICAL PRACTICE

Social responsibility and ethical practice should lead marketers to be concerned with this area of activity and thought. The consumer movement, an umbrella term for the many organisations concerned with consumer protection (see consumerism later in this chapter), is generally in favour of legislation to provide consumers with information (data, especially comparative), education (knowledge and how to deal with companies) and protection (against deception; health and safety). Basically self-regulation is not trusted by all players. Marketing is seen by some advocates, for example people in businesses or marketing but from all walks of life, as being a positive force. It serves to educate, inform, to provide lower prices and improve quality, to stimulate the local economy and provide jobs. These advocates generally see marketing and marketing communications elements, such as advertising, being used for the social good, as with the many social marketing campaigns that have been undertaken over time, for example the AIDS/condom campaigns or in the UK the Full Stop campaign by the NSPCC (the National Society for the Prevention of Cruelty to Children), a campaign aimed at stopping cruelty to children once and for all.

Others see some marketing activities in a negative light. Advocates again come from all walks of life but there are many within the consumer movement who are sceptical of marketing, particularly advertising. Some see advertising as a negative force that engenders cultural imperialism, raises expectations and causes agitation, mitigates against consumer protection and hits local competition hard, especially where status is attached to having the big brands. Advertising in this view is responsible for exaggerated claims and even deceit (deception is considered a crime in most countries). There is a distinction that can be made between hard and soft advertising issues. The use of sex appeal might be relatively soft unless it becomes indecent, tasteless or sexist. The use of race may be appropriate but racist messages are unacceptable and illegal. Advertising can become demeaning through the use of stereotypes, violence against woman and objectification of women (where there is no relevance) or obscenity; these are all problematic and do vary between cultures and markets (see Chapter 18 of this book). Some of these practices are discussed below.

Subliminal advertising

Subliminal advertising involves subliminal messaging through advertising media. Sensory stimuli that are below the threshold of conscious perception are used in the creation of a message by the marketer. Subliminal perception refers to the perception of things below the conscious level. The use of subliminal messages in advertising and marketing is controversial and has been banned in some countries. Subliminal messages can be found everywhere and not just in marketing materials. Indeed such messages were used in advertising long after they were used for political propaganda purposes across the centuries, but in particular the 20th century, by many political movements from fascism to Soviet socialism to capitalism. Over many years psychologists have studied the influence of subliminal messages on behaviour. The use of subliminal advertising and messaging still persists despite psychological research showing that subliminal messages do not produce the powerful and lasting effect on behaviour that marketers might wish, although there are those who think it might.

Since 1957 and the US market researcher James Vicary who claimed to be able to 'get moviegoers to drink Coca-Cola and eat popcorn' (Alleyne, 2009) there have been concerns about what governments and other organisations could do with such 'hidden persuader' techniques. A key issue is not only whether the subliminal image registers with the audience but also whether it has any effect. Sex sells, but embedding the word sex or some other related image such as a phallic object does not necessarily guarantee success. The objective behind subliminal advertising is emotional manipulation by suggesting that there will be satisfaction of emotional need, and the brand is then associated with this need satisfaction. According to Alleyne, research from University College London suggests that subliminal advertising can be effective in terms of changing thinking where negative images and words can alter mood: 'The researchers found that the participants answered most accurately when responding to negative words – even when they believed they were merely guessing the answer.' This could be particularly useful in safety campaigns and other public service announcements whereby negative words may have a quicker impact.

Subliminal product placement

Product (or more accurately brand) placements in television programming and other media and contexts have, to some extent, replaced use of the subliminal approach in advertising. The more natural setting for a brand to be seen is in a piece of drama or within a gaming environment, such as cleaning fluid or a jar of coffee in a kitchen scene. Subliminal product or brand placement is also referred to as embedded marketing. As discussed in Chapter 15 of this book, there is no doubting the value and realism that product placement brings to entertainment and why producers are attracted to it. The Snapshot in Chapter 1 of this book on product placement highlighted recent changes to product placement on television in the European context (Hauck, 2011; Robinson, 2010) and there is clearly a need for regulatory frameworks. As will be returned to in Chapter 15, there are differing layers of concern over what some see as 'covert advertising' and the powerful effects this can have on consumers, especially in terms of health if unhealthy food and drink brands dominate television product placements in particular, especially when the consumer is not consciously aware that they are noticing a brand.

Stereotyping

Stereotyping is used in marketing communications, predominantly in advertising, whereby generalised and therefore simplified images of reality are used to portray some aspect of a larger group in order to target that group as a whole. There are clear dangers in this practice. If the marketer gets the stereotype wrong then brand damage could ensue and the use of stereotyping can lead the marketer into the realms of deceptive or misleading images. For example, with gender stereotyping males are often depicted as macho 'real men' and practical or even expert while females are depicted as mere decoration. In a different scenario women might be portrayed as strong and independent or 'real women', in the sense that the Unilever brand Dove used 'real women' of all shapes and sizes as a counter to accusations in the health and beauty sector that airbrushed or now Photoshop images (often of thin models) are being used that are unrealistic and even misleading and deceptive since the portrayal of an 'ideal type' that could never be attained might fall foul of a regulator's code of conduct.

Such stereotypes are often in the first instance at least culturally driven. Here care has to be taken with the marketer's perception of traditional culture where the assumption might be, for example, that a homely image of a young woman might fit the cultural beliefs and values. However, if young women in a particular sector, for example luxury perfume, are influenced by international magazines such as *Cosmopolitan* or *Vogue* and the models and celebrities used to represent the luxury brand, then traditional culture may have little or no influence. In this example the philosophical debate over whether advertising shapes a society or merely reflects that society's norms and values comes to life in a practical way.

Many other examples exist beyond the gender stereotyping used in advertising. Older people or 'senior citizens' are often portrayed as 'past it' in some way whereas in many countries such the USA many 'seniors' are highly active with high disposable income and may very well have many leisure pursuits. In such cases marketers cannot afford to miss a trick and get it wrong through the use of misguided stereotypes. Many other groups have to be treated with care and attention. Single parents, gay men, ethnic minorities, the unemployed and others often form substantial market segments for certain products and services. The use of inappropriate or even offensive stereotypes should clearly be avoided. There is further discussion on the opportunities and dangers of the use of national stereotypes in Chapter 18 of this book.

Products

Depending upon societal conditions and cultural influences certain products are, by their very nature, problematic. This varies from society to society (see Chapter 18 of this book) but generally products associated with gambling, betting and lotteries, tobacco, alcohol, pharmaceuticals, financial services, children's products (especially toys), baby food, and cosmetics can be problematic in themselves. Specific laws and regulations usually exist with these and products associated with health and safety. For example, with tobacco, much is debated here but basically there are two viewpoints: that a ban on advertising will cut cigarette consumption and is therefore a good thing for a nation's health; or that advertising only affects brand differentiation, not the number of smokers, and therefore there is no advantage to a ban on advertising. Attitudes towards this vary between countries but generally healthcare professionals support the former and the tobacco industry and lobby support the latter.

Creative message content

The much referenced and infamous 1980s international advertising campaign for Seiko that ran the strapline 'Man invented time, Seiko perfected it' fell foul of religious sentiment in countries like Malaysia simply because of the belief that God invented time. The strapline was adapted and became 'Man invented time keeping...', and changes were made to outdoor and press advertisements. This is a good illustration of the adaptations that companies may have to make in different marketplaces around the world (see Chapter 18 of this book). The Seiko example illustrates a genuine mistake that had to be rectified. More generally there are a number of creative content issues that can fall within the area of unethical practice that are not necessarily mistakes but are deliberate attempts to go to the margins of taste, decency, what is legal, what is truthful, and what is honest. Some may even go well beyond the margins.

In many instances it is not the products themselves but blatantly offensive advertising that causes complaint, furore and mistrust. There are many examples of such campaigns that use the various appeals that are at the communicator's disposal, including fear, shock, sex and sexual innuendo. One such example is the poster campaign in the UK in 1995 for the Club 18–30 packaged holiday brand aimed at the 18–30 (or slightly younger) demographic. This used sexual innuendo in the form of 'Beaver Espana' and 'The summer of 69'. This fell foul of the UK Advertising Standards Authority (ASA) adjudication after complaints from the public were made. The advertising was withdrawn but much was made of the publicity, particularly when the complainants were not part of the 18–30 target group. A more recent example is that of Carlsberg, the leading international brand of lager beer, who began a series of viral advertisements. One piece of viral advertising, released in 2013, tested the limits of friendship in a form of shock appeal that used hidden cameras. In this film there is a gambling den where the protagonist phones a friend to say that he has lost his money and needs instant cash. The friend comes up trumps in what seems to be a dangerous and hostile environment. It is then revealed that it is a test and is in fact a hoax. The film ends with lots of happy people consuming the brand. In another film in 2011, cinemagoers found themselves apparently surrounded by a gang of bikers. Those who stayed with it were rewarded with free Carlsberg beer and can be seen enjoying a drink – along with the 'bikers'. Some might find this enjoyable; others may feel that it is a worrisome trend in pranks that could get out of hand.

Targeting sensitive and vulnerable groups

A key vulnerable group is young consumers, although in reality there is more than one group within the young consumer coverall. Demographically, children as consumers have been grouped by age in the 3–7, 8–12 and 12+ brackets by marketers, although the age ranges will vary depending upon, for example, the nature of the product. Descriptors are often applied to these groups, the most obvious being teenager, a label that emerged in the USA in the 1950s but in concept form much earlier, probably about the 1920s. This development has been linked to the development of transport and the automobile that created social change. Since that time younger children's groupings have been given labels such as tweenie (or tween), a term that variously describes a pre-teen child between the ages of about 8–12 or 9–12. Younger children have also been labelled, for example, tots.

Psychologists have been involved with marketing and in particular, of course, consumer behaviour throughout its development in the modern era, and this includes the ways in which advertisers in particular target young consumers. Clay (2000) has suggested that there has been a rift among psychologists because of the continued pursuit by some of ever-more sophisticated approaches to such consumers and the damage that might be done through the creation of materialistic values in children that is contributing to their felt need for certain products and resultant problems relating to feelings of inferiority if they do not have such products. The dangers of children becoming narcissistic and dissatisfied with their lot are real. Many companies from McDonald's-type restaurants to actual toy manufacturers like Mattel or film-makers like Disney are involved in marketing a vast range of collectables, toys, food and drink and many more products in the form of brands. There is concern about 'psychologists' use of their knowledge and skills to observe, study, mislead or exploit children for commercial purposes'. It is not surprising that marketers want to market to children given the value of such marketing activities, estimated to be hundreds of billions of dollars in the USA alone if the money spent by adults on children, including through pester power, is added. The argument, however, goes beyond what psychology has to offer, which is substantial and invaluable to marketers. It is also about what psychologists become involved in regarding the kinds of product and service targeted at children, and whether they should 'turn down assignments dealing with violent video games, action figures armed with weapons and other products they believe are bad for children' and focus instead on products that they consider either good for children or are at least neutral (Clay, 2000).

It is worth noting that the regulatory authorities have particular structures in place to deal with advertising and children. For example there is the ASA in the UK, who say there will be no hesitation in banning any advertising that could result in physical, mental or moral harm and they have in place Ad:Check, which is a resource for schools that helps children and young people make a critical assessment of advertisements; they are also exploring how to address the findings from the ASA's Harm and Offence research, which has already looked at issues such as violent and sexual content, body image and also charity advertising, most likely to be the source of distress. In the USA there is CARU (Children's Advertising Review Unit), which is the children's arm of the American advertising industry's self-regulation programme. CARU evaluates advertising and promotional material in all media that is targeted at children in terms of truthfulness, accuracy and consistency in the context of self-regulation codes and relevant laws.

Spamming and cookies

Spamming is an Internet 'flooding' activity whereby many copies of the same message are sent to many people at the same time. This is the use of unsolicited messages, usually some form of advertising for products and services that might be dubious in nature, by various means.

Spamming costs little to send and in this sense is a modern version of leafleting or direct mail marketing where the rate of return was expected to be low, but the exercise could be profitable on a few percentage points of the total number of recipients of the message. There is Usenet spam that is sent to Usenet newsgroups where the likelihood is that the message will be irrelevant to many in those groups. The message is aimed at the type of people who observe but do not participate (lurkers). They are bombarded with messages that also affect the management of the Usenet groups. Email spamming targets users with direct email messages and is usually conducted using mailing lists that can be generated from scans of Usenet posts or other means of list building, some of which might involve theft. This can cost time and money for all parties concerned – the spammer, the recipient, and the Internet service provider.

Cookies are seen by some as intrusive spying devices and by others as harmless text files. Many sites tell the user when they enter the site that the site uses cookies and the user will then be in the know about cookies being used if they choose to proceed. This is the case in the EU but until May 2012 it has been up to individual users to block or allow them. The new

EU law means that sites that use cookies now have to ask the user's permission to retrieve and store data about website browsing behaviour. Cookies are tracking mechanisms that track the user's movements around Internet sites. Cookies are files not programs and they contain both a site name and unique user ID. When a site is visited the first time a cookie is downloaded onto the computer, and the next time the site is visited by the user of that computer there is a check to see whether there is a relevant cookie. If so then the website then recognises that the computer has been on the site before. Depending upon the type of cookie, more sophisticated data will be collected such as site design preferences. The use of cookies is seen as a double-edged sword. Some view this as beneficial because if a user is a frequent visitor to a site then interacting with it is made easier. On the other hand this kind of data collection is seen by some as potentially dangerous in terms of data security and privacy issues in a Big Brother-like way. Or it may be that there is a nuisance factor of users ending up on mailing lists, hence laws such as the aforementioned EU law. In the UK, the Information Commissioner's Office (ICO) monitors sites to make sure of compliance (go to www.ico.org.uk/for_organisations/privacy_and_electronic_communications/the_guide/cookies) for more information.

Guerrilla and stealth marketing

Guerrilla marketing is so called because of its non-conventional marketing nature. The conventional marketing objectives of sales turnover, profit or growth remain but it is the means to achieving the objectives that are different. Rather than simply spending money, guerrilla marketing involves the investment of time and imagination to create marketing that is relatively much less costly than conventional marketing activities, making it very attractive to smaller firms and other organisations on tight budgets. The term guerrilla marketing was coined by Jay Conrad Levinson (www.gmarketing.com/) who has worked with some of the biggest brands around, e.g. Microsoft, Pillsbury and Marlboro. Guerrilla marketing is an umbrella term or label for myriad activities such as the use of graffiti and other 'street' techniques. Guerrilla marketing in itself is not necessarily unethical. However, some practices do border on unethical if not illegal practice.

Stealth marketing is often seen as a subset of guerrilla marketing and is a potentially dangerous way to practise marketing. Stealth marketing practices are often called 'undercover' marketing or 'buzz' marketing, because consumers often do not know they are being targeted. A person might be paid to use a brand in a social setting, exposing other people within that context to the brand. Another example is the use of public benches as a way of creating advertising messages on the legs of people via a small plate placed on the seat that then embosses a temporary mark on the skin on the back of the legs. Stealth marketing has attracted academic attention. For example, Roy and Chattopadhyay (2010) present stealth marketing as a strategy in its historical context and suggest that it has gained attention in the last few years as it has been practised in myriad ways: they also suggest that it can be used for 'doing good' in society as well as posing problems with regard to both consumers and other businesses who might be competitors. The overall risk, however, is that people generally do not like being deceived and such activities might easily backfire.

Ambush marketing

Ambush marketing is the well-established practice of a company or brand being associated with, for example, a team or an event such as the Olympics without paying for the right to do so, whereas a competitor who is an official sponsor has done so, often at great expense. The objective may be to detract attention away from the competition and neutralise a competitor's legitimate marketing effort. Chadwick and Burton (2010) suggest that ambush marketing assumes many forms these days and is set to continue, especially in the area of sports marketing where sponsors pay 'millions of dollars for their brands to bask in the publicity surrounding certain teams and events' while 'a growing number of companies … crowd into the spotlight without paying – sometimes by bending, or breaking, the rules'. Examples are attempting buy-in to an event by sponsoring an individual player or athlete rather than the event itself.

Sponsorship (see Chapter 15 of this book) and especially sports sponsorship are big business and a vital part of sports organisations' revenues, and there is concern that ambush marketing is a damaging practice. Merrit (2010) suggests that 'contemporary ambush marketing appears to have evolved into a marketing tool all its own' so that the use and understanding of the tool have changed in recent times as it has become simply another way to gain publicity and market goods or services generally. Accordingly, more is being attempted to protect investments, for example 'street vending will be eliminated and outdoor and public transport advertising controlled from two weeks before the opening ceremony until the official closing'. Merrit concludes, however, that in general 'efforts to prevent ambushing continue to enjoy limited success as the strategies ambushers use continue to multiply'.

The Snapshot below discusses the problematic area of short-term, high interest 'payday' loans and the controversy that emerged as the leader of the Church of England attempted to intervene. These are legitimate products but potentially with social consequences.

Snapshot Payday loans, Wonga, the Archbishop and the money expert

Martin Lewis, founder and editor of moneysavingexpert.com (www.money savingexpert.com/), in an article titled 'Dear Archbishop … why I disagree with you over Wonga', showed opposition to Archbishop of Canterbury Justin Welby's suggestions and ideas on how to counter the activities of payday loan companies such as Wonga. According to Lewis (2013) 'Wonga and other 6,000pc APR loans are the crack-cocaine of the money-lending world'. Short-term, very high interest loans are clearly a problematic product for many, but not all, people. Lewis describes the archbishop's efforts as 'laudable but blundering' and he trusts 'doesn't hurt more than it helps'. As it turns out, some of the Church's own investments involved Wonga, which appeared in the media somewhat as an own goal, but in Lewis's view this aspect is a sideshow since the original attack on Wonga involved the archbishop saying that the Church wanted to compete with Wonga (compete them out of business), not seek legislation against such companies – and do so by the use of cheaper loans including the activities of credit unions.

Payday loan products have been linked to social problems in the same way as alcohol, tobacco and gambling, with some people becoming addicted. According to Lewis 'Lenders use instant apps and fast clicks to target the impulses of the "must have it now" generation. Loans are processed at lightning speed, quick enough for some to apply and receive while drunk.' Lewis has nothing against credit unions (he says he is a fan) and he applauds the fact that the archbishop invites them in; this is 'unlikely to scratch this 21st century problem's surface. Many payday loan customers are as likely to visit a church as the archbishop is to win Olympic gymnastics gold. These loans are about speed and ease.' However. the problem is deeper than this. If people cannot afford the loan, even at a low or no rate of interest, then the Church have said they will not lend – but payday loan companies will and such people will go to them. According to Lewis the UK is a place that is not regulated in terms of such loans, although companies like Wonga might disagree. It was clear, several weeks after the Archbishop's comments in July 2013, that the Church could not compete with these companies as it would take several years if not over a decade to set up a proper system. Lewis therefore advocates tighter control rather than a free market: 'We do need tight controls on this industry. Competition from the Church is not enough.' As a campaigner for government to intervene, Lewis is concerned that the archbishop is letting the politicians off the hook. Instead he suggests:

- a ban on advertisements for such loans on children's television. 'This is an attempt to target hard-pressed families – even though lenders claim they are not their target market.'

- a restriction on the nature of other advertising content: 'Payday loan advertising is pervasive. They make it look like this is a fun, little transaction rather than a hardcore form of debt.'

- they introduce a total cost cap rather than capping APR rates, which is meaningless for short-term lending.

- a delay between applying for and receiving cash (a cooling-off period) because the loans are based around convenience, speed and ease. This would at least give 'people a chance to reconsider.'

- mandatory affordability and credit checks because at present 'some advertise their loans predicated on the fact that they do not credit check you. It should be mandatory for all payday loan lenders.'

The controversy deepened somewhat when Wonga became shirt sponsors of the English football Premiership team Newcastle United, and striker Papiss Cisse said he would refuse to wear the shirt on personal and religious grounds during the pre-season at Newcastle following a dispute over the club's sponsorship deal. The player later relented to concentrate on the football rather than the kit having missed out on the club's pre-season tour of Portugal. Wonga are also shirt sponsors of fellow Premiership side Blackpool and of Scottish Premiership side Hearts, among many other related activities.

Stop Point

Much has been written, said, debated and argued in the media and maybe even on the football terraces about payday loan companies and the kind of products they offer. Undertake the following: 1. Discuss the notion that if a product is legal then within the law and code of conduct it should be allowed to get on with its marketing and marketing communications efforts without hindrance; 2. Explain the merits of 'cooling-off' periods in this and other contexts that you are aware of.

CONSUMERISM AND REGULATION

Marketers and marketing communicators should be interested in regulations, restrictions and the monitoring of any changes that may affect their activities. It is inevitable that regulations and restrictions will exist, especially in market economies, in order to protect both citizens and companies. Most companies support the idea of regulation but at the same time they are in favour of self-regulation. Communications and in particular advertising regulations are developed to a reasonable extent in many countries and this aspect continues to grow; most countries have at least some regulation (see Chapter 18 of this book).

Consumerism and the consumer movement

Growth of public interest and pressure groups and the advent of the consumer movement as a major social force have been happening for the last six decades. Ralph Nader, who first came to prominence in the USA in 1965 with the publication of his book *Unsafe at Any Speed*, a critique of the automobile industry's safety record (in particular the Chevrolet Corvair), was hailed as the founding father of the movement that questioned the true nature of the 'sovereign consumer' with many examples of exploitation in many markets, such as those for cars, meat, loans, car repairs, insurance, the environment and many more. There are many organisations that could be included under the umbrella of the consumer movement, with consumer magazines like *Which?* and television programmes like the BBC's *Watchdog* carrying the flag in the UK.

Government regulation

The early forms of communication were often trade depicters such as inn signs, the barber's pole or an apothecary's jar of coloured liquid intended to advertise the products and services of a particular trade in the simplest of ways. Today advertising by itself is a large (and powerful) industry in its own right. There are many and varied areas of communication where some form of regulation is deemed necessary, but it can be said that the marketing communications industry and their clients have come a long way since the now infamous Carbolic Smoke Ball advertisement of the Victorian 1800s. This was an advertisement for a remedy for many ills, placed in the *Pall Mall Gazette* in 1892 by the Carbolic Smoke Ball Company. This case is seen by some as 'the birth of modern consumer protection – as it helped to define in law the trading relationship between a company and its customers' (Coleman, 2009). The company had offered a reward of £100 to anyone who used the product correctly but then caught the flu. A Mrs Carlill claimed that is just what happened and after the company refused to hand over the money she sued and won, despite the company protesting that there was no contract between the parties. As Coleman suggests the 'company failed largely because they had deposited £1,000 to show that they were serious' and yet 'they maintained there was no way of knowing whether Mrs Carlill had followed the instructions correctly. That would have been a good argument had the court not simply dismissed it out of hand.'

Self-regulation and codes of conduct

Regulations made by a country depend on the cultural and otherwise make-up of that country as to whether advertising is seen as negative or positive (see Chapter 18 of this book). There are different types of regulatory controls and regulation involves an increasing and changing amount of legislation, for example the protection of companies from each other, the protection of consumers from unfair business practices, and the protection of the larger interests of society against unbridled business behaviour. Many governments and their agencies are active with regard to such issues. For example the Antitrust Law in the USA is an umbrella term for many pieces of legislation. The Monopoly and Mergers Committee (UK) was set up to prevent unfair competition and is now the Competition Commission, an 'independent public body which conducts in-depth inquiries into mergers, markets and the regulation of the major regulated industries' (Competition Commission, 2013). There are plans to create a new single Competition and Markets Authority that 'will take on the functions of the Competition Commission and the Office of Fair Trading's competition functions and consumer enforcement powers. The current intention is that the new authority will be established in October 2013 and fully functioning in April 2014.' This reflects the ever-changing and evolving nature of regulation in the marketing arena. There are, therefore, changes in roles and changes when new governments are elected that might have differing leanings toward regulation and deregulation. National governments should be able to control the operations of enterprises through their own laws as passed in the legislative body such as the parliament in London. Many decisions are made through legislation when it is felt that this is the only way to achieve safe and fair business practices. The international context poses many issues and there is further discussion on this in Chapter 18 of this book.

Self-regulation and codes of conduct

There are three objectives to self-regulation in marketing communications:

1. To protect consumers against false or misleading communications or communications that intrude on privacy or are of an offensive nature.
2. To protect legitimate companies against false or misleading communication by the competition.
3. To promote the public acceptance of communications, particularly advertising, so that they can remain effective.

The marketing communications industry established its own codes of practice to prevent the interference of governments in its affairs. The ICC (International Chamber of Commerce) was established in 1919 and by 1937 had established Codes of Standards of Advertising Practice (see Chapter 18 of this book). Since that time the self-regulatory system has developed and other regional and national bodies have been established in an organised international network. However, restraint is still very much domestic driven. In the UK the Advertising Standards Authority (ASA) is a typical domestic body. It is the independent regulator of advertising across all media and it applies the Advertising Codes, which are written by the Committees of Advertising Practice. The work of the ASA therefore includes acting on complaints and proactively checking the media to take action against misleading, harmful or offensive advertisements. Although independent, the ASA does not stand alone; for example, EC Directives are becoming increasingly important and there are other affiliations such as to the European Advertising Standards Alliance (EASA) as discussed further in Chapter 18 of this book.

A fundamental question is whether or not the business community is capable of self-regulation or, left to their own devices, whether some firms break the rules. After all, business exists to make money not moral or ethical judgements. On the other hand intervention is justified for consumer protection. Self-regulation is about voluntary control by the industry for the industry in order to keep up standards. Many countries have laws but also controlling bodies involved in the regulatory process. The nature and administration of the codes practitioners are expected to adhere to usually mean that such bodies are actively involved in the development of communication before it is executed. For example, in the UK as well as the ASA there is Ofcom, the official body that regulates the television and radio sectors, fixed-line telecoms, mobiles, postal services, plus the airwaves over which wireless devices operate.

The Snapshot below discusses what some have described as the commodification of water and how bottled water in particular has prompted pressure (or accountability) groups to take action.

Snapshot   Bottles, bottles everywhere ... so think outside the bottle?

Baskind (2010), on the Mother Nature Network (an environmental and social responsibility online network), provides five reasons why not to drink bottled water, including that it is expensive and wasteful, not actually any healthier than tap water, and produces up to 1.5 million tons of plastic waste per year in the USA. Images of 'cool mountain streams' are used to advertise the product, or as Baskind puts it, marketers would have consumers believe in the health benefits: 'Just look at the labels or the bottled water ads: deep, pristine pools of spring water; majestic alpine peaks; healthy, active people gulping down icy bottled water between biking in the park and a trip to the yoga studio.' It is worth a lot of money in the USA alone, up to $100 billion annually with a growth rate of 7 per cent, according to Baskind, who suggests that it is not good value, costing many times more than municipal tap water, and yet brands like Dasani (Coca-Cola) and Aquafina (Pepsi) are filtered tap water. It is no healthier than tap water and it even falls below the US Food and Drug Administration standards, yet tap water is regularly inspected by the US Environmental Protection Agency and is regularly inspected for bacteria and toxic chemicals. Baskind admits that 'many municipal water systems are aging and there remain hundreds of chemical contaminants for which no standards have been established', but the point is made that there is 'very little empirical evidence that suggests bottled water is any cleaner or better for you than its tap equivalent'. As suggested, bottled water means garbage and the 1.5 million tons of plastic waste per year require up to 47 million gallons of oil per year to produce. And while the plastic used to bottle beverages is of high quality and in demand by recyclers, over 80 per cent of plastic bottles are simply thrown away'. A lot of this is not recycled but ends up in water systems representing 'a great risk to marine life, killing birds and fish which mistake our garbage for food'. Bottled water has also meant less attention being given to public systems: 'Once distanced from public systems, these consumers have little incentive to support bond issues and other methods of upgrading municipal water treatment' according to Baskind. Lastly, water has been corporatised, which is a problem worldwide where water resources are effectively privatised and thanks to 'increasing urbanization and population, shifting climates and industrial pollution, fresh water is becoming humanity's most precious resource'. Baskind suggests that the multinational corporations have 'commoditized what many feel is a basic human right: the access to safe and affordable water'.

Corporate Accountability International, a leading US-based corporate accountability organisation for the last 35 years, has begun the 'Think Outside the Bottle campaign whereby people across the USA are asked to pledge to "Think Outside the Bottle"', meaning that US citizens are being asked to challenge the idea that bottled water is necessary: 'Bottled-water corporations have attempted to convince us that the only place to get clean, safe water is from a bottle. It's just not true'. The campaign in the USA is a 'national action and education campaign' that sets out to challenge 'the marketing muscle of bottled-water corporations'. The organisation says it works with communities across the country in a bid to get people to opt for tap water rather than buying and consuming bottled water. The organisation claims that since 2006 'we have asked public officials, faith groups, restaurants, celebrities, campuses and individuals to Think Outside the Bottle. And they have!'

Stop Point

Much can be said about plastic and packaging, especially the sort that is non-biodegradable, but this bottle and tap water story is more than just about the plastic, although a hugely important issue. Undertake the following: 1. Examine the accountability issues around packaging and the use (or not) of recyclable materials for products such as water and other soft drinks; 2. Critically assess the use of images such as mountain streams or alpine peaks when marketers advertise bottled water brands when the actual product is essentially filtered tap water.

Assignment

The rise of Sustainable Development (SD) and Corporate Social Responsibility (CSR)

Sustainable development (SD) and corporate social responsibility (CSR) are different but interrelated concepts, even though some commentators might use them interchangeably. In the business context CSR is about mission and vision, about the responsibilities of the company, its reason for being, and its behaviour. SD in the business context is about how the company will operate and how it views and consumes natural resources directly or indirectly. It is about how the company can be profitable while not compromising the needs of future generations and how the company itself can build a long-term future. This is an ethical stance based on the belief in give and take, in a commitment to protecting the environment and reducing the company's carbon (ecological) footprint, and gaining acceptance of its corporate behaviour by society. CSR is a strand of the SD concept, which is a stakeholder approach that requires the company to meet its responsibilities as a member of society. It is therefore a social strand that is affected by the external (or macro) elements of the marketing environment as discussed above.

Your task

For a company of your choice discuss, in a 2,000-word paper, the key elements of the external/macro marketing environment in terms of the sustainable development concept. Outline, on a macro level, the likely sustainability orientation of the company's corporate social responsibility.

Summary of Key Points

- The marketing communications mix elements have relationships with and influence on aspects of society.
- Marketing communications as a function can be placed within an ethical context.
- Corporate social responsibility is a positive step forward and can involve cause-related marketing, fair trade and environmental marketing.
- Business, especially big business, is often perceived and portrayed as being unethical.
- For the most part organisations are ethical but there are instances of unethical, poor practice.
- There is a need for organisations to appreciate that unethical practices can lead to brand damage or loss of reputation.
- Marketing communications, particularly advertising, is sometimes seen as misleading, dishonest, deceptive and even illegal.
- Companies and other organisations have been accused of targeting vulnerable groups such as the very young or the elderly.
- The use of some appeals such as shock tactics can be too strong and cause an outcry.
- The use of stereotyping can be successful but it is also a dangerous practice that can lead to brand damage.
- Subliminal images that are covert and for the most part illegal or use brand placement in a deliberate attempt to get around bans on other forms of communication can also result in complaints and regulatory or even legal action.
- Consumerism and the role of pressure or accountability groups have important roles to play in society.
- Self-regulation, although not a concept entirely trusted by all players, is at the centre of ethical standards and practice.
- In most cases organisations are honest, truthful, legal and decent but need to have frameworks that enable them not to fall foul of the laws and codes of conduct.

Discussion Questions

1. In terms of ethical standards, discuss the differences between being legal, decent, honest and truthful, using examples to illustrate.
2. Critically assess the similarities and differences between the marketing communications mix of elements when it comes to influence on society.
3. Explain what is meant by corporate social responsibility (CSR). Discuss the importance of understanding CSR for companies wishing to become involved with cause-related marketing.
4. Explain what fair trade is as a concept, using examples to illustrate.

5. Critically assess environmental marketing as a marketing tool, illustrating this with both positive and negative examples of actual practice.

6. Outline the reasons why business, especially big business, is often perceived as being unethical using examples of your choice to illustrate.

7. Discuss the dangers of brand damage or loss of reputation when organisations are seen to use advertising that is viewed as misleading, dishonest or deceptive using examples to illustrate.

8. Outline the reasons why *either* targeting vulnerable groups *or* using shock tactics in advertising can cause an outcry using examples to illustrate.

9. Explain *either* why the use of stereotyping in advertising can be dangerous practice *or* why subliminal images in advertising are not allowed in most cases using examples to illustrate.

10. Critically assess the role of consumer and accountability groups in the context of regulation and self-regulation. Illustrate your assessment with well-chosen examples.

Further Reading

Bush, V.D., Korthage Smith, R. and Bush, A.J. (2013) 'Ethical Dilemmas and Emergent Values Encountered by Working College Students: implications for marketing educators', *Journal of Marketing Education*, 35 (23: 107–18. http://jmd.sagepub.com/content/35/2/107

This article is about entry-level, frontline employee positions and ethical dilemmas as opposed to the upper-level manager and CEO-level positions with respect to ethics education and training. Its aim is to contribute to an area where there is a paucity of research, especially since many college students work while studying. The article considers ethical decision-making models and corporate ethical values. This piece of qualitative research concludes that working college students are faced with a plethora of ethical dilemmas even before they graduate and that they seek guidance from their managers and co-workers rather than within their academic context. The article therefore reveals a pedagogic opportunity in terms of programme development in order to bridge this divide.

Campelo, A., Aitken, R. and Gnoth, J. (2011) 'Visual Rhetoric and Ethics in Marketing of Destinations', *Journal of Travel Research*, 50 (1): 3–14. http://jtr.sagepub.com/content/50/1/3

This article is about the visual rhetoric of advertising within destination marketing and branding. The study is naturally concerned with the ways in which advertising creates and reinforces meaning, especially in terms of people and place representation. The context is New Zealand (the 100% New Zealand campaign) and the purpose is to discuss the ethics involved in this kind of representation, which also involves communities and culture. The authors call for a theory of visual rhetoric that is concerned with ideological and ethical rather than simply systemic and operational issues.

Donoho, C., Heinze, T. and Kondo, C. (2012) 'Gender Differences in Personal Selling Ethics Evaluations: do they exist and what does their existence mean for teaching sales ethics?', *Journal of Marketing Education*, 34 (1): 55–66. http://jmd.sagepub.com/content/34/1/55

(Continued)

(Continued)

This article is about the divergence between men and women when facing ethical sales dilemmas. The study measures the impact of idealism and relativism on sales ethics evaluations of both men and women and suggests that it is women who see sales scenarios as less ethical than men. These findings have meaning for sales educators with respect to moral idealism, which can, if necessary, be supplemented by the use of cognitive moral development frameworks.

Golding, K.M. (2009) 'Fair Trade's Dual Aspect: the communications challenge of fair trade marketing', *Journal of Macromarketing*, 29 (2): 160–71. http://jmk.sagepub.com/content/29/2/160

This article is about communications strategies and sustainable consumption in the context of whether this can be achieved within the existing social paradigm or whether a new paradigm is needed. The article involves the Divine Chocolate Company and its campaign that transcended the polarisation of radical and pragmatic visions of fair trade and the synergism thus achieved and what this might mean for other sustainable consumption contexts.

Kendrick, A., Fullerton, J.A. and Kim, Y.J. (2013) 'Social Responsibility in Advertising: a marketing communications student perspective', *Journal of Marketing Education*, 35 (2): 141–54. http://jmd.sagepub.com/content/35/2/141

This article is not only about the role advertising has played in promoting social responsibility but also about social responsibility in advertising. In this study marketing students were asked for their take on corporate social responsibility. The authors suggest that the respondents have 'message myopia' with many other ethical and social responsibility issues being neglected and that there is a role for educators in this area of activity.

REFERENCES

Alleyne, R. (2009) Subliminal advertising really does work, claim scientists', *The Telegraph*, 28 September, available at: www.telegraph.co.uk/science/science-news/6232801/Subliminal-advertising-really-does-work-claim-scientists.html

Balabanis, G., Stables, R.E. and Phillips, H.C. (1997) 'Market orientation in the top 200 British charity organisations and its impact on their performance', *European Journal of Marketing*, 31 (8): 583–603.

Baskind, C. (2010) '5 reasons not to drink bottled water', *Mother Nature Network*, 15 March, available at: www.mnn.com/food/healthy-eating/stories/5-reasons-not-to-drink-bottled-water

Bush, V.D., Korthage Smith, R. and Bush, A.J. (2013) 'Ethical dilemmas and emergent values encountered by working college students: implications for marketing educators', *Journal of Marketing Education*, 35 (23): 107–18.

Campelo, A., Aitken, R. and Gnoth, J. (2011) 'Visual rhetoric and ethics in marketing of destinations', *Journal of Travel Research*, 50 (1): 3–14.

Chadwick, S. and Burton, N. (2010) 'Ambushed!', *The Wall Street Journal*, 25 January, available at: http://online.wsj.com/article/SB10001424052970204731804574391102699362862.html

Clay, R.A. (2000) 'Advertising to children: is it ethical?', *American Psychological Association*, 31 (8), available at: www.apa.org/monitor/sep00/advertising.aspx

Coleman, C. (2009) 'Carbolic smoke ball: fake or cure?', BBC Radio 4, 5 November.

Competition Commission (2013) 'Welcome to the Competition Commission', available at: www.competition-commission.org.uk/

Copley, P., McLean, A. and Baker, J. (2012) 'A CSR-driven strategic alliance case study of the launch of the small business children's clothing brand Baggers and Tyne Gateway, a local North East England children's charity', ISBE Conference 2012, Dublin, 7–8 November.

Corporate Accountability International (2013) 'Think outside the bottle: people across the country pledge to think outside the bottle', Corporate Accountability International, available at: www.stopcorporateabuse.org/think-outside-bottle.

Donoho, C., Heinze, T. and Kondo, C. (2012) 'Gender differences in personal selling ethics evaluations: Do they exist and what does their existence mean for teaching sales ethics?', *Journal of Marketing Education*, 34 (1): 55–66.

Fairtrade Foundation (2013) 'What is Fairtrade?', Fairtrade Foundation, available at: www.fairtrade.org.uk/

Fraj-Andres, E., Lopez-Perez, M.E., Melero-Polo, I. and Vazquez-Carrasco, R. (2012) 'Company image and CSR: reflecting with SMEs' managers', *Marketing Intelligence and Planning*, 30 (2): 266–80.

Golding, K.M. (2009) 'Fair trade's dual aspect: the communications challenge of fair trade marketing', *Journal of Macromarketing*, 29 (2): 160–71.

The Guardian (2001) 'So close – but children are the real winners', 20 January, available at: www.guardian.co.uk/theguardian/2001/jan/20/jobsmoney

The Guardian (2012) 'How community groups can use existing assets to develop local projects', 2 May, available at: www.guardian.co.uk/voluntary-sector-network/community-action-blog/2012/may/02/nesta-neighbourhood-challenge-mapping-assets

Hainmueller, J., Hiscox, M.J. and Sequeira, S. (2011) 'Demand for the Fair Trade label: evidence from a field experiment', MIT Political Science Department Research Paper No. 2011-9B, MIT, 1 April.

Hauck, B. (2011) 'Will product placement change TV?', available at: www.bbc.co.uk/news/magazine-12449502

Kendrick, A., Fullerton, J.A. and Kim, Y.J. (2013) 'Social responsibility in advertising: a marketing communications student perspective', *Journal of Marketing Education*, 35 (2): 141–54.

Kolk, A. and van Tunder, R. (2010) 'International business, corporate social responsibility and sustainable development', *International Business Review*, 19 (2): 119–25.

Lewis, M. (2013) 'Dear Archbishop … why I disagree with you over Wonga', *The Telegraph*, 30 July, available at: www.telegraph.co.uk/finance/personalfinance/borrowing/10209475/Martin-Lewis-Dear-Archbishop...why-I-disagree-with-you-over-Wonga.html

McAlister, T. (2010) 'UK/Canada: Tar sands crude is reaching British petrol stations, Greenpeace say', *The Guardian*, 9 May (posted on CorpWatch) available at: www.corpwatch.org/article.php?id=15579

Merritt, J. (2010) 'Mastering the art of ambush advertising', *The Wall Street Journal*, 25 January, available at: http://online.wsj.com/article/SB10001424052970204731804574391102699362862.html

Murillo, D. and Lozano, J.M. (2006) 'SMEs and CSR: an approach to CSR in their own words', *Journal of Business Ethics*, 67 (3): 227–40.

Nielsen, A.E. and Thomsen, C. (2009a) 'Investigating CSR communication in SMEs: a case study among Danish middle managers', *Business Ethics: A European Review*, January, 18 (1): 83–93.

Nielsen, A.E. and Thomsen, C. (2009b) 'CSR communication in SMEs: a study of the attitudes and beliefs of middle managers', *Corporate Communications: An International Journal*, 14 (2): 176–89.

Nijhof, A.H.J. and Jeurissen, R.J.M. (2010) 'The glass ceiling of CSR: consequences of a business case approach towards CSR', *International Journal of Sociology and Social Policy*, 30 (11): 618–31.

Perrini, F., Russo, A. and Tencati, A. (2007) 'CSR strategies of SMEs and large firms – evidence from Italy', *Journal of Business Ethics*, 74 (3): 285–300.

Robinson, J. (2010) 'Ofcom confirms product placement on UK TV', available at: www.guardian.co.uk/media/2010/dec/20/ofcom-product-placement-uk-tv

Roy, A. and Chattopadhyay, S.P. (2010) 'Stealth marketing as a strategy', *Business Horizons*, January, 53 (1): 69–79.

Seitanidi, M.M. (2009) 'Missed opportunities of employee involvement in CSR partnerships', *Corporate Reputation Review*, 12 (2): 90–105.

Seitanidi, M.M. and Crane, A. (2009) 'Implementing CRS through partnerships: understanding the selection, design and institutionalisation of non-profit-business partnerships', *Journal of Business Ethics*, 85: 413–29.

7 Advertising and Branding

CHAPTER OVERVIEW

Introduction

The main concern in Chapter 2 was for the fundamental use of the very basic model of the (marketing) communication process. The critique of communications theory used in Chapter 2 applies equally here in terms of advertising, so that advertising practice without theory (and vice versa) is problematic. In this chapter the theoretical and practical nature of advertising is explored, particularly in relation to branding. Three key practitioners' views that have been influential over the last five decades or so are examined and explained. As with the broader communications argument, in this chapter there is concern for practitioners and what they can gain from theoretical stances. The nature of this, of course, will be dependent upon the type of product and whether it is new or established, a physical product or service, low cost or expensive, consumer or industrial. This will determine the importance of advertising in the communications mix in any given context. It will also depend upon the type of market, whether it is a growth or mature market for example, which will also impact upon the use of advertising. The product/brand/market life cycle, objectives and policies of the organisation, economic outlook, competitive activity, promotional resources and many other parameters will determine the nature and importance of advertising activities.

Learning objectives

This chapter considers advertising and branding in the context of what theory has to offer advertising and branding practice. More specifically, on completion of this chapter, the student will be able to:

- discuss the nature of advertising in the 21st century in terms of theoretical development;
- define advertising in comparison with other elements of the communications mix;
- explain the relationship between advertising and branding decisions and how advertising is used to create brand value;
- outline the major practitioner influences on current day advertising and establish a link between past and present.

ADVERTISING THEORY

Advertising as the art of persuasion

Advertising is by and large seen as an art – the art of persuasion – and can be defined as:

> Any paid-for communication designed to inform and/or persuade.

It is much more than this though, as alluded to in Chapter 1 of this book. It is part of the fabric of everyday life. Television advertising in particular has changed from being exclusive and even exotic to being prosaic and 'everyday'. This underscores the importance of the McCluhanism 'the medium is the message', or at least part of it (McLuhan, 1964; McLuhan and Fiore, 1967). Advertising has been seen as both a positive and negative force in society. As indicated above, it is not the intention here to get too deeply involved in the ethical debate that surrounds what has been called the 'second oldest profession'. Since the 1960s the debate has been about whether advertising shapes society or whether it merely reflects societal norms in order to do its job and sell things. In fact, concerns had been expressed earlier than this. The manipulation of consumers by corporations through the use of motivational research and other techniques such as subliminal advertising were explored by Packard (1957) who was interested in consumer expectations and the way these were influenced by the desire for products. This, for Packard, was driven by compelling needs created by advertisers with a promise to fulfil them. Such debate has not gone away and can be seen in the controversial advertising of Benetton or the pester power of children where parents' lives may be made difficult because of an advertisement they have seen for expensive trainers or the latest console game.

Advertising can be said to be art in the sense that it is part of a creative industry and of society. It can be seen as 'pop art' in the same sense as, for example, popular music, dance or theatre. The old adage of Lord Leverhulme – founder of Unilever – which is something like 'Half the money I spend on advertising is a waste. The problem is I don't know which half' (also attributed to others such as John Wanamaker, the US store owner) underscores this notion. The corollary to this is that advertising is not an exact science. Pure transfer of meaning is difficult if not impossible to achieve and this is true of mere information-giving, leaving aside the problems associated with persuasion. As communication strategies are developed the organisation, as we have seen in Chapter 1 of this book, has a number of alternatives available in terms of the communications mix. The elements of the mix can be described and grouped in a number of ways. For example communication can be mass (as with advertising) or personal (as with selling). Alternatively, communication can be paid for (for example advertising or exhibitions) or free (publicity or word-of-mouth). Communication can also be a mix of these, that is:

- mass and free (publicity);
- mass and paid for (advertising);
- personal and free (word-of-mouth);
- personal and paid for (selling).

There has always been confusion over the difference between advertising and publicity. Also, confusion still remains over what is paid-for sponsorship rather than advertising. The sponsorship by, for example, Emirates or Etihad airlines of English football clubs can, however, be seen to be very different from an Emirates or Etihad advertisement through the objectives behind the different forms of communication. As well as this, the comparative advantages and limitations of personal as opposed to mass communication can be expressed in terms of other factors. Mediated communication like advertising has long been recognised as a fast medium that has a low cost per contact. It can attract attention and engage people with a message but has to try hard to do so. Advertising has so far been a one-way flow of message content (although this has changed somewhat with the advent of online and other digital forms) and its effects have been difficult to truly measure. Compare this with personal communication, which is often face-to-face, provides instant feedback, and allows messages to be tailored to individuals. Advertising is a paid-for communication that usually involves mass media such as television. However, as technology changed, advertising became less mass and more personalised, introducing media such as mobile phones utilising text messages. Compare the strong degree of control that the advertiser who is paying for the communication has as opposed to seeking publicity where messages have to be filtered through editors and others.

The advantages of advertising over other forms of communication centre on control. The sender pays for the space and can therefore say what he or she likes, where and when to say it and to whom, providing this is within legal and regulatory frameworks. The low cost per contact and the creative power of advertising mean that it can be very cost-effective, especially in consumer markets where there is little between brands other than the ingenuity of accompanying advertising that becomes part of the brand's architecture. On the other hand the disadvantages of the non-personal nature of advertising mean there is no opportunity for immediate feedback, and the costs of production and media can be very high yet credibility can be low. Most people know that advertising exists to persuade (or at least they perceive it so) and if they so wish viewers, listeners and readers can 'screen out' messages either psychologically through selective perception or physically by, for example, leaving the room when a television commercial break is on. Another disadvantage of advertising as mass communication is that messages were thought to have to be very general in their appeal. These days, however, the fragmentation that has occurred in the various media means that there are smaller groups of recipients of messages and marketers and therefore they have the ability to target these more with more specific messages. Also, the idea of narrowcasting within broadcasting whereby a mass medium such as TV can be used by employing audience research and analysis has been with us for some time.

How advertising works

The hierarchy of effects model

The hierarchy of effects model was discussed generally in Chapter 3 of this book. For advertising to work at all it has first to be seen, read and listened to, and then comes belief, being remembered and even acted upon (Crosier, 1999). Thus as discussed in Chapter 3, various models from fairly early on in the 20th century were developed to try to understand the processes involved in moving from states of unawareness to awareness through to actual behaviour to try to measure communications' effects. Thus, from Strong's 1925 AIDA through to Colley's 1961 DAGMAR, there were the think-feel-do sequence and its derivatives. Also as discussed in Chapter 2 of this book, there has been developed an attempt to show the problems of measuring the actual effect of a particular form of communication, not least advertisements. This is descriptive, and does not say why people respond as they do to advertisements, yet is consistently used to help form objectives. The AIDA model and those similar to it are still the implicit conceptual underpinning of much of present-day advertising strategy. Indeed, as Crosier (1999) points out, it has to be conceded that some form of basis for objectives formation, even if deficient, is preferable to none. Crosier concludes that the measurement of cognition is possible, of affectation possible but difficult, and of behaviour possible after the fact, but to predict accurately is very difficult.

The communications process model

The advertising process follows the communication process that was dealt with generally in Chapter 2. However, this model was originally developed to deal with the problems of one-way mass communication. The sender or source of the message in advertising terms is usually the organisation. The message may be handled by some form of communications company. The sender/source itself is usually part of that message. The source characteristics outlined in the Kelman model in Chapter 2 of this book apply here also. Advertising may have elements of trust, likeability, attractiveness and power in order to influence and persuade. The celebrity endorser may be used to get across, for example, enthusiasm or likeability. Encoding deals with problems where the advertiser's job is to perceive correctly the problems to be solved, create the right concept, and develop the advertising in terms of the right sentences, words, symbols or whatever else from the vast array of verbal and non-verbal elements. The advertising message is the symbolic representation of the sender's/source's thoughts/ideas. Decoding involves deriving meaning from the received message that is a composite of the actual message sent and any influences the medium may have had upon it. Feedback is the loop of the process that provides the sender/source with a channel for evaluation of the encoded message. Most feedback activity occurs in the area of advertising research. Noise (interference or impedance) is the blocking or distortion of the message and this has a particular bearing on advertising. It might be the lack of knowledge that causes a consumer to be unable to fully understand. This can therefore be physical or cognitive and anything from interruption though channel flicking to the sheer amount of clutter in a newspaper or magazine. Realm of understanding/field of experience is used to indicate the possibilities of overlap between sender and receiver so that there is 100 per cent commonness of field of experience. In advertising terms prior knowledge of a particular brand or the residual effect of a previous campaign would be part of this.

Other communication models

Step flow/personal influence models, innovation theory, and hierarchy of effects all have a resonance with advertising. It is the latter, hierarchy of effects, that has been paid most attention and yet is the most problematic. Clearly advertising has been the most prolific communications tool used to gain awareness and interest, within the think-feel-do sequence of events regarding the cognitive (awareness, knowledge), the affective (interest/liking, desire/preference/conviction) and the behavioural (action/purchase). This has been subjected to the usual criticism (see Chapter 2 of this book) that is applied to stage models but also knowing that the level of communication input in order to facilitate change is difficult to measure. Until this is known an optimal communications mix cannot be devised and implemented.

Another common model referred to above and applied to advertising is the Kelman Source Characteristics Model. The ways in which sources obtain and retain their characteristics that can be used in message strategy were discussed generally in Chapter 2 and the use of a celebrity endorser is discussed in Chapter 6. The model elaborates how credibility (for objectivity, relevancy, expertise, trustworthiness and so on), attractiveness (through identification with the source) and power (when the source can reward and punish and therefore involves compliance) can be used in communications but especially in advertising. High credibility is not necessarily as effective in certain situations as might be expected. The use of a high credibility source is of less importance when receivers have a neutral position. This is clearly plausible with regard to low and high involvement and where risk is involved. Everyday products like insurance can be promoted in this way. Empathy or a correlation between source and recipient means that the receiver will find the source attractive and a relationship can then develop. The latter sees him-/ herself in the situation depicted, say, through slice of life advertising, i.e. he or she relates to and identifies with it and the problems it appears to solve. Many advertising examples of credibility and attractiveness exist. However, the use of power characteristics is rarer and is more easily seen in personal communications situations where both the stick and carrot are in evidence; for example expense accounts, type of car allowance, bonus rewards or penalties.

The context of advertising

The context of advertising determines much of what is eventually practised. The industrial setting is often radically different from that of the consumer but within the notion of 'consumer advertising' there are very different contexts. Fast-moving consumer goods (fmcg) advertising may be very different from that of consumer durables. The business to business (B-to-B) situation has many contexts and it is erroneous to assume that industrial equates to B-to-B, or that all non-consumer advertising can be grouped under the umbrella of 'organisational'. It is believed that it is far better to look at advertising within specific contexts, perhaps on a market or industry basis.

The Snapshot below discusses the crucial role of packaging and pack design in the development of brands and in particular the luxury brand that is Harrods in terms of three new tea products. It also discusses the impact that the award-winning restaurant The French Laundry has had on the Harrods' brand through a co-branding pop-up restaurant project that allowed Harrods to further its food brand reputation.

Snapshot A place for design in the Harrods' brand communications mix – Harrods Herbal Teas

According to the agency Honey Creative (2008), the redesigning of packaging, in this case for Harrods Herbal Tea, demonstrates design effectiveness. The Knightsbridge (London) store and brand undertake many initiatives that help build and maintain

(Continued)

(Continued)

brand equity. Honey Creative report that Harrods view branding and design as having been the most significant change that has impacted on sales, profit and performance. Harrods made the decision to expand their products to meet demand. This required a design solution in order to tap into the untapped value inherent in its brand equity. The brief for Honey Creative consisted of five things: to create an eclectic packing range for three herbal teas (peppermint, camomile and lemon verbena); attract premium food lovers beyond the usual tourists; create a real standout; inspire multiple purchases; and bring to life the core values of Britishness, innovation, sensation and luxury. The project was based on research that indicated a significant unfulfilled demand for premium-badged goods.

The key with Harrods was to offer a wider and more complementary range of herbal tea to a higher demographic as well as international and UK tourists. The Honey Creative campaign also managed to convert footfall into sales, create a cool brand in order to rival Fortnum and Mason and also Waitrose, invigorate pride and passion through product and packaging development and stimulate multiple purchases, especially with the discerning 'foodie' buyer. The results of this campaign have been impressive. From September 2007 to March 2008 volume rose by 135.4 per cent and value by 161.5 per cent, despite a decline in footfall during the previous year (down by 2 per cent), the sale of tea (down by 25 per cent between 1999 and 2007) and visitors to London (down 20 per cent during the period 2000–6). There was also an increase in export sales, for example to Japan and Australia, and sales in Harrods' airport stores.

According to Honey Creative (2008) the budget for this campaign (actual figure undisclosed) represented a saving of 15.5 per cent on costs through purchasing economies, improvements in staff morale, changes in staff behaviour and productivity, and 'economies of scale on Harrods projects'. This covered 'research, design concept, development, copy writing, illustration and artwork'.

The three packs had to look 'stunning' individually but, as per the brief, they had to 'eclectically sit together'. The design team, in order to achieve this, drew 'upon Harrods extensive heritage' and raided 'their amazing archive'. Inspiration was found in the architecture of Harrods' food halls, which, according to Honey Creative, are 'unique art-nouveau/deco'. The team was able to create 'design language' that enabled 'products and ranges to tell their individual stories'. This is a 'herbal story' involving flowers and leaves, 'Middle Eastern inspired graphic reflecting the tea brewing ceremony', fonts 'borrowed from history', 'strong uncoated colours' that 'contrasted with foil blocking by printing on reverse of carton-board' and 'intensity of spot colour out of 4 colour process". According to Honey Creative, 'The new design will continue to build Harrods' name and reputation for the best ingredients money can buy"'

Harrods' internal research revealed the effects the new packaging had on staff and customers. This included an appreciation of the new tea range, a perception that the new packaging sells itself, closer partnerships with vendors, a feeling that anything is possible, improved recruitment, renewed confidence, higher morale and, with customers, improved conversion rates from merely looking to actual sales.

Reflecting upon the Harrods' tea packaging project Honey Creative suggest that the Harrods' brand of teas were 'in line with a trend towards exotic and unusual flavours for the more adventurous consumer … Although more expensive, speciality and herbal/fruit teas are gaining share' and the packaging project addressed 'opportunities and challenges from a strategic perspective'.

Stop Point

Harrods is clearly intent on maintaining and developing what is already an iconic, international brand. Undertake the following: 1. Consider and discuss the impact of pack design on the Harrods' tea brand both in the UK and internationally; 2. Examine and discuss the opportunities for Harrods and other potential partners in terms of co-branding.

BRANDING AND ADVERTISING

The meaning of 'to brand'

Just as mass marketing is a thing of the past so too is the generic product. Even at supermarkets where there are products that are not labelled as individual brands per se, they are often still branded in a particular basic fashion, such as Tesco's own-label 'Everyday Value' range, which has superseded the 'Tesco Value' range. The Tesco Everyday Value is, for Davidson (2012), 'a new sub-brand for changing times' (see the Snapshot later in this chapter). The brand image is a perception on the part of the consumer. It is a perception of what the marketer has created in terms of brand identity. Chapter 14 of this book provides a more detailed discussion on the relationship between identity and image (at the corporate level). The consumer has a perception that is called the brand image and uses this as shorthand in order to aid decision making. The benefits of branding are, according to marketers and those who are pro-branding, myriad. These include providing choice, saving time and money, and guaranteeing product quality, while those against point to waste, particularly with packaging and high prices.

Brands are configured from a basic product but are added to with tangible and intangible attributes. Another way of looking at this is to take the view of David Bernstein (1984), who sees the brand as a product with clothes on that grows and matures in much the same way as a baby comes into the world and grows up. Levi, Lee and Wrangler offer similar denim jeans, but they are very different brands with different personalities. This is because of the symbolism used, the communications (particularly advertising) created and the behaviour of the parent and brand itself. Blind testing is a testament to the power of the brand and when a brand is stripped of its 'clothes' back to the original product this can be very revealing.

Brands as illustrated in Figure 7.1 therefore consist of the following:

Core product – the actual, physical product or service that is generic and easy to copy, which is a basic product that might easily become a basic brand of, for example, a chocolate bar, a soft fizzy drink or fruit juice. It is interesting to note that there may well be exceptions to the tried and tested model of branding. Where fashion comes into it, it may well be that the designer, Jean Paul Gaultier, Stella McCartney or Donna Karan, may be at the core, and the physical product does not matter. Some believe that designers of this stature could put their name on almost anything, and it would be the name that counted.

Tangible attributes – these are design, performance, ingredients, parts, size, shape, pricing and harder to copy.

Intangible attributes – these are value, image, distributor's image and much harder to copy.

Brands are therefore built through the use of names and other signs and symbols to create a symbolism that becomes an identity. This makes the brand memorable and may describe the benefit sought by the consumer, as with Slim Fast or Head

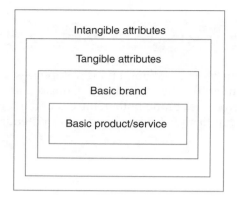

Figure 7.1 A simple brand configuration model

& Shoulders. It may use association with activities, such as Range Rover, or it may be distinctive, such as Apple's distinctive coloured apple logo. Pronunciation and phonetics are important, as recognised many years ago by Kodak, which is acceptable in many markets throughout the world without alteration or adaptation. Other brands may not have at the core a bare or basic product that is then built upon to create a brand. Other issues surrounding branding are beyond the scope of this chapter and indeed book, but some are returned to in Chapter 13 from a corporate communications perspective.

Brand strategy (in terms of monolithic, family and umbrella branding), brand extensions (in terms of resource saving and IMC) and co-branding (in terms of relationship marketing and collaborating partners such as Visa and banks such as HSBC and others) are important and should be pursued outside of this text.

Advertising, brand image and objectives

For some time the primary role of advertising has been to help build brands. Many years ago shopkeepers knew their customers personally. Then, they saw customers on a daily basis and would have known them by name but now this relationship has to be simulated, especially by the large retailers. One way of achieving this is to use branding. If the object is to bring product/company and customer together in a relationship of trust, commitment and perhaps even loyalty, this poses real difficulties/dilemmas for the use of certain tools. For example, the use of sales promotion (see Chapter 9 of this book) might be seen as some form of bribery but if used more subtly can be a real relationship management tool in order to keep customers, for example the loyalty or bonus card. In order to achieve this, objectives have to be clear.

Advertising Objectives

In Chapter 4 of this book, marketing communications objectives are discussed in relation to their role in the marketing communications planning process. In essence advertising objectives can be viewed in the same way, as part of a planning process, and may take the following forms:

- First in a hierarchical form, from mission down to marketing communications and then advertising.
- Second, they should be viewed as being SMART, that is to say specific, measurable, achievable, relevant and timed.

The role of objective setting is to constrain strategy and help eliminate the large number of strategic options. MBO (management by objectives) is as old as time but the 1950s saw the start of its use in business and marketing and this was true of marketing communications also. For example Rothschild's (1987) list of reasons why we should use the MBO approach includes the idea that objectives give direction, are a means to performance measurement and are consistent with time management. This still holds today. In marketing communications or more specifically advertising terms, the DAGMAR model (designing advertising goals for measured advertising results) is typical of such an approach, since it looks to measure the results of a specific advertising task in terms of the hierarchical 'think-do-feel' cognitive/affective/behavioural system on a defined audience. There is therefore an attempt to measure the degree of change in a given period of time as one moves through the hierarchy. An example might be to make 70 per cent of the target audience aware of the new product and to achieve a 50 per cent understanding of the proposition, with 40 per cent convinced, but with the expectation when it comes to it that only 20 per cent will purchase in the first period (see Chapter 3 of this book for more on buyer behaviour and hierarchy of effects models). The distinction between marketing, marketing communications and advertising objectives within this context should be clear. In the above example the marketing objective is to achieve a 20 per cent market share in the first trading period, say, one year. The marketing communications objectives to help achieve this could be many and varied, with the first being the creation of 70 per cent awareness. This might be achieved solely through advertising but for conviction other forms of communication, let's say Public Relations, might be used. Towards purchase, sales promotion may become appropriate.

Advertising is used not only to build brand awareness but also to provide information if necessary. Brand image and identity cannot be built and sustained without some form of advertising. In Chapter 4 of this book the management model used placed objectives and dir   clearly at the start of the communications' management process. Advertising
objecti   ferent in this regard, as advocated earlier. Advertising objectives should
be de   with influence during a campaign. This requires that the objectives
behi   be explicit rather than implicit, since without this kind of precision
a v   be filled with ambiguous creative media outcomes. Most writers
ar   ould therefore advocate SMART to avoid any vagueness and provide
a   y objectives can be measured. Perceptions, attitudes and predisposi-
          some form of measurement otherwise they are of little use in terms of
          d in particular advertising effects.

          en (2000) go further and move away from mere communication effects
          urn on customer investment). Key to this concept is that of incremental
          f calculating ROCI. This system is self-explanatory and a simple formula
          marginal analysis) and works at a very superficial level unless, as Schultz
          nt out, 'hurdle rates' for investments are set, i.e. minimum percentage
          Also advocated is the notion of short- and long-term brand aspect measure-
          roach means not only investment in brands but also measurement of brand
          of price willing to pay, advocacy and so on. Interestingly, Schultz and Kitchen
          attitude and behavioural measurement, albeit in an explanatory rather
          ive manner. The new acronyms of ABC – activity-based costing, which means
          osts directly to customers/potential customers – and EVA – economic value
          i.e. economic worth – suggest an investment in communications approach
          n treating communications as a cost. This argument can be extended to create
          urn on brand investment), i.e. return that comes from the investment made in a
          There are many ways to measure ROBI, some of which are qualitative while others

are quantitative. Examples are awareness, recognition, positioning, the number of customers found or lost, market share, purchase patterns or customer satisfaction. As many as 20 such measures might be applied to give a clear picture of before and after the investment.

Brand image and trust

By creating satisfaction and attempting to gain loyalty the marketer enters into a binding contract in the marketplace. This is achieved through being courteous, accessible and responsive and so that produces an affinity with and liking by the customer of the brand owner. The intensity of the relationship that then follows will affect the degree of loyalty. For Duncan (2002) this is about expectations, and provides a scale from awareness through to identity, being connected, continuity and finally advocacy, that a consumer might move up or down. Duncan reminds us we should not forget the negative, i.e. if a consumer is disappointed, then not only is he or she not an advocate for the brand, but also may very well be a vocal disparager of it.

Total brand loyalty may only exist with the less fickle Bon Jovi or Rolling Stones rock band follower or Newcastle United or AC Milan football fan so that brand loyalty is, these days, an unrealistic prospect, but this does not negate branding. Indeed this is far from the case, with estimates hovering around some form of the 'Pareto Principle' of 80/20 i.e. 80 per cent of something provides 20 per cent of something else. In this case 80 per cent of turnover might be produced by a brand that represents just 20 per cent of a company's products while the rest, 80 per cent of products, only produce 20 per cent of turnover. In some instances brands can be worth a considerable percentage of the worth of the parent, as with Apple and Coca-Cola.

Brand awareness, association, perceived quality, proprietary assets such as trademarks and to an extent loyalty can all be measured in some way, leading to brand equity. While the customer/consumer gets the benefit such as less risk or easier decision making, the company benefits from, for example, reduced costs and increased sales and revenue since it costs less to sell to existing customers who are likely to be heavier users.

For some years now there has been an interest in relationship quality that stems from trust and the high degree of certainty of predictable and obligatory behaviour that leads to sales, giving the seller integrity and the process a high degree of certainty (Crosby et al., 1990). The process proposed by Morgan and Hunt (1994) is central here, i.e. that trust leads to commitment which leads to loyalty and that this is essential for successful relationship marketing. What is proposed is that this process is transposed to the consumer/brand relationship, thus the brand inspires the same degree of relationship quality that is usual in human relationships. This trust in brands requires investment that carries with it some degree of risk that consumers will cease to cooperate and cease resisting attractive alternatives.

Trust for some writers (for example Delgado-Ballester and Munuera-Aleman, 2001) within the consumer/brand context has not been adequately explored and lacks suitable definitions and measurement. McDonald's (1981) analogy of marriage – mutual social trust leading to commitment and the establishment and maintenance of exchange relationships – is helpful in conceptualising how consumers might choose brands, as are the ways in which people choose friends based on personality. The resultant loyalty to brands is rather more than the simplistic notion of repeat purchase over time. There is a much more complex notion of brand loyalty, involving frequency of usage, share of portfolio and attitudinal loyalty. In other words brand loyalty is commitment. Rather than a formula of trust + commitment = loyalty, there is a holistic process where trust, commitment and loyalty become one and the same. What has been suggested is a modification of an existing model that will then reflect key areas of the consumer/ brand relationship.

Trust (and reliance) is the key variable within the consumer/brand relationship but this is shaped by:

- opportunistic behaviour (a negative influence on the relationship since it is deceit-oriented);
- consumers' predetermined set (recognition that consumers can be influenced by factors not necessarily within their direct control, i.e. parental influence and life stage);
- communications (formal and informal sharing of meaningful and timely information).

Commitment exists when the consumer believes that an ongoing relationship with the brand (from a repertoire) is so important that they wish to maintain it through maximum effort and believe that buying the brand will result in a positive outcome. Commitment can be deemed to be attitudinal and is influenced by:

- shared values (extent to which both the consumer and the brand have common behaviours, personalities, goals, functions, ideals, representations, attitudes, and policies);
- relationship benefits (brand should consistently satisfy the consumer both in its functionality and the way in which it represents the consumer to others);
- relationship termination costs (expected loss suffered, both financial and emotional).

It is posited that trust and commitment reinforce one another within this process towards loyalty. If this bond weakens then naturally loyalty will weaken. It has also been suggested that where consumers trust in, and are loyal to, a repertoire of substitutable brands (Erhenberg, 1991; Hallberg, 1995) this is largely dependent on perceived involvement. Naturally where involvement in a product category, or the brand itself, is high the costs and benefits are high and the consumer may give more thought to the other variables.

The components of brand or corporate image are seen by many as being both rational and emotional, as explored further in Chapter 8 of this book, which is fundamental to the notion of what a brand or organisation really is in any given situation. Bhat and Reddy (1998) use the terms functional and symbolic in terms of brand or corporate positioning where a brand can be both or one or the other. The symbolic offers either (or both) prestige and self-expression. The functional meets immediate practical needs. Whatever facets there are to a particular brand, it seems likely that trust plays a vital part in the process that leads from consumers' perceptions and experiences of a brand to brand loyalty.

Trust, pragmatically, is seen as a powerful marketing weapon in the armoury and is something that can be lost and won (Bainbridge, 1997) and something for both parties to win with. There can be a win-win mutual benefit bargaining rather than the win-lose adversarial bargaining where consumers expect information and to be taken seriously otherwise the relationship will be damaged (Fletcher and Peters, 1997). Trust in this light becomes an important brand attribute making major fmcg brands more powerful than the Church (according to the Henley Centre's Planning for Social Change 1998 report). Marks & Spencer have trust and this enables them and others, such as Virgin, to extend into hitherto unknown (to them) areas but where consumers welcome brand extension under certain conditions. Marks & Spencer or Tesco in this sense have become choice editors, manufacturers in their own right (own label) and service providers. They know, however, that trust can be just as easily be lost as won and is best kept by a philosophy that runs across the whole organisation, not just the marketing department. Academic research recognises the importance of trust and hence the building and maintenance of a brand personality that affects both brand trust and brand affect, with some personality dimensions relating more to one and some to the other and some to both. With brand trust, sincerity and ruggedness are likely dimensions, but with brand affect, excitement and sophistication are more likely dimensions. With both trust and affect, competence is a likely brand personality dimension with influence (Sung and Kim, 2010)

Brand systems

Many of the advertising agencies or communications companies have developed, over the decades in some cases, brand or branding systems. Such systems are designed to help the client develop brands and are to do with brand architecture of one sort or another. Most of these systems are based around the idea of a brand facet model, which when applied to a particular brand would yield a mix of facets. Branding systems, or architectures, can take various forms that might highlight the corporate name to endorse the brand (sometimes referred to as umbrella branding). Alternatively the system might dictate that the brand stands alone (sometimes called mono brands) as an entity in its own right. Combinations of these two approaches are clearly extant.

A strong corporate image is usually synonymous with product class. This is not common in packaged goods but can be clearly seen in technology-associated products. For example a brand such as Toshiba can be said to have saliency (emotional closeness/distance of consumer to brand) and its corporate brand personality (personification of the organisation that demonstrates how the corporate brand's core emotional character has been projected to the consumer). Another example is Dyson with its Dyson Digital Slim vacuum cleaner. Other ways to branding are through licensing (popular in fashion accessories), house branding (usually involving diverse brands), dual branding that combines a corporate brand with a strong sub-brand (sometimes referred to as a family and could be said to be corporate or umbrella branding) and co-branding that allows synergy and might introduce a brand to a market that it could not enter in its own right. There are branding systems such as Lovemarks (Saachi and Saachi's/CEO Kevin Roberts' attempt to suggest a branding system that is beyond mere branding, the future beyond brands, at www.lovemarks.com/). The claim is that certain products create such an emotional bond that they are more than mere brands.

Mission, vision and international brands

The importance of corporate mission and vision, which deal respectively with 'what the company is doing' and 'where and what the company wants to be' as an organisation, at some time in the future, cannot be overlooked. Mission should be viewed as a strategic discipline, part of the intellect of the organisation, the cultural glue that binds the organisation's often-disparate elements – in essence the soul of the organisation and the reason for being (see Chapter 13 of this book). This plays an important role in brand development and can contribute towards competitive strategy and comparative advantage. International and global branding and advertising will be addressed in Chapter 18 of this book but it is worth addressing it briefly here. This clearly involves some discussion on the benefits of advertising that include the encouragement of competition, economies of scale, product development, stimulation of economic growth, improved products due to competition among brands, lower prices and greater variety. Conventional wisdom seems to say that no amount of advertising, however good, will enable a poor product to succeed. However, besides being used to communicate the benefits and availability of a product, it can explain how a product may be used to best advantage.

The Snapshot below looks at the importance of meeting the needs of the target market and communication that is meaningful within the context. It therefore looks at the brand essence for the Unilever brand Lynx.

Snapshot The Lynx (or Axe) effect – why using sex to sell may (or may not) cause problems for brands

The Lynx/Axe brand (Lynx in the UK, Ireland, Australia and New Zealand and Axe elsewhere) uses a version of sex appeal in its advertising that at times takes its owner Unilever to the edge of what is and what is not acceptable. In 2011 two separate commercials were banned by the UK Advertising Standards Authority (ASA) for being 'degrading to women' and being 'unsuitable for children'. In response an online video was posted featuring Lucy Pinder, the glamour model, apologising for any offence caused (O'Reilly, 2012). In fact the advertising had starred Lucy Pinder and had attracted more than 100 complaints to the ASA. The advertising was deemed to be likely 'to cause widespread offence' with its 'The cleaner you are the dirtier you get' headline for shower gel in July 2011 featuring bikini-wearing women. A much smaller number of complaints (15) were made about an online advertisement in the summer of 2011 for deodorant that 'featured Lucy Pinder in a series of provocative poses' and showed the 'glamour model eating an ice lolly, stripping wallpaper or bending over an oven door'. These advertisements were on sites such as Yahoo but the ASA adjudicated that they were also 'irresponsible', 'because they had been placed on two websites, Rotten Tomatoes and Anorak', which 'were not protected through age verification or other similar targeting' (Mirror Online, 2011). A Lynx spokesperson is reported as having said 'As an advertiser we strive to be responsible and observe strict guidelines for all brand communications. Lynx adverts often provoke diverse reactions and opinions but it is never our intention to cause offence' (Mirror Online, 2011).

Moving into 2012, in the UK the Lynx Attract brand was again the subject of complaint, this time for television advertising that was said to be too sexual. Unilever managed to avoid censure from regulators, however. The advertisement that was the subject of complaint was styled in a news bulletin format that reported on the chaos caused by people using the Lynx Attract brand, which resulted in chaos in New York, an emergency landing by an aircraft and animals escaping from a zoo. The mock reporting style appeared to be as much of a problem as the sexual allusions. The effect of Lynx Attract that caused people to tear their clothes off and rush towards the opposite sex appeared misleading to some because of its news reporting style. Others felt the sexual content was, as in previous Lynx cases, problematic in terms of children watching. Apart from the sexual content including kissing there was also 'a gorilla holding a bra on top of a bus with a "69 BERLIN" display' and 'viewers also complained the ad was offensive because it made light of serious issues including aeroplane crashes and epidemics. In response, Unilever said it used a "fantastical and humorous tone" interspersed with regular references to Lynx Attract, which made it immediately obvious to viewers that it was an ad and not a real news bulletin' (O'Reilly, 2012). As in previous defences of the brand and its communication Unilever suggested that "audiences have come to expect and are comfortable with the type of 'playful, sexy, tongue-in-cheek' tone it takes with Lynx advertising and 'went no further' than previous campaigns that featured sexual but light-hearted treatments" (O'Reilly, 2012). Clearcast (www.clearcast.co.uk, the UK broadcast clearance service) had given the advertisement a post 7.30pm rating but 'Unilever also instructed broadcasters only to show the ad after 9pm to ensure the ad

(Continued)

(Continued)

was not scheduled to be shown when children are watching' and 'Unilever also made efforts to ensure nobody in the ad was shown to be hurt or frightened as a result of the "epidemic" and that the spot made it clear the plane had landed safely because the passengers needed to undress, not because of a problem with the plane' (O'Reilly, 2012). The ASA concurred with Unilever and there was no action required (www.asa.org.uk/ Rulings/Adjudications/2012/7/Unilever-UK-Ltd/SHP_ADJ_189445.aspx).

Stop Point

Unilever has invested a great deal of time, effort and money in the Lynx/Axe brand to make it a success. Undertake the following: 1. Consider and discuss the use of sex appeal by Unilever for the Lynx brand; 2. Discuss the difficulties, problems, and pitfalls but also the rewards of using creative ideas that perhaps move toward the edge of corporate social responsibility and the ethical dimension when advertising to younger target audiences.

ADVERTISING PRACTICE

Practitioners' views on how advertising works

Most advertising practitioners have some form of system as to how advertising should work. This helps to resolve the potential conflict between communication planning, effectiveness and creativity. The idea that creativity (see Chapter 4 of this book for the marketing communications planning framework used in this book, including for creative strategy considerations) can be planned or harnessed in some way may not sit quite right with some people, but this is what advertising practitioners have to try to achieve. They, along with brand and marketing managers, are responsible for the message (what is said), the media (how the message will be carried) and the timing (or manner in which the message will be carried), among other things. This might be called creative planning, since it deals with strategy, execution and production.

Historically, at least three strains of thought associated with certain individuals have established themselves as cornerstones as to what advertising is or should be. Central to this apparently is the search for the 'Big Idea', for example a strapline with endurance and longevity such as Nike's 'Just do it'.

The unique selling proposition (USP)

The USP was a concept developed by Rosser Reeves (1961) of the Ted Bates agency where he rose to be chairman. He suggested there are three characteristics of a USP:

1. Each advertisement must make a unique proposition to the consumer rather than simply words or product puffery or window dressing. Each advertisement must provide a tangible benefit to the consumer so that they can say 'If I buy this product I will get this benefit'.
2. The proposition must be one that the competition either cannot or does not offer. It must be unique either in the brand or in the claim.
3. The proposition must be strong enough to move people. That is, pull over new customers to the brand, either through taking market share from competitors or expanding the size of the market or both.

Reeves, a controversial figure whose direction for advertising was eventually to fall out of favour, felt the attribute, claim or benefit that forms the basis of the USP should dominate the advertisement and other communications and be emphasised through repetition. For example Volvo, originally at least, had a USP that meant safety because of the quality and strength of the materials used in the car's body construction. However, for this approach to work there must be a truly unique attribute or benefit. The position must give them a sustainable competitive advantage, i.e. one that cannot be copied too easily. This of course is based on the premise that the consumer thinks rationally and the advertising must also operate in a rational way. Something as mundane as a soap powder or surface cleaner can be given a USP, for example speed, which has concrete benefits to the consumer (time saving or work that is not too hard or boring). The advertising's task is then to get this benefit across and it may simply utilise a colour change to demonstrate the speed of the brand's action. However, a USP may be achieved by other means. A change in product form (from powder to liquid) or packaging (a new way to get the product out of the container) can be the basis of the USP. It is also the case that the USP will not work on certain products where emotion is involved. This can occur in the seemingly rational world of industrial marketing where prestige of supply is involved. One thing that can be said, for a while at least, is that the USP worked for Ted Bates as an agency, where the USP for the agency's services was the USP.

The brand image

The brand image is almost the opposite of the USP and appears to work in many product/service categories where competing brands are very similar and the USP may not, or at least it may be difficult to implement. Brand image was championed by David Ogilvy, founder of Ogilvy, Benson and Mather and sometimes affectionately often referred to as 'the Pope of the profession'. Ogilvy advocated that advertising's task was to develop a strong, memorable identity for a brand through 'image advertising' where an image is developed that will appeal to product users. Thus Ogilvy, contra Reeves, comes down largely on the side of emotion rather than reason, but not exclusively so. Ogilvy was interested in brands and personality, seeing the job of advertisers being to match a brand's personality to that of the target. There was a need to give the brand a 'first class ticket through life' and the consumer a 'first class ticket to product quality'. To achieve this, the brand must first be given a personality. If a brand is a product with clothes on, then personality is what it wears. This is a set of associations, favourable connotations or positive psychological overtones, or what Ogilvy (1983) called chemistry rather than the literal product. Put the same whisky in two milk bottles and blind test them. The drinker will think the drinks are quite different if they are told they are, even though it is the same whisky. They are in fact 'tasting images'.

Positioning

In practice, the rational and emotional approaches are often used in conjunction to form creative strategy (see Chapter 4 of this book for consideration of creative strategy within the marketing communications management process), and as David Ogilvy rightly said there is not necessarily a conflict between image and fact. This was not lost on John Hegarty, of the British agency Bartle, Bogle and Hegarty, when creating the magazine advertising for the super-premium ice cream brand Haagen Dazs. Here double page spreads were used with imagery on the right-hand page (emotional, sexual and sensual) and factual information on the left (rational, quality of ingredients, etc.). The positioning attitude towards advertising favoured by many, including Reis and Trout who championed this in the 1970s, has become a popular basis of creative development. The basic idea is that communications activity is used to 'position' the product or service in a particular place in consumers' minds. Positioning can be on the basis of the brand in relation to, for example, the competition, product attributes, price or quality. A brand can be positioned on rational or emotional bases or both (Trout, 1969).

The ideas in Ries and Trout's (1981) book *Positioning: The Battle for Your Mind* took the reader away from internally conceived benefits of the product to the mind of the prospect and how they perceived the product or brand, underlining the need to think about how the consumer and not the marketer sees it. The product has to be placed in the consumer's mind to create an image based on an identity for a product, brand or company, i.e. as perceived by the target market in relation to the competition. This requires an understanding of such perceptions through the use of marketing research to enable the construction of perceptual mapping – product features and related benefits that meet needs and provide solutions to problems and issues (functional or emotional/symbolic, for example self-image enhancement).

According to the agency D'Arcy, Masius Benton and Bowles (subsumed by Publicis, one of the three largest advertising and related activities groups worldwide, in 2002), the position must first be clear and the target must be able to see what the product is for and why they should be interested in it. Benefit(s) should also be clear and compelling. Uniqueness on its own is not enough. This means the offering should be 'describable in a simple word, phrase, or sentence without reference to any final execution', and 'be likely to attract the prospect's attention'. There should be a clinching benefit and the advertising should allow branding advertising through which the prospect can vividly experience the product or service. In this agency's opinion, brand personality gives the product an extra edge where 'all brands do something, but the great brands also are something'. D'Arcy, Masius Benton and Bowles also proclaimed that agencies 'must dare to be different' where the agency itself must 'stand out' and 'not emulate but annihilate' the competition. The Big Idea, championed by David Ogilvy, was also advocated by this agency, where the advertising must be single-minded, and 'should be all about that one big thing'. This may be emotion rather than reason. A 'tear, a smile, a laugh … an emotional stimulus' that the viewer will want to see 'again and again'. However, the advertising should also be 'visually arresting … compelling, riveting, a nourishing feast for the eyes'. Finally D'Arcy, Masius Benton and Bowles advocate 'painstaking craftsmanship … go for the absolute best in concept, design and execution'.

The Snapshot below looks at rebranding in the context of the value brand. It discusses how Tesco was successful, particularly in the UK, with its Tesco Value range of budget, own-label, branded products, but then how the retailer had to change to meet the changing needs of its target customers.

Snapshot   Everyday Value – Tesco's rebranding of the notion of the value brand

The rebranded brand

In April 2012 it was reported that Tesco 'has abandoned its famous Value range of goods, in favour of an updated line of products, as it continues its fight back against rivals' (Wallop, 2012).

The new range is called 'Everyday Value' and this is Tesco's attempt to move the concept of value in supermarkets up-market; the brand is, for Wallop (2012), 'quite similar to Waitrose's Essentials range of goods'. For Davidson (2012), the Everyday Value range is not 'a back-of-the-envelope decision' but is, as the company insists, 'part of a carefully thought-out strategy'.

Tesco maintain that they have listened to what customers say they want and claim that the same low pricing remains, and yet Everyday Value products taste and look better (Davidson, 2012). In typical rebranding fashion the 550 lines of the old Value range have been repackaged. The new packaging has perhaps a retro, warmer and more homely feel than the 'stark blue and white stripes' of the Tesco Value range. So the old packaging is gone 'in favour of more upmarket, colourful packaging which features 1950s-style line drawings of kitchen equipment and food' (Wallop, 2012). The new packaging is 'more stylish with retro 1950s artwork rather than stark blue-and-white lines, which did rather scream "budget!" from shoppers' baskets' (Davidson, 2012). Lawson (2012) suggests that the packaging itself has 'a kitsch design, modernising the brand from Tesco Value's stripes'.

For Chapman (2012), Tesco is 'running ads that mimic the launch campaign for Waitrose's Essentials'. Chapman therefore suggests that it has taken three years for Tesco to match Waitrose. The Tesco campaign in mid-2012 was led with press advertising and was supported by television commercials. The campaign message was about quality, healthier options and improved packaging. Lawson (2012) warns that while Tesco have the new Everyday Value brand it still needs more initiatives 'to get its UK like-for-likes back on track'.

The products

The healthier options and improved quality clearly needed to become a reality in terms of the actual product. The Tesco Value range therefore was revamped to become the Tesco own-label Everyday Value brand. The products in the new range 'include no MSG, hydrogenated fats, artificial flavours or genetically modified ingredients'. A number of products have also been reformulated to contain less sugar and fat, while the fish fingers product will contain a 100% fillet of fish (Chapman, 2012). Other improvements to both product and packaging include changes to apple sauce, which contains 33 per cent more apples, cheddar that comes in a re-sealable bag and mince that contains less fat (Wallop, 2012). Davidson (2012) comments on these and that the 'lemon curd will be more lemony', then rather sceptically asks 'Radical stuff. What ingredients, you might wonder, have been removed from Tesco's apple sauce to make way for extra apples? It doesn't bear thinking about'.

The Tesco move from the Value range to the Everyday Value range with products that are of better quality, healthier and have better packaging, yet are still budget prices, does raise a question as to why Tesco might not have done the latter in the first place. As Davidson points out, Tesco may have launched the Everyday Value range 'but it is still the supermarket's budget option. The fact is that 99 per cent of shoppers, presented with a range of products, will opt neither for the very cheapest nor the most luxurious, but for something in between. Supermarkets need to strike a balance between quality and value for money, and reflect that in their branding'. As Lawson (2012) suggests, 'Tesco has been accused of attempting to be all things to all men on a number of occasions and it must ensure the range is not too expansive. The core of Tesco's customers is still likely to put good value at the top of its criteria'.

Stop Point

Tesco's original Value range was clearly successful for some years. As is well known, however, markets evolve and change is constant. Tesco's fight-back with Everyday Value appears to be a classic marketing response to changing customer needs. Undertake the following: 1. Consider and discuss the importance of own label in markets around the world; 2. Discuss the importance of monitoring the environment and in particular listening to customers in order to ascertain real needs and wants in the marketplace.

Assignment

Choose a city – Milan, Glasgow, Kuala Lumpur, London, Newcastle, Athens, Rio de Janeiro or another that you prefer – and apply the branding framework that would help reshape its image. Make a list of the things that would allow you to effectively brand the city. For example, is the city 'green' in the environmentally friendly sense, or is there some other part of the marketing environment that allows you to use the city's attributes? Follow this through with basic ideas on the role of advertising in the promotion of the city. Devise some form of symbolism and slogan that would be appropriate to the new brand.

Summary of Key Points

- Advertising can be seen as a positive or negative force in society. On balance it is probably seen by most as positive.
- Advertising is seen by many as art not science, where the transfer of pure meaning is difficult if not impossible.
- Different objectives drive different communications, and the difference between elements of the communication mix is reflected in such objectives, which should always be SMART. For example a fundamental difference between advertising and publicity is the degree of control.
- Measurement of communications (especially advertising) effects has to an extent been superseded by models such as ROCI or ROBI, but it is still fruitful to apply the basic communications process to advertising.
- The context of advertising is important. Advertising has a different role in different contexts and is more important in some rather than others.
- Advertising can emphasise brand values and explain what the brand proposition is.
- Branding appears to be here to stay. Core, tangible and intangible attributes make the brand and create brand equity.
- Brand loyalty is something of a myth but trust and commitment and perhaps loyalty are worth striving for.

- There is a link between mission, vision and branding. There is an intimate link between branding and culture.
- Practitioner views as to how advertising and branding work are important and influential. The USP and brand image stances have produced a rational versus emotional myth. Positioning has been prevalent for over three decades.

Discussion Questions

1. Discuss the notion that advertising can be said either to shape society or merely reflect societal mores.
2. 'Advertising is not and could never be a science. At best it is managed art'. Discuss this statement using examples to illustrate why you agree or disagree.
3. Explain the characteristics that distinguish advertising from other elements of the marketing communications mix. In particular highlight the differences between advertising and publicity.
4. Distinguish between business, marketing and advertising objectives by using examples of your choice. Discuss the requirement to be SMART with advertising objectives.
5. 'Return on communications investment is more important a measure than the effects of communication on behaviour'. Explain what this means.
6. Explain, using examples to illustrate, why the context of advertising makes advertising more or less important in the communications and marketing mix.
7. Brand values and proposition are fundamental to advertising. Explain the role, if any, that advertising might have in this area.
8. Explain what is meant by core, tangible and intangible attributes in relation to brand equity. Explore the relationship between loyalty, trust and commitment for a consumer brand of your choice.
9. Explain the link between mission, vision and branding in the context of a major consumer brand such as Levi.
10. Explain what USP, Brand Image and Positioning mean and provide examples from each of these practitioners' views on how advertising works.

Further Reading

Ashton, A.S. and Scott, N. (2011) 'Hotel restaurant co-branding: the relationship of perceived brand fit with intention to purchase', *Journal of Vacation Marketing*, 17 (4): 275–85. http://jvm.sagepub.com/content/17/4/275

This article is based on a study that investigates perceptions of brand fit and purchase intentions in this co-branding context. Overall perceived fit and complementary fit in terms of product usage and goals were found to be positively related to purchase intention. The

(Continued)

(Continued)

authors conclude that complementary fit can be found between two products that do not have the same attributes, such as in this case accommodation and restaurant, with the key aspect of influence being the synergy effect whereby the two brands representing the hotel (accommodation) and the restaurant (as part of a different branded chain) are complementary to each other.

Kaneva, N. and Popescu, D. (2011) 'National identity lite: nation branding in post-communist Romania and Bulgaria', *International Journal of Cultural Studies*, 14 (2): 191–207. http://ics.sagepub.com/content/14/2/191
The article deals with the reinvention of national image through 'nation branding'. This is effectively the development of a new image for external consumption. The article provides a comparative study of symbolism in the branding campaigns for the two countries. It deals with the politics of image creation and symbolic commodification in this particular political context. The study findings suggest that national identity can be used within neoliberal globalisation, resulting in what the authors call a 'national identity lite'.

Kemp, E., Williams, K. H. And Bordelon, B. M. (2012), The impact of marketing on internal stakeholders in destination branding: the case of a musical city, *Journal of Vacation Marketing*, 18(2): 121–33. http://jvm.sagepub.com/content/18/2/121
The authors discuss the importance of brand image in destination marketing. The needs of internal stakeholders (city residents), however, are the focus of this article, which recognises that an understanding of such needs is necessary for brand strategy success. The study suggests that if internal stakeholders are committed to the brand and branding efforts the brand strategy is likely to be more successful. Once committed, the brand becomes aligned with their self-concept and such stakeholders can become evangelists for the brand. They will actively promote the brand via word of mouth, resulting in a civic consciousness that becomes part of the brand management system that deals with external constituents such as tourists.

O'Boyle, N. (2012) 'Managing indeterminacy: culture, Irishness and the advertising industry', *Cultural Sociology*, 6 (3): 351–66. http://cus.sagepub.com/content/6/3/351
The author looks at discursive practices involving the Irishness of advertising people working in Ireland. Irishness can be seen as both fixed/essential and fluid. Practitioners can therefore shift between these two positions. Irishness is looked at as an old idea of culture that is seen as objective, knowable and actionable. The author looks at the work of John Fanning (the 'grandfather of Irish advertising') as an advertising industry account of and response to cultural change, and concludes that the tendency to objectify (Irish) culture makes it more measurable and actionable. At the same time the author maintains that if the practitioners are hesitant to define Irishness this does not prevent them from claiming 'truths' about it.

Rossiter, J.R. (2012) 'Advertising management principles are derived mostly from logic and very little from empirical generalisations', *Marketing Theory*, 12 (2): 103–16. http:// mtq.sagepub.com/content/12/2/103
This article tackles the strategic principles of advertising management and the logical, deductive process upon which management frameworks are based, as opposed to the inductive empirical approach which provides generalisations that are useful if translated into strategic principles. The author claims that this article comprehensively demonstrates that strategic principles in advertising depend on either entirely logical thinking or logical thinking about causality designed to 'ungeneralise' general empirical findings in order to be more specific and helpful to the brand by helping out in the area of strategic principles that allow managers to perform better.

REFERENCES

ASA (2012) 'ASA Adjudication on Unilever UK Ltd', Advertising Standards Authority, 11 July, available at: www.asa.org.uk/Rulings/Adjudications/2012/7/Unilever-UK-Ltd/SHP_ADJ_189445.aspx

Ashton, A.S. and Scott, N. (2011) 'Hotel restaurant co-branding: the relationship of perceived brand fit with intention to purchase', *Journal of Vacation Marketing*, 17 (4): 275–85.

Bainbridge, J. (1997) 'Who wins the national trust?', *Marketing*, 23 (October): 21–3.

Bernstein, D. (1984) *Company Image and Reality – A Critique of Corporate Communications*. London: Cassell Educational Ltd.

Bhat, S. and Reddy, K. (1998) 'Symbolic and functional positioning of brands', *Journal of Consumer Marketing*, 15 (1): 32–43.

Chapman, M. (2012) 'Tesco mimics Waitrose with Everyday Value range push', *Marketing*, 30 April. Available at: http://www.marketingmagazine.co.uk/article/1129342/tesco-mimics-waitrose-everyday-value-range-push (accessed 03/04/14).

Crosby, L., Evans, K. and Cowles, D. (1990) 'Relationship quality in services selling: an international perspective', *Journal of Marketing*, 54 (3) July: 68–81.

Crosier, K. (1999) 'Advertising', in P.J., Kitchen (ed.), *Marketing Communications*. London: Thomson International Publishing.

Davidson, M. (2012) 'Every little hurts – Tesco's new budget brand lacks snob value', *The Telegraph*, 5 April, available at: www.telegraph.co.uk/foodanddrink/9188573/Every-little-hurts-Tescos-new-budget-brand-lacks-snob-value.html

Delgado-Ballester, E. and Munuera-Aleman, J.L. (2001) 'Brand trust in the context of consumer loyalty', *European Journal of Marketing*, 35 (11/12): 1238–58.

Duncan, T. (2002) *Integrated Marketing Communications: Using Advertising and Promotion to Build Brands*. New York: The McGraw Hill Companies Inc.

Ehrenberg, A.S.C. (1991) 'New brands and the existing market', *Journal of the Market Research Society*, 33 (4) October: 285–99.

Fletcher, K.P. and Peters, L.D. (1997) 'Trust and direct marketing environments: a consumer perspective', *Journal of Marketing Management*, 13 (6): 523–39.

Hallberg, G. (1995) *All Consumers Are Not Created Equal*. New York: John Wiley & Sons.

Henley Centre (1998) *Planning For Social Change*. London: Henley Centre.

Honey Creative (2008) Harrods Herbal Teas, Design Business Association, Bronze Design Effectiveness Awards, www.dba.org.uk

Kaneva, N. and Popescu, D. (2011) 'National identity lite: nation branding in post-communist Romania and Bulgaria', *International Journal of Cultural Studies*, 14 (2): 191–207.

Kemp, E., Williams, K.H. and Bordelon, B.M. (2012) 'The impact of marketing on internal stakeholders in destination branding: the case of a musical city', *Journal of Vacation Marketing*, 18 (2): 121–33.

Lawson, A. (2012) 'Tesco Everyday Value: What does this mean for the grocer?', *Retail Week*, 4 April. Available at: http://www.retail-week.com/sectors/food/tesco-everyday-value-what-does-this-mean-for-the-grocer/5035516.article (accessed 03/04/14).

McDonald, G.W. (1981) 'Structural exchange and marital interaction', *Journal of Marriage and the Family*, November: 825–39.

McLuhan, M. (1962) *The Gutenberg Galaxy: The Making of Typographic Man*. Toronto: University of Toronto Press.

McLuhan, M. (1964) *Understanding Media: The Extensions of Man*. New York: McGraw Hill.

McLuhan, M. and Fiore, Q. (1967) *The Medium is the Message: An Inventory of Effects*. New York: Random House.

Mirror Online (2011) 'Lucy Pinder raunchy Lynx advert banned for being "degrading to women"', 23 November, available at: www.mirror.co.uk/news/uk-news/lucy-pinder-raunchy-lynx-advert-278840

Mohammad, A.A.S. (2012) 'The effect of brand trust and perceived value in building brand loyalty', *International Research Journal of Finance and Economics*, 85: 111–26.

Morgan, R.M. and Hunt, S.D. (1994) 'The commitment-trust theory of relationship marketing', *Journal of Marketing*, 58 (3) July: 20–38.

O'Boyle, N. (2012) 'Managing indeterminacy: culture, Irishness and the advertising industry', *Cultural Sociology*, 6 (3): 351–66.

O'Reilly, L. (2012) '"Sexual" Lynx ad escapes ban', *Marketing Week*, 11 July. Available at: http://www.marketingweek.co.uk/news/sexual-lynx-ad-escapes-ban/4002643.article (accessed 03/04/14).

Ogilvy, D. (1983) *Ogilvy On Advertising*. London: Pan Books.

Packard, V.O. (1957) *The Hidden Persuaders*. London: Longmans Green.

Reeves, R. (1961) *Reality in Advertising*. New York: Alfred Knopf.

Ries, A. and Trout, J. (1981) *Positioning: The Battle for Your Mind*. New York: Warner Books/McGraw Hill Inc.

Rossiter, J.R. (2012) 'Advertising management principles are derived mostly from logic and very little from empirical generalisations', *Marketing Theory*, 12 (2): 103–16.

Rothschild, M.L. (1987) *Marketing Communications: From Fundamentals to Strategies*. Lexington, MA: D. C. Heath.

Schultz, D. and Kitchen, P. (2000) *Communicating Globally: An Integrated Marketing Approach*. London: McMillan Business.

Sung, Y. and Kim, J. (2010) 'Effects of brand personality on brand trust and brand affect', *Psychology and Marketing*, 27 (7) July: 639–61.

Trout, J. (1969) 'Positioning is a game people play in today's me-too market place', *Industrial Marketing*, 54 (6) June: 51–5.

Wallop, H. (2012) 'Tesco ditches £1bn Value range', *The Telegraph*, 4 April, available at: www.telegraph.co.uk/finance/newsbysector/retailandconsumer/9185356/Tesco-ditches-1bn-Value-range.html

Message Creation and Execution

CHAPTER OVERVIEW

Introduction

Creative strategy is a key stage in the communications planning process, and should determine what action is required from the audience, what the messages should say or communicate and what is the 'big idea', alluded to in the previous chapter of this book, if indeed one exists. Creative tactics need to be executed and this usually involves media considerations as well as the actual design of an advertisement, a piece of packaging or a press release.

Learning objectives

This chapter seeks to explore the nature of creativity in relation to communication. More specifically, on completion of this chapter, the student will be able to:

- discuss creative strategy and explain the nature and role of the creative brief;
- highlight the commonest creative appeals available to marketers;
- discuss the execution of creative ideas;
- examine message strategy design considerations including message style, pattern, presentation order, source and integration;
- appreciate an evaluation of creative strategy and creative work, including conventional brand and communications research and also the role of less conventional tools of analysis such as projective techniques and semiotics in brand and communications research.

THE IMPORTANCE OF CREATIVITY IN MARKETING COMMUNICATIONS

The nature of creativity

Creativity is an important factor in our over-communicated society, especially when developing a position to differentiate products/services. Just because a promotion or an advertisement is creative or popular does not mean it will achieve the objectives set. Communication should be effective and not necessarily creative in this sense. Creativity is about finding new and appropriate ideas or directions in order that communications problems can be solved. There may be tension between effectiveness and creativity but creativity needs to be harnessed from a management perspective. For this reason alone much attention is paid to the question of how to manage creativity. Pickton and Broderick (2005) rightly suggest, for example, that creativity in marketing communications is not just about creative ideas for 'ads' but that creativity is part of the management and planning process. Schultz and Kitchen (2000) have suggested the idea of 'creative templates', where there are four drivers of creativity in communication. These are the consumer, the competition, the environment and the product/brand. Generating ideas through some form of research in these areas has been commonplace for many years.

Everything is capable of receiving creative treatment. There may be opportunities in the way things are done creatively in certain contexts but where the same creative ideas cannot be used in other contexts. This is often for cultural reasons of one sort or another, for example, aspects of religion or language, so that there are certain words or representations (for example through the use of nudity or sexual images) that prohibit the transference of a creative idea from one context to another. It may be difficult, if not impossible, to transfer an idea generated in a consumer context to an industrial or business-to-business one. Humour, sex or fantasy, for example, might never be used in the context of communicating the benefits of certain medical products, such as urological catheters. Similarly it is unlikely that facts, figures and logic would be used in the context of tobacco products. Some commentators suggest that it is the personality of the brand and not logic that is important. In short, despite a certain creative approach being successful, it cannot always be re-used. However, Schultz and Kitchen (2000) emphasise the notion of patterns or templates that can help screen out unproductive ideas and establish productive creative ideas. Six 'Creativity Templates' were derived from research involving a sample of 200 advertisements. Rather than deriving a creative approach from more research, the use of these templates can help the creative function to replace, for example, the cultural driver in one marketplace with another for a different context. In this way symbols can be changed and extended to existing and new products.

Creative planning

The message is what is to be said through media of one sort or another in a particular manner at particular times. It may appear a contradiction in terms to talk about 'creative planning' since one might assume that to be creative one must be free to do as one pleases. This is not the case at all. Creativity has to be harnessed and managed. The communication has to position the product, company or brand for the target audience so that they know what it stands for, what it is for, whom it is for, and why they should be interested in it. Then creative work can begin to show, for example, benefits or the 'big idea'. There should be a development of a dynamic, creative communications concept that utilises all tools and techniques including brand personality (as discussed in Chapter 7 of this book), doing something different and even outstanding. Perhaps this means providing something that is visually or aurally arresting that becomes compelling viewing or listening.

Creative strategy development

Creative strategy is based on several factors:

- First, the identification of the target market must be made.
- Second, the basic problem, issue or opportunity the communication must address has to be identified.
- Third, the major selling idea or key benefit needs to be communicated.
- Last, any supportive information that is required should be included.

Once these factors are determined a creative strategy statement should describe the message appeal and execution style. This will necessarily include a copy platform or creative brief, i.e. the platform for creative strategy in the form of a document that underpins the rationale behind the message, the creative concept and execution. This written document thus specifies the basic elements of the creative strategy, including the basic problem or issue, communications objectives, target audience(s), the major selling idea or key benefits, a creative strategy statement and supporting details, encapsulating all important points. The USP, Brand Image (including the ESP, emotional selling proposition) and Positioning in relation to advertising and branding were discussed in Chapter 7 of this book. The creative 'Big Idea' will either:

- be rational (a Unique Selling Proposition);
- be emotional (Brand Image);
- deal with the position of the brand in the marketplace;
- deal with a mixture of these approaches.

Creative ideas can be arrived at by a variety of means from the use of free association and juxtaposition of ideas to form new ideas to convergent, divergent and lateral thinking in the search for new ideas. Brainstorming sessions, usually run in a focus-group way by a trained interviewer or psychologist, are another form of free association that can be used as a vehicle for arriving at new, creative approaches. These kinds of technique allow marketing people to produce 'rough roughs' – crude but effective drawings or computer-generated visuals – and also scripts and/or storyboards that help improve the communication process between company/organisation and agency/communications company. In many instances it is the creatives who develop such techniques. For example Catling and Davies (2002) report on the briefing given by Cadbury Schweppes to consider new toppings for ice cream. They proceeded by inviting lots of the eventual target (kids) to try the products out and listened to their views on what was 'ugh and what was yum' in order to get a new perspective on the product. In this way ideas can emerge from a process of generation to the selection/discarding and verification of final idea(s). As Hallward (2007) points out, the 'Big Idea' must 'undeniably involve the brand' and 'with strong brand integration'. This is a sentiment echoed by McKee (2010) who talks of wrapping brands around 'big, everlasting ideas', whether this be innovation (Apple), performance (Intel), savings (Wal-Mart) or motivation (Nike). McKee notes that the word used to describe the big idea may not be used in advertising and communications, as with Nike, but the idea will be embodied in the brand as in 'Just Do It', which is of course Nike's enduring strapline. It may not be, as McKee suggests, everlasting but it may certainly endure, as with the BMW example of 'The Ultimate Driving Machine' being brought back after a six-year 'rest'.

The 'Big Idea' is discussed below in terms of appeals. The creative sequence becomes:

STRATEGY
BRIEFING
OUTPUT

The contents of the brief should be just that – brief. This document should be a short account of:

- why the campaign is necessary;
- the objectives;
- the target(s);
- the main idea;
- the tone of voice;
- expected reactions of the target(s);
- production, traffic or media requirements.

This latter point might include ideas on, for example, 'triggers' (words or other useful devices) or facts. The brief should not be too prescriptive so as not to constrain too much the people who have to work on it.

The Snapshot below explores the nature of creativity and how changes to the understanding of this concept through the effects of the pace of technological change have occurred.

Snapshot   If creativity never stops or pauses does this mean that advertising is always a work-in-progress?

There are many definitions of creativity in advertising and marketing communications more generally. A relatively recent one comes from Shimamura (2013) who takes the reader back to the 1984 Super Bowl advertisement for the Apple Macintosh, effectively a short film depicting an 'Orwellian future' image (well, it *was* 1984) that is shattered by 'an emboldened woman who rushes up to the screen with a large sledgehammer, launches the weapon in hammer-throw fashion, and shatters the image of the dictator. Amazingly, the computer itself is never shown in the commercial'. Shimamura suggests that creativity is 'often described as moving against the flow of the standard or familiar'. If the 'flip side of familiarity is novelty then 'creative events – such as those commercials that turn our heads and become part of our living culture – can be viewed as moments that make us think and feel in new and refreshing ways'. Shimamura uses the 2013 example of Yahoo, whose creative strategy was to change the logo design each day until finally arriving at the new and permanent logo after a period of time, allowing the viewer to take notice of the change and allowing 'us to become accustomed to change itself'.

Another view is that of Tutssel (2013) who suggests that the 'marketing industry is at a zeitgeist moment' whereby creativity has been democratised and therefore the ways in which ideas are created and consumed have changed. This has been brought about through the (speed of) technological changes that have occurred in society generally but in particular in the marketing communications and especially the advertising industry. Tutssel maintains that brands are no longer competing against brands but against the whole of pop culture, with the resultant re-invention of the advertising industry from the inside out.

On the surface technologically-driven change means that many people (but by no means all) around the world are now online and have smart phones but there is a need to look more deeply than this to find real impacts. With creativity in marketing communications a key impact has been a move from professionals such as designers creating images and passing these down as a way of earning a living. As Tutssel suggests there has been a combination of technology and globalisation that has dramatically transformed 'our industry … Technology barriers prevented others from entering the creative game, ensuring we didn't have much to compete with in terms of content'. This meant that the industry image (and other things) creators had control. This has now changed and the industry has to change in order to deal with the interactivity and engagement on the part of the ordinary citizen that has seen the emergence of, for example, user-generated content.

Tutssel suggests that 'we are amazingly placed to benefit from these ever-changing technological, social and cultural shifts' and puts forward four tenets 'that together will set the benchmark for cultural communications'.

The first, cultural fluidity, suggests that creativity is 'rooted in compelling human insights and mobilised by technology'. Tutssel cites, for example, Dove's 'Real Beauty Sketches' as an example of a 'beautiful' idea that 'resonate[s] with people all around the world'.

The second, the democratisation of creativity, means that anyone can be creative and take part in the process whereby the 'means of production and the channels of distribution have been turned over to the masses. Every single one of us has access to a potential audience of millions on social media channels'. Control has to be relinquished and ideas re-imagined in order to 'reap the benefits of global participation'.

The third, the notion of being 'always on', means that there is a 24/7/365 world of constant activity whereby 'people are living their digital lives in real-time, so we're constantly consuming bite-sized content' and as a result 'we're seeing shorter and shorter pieces of online content' so that tools like Twitter's Vine mean that there is more capturing of real-time moments.

The fourth, global collaboration, means that 'remarkable possibilities have opened up' in terms of the ways in which organisations operate and 'ultimately deliver for our clients'.

Stop Point

Creativity is central to the advertising and marketing communications industry, has been from the start and will continue to be so. Undertake the following: 1. Discuss the notion that being allowed to view change can be part of the creative process in an advertising campaign; 2. Expand and comment upon Tutssel's four tenets of cultural communications.

COMMUNICATION APPEALS AND EXECUTION

Communication appeals

Having developed a creative strategy that clarifies what the communications should say, marketers and their agents need to decide how this message can be executed. An appeal refers to the approach used to attract the attention of consumers and/or influence their feelings towards a product, service or cause. The creative execution style refers to the way a particular appeal is turned into a message that can be presented to the consumer.

Creative strategy should strive to achieve successful communication. A number of approaches can be taken either individually or in conjunction with others, using the product/brand to explain and compare vis-à-vis the nature of the proposition and the competition. For example, a visual technique or some form of demonstration may be used to make clear and simple what would otherwise be a complicated proposition. The use of visuals to show liquid flowing into an engine (oil), a body (a heartburn remedy) or a washing machine (a liquid detergent) is commonplace. Direct comparisons with other, competitive brands are commonplace in the USA but less so in Europe. However, even in Europe, increasingly 'knocking copy' is being used to show a brand in comparison with that of a competitor. Comparison comes in other forms such as a 'challenge' or direct price comparisons. For example, in the UK the comparison might involve Tesco versus Sainsbury or Aldi versus manufacturers' brands rather than Tesco or Aldi simply declaring low or lower prices.

A before/after demonstration such as that for Head & Shoulders anti-dandruff shampoo or 'torture tests' using extreme examples to prove a product feature, such as strength, are commonly used. Very strong glue shown to be able to hold the weight of a man or machine is one example. Also the brand or product may be portrayed as a hero, where it is the star and is given an identity and personality as with, for example, Mr Muscle. Using people is common in communication. This can be either direct or indirect in its approach. The former uses a medium on a one-to-one basis, with someone talking directly to the audience. The presenter may be a celebrity, an unknown, an animated character or a puppet. An example of the use of this is in a selling situation or in advertising that uses a presenter where a testimonial is employed, usually underscoring a feature such as safety. The indirect approach involves techniques such as enacting a story as with the many slice-of-life/soap operas over time, such as 'The Oxo Family', British Telecom's (BT) long-running 'Adam and Jane family' and then subsequently 'Student' tribe, or the earlier Nescafé 'Couple'. The use of brand properties should result in identification with the brand, the difficulty being having the brand remembered and not merely the creative treatment such as a humorous sketch or the actor/comedian him-/herself. *Marketing Week* (2011) provides a reminder that if done well humour can be used, for example, in television advertising effectively. This may vary by sector. Health and beauty and food brands such as Heinz have had success with 'straight' advertising while car brands have used humorous advertising successfully. On balance, the jury may be out however. For example Tuttle (2012), writing in *Time* magazine, suggests that advertising that makes you laugh might not make you buy, i.e. funny advertisements can achieve the attention or likeability objective but ultimately the measure in most cases is whether or not sales, profit or market share have increased.

Types of appeal

There are a great many types of appeal that can be utilised by the marketer, but not every appeal is suitable for every occasion. Animation can make a brand come to life and a cartoon character can symbolise a brand or organisation. Kellogg's Frosties' 'Tony the Tiger' (www.frostedflakes.com/) is typical of this treatment and there are many others such as Green Giant (formally the Jolly Green Giant, part of General Mills, the US frozen and canned vegetable supplier: www.generalmills.com/Brands/Vegetables.aspx). Others include humour, shock and various devices that play on the emotions. At the broadest level, appeals are broken down into two categories – rational/informational and emotional. Involvement plays a vital role here where generally speaking the higher the involvement the more likely it is that the appeal will be rational, using product characteristics and subsequent benefits and information. Where low involvement is prevalent emotional and image-based appeals are likely to work, especially where there is hedonic consumer behaviour on display.

Emotional appeals are often referred to as 'soft sell' and include many techniques such as fear, humour, sex, music, fantasy and surrealism. These can be used to play on personal states such as safety and love or on social states such as status or rejection. Marketers use emotional appeals to produce positive feelings that cause a favourable evaluation of the brand in the mind of the audience. The negative consequences of an action or inaction can be presented in a 'fear appeal'. For example, a person may be perceived as being someone stranded in a flood-affected house but who has not taken out insurance. Fear can also be used with the threat of social rejection if the product is not used. For example a deodorant or sanitary protection products can be depicted as a heroic problem-solver – but the communication tells the viewer that if they do not use the brand the implication is that they could be in trouble. Fear appeals need to be used with caution since the recipient of the message will selectively screen out a message that is too strong and that causes cognitive dissonance as with, for example, anti-smoking or drink-driving campaigns. Humour is well known for its ability to attract attention and interest. It also creates a favourable and positive mood. However, ironically, the success of humour in doing this can detract from the message/brand, i.e. the humour works but not to the benefit of the brand. The comedian/celebrity used may be remembered and liked but the brand/brand name may be lost and not recalled or recognised. The trick then is to have successful humour that is associated with the brand. Sex is good at getting interest, and can be used more subtly or openly if in the guise of sensuality. Music of various denominations can be a psychological cue for gaining attention, enhancing visual images and generally reminding the target that the brand is still out there. Fantasy and surrealism have been used by, for example, Guinness to stimulate and interest the audience. This is particularly useful where the brand proposition is such an experience, for example, where the suggestion is one of a magical experience with Disney.

Rational appeals focus on the consumer's practical, functional or utilitarian need for the product/service. They often emphasise features and benefits and facts. In an informative way the message tries to persuade consumers to buy the brand because it is the best available at meeting their needs. Common rational appeals include: comfort, convenience, economy, health, touch, taste, smell, quality, dependability, durability, efficiency, efficacy and performance. Information appeals tend to be very factual where higher levels of involvement mean that information will be processed.

Combining rational and emotional appeals

Of course, many messages will contain both rational and emotional elements. Advertising for the brand Haagen Dazs is a classic example where, after specific public relations and sales promotion tools were utilised, the advertising campaign was launched in the UK using magazines as the main medium. On one side of a double page spread there was a sensual image of near naked couples embracing in erotic clinches but always with the brand in full view. On the other there were facts about the quality of the ingredients use to produce the super-premium brand, thus showing that emotion and reason could work well together. This echoed the words of David Ogilvy, who famously said that there should be no conflict between images and facts.

Communication execution
Ways to execute rational appeals

Rational appeals can be presented in a number of ways. They could be presented as slice-of-life where a problem is presented in a factual way together with the solution, usually the brand. Demonstration is another means to this end as is comparison with other products or brands, where appropriate technical features can be turned into benefits and a favourable price can be used as leverage. Other ideas include the announcement of new products, service or extensions in the range and this can, for example, give the audience reassurance of caring, inventiveness, quality, value or reliability. It may be that a simple straight or factual message or a straightforward presentation of information concerning the product/service is appropriate.

Ways to execute emotional appeals

Emotional appeals are more likely to be executed through other means such as animation, especially with children but increasingly more with adults since the advent of the 'adult cartoon' in television programming and other media forms. Also used are characters or personality symbols that might be represented by actors (for example the long-running but evolving figure of Captain Birdseye/Iglo as discussed in the Snapshot below) or cartoon characters such as Kellogg's Frosties' Tony the Tiger or the more controversial Kellogg's children's brand Froot Loops. Toucan Sam is the Froot Loops mascot and has been for decades in the USA, but is relatively new to the UK having only recently been introduced to the market in the summer of 2012 on a limited basis in the first instance, being more restricted by European legislation that requires different specifications to those for the US product, i.e. formulations vary, for example in the UK with sugar and salt levels and the requirement for natural colour and flavour that affect appearance and taste. Froot Loops was, in September 2012, removed from the UK market, apparently due to a lack of demand for the product. All manner of characters have been developed from people in costume (the Honey Monster for the Sugar Puffs brand of breakfast cereal, which for many years was owned by the Quaker Oats Company before being sold in 2006) and line drawings (for example Prudence from the Prudential). As Kemp (2007) points out, the Prudence character was famous for her red bandana, which stood out in the drawing and was created in 1986 to replace 'The Man from the Pru', only to be replaced by 'The Man from the Pru' in 1998, but then resurrected in 2007 to bolster its position in the retirement market for financial services. The Tetley Tea Folk can, these days, be found on Twitter (https://twitter.com/tetley_teafolk) and Facebook (www.facebook.com/TheTetleyTeaFolk). The Tetley brand of British/English/Yorkshire beverages is interestingly now part of the Indian-owned Tata Group but in the UK can be found at www.tetley.co.uk/. As Bold (2010) points out the cartoon images and characters that were dropped early on in the decade were brought back in 2010 with a £9m campaign. The animated Tetley Tea Folk were given a makeover and featured in a 'through-the-line campaign' that included television advertising. Seemingly the Great British Public loved the characters with thousands of demands for their return, and the key characters of Gaffer, Sydney and Tina included. The Disney-like animated stories, it seems, were dearly missed. Such stories fit well with family-time television viewing (see the Snapshot later on in this chapter on the Tetley Tea Folk).

Earlier stories involving the Tetley Tea Folk had suggested not only emotional bonding but also a rational appeal through the use of the strapline 'Lets the Flavour Flood Out', a reference to the tea-bag design that allegedly did what the strapline suggested. On an emotional level these devices can create interest for many low-involvement products but this is not always the case, as the Prudence example illustrates. Fantasy and surrealism are used in the execution, as with the now famous campaigns for Benson and Hedges cigarettes. Similarly drama, slice-of-life and demonstration can be used to deliver emotional appeals as well as rational ones.

The Snapshot below explores the Iglo brand Captain Birds Eye with origins in the use of an old sea captain as the main character that represented the brand for decades. It tells of the move to a different character, Clarence the polar bear, as the campaign became more one of education around the value of and benefits offered by frozen foods as more nutritious and healthier options than some fresh foods.

Snapshot   From sea captain to polar bear – the evolution of Clarence Birds Eye

During the 1960s the Birds Eye brand in the UK was beginning to be developed around its fish products, and by 1967 'Captain Birds Eye, the white-bearded seaman with a strong seafaring accent, became the Birds Eye advertising mascot' (Willis, 2010). Owners Iglo have not got rid of the Captain totally; the character has not been killed off in the UK and is still used in Italy and Germany where there have been other actors playing the Captain. In the UK the Captain was felt to be overly nostalgic and a fresh approach was needed – so enter Clarence, named after Birds Eye of course. The polar bear has been the centre of Birds Eye's marketing (television and digital) since 2010. Clarence appears in the home freezer 'to give advice on the benefits of frozen food and the quality of Birds Eye's range', and there is also the 'Give a Bear a Home' campaign, which includes an on-pack promotion and a digital TV ad that sees Clarence open the door of the freezer to find a toy version of himself (Baker, 2011). The 'giveaway' cuddly toy versions of the Birds Eye brand character follows in the successful footsteps of 'Comparethemarket.com, which is currently running a campaign to give away its meerkat characters' (Baker, 2011).

Fernandez (2010) reports on the £9m campaign in the UK, suggesting that part of the purpose of the campaign is to 'further educate consumers on the benefits of frozen vegetables that will also help 'rebuild trust in the frozen category and re-establish a benchmark standard by championing the quality of ingredients used in Birds Eye'. Birds Eye claims, 'for its family favourite lines: Fish Fingers that are made from 100% Fish Fillet, Chicken Dippers that are made from 100% chicken breast and Garden Peas that are 100% perfect'. There is a 'prominent 100% rosette''' on the pack and of course the straight-talking polar bear, Clarence will front it. Clarence is 'voiced by Hollywood actor Willem Dafoe', lives in the freezer, and is 'a big fan of Birds Eye. He will remind mums of the convenience, quality and taste that the brand provides'. Clarence is effectively railing against poor quality and according to Birds Eye the campaign aimed to lift the debate over the quality of frozen food generally. The campaign included television and radio initially and then extensive multimedia activity involving PR, direct mail, digital media, social media, display and promotional in-store materials (Fernandez, 2010).

This new approach has not all been plain sailing, however. Clews (2011) reports that part of the campaign has run into trouble for 'claiming its frozen vegetables contained more vitamins than fresh equivalents. The spring poster and press campaign showed a toy bear holding a clipboard seated next to a pack of Birds Eye Field Fresh Broccoli Florets. Text at the top of the poster stated "30% more vitamins than fresh vegetables. I've just read the research". The Advertising Standards Authority upheld five complaints that the ad was misleading and it could not be substantiated because the research it cited mentioned in small print on the ad, only studied vitamin C and so could not be applied to other vitamins'. The ASA justified its decision on the grounds

(Continued)

(Continued)

of breaking rules on health claims in terms of exaggeration, misleading and unsubstantiated claims: 'It also said Birds Eye should not make comparative claims between frozen and fresh vegetables in future as European rules on health claims forbid products being compared to products of a different category' (Clews, 2011).

The intention, according to Birds Eye, was to 'educate consumers about the health benefits of frozen food and directed them to further information about the study on its website' and later 'launched a new campaign featuring TV personality Myleene Klass ... to promote its fitness initiative "100% active"' (Clews, 2011). Ebrahimi (2013) suggests that the 'company has worked hard to shimmy its image from cheap and cheerful to "convenience" and "wellness", hence the demise of the dated old sailor who appealed to nostalgia' which is 'an emotion ... not that useful for winning over new generations of consumers'.

Stop Point

The Iglo Group has clearly done well in the past few years. The success in the past was helped with the advent of Captain Birds Eye and his various alter egos, but more recently in the UK by the introduction of Clarence the polar bear. Undertake the following: 1. Discuss the importance of being current and the reasons why Iglo decided, in the UK at least, to replace the Captain with Clarence; 2. Consider and comment upon the need at times to educate the market and in this instance about the process and benefits of frozen foods and the need to stay ahead in terms of brand essence and message strategy.

MESSAGE STRATEGY DESIGN CONSIDERATIONS

The message style

Linked to appeals is the design of the message. A consideration of the need to provide information or the use of pleasure and enjoyment in consuming the message should be made through an emphasis on rational or emotional appeals (or a combination of both). The amount and quality of the information that is communicated, and the overall judgement each individual makes about the way a message is communicated, have to be considered. Messages might be product-oriented and rational, or customer-oriented and based on feelings and emotions, or indeed both. As a 'rule of thumb' (a general rule) high-involvement decisions are likely to require an information emphasis – key product attributes and benefits – and low-involvement decision making requires the message to create images in the mind of the consumer and an emotional response. However, high-involvement decisions, although requiring an information search, might well have an emotional side and there may well be room for an emotional element within the message. Whichever, the more a receiver likes a message the more likely there is to be a positive response to it. Likeability then is linked to a favourable attitude or predisposition towards the brand or the organisation, which is a desirable state. To achieve this, the marketer is likely to choose some form of entertainment, for example humour, in order that the target likes the communication and hopefully the brand or organisation.

Message pattern

Messages can be designed so as not to cause problems or confusion for the audience. Conclusion drawing (as opposed to the audience interpreting what they want) can be considered. This is explicit rather than something implicit and will only work if the issue is complex enough to warrant it where the audience will welcome it, or if the audience education level is relatively low so that they will accept a conclusion. Better-educated audiences prefer to draw their own conclusions and less well-educated audiences may have to be told what to do, i.e. a need for conclusions to be drawn for them. The urgency of the situation may make it sensible to draw conclusions, but the level of involvement probably overrides most considerations since if a lot of information gathering is going on, this negates the idea of conclusion drawing. One- and two-sided messages can offer arguments for and against a particular benefit or issue.

A one-sided message, for example 'Guinness is good for you' or 'Philips, simply years ahead', will work to reinforce the brand on those who already believe in it, especially in situations where the targets are less well educated. These are messages that present just one argument, in favour of the product or issue. For example, Foster's Lager in the past has used several campaign straplines that are of this nature, such as 'Foster's, he who thinks Australian drinks Australian'. Latterly Fosters have been provided with the 'Good Call' campaign (featuring agony uncles Brad and Dan), which uses comedy and taps into what Foster's call a universal insight into the relationships between men and women (*The Drum*, 2012).

The two-sided message can be used when trying to explain and persuade. The target is likely to be better educated and willing to consider the argument, where the good and bad points of an issue are presented, and are more effective when the receiver's initial opinion is opposite to that presented in the message or when scepticism exists. With a sound argument, credibility is improved (Becker-Olsen, 2006) and a more positive perception of the source can occur. An example of the two-sided message is that of Domino's (pizza). Marafiote (2012) reports on the challenge to differentiate this brand from the rest in the US marketplace. By employing a two-sided message approach, Domino's managed to turn around a negative response to advertising brought about because of the brand's perceived product quality. As Marafiote puts it, customers were complaining that the product was like 'cardboard' and that it was 'mass produced, boring and bland', and even that 'microwave pizza is far superior'. Domino's response was to tell the brutal truth, that they had 'screwed up' and were 'trying to improve', and plead with consumers to 'give their pizza another chance. This not only provided a means to differentiate Domino's from the rest but also provided the all-important credibility that can be had from two-sided messaging. The problem, as Marafiote points out, would have been exacerbated had a one-sided 'new-improved' campaign been launched. The advertising was more believable because of the admittance of issues around quality. Three things are needed according to Marafionte: volunteer information; relatively easy context in terms of cognitive load; and the positive side of the message must be unique and meaningful to the audience.

The presentation order

The presentation order of points, issues or benefits is important. The *primacy effect* uses messages that make the strongest claim first, and therefore uses anti climax. This is the direct opposite of the *recency effect* where the strongest claim is made last, which uses climax. Generally speaking (although the approach usually depends on degree of involvement), personal communication techniques use the recency effect. This means that a persuasive build-up via argument allows the key selling point to be made at the end. Where fast attention grabbing is the goal, the use of key points at the start is more appropriate. The decision to place main points at the start or end of the message depends on the audience involvement. A low level of involvement will require an attention-getting message component at the beginning. For high involvement the audience will be interested enough in the information to stay with the message until the end, so building up to the key selling points can be very effective. Television advertising is more likely to involve the primacy effect; personal selling the recency effect. Repetition either within the message or the message as a whole has been proven to work but can be expensive and the danger is one of brand damage if the frequency of the message is too high. Music and jingles in particular have been used successfully within advertising and elsewhere. For example, existing songs and specially created jingles have been used in advertising and sometimes in-store by the international DIY and builder's merchant chain B&Q (owned by the Kingfisher Group) for a number of years, with pop songs such as *Our House* (by Graham Nash and performed by Hazel Tratt), *Let's Do It Together* (performed by Adelphoi) and *Your Love Keeps Lifting Me Higher and Higher* (performed by Pixie Lott) with a voiceover from Rob Brydon for the 'Unloved Rooms' commercial in 2013. Slogans and taglines/straplines similarly are used with frequency to work on the memory, often employing mnemonic devices such as rhymes and rhythms.

Source of the message

The importance of source credibility, attractiveness and power was discussed in Chapter 2 of this book and is part of the message strategy. The decision needs to be made about who will be the presenter of the message. For example it might be the organisation itself, a spokesperson, the CEO, or a celebrity. The key to source credibility is trust and the audience must believe the source and their motives. The key components to developing credibility/ trust are expertise, knowledge, motives, likeability and similarity to consumer. Often corporate or brand names will carry a good reputation so these are included as part of the source.

Message integration

Message integration is similar to the integration of IMC discussed earlier in Chapter 1 of this book in terms of 'the single voice' or the 'Gestalt', the whole being 'greater than the sum of the parts'. A marketing communications message can be made up of many components: the headline, copy, layout, illustrations or photographs, strapline/tag line, brand/organisation or logo. Obviously the better these components work together, the more likely it is that effective communication occurs. Thus the components of any message have to work together.

In print headlines (the words in the leading position that are read first and positioned to get attention) have to work with body copy (the detailed text with the key message). Visuals are often used to attract attention and support the headline and copy. They also make the message more interesting to the target. Layout refers to the physical arrangement of the elements.

With broadcast media there is usually an audio element. This may be in the form of a voice-over, or a presenter talking to the audience directly, or an indirect message carried through, for example, a 'slice-of -life'-type advertisement. Music can work to create positive emotions and mood. This can be associated with a brand and used as a background element in store or within an advertisement. Jingles are a variation from a more subtle background and mood-creating music, and are often used for low involvement type products or services. Jingles can become very much a part of the brand.

Advertorials and infomercials

Another device invented in order to escape message clutter is the *advertorial*, i.e. an advertisement plus an element of editorial. Obviously this would be a longer slot – say, for two minutes on television – that would not only advertise the brand but also combine it with a story. For example the viewer may be taken into the world of classical music with facts about the life and works of classical composers. Later in the piece the actual product on offer – a classical music compilation CD set – can be introduced, as can an extra CD at a special price. In this way the viewer is drawn into the message. This technique does bring into question the ethics of the use of such communication.

In a similar fashion the *infomercial*, i.e. information plus commercial, has been criticised as a potentially unethical way of doing business. Informercials are usually much longer pieces whereby the viewer is urged to 'pick up the phone', having been introduced to the product by way of demonstration and then urged to buy it, thus moving the viewer from zero information to purchase in a relatively short space of time.

Such techniques are linked closely to 'cooling off periods' where refunds, by law, have to be made within a given space of time.

The snapshot below discusses one of the tools that can be used as the spokesperson for the brand, the spokes-character, and how the Tetley Tea Folk first appeared in this role in the UK and were used for nearly three decades. The discussion tells how, after the Tata acquisition, the Tea Folk were then dropped for nearly a decade and reprised again for two years only to be dropped again, albeit not completely.

Snapshot   The spokes-character for the brand – why the Tetley Tea Folk came and went and came and went

Who are the Tetley Tea Folk?

The Tetley Tea Folk first arrived on television in the UK in 1973 in a campaign that expanded across a range of communication activities, including Tetley Tea Folk Collectables (a set of collectable Tea Folk figures and other related items), and lasted until 2001. The Tea Folk are a set of animated characters whose number includes two key characters, Gaffer and Sidney, and various supporting characters.

The end of the Tetley Tea Folk

Tetley began in Yorkshire, England, in 1837, and by 1856 had relocated to London as the Joseph Tetley Company. The first tea bag was launched in 1953. The company was bought by Indian tea giant Tata in 2000. By 2001 Tetley announced a change in the marketing approach to the Tetley Tea brand in the UK. At that point Tetley were unsure about the fate of the Tea Folk but shortly after that they were gone and replaced by a campaign aimed at younger tea drinkers which centred on the 'health credentials of tea' (Harmsworth, 2010).

Return of the Tetley Tea Folk

In mid-2010 it was announced that the Tea Folk were coming back. Tetley Tea in the UK is second in the marketplace to PG Tips, the number one Unilever tea brand. Unilever

(Continued)

(Continued)

have an established animated character called Monkey (a knitted sock monkey) who has a double act with comedian and actor Johnny Vegas. Later in 2010 a £9m through the line (including television advertising, digital, direct marketing and PR) campaign in the UK began with the 'reawakening' (someone spilt some tea) of the Tea Folk and their return to the factory where they are greeted with a degree of fame by the workers there. This was described as a 'nostalgic, emotional, tearjerker of a TV ad' (Harmsworth, 2010).

New products included Pure Green Tea and Tetley Pure Redbush. The Tea Folk characters received a makeover and were re-introduced after 10,000 enquiries 'from people demanding their return' (Bold, 2010). Once again the key television characters were Gaffer and Sydney, joined by major character Tina and regulars Archie and Clarence. The Tea Folk were thus introduced to what Tetley called 'a new generation of fans' (Burrows, 2010).

Tetley Tea Folk gone again?

O'Reilly (2012) reports that in 2012 Tetley Tea 'dropped its long-running Tea Folk brand ambassadors in a new £10m campaign that repositions its marketing to focus on championing quality time with friends and family'. Apparently the rationale for this has been to target a younger audience, who presumably live fast lives and where time is precious, with a message that resonates with them. This is seen as a move to modernise the brand and it 'includes a TV ad, created by Dare, which uses the strapline "Make time, make Tetley"', and Tetley 'will also become the first advertiser using Channel 4's catch up service 4oD's "Ad Pause" digital ad format, which serves up ads when viewers pause programmes … the ad will play more than 3 million times in the three month tenancy period on 4oD' (O'Reilly, 2012).

The Tea Folk, however, have not entirely left the building. They are still being used in the Tetley Tea range pack design and consumers, if they are inquisitive enough, can scan the QR code for more information about the product. Other activity includes radio and 'the creation of a Tetley Tea Table Book, which commemorates the brand's 175th anniversary and was developed in partnership with children's cancer charity CLIC Sargent and PR agency Emanate' (O'Reilly, 2012). The Tea Folk are also online in the UK on the Tetley Tea website at www.tetley.co.uk/ (but do not appear in other countries) and on Twitter, Facebook and the Tetley YouTube channel – https://twitter.com/tetley_teafolk, www.facebook.com/TheTetleyTeaFolk and www.youtube.com/user/thetetleyteafolk.

Stop Point

The Tetley Tea Folk have served the brand well over the years as spokes-characters for the Tetley Tea brand, but clearly the company felt a need to modernise the brand and have attempted this by tapping into the idea of precious time. Undertake the following: 1. Discuss how animated characters can be used in advertising for brands, whether for products such as tea, insurance services or mobile phones; 2. Consider and comment upon the broader communications mix and how such characters can work in different media and in different forms of communication such as PR or sales promotion, online or in traditional media.

Assignment

Complete the following tasks:

- Watch a series of current TV advertisements and analyse what you see with reference to objectives, source and style (whether rational/informational, emotional or both).
- Watch out for patterns, i.e. conclusion drawn, one- or two-sided order of presentation, primacy or recency effects.
- Look also for appeals being used, for example, via slice-of-life, fear, animation, humour, music, sex or fantasy.
- Now do the same with newspaper advertising.
- Now look at magazines in the same way.
- Review a selection of packaging and consider what the communication effects might be.

Think about the research opportunities within all of this and to what use could be put conventional research and less conventional research involving projective techniques.

Summary of Key Points

- Creativity is an essential factor in overcrowded marketplaces but tension can exist between creativity and effectiveness.
- It may be difficult or impossible to transfer creative ideas between contexts but unproductive creative ideas can be screened out. Creative ideas must be planned and managed. A good creative brief will assist in this.
- Creative appeals are used to attract attention and/or influence feelings, or indeed move the customer towards a particular behaviour.
- The product or brand and people can be used in the creative process so that brand characteristics, celebrities, reference group images and so on become an integral part of the process.
- Appeals are broadly either emotional or rational but a combination of the rational and emotional is not only possible but in many cases also desirable.
- There are many creative executions to choose from, for example the use of the surreal in an animated form.
- There are also design considerations such as conclusion drawing and one- or two-sided messages. The presentation order involves decisions on primacy/recency effects. Repetition, music, slogans and straplines are other considerations.
- The source of the message clearly has characteristics that can be invaluable.
- Message integration, as with IMC generally, requires a Gestalt-type approach with elements of the message working together.
- Advertorials and infomercials are alternative choices to get consumers to take action 'on the spot' but there is clearly an ethical and legal dimension to this approach.

Discussion Questions

1. Explain what you understand creativity to be. Discuss the idea that creativity can be planned and managed, using examples to illustrate.

2. Discuss the notion of planning and managing creative ideas against the notion of creative freedom.

3. Outline what you consider to be the important elements of a creative brief. Say why, using examples, it might or might not be possible to transfer creative ideas from one context to another.

4. Discuss the kinds of creative appeal that are available to communicators. Consider the usefulness of combining emotional and rational appeals in some instances. Illustrate your response with an example of one such combination.

5. Explain the range of creative executions available to marketers. Choose one such execution in particular and discuss its pros and cons in relation to a particular brand.

6. Examine advertising message design considerations and comment on tools such as conclusion drawing and one- or two-sided messages.

7. Examine the advertising message presentation order and discuss the notions of primacy and recency effects.

8. Creative decisions may include use of the source as part of the creative effort. Explain why this might be so and provide examples to illustrate.

9. Discuss the importance of the integration of elements of a message with particular reference to creative appeals and brand recall. Illustrate with examples.

10. Distinguish between the advertorial and infomercial. Using examples to illustrate, explain the advantages and disadvantages of their use.

Further Reading

Branchik, B.J. (2007) 'Pansies to parents: gay male images in American print advertising', *Journal of Macromarketing*, 27 (1): 38–50. http://jmk.sagepub.com/content/27/1/38
According to the author, images of gay men in US print advertising are a recent phenomenon. Such depictions date back to the mid-1990s but images of gay males can be found from the early part of the 20th century. The author adapts a framework for categorisation from work on the depictions of minorities in media to develop a chronological series of 25 print advertisements (1917–2004) that are then analysed in terms of one or more of the 10 criteria established for the study. The images were found to evolve over time. The authors place these in the four stages of targeted recognition, ridicule/scorn, cutting edge and respect, showing the link with US society's changing view of homosexuality. The study also shows the media's changing role in portraying gay men and also the media's relationship with the history of the gay community in the USA.

Keller, H. and Thackeray, R. (2011) 'Social marketing and the creative process: staying true to your social marketing objectives', *Health Promotion Practice*, 12 (5): 651–3. http://hpp.sagepub.com/content/12/5/651

The authors discuss health communication and social marketing that involves mass media and health-related products such as sun protection. The article is a brief but useful discussion on social marketing communication planning, especially the creative process, and health practitioners working with creative professionals to ensure that objectives are met through creative development and the execution of promotional messages and materials that stay 'on strategy'.

Moeran, B. (2009) 'The organisation of creativity in Japanese advertising production', *Human Relations*, 62 (7): 963–85. http://hum.sagepub.com/content/62/7/963

An ethnographic participant observation study is used by the author to look at how creativity is organised in this advertising context. The author suggests that advertising is produced on behalf of clients by a 'motley crew' of personnel from within and without the agency. The author uses the concepts of 'frame analysis' and 'art worlds' to analyse the symbolic space of the studio and the 'transformations' that occur in that space, but also the concept of 'field' that allows for a comparative analysis of the 'space possibilities' in advertising where different actors position themselves and clients' products. The author argues that creativity is used to establish power relations not only among the 'motley crew' of personnel but also among consumers by the process of positioning or re-positioning products conducted on behalf of the client by the 'motley crew'.

Philips, B.J. and McQuarrie, E.F. (2011) 'Contesting the social impact of marketing: a re-characterisation of women's fashion advertising', *Marketing Theory*, 11 (2): 99–126. http://mtq.sagepub.com/content/11/2/99

This article focuses on the prevailing view about fashion advertising being idealised. The gap between what is real and what is ideal is toxic to women's self-esteem according to the authors, who challenge what they call this 'ideological' view by means of empiricism through content analyses, a survey and interviews. The authors conclude that fashion advertising has been confused with different product categories and once fashion advertising is cleared of its 'ideological debris' there is an opportunity to extend marketing theory to account for a broader range of consumer responses with goods that cover 'taste' rather than fashion. The authors concluded, among other things, that women do not report negative emotions that might undermine their sense of self and instead respond positively towards fashion advertising.

Smith, R.E. and Xiaojing, Y. (2004) 'Towards a general theory of creativity in advertising: examining the role of divergence', *Marketing Theory*, 4 (1/2): 31–58. http://mtq.sagepub.com/content/4/1-2/31

This article is about advertising creativity and advertising effectiveness. The authors define what they mean by creative advertising in terms of an advertisement being divergent (novel or unusual) and relevant and the effects on consumer processing and response. A general theory should contain, in these authors' view, five primary areas – communication process, management process, social process, group process and personal process. The authors conclude that a conceptual understanding of advertising is needed before the creative goals can be achieved.

REFERENCES

Baker, R. (2011) 'Birds Eye creates polar bear toys', *Marketing Week*, 26 August. Available at: www.marketingweek.co.uk/birds-eye-creates-polar-bear-toys/3029614.article

Becker-Olsen, K. (2006) 'Music-visual congruency and its impact on two sided message recall', in C. Pechman and L. Price (eds), *Advances in Consumer Research*. Deluth, MN: Association for Consumer Research, 33: 578–9.

Bold, B. (2010) 'MCBD confirms the return of the Tetley Tea Folk', Brand republic.com, 23 August. Available at: www.brandrepublic.com/news/1024881/MCBD-confirms-re turn-Tetley-Tea-Folk/?HAYILC=RELATED

Burrows, D. (2010) 'Tetley Tea Folk return', *Marketing Week*, 23 August. Available at: www. marketingweek.co.uk/tetley-tea-folk-return/3017330.article

Catling, T. and Davies, M. (2002) *Think!* London: Capstone.

Chandler, D. (2007) *Semiotics – The Basics*, 2nd edn. New York: Routledge.

Clews, M.-L. (2011) 'Birds Eye rapped over misleading health claim in ads', *Marketing Week*, 17 August. Available at: www.marketingweek.co.uk/birds-eye-rapped-over-misleading-health-claim-in-ads/3029323.article.

The Drum (2012) 'Latest Fosters ad sees Brad and Dan take a call from Lucy in Manchester', 3 May. Available at: www.thedrum.com/news/2012/05/03/latest-fosters-sees-brad-and-dan-take-call-lucy-manchester

Ebrahimi, H. (2013) 'Martin Glenn, Birds Eye's "codfather", aims for frozen food sweet spot', *The Telegraph*, 7 January. Availanle at: www.telegraph.co.uk/finance/newsbysector/retailandconsumer/9277975/Martin-Glenn-Birds-Eyes-codfather-aims-for-frozen-food-sweet-spot.html

Fernandez, J. (2010) 'Birds Eye highlights 100% quality message in latest ad push', *Marketing Week*, 10 May. Available at: www.marketingweek.co.uk/birds-eye-highlights-100-quality-message-in-latest-ad-push/3013256.article

Hallward, J. (2007) 'The creative BIG idea must link to the brand … or else!', Lessons Learned in Evolutionary Marketing – Lesson No. 8, Ipsos ASI available at: www.ipsos.com/asi/sites/ipsos.com.asi/files/pdf/Ipsos_LL8_CreativeBigIdea.pdf

Harmsworth, A. (2010) 'It's a tea-jerker as Tetley tea folk return', *Metro*, 30 June. Available at: http://metro.co.uk/2010/06/30/its-a-tea-jerker-as-tetley-tea-folk-return-428710/

Kemp, E. (2007) 'Prudential plots return of Prudence character', *Marketing*, 11 July. Available at: www.brandrepublic.com/news/670282/

Kitchen, P.J., Kim, I. and Schultz, D.E. (2008) 'Integrated marketing communications: practice leads theory', *Journal of Advertising Research*, 48 (4): 531–46.

McKee, S. (2010) 'How to create better advertising', *Business Week*, 16 April. Available at: www.businessweek.com/smallbiz/content/apr2010/sb20100416_222501.htm

Marafiote, F. (2012) 'Dominos increases ad effectiveness with two-sided messages', 30 March, available at: www.fmwriter.com/2012/03/30/dominos-increases-ad-effectiveness-with-two-sided-messages/

Marketing Week (2012) 'Make 'em laugh – humour boosts the effectiveness of TV ads', January. Available at: http://knowledgebank.marketingweek.co.uk/monthly-insights/2011-jan.html

O'Reilly, L. (2012) 'Tetley brews £10m marketing push', *Marketing Week*, 9 August. Available at: www.marketingweek.co.uk/news/tetley-brews-10m-marketing-push/4003184.article

Pickton, D. and Broderick, A. (2005) *Integrated Marketing Communications*, 2nd edn. Harlow: FT Prentice Hall/Pearson Education Limited.

Schultz, D. and Kitchen, P. (2000) *Communicating Globally: An Integrated Marketing Approach.* London: McMillan Business.

Shea, Carol (2013) 'Harness the power of projective marketing techniques', Olivetree Research, available at: www.olivetreeresearch.com/sidebar/techniques.pdf

Shimamura, A.P. (2013) 'The creativity of advertising, media, and movies: got art?', *Psychology Today*, 28 August, available at: www.psychologytoday.com/blog/in-the-brain-the-beholder/201308/the-creativity-advertising-media-movies-got-art

Tutssel, M. (2013) 'Creativity without borders: 4 Trends and a new vision for global marketers', *Forbes*, available at: www.forbes.com/sites/berlinschoolofcreativeleadership/2013/09/06/creativity-without-borders-4-trends-and-a-new-vision-for-global-marketers/

Tuttle, B. (2012) 'Ha! Ads that make you laugh don't really make you buy', *Time*, 18 July. Available at: http://business.time.com/2012/07/18/ha-ads-that-make-you-laugh-dont-really-make-you-buy/

Willis, A. (2010) 'Birds Eye: a timeline and history', *The Telegraph*, 4 July. Available at: www.telegraph.co.uk/foodanddrink/foodanddrinknews/7867792/Birds-Eye-a-timeline-and-history.html.

Zakia. R.D. and Nadin, M. (1987) 'Semiotics, advertising and marketing', *Journal of Consumer Marketing*, 4 (2): 5–12.

Traditional Media: Characteristics and Planning

CHAPTER OVERVIEW

Introduction

In this chapter, the three broad areas concerning media characteristics, media planning and spend issues are addressed. The changes that have taken place in the media in recent times are immense. The Internet and other technology-driven media and influences are of course remarkable but the media themselves are not the only consideration as targeting and fragmentation has evolved. However, the characteristics of these media can be seen in sharp relief against the more traditional media types (see Chapter 10 of this book on digital technologies and media). The changing characteristics of target audiences have created even more challenges when matching media to targets. Planning media in a strategic fashion is addressed to a point that prepares the reader to be able to carry on with the more detailed aspects of media planning. Allocation and budgets are addressed in a theoretical as well as a practical manner.

Learning objectives

This chapter considers the nature of media characteristics and how media can be planned in relation to the amount of money available. More specifically, on completion of this chapter, the student will be able to:

- appreciate the nature and role of traditional media within marketing and marketing communications;
- explain the role of media planners and buyers;

- outline the media planning process and explain this in relation to other marketing communications elements;
- explain reach, frequency and weight of media and discuss the relationship between these;
- discuss scheduling in relation to cost and cost per thousand (CPT);
- explain the theoretical and practical approaches to allocation and budget setting.

THE CHARACTERISTICS OF TRADITIONAL MEDIA

In the 'medium is the message' assertion, McLuhan (1962, 1964) and McLuhan and Fiore (1967) suggested that different media can have differing effects on recipients. Over time, the effects of the media have changed as the move from the more passive to the more active, interactive or engaged recipient of messages has happened. Television in the past may very well have washed over audiences fascinated by the new medium and its stars of varying sorts depending upon type of programming. Advertising on television was particularly attractive and could lull consumers into consuming, or at least buying. Now (and without ignoring the technologically-driven media developments discussed in Chapter 10 of this book), although general interest magazines, newspapers and programming still have a place, special interest magazines, newspapers, television and radio programmes have evolved to meet the needs of specialist groupings that were perhaps once part of a mass audience. This gives rise to issues of duplication and repetition. The criteria for choice lie within the characteristics or qualities of different media and media vehicle types. Quantitative measures of how many of the target are reached are important. However, more qualitative measures as to how the media are consumed and the technical characteristics of the various media such as colour reproduction or quality of print have to be considered also. The various media at the communicator's disposal quite obviously have certain characteristics that were briefly discussed in Chapter 4 of this book under media strategy and tactics within the marketing communications planning model.

Wading through all of the various good and not so good points about various media can be pedantic but knowing the media is essential grounding in order to complete the real task of choosing the right media categories and vehicles. This necessarily includes the Internet and other digital means of delivering messages such as the ubiquitous CD or DVD. Those media at the cutting edge of technology can now be viewed in much the same way as previous generations viewed television, radio and print (see Chapter 10 of this book). A key question might be whether or not the idea of 'narrowcasting' (in essence effective targeting) is more achievable with these new tools. Another question is how much longer will it be before we have available to us a truly in-home multimedia environment? The various media are often selected for, for example, their geographical reach, the ability to dramatise or frequency of exposure.

The overall goal within this area is to devise an optimum situation for the delivery of promotional messages to particular target audiences. The structure of the media industry itself has changed, while there are obvious media specialists now there have been media independents since the 1970s. As advertising agencies mutated into the communication companies of today, one of the first changes was the creation of media companies and brokerages, the owners of which were often the old media departments of the larger agencies who decided to shed this function and to use such independents. As multimedia schedules became the norm, so too did computer software that could handle such complexities, but this has not seen the demise of the media buyer as a function as some had predicted. Organisations strive to be more effective and efficient in many other areas and this includes the media context (see Chapter 5 of this book on the structure and workings of the marketing communications industry).

The traditional electronic media

Television and radio

Traditionally the two main forms of electronic broadcast media have been television and radio. They are mass media that can reach large audiences at a relatively low cost per target. There has been a large growth in the number of electronic vehicles recently due to the development of cable and satellite television, and also the introduction of many more commercial radio stations (including online stations – see Chapter 10 of this book).

Developments in satellite, cable and digital transmission are here and still happening. As with advertising media there are problems but also opportunities. On the down side television's absolute (i.e. for the actual, say, 30-second spot) costs are high but relative (i.e. per contact) costs are low. Audiences have been encouraged in a way by the advent of the handset. There is a high level of repetition and the message has a relatively short life. There is also a lot of 'clutter' and fragmentation as the medium has gone through rapid change. On the plus side the medium is flexible, still has prestige (although some might say it is too prosaic now for this to be a characteristic), can allow dramatic effects and can have highly creative outputs. There is scope still to reach relatively mass audiences, with major soap operas reaching many millions, to more specialised programming with perhaps only a few thousand. Commercial radio was strongly regional in countries such as the UK. National and to an extent international coverage such as Virgin and Classic FM is now firmly secured. One of the down-side issues in the past was the perception that radio would not capture attention or would have a very big span of attention. It was thought that because it was not a visual medium it would be 'aural wallpaper'. Couple this with the low prestige of especially local radio and it is not surprising that radio was a much under-utilised medium, especially when no real national possibilities existed. However, on the up side, costs have been much less than television and radio offers international, national and regional coverage. It also provides the ability to target via programming such as 'drive time' or sports coverage slots. The realisation that radio's key characteristic is the use of imagination has made radio a popular choice for particular campaigns. Used cleverly it can become a visual (pictures in the mind) medium and not just background noise. It is also a portable medium that can be listened to in a variety of locations and is therefore both flexible and capable of involving the audience.

Other electronic media

With other electronic media interactivity is considerably higher and in many instances there are immediate responses. Targeting is possible and there are relatively low costs and a good degree of flexibility. On the down side there are often high set-up costs, poor security and slow developments (despite the pace of technological change) and targeting might be segment-specific in some instances. Developments online and with mobile technology are discussed in Chapter 10 of this book. Teletext and the facsimile (fax) machine are still available to marketers who can either keep in touch in a regular way with customers or use random messaging, but this technology is in danger of being perceived as obsolete as email has taken hold. The ubiquitous CD-ROM has an uncertain future but this is currently still an option, more likely in DVD form, for consideration when reviewing the various media and their qualities. The Internet and e-commerce is now here with the Web as the main commercial arm of the Internet. The number of users is now into billions, and its use in the business-to-business marketing context has until now outpaced that of the consumer. However, consumer e-commerce is catching up. There are still problems with security and also the cost of access, but there is no doubt that many things are going online so that through websites both the organisational customer and consumer can 'shop' for 24 hours a day, 365 days a year, anywhere in the world – or at least the cyber world. Direct sales, public relations and other marketing communication forms such as couponing as part of sales promotion are fast developing (see Chapter 10 of this book).

Other media

Direct marketing

Direct marketing of one form or another has been around for many years but in recent times, largely due to information technology and data handling, this kind of activity has grown considerably. Direct marketing (considered more closely in Chapter 12 of this book) includes direct mail, telemarketing, and direct response to press or broadcast media advertising and online. Where appropriate, more sophisticated interactivity will take place such as with satellite television advertising. Direct marketing is often used to make an offer then and there but can also provide more detailed information. This might be in the form of a reader/viewer offer with the media vehicle and marketer sharing profits. In this case no charge for space taken would be made but the marketer would, of course, supply the product. It has been successfully used in many integrated campaigns but on the down side it has been associated with 'junk mail', i.e. unsolicited and often unwanted mailings viewed as rubbish to be 'binned' (often unopened) by recipients. If used properly through good database management then it can be a very cost-effective way of maintaining contact with customers. The same logic applies to telemarketing where prospecting calls can be viewed as 'junk calls' if they are not relevant to the recipient or indeed interrupt them at inconvenient times. This is different from calls from prospective customers who respond to the marketer's stimuli via the telephone when it is convenient for them so that they can place an order or gather information. Again, the same logic applies to email.

Print media

Despite the impact of the Internet and online and mobile activity, newspapers and magazines are still popular, although it is clear that the traditional printed newspaper generally is in trouble with some commentators predicting a slow but inevitable death. Branding, however, is strong and behaviour often habitual. Here the classic lifestyle activities, interests and opinions can be clearly seen. Magazines in particular reflect interests and lifestyles so that targeting can be very accurate, allowing marketers to understand the characteristics of the target and work on this through advertising, editorial (where effective PR and press relations are at work) and offers and other sales promotions such as competitions. Generally, the printed word allows for detailed explanations, and the supply of facts and figures if appropriate, which can be particularly useful where there is high involvement. From a PR perspective, editorial in print has high credibility among readers of newspapers and magazines, the logic being that if a reader buys and trusts a particular periodical, then he or she will trust any PR-based write-ups or feature articles.

Newspapers have a wide reach and high coverage and are of course national and regional vehicles, and while many are published daily some are weekly or Sunday newspapers. The reader controls the speed of consumption and chooses what they want to read and ignores other parts of the paper in the time frame that they dictate. Detailed information can be provided and coupons used at a later time. Newspapers have short lead times, usually a day or two, and now most offer colour, different sizes of adverts and varying placements, for example back page. On the down side they are disposable, often only skim-read and have a very short life span, therefore exposure can be at best a fleeting glimpse. There is much clutter and newspaper can often end up with poor reproduction and this can lessen impact or even damage the brand.

Magazines, especially hobby, lifestyle or special interest (SIMs), usually have targets with a high attention regarding what is on offer. There are titles targeted at male and female readers and other targets such as the lesbian and gay community. As well as SIMs there are general interest magazines, or GIMs, that appeal to a wider spectrum of reader. Visually, the quality of magazines is usually very high. Certainly with the 'glossies' this is deliberately so to offer the quality required by advertisers such as Chanel or Boss. This might be less appropriate in other contexts but generally with good-quality paper and colour print the norm. Magazines have longevity, i.e. a much longer shelf life than newspapers and readership is usually higher than circulation, i.e. there is more than one reader per copy. On the down side lead times are long, namely weeks or months as opposed to days. Special editions are common. With business-to-business magazines there is often an edition tied to a particular event, such as a trade show at a particular time, and space has to be booked well in advance. Using inserts may help this situation but although most magazines offer little wastage in terms of hitting the target, absolute costs can be very high, especially with consumer magazines. It would be wrong to assume that magazines are a visual-only medium since sampling has been successfully done, especially for perfumery but other products too, for a number of years now so that the tactile nature and other qualities of the product or brand can be conveyed.

Out-of-home media

This category is now very wide with many media and vehicles including cinema, billboards or poster hoardings, transport (outside as well as in), in-store promotions, shopping trolleys, parking meters, window displays, sports arena and sports apparel, banners from planes and projections onto buildings. Apart from cinema these media are mostly used as support media to other lead media such as television. Out-of-home media can provide triggers that jog the memory by using short, simple messages.

The characteristics of cinema can be very similar to those of television but it is an out-of-home medium. Therefore, recipients of any marketing communications (in particular advertising of course) will have selected a particular cinema and a particular film, possibly in a social setting but certainly a context that has a different atmosphere, mood and other qualities. The creative impact of cinema advertising can be extreme in comparison to the 'box' (still a nickname for television despite technology bringing much larger and flat screens into the home and into pubs, cafes and other outdoor events, especially for sports). Darkened auditoriums, large and wide screens and stereo or even surround sound; the advent of some of these cinematic qualities as part of home viewing is also here with, for example, surround sound and in effect mini-cinemas available.

Outdoor media such as posters are limited in scope but have high reach and frequency, low cost, good coverage nationally and regionally, and provide targeting opportunities. They also have a 'poor relation' kind of image in comparison with other media, long production times and impact is difficult to measure. Transport media have high length of exposure and low costs but biased recipients of messages since many are travellers of one sort or another. There is also a lot of clutter around such media. In-store opportunities are numerous including shelf screamers and point-of-purchase. These are inexpensive and flexible and can be persuasive and attention grabbing. However, if not done well they can cause damage to the retailer and manufacturers' brands, especially if they appear tatty and cluttered. They are also biased towards shoppers as might be expected in the context in which they are used.

The Snapshot below discusses the influences of technological change and the pace of that change on the way people consume news and seek and access information. The question on the fate of traditional news print, especially newspapers and, to an extent, magazines, has been a perennial one for the last few years. The fate of traditional news print is discussed in relation to a number of different titles.

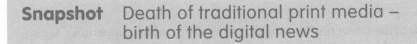

Snapshot Death of traditional print media – birth of the digital news

More and more news and information is being delivered by different means and often free of charge. Newspapers 'need to deliver something that is distinctive', especially with the constant arrival of new, digital means of obtaining news and information. People will 'pay for news if they think it has value. Newspapers need to focus relentlessly on that' (*The Economist*, 2010).

Dead by 30? *USA Today*

Gillin (2012a) suggests that the relatively young, 30-year-old *USA Today* newspaper is in danger of dying young as 'columnists are wondering if it'll see 40. Or even 35'. Commentators in the industry think this lifespan has had three stages:

- Growth and massive disruption – *USA Today* 'challenged many of the industry's assumptions about how and what people wanted to read'.
- A decade of prosperity, 'when *USA Today* became the most widely circulated newspaper in America'.
- A decade of decline, with competition from *The New York Times* and *Wall Street Journal* and with 'changing reader habits and all the economic pressures that have hit the industry'.

USA Today was innovative and recognised changing audience needs. It was targeted towards business travellers, in line with an explosion of deregulated air travel. Advertising revenues came from this source and the hotel and hospitality sector. *USA Today* was first in this, but inevitably, it was not to last. Online activity also started competing with print, for example with sports coverage: 'Even *USA Today*'s once-prominent full-page weather map is now an artefact, thanks to smart phone apps' (Gillin, 2012a). Another problem was the drift towards almost free distribution via hotels which might have damaged *USA Today*'s image in relation to its two main rivals.

So, despite being innovative and anticipating 'many of the changes in reading habits that other newspapers grudgingly adopted … their reluctant move toward shorter stories, more graphics and full-color production', which Gillin suggests 'probably staved off the industry's decline by a few years', *USA Today*, according to industry commentators, may find it hard to survive. Gillin adds that *USA Today*'s continuance with its free access online via its websites and its resistance to the paywall trend is problematic, especially when combined with the long-term decline in advertising revenue: 'it's hard to believe that free will be a virtue in a crowded market. Unfortunately, *USA Today* may have little choice. If more people are willing to pay $2.50 for a copy of the *Times* or $2 for the *Journal*, then it's hard to imagine that a paid website strategy will get much traction.'

The fate of *Newsweek*

The example of *Newsweek* going out of print in 2012 after 79 years is reported by Gillin (2012b). December 2012 was the last issue in print, with a digital format in place

(Continued)

(Continued)

from 2013 onward. In the USA only *Time* magazine remains, other competitors having already gone. *Newsweek* has had different owners recently and has seen its circulation fall by more than half from 'over 3 million to 1.4 million'. Again, changing the brand's offering did not apparently help the situation. According to Gillin, the editor 'tried to enliven the print magazine with provocative tactics like a July 2011 cover depicting what Princess Diana would have looked like at age 50, but some media observers thought the racier fare was out-of-step with the magazine's buttoned-down tradition'. At the same time the US magazine industry is not necessarily a bad place to be. According to Gillin there has actually been 'a resurgence over the last three years, with revenues growing modestly and print start-ups exceeding closures by a three-to-one margin in 2012'. On the surface it would appear that *Newsweek* has been a victim of the 'death of newsprint', but this is not the case and it would seem that the situation has simply not been well managed. Gillin (2012b) stated that while *Newsweek* would still be printed for a while outside of the USA it would, by the end of 2013, be fully digital, and 'subscribers will next year find ... the all-digital *Newsweek Global*, with a single, worldwide edition that requires a paid subscription'.

Stop Point

There is no doubt that technology is changing the way people gather news and information. More importantly the pace of technological change is, at times, breathtaking. From a marketing perspective, consumers' consumption habits are central. Undertake the following: 1. Examine and comment upon how news and other information are being gathered and consumed today; 2. Consider and discuss what newspapers and magazines may have to do to survive and even thrive against this backdrop of constant and continual technological innovation and change.

MEDIA PLANNING

Traditionally up to 90 per cent of appropriation was spent on buying actual space or slots (Donnelly, 1996) but more latterly, with online and other digitally-driven activities on the rise, traditional media space has declined in favour of the adoption of these newer forms (see Chapter 10 of this book). Choosing appropriate traditional media, however, is of crucial importance. There clearly is a link between marketing activity and media planning i.e. from marketing planning down a hierarchy to media and creative planning (see Chapter 4 of this book for the marketing communications framework that includes media choice and planning).

Role of the media planner

Armed with the characteristics information as described above, the planner has to decide which media are feasible, pick the main medium and decide how it should be used. He or she then has to decide on support media based on:

- creative suitability (such as the ability to dramatise);
- experience of effectiveness;
- availability and lead time (long/short copy deadlines);
- regional availability;
- the competition (where do they advertise);
- the effect on trade and the sales force;
- audience coverage;
- cost per thousand (a key measure of the costs of opportunity to see an advertisement).

Media planning is therefore about matching the media to the target audience after careful consideration of many things but especially audience characteristics. International campaigns are shaped by strategy, i.e. whether the multi-local or global (or something in between) approach is taken. For a number of years international media vehicles such as the *International Herald Tribune*, the *Wall Street Journal*, *Time*, *Fortune*, *Newsweek*, *Readers Digest* and *Cosmopolitan* – to name but a few – have been available to marketers, even if some have been English only. In short the planner has to understand the media planning process through to evaluation and within this must intertwine creative and media work.

For many years now the marketer has had to consider 'zapping' (the 'do they watch or make a cup of tea' debate) as a major problem that may be solved by the creation of striking, strong advertisements that will gain and hold attention and break through the clutter. The number of television sets per household, time-shift viewing and zipping along video tape (and now DVDs) are currently still a problem so it is up to the creatives to solve problems if they can. There is also concern for things such as changes in media technology, the development of mass markets, the standardisation of brands, and changing life styles of consumers. This adds up to the central dilemma of narrowcasting, i.e. using highly selective media for special target groups. For example, MTV was launched more than three decades ago and is now an international commercial channel that carries advertising. It has a target audience of 12- (originally 14-) to 34-year-olds and is therefore to some extent an opportunity for international if not global narrowcasting, especially since within this age band further refinement can be made. For example 15-to 17-year-old young adults can be targeted through particular programming within MTV.

Reach, frequency, gross rating points, placement and cost of that placement are all important and are discussed more fully below. These quantitative measures are relatively simplistic, but not virtuously so. Many practitioners now believe that these are not enough on their own for effective media planning and are using focus groups to help understand target audience behaviours and consumption more fully – the simple notions of how many of the target audience (reach) and how many times (frequency), which if multiplied together provide a measure of weight of advertising expressed in gross or television rating points. The costs of reaching that many of the target audience, usually expressed in cost per thousand (CPT or CPM), are of little use on their own. Typically, for example, creative content has an effect on advertising effectiveness and would have to be weighted in some way to be entered into any calculation. This is clearly problematic. Audience duplication is another problem that needs to be addressed.

Role of the media buyer

There is a view that the roles of the media planner and buyer have been diminished by the introduction of even basic software. A counter view is that the role has merely changed because of the increased use of technology and is just as important as ever, if not more so. Media costs can be extremely high. Buyers must be aware of how to reach target audiences via the best and most advantageous media, negotiations for favourable rates, size, length and frequency. The buyer must also be aware of traffic and production, artwork, scripts and associated deadlines. Timings have to be controlled; for example printing from artwork. Supporting publications for wider coverage and experience of such media are also important considerations. In short they should be able to choose the channel(s) of communication that can give the message the best chance of being clearly expressed. The marketer will want to communicate to as many of the selected audience as possible at the lowest cost and eliminate the problems of judgement via supporting facts and figures. Buyers therefore must have information, authority, respect and persistence.

Situation analysis for media decisions

Media planning is a central part of communications (and particularly advertising) management. Media planning decisions are influenced by a number of factors in the marketing environment as expressed in Figure 9.1 below.

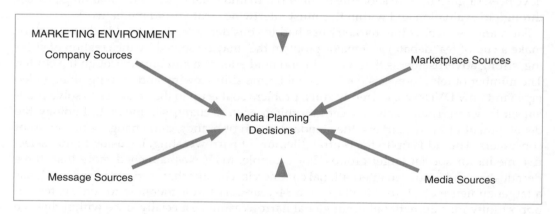

Figure 9.1　Marketing environment factors that influence media planning decisions

Taking each of these in turn:

COMPANY SOURCES – an understanding of the company in terms of, for example, targets/prospect profiles, purchase cycles and distribution patterns and so on. Clearly it is important and even necessary to know the target audience early on in order that matching with readership/viewing/listening profiles can take place.

MARKETPLACE SOURCES – an understanding of the marketplace, for example, monthly sales (past and projected), sales areas or rival advertising.

MESSAGE SOURCES – knowing what to say and how, through, for example, knowledge of themes, copy platform or levels of awareness derived from research.

MEDIA SOURCES – knowing the media. This is an industry in its own right led by research companies such as Nielsen and Taylor Nelson Sofres (TNS) globally and in the UK by, for example, the British Audience Research Board (BARB) that operates a 5,000+ strong sample with 'Peoplemeter'. The British Market Research Bureau (BMRB) has a 24,000 strong sample in the UK with TGI (Target Group Index). The figure for TGI worldwide is nearly ¾ million people in 60 countries. Many media companies and agencies such as Nielsen Media Research help clients understand advertising expenditure. Media sources involve more than broadcast media and older instruments are still used; for example telephone and face-to-face surveys and also diaries. Increasingly this kind of research, like a lot of marketing research generally, is being conducted electronically and online. With print media in particular the ABC (Audit Bureau of Circulations (www.abc.org.uk/) service is highly valued in order to be best placed to find the best place and time when the audience are likely to use the message (often called the aperture or window of opportunity). The net result is that good use of media sources puts the marketer in the position to be able to say what their audience profile is. It may be that 70 per cent of ABC1 men watch a particular programme but only 3 per cent of C2DE men watch the same programme. This kind of analysis is only possible with good media source information.

Objectives

Reach involves the opportunity to see (OTS), sometimes referred to as exposures or impressions, and this helps advertisers to measure how many people have a chance to view the advertisement but does not indicate how they react to it. This is usually measured in a four-week time period. There are complications regarding multimedia (most examples given in textbooks are of the single media vehicle variety for simplicity, as illustrated below) and duplication. Also, placement is very important whether this be different times of day for a TV channel or within a magazine or newspaper. When the goal is cognitive (attention/awareness) then the reach objective will be high and therefore an attempt to minimise duplication will be made. When the goal is affective it may not be possible to achieve the same level of cover because of costs. A simple example of reach is that if 70 per cent of the audience of 10 million viewers that watch a particular news programme are ABC1 men, and if 9 million ABC1men exist in a particular market, then 78 per cent of the target can be reached, (see Figure 9.2).

$$\frac{\text{No. of target viewers}}{\text{Size of target market}} = \frac{7}{9} \times 100\% = 78\%$$

Figure 9.2   A simple example of reach

Put another way, 78 per cent of the ABC1-men market can be covered using advertising around such programming. Reach will always be lower than coverage unless the universe is reached, i.e. 100 per cent of the target. The marketer can build towards achieving this but often through repetition and duplication where a complex media and media vehicle mix may exist. It may be possible to reach 100 per cent of the target but the marketer has to ask the question 'At what cost?'. *Effective reach* in the end must be measured not just in OTS or exposures but also, at the very least, awareness of the message. A way to tackle this issue is to think in terms of gross versus net reach. With the former a person will be counted twice and with the latter only once. As a simple illustration let us suppose we have two media types that overlap as illustrated below in Figure 9.3.

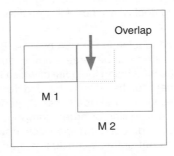

Figure 9.3   A simple illustration of gross versus net reach

The first medium, M1, and the second, M2, have a common overlap area O. Gross reach and net reach can be expressed as shown in Figure 9.4.

Gross reach, GR = (M1 + O) + (M2 + O) where a person in the overlap area would be counted twice.

Net reach, NR = M1 + M2 + O where a person in the overlap area would be counted only once.

Figure 9.4 Expressions of gross and net reach

Effective reach is generally accepted to be achieved between 3 and 10 OTS (and exposures/impressions) during this four-week period (Murray and Jenkins, 1992, but see frequency below). As usual cost considerations dominate and the use of television may well deny this number of exposures in a schedule. However, consideration of reach in this way coupled with effective targeting can improve the efficiency and effectiveness of reach. A large reach can be had using television but in terms of the target specialist magazines may be more effective. De Pelsmaker et al. (2004) cite Morganstern's B-coefficient analysis, suggesting that different media require a different number of exposures to achieve the same levels of memorisation where the lower the co-efficient then the higher the number of exposures. It is suggested that cinema has a B-coefficient of 70 per cent, requiring only two exposures, whereas radio only has a coefficient score of 5 per cent and requires 5–14 exposures in order to achieve the same level of memorability.

Frequency involves the ideas of 'wear-in', i.e. starting with one exposure and building more, and 'wear-out', whereby the optimal number of exposure has been achieved and wastage is occurring. Frequency therefore deals with how often, or the number of times, the target audience is exposed in that period on average. There is no real consensus in this area as to what is best. Over-exposure is seen both as a waste and potentially brand damaging. The target might read the cost of frequent exposures as being paid for by them, in the price of the brand. Under-exposure is seen as ineffective in achieving objectives and moving people. Repetition can be beneficial but only in a balanced way. The deliberate repetition of some advertising is so that the audience sees the message more than once. Effective frequency is a measure of the number of times the target needs to be exposed in order to achieve the objective and several practitioners/writers have estimated this. A key question therefore is 'How many exposures do we need to achieve our objectives?', the answer to which will depend on the nature of the objectives within a particular marketing context. Below are three examples:

- *Krugman (1972)*. Krugman estimates that three opportunities to see is the optimum, with the first providing understanding as to what is being advertised, the second relating to recognition and what the communication means, and the third stimulating some form of action. Krugman's upper limit is apparently 10 exposures, anything beyond being wasteful. Krugman's 'rule of thumb' of three exposures is one to get over 'what it is', two to deal with 'what of it', and three to 'remind'. This is still only dealing with opportunities to see.

- *Naples (1979)*. Definitive work conducted in the USA by Lever Brothers via Naples concluded that the optimal frequency of exposure must be three – one exposure having no real lasting effect, two being the threshold, and the third being the point at which the advertisement has the greatest effect. After that the advertisement can be effective but at a decreasing rate so that three becomes the benchmark. This led Naples to the 'S' shape curve. Opponents argue that other factors such as the residual effects of other advertising or brand/company image mean that advertisements have an effect immediately, rise to an optimum, then slow down, producing a convex curve. The one clear message that comes out of this inconclusive area is that frequent exposure brings positive results.

- *Jones (1995).* A diversion from this consensus comes from Jones with his Short Term Ad Strength (STAS) scan data approach. This contends that in the short term, rather than advertising for longer-term brand building, advertising can be used to get sales. The effect may be small and temporary but enough to warrant the expenditure on advertising rather than a potentially brand-damaging sales promotion tool. Here the first exposure is the greatest part of sales, therefore the most effective frequency is one. After this the impact gets smaller so that it is uneconomic to use heavy bursts because of diminishing returns. The recommendation is to have a low frequency over a longer period. Critical to this is the idea of the STAS differential. This is the difference between market shares achieved with and without the exposure and this must be large enough to justify the frequency of one.

Average frequency refers to the number of times a target is exposed to an advertisement over time within a schedule (see Figure 9.5).

10% of the target is exposed 10 times so this equals	100
25 % of the target is exposed 7 times so this equals	175
65% of the target is exposed 1 time so this equals	65
Total	340

Figure 9.5   The average frequency of exposure to an advertisement

The average frequency of exposure in this scenario would be 3.4. The use of average frequency figures can be misleading since it is clear from the example above that nearly two thirds of the target would have been exposed or, worse still, had the opportunity to see the advertisement only once. Added to this is the complex nature of most scenarios where unwanted duplication has to be accounted for.

Weight is how much the target is exposed in a given period and is the product of reach and frequency. This is usually expressed in rating points. This in reality is not discrete but involves complex viewing, listening and reading habits, and therefore effects on consumption can only be established through the use of qualitative research.

Typically a rating will be assigned a monetary value and this has to be added to production and commission costs. Television Ratings (TVRs) are a percentage of households tuned in to a specific programme (see Figure 9.6 below).

$$TVR = \frac{\text{number in target TV households tuned} \times 100}{\text{total number of target TV households}}$$

$$TVR \text{ for news programme} = \frac{7}{9} \times 100 = 78 \text{ i.e. } 78\% \text{ coverage}$$

1 TVR = 10% of all TV households in an area tuned in to a specific programme, here the news programme, therefore the news programme has a TV rating of 780 i.e. 78 x 10 = 780.

$$\text{Cost per TVR} = \frac{\text{absolute time cost}}{TVR}$$

If the cost of the slot is £100000 then cost per TVR is $\frac{100000}{780}$ = £128 (CPTVR = £128)

Figure 9.6   A simply example of television ratings (TVRs) costing

Another measure that can be applied is the combination of CPTVR + CPT to combine the two measures and form a bridge. The higher the rating then the higher the cost of the slot will be.

If there are a number of targets and one target does not get exposed, this means only a percentage is reached. If the average frequency is 3.4 this yields 310 (rounded) Gross Rating Points that are the sum of all vehicle ratings in a media schedule. This figure is of course gross and usually takes into account the whole audience and not necessarily the target audience, but this could be done in terms of target rating points (TRPs). This coupled with the point made above under reach regarding objectives might present the planner with a superior choice even though less rating points are provided because the frequency is higher. Cumulation is a result of the first impact being potentially more powerful than the next, where effective as opposed to empty reach is important.

The average rating is said to be 400. A burst campaign with 8 OTS might be designed to gain 85 per cent coverage. The rating would then be 680. This might be considered heavy, but would not be unusual if the campaign had the prime objective of gaining awareness. The notion of recency might be an almost diametric opposite stance. Messages might be targeted at those who are known to be in the market and are prepared to buy and may be running out of stock/products. In this case reach is of more importance than frequency and the objective would be to reach as many of these as possible in as many weeks as possible. This would then lead to a low weekly weight and a long, continuous campaign with frequency spread.

The complexity of what appears to be a simple scenario should not be underestimated. Some useful points are:

- The atmosphere and environment surrounding the vehicle. Editorial tone, experience, credibility of journalists and prestige are all of importance. Two very similar-looking magazines such as *Cosmopolitan* and *Marie-Claire* are different in some way or other. Different market versions of the same magazine will be different by the same logic, i.e. the environment will be different for *Marie-Claire UK*, *Marie-Claire Malaysia* and *Marie-Claire France*.

- Repetition is beneficial because it helps to limit brand switching and aid believability in the brand. It works through top-of-the-mind awareness and if done properly can be a cue for brand quality. If not, then repetition can be a costly way of damaging the brand.

- Technical and reprographic characteristics. This involves the usual characteristics of colour, movement or sound but also whether, for example, there is front page, back page, or particular slots available on TV.

- Vehicle fit. Where a complex audience profile exists it may be difficult to match with just one vehicle. Here the marketer might think in terms of segmentation bases so that some of the target is reached through demography, some through psychographics and some through product usage, or a combination of bases.

- The nature of the product. Clearly some products automatically match particular media and vehicles. Major consumer brands are well suited to peak-time viewing of soap operas and situation comedies. Indeed this is the starting point of the 'advertisers control programming' debate. It is argued by some that television programmes, for example, have to be 'dumbed down' in order to match the ordinary everydayness of consumer products such as toilet rolls. In this way major players such as Procter and Gamble control television output.

Media scheduling

Scheduling is linked to whether or not objectives are short, medium or long term, and achieving these is linked to the frequency of exposures as discussed above. Because of the cost there are problems with the frequency of advertisements. Methods of scheduling are illustrated below.

There are two basic strategies to consider when deciding upon schedules, which can be adjusted in a number of ways. These are *burst* and *drip* as illustrated below in Figure 9.7.

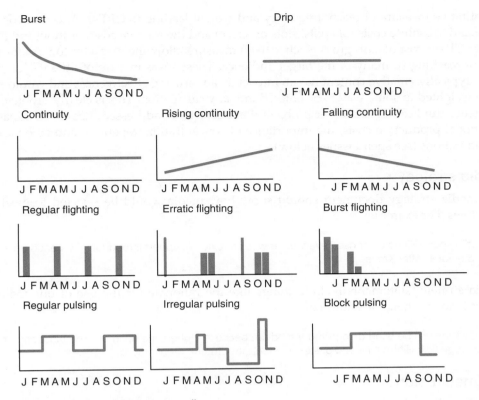

Figure 9.7 Methods of scheduling media

A burst at the start of a campaign means there is a requirement to achieve high reach, making as many of the target aware of the brand but frequency in particular media relatively low. As the campaign progresses less reach but increased frequency may be required, through a much more continuous, regular drip or continuity campaign.

Certainly this would be the case with more mature products, especially cash cows, where regular maintenance is required. Rising or Falling Continuity may be employed when the campaign is linked to an event, such as a cup final or marathon where scheduling builds towards it in a controlled, continuous way, or indeed away from it, with the dissemination of information on the product, product modifications and so on. Flighting may be chosen when the marketer wants to use resources over a longer period but not all of the time. Flighting may be erratic, regular or used in a burst-like way for the start of a campaign. Schedules will often be constructed around the idea of pulsing, which is a combination of continuity and flighting where there is a constant presence coupled with the occasional flight or pulse. Flighting is a flexible way of dealing with seasonality and other such issues and may be regular, irregular or blocked.

Costs

Media and media vehicle selection and the choice of other forms of communications in the mix are governed, or at least tempered, in the main by cost. Since many media forms have witnessed fragmentation, this has made it more difficult to generate consistency. Placement and the cost of that placement are important regarding relative simplicity. However, it is not a case of simplicity being a virtue necessarily. As mentioned earlier, focus groups are now used to help understand targets more fully, rather than simply rely on the aforementioned quantitative measure of reach, frequency and weight leading to GRPs/TVRs and cost per thousand. Absolute costs (of spots, slots or space) and the relative cost per thousand (CPT, where CPT = cost of slot/gross reach x 1000) measure allow the marketer to work out the cost of reaching so many of the target audience. These measures are of little use on their own. Typically, creative content has an impact on advertising effectiveness and would have to be weighted in some way to be entered into any calculation. This is clearly problematic. Audience duplication is another problem that needs to be addressed. Loss of domination, additional production costs, the importance of concentration, repetition and so on are all considerations (see spend issues below).

Media strategy

The media strategy document should show how media would be selected to meet the objectives. For example:

> 'Radio spots will be purchased every other week to extend support throughout the period up to and immediately after Xmas.'

Media strategy statements include things like the rationale for the use of one medium rather than another. For example:

> 'Television will be used as a primary medium because it offers the optimum combination of mass coverage flexibility in time and place and meets the creative requirements.'

The media plan

This shows how media strategy is to be executed in terms of specific purchases. For example, six one-half pages are recommended in *Good Housekeeping* magazine because:

- it provides concentrated coverage of the target market;
- it has minimal duplication with other recommended media;
- the *Good Housekeeping* seal of approval is an asset in this product field.

Another simple example could be around the sport of golf whereby a particular magazine would offer a similar rationale around the reader demographics of:

- average age of 47 years;
- 73% social class ABC1;
- average annual income of £25,000 set against the average UK adult salary of £14,000;
- 95% male;
- average handicap of 11;
- 76% playing golf for 10+ years.

When evaluating the media plan two areas for consideration are important, as alluded to earlier, i.e. the suitability of the various media types and media vehicles and audience research. This should be an on-going process, especially in view of new technology and fragmentation. Evaluation as a whole and including audience research is dealt with in Chapter 17 of this book.

The Snapshot below discusses media planning in terms of what is required to put an effective media campaign together. It then relates this to a particular context, that of the cider industry, and the effective use of research in planning a marketing communications campaign's media usage.

Snapshot — Effective media planning with the aid of research – a case of UK cider and the Ipsos ASI Media Planner 360

A role for research in the media planning process

According to its website, 'Ipsos MORI is one of the largest and best known research companies in the UK and a key part of the Ipsos group, a leading global research company' (Ipsos MORI, 2013). The company has a presence in 84 countries with five global practices of public affairs research, advertising testing and tracking, media evaluation, marketing research and consultancy, customer satisfaction and loyalty. Mohamed and Glasspoole (2012) provide a case study that illustrates this claim. This involves premium cider and the use of research to aid effective media planning. The authors suggest that while the creative side is crucial to advertising success, the 'importance of getting the media strategy right should not be underestimated. In today's cluttered and constantly evolving media environment, the plethora of choices can be daunting. Get it wrong, and the power of great creative might not be maximized'. Coming from a research company might make Mohamed and Glasspoole appear biased but they are not wrong when they suggest that 'research can help guide the media planning process'. According to the company, the Ipsos ASI's Media Planner 360 approach has been developed to shape strategy.

Magners' cider as the leading brand

The leading brand of cider in the UK had been, until 2011, Magners, which is well documented as having been majorly responsible for the renewal of the UK cider market (see for example Stokes et al., 2007). However, and as might be expected when there is success in the marketplace, new entrants came in and took some of the share 'despite a 9% year-on-year increase in its marketing budget' (Mohamed and Glasspoole, 2012). By applying the rationale regarding different kinds of media, however, the 'potential for optimisation' can more easily be seen. The media analysis showed that in-store presence worked but that television, on-trade and packaging could be better. The research also showed where low-spend activities appeared not to be working very hard for the brand, 'suggesting an opportunity to review whether and how they are used' and if there is a possibility of increasing recall of television advertising that increases sales by a larger sum than the increased advertising costs then the advice from Mohamed and Glasspoole is 'buy this media!' The research suggests that once high brand recall is achieved then this plus television advertising and word of mouth are 'amongst the most important for generating brand impact, both short and long-term. This paints a clear picture for where strategy should focus within this category'.

Online possibilities missed?

It may appear that Mohamed and Glasspoole are omitting the possibilities of online communication but this is not the case: 'What we've seen in this case study is a glaring absence of online advertising as a key influencer of visibility or brand impact. Digital touchpoints cannot be realistically expected to gain the same level of exposure as TV given the relative levels of spend'.

(Continued)

(Continued)

However, these researchers question the way in which digital was used and not the role that digital tools might play. They suggest that 'the low rankings for brand impact raise issues about whether Digital is being used to best effect … we firmly hold that for Digital, content is king. Good online and mobile content is capable of creating a unique and engaging branded experience for consumers, through participation and engagement. This in turn can transform opinion and create buzz'.

A case of spending money on researching the media

Mohamed and Glasspoole (2012) conclude that 'the results of the Media Planner 360 provide a clear recommendation for this category in terms of where to invest. Carrying a TV campaign to point-of-purchase can convert an implicit impression to brand choice. In a cluttered media environment, the substitutability battle is most fiercely fought at the point-of-purchase. Differentiating your brand from a host of premium ciders is vital for your brand to stand out'. This case study is a good example of spending money (on research) in order to save money: 'The approach is highly adaptable, helping advertisers to save money or generate more brand impact from the same spend' (Mohamed and Glasspoole, 2012).

Stop Point

The case of the use of the Ipsos ASI Media Planner 360 media research approach illustrates that media planning is not as straightforward as it might seem. The ability to understand which media are working efficiently and effectively and which are not – and why – would appear to make common sense and a sound investment in marketing communications campaigns. Undertake the following: 1. Discuss planning the media with and without this level of analysis as to what and how consumers consume media and messages; 2. Comment on the notion of the sense it makes to provide some of the marketing communications spend for research and the folly of not so doing.

SPEND ISSUES

Traditional attitudes towards spend (or funding) are used by most text authors and this book is no exception. What is clear is that it is still notoriously difficult to arrive at optimal spend figures. Something that does not help the situation is the lack of certainty as to what the money actually does. It is worth recalling the Lord Leverhulme (William Lever, also attributed to John Wanamaker of the Wanamaker store fame, one of the first US department stores) quip to the effect of 'half the money I spend is a waste – the problem is I don't know which half'. Measurement is the key to understanding this but it is clear that senior management, while recognising the need for communications, have treated it with a certain amount of caution (and in some cases derision). Arriving at 'spend' is difficult because it is hard to quantify, attitudes toward advertising in particular have been in the 'cost' not 'investment' mould, and comparisons between different communications tools have been difficult.

Appropriation

Appropriation is the term used to describe the total sum of money available. There are tried and tested methods for arriving at how this money should be split into various pots to form budgets. Appropriation refers to how this money is spent in total. The conclusion drawn by most if not all writers in this area is that no one method prevails or is best at any given time. Things have changed since the 1980s. Advertising expenditure has fallen at the expense of other forms of communication, such as direct marketing and sales promotions, as accountability held sway during the 1990s and into the new millennium. Sponsorship and product placement have gained in popularity. Even so, advertising expenditure on the part of the likes of Procter and Gamble is still huge. However, it has to be said that the easiest thing for accountants to chop when things are tight is advertising expenditure. It is therefore argued that spending on promotion is an investment and should be viewed as such – and not a cost or expense as others in a company, for example accountants, might have it. What is clear is that investment is crucial to brand equity protection.

Budgets

Budgets are to do with timing the spread of financial resources. Budgeting in marketing communication terms deals with how much money is allocated to the elements of the communications mix. Appropriation is therefore the total sum allocated while a budget is specific to the media or a market. These are the two broad tasks the organisation faces in terms of resource allocation. The size in the end depends on objectives that of course may have to be revised in light of the amount of money available. It also depends on the stage in the PLC and the competitive environment. Costs depend on which media slots are bought and how much is spent on production, administration and research. A reserve of some sort should be considered. Budgets are necessary for planning activities. This means co-ordinating efforts across the organisation, taking an integrated approach and seizing on the opportunity for mutual support. This also means it is part of the planning approach since the marketer can return to the objectives to check the feasibility and viability of the campaign.

The overall conclusion must therefore be that there is no simple answer to the question 'How much do we spend?' A simple solution for many small businesses is to take the percentage of predicted turnover based upon the sector norm. This is by no means ideal but can be put into practice. The theoretical ideal only serves to complicate matters since it is impossible to put into practice for most organisations and probably not much use in reality for anyone. It should be noted that much of this applies to advertising only. Personal selling is mostly kept out of marketing communication and treated separately in this context. Some of the approaches such as objective/task and competitive parity can be used for sales promotion and PR. Often a predetermined ratio based on 'what works' for a sales promotion campaign might be implemented with a maximum percentage of sales being used accordingly. The key practical methods employed are:

1. Strategy-based approaches (bottom-up)
   Task/objective. This method may not be usable if unrealistic in terms of resources. Objectives have, therefore, to be revised in light of this, as per the analytical nature of the decision sequence model approach. This usually takes an AIDA-type approach, i.e. cost of achieving varying levels of awareness and the cost of moving through the AIDA-type sequence. This is the only bottom-up approach and is generally thought to be the most desirable. Often the costs are not all known until the task is complete. There is an appearance of unrealistic budgets needing constant revision and budget setting might be seen as farcical. A compromise

might be had in a 'sensitivity analysis' approach with adjustments being made incrementally and where it is easier to measure the time scale for recuperating expenditure. Another term for this is 'experimental allocation'. There are many ways in which one might experiment with differing levels of allocation. Different areas of the market can be treated differently and this can use a control area approach to keeping some things the same while levels of spend are experimented with. This is rather like a test market and as such similar problems occur in reality. For example there may be different levels and kinds of competitive action and reaction, differing regional media and differing levels of impact for national media in different areas. There is a positive aspect to budgets being evaluated and revised year on year and it is sensible to take feedback in order to gain improved performance. However, it is recognised how difficult it can be to estimate all of the cost likely to be incurred and to arrive at an accurate, final cost.

2. Predetermined approaches (top-down)

There are several, established approaches that are predetermined and top-down:

- *Inertia* i.e. to keep the budget at the same level, which is rare since most organisations, unless in crisis, are at least usually willing to keep in line with inflation.

- *Affordable* is just that – what is affordable after all the costs and required profit. This is hardly analytical and may be used by organisations that view communications as a cost and not an investment. There may be some form of product orientation where there is a belief that the product or the cause (if a charity) will self promote. This is often used by smaller organisations such as some charities, micro businesses and SMEs.

- *Arbitrary*, or the 'chairman's rules', is 'budgeting on the hoof'. This has flexibility but is in no way analytical or driven out of customer consideration. Again, this is often a feature of smaller organisations.

- *Historical*, what has been done in the past and possibly what the boss says. The only increase may be where media costs have to be followed, or must keep in line with inflation. This might be allied to the 'all we can afford' approach, which has clear drawbacks, and is based on what is left after the costs and profit are subtracted from revenue.

Two other, linked methods are worthy of consideration; percentage of sales and share of voice:

Percentage of sales

This method can be set either through advertising industry or industry (norm for the) sector sources. The *Advertising to sales ratio* is a measure of the effectiveness of an advertising campaign. The figure is calculated by dividing the total advertising expenses by sales revenue and is therefore based on the relationship between advertising weight (expenditure) and sales volume and value. The sector, therefore, is important as can be seen in the big difference between cosmetics (up to 20 per cent of sale turnover on promotion) or retail generally (around 2 per cent) and other sectors, and the method offers a solution to the problem (or at least a rough guide) of deciding how much to spend by following the industry or sector average. The ratio is designed to show whether the advertising resources a firm spends on a campaign have helped to generate new sales. A high ratio indicates that high advertising expenses have resulted in relatively low sales revenue, which could mean that the campaign has failed. A low ratio may indicate that the advertising campaign generated sales. The lower the ratio the better, given that a low value for the ratio will mean the money spent is likely to be working harder. It is therefore possible to compare sector averages and competitors' ratios and determine spend figures. For example the ratio for women's perfumes (around 14 per cent) can be several time higher than, say, for off-the-peg clothing (around 5 per cent) and about the same as that for spirits such as whiskey (around 15 per cent). Figures do vary depending upon the market and the way in which they are compiled. For example the Illinois-based business information company Schonfeld & Associates would group perfume in with cosmetics and toiletries preparations and give a ratio figure of 20.0 per cent in 2012 (19.8 per cent in 2011, down from 20.1 per cent in 2010) and for wine, brandy and brandy spirits one of 4.8 per cent in 2012 (11.8 per cent in 2011, up from 3.3 per cent in 2010).

The above figures are for the USA and are general to advertising but not to marketing communications so that a campaign may have been successful at least in part because of the success of other communications tools. Another issue is that of different media being used in the advertising campaign whereby the marketer may not know which media were responsible for new or falling sales. Not all companies, of course, will rely on or even use advertising. Some campaigns are not about sales in the shorter or medium term but are about achieving longer-term objectives. This method puts a focus on sales rather than profit and is often based on past rather than current or future sales. However, the marketer does not have to base the percentage on past sales. Every effort should be made to base figures on realistic projections. Year on year therefore it is unlikely that *ceteris paribus* will prevail, i.e. that all things will be equal. This can result in a downward spiral in terms of sales decline, which in turn will result in a decline in allocation if based on the percentage of sales. This is a cost-oriented approach to communications and in particular advertising, rather than one of investment. If the latter orientation prevailed, clearly if sales declined a consideration of spend as investment to halt the decline and rebuild sales would be an option worth exploring. Another issue is that this method is actually effect and cause rather than cause and effect in nature, where the latter may be the preferred approach. The marketer may wish to take into consideration other variables including the other forms of marketing communications available, which may, in any event, be more relevant than advertising to the type of organisation and sector where less advertising is used than in other contexts.

The advertising to sales ratio, according to Fill (2009: 427), is likely to be higher in sectors where the offering is standardised and where there are many end users whose financial risk is small. The same can be said if marketing channels are short and a premium price is charged with high gross margin, and if the particular industry is characterised by surplus capacity and a high number of new product launches.

Share of voice (SOV), share of market and competitive parity

Using the advertising to sales ratio helps the marketer to control 'spend' and if so required to set budgets against the competition or sector average. This leads to the idea of 'share-of-voice', the voice being the whole of expenditure in a particular context. If this SOV is greater than all the other SOVs then in theory this voice has a better chance of being heard. This relies on weight being the important factor and it is this premise that has been challenged by numerous agencies that have produced successful campaigns for clients by cleverly using the media and/or creative ideas that give the client's brand the edge.

SOV can be an objective tool, especially if used in conjunction with *competitive parity*. If the data are available the marketer can spend the same as the competition, an action that tends to stabilise the market. But the trade/consumer mix has to be taken into consideration so that like with like is compared and similarly with the qualitative aspect of the message. If this is equal then share of voice may be considered the best option since the weight of advertising spend will be the important factor. This can then be linked to *share of market*. When SOV = SOM then equilibrium exists. Competitive equilibrium exists when key players make it so in order that the status quo is maintained. This might well be collusion on the part of competitors. At the same time it can be viewed as part of strategy with decisions to attack or defend, assuming reliable data are available. This may well lead to more being spent to defend or attack a position than would be the norm. To use the Boston Consulting Group categories Cash Cows are generally high price and low maintenance and therefore have an SOV less than that of an SOM. A market leader may well have economies of scale and achieve this position above the equilibrium line. Also above this line might be niche players. Below this line are market followers that may well be Stars that need investment if the SOV is less than the SOM in order to reverse this and move Stars toward Cash Cow status.

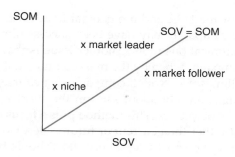

Figure 9.8 The SOM/SOV relationship

Other factors may well influence budget setting that overrides the SOV/SOM and competitive parity machinations, such as resources or difficulties within product life cycles.

Theoretical approaches to setting budgets

Theoretical approaches include marginal analysis and sales response curves. Overall these are of questionable practical use, principally because they are not real and in any event the information required is impossible or too expensive to acquire. The simple, concave sales response curve follows the law of diminishing returns where the sales and expenditure relationship is expressed as shown in Figure 9.9.

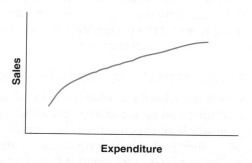

Figure 9.9 The concave sales response curve

Thus the incremental value of sales decreases as a new unit of expenditure is added. Beyond an optimal point there will be no communications effect and therefore, theoretically at least, a smaller budget can achieve the same results as a larger one, and be just as effective for less expenditure. This also implies that when the communications effort is zero sales will be zero, which may not be the case at all. This gives rise to the S-shaped sales curve. Here the sales produce a concave curve, but after an optimal point (A) the curve will plateau and may even decline as a result of irritation or other negative customer perceptions (see Figure 9.10).

The marginal approach revolves around the idea that it is possible to predict how many extra sales can be had from an extra unit of spend where the point will be reached where there is equilibrium, i.e. marginal revenue = marginal costs, and P1 is the optimal level of promotional expenditure.

However, there are too many assumptions not least of all that promotion is the only cost or influence on sales, that there is no influence from competitive action and reaction. Communications cannot be varied smoothly and continuously as assumed and not all messages are standardised.

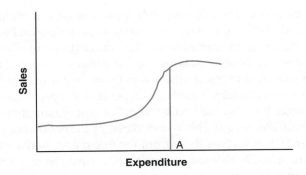

Figure 9.10   The 'S' shaped sales curve

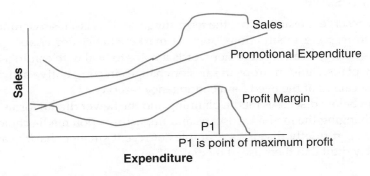

Figure 9.11   The sales value/expenditure relationship

Costs of other elements of the marketing communications mix

The marketer has to decide what the money allocated to this area of activity is be used for since clearly advertising is not the only communications tool in the box. The marketer also has to consider the best ways of achieving objectives such as building brand images or selling products. Such objectives are likely to be achieved by particular elements of the communication's mix. This has a bearing on how much is spent on other elements such as sales promotions and PR. Sales promotions' costs are relatively easy to measure and it is easy to predict the point at which costs will be covered. Similarly, PR approaches can be costed with a degree of accuracy since mostly it is fixed costs being dealt with such as fees, retainers or expenses and not buying media space or particular production costs as is the case with advertising. Personal communication is often but not always associated with fixed costs and the rest of the mix with variable costs. The former applies to sales management and the latter to brand or product management. Fixed costs are relatively high and easy to calculate but the relative cost is a more difficult variable to measure. Absolute costs can be known, but the relative costs of achieving impact are more problematic and are usually based on experience and are therefore subjective. However, this does not rule out anything other than a task approach and in a similar way, as with advertising for example, ratio approaches could be used.

There is a common belief that 80 per cent of new products fail (for example Howells, 2011). This follows a version of the Pareto Principle (or 80/20 law) i.e. 20 per cent of products will produce 80 per cent of sales revenue leaving 80 per cent of products only producing 20 per cent of sales revenue, resulting in many product failures and deletions. If this is the case then it is necessary to invest and spend to get the 20 per cent to succeed at the same time as bringing down the product or brand failure rate. This is allied to brand building in the longer term. A combined approach to allocating and setting budgets may very well be taken in order to get the best out of all of the above when dealing with appropriation and budgeting. Many would argue that the most used method is percentage of sales. For example De Pelsmaker et al. (2004), maintain that across the consumer market board this is so (50 per cent of all situations) but that 30 per cent of consumer goods organisations use the affordable method and 12 per cent the arbitrary method. However, in terms of business-to-business the arbitrary method is used by 34 per cent of concerns, the affordable method by 26 per cent, the percentage of sales method by 28 per cent, and the objective/task method by 40 per cent of organisations (clearly more than one method having been employed). This is underlined by the notion of a combined approach. Especially since other factors such as those from the micro and macro environment are constantly present and changing, a crisis may occur or a new situation may arise; for example, the opportunity to develop a new product.

Contingency reserve

A contingency reserve is exactly what the term suggests. This is a reserve fund that enables the marketer to respond to situations, such as market changes or crises, quickly and to finance actions where necessary. In other words it helps to deal with contingency measures in contingency plans. Sudden drops in sales or changes in competitive activity are two of the commonest causes of the need for a contingency reserve.

The Snapshot below discusses media planning and the newer digital forms of media that are radically changing the media landscape and impacting upon media choices within the planning process. It briefly discusses examples of recent smaller charity campaigns that were exclusively digital in their use of media.

Snapshot   When traditional media are cost-prohibitive – how causes such as small charities can use social media in planning the media

Alternative approaches to 'spend' in the digital media for smaller organisations

Smaller charities do not have the resources, of course, to run a large media advertising campaign in the first place but they can endeavour to find ways of creating publicity that is relevant to their raison d'être. Things, as they say, have changed. According to the *Third Sector* (2009), the magazine for Australia's non-profit and not-for-profit sector, the 'Connecting Up Conference in Sydney recently heard that Australia's charities and community groups are surging towards free and low cost social media and mobile technologies to reach their clients and donors'. This illustrates a sea change for charities, especially smaller ones, whereby innovative approaches to media coverage will be mixed in with and even supersede traditional ones. The *Third Sector* (2009) reported that 'Innovative initiatives ranged from Starlight Foundation's Livewire project for kids living with an illness to the individual fundraising web pages of Everyday Hero' and that the Connecting Up conference saw the use of 'leading edge online tools to actively embrace those who couldn't make it to the venue, including live blogging and Twitter feeds', with a range of charities represented in the conference presentations that involved, for example, Google's web tools, stories to develop a community website in New Zealand and web philanthropy. Issues such as web piracy were said not to matter, the feeling being that not-for-profit organisations that fail to embrace social media fully 'will cease to be relevant'.

The Child's i Foundation

It would appear that a transition has to be made on the part of all organisations in terms of moving away from a situation of traditional media only, to one of embracing newer, digital and interactive media and getting used to the idea of utilising things such as blogs and bulletin boards and basically being connected. This is especially beneficial to those smaller organisations that need to invest time and effort into understanding how to create low-cost online strategies and plans. Pati (2011) reports on the idea that 'social media can reach more people, raise funds and attract more volunteers'. The Child's i Foundation (www.childsifoundation.org/) was set up in 2008 by Lucy Buck, who 'used her experience of working in television to set up an interactive charity helping children in Uganda' (Pati, 2011). Buck apparently got the inspiration to set up a campaign that had connectivity and real-time engagement while working on Channel 4's *Big Brother* where television and audiences connected in real time: 'As one of the series' producers for seven years, Buck decided to quit her job to set up an interactive charity for abandoned Ugandan children'. According to Pati the charity has a reach 'that most small charities can only dream about' through its interactive nature and an annual income of 'approximately £340,000, 28% of which is generated online using sites such as JustGiving, where supporters can donate and arrange fundraising events'.

The 'save Baby Joey' appeal

Pati highlights the case of the appeal for 'Baby Joey which raised over £10,000 in 38 hours entirely online'. This was an appeal to save the baby's life in August 2010: 'Baby Joey was the first baby put for adoption but just a few weeks later, his adoptive parents discovered he needed critical heart surgery'. The money was raised using a 'zero budget multi-media strategy across all its available online platforms and social media channels'. In just 38 hours the story was published on 'Facebook, Twitter and JustGiving' and the charity 'emailed a newsletter to over 1,000 supporters using mailing list MailChimp'. Joey's progress was made available through 'tweets and Facebook posts throughout the appeal'. Supportive messages were sent to Joey's adoptive parents and video was used to show his journey from adoption through to the discovery of the condition and successful return to home: 'The charity and parents also thanked supporters through video' (Pati, 2011).

Stop Point

The future of media planning is uncertain. Although traditional approaches to media planning will no doubt continue in many cases, there is a growing and inevitable use of digital forms of media by most organisations. Undertake the following: 1. Consider and discuss the future of purely traditional media campaigns and the likelihood of this type of campaign disappearing altogether; 2. Comment on how traditional and newer, digital forms of media can be used in unison and how together they can best serve organisations' marketing communications management needs.

Assignment

Choose a large company such as Procter and Gamble, Unilever, Tata, Nestlé, Nissan or L'Oreal. Research one of this company's brands with a view to determining which media are used and why, and how such media might be planned and budgets formulated. In comparison, place alongside your chosen company a typical smaller enterprise (say with a turnover of £1 million) and write a comparative report that teases out the differences at each stage of media selection, planning and spend.

Summary of Key Points

- The characteristics of the various media are fundamental and should be understood by marketers.
- The media industry has changed and independent media specialists are now the norm.
- The media need to be planned in a way that fits in with IMC philosophy, the roles of the planner and buyer being crucial still to this process.
- There are a number of external and internal sources of data that inform media planning and facilitate media decision making.
- The key objectives within media planning are reach, frequency and weight resulting in the use of gross rating points (GRPs) and TVRs (television ratings) to help establish which particular spots/slots might be purchased and used to develop media schedules.
- Cost is always a key factor.
- Budgets are to do with timings and spend of financial resources.
- There are top-down and bottom-up practical approaches to setting budgets.
- There are also theoretical approaches that are available to the marketer but which in practice are of questionable value.

Discussion Questions

1. Explain why the various characteristics of the media such as interactivity, dramatic effect or imagination are important considerations during the process of media selection. Use examples to illustrate.
2. Write a job specification for media planners and media buyers, outlining the main tasks facing each.
3. Explain the terms 'reach', 'frequency' and 'weight' in the media-planning context. Explain what a GRP is and illustrate this in terms of TVRs.

4. Explain why the cost-per-thousand method is extensively used despite being so flawed.

5. Explain how scheduling can use the ideas of continuity, flighting and pulsing.

6. Explain the difference between appropriation and budgets. Outline the theoretical and practical approaches available to the marketer when dealing with marketing communication appropriation and budgeting. In terms of setting budgets, explain why the objective/task/method appeals to marketers.

7. Theoretical approaches continue to haunt the media planner as an ideal that is unreachable but so desirable. Explain in depth marginal analysis in the media planning context.

8. Explain why the advertising to sales ratio method is limited to particular contexts and cannot be used by the marketer setting budgets across the board.

9. The valuation of brands has finally arrived with brand equity on the balance sheet. Discuss this in relation to the view that communication is an investment rather than a cost.

10. Despite the wonders of technology the effects on communications are evolutionary rather than revolutionary. Explain why this is the case using examples to illustrate.

Further Reading

Chang, B-H. and Chan-Olmsted, S.M. (2005) 'Relative constancy of advertising spending – a cross national examination of advertising expenditures and their determinants', *Gazette: The International Journal for Communication Studies*, 67 (4): 339–67. http://gaz.sagepub.com/content/67/4/339
This article is based on an empirical study across 70 countries over time. The authors look at the principle of relative constancy (PRC, based on the relationship between level of advertising spend and the general state of an economy) and the relationship between advertising spending and GDP as a variable within national economies. The results suggest that this relationship is not proportionate and therefore there is potentially a different variable or variables at play that affect a country's advertising expenditure. The authors also suggest that the degree of applicability to the PRC might be different depending upon media types and characteristics of nations, especially since the PRC seems more apparent in developing nations.

Kawashima, N. (2006) 'Advertising agencies, media and consumer market: the changing quality of TV advertising in Japan', *Media, Culture and Society*, 28 (3): 393–410. http://mcs.sagepub.com/content/28/3/393
The idea that people are surrounded by edited material such as newspaper articles but also advertisements is not a new one. This article looks at advertising within media culture and the immediate economic and industrial framework in which advertising is produced, such as in commercial broadcasting and newspaper publishing. In particular, as the title suggests, the article addresses the issue of quality in Japanese television commercials which involves fragmentation and a loss of revenue to a shift towards sponsorships, as well as the influence of technology on the TV medium itself, which is allowing consumers

(Continued)

(Continued)

to take more control of what they actually watch. The interface between the TV medium in Japan and creativity (and especially the use of celebrity endorsers as the creative platform) is explored and critiqued. The argument is extended into media culture and more generally consumer society.

Overby, L.M. and Barth, J. (2006) 'Radio advertising in American political campaigns – the persistence, importance and effects of narrowcasting', *American Politics Research*, 34 (4): 451–78. http://apr.sagepub.com/content/34/4/451

This article is based on a study of US electoral dynamics through the use of radio (rather than television) campaigns and the possibilities for narrowcasting. The authors explore, through the use of empirical data to look at the factors that influence exposure to radio advertisements, the public's perception of the importance of such advertisements and the impact of exposure on public perception of the quality of the democratic process. The authors conclude, among other things, that the US public appear to like the idea of narrowcasting and customised messages that speak to them about local issues, which appears to be in opposition to the notion of an open dialogue.

Reid, L.N. and King, K.W. (2003) 'Advertising managers' perceptions of sales effects and creative properties of national newspaper advertising: the medium revisited', *Journal of Mass Communication Quarterly*, 80 (2): 410–30. http://jmq.sagepub.com/content/80/2/410

Sales effects of newspaper advertising through the eyes of advertising managers are the focus of this article. The study looks at delivery effectiveness, sales effects and creative properties of advertising and finds that in comparison to network TV, newspapers fared poorly in terms of effectiveness on these three parameters but were judged to be effective in terms of immediate sales and the ability to deliver both simple and complex messages. The authors conclude that the more spent with national newspapers by the manager's company the more effective the medium was perceived to be.

Soh, H., Reid, L.N. and King, K.W. (2007) 'Trust in different advertising media', *Journal of Mass Communication Quarterly*, 84 (3): 455–76. http://jmq.sagepub.com/content/84/3/455

This article looks at consumer trust in advertising media and the relationship with media credibility. The study on which it is based found that consumers appear neutral regarding this issue, neither trusting nor distrusting advertising media, but that this level of trust does vary across different media. Education and income appear to be parameters and trust and credibility appear to correlate.

REFERENCES

Chang, B.-H. and Chan-Olmsted, S.M. (2005) 'Relative constancy of advertising spending – a cross national examination of advertising expenditures and their determinants', *Gazette: The International Journal for Communication Studies*, 67: (4) 339–67.

De Pelsmaker, P., Geuens, M. and Van den Bergh, J. (2004) *Marketing Communications: A European Perspective*, 2nd edn. Essex, England: FT Prentice Hall/Pearson Education Limited.

Donnelly, W.J. (1996) *Media Planning, Strategy and Imagination*. New Jersey: Prentice Hall.

The *Economist* (2010) 'American newspapers: not dead yet', 10 June.

Fill, C. (2009) *Marketing Communications*, 5th edn. London: Prentice Hall/Pearson Education.

Gillin, P. (2012a) 'As *USA Today* turns 30, columnists write its obituary', 26 September. Available at: http://newspaperdeathwatch.com/as-usa-today-turns-30-columnists-write-its-obituary/

Gillin, P. (2012b) 'Newsweek to go out of print', *Business News*, 20 October. Available at: http://newspaperdeathwatch.com/newsweek-to-go-out-of-print/

Howells, R. (2011) 'Why good products fail and what you can do about it', *Forbes Magazine*, available at: www.forbes.com/sites/sap/2011/07/12/why-good-products-fail-and-what-you-can-do-about-it/

Ipsos MORI (2013) 'Welcome to Ipsos MORI', available at: www.ipsos-mori.com/

Jones, J.-P. (1995) 'Advertising's impact on sales and profitability', March IPA Conference Paper, London.

Kawashima, N. (2006) 'Advertising agencies, media and consumer market: the changing quality of TV advertising in Japan', *Media, Culture and Society*, 28 (3): 393–410.

Krugman, H.E. (1972) 'Why three exposures may be enough', *Journal of Advertising Research*, 12 (6): 11–14.

McLuhan, M. (1962) *The Gutenberg Galaxy: The Making of Typographic Man*. Toronto: University of Toronto Press.

McLuhan, M. (1964) *Understanding Media: The Extensions of Man*. New York: McGraw Hill.

McLuhan, M. and Fiore, Q. (1967) *The Medium is the Message: An Inventory of Effects*. New York: Random House.

Mohamed, S. and Glasspoole, K. (2012) 'Using Research for Effective Media Planning: Cider Advertising UK Case Study', IPSOS/ASI, September.

Murray G.B. and Jenkins, J.G. (1992) 'The concept of effective reach in advertising', *Journal of Advertising Research*, 32 (3): 34–44.

Naples, M.J. (1979) *Effective Frequency: The Relationship between Frequency and Advertising Effectiveness*. New York: Association of National Advertisers.

Overby, L.M. and Barth, J. (2006) 'Radio advertising in American political campaigns – the persistence, importance and effects of narrowcasting', *American Politics Research*, 34 (4): 451–78.

Pati, A. (2011) 'How small charities can make a big impact with social media', *The Guardian*, Guardian Professional, 21 September.

Reid, L.N. and King, K.W. (2003) 'Advertising managers' perceptions of sales effects and creative properties of national newspaper advertising: the medium revisited', *Journal of Mass Communication Quarterly*, 80 (2): 410–30.

Soh, H., Reid, L.N. and King, K.W. (2007) 'Trust in different advertising media', *Journal of Mass Communication Quarterly*, 84 (3): 455–76.

Stokes, M., Jenkins, S. and Nolan, M. (2007) 'Magners Irish Cider – The Magners Effect: how Magners single-handedly re-invigorated the cider category', Institute of Practitioners in Advertising, IPA Effectiveness Awards.

Third Sector (2009) 'Charities ride the new wave of social media', July.

Digital Media – Interaction and Engagement

CHAPTER OVERVIEW

Introduction

This chapter explores the demise of the monologue and the rise of the dialogue in marketing communications. Perhaps more than this, the fragmentation of markets and that of the media that has followed targeting and the interactivity and engagement that has intensified in recent years has led to what might be called the electronic or digital frontier, where digital media have arrived and begun to flourish. In practice marketing communications is a mix of old and new media elements that now includes websites, social media and developments in mobile applications. Today there is a mix of traditional and interactive media involving e-commerce and many types of relationships. This chapter therefore explores the meaning of interactivity and engagement and discusses the emergence of digital media, and in particular the Internet and its associated developments, that have had an enormous impact on the integrated marketing communication mix in recent times. These newer, digital mix elements are therefore considered, particularly in relation to the Internet and developments in e-commerce that have had such a profound effect on many people's daily lives.

Learning objectives

This chapter seeks to explore the newer forms of digital media and the importance of interactivity and engagement in marketing communications. More specifically, on completion of this chapter, the student will be able to:

- understand the relationship between technology and communication;
- discuss the nature and importance of interactivity;
- explain the nature of online marketing and e-commerce;
- understand how new digital media forms have become part of IMC;
- explain issues surrounding website design, characteristics and management;
- appreciate the relationship between online advertising and the brand;
- appreciate online design and management issues including search engine optimisation;
- understand the use of advertising and other forms of communication activities online;
- understand the nature of communication networks and relationships with social media and mobile marketing;
- explain the measurement of digital activities and the need for effective monitoring.

TECHNOLOGY AND COMMUNICATION

Background

If the Industrial Revolution took workers from farm to factory, the 'Information Age' is a time of migration for workers from manufacturing to service industries. Changes in technology have had an immense impact on communications whereby, for example, news about companies, brands or individuals can be spun around the globe in many cases instantaneously or, if not, within a day or days rather than weeks, months or even years, via the Internet in the form of social media, blogs and other such inventions. The use of direct response television was, at the dawn of the new millennium, indicative of the changes that had taken place in terms of the ability to process information and the improvements in database creation and maintenance. Since then the introduction of broadband in many countries such as the UK is an example of the amount of digital information that can be sent backwards and forwards despite the increasing complexity of messages and the space required to handle them.

The growth of videotext, the Internet and other important areas such as mobile phone technology, in particular 'smart' phones with all of their applications including texting, photo messaging and Internet access, is evident in everyday life. Somewhat ironically, this has led to a decline in television advertising, yet at the same time radio, which was in decline, has been revived and has survived and now flourishes around the world. Radio is a very personal medium that had at its core a local personality which it now has back having moved away from this position. With the advent of television and then cable it looked as though radio would fade away but instead it has been transformed, despite iPods and similar devices. Satellite and Internet radio are part of this transformation but it is radio's ability to hit niche (such as talk radio and sports coverage) and local targets that means it continues to survive and thrive. Some would argue that there is no reason why this cannot continue as long as there is an understanding of the values, interests and things that are of import to listeners. Local advertisers like local radio because of its cost but also because of its ability to target, its intimacy and other creative qualities such as an ability to tap into the imagination and create mental pictures and images. It is this latter quality that may help in targeting a younger demographic and lure them away from portable media players such as iPods and iPads.

The future of newsprint was discussed in Chapter 9 of this book in relation to changes online, but basically as online has grown, inevitably the increase in spend online has been at the expense of other media, particularly print. Newspapers and magazines are often available both on- and offline, with newsprint surviving but with radically changed offerings.

Direct marketing has moved to an extent from traditional mail to email in a similar fashion to the way classified and recruitment advertising has moved online. The changes in technology have meant that to be cost effective enough to be profitable, the market has fragmented with much smaller (often special interest group) audiences. Online newspapers, magazines and radio have threatened traditional forms, offering the same kinds of content from gossip to serious news to the weather report. Outdoor displays are not immune from technological advance with the marketer's ability to throw images almost Batman-like into the skies, or at least on to buildings such as the Houses of Parliament for dramatic effect. Electronic displays, database technology and swipe cards that allow for loyalty programmes, EPOS systems and in-transport communication are all evidence of the effects of technology on daily life in many countries. It is possible that other forms of business communication, such as the ubiquitous fax machine, will soon be obsolete, although there appears to be a form of online faxing – the infographic – that is popular when signatures are required. The fax machine, pre-Internet, had replaced the previous technology to become the most popular and efficient way to send documents and information electronically and was seen as cutting edge. Some people still like the idea of paper rather than an electronic file for trust reasons.

The digital not analogue age

Broadcast media

A number of activities are now possible because of the way technology and in particular digital technology has transformed the marketer's arena. The broadcast media are still available in analogue form but in many countries the digital form is now dominant. For example the UK switched from analogue television to digital in 2012 and many European states switched earlier than that. The interactive media are driven by digital technology. The delivery of television and radio is now via satellite, cable but still terrestrial means. Digital television offers much-improved picture quality but it is the future impact of inter-activity in terms of home shopping, home banking and many other activities in life that makes the prospects of this mouth watering to marketers. Some would argue that it is digital television and not the Internet that will lead commerce. Others suggest that business and marketing will be integrated activities anyway so that it is the integration and not the medium that is important. Videotext is a system whereby text and pictures are displayed on a television screen. Teletext uses broadcast information through ordinary television signals. Viewdata uses a central data bank and telephone network and both require the use of a television receiver with a special decoder. Such systems provide two-way communication. In the past the failed Prestel system (UK) was never a match for the impressive French government-sponsored 'Minitel', still used up until 2012 and phased out due to a lack of interest. Many other countries had similar systems but none as developed as the French.

CD and DVD

The CD as a medium has not been passed over totally yet and the DVD is still relevant. Its predecessor, vhs video tape, has largely become defunct.

Telephone, video and messaging services

Video conferencing, whether with PC or room-based, still has potential but has equipment and time-zone problems. Skype, now owned by Microsoft, is an instant messaging service that allows users to communicate by voice or video over the Internet. The Skype service is free but telephone calls to landlines and mobile phones are not. Importantly, it can be used for video conferencing. Skype now has growing competition, for example from Google

Voice that has a range of services including telephone calls (some of which are free or inexpensive) and video conferencing.

Call centres and automated answering systems

The telephone systems that are fully automated in call centres can be viewed either as an asset that helps builds relationships or as a hindrance to this process if the 'annoyance factor' is real. Successful automated answering systems are still required to meet customer need and not least the interactive voice response (IVR) has to be supported by good design and a system with response capabilities and menu options. The system must be able to capture customer response and be monitored and up-dated continuously.

The call centre may be part of a contact or customer support centre (and part of customer relationship management) that handles other forms of communication such as the traditional mail, email or faxes. The call centre uses the telephone and is now an established form of centralised office capable of either receiving (inbound) and/or transmitting (outbound) enormous numbers of requests by telephone. Inbound messages are usually from customers or potential customers and about things such as inquiries, complaints, information-seeking or product support. Outbound involves activities such as telemarketing and marketing research. The call centre may operate independently or be networked.

Technological innovation and advancement have meant that computer telephony integration (CTI) allows the integration of telephones and computers. This has seen the advent of different levels of customer support with inbound communications in terms of options and routes to the appropriate person, which is supposed to create greater efficiencies in terms of wait times. However, there are problems that tend to centre on the work environment, monitoring of staff and low pay rates related to the skills and motivation of operatives where there has been much academic research done. Critics also point to the automated responses from operatives that are 'scripted', or overseas locations that may reduce staffing costs but cause problems with language. Wherever situated geographically, long queues can be off-putting. On the plus side is the development of outsourced contact centres that can be bought into by SMEs and micro businesses for affordable rates that at least provide the firm with a point of contact, even if only a telephone answering service whereby a firm is allocated a dedicated operative who is a proxy employee rather than an answer machine.

The nature of interactivity

The technological advancements alluded to above have ensured that communications have become operationally interactive. The advent of the Internet is important but so too are other developments. Digital television in particular and broadcasting more generally have seen and still see interactive services arriving at a rapid pace. The Internet, discussed in more detail later in this chapter, has stimulated commerce in many ways, including locally with, for example, online shopping and delivery from supermarkets such as Tesco in the UK. In this instance, and somewhat ironically, the shopping may be conducted online but delivery still has to be conducted in a conventional way. In this sense making a list online at Tesco and having it delivered is not that different from drawing up a list for the local department store or supermarket and placing it with the store on a regular basis, a practice that harks back to decades earlier. 'Click and collect' appears to be a popular option with consumers.

The desirability of one-to-one targeting in marketing and the dream of two-way transactions approach reality as the passive audience become active in real time, where targets are not only accessible and recognisable but are also responsive. Interactivity in essence is adding and facilitating two-way communication to one-way communication to achieve connectivity with the target whereby messages can not only be retained but also engaged with. One-way communication is about awareness but two-way is about relationships that are personalised, social and responsive.

Marketing online and e-commerce

The Internet

The Internet is made up of websites, bulletin boards, forums and chat rooms to variously send email and attachments, post notices, or engage in real-time interaction with others. The part of such activities that is actually involved with selling is usually referred to as e-commerce. Many people use the Internet to look for information, use email or visit chat rooms. Some companies are strictly online only such as Ebay or Amazon. Bricks and mortar organisations such as Argos, IKEA or Tesco do, of course, engage with traditional and online commerce. The key to successful e-commerce has been developments in navigation, the design of home pages and the use of search engines such as Google, Bing or Ask Jeeves. Such engines find websites based on key words. A portal is a search engine for a selected number of sites so that, for example, Yahoo is both this and an online shopping centre. Such organisations have helped to develop navigation across the 'world wide web' that has become a graphical communication medium that uses hypertext mark-up language (HTML) which allows text images, icons and sounds to be shared in a user friendly way.

Interactivity

Interactivity is dependent in the first place on the accessibility of the Internet, the increase in and range of information available, and the fact that the Internet is 'fast and vast'. Business-to-business commerce on the Internet had led the way but as consumer access has risen so too have the number of websites and other usage. However, any general comparisons between consumer and business use have to be qualified and contextualised since there are huge variations in access possibilities around the world. The Internet has been about interactivity and about real time, targeted, personalised brand messages. By the mid-1990s it had moved from being a leisure pursuit for 'anoraks' and before that the tool of academics and before that a military tool. The Internet soon became a commercial necessity with many companies, without understanding its true nature, rushing to be on 'the web' or 'the net' if only to be able to say 'visit our website'. Having a website became a 'must have', even if the site was little more than a simple leaflet on a screen. There was kudos to be had from being 'on the web', thus following the Marshall McCluhanism 'the medium is the message' whereby merely being on the Internet said something about the organisation in the order of 'progressive', 'up-to-date' or 'go-ahead'. The converse would be that not being on the Internet suggests a slow, non-progressive and not up-to-date organisation.

Although traditional tools of commerce are clearly still extant, online marketing has become an important part of organisations' marketing and of IMC. What started with website addresses being communicated via conventional advertising has evolved into something completely different as it was soon realised that the Internet had a social dimension with a style reminiscent of television but somehow more synchronised. The most important aspect is of course the way the customer or consumer has control of content and contact. The Internet was quickly characterised by banner advertising; boxes that were the commonest way of alerting the user to a facility that provides a click-through to a relevant page on a website. These were often animated and, when in a pop-up form, could be irritating and the cause of overload on the user's system. This led to 'freezing' of screens and the necessity to reboot the system.

The value of Internet trade

Despite industry predictions of big business the Internet was relatively slow to grow and worth only $4.2 billion in 2000 according to O'Connor and Galvin (2001). Since that time it has become clearer what the size of trade is in different product categories and industries. For example *The Week* (2011), using *The Atlantic*, *Economic Times* and McKinsey Global Institute sources, suggests that the online activities of the G-8 countries plus those of China, India, South Korea, Sweden and Brazil are worth much more. Using the McKinsey Global Institute information that slotted Internet activities into four categories of private consumption, private investment, public expenditure, and trade, the estimate of the 'Internet economy' was $8 trillion (with 30 per cent of this coming from the USA). Other figures provided by *The Week* from these sources suggest that in 2011 the Internet constituted 3.4 per cent of the GDP of large, developed economies. The Internet was also responsible for 2.2 per cent and 3.9 per cent of the GDP of the agriculture and transportation sectors respectively of large, developed economies.

The Internet accounted for 21 per cent of GDP growth in the world's largest economies over the five previous years. In terms of Internet users *The Week* (2011) uses *Economic Times* figures to suggest that 246 million were added between 2007–10 from India and China and the total number in the USA alone in 2010 reached 244 million, while in China the figure was 485 million (the biggest Internet user base) in 2010. *The Week* also suggests that for every job lost because of the Internet 2.6 have been created, with the example of 31,353 people employed by Google as of September 2011 in its 13 years of existence up until that point. E-commerce continues to grow with the march of technology, access and the relatively recent introduction of broadband to many areas of the world which has enhanced capabilities. The Internet is now a daily reality for many people (but by no means all as yet) that has changed the ways in which those people live and work, including the sharing of information and knowledge. Trade figures are expected to be much higher online but this will be dependent upon other advances such as challenges arising from the convergence of the Internet and digital television.

Smart television and connectivity

Woodward (2012), writing on the challenges facing connected television, suggests that there are still 'substantial issues to address before the true potential of online content is realised and switched on in every home', one being educating consumers so that they are able to get the most out of 'smart television' in the first place. Although there are several big players already, such as Netflix and LoveFilm, connected television still has a long way to go before the full potential is met. This is not helped by over half of televisions that could be connected left unconnected either because it is perceived as being too complicated a process to connect or simply that it is not worth the effort or justification to change. This situation for Woodward could be helped by the industry offering a more 'TV-centric experience' and adding value by 'tailoring online content and on-demand programming for the TV'. This means 'delivering enhanced TV services across multiple devices while remembering why consumers turn on their TV in the first place: to sit back and relax'. This, for Woodward, is hampered by the lack of standards across television devices whereby applications have to be tailored to each manufacturer's range of products, but progress has been made in this area in France and Germany. Television viewing as an experience is changing as consumers want more from the experience. The solution to this is achieving a converged service 'that combines the best of TV with the best of tablet and smartphone functionality. In turn this will provide truly personalised services to the viewer', but before this can happen the devices need to be 'talking' to each other: 'We'll also start to see set-top boxes and

TVs streaming live and recorded programmes directly to tablet and smartphones creating another TV screen in the home' (Woodward, 2012).

Communications networks

Intra- and extranets

Web-based technology has had a high impact on networking and networks in terms of customers, employees, business partners and any other significant stakeholders. The key of course is interactivity. Intra- and extranets are related to the Internet. Intranets preceded the Internet and were expensive but relatively secure. These internal, password-protected systems were used for document management, project management, knowledge management, training and other support. The material shared could be calendars, newsletters, discussion documents or even a cafeteria menu. An extranet takes this outside to other stakeholders. Again this network would be password protected. Both could be Internet-enabled and allow access from home. The benefits of networks are in the areas of speed, cost-reduction and a more integrated approach to issues and concerns. Improved records, information, knowledge, flexibility and barrier-reduction are other benefits that can be had and the Internet can be said to have contributed greatly to globalisation, not least for smaller businesses. Wireless communication is of course a new infrastructure that for some developing nations means that they can skip the old (for the developed nations) infrastructure and put investment into the newest generation, unhampered by the 'baggage' (i.e. cables and wires) of the past.

The Snapshot below discusses the smart television and its relationship with connectivity and interactivity. Those consumers who have already bought a smart television appear to use them to go online but the challenge appears to be to get consumers to buy a smart television in the first place.

Snapshot   Just for pay TV? Smart TV, interactivity and connectivity

According to Clover (2013), Smart TV is 'failing the connectivity test' and 'lagging behind laptops, desktops and set-top boxes when it comes to consumers deciding how to connect their TV sets to the internet'. Clover uses the UK YouGov's Connected TV tracker statistics to show that the idea of accessing online content via television is liked by half of UK consumers but only 13 per cent owned a smart television (as of the first quarter of 2013) – laptops (24 per cent), desktops (12 per cent) and set-top boxes (23 per cent, made up of 12 per cent Sky+, 6 per cent Virgin Media, 3 per cent Freeview and 2 per cent BT Vision). 'Catch up' television is watched by over one third of people in the UK via a set-top box but only 7 per cent do this using a smart television.

The issue seems to be that about half of the consumers who buy a smart television do not do so to go online but to simply update the set and about a quarter because the set was broken, leaving just under a quarter who actually buy a smart television to use it to go online. Clover suggests that the challenge is for smart television manufacturers to make it easier to go online through the use of apps but that it appears that only pay television subscribers are likely to take this up currently.

Perhaps this step in the connectivity process is a while away. Broadband TV News (2013) reported that in late 2013 it looked like 73 per cent of US consumers were not interested in smart TV, or at least not for another year. Part of this may be the recession but part of it might be to do with educating the market: '… demand rises markedly when consumers are aware of what smart TVs are, showing that the product's chances of success can improve with just a little market education' say *Broadband TV News* (2013), using the results of a survey conducted by the TV Systems Intelligence Service. It would seem that there is no stampede to purchase smart televisions and it is up to manufacturers in the US marketplace to help stimulate sales by education. Consumers need to see the benefits of smart television over what they already have. Such benefits lie in features such as online interactivity and on-demand video streaming and again apps appear to be key, just as with smartphone usage. Most people with a smart television connect to the Internet with it, enabling them to access services such as Netflix.

The challenge is to get more people to buy a smart television. Broadband TV News suggests that the 'survey also revealed that 75% of smart TV owners possess a smartphone, and 65% have a tablet, which creates an opportunity for secondary-screen applications, including content discovery, content sharing/mirroring and remote control' and that 'consumers love big screens, but are getting more price sensitive'. The opportunity appears to exist, however, because of the growing desire to be connected online so that the impetus appears still to be there to acquire an interactive but integrated home entertainment centre. Apparently smart televisions have two to three times more pulling power than 3D television because of the interest in high definition and ultra high definition television once these become affordable.

Stop Point

Consumers are still buying televisions but the demand for smart televisions needs to be stimulated and cultivated. Undertake the following: 1. Outline what you think smart television marketers should do in marketing communications terms to stimulate this demand; 2. Discuss the future of interactivity and connectivity in terms of what the home entertainment system might be within a few years' time.

ONLINE DESIGN AND MANAGEMENT ISSUES

Managing websites

A webmaster or web developer is normally hired to manage a site. This includes analysis and monitoring of site activity and checks on navigation and connectivity. Servers, required to link a user's computer to the Internet, involve software so that an Internet Service Provider (ISP) can then provide this service. Many of the problems of going online are technical and technological. Many Internet difficulties are quickly resolved but just as this is done other difficulties pop up. Such is the ever-changing nature of this particular (technological) beast. From an organisational perspective, there should be clear links to marketing strategy when considering the use of the Internet and not just the 'number of visitors on our web site' mentality that appeared to be extant in the mid 1990s. As with the rest of the marketing communications management process, and as advocated in this book in Chapter 4, a decision sequence model approach to managing Internet activity should be taken. In the past an online brochure may have been the requirement, but much more is desired now and this demand is set to continue to increase.

The inter communications process

Websites and e-commerce as a complement to other activities, quite common by the end of the 1990s, are now the norm. The Internet was originally weak on awareness whereby in the first instance there was a requirement for more traditional forms of communication such as television advertisements that could create initial awareness and guide the viewer to a web address. For example, television advertising might be used to create awareness of the brand and its potential benefits and take the prospects to a website where they could buy online. This was the case with Esure, an online insurance company who typically offered a 10 per cent discount if the prospect bought online rather than offline (the option was there to use the telephone if needs be). The integrated marketing communications campaign drew attention to the offering of the company with conventional television advertising, but by way of a special online promotion a prospect was potentially turned into a customer. This allowed for greater use of the creative platform to work cognitively and affectively until an action was taken, since once on the site the prospect was involved with something that was interactive, flexible and targeted. Campaigns like this are still extant but as access and use of online facilities have increased things have changed. For example social media might well be employed, with the use of, say, video, as lead media rather than conventional media leading, perhaps with the mention of a web address. The Internet has been and is, clearly, a medium that is good on product and company information but it is now much more than it was in the early days. It can also still be a cost-effective way of doing business despite becoming more expensive as it has developed over the last two decades.

Website design

Characteristics

The key to successful Internet use is interactivity and the key to interactivity is ease of use. The characteristics of web design are crucial to the length of stay and activities undertaken and potential for a return visit. This applies whether dealing with corporate or marketing/product/brand issues. Key to this is customer search. The prospect is searching and apart from cross-cultural issues and variances such as language, speed is of the essence as are accessibility and the incidence of devices that enable online access. Personal computers and laptops, but also now mobile phones and tablets, are such devices that are key. Wireless connectivity for social and business use has grown, so much so that its availability at airports, railway stations and other venues is an expectation.

Visitors to websites can be categorised by type. Experienced users need directed information but there are those who require this less. The experienced buyer may need no information. Other visitors might need more in order to navigate a website. If the visitor is a professional buyer then they are likely to have very different needs from consumer types who seek entertainment, for example. Just as with traditional marketing and media, these types could be classified as active or passive. The quantification of hits on websites is useful but the quality of the hit is important, which is rather like the argument about the quality of visitors to an exhibition stand.

There are now many companies that offer website or web design services and there is much advice also, often in the form of tips to get the most out of a website design. The designer has to take account of the relevancy of the material in meeting need and not simply using design as an end in itself. However, the site has to excite and might engender curiosity, if this is appropriate. In a similar manner to advertising or packaging the website design will have characteristics such as being visually interesting or arresting and being likeable. The site should be user-friendly and the interface interactive. Messages should not be concealed by overuse of gimmicks or graphics. Navigation will become difficult if the site is too complex or has too many levels. Menu options should be clear and complete with easy return and exit buttons. As ever, irritation should be considered carefully. Mokhov (2013) of Hongkiat.com, an online design and development company, offers five tips to simplify web design:

1. Focus only on essential elements – identify what needs to be a focus just as with any good visual design.
2. Get rid of all unnecessary elements – do this by using the 80-20 rule (if 20% of the design gives 80% of the value then use the 20%).
3. Reduce the number of pages – have fewer places to explore and click around by trimming the page count: make sure that the pages facilitate what is necessary and nothing more.
4. Get more content above the fold – studies have shown that a majority of people spend most of their time above the fold on web pages (what shows up on the screen without scrolling down) so have the main content and call-to-action elements above the fold.
5. Limit your colour scheme – if more subtlety and texture to visual design are needed use shades of the same colour.

Online branding and advertising

Branding and brand loyalty are part of the marketing communications process online just as offline. Branding can bring with it a greater use of emotional elements as well as the use of rational/informational elements that the Internet was used for in the early days. Once on a site delivery can be a simple click-through, the method used to get on the site in the first place in many instances. Delivery is therefore consistent and getting a sale and then improving retention to achieve some degree of brand loyalty the objectives. Online advertising is said to have four times the growth of offline advertising globally and online spend is expected to exceed 20 per cent of all advertising by 2015.

Cookies

Cookies are text files that are embedded on the hard drive of a site visitor and which allow companies to repeat offers to that visitor once the cookie is established.

Display

Display advertising online has been there effectively since the start in a basic form and has mutated from being on a static web page with text (or copy), a logo and photographs to much more interactive items such as location maps, banners and similar items, an audio or video link, and also billboards, posters and fliers. According to Glenday (2013), expenditure on Internet display advertising 'has risen by 27 per cent on a year over year basis, complementing a rise of 4.2 per cent in global TV ad expenditure and a 5 per cent increase in outdoor spend'. Glenday uses data from the Nielsen's quarterly *Global AdView Pulse* reports, 'which showed that in the first half of 2013 global TV ad expenditure was the leading advertising format with a 57.6 per cent market share', reflecting growth in spend globally 'with the notable exception of Europe' on television and online at the expense of print.

Banners, buttons, billboards, skyscrapers and wallpaper

Banner advertisements are an option and can be static or more interactive as the medium has moved towards a more television-like presentation. Banners can be placed at the top, side or bottom of the screen and click-through takes the prospect elsewhere. As banners developed, sound and animation were added for effect, such as a car and the 'vroom' sound associated with starting off. The costs of banners are relatively low but so too are response rates, although involvement is a factor that leads to more effective targeting;

however, there is an annoyance factor. Animation and other novelties can lift the rate of click-through on low-involvement situations but have little effect on high-involvement situations where novelties might only serve to annoy. Banner advertising is embedded into a web page and the intent is to attract traffic to a website. Unlike traditional advertising, banner effects can be monitored in real-time. Buttons are smaller versions of banners that take the prospect straight to a site. As the technology has developed and banner advertising reaches its 20th year, other options have become available such as billboards, skyscrapers and wallpaper. According to Haggerty (2013), industry sources are suggesting that 'banner ads are dead and wallpaper ads are in' as 'internet users are becoming increasingly banner blind' where 'click through rates for wallpaper ads reach up to two per cent while banner ads achieve an average 0.014 per cent'.

Front pages

Front or home pages have been designed with some of the above considerations on sound or animation. This first or main website page usually has visual displays or video and a click-through facility to other pages.

Pop-ups, interstitials, superstitials and multi-screen

Decisions to use the interstitials, superstitials or pop-ups have to be balanced against the irritation factor that can do damage and drive prospects away. A similar consideration has to be made with the use of multi-screens. *Pop-ups* are online advertisements such as an interstitial (a small space in between), which is displayed in a new browser window when the user clicks through from page to page and the page is still loading. Interstitials are likely to contain larger graphics, streaming media or applets that do not appear in banners because of restrictions on size. Interstitials can be seen as anti-permission marketing that can have a negative effect if users get irritated or worse. Similarly with the superstitial, which is the advertisement that is launched in a new browser window while the user is waiting for a page to load. These days, online shoppers use a variety of devices to go online so that online marketers have responded by using a multi-screen strategy because increasingly consumers are using more than one device to shop with, so that the paths (or screens) to purchase might be multiple and commonly start from a smart phone. Apps are an important part of this process because responsive sites are necessary for holding a prospect's attention.

Video

With the widespread use of broadband access to the Internet have come speed and video use online. Video clips have become very popular in many different forms. Video can be used on, for example, websites, YouTube-type social media channels or blogs. All manner of video types are used online from news to humour to music. The online video as an advertising tool has emerged as a powerful way to deliver a message, whether this is on an organisation's website or through social media of one sort or another.

Other online marketing and corporate communications

Sales promotion

Chapter 11 of this book discusses the nature and role of sales promotion in detail. Sales promotions rely on interest and involvement that will encourage return to a site where a prospect may have registered online and be part of a database. Emailing is then possible so that, for example, Amazon or Ebay typically email offers and attachments. QR (quick response) codes can be used to take the user directly to a brand's website. The ideas behind online promotions are the same as offline and many of the techniques are the same – for example, contests, sweepstakes, competitions or prizes – so that many of the outcomes of using promotions online will be the same. For example, with contests, the interest and involvement online can be high and databases can be built in this way as long as the right type of person is attracted to the promotion. Offline communication such as television advertising or packaging may be used to drive the person on to the website. Promotions online may get visits and clear stock or offer the potential customer a price reduction through the use of a code but, as with traditional promotions, this is not usually part of a brand-building exercise but can be brand recognition or rewards for regular customers.

Sampling and couponing have quite logically gone online and are potentially targeted in a better, more efficient, way. If the user is willing to leave forwarding address details then actual sampling can take place. Of course, if the product is downloadable then this can be carried out instantly. Coupons can be redeemed then and there on a website or printed and then used in store. Groupon is a company that is typical of the 'group coupon' (i.e. a portmanteau of these two words) that has at its core the idea of the 'daily deal' sales promotion that companies can sign up to, offering anything from local restaurant meals to facials at special rates if enough people (the group) sign up.

Direct marketing, online events and 'webinars'

Direct marketing online using email is the same in logic as direct marketing offline, as discussed in Chapter 12 of this book. As mentioned above, direct email can be used to contact prospects with promotions and attachments or with offers. Viral marketing and ewom, the electronic form of the original word-of-mouth, have a relationship with opinion leadership (as discussed in Chapter 2 of this book) and might also be viewed in the same way as a chain letter, whereby a message is sent to a small number of people who then send it on to others. This might be a humorous message or one with special interest. Such special interest groups may, or may not, be interested in commercial offers so that this is a kind of permission marketing where affinity groups and even affinity sites exist to share information and ideas. Online events are possible that equate to an exhibition or (trade) show and online seminars (often called webinars) are also possible. These usually have to be made known through more conventional means of communication and like their offline counterparts have a certain shelf-life and are perishable.

Public Relations

The Internet provides the ideal context for information to be posted about the organisation, the company and its brands. Both marketing/product and corporate levels benefit from Internet PR activities that are used in traditional PR (as discussed in Chapter 13 of this book), such as investor and corporate relations through published accounts and press releases, past press releases, history, newsletters or images/photography. The organisation can now use the Internet and digital technologies such as podcasts and video to communicate with its various publics to deliver the organisation's key messages.

Sponsorship

Sponsorship deals and materials can be announced but there is also the prospect of sponsorship opportunities online such as the sponsorship of a good cause's website. The usual goals such as targeting particular groups with the brand and achieving goodwill are the same as discussed in Chapter 15 of this book. The means are different since online communities, special interest groups and chat rooms for real-time interaction can be used. Diffin

(2010) adds that fundraising websites are 'now a popular way of collecting money for a good cause' but questions their impact on sponsoring people and whether or not they have helped the cause. Diffin concludes that such sites have raised millions. For example, 'Children like Charlie Simpson have ridden bikes to raise money for charity for years but few have ever made national headlines. Of course, few of them have ever raised more than £173,000 from people around the world either. The tale of the boy from London who rode his bike to raise funds for earthquake survivors in Haiti is now well-known, and heart-warming. But "little Charlie" is only one of millions of charitable folk who raise money through their exploits to help worthy causes'. As Diffin suggests, in the past a sponsor-ship form would be sent around parents, friends or the office but this activity has now 'migrated online' and 'sponsorship websites are changing the ways charities work'. This is because of their reach, ease of use and the fact that it is not necessary to handle actual money: 'Some organisations have seen as much as a 40% increase in donations as a result of being on such sites – and that's during a recession'. Diffin adds that Charlie Simpson raised more than £170,000 on JustGiving, said to be the largest charity support and fundraising site in the world.

Virtual reality, simulation and animation

Virtual reality online is a computer simulation of a real or imaginary situation used in gaming, advertising and other online applications in 3D. Virtual reality enables the perfor-mance of actions operations in real time. Virtual reality is now a reality because broadband is established and able to carry much more information. Virtual, rich media technologies have been in place for some time but the means of delivering these have only relatively recently been established in much of the world though of course not all of it. Virtual towns, stores and other venues or contexts are an interesting marketing prospect (see below under 'social media – virtual game worlds and virtual social worlds').

Email, permission marketing, spam and phishing

In Chapter 12 of this book the use of direct mail is discussed in terms of response rates and a similar argument can be transferred into the email domain. Unsolicited email can cause simi-lar problems to those generated in the more conventional field and 'permission marketing' is a possible part of the solution to such problems. Once an organisation has an email address an advertisement or promotion of some sort can be sent, although this would be inherently risky if unsolicited. Opt-in email makes this means of communication a different prospect. As mentioned above, email marketing is often used within direct marketing that utilises lists or databases, and like traditional mail can be used to deliver promotional messages but also links to websites, newsletters, ezines (electronic magazines), product information, sales promotion offers or catalogues. The main advantage is immediacy followed by the ability to easily track effects, reach and cost. The main disadvantage is invasion of privacy and nuisance effect.

With the electronic form, spam (or spamming) is a tempting prospect but is a practice that does not fit in well with the IMC approach advocated in this book and many other places. Spam is 'junk' or unsolicited email whereby the same message is sent to many recipients at the same time and may involve recipients being sent to phishing websites. Phishing is a method of email fraud when a legitimate-looking email (for example from a bank) is sent in an attempt to gather personal and financial information from recipients. If the situation is an 'opt-in' one whereby the recipient is happy to receive email and attach-ments, then advertising messages can be sent via rich media such as video, newsletters or press releases. Specialist companies can handle this work and there is a relative low cost associated with it if compared with conventional media. Potentially, there will be a better response from email than from banner advertising, provided permission is granted.

Mobile marketing and advertising

Mobile phones, tablets and other mobile devices

Perhaps the most exciting area is that of mobile technology, where the wonders of WAP (Wireless Application Protocol) technology led to mobile email, text and photo messaging, among other things. As ever, however, the commercial viability aspects of applying such advances have a bearing but the advance of this kind of technology and applications appears relentless, with possibilities, for example, around security involving face recognition and finger print and retina scanning, as mobiles encompass 'virtual wallets'. Soon people may be wearing phones that appear as fashion accessories such as watches, glasses or even something that is worn all of the time so that people are connected as convergence becomes a reality that includes video (rather than telephone) calling, such as FaceTime from Apple.

Mobile technology in particular is at the forefront of an increasingly wireless world where wireless messages can be used to redirect customers to websites. It remains to be seen if consumers will revolt against commercial text, photo and video messaging, especially in the light of a number of scams that have been exposed. An industry has grown up around this whereby the phone user is willing to pay for software that will block messages that are either 'spam' and meaningless or 'spam' for commercial gain of some sort.

With the advent, development and ubiquity of mobile phones and especially smart phones, the reach of marketers' messages has been vastly increased. Consequently there is much interest in mobile phone marketing and advertising, although advertising spend is relatively low despite there being many more mobile phones than other devices capable of accessing the Internet. This, of course, is developing rapidly as marketers work out how best to use this technology, with mobile advertising growing rapidly and expected to be worth more than £20 billion worldwide by around 2015.

Messaging and changing technology

Rich media advertisements are now available as are banners and posters, but mobile marketing is still dominated by SMS (short message service) advertising. Some in the industry reckon that this will not last for much longer. While recipients of messages are more likely to view a text message than an email, a picture or image is a tempting prospect and can speak volumes. MMS (multimedia message service) is developing rapidly and there is the development of advertising and product placement within mobile games and mobile audio and video. As mobile marketing has developed and is developing so too is the infrastructure around it, such as the Mobile Marketing Association (MMA, www.mmaglobal.com/), the mobile marketing trade body whose goal is to help develop mobile marketing as an indispensable part of the marketing mix as well as guide and protect the industry. The measurement of the effectiveness of mobile marketing is also developing as mobile marketing develops. The main measurement currently is the quantitative measurement of impressions or opportunities to see (OTS) and click-through rates, but other measurement is needed such as that of interaction and engagement, which needs a more qualitative approach. Issues such as the nature of the message sent to particular targets are important. For example, if the target market is relatively young then mobile advertising could be particularly attractive to marketers since younger people have an intimate relationship with their (usually) smart phone and the ability to send and receive text and other messaging. At the same time they are likely to appreciate commercial messages that appear to build a relationship with them with their permission rather than a message that ignores the option to opt-in and is too direct.

Search engine marketing (SEM) and search engine optimisation (SEO)

Search engine marketing (SEM)

SEM is a marketing tool that helps to build traffic and visibility from search engines in their results pages (SERPs) through paid-for efforts, based on bidding on keywords or 'pay per click'. It involves buying traffic through paid search listings. The most famous and largest supplier is Google AdWords as SEM has grown much faster than traditional advertising or any other online marketing tool. SEM works through the enabling of potential customers when they are looking to buy (when they are in 'hunt mode') and are searching the Internet. Most people who use the Internet use search engines and for most the choice is Google, to the extent that Google has become synonymous with this activity rather like Hoover was to vacuum cleaning. This is a unique situation because there is clear intent shown, like a buying signal in personal selling, and the potential customer is at least at some point in a buying cycle and decision-making process. It may be that they are only at the stage of researching a product or service for an immediate or future need but 'this makes search engine results some of the best sources of targeted traffic' (Lee, 2013).

Search engine optimisation (SEO)

SEO is about obtaining traffic through unpaid for, free listings. This has great potential to improve the effectiveness of a website but like email it can also be risky in terms of brand damage and reputation. SEO is involved with the re-writing of website content to achieve a higher ranking in SERPs.

The Snapshot below discusses SEM and SEO and the reasons why marketers have to gain an understanding of how the search engine can work within their marketing mix and how to make it a powerful tool for the organisation.

Snapshot   Why search marketing, paid for or free, should be part of any marketing mix

Search marketing, as search engine marketing is often referred to, 'has already proven itself a valuable part of an overall integrated campaign, for both branders and direct marketers. All kinds of marketers can easily benefit from a dialogue with a searcher; whether that searcher is facing a crisis, is in need of information, or is ready to purchase' (Lee, 2013). Lee, writing for SEMPO, the not-for-profit trade organisation which stands for Search Engine Marketing Professionals' Organisation, which is USA-based, suggests that 'information retrieval search engines existed long before the internet', citing Electronic Card Catalogs and Lexis/Nexis, travel reservation systems and private search databases that 'have existed for almost as long as computers have'. Lee suggests that early search queries go back as far as the punch card and pre-date web browsers: 'After the browser was invented as a graphical way to displaying information, it became an interface for search.'

Marketers need to understand how both paid for SEM and unpaid for SEO can be used effectively in order to take advantage of this powerful tool. Lee (2013) suggests that search engine traffic is unique because it is:

1   Non-intrusive and taps into a searcher at the exact moment they are seeking knowledge or a solution – it is just-in-time marketing.

2   It originates from a voluntary, audience-driven search.

3   It results from a fixed inventory of searches that the searcher must choose from.

Lee discusses 'organic' (free) search engine marketing that 'combines the best practices of technology, usability, copy/linguistics and online PR' because text on a page or site is combined with external things such as links and user behaviours and preferences. Since marketers can buy text-link search results, paid for search results through buying advertising that results in high value traffic, there has been a great deal of interest in such a marketing tool. The unpaid for side of things has become increasing difficult as it was 'once fairly easy to garner – before there were 3 billion documents competing for attention in the search engine databases'. Still, it would seem that organic SEO, 'particularly efforts in site design, HTML formatting, copy optimization and server platform adjustments', is worthwhile, but paid listings such as paid placement, directory paid inclusion, XML (per-ULR paid inclusion, shopping search and graphic (rich media) search inventory are, according to Lee, playing 'an ever-increasing role in most marketers' minds, due to their increasing screen real estate'.

SEO can be compared with public relations because it is basically about getting free long-term exposure for a business or a brand but this does depend on the way in which SEO is conducted. There is a difference between honest practice such as making a website easy for the likes of Google to read, whereby building links and using valuable content and relevant keywords are good and honest, but trying to trick the search engine or being dishonest can lead to the kind of bad PR that would happen offline if a similar attitude prevailed. Hidden keywords and multiple domain names can be used to influence the 'ranking game'. Getting ranked well is extremely important but the way the ranking happens is important too. There are numerous ways to enhance websites and optimise a search. Since search engines read text, textual content is good so that images should be labelled, have a URL for each page and have search words in each URL. A search engine will rank content so that each part needs to be given relative importance and of course having quality content is important as are key words that are relevant to the organisation or brand. Links are important too but they need to have authority, credibility and trust (link quality) for the search engine to be influenced in terms of rankings.

Stop Point

Working on the design of a website in order to make it better and more user-friendly while at the same time making it the kind of website that will do well when a user of a search engine makes an inquiry would seem a logical proposition. Undertake the following: 1. Comment on the difference between the terms search marketing, search engine marketing and search engine optimisation; 2. Choose a website and explain why it is a good, bad or indifferent site in terms of search engine optimisation.

SOCIAL MEDIA

Gupta et al. (2013) place social media into six types: collaborative projects such as Wikipedia; blogs and micro blogs such as Twitter; content communities such as YouTube; social networking sites such as Facebook; virtual game worlds such as World of Warcraft; and virtual social worlds such as Second Life. These authors are interested in the promotion of health and in education and argue that social media are a communication boon for the public health community with the ability to promote behaviour change, particularly in times of crisis. Social media in their varying forms, including consumer-generated content, are of course being used by most organisations such as those that are public and private, small and large, or for-profit and not-for profit. Social media are certainly being taken seriously by many organisations as a key tool, so much so that many have allocated resources such as dedicated staff employed full-time, with coverage and monitoring 24/7/365. Companies in particular, but all forms of organisation, have realised that social means social and personal and not corporate, which has major ramifications for message construction. They also realise that consumers using social media expect something from organisations, especially companies and brand owners, to offer something extra, by way of, for example, a promotional offer or product/brand information, but which has to be credible.

Social networking

There are now many social networking sites. Social networking is a global phenomenon with billions of users worldwide. It is all about people staying in touch with other people, and exchanging experiences, images and other personal content including sending emails. Being on Facebook or MySpace has become part of the daily lives of many people around the world, despite warnings about private information disclosure and other activity that involves interfacing with people, often through clicking on links of one sort or another. Social networks are seen by many organisations as valuable tools that allow marketing to take place with more and more contacts, but there are risks involved. Grooming on Internet chat rooms has been in the news generally for some time and this and other activity such as peer pressure have been exacerbated by the advent of social networks. Many of the issues around social networks are to do with the individual and what they post on a site and how this is then used.

Facebook

Lee (2012), for the *BBC News*, declared that Facebook 'surpasses one billion users as it tempts new markets', with North America having 238m users, its biggest market, but with regions like Europe having 243 million. This billion-plus user base is apparently responsible for 1.13 trillion 'likes', 219 billion photos and 17 billion location check-ins. However, despite moving into new markets, just what the commercial potential of Facebook and other social network sites has not as yet been determined. Certainly its share price nearly halved from a starting point of $38 to $20. Zuckerberg, however, was in Moscow shortly after that to promote his creation there: 'The competition in this region comes from the likes of VKontakte, which is far in the lead with an estimated user base of almost 300 million'. So it goes around the world with 258 million Facebook users in Asia, excluding of course China (see Renren below), where the biggest market is India (60 million users) and Facebook's third biggest country. Lee (2012) provides other user figures from around the world such as South America (135 million), Australia and Oceania (15 million) and Africa (48 million), reflecting the challenge of technology, connectivity and accessibility. As Lee points out, however, many 'Africans use mobile payment as their primary way of spending and earning cash – a trend the wider world is slow to follow up on'. Facebook has a range of enabling tools such as Every Phone that allows Facebook to run on basic handsets. By mid-2012 there were 600 million users accessing Facebook via a mobile device.

Facebook's presence in a country is primarily around selling advertising with local brands ranking highly among the most engaged pages, but the value of such advertising that is based on 'likes' is still uncertain. However, with the power of sites like Facebook recognised by companies and governments alike, Facebook continues to march on. According to Lee (2012), in the UK 'ministers are said to be considering using Facebook, among other services, to act as official identification for accessing public services online'. With advertising on Facebook regulated by local bodies such as the ASA in the UK, any other activities will surely come under scrutiny as well, and as Lee notes 'Such advancements are being noted by data regulators. In Europe in particular, Facebook has been faced with increased demands to tighten data privacy practices'. In Europe Facebook has its HQ in Ireland and as such in April 2012 was told to amend its Phototag feature (a tool powered by facial recognition software) and following an extensive audit by the Irish Data Protection Commission extra assurances were sought from Facebook 'over issues surrounding account deletion and targeted advertising'. Facebook may also be losing younger users to newer social network sites such as Pinterest, Foursquare and Instagram, the latter having been acquired by Facebook for $1 billion in 2012 and which is 'attempting to build momentum in key verticals such as fashion, sport, food and celebrities as it seeks to build its global user base of 150 million' (Barber, 2013).

Facebook continues to evolve with additions such as Timeline that allows for a history of brand events in Brand Pages in September 2011, which enhanced the ability for marketers to have engaging content to help cut through the clutter. This was a response to marketers' complaints that posts were getting lost in the milieu of activity. Peterson and Heussner (2012) report that Timeline 'shares many features with the consumer version, such as the vertically oriented content timeline and addition of a widescreen image atop the page', but there are additional features. For example 'Companies can star posts to expand their appearance to widescreen or pin posts to appear in the Timeline's top-left area for seven days. The latter feature is not unlike what Twitter has done with its enhanced profile pages that brands can use to dock a specific tweet atop their feed, regardless of when it was first posted'. Facebook also offers 'milestones', content boxes that can feature photos and text that can 'detail specific points in a brand's history'.

Renren (previously known as Xiaonei from 2005 until 2009)

By way of comparison to Facebook, Renren is considered here as what has been called the 'Chinese Facebook', a label that many people dispute. In 2011 Renren raised $743 million on the New York Stock Exchange with an opening price of $14. The way Renren works is like Facebook with people doing the same kinds of things as they would if they could on Facebook such as status and photo sharing. However, by 2013 Renren's share value was just $3. While Facebook is still growing and broadening its user base, Renren appears to be narrowing and contracting with its main user base in China. After its initial college-based creation (Xiaonei), younger users have left and fewer have been recruited and it appears that it is less of a social site than a commercial one with charges for additional features, which some users do not like. Renren has also been accused of a lack of innovation and of simply copying the technical ad-ons of Facebook. Users have apparently moved on to micro blogs like Weibo, which is akin to Twitter (see below).

Myspace

As Costill (2013) reports, MySpace, 'the once dominant social media platform, has been gaining users'. According to Costill 'within the last four months (since the summer of

2013) 24 million people have signed up', bringing MySpace's total users to around 36 million. The new MySpace is a re-launch of the old but with a music twist. It has been overhauled with full screen video and 'drag and drop' content facility and can be used for multimedia playlist creation that then can be shared via ties with Twitter and Facebook. The move towards music came about through the buy-in by Specific Media, the global interactive media company, and actor and singer Justin Timberlake. For organisations there are opportunities to create engaging ways to contact consumers, but MySpace have work to do to attract such companies and of course more users. As Costill suggests: 'Since the site is geared towards music, you would think that almost anyone in the industry would latch on. For example, publications like *Rolling Stone* and *Billboard* aren't on MySpace, which is a shame'. Costill is of course referring to the obvious link between music magazines/papers and a music-oriented social networking site as MySpace now is: 'Obviously both magazines are involved with music, but the layout, large images and multimedia content could expand their market by connecting with fans through a new medium'. Clearly other sorts of brands will have a use for a site like MySpace, which is concentrating on a younger demographic. Costill suggests that a brand like Gap have lost an opportunity in not using MySpace as part of their recent campaign, which 'features the children of iconic musicians covering classic songs originally performed by their parents. Gap could have used MySpace to not only showcase the new clothing items and music videos, but they could have had the artists create playlists on their MySpace pages which relate specifically to the ads. It's just a simple way to reach new consumers who may not have typically invested time in your brand'.

LinkedIn

LinkedIn is the best-known social network site for professionals. It has been up and running since 2003 and by summer 2013 had about 260 million users around most of the world. It is available in 20 languages and, according to the *BBC News* (2013), LinkedIn is, as of 12 September 2013 'dropping its minimum age for membership from 18 to 13', whereby children's profiles 'will have default settings making less of their personal information publicly visible, with more prominent links to safety information. Support requests from child members will also be dealt with separately'. This has come about after LinkedIn launched University Pages that have allowed higher education institutions to set up profiles. The aim is to help children differentiate between their personal Facebook-type profile and a profile for employment. This may come with some problems with children being children and, for example, creating profiles under false names. Already set up on LinkedIn are New York University, the University of Michigan and French university Insead. Companies, of course, are big users, not least for recruitment. Macleod (2013) reports on LinkedIn's most engaging FTSE 100 marketers. This ranges across sectors from finance to hotel groups. LinkedIn's Most Engaged Marketer 2013 'highlighted the UK marketers that are using the platform to their best advantage, not only for their personal brand, but also being advocates for the company they work for'. Top of the list was Reckitt Benckiser's (consumer goods with brands such as Dettol, Durex and Cillit Bang) Marco Augugliaro who works with digital media. Augugliaro uses LinkedIn for its 'unmatched aggregator' of marketing/business/social knowledge and news, lead generator for suppliers in marketing agencies and as a job searcher in marketing. Others on the list of LinkedIn's most engaged FTSE 100 marketers cited LinkedIn as the first place to go for new insights, inspiration, to learn from experts, to check up on competitors, to maintain contact with colleagues, peers and friends, and as a vehicle from which to sent messages to customers or sales colleagues.

Macleod lists the 10 Most Engaged FTSE 100 Marketers on LinkedIn as:

1. Marco Augugliaro, Digital Media, Reckitt Benckiser
2. Paul Hudson, Global Marketing Consultant, RSA
3. Claire Whitehead, former Head of Global Brand Strategy & Marketing
4. InterContinental Hotel Groups
5. Craig Chadburn, Social Media Manager, BT
6. Marghaid Howie, Chartered Marketer, Capita
7. Americo Campos Silva, Global Media Manager, Shell
8. Vinne Schifferstein Vidal, Market Development Director, Pearson plc
9. George Cairns, Acting Head of Digital Marketing Strategy, Lloyds
10. Jon Coulson, Marketing Consultant, B&Q
11. Rebecca Heptinstall, Social Media Manager, *Financial Times*

Blogs and micro blogs

There are hundreds of millions of blogs online. A blog (a portmanteau from the words web and log) consists of entries or posts, usually in reverse chronological order. They can be written by individuals, groups of people, by the media, interest groups, or indeed organisations such as companies or charities. There are 'professional bloggers', often journalists or 'think tank' members. Blogs are usually interactive with the ability of the reader to add to the blog via a post, which is a commonplace occurrence. In a sense blogs are a form of social networking because of this interactive nature. Bloggers build relationships with regular readers but some blogs remain static and are non-interactive. Blogs function in different ways. Some provide a running commentary on a particular subject while others are more like personal diaries. Companies and brand owners use the blog as a form of advertising or PR and since blogs can contain more than mere text, rich media can be used within a blog such as artwork, video, photography and music. Some blogs become video or podcasts.

Micro blogs feature very short posts that are short text updates. Bloggers usually have access to instant messaging or email depending upon the site used (see, for example, Twitter below). Posts are therefore micro posts and micro blogging is used within other social networking sites such as Facebook that feature in profiles, and in Facebook's case this is 'Status Updates'.

Twitter

In 2006 Jack Dorsey and Biz Stone founded Twitter, the most used and famous micro blogging service in the world. On 7 November 2013 Twitter was floated on the New York Stock Exchange with a value of $14.2 billion from a raised price beyond its initial public offering to $26 a share (*The Telegraph*, 2013). The rise of Twitter and other micro blog sites created social news streams from what were originally singular, micro posts or 'tweets'. A tweet is a short burst of characters up to the 140 maximum allowed. Links can be included to other content. Many different kinds of people tweet, with celebrities often having millions of followers on Twitter. According to *The Telegraph* (2013), pop star Katy Perry has more than 46 million Twitter followers and other celebrities are anxious that they are being defined by their popularity on Twitter. Breaking news is often found on Twitter first and certainly journalists and politicians use Twitter as a fast means of communication. Companies and other organisations can use the service as a free way to engage customers and consumers since tweets can contain promotions and special offers. Small businesses may not have followers into the millions but certainly building such a base, even if only in the hundreds and then thousands, can be a worthwhile endeavour.

Weibo

Sina Weibo started life as a Twitter clone but has since grown and according to Tan (2013) 'has since innovated to morph into an offering that surpasses the original site'. Weibo has more than '500 million registered users worldwide with more than 46.3 million daily active users'. The popularity of the Chinese micro blogging site cannot be denied, but it is Weibo's aim to go for 'a slice in the Southeast Asia market' and its recent expansion into the Singapore and Indonesian markets that concern Tan because 'these markets are dominated by Silicon Valley companies such as Facebook and Twitter' and it is 'unclear if Sina Weibo can succeed in penetrating and reaching out to its targeted Chinese speaking audience in the two countries, or even Southeast Asia'. Apparently, Sina Weibo has a goal of getting 1.5 million daily, active users in Singapore and plans and strategies for tackling the market were revealed in late November 2013.

Collaborative projects

Wikipedia is probably the most used and most famous online collaborative project. As the name suggests, collaborative projects mean that 'many hands make light work'. While Wikipedia is an online encyclopaedia there are many other projects that are more specific to an industry, sector or profession. For example, The Teachers Corner (2013) aims to engage learners in creative ways while ensuring that both curriculum and technology standards are met: 'Collaborative projects offer learning experiences that are authentic, purposeful and engaging'. The collaboration is between two or more classrooms that are in 'various locations around the world and use the Internet to interact with one another … The students enrolled in a project are all working on a similar topic for a specific length of time. They use the Internet to share their activities, findings and reflections. In addition to student collaboration, teachers are also being provided with the necessary tools to collaborate with one another'. Each project has a focus and an example is Project Pumpkin, where the area of focus is maths and the project will 'allow students to celebrate the fall, Halloween and/or the harvest season. Classes will be collecting, sharing and analyzing pumpkin-related data'.

Content communities

YouTube is perhaps the most famous of such a community where there is sharing between users, especially of course video but also comments. Such communities are content-specific within which there are individuals and groups focusing on areas of common interest. Many content communities are usually free to users but organisations, especially companies, have to pay for additional benefits. Key words are used and if the organisation's materials are tagged this can attract an audience that should be of similar mind within a particular community so that members will be able to view things like videos and photographs. Marketing materials like this can be uploaded, especially if the site is a presentation or document-sharing one. Original material can, of course, be created for the particular purpose, making it easy for the community members to access and use. There are millions of content communities. Three of the more famous ones are discussed below.

YouTube

YouTube (owned by Google since 2006) is primarily a video-sharing site although there are comments that are effectively micro blogs. Users upload and share a huge variety of video content. This can be anything from television or film clips, music videos or video blogs. People are able to make videos of themselves and others in short original videos. Organisations can do this also, but videos have to be suitable for online streaming. Once established a YouTube channel can carry advertising, the money from this is shared and there are other marketing opportunities. Videos can be shared on web pages outside the site by embedding them in other social media sites, pages and blogs. There is some mobile access to YouTube, depending upon the nature of the video. Alexa, the web information company and a subsidiary of Amazon, ranks websites and ranks YouTube third top site.

Flickr

Flickr is a content-sharing site for photographs and now video. Flickr has been used as a repository with billions of images housed. At a basic level Flickr is free to users and one useful feature is the ability to tag an item as a favourite. It also has a group facility with discussion board. There are also privacy, usage and safety features.

Slideshare

Alexa ranks the Slideshare site at number 121. Slideshare basically shares presentation content and as such is much more geared towards professionals and students than the general populous. It is the largest presentation-sharing community worldwide and allows many formats to be uploaded including PowerPoint, PDF, Word, Keynote and OpenDocument. Views, ideas, concepts or models can be shared and contacts made and developed, making this a kind of social network as well as a community. As with other social networks, presentations can be shared with the general populous or a specific group of people. Groups can be joined and there are marketing opportunities for organisations. Presentations are tagged and can be embedded into blogs and other websites. In this sense Slideshare has been compared with YouTube.

Virtual game worlds and virtual social worlds

Gupta et al. (2013) suggest that 'World of Warcraft' is typical of the type of online game that attracts millions of subscribers. Gamers can now join others in virtual worlds of games of all sorts. These authors also mention 'Second Life' as a virtual social world but there are many other forms such as 'The Sims', which is a real-time simulator where characters have feelings (sentiments) and can be confident or depressed and many other things. Gaming and social worlds apart, the marketing opportunities include advertising, sponsorship and product placement.

PRIVACY, SECURITY AND MEASUREMENT ISSUES

Privacy and security issues

Privacy in terms of personal data sold to others and third party involvement is clearly an important management issue as it has been with traditional database management for decades. Similarly, security remains as one of the biggest barriers to e-commerce and the use of the Internet generally. Despite industry claims, perceptions especially of credit card fraud remain and this is not surprising when this kind of fraud regularly crops up in more traditional telephone and over-the-counter contexts as well as, nowadays, in online transactions. The Internet at this point is therefore not seen as a medium that is adequately protected against theft and there is still no great confidence regarding credit card fraud. Customer expectation seems still to be that a transaction should be comprehensible, flexible, adaptable, predictable, easy to understand and transparent. These expectations may very well mitigate against being secure transactions.

Measurement issues

In terms of digital activities, there should be no philosophical difference in management attitude towards measurement of effectiveness, efficiency or performance than with other communication forms. As with the management model outlined in Chapter 4 of this book and as discussed in more detail in Chapter 17, achieving corporate, marketing or marketing communications objectives can only be realised if some attempt is made to measure effects not only in terms of communications but also financial performance. It has been recognised for some time that sales promotions and direct marketing are marketing communications activities that are relatively easier to measure than other elements of the marketing communications mix. Digital activities, because of their nature and in terms of websites' log server files and retrieval of information, are said to be easier too in this respect.

In terms of practical measurement and feedback, common activities include asking visitors to provide email contact information or feedback forms. This information will hardly be representative but will be of some value, although care should be taken with bias. Many of the techniques used in monitoring, evaluation and measurement of traditional marketing communications can and are applied in the digital arena. On-and offline surveys can be carried out, but unless the organisation has the ability and resources (financial and/or human) to do this work properly then they are advised to use the specialist website and other digital research companies that have been established and emerged and who can handle both on and offline as well as both qualitative and quantitative research if required. If so, this would involve not a simple quantitative measure of the number of hits, duration of visit or 'likes', but would use a range of techniques including in-depth interviews, focus groups or panels to investigate design issues such as positioning of banners, effectiveness of click-through, or quality of classified advertising lists in relation to key words. Profiles of visitors can be measured in terms of demographic and psychographic characteristics, but also satisfaction, usage, attitudes, values and more generally lifestyle. Research companies offer services that measure the quality of website content, navigation performance, website design, interactivity, attractiveness or likeability.

Organisations with a research budget can buy-in to services offered by a large range of research companies such as FlexMR (www.flexmr.net/) who have a series of research suites on offer including survey, panel, focus group, diary, interactive, community and analytic. This research company claims that these suites span the full spectrum of the online qualitative and quantitative research and community. FlexMR clients include Iceland Foods and ITV (Independent Television). Organisations can also buy in to what Google Analytics have to offer (www.google.com/analytics/). Google Analytics suggest that through its services companies can boost sales, find more visitors, improve mobile applications, and gain insights that can be turned into action.

The Snapshot below discusses the social networking sites of Facebook and Tencent and some of the issues around the rise of mobile connectivity and the demise of the desktop.

Snapshot   From Facebook to Tencent – what a difference mobile connectivity makes on social networks

The Economist (2013) questions whether Tencent is one of the world's greatest Internet firms, maintaining that there are 'grounds for scepticism'. Tencent is the Chinese gaming and social media firm that is a copy of 'Western success' with, for example, QQ, its instant-messaging service (a clone of ICQ, the Israeli invention acquired by AOL in the USA). *The Economist* points out that Tencent is still making its money in the (protected) Chinese market. It has a stock market valuation of $100 billion that is similar to

Facebook but has bigger revenues and profits than the US firm: 'In the first half of this year Tencent enjoyed revenues of $4.5 billion and gross profits of $2.5 billion, whereas Facebook saw revenues of $3.3 billion and gross profits of $935m'. The phenomenal rise in its share price means that Tencent had a higher shareholder return by 2012 than Amazon or Apple and according to *The Economist*, 'Tencent has created a better business model than its Western peers', pointing to the ways in which Tencent has been able to sell online games and other money-making products, unlike the Western model that gives things away and then seeks to 'monetise' users through online advertising, as with Google and 'revenue-rich but profit-poor Amazon'. According to *The Economist* QQ is used by 800 million people, and WeChat (the social networking app) has several hundred million users. It makes 80 per cent of its money from 'value added services'; for example add-ons in games such as weapons or costumes for avatars.

China is now the world's biggest e-commerce market and also the biggest for smart phones and m-commerce (mobile commerce) so that Tencent is dealing with the biggest market in the world, i.e. its home market. This is *The Economist*'s key point; that Tencent is investing heavily in rather unimpressive e-commerce offerings that will 'eat into profits' and worse still that its m-commerce activity 'risks distracting it from gaming and value-added services, the cash cows that are paying for everything else. A $100 billion valuation might then seem too rich'. Tencent's rivals in China (Baidu and Alibaba) as well as Tencent 'have gone on acquisition sprees, in an attempt to lead the market'. For example, Alibaba 'recently invested $300m in AutoNavi, an online-mapping firm, and nearly $600m in Sina Weibo, China's equivalent of Twitter'. Baidu has gone further with $1.85 billion to buy 91 Wireless (China's biggest third-party store for smart phone apps) and $370m for PPS (online video). Despite the popularity of WeChat, Tencent has bought into Sogou (an online search firm) with $448m and it 'plans to merge its own flagging search engine (aptly named Soso) into the venture. It had previously invested in Didi Dache, China's largest taxi-hailing app, and is rumoured to be interested in online travel and dating firms too'.

Since Facebook is not strong in mobile products and has not had the advantage that Tencent has of starting from a mobile base, the US firm is at a distinct disadvantage. Mobile connectivity is very different from that of desktop and as McKenzie (2013) comments, Tencent 'has shown Facebook how to reinvent itself for a mobile era'. The difference in connectivity means a move from 'friending' people on Facebook to building your 'social graph' around 'your address book'. The irony is that Facebook 'while an immense media network with a strong mobile presence, has become vulnerable to mobile threats, not only from Google, whose apps dominate the user experience on mobile and whose Android operating system is dominating handsets globally, but also from messaging apps, including Snapchat, WhatsApp, Kik, and, in Asia, Line, KakaoTalk, and China's WeChat'.

Stop Point

The 'winds of change' in the mobile era, as in many other contexts, mean that nothing stays the same. In the context of the social networking arena many factors are present such as payments and changes in operating systems and new gaming platforms. Undertake the following: 1. Comment on the differences and similarities between Facebook and Tencent; 2. Discuss the likely issue that will emerge in the next year or so in mobile marketing using social networks.

Assignment

You are required to write a consultative report for an organisation of your choice. Assume this organisation's managers have no knowledge of interactivity and especially Internet websites, search engines, web design issues or social media. The report should cover all aspects of interactivity and highlight the options available to the client, given the context in which that client operates. The report should include commentary on two websites of your choice. One of these sites must be what you consider to be best practice and the other site should be what you consider not good practice.

Summary of Key Points

- Technological change has led to an increasingly complex situation with the Internet but also with intra- and extranets, WAP technology and wireless communications.
- Interactive media have evolved into digital technology and an 'electronic frontier'.
- The newer electronic media are not in conflict with more traditional media and at present IMC is perfectly feasible using all forms of media.
- The Internet and especially website design have been key drivers in IMC.
- E-commerce has over time gained momentum and as long as the Internet can deliver customer service this will threaten more traditional commerce.
- The Internet and e-commerce can enhance brand loyalty because of positive relationship building.
- The electronic frontier is an exciting and daunting prospect at one and the same time. 'Traditional' Internet advertising has changed at a pace, with search engine optimisation threatening to overtake website design as the key driver.
- Social media offer places where people can go to share their status, upload photographs, and get news feeds from friends and many other activities. As such, social media have become important tools in the marketer's armoury.
- Effective evaluation will still be required, regardless of which form of technology dominates.

Discussion Questions

1. Define interactivity in marketing communications terms using examples to illustrate.
2. Examine the Internet and its relationship with intra- and extranets. Use examples of each to illustrate this relationship.
3. Highlight the benefits of the Internet in terms of branding and relationships, illustrating these with pertinent examples.

4. Briefly explain IMC in relation to online marketing. Use examples to illustrate the role of two online marketing communications tools such as email, search engine marketing or video.

5. Discuss the importance of the 'electronic frontier' in terms of technological change.

6. Assess the impact of the transient nature of advertising on the Internet using relevant examples.

7. Explain, in broad terms, the strategic options available to marketers regarding advertising on the Internet. Discuss in particular the difference between banner advertising and pop-ups and how these work in relation to click-through and web pages using examples to illustrate.

8. Discuss website creation in terms of design and the practical implications for navigation, using examples to illustrate.

9. 'Search engine optimisation is now a key issue for any organisation, large or small, from a marketing perspective.' Discuss the veracity of this statement using examples to illustrate.

10. Examine the use of social media by marketers seeking to target a particular type of customer, using examples to illustrate.

Further Reading

Cheung, M. (2008) '"Click here": the impact of new media on the encoding of persuasive messages in direct marketing', *Discourse Studies*, 10 (2): 161–89. http://dis.sagepub.com/content/10/2/161

This article looks at the impact of 'new' media on the encoding of persuasive messages in sales emails as part of direct marketing. The Hong Kong study examined equal numbers of email and print sales letters and found differences and similarities in discourse structures. The study also included interviews with specialist and corporate informants involved with sales promotion that verified the results.

Gupta, A., Tyagi, M. and Sharma, D. (2013) 'The use of social media marketing in healthcare', *Journal of Health Management*, 15 (2): 293–302. http://jhm.sagepub.com/content/15/2/293

The authors begin by placing social media into six types: collaborative projects such as Wikipedia; blogs and micro blogs such as Twitter; content communities such as You Tube; social networking sites such as Facebook; virtual game worlds such as 'World of Warcraft'; and virtual social worlds such as 'Second Life'. The authors' objective with this article is to explain the use of social media in health promotion and education, arguing that social media are a communication boon for the public health community with the ability to promote behaviour change, particularly in times of crisis.

Khang, H., Ki, E-J. and Ye, L. (2012) 'Social media research in advertising, communication, marketing and public relations, 1997–2010', *Journal of Mass Communication Quarterly*, 89 (2): 279–98. http://jmq.sagepub.com/content/89/2/279

This article is based on a study of patterns and trends in social media over the time period specified across four disciplines. The article reports an increasing number of social

(Continued)

(Continued)

media-related studies. This has happened in an incremental way whereby scholars have been keeping pace with increased social media usage. The authors conclude that there is a need to focus on prospective aspects of social media and outline some of the future directions for research.

Wong, W. and Gupta, S.C. (2011) 'Plastic surgery marketing in a generation of "tweeting"', *Aesthetic Surgery Journal*, 31 (8): 972–6. http://aes.sagepub.com/content/31/8/972 This article is about the increased use of social media such as Twitter, Facebook or MySpace and the need to apply website-building ethics. The authors recognise the use of social media in the promotion of plastic surgery services that is in addition to the use of traditional media such as television or feature articles in magazines.

Wymbs, C. (2011) 'Digital marketing: The time for a new "academic major" has arrived', *Journal of Marketing Education*, 33 (1): 93–106. http://jmd.sagepub.com/content/33/1/93 This article acknowledges the arrival of digital marketing and the digital economy and basically argues for a radical redesign of the marketing curriculum to make it consistent with and relevant to the real world. The author puts forward the rationale for change after performing a curriculum audit and also puts forward a new curriculum that is reflective of marketing in the digital age. There is an approach suggested to implement such change as well.

REFERENCES

Barber, L. (2013) 'Facebook UK PR head Sophy Tobias moves to lead Instagram EMEA comms', *PR Week*, 7 November.

BBC News (2013) 'Children to have LinkedIn profiles', *BBC News*, 20 August, available at: www.bbc.co.uk/news/technology-23766251

Broadband TV News (2013) '73% of US consumers not interested in smart TV', *Broadband TV News*, 28 October, available at: www.broadbandtvnews.com/2013/10/28/73-of-us-consumers-not-interested-in-smart-tv/

Cheung, M. (2008) '"Click here": the impact of new media on the encoding of persuasive messages in direct marketing', *Discourse Studies*, 10 (2): 161–89.

Clover, J. (2013) 'Smart TV failing the connectivity test', *Broadband TV News*, 21 May, available at: www.broadbandtvnews.com/2013/05/21/smart-tv-failing-the-connectivity-test/

Costill, A. (2013) 'Should your brand be on Myspace?', *Search Engine Journal*, 5 November, available at: www.searchenginejournal.com/should-your-brand-be-on-myspace/71917/

Diffin, E. (2010) 'How online sponsorship changes the way we give', *BBC News Magazine*, 29 January, available at: http://news.bbc.co.uk/1/hi/magazine/8482750.stm

The Economist (2013) 'Tencent's worth: a Chinese internet firm finds a better way to make money', 21 September, available at: www.economist.com/news/business/21586557-chinese-internet-firm-finds-better-way-make-money-tencents-worth

Glenday, J. (2013) 'Internet display ad spending registers 27% global year on year', *The Drum*, 22 October, available at: www.thedrum.com/news/2013/10/22/internet-display-ad-spending-registers-27-global-year-year-increase

Gupta, A., Tyagi, M. and Sharma, D. (2013) 'The use of social media marketing in healthcare', *Journal of Health Management*, 15 (2): 293–302.

Haggerty, A. (2013) 'Banner ads are dead and wallpaper ads are in, says WeTransfer as it reaches 16 million users', *The Drum*, 23 July, available at: www.thedrum.com/news/2013/07/23/banner-ads-are-dead-and-wallpaper-ads-are-says-wetransfer-it-reaches-16-million.

Khang, H., Ki, E.-J. and Ye, L. (2012) 'Social media research in advertising, communication, marketing and public relations, 1997–2010', *Journal of Mass Communication Quarterly*, 89 (2): 279–98.

Lee, D. (2012) 'Facebook surpasses one billion users as it tempts new markets', *BBC News*, 5 October, available at: www.bbc.co.uk/news/technology-19816709

Lee, K. (2013) 'Introduction to search engine optimisation', *SEMPO*, available at: www.sempo.org/?page=intro_to_sem

Macleod, I. (2013) 'LinkedIn's Most Engaged Marketers 2013: Reckitt Benckiser, BT and Lloyds top the list', *The Drum*, 7 November, available at: www.thedrum.com/news/2013/11/07/linkedin-s-most-engaged-marketers-2013-reckitt-benckiser-bt-and-lloyds-top-list

McKenzie, H. (2013) 'Tencent shows Facebook how to reinvent itself for a mobile era', *Pandodaily*, 18 October, available at: http://pandodaily.com/2013/10/18/tencent-shows-facebook-how-to-reinvent-itself-for-a-mobile-era/

Mokhov, O. (2013) '5 tips to simplify your web design', Hongkiat.com, available at: www.hongkiat.com/blog/5-tips-to-simplify-your-web-design/

O'Connor, J. and Galvin, E. (2001) *Marketing in the Digital Age*. London: FT/Prentice Hall.

Peterson, T. and Heussner, K.M. (2012) 'Facebook rolls out Timeline to Brand Pages', *Adweek*, 29 February, available at: www.adweek.com/news/technology/facebook-rolls-out-timeline-brand-pages-138637

Philips, B.J. and McQuarrie, E.F. (2011) 'Contesting the social impact of marketing: a re-characterisation of women's fashion advertising', *Marketing Theory*, 11 (2): 99–126.

Tan, V. (2013) 'Sina Weibo enters Twitter's turf in Southeast Asia. Suicidal or genius?' (Startup Asia preview), *TechInAsia*, 7 November, available at: www.techinasia.com/sina-weibo-sea-startup-asia-preview/

The Teachers Corner (2013) Online Collaboration Projects, available at: www.theteacherscorner.net/collaboration-projects/

The Telegraph (2013) 'Twitter IPO; shares hit the stock exchange – live', *The Telegraph*, 7 November, available at: www.telegraph.co.uk/technology/twitter/

The Week (2011) 'The $8 trillion Internet Economy by the Numbers', 7 November, available at: http://theweek.com/article/index/221181/the-8-trillion-internet-economy-by-the-numbers

Wong, W. and Gupta, S.C. (2011) 'Plastic surgery marketing in a generation of "tweeting"', *Aesthetic Surgery Journal*, 31 (8): 972–6.

Woodward, S. (2012) 'The challenges facing connected TV', *The Guardian*, 12 March, available at: www.theguardian.com/media-network/media-network-blog/2012/mar/14/challenges-facing-connected-tv

Wymbs, C. (2011) 'Digital marketing: the time for a new "academic major" has arrived', *Journal of Marketing Education*, 33 (1): 93–106.

11 Sales Promotions

CHAPTER OVERVIEW

Introduction

Traditional sales promotions were, until the mid-1990s, growing in status, especially when compared with traditional media advertising. Sales promotions, especially money-off coupons, have been with us for a very long time. Premiums, especially those that are self-liquidating, i.e. an offer for a sum of money that covers costs, including handling charges, so that the marketer makes neither profit nor loss on the offer, have been around since the turn of the 20th century and many a child has enjoyed the 'free' toy in the cereal box over the decades even if parents have not. As many writers point out, it was Ovaltine that first went 'interactive' way back in 1930 with a decoder ring that required the participant to get information from the *Little Orphan Annie* radio shows (radioarchives.com, 2013). Elliot (2006) adds that 'code-centric promotions' have been with us for some time when brands like Ovaltine in the 1930s offered radio listeners 'secret decoders' and other prizes in exchange for proof of purchase savings. This kind of promotion re-surfaced in the 1950s when television became the new mass medium and the decoder rings were used with the *Texas Rangers* TV shows (English Articles, 2011). However, it is not just consumer brands like McDonald's and Pepsi that use promotions and this chapter provides coverage beyond the consumer, where admittedly most ideas have been developed and most money spent. Industrial sales promotions and those within channels of distribution are also addressed as are the problems and benefits of using sales promotions.

Learning objectives

This chapter seeks to explore the nature and role of sales promotions in relation to the rest of the communications mix. More specifically, after reading this chapter, the student will be able to:

- critically discuss the changing, dynamic role of sales promotion within the integrated marketing communications mix;
- understand the advantages and disadvantages when using sales promotions;
- appreciate the objectives behind the use of sales promotions;
- appreciate the role of creativity in providing the key notion of added value through promotions;
- understand the various types of consumer promotion available to marketers (both consumer and trade) and also those available in the organisational (business-to-business/industrial) marketing context;
- critically consider sales promotions beyond the usual tactical level and consider how sales promotions are implemented strategically.

THE NATURE OF SALES PROMOTION

The nature of sales promotions

It is hard to say in percentage terms what is spent on sales promotions. Sales promotion's role in the communications mix is very much dependent upon the context in which it is used. Consumer packaged goods from the likes of Kellogg's, Heinz, Pepsi or Coke are big players in consumer and trade sales promotions and a simple description would be that sales promotions are used to differentiate brands on a shelf in a retail environment. However, other consumer sectors, consumer durables, business-to-business and industrial marketers use sales promotions in one way or another. Estimates vary but a typical promotional budget of a fast-moving consumer good (fmcg) campaign would be 60–70 per cent spent on sales promotions with most of the rest on advertising. However, during the early 2000s this has perhaps risen to 75 per cent. Added to this is the fact that advertising often has as a platform a sales promotion message with up to 20 per cent of all advertisements being of this nature. An example is that of supermarket chain ASDA (part of Wal-Mart), known for its food grocery proposition of 'everyday low prices' (*Marketing Week*, 2012), running a UK television campaign to advertise their £1 range of hundreds of brands to help counter, say ASDA, the reduction of family disposable income in recessionary times. It can be argued that this sort of communication can be both an incentive and brand image building if done properly.

Marketing spend during the first quarter of 2011 fell (Warc, 2011) but the picture remains unclear going forward (Warc, 2012). In the UK media advertising has seen a decline in its use since the 1980s so that spend has fallen as a direct consequence of the increase in spend on consumer sales promotions, particularly in packaged goods. About half of all promotional spend on consumer packaged goods is allotted to trade promotion and roughly one quarter each to consumer sales promotion and consumer media advertising. Other sectors vary but spend on sales promotion across the board is on the increase whereas advertising spend is not. An Institute of Practitioners in Advertising (IPA) poll in the UK of 300 companies found that in the last quarter of 2011, 20 per cent had boosted their marketing budgets but 19 per cent had cut back (Warc, 2012). From the same poll it can be seen that traditional media spend was down by 1.2 per cent while sales promotion and direct marketing spend was up by 0.8 per cent. Online spend was 13.4 per cent of the total marketing spend, rising to 14.9% for paid search alone. Such trends according to Warc (2012) are indicative of the changing priorities of brand owners. It would seem that money is being spent out of necessity to protect market share but the rise predicted for 2012 was weaker than in previous years.

Sales promotion can be seen as an acceleration tool to speed up the buying process, to drive up the rate of sale. Ideally sales promotions should generate sales that cannot be generated by other means and the marketer needs to ensure that they are not selling product through an inducement and at a cost on a product that would have been bought anyway. Also, the marketer needs to make sure that the customer is not merely stocking up on non-perishables without this being part of a planned communication campaign, for example to defend against competitive action.

For some academics and practitioners, sales promotions are a range of tactical marketing techniques designed within a strategic marketing framework to add value, usually monetary, to a product or service in order to achieve specific sales and marketing objectives. In this way of thinking sales promotions should be short term and used to trigger or induce immediate behaviour, or at best to accelerate the consumer decision making as with 'buy now, pay later' schemes. However, this book argues for a strategic and integrated marketing communications approach so that this sentiment alone does not fit. Sales promotions, advertising and the rest of the communications mix should be operating together in an integrated fashion. The view that advertising provides added value that is intangible and other promotions provide added value that is temporary and tangible is rather naive and restricting. For sure, a sales promotion is a direct inducement that offers added value and often the objective will be one of creating a sale but the term 'sales promotion' has a broader meaning than this. Sales promotion then can be defined as:

> the marketing function that induces the customer to buy through offering something that adds value above and beyond a product's or brand's original value.

In other words sales promotions add value of one sort or another such as the chance to win a prize or extra product for the same price. But this has to be real value as perceived by the target customer and not by the company or agency people. Sales promotions can be used in such a way as to help build brand equity and image, as discussed later in this chapter.

Buyer behaviour theory and sales promotion

Chapter 2 of this book deals with communication theory and Chapter 3 with behaviour. More specifically, learning theory is very useful when attempting to understand the role of sales promotion in the customer decision-making process. Much of what the behaviourists wrote that has been applied to marketing has also been applied to the sales promotion area. Classical and operant conditioning, as discussed in Chapter 3, are about predicting behaviour as determined by reward and punishment. It is therefore useful in that sales promotion reinforces the reward that the use of the product produces and should increase the likelihood of repurchase. Pavlov, the Russian physiologist, had developed respondent conditioning with the now famous dogs salivating at the sound of a metronome, associating this with the meat powder that Pavlov had rubbed into their mouths to the sound of a metronome.

Although it would be John Watson, an American psychologist, who would become the founding father of American Behaviourism and S-R (stimulus-response) Psychology, despite being sacked from his university, it was Edward Thorndyke who created the 'law of effect' that is to do with positive and negative consequences. The 'law' states that the consequences of behaviour will govern the frequency of that behaviour in the future. Using cats as subjects, Thorndyke showed that a cat could learn to do the behaviour repetitively in order to achieve the favourable outcome of food by hitting a lever to open the cage, thus demonstrating operant or instrumental conditioning. Fred Skinner distinguished between operant and respondent behaviour, and introduced psychology to the worlds of managing people's lives and managing children, leading to behaviour therapy to deal with phobias and anxiety disorders.

However, from a marketing perspective, it would be Watson who would be most influential. It was he who would, post-university, move into advertising and become responsible for shaping, as discussed in Chapter 3 of this book. Shaping is the concept of diminishing reward. Watson had used this in advertising terms to show how, over time, he could manipulate images of cigarette packs and women to gain acceptance of the idea that a woman could smoke. It was no longer taboo for a woman to smoke since the public could be shaped, over time, by moving the cigarette pack closer to the woman, i.e. reinforcement of successive acts, whether by advertising or sales promotions. Shaping therefore breaks the desired behaviour into a series of stages and the parts are then learned in sequence. This process is useful for complex decision making as these behaviours rarely occur by chance. It is also extremely useful when introducing new products because the initial purchase of any new brand involves a complex set of behaviours. Shaping is a process from gaining trial to gaining repeat purchase to regular purchase. Marketers have to distinguish between the inducement and the product. Shaping should move the customer away from the inducement towards purchase of the product at a normal price and quantity. The marketer might begin with free samples to achieve trial, followed by coupons to induce purchase for a small financial outlay and then a larger one until finally the consumer purchases without inducement. The use of such techniques is the foundation of sales promotion strategy for new brands but over-use of them can have a disastrous effect on brand image.

Reasons for the increased growth of sales promotions activities

Sales promotions are no longer just an afterthought in strategic planning terms and therefore also no longer simply short-term tactical tools to 'shift stock'. The sales promotion industry has matured and communications companies have the expertise to fully integrate the communications mix. The shift in the power of retailers as discussed in Chapter 1 of this book led Schultz (1996) and others, for example Schultz et al. (1994), to conclude that retailers at one time did very little but now take a more than active part using sophisticated in-store equipment. The 70 per cent or more decisions being made in-store from a repertoire of brands have made in-store displays and other promotions all the more important. Retailers know what is working and so do most manufacturers, but it is the strength of Wal-Mart and others within a consolidated industry with big companies' own or private labels having such an impact that dominates currently. More specifically:

- Advertising costs rose dramatically forcing marketers to seek other forms of communication.
- There has been a decline in brand loyalty and there is now a 'repertoire of brands' approach with greater consumer choice and a willingness to experiment and seek variety.
- Consumers like incentives and rewards and because of time pressures in busy lives, sales promotion works in store, on the spot.
- The proliferation of brands means that sales promotions can use trial and shape behaviour over time to achieve repeat purchase in conjunction with retailer shelf space.
- The fragmentation of markets and increased importance of the target have meant a move away from the mass and a move toward one-to-one marketing, often at a local or special interest group level. Sales promotions are often tied to direct marketing activity that uses personalised incentives.
- Short-termism became a problem with brand managers shifting stock to meet goals and this is part of the reason why P&G moved to category management. Companies with perhaps lots of 'cash cows' in slow or no growth markets might be tempted to use sales promotions as a quick fix solution but with deeper problems remaining. The creativity that is needed to solve such problems can be hindered.

- With increasing accountability expected sales promotions are a direct way of knowing what works, especially with the technology available.

- Sales promotions can work fast and there is pressure from the trade end on manufactures to provide them in the mix.

- Competition is intense and relationships or co-marketing alliances with particular retailers have developed. Possibly half the sales promotion money is spent in this way.

- Clutter breakthrough can be achieved through promotional messages but these may work better than non-promotional messages in some media rather than others.

Advantages and disadvantages of sales promotions

The *advantages* associated with sales promotions are that they provide an easy to measure response and are relatively inexpensive, fast and flexible. The *disadvantages* are that they may appear a short-term 'quick fix', cheapen the brand, and may not work unless retailers cooperate, and this may have a high cost in terms of allowances. Sales promotions should be about adding value but problems with brand damage and effect on worth of the brand in terms of equity can be real. US practitioners Ganiear and Martin (2012) suggest that an addiction to discounts 'is costly for retailers, but in moderation, promotions can boost profits and brand value'. In a time of changing in-store shopping experience and tough economic conditions, the temptation to carry on discounting is huge. However, as many writers point out, short-termism can make things worse longer term with brand damage the ultimate price of short-term survival. Ganiear and Martin use the example of the J.C. Penney Corporation's failed attempt in early 2012 'to purge the word sale from its marketing playbook in favor of everyday low pricing'. However, since customers were 'conditioned to expect frequent, heavily advertised discounts at J.C. Penney' they stayed away, and within three months sales had fallen by 20 per cent and store traffic by 10 per cent.

Advertising may be best for a long-term franchise where a marketer can build image rather than sell volume. Image and position are key, but this depends upon whether sales promotions are being used to build brand franchise or simply as a short-term tool. Certainly trade sales promotions can be used to promote the brand to the trade in a 'look what we offer you in terms of partnership/relationship' kind of way. Plus loyalty schemes such as air miles or redemptions against other things can help build the consumer brand franchise. In addition, offers consistent with brand image such as a competition to win a holiday are a consideration. Some sales promotions are short term and damaging and some good trade allowances may not be passed on in the way intended, but this is simply bad practice. Without due care and attention actions in the sales promotion area can cheapen the brand in the eyes of the industry.

The Snapshot below discusses the origins of the sales promotion code and its early, interactive use with the malted drink brand Ovaltine.

Snapshot   Sales promotions over the decades – Ovaltine radio codes

Sales promotions were originally designed to bring action by providing an incentive for the consumer or customer to behave in a desired way. But some sales promotions have also been about involvement rather than the more simple behaviour that leads, almost mechanistically, to a short-term sales increase of one sort or another. Sales promotions, like advertising, have a long, interesting and rich history and, like advertising, have become part of the everyday lives of consumers, providing, as they do, an extra incentive to buy one brand over another or to buy more of a product than they might normally do. One of the oldest and most-used sales promotion tools is the money-off coupon. Companies such as Procter and Gamble (P&G) soon became involved with the technique, issuing coupons in the 1920s, initiated by the issue of a metal coin which was soon followed by the familiar paper coupons. A first in an in-box premium was the brand Cracker Jack that in 1912 offered 'a prize in every box'. Many examples exist of marketers taking promotions to customers, from 13-foot-long mock-ups of German-style sausages in the 1930s in the USA to the Pepsi challenges worldwide of the 1970s. What started as a simple 'bake-off' in 1949 as a contest for Pillsbury became a yearly, prestigious competition for cooks. By 1981 the first 'frequent flyer' programme was launched by American Airlines (English Articles, 2011).

In the 1930s the Ovaltine brand began offering its interactive decoder rings 'that were needed to decode secret messages broadcast in Little Orphan Annie radio shows ... brought back 20 years later as television became the new mass medium and the rings were used to decode messages in the Texas Rangers TV shows' (English Articles, 2011). Taylor (2004) reminisces about being a child of the 1950s where 'Saturday morning television was a rite of passage', with the likes of *The Adventures of Rin Tin Tin*, *The Lone Ranger* and *Tales of the Texas Rangers* shows being prominent (and international) examples. This being the USA at the time, sponsors came with these shows, but it is the Swiss-originated malted drink Ovaltine that stands out on engagement. Originally created as a drink that might combat malnutrition in children and initially called Ovomaltine, the brand became an energy drink that was successful at Swiss ski resorts. By the time it was introduced to the UK in 1909, and by mistake, it became Ovaltine. Soon a cocoa version of the brand was added and 'the definitive identity of the brand was locked. From a taste standpoint, Ovaltine was to chocolate milk what coffee was to tea: similar in style, but radically different in taste' (Taylor, 2004). Marketing was key to Ovaltine's success with children's radio show sponsorship in the 1930s and the creation of the 'Ovaltineys', which, as Taylor (2004) points out, was a phenomenon with the 1935 action-adventure show in the UK *The League of Ovaltineys* – essentially a 'secret club' for children who engaged through collecting coupons in the jar which they then posted in. According to Taylor 'by 1939 five million British children — more than 10% of the total U.K. population — were card-carrying Ovaltineys'. The children's radio show *Little Orphan Annie* was a success and sponsored by Ovaltine from 1930 to 1941, and this was followed up in the 1950s with children's television show sponsorship. Taylor (2004) also notes an important point about premiums:

> In the 1930s, the company solved a frequent complaint, product solubility, by creating the wildly popular Little Orphan Annie Shake-up Mug as a mail-in premium pitched directly to kids during commercial broadcasts. The success of this early premium seemed to convince the company that it could drive sales with mail-in premiums themed around its entertainment properties. Ovaltine presaged McDonald's wildly successful Happy Meal program with Walt Disney Co. by a good 50 years.

Stop Point

The way sales promotion codes were developed for the Ovaltine brand way back in the 1930s saw an early recognition of the importance of interacting and engaging with consumers. Undertake the following: 1. Consider and discuss the possibilities of a brand becoming more engaging through the use of sales promotions rather than simply being about short-term selling; 2. Outline the possibilities of a brand owner utilising sales promotions in order to help build relationships with customers, rather than simply seeking short-term sales.

TARGETING AND OBJECTIVES

Targeting

The essence of targeting was dealt with in Chapter 4 of this book. Targeting involves the break-up of mass markets and the creation of target groups, each of which has potentially different needs to be met. Target needs and wants rather than market needs and wants are a requirement that will only be determined by research and/or experience. Quantitative research is required to establish targets and qualitative research to determine what motivates the people in them, including the kind of sales promotion, if any, to which they will respond positively or negatively. This will determine things such as loyalty towards brand or trust in companies, as well as how a particular sales promotion will work and what is required to make it work.

Objectives

Chapter 4 also discussed in general terms what marketing communications objectives are and their place in planning communications, so they should be specific, measurable, achievable, realistic and timed (SMART). The short-term quick fix is often the objective of the sales promotion but by no means the only one and there is often more to it than inducing a sale. As mentioned above, sales promotion operates at the action end of the awareness, interest, desire and action (AIDA)-type process and so usually the purpose of a sales promotion is to make the recipient move in a particular direction and it is therefore behavioural. Usually the recipient is being induced to try a brand, continue using it or to increase use of it, and the trade are encouraged to engage in pushing through the channel to the consumers. Objectives can be *offensive*, for example to gain trial or distribution, or *defensive*, for example to defend against competition. Objectives can therefore be short term or longer term. The latter is less likely but it can be a case of keeping in touch with customers and adding to the brand in some way, such as rewarding loyalty. Objectives should be clear and the company should have a firm idea as to what is to be achieved and why, who the targets are and what benefit they will receive, and the length of time and money involved.

Examples of sales promotions objectives are as follows:

- Get a trial among first time or non-users with an associated reduction of risk. This can be done through, for example, sampling, money-back guarantees or using introductory offer coupons. This can help ensure that a brand is 'right' in situ and encourage repeat purchase. The latter is important since the objective of gaining trial on its own would lead to product failure without repeat purchase at the normal price.

- Following on from this the objective would be to increase repeat purchases or gain multiple purchases by existing users for a now established brand. New uses may then be found for existing users while incentives can continue for new users and act as a reward for existing users.

- Sales promotions can be used to introduce an improved product (new improved) or line extension. 'Buy the shampoo and get the new conditioner free' is a common bound-to-pack way of achieving this objective, which of course encourages trial.

- Defend share against competitive activity by using sales promotions to take users of the product out of the market for a considerable time. By encouraging stocking up through the use of, for example, coupons they are then unlikely to switch to a competitive brand, even though it is being promoted.

- Target a specific segment through sales promotions using geodemographic, psychographic or allied techniques such as light users, heavy users or non-users. Competitions, contests and sweepstakes are useful to target special interest groups.

- Help build brand image and equity through, for example, association with a top prize in a competition.

There are many other, fairly simple, objectives such as easing price increases or introducing a new way of working with the product. Sales promotions can be part of a bundle of offerings to a client, especially on the business-to-business/industrial side of things.

The Snapshot below discusses the use of codes as price reducers or for use with other activities such as competition entry or the activities of daily deal websites such as Groupon.

Snapshot Online codes, engagement and interactivity – Groupon

Codes have been with us for some time and are used as price reducers or to enter competitions, contests and sweepstakes, and can be found in- and on-pack on coupons or cards, on neckties around bottle necks and increasingly in a variety of web-based forms. This usually involves code promotions being 'redeemed', not at a store or on the telephone, but online on websites or through texting, where codes are processed far quicker, and of course come with a range of data collection opportunities. Codes now are part of a wider marketing effort beyond mere proof-of-purchase for a reward. Sales promotions are now much more than one-offs. As Elliot (2006) points out, websites have been used to allow consumers on a large scale to 'open accounts, accumulate points by entering codes' and 'redeem the points for prizes from Coca-Cola or other companies including Adidas, Delta Air Lines and Hilton'. The online nature of such promotions is essential for this facilitation and for the larger players this involves millions of accounts and hundreds of thousands of prizes with redemption extremely frequent, involving of course other brands as rewards and prizes.

This kind of sales promotion activity is truly about engagement with and immersion in brands of all kinds. The use of technology and data collection is crucial whereby online activity is more than a website being used as a mere redemption centre. According to Elliot (2006) consumers have been successfully spurred on to visit websites as the promotions begin by sending email messages containing starter codes 'to those who took part in previous online programs' and that it was 'DaimlerChrysler who have also recognized how the internet can jump-start code promotions' by adding 'sweepstakes to its current ad campaign featuring its chief executive, Dieter Zetsche, as Dr. Z', whereby users 'were directed to local dealerships to receive cards bearing five-digit codes and to enter the sweepstakes at the campaign's Website'. This resulted in broad exposure for the brands (Chrysler, Dodge and Jeep) with millions of impressions

(Continued)

(Continued)

in what was a large-scale and cheaper (than conventional direct marketing) campaign with more than double the average registrations.

Elliot (2006), however, alerts us to the inevitable drawbacks with online code use around privacy and personal data, which can lead to problems, and suggests that marketers should make sure that 'there are opportunities to opt out of providing information'. This said, perhaps the magic does lie in the winning rather than just a give-away, whereby a participant does not know of the outcome until the code is entered online. The same can be said of a scratch card where the excitement is still maintained, which cannot be said of a guaranteed money-off such as those provided by Groupon, which negotiates discounts with other businesses and then emails offers on various deals each day. If enough people take this up then a voucher can be presented to the business, having been printed off by the consumer, and the discount claimed. Groupon is part of a new concept in collective buying and despite some issues already whereby, in the UK, the OFT (the Government's Office of Fair Trading , superseded by the Competition and Markets Authority in early 2014) have been involved as a 'watchdog' in this area, the outlook appears positive for such sales promotions. Concerns over exaggerated discounts and non-existent products or services in the end will fall under the same scrutiny as do other forms of marketing and communications; honesty and accuracy will feature prominently, as will applying the rules and paying attention to unsubstantiated claims. But according to the OFT there are real benefits for consumers and marketers in collective buying and discount schemes (*BBC News*, 2012).

It is interesting to note that codes used for marketing are not a new phenomenon, but that somewhat ironically the original codes for the likes of Ovaltine (see the previous Snapshot) way back in the 1930s might be considered more interactive and certainly more engaging than the online-driven sales promotion codes of today, many of which are much more about short-term selling and much less about relationship building.

Stop Point

The online activities and developments that can be seen today show that companies have not given up on sales promotion as a marketing communications tool. Undertake the following: 1. Discuss the prospects for more engaging online sales promotion but also about dilemma of pre-testing ideas when you do not wish to inform the competition; 2. Consider relations with other players such as dealers and retailers and what might be expected of them and comment on the possibilities for last-minute collective deals, especially for businesses such as restaurants and travel companies who constantly face the dilemma of decay and the impression given by an empty space.

TYPES OF SALES PROMOTION

Sales promotions can be targeted at consumers or any part of the supply chain. Consumer promotions are typically coupons, premiums, sampling, price-offs, offers, contests, sweepstakes and competitions. Trade promotions include allowances, display materials and sales contests. There are also different promotional activities recommended for product launches and established product and for consumers and retailers. Then there are other sales promotions that are used in the business-to-business and industrial marketing contexts so that this can be viewed in a number of ways, as discussed below.

Consumer sales promotions

Sampling

If the objective is trial then sampling is a key tool in inducing this and to break old loyalties. Sampling is associated with products of low unit value and can only be used if the product is divisible and the brand features and benefits can be adequately demonstrated. Purchase cycles have to be relatively short otherwise consumers will forget. Sampling therefore is much used by FMCG packaged goods manufacturers. Sampling can be very effective but will not make consumers re-try a product that is somehow inferior. Clearly it is difficult if not impossible to sample many products such as forklift trucks or consumer durables like washing machines. Even on the faster side of consumer marketing some products will take longer to work or try out, such as a brand of moisturiser, the effects of which may take some time and trial to assess, and sampling may not be a possibility.

The means of delivering the sample are many and varied. Door-to-door or through the use of newspaper-type delivery is effective but expensive. Through the mail or post is a common method but clearly only relatively small, lightweight samples can be delivered. Geodemographic systems such as ACORN (A Classification of Residential Neighbourhoods, from CACI) or Mosaic (by Experian), are two UK commercial examples but there are many others around the world. These systems can be used as a database for mailings generally but for samples also. In-store sampling is common for food and drink and is used in conjunction with money-off coupons for instant purchase. Related to this is the in-store demonstration that is often food-related, such as kitchen equipment or knife sharpeners. Such activities can be expensive and need careful planning as well as, in many cases, the co-operation of retailers. Sampling can take place in a similar way at different events such as sports matches and samples can be strapped to packs of products that would have the same type of buyer. Samples of perfumes have even been placed in magazine advertisements whereby the reader could scratch the paper to release the fragrance. With technology moving forward and the Internet's pace of development, more and more opportunities for creative sampling distribution are being found. Certainly, minus the coupon, sampling avoids the potential brand damage associated with couponing.

Couponing

The coupon is the oldest sales promotion device and now probably the most problematic in terms of cheapening the brand and also of misuse. For these reasons couponing has declined in recent years having peaked in the 1990s. However, it is still a major tool and apparently most Americans use coupons and one-quarter apparently always use them. These effectively lower the price to encourage trial and they also encourage re-trial, but once price-reductions through couponing start the problem is where to end the process. This is a problem for both new and existing products where for the latter sales promotions can be used to attract non-users or reward existing ones. This, however, does not necessarily make sense in terms of margins. Couple this with the length of time it takes to redeem coupons and the problem is magnified. Digital couponing has accelerated the process as email has grown in acceptance.

Abuse of coupon redemption is one of the reasons for the demise of the coupon. Coupons have even been forged and passed on as the real thing. One of the more common occurrences is redemption by retailers without the product being sold. Coupon distribution is by similar means to that of sampling, i.e. through the mail, door or online in various forms, but often through advertising and inserts in newspapers and magazines. However, there is a lot of clutter because of the costs and quality that can be achieved. Direct marketing is increasingly being used because of the benefits of this medium (see Chapter 12 of this book) and as said previously can be used with a sample as well as the coupon, but it is expensive. There are other forms of coupons such as the instant coupon, which is redeemed there and then at the till. These can be placed in-store or on packs.

Competitions (or contests) and sweepstakes

Competitions are also quite popular, and can incorporate product knowledge tests, which can assist in the learning process. Competitions can be fairly low-cost promotions, and often have retailer support, or it may be a competition among staff (see Chapter 16 of this book). These promotions can add excitement and if designed well tie-in with brand management to contribute towards brand image and development. Awareness, attention and interest can be created among a large proportion of the population but this is not necessarily useful in the targeting sense. The difference between a competition and a sweepstake lies in the skill or some other form of ability required for the former. Some sort of judging goes on in competitions but with a sweepstake the winner is determined by chance. Sweepstakes come in many forms, one popular one being a scratch card. These are used a lot at the till and in direct mailing. These promotions have a fixed, known cost and they may allow the marketer to develop the brand by getting consumers so involved that, for example, the essence of a competition may be to engage consumers with naming a brand. This is quite a clever way to suggest that the brand belongs to the consumer.

These promotions are now having billions spent on them and they continue to be popular in many markets, especially with the popularity of game shows and the continued growth of reality television, which promote the idea of gaming and involvement generally. Alongside this are the growing problems on the legal side of things, which is why marketers rely on specialist firms and the appropriate regulatory body when designing such promotions. For example, in the UK the Code of Advertising Practice (CAP), administered by the Advertising Standards Authority, includes a code for sales promotion practice that runs alongside legislation as laid down in Acts of Parliament, typically the Gambling Act (2005) whereby almost all such legislation going back to 1845 is incorporated that deals with levels of skill involved such as the need for 'substantial skill' required in a particular competition.

Money refunds

Refunds, rebates or cash-backs involve the consumer purchasing the product in the knowledge that there will be the facility of a refund. Typically this will be 'no fuss money back if not entirely satisfied'. This minimises the risk to the consumer and encourages repeat purchase. Refunds are subject to codes of practice and law also. In the UK the Sale and Supply of Goods Act (1994) is typical of such legislation, which is linked to the Sale and Supply of Goods to Consumers regulations that took effect in 2003 after some delay following an EU directive in 1999. Another form of refund or rebate involves saving coupons or till receipts but these can be problematic especially where more than one proof of purchase is needed. Redemption rates are low, indeed as low as 1–5% per cent, depending on the medium of delivery, print being lower than in-store or in-/on-pack offers.

Premiums, bonus packs and price-offs

Often the main tool used for promoting existing products is a premium, which would not normally be used for new products to induce trial. A premium is an extra item offered at a low price or for free. They can be effective at increasing sales but can also be a distraction from the brand properties. Premiums can attract brand switchers and used with current users to increase repeat purchases. A premium can be free or have some cost to the consumer. A self-liquidating premium is one where the consumer covers the cost of the promotion but this will only work if there is an incentive for that consumer. Many marketers have moved away from gimmicky toys and the like towards real added value with quality premiums, although McDonald's is the epitome of the former. With the latter, Philip Morris's Marlboro is typical, whereby part of an 'in-the-mail' promotion included various merchandise offers such as a cigarette lighter. Premiums are subject to tight restrictions, not least because of the obvious link with children and television advertising and other promotions.

The bonus pack is an uncomplicated way of giving extra value and this can be attractive to the consumer who may switch brands. Apart from rewarding existing consumers, giving them extra may very well take them out of the market and away from the competition but the consumer may very well stockpile since they would probably have bought the brand anyway. A price-off price reduction may create the wrong perception of the product. Price-off deals normally involve on-pack price reductions. Bonus packs and price-offs are closely linked. Link-saves are now common in supermarkets because the technology allows for easy stock control and operation. Two for one or 'buy one get one free' is now commonplace. The 'buy one get one free' phrase now appears to have the acronym 'BOGOF' attached to it. 'Bog off' is British slang and an impolite term for 'get lost' or 'go away' and now seems to have crept into ordinary English language. In the UK supermarkets, for example Tesco, have tried to introduce the BOGOL – buy one get one later – concept aimed at reducing consumer waste, especially on perishables, by providing the inducement of a coupon that goes with the product (for example a pot of yogurt) whereby the coupon can be redeemed at a later time when the consumer is ready to consume rather than have two products, one of which potentially goes past a sell-by date before it can be consumed and is therefore wasted. The BOGOF is also potentially off-putting as a promotion since the consumer knows that there is a good chance that waste will occur with certain types of product.

Loyalty schemes

Many organisations now have a loyalty scheme of one sort or another. Most involve some sort of point system and the ability then to trade points for merchandise such as wine or other less tangible things such as air miles that are potentially harder to 'spend'. Clearly the objective is to create and sustain that most illusive of things called loyalty, so that it is about relationship and database marketing. The 'loyalty scheme' is somewhat of a misnomer and they should perhaps be called a 'frequent purchaser scheme', as with Flying Blue, the Air France/KLM (and other partners) frequent flier programme.

Exhibitions

Exhibitions are important forums that are a shop window where actual and potential customers can see, touch and feel products. These are interlinked with trade shows (see below). They provide the opportunity to interact with customers and consumers, to answer questions and more often than not to sell merchandise. Typical of the large consumer exhibition that is also a tradeshow are the motor shows, which occur, like fashion shows, around the world such as in London, Geneva, Detroit or Bangkok. Technically this is not a place to actually sell directly but it is a vehicle that is part of many companies' integrated marketing communications and as such is a powerful way of reaching a large number of people.

Ordinary people who visit the Motor Show may not do so because they are on the point of purchasing a new car but clearly they at least have an interest in the products of that particular industry and will gather information to be used in the future. Some exhibition venues are static such as London's Earl's Court, the Birmingham (UK) NEC, the Palais de Congress in Paris (France) or the many others in, for example, Thailand or China. Non-static 'road shows' are quite common where the product is taken to the buyer and these can be held in hotels, football grounds and arenas (such as the various arenas in the UK and elsewhere). An advantage with road shows is that whereas a consumer might find it too much hassle to visit a London-based exhibition, they might be willing to visit a local hotel or some other accessible venue to view the latest ideas and offerings from a particular industry.

Packaging

Packaging is a much-neglected area of marketing communications that has functional and emotional properties that are important to brand image. Packaging has often been referred to as 'the silent salesman' that sits on retailers' shelves and sells products. But it is so much more than this. Just look at the ingenious way perfume is packaged for an immediate appreciation. Take a look at the malt whisky section of any supermarket and there you will see a number of different images from tartans and bagpipes to ship-wrecks and sailors. What you will look at though with most brands is a tube that holds the bottle that holds the whisky/whiskey. This is little more than an oversized version of the cardboard tube that holds the tissue paper on a toilet or kitchen role and yet these tubes are designed in such a way as to be extremely attractive items that can scream and shout from the shelves. Packaging, therefore, is much more than the information that must be, by law, provided on it. It has been referred to also as the part of the clothing the product wears in order to become the brand. As such, packaging is an essential, visual part of the brand's identity. Indeed it is part of the brand's personality and therefore contributes towards meaning (in the sense discussed in Chapter 8 of this book) and therefore is part of the expression of brand values. Packaging can be used in a number of different ways. Certainly it can be designed to work well on display but that is not to say it will be 'silent'. Agariya et al. (2012) summarise the elements of good packaging design as:

1. Attraction of the buyer. To achieve this, the packaging must have strong visual impact so that it stands out and draws attention to itself through the use of effective choice of colour, shape, logos and other features.
2. To communicate a message to the buyer. The packaging has to fit with the brand image and reflect what the brand stands for in terms of brand values.
3. To create desire for the product by adding value whether this is through functionality or being aesthetically pleasing.
4. To sell the product and create the desire for repeat purchase.

A package has to be attractive, recognisable and different. To achieve this the designer has a number of tools at her or his disposal including colour, form and surface but also the use of logos, typography, and different materials from tin to plastic and from cardboard to paper. Labels can be stuck or printed on, or indeed engraved, and size does matter, whether this is to encourage product use (larger) or to sample (small).

Packaging is to do with more than appearance. It can have a tactile element to it as well as being visually attractive in appearance. The *functional* aspects of packaging are to protect the product inside, often to hold the product, as with liquids for example, and more lately

to be in many instances easy to dispose of and in some cases have biodegradable properties. Cost, of course, as always comes into play at some stage.

Trade/retailer sales promotions

A key objective with trade sales promotions is to increase distribution and this means gaining shelf space, especially for new products. Ideas that have developed over the years are
discounts, extended credit, point-of-sale or purchase (POP) materials, tie-ins, shelf facings
and screamers and displays. These are used in conjunction with advertising, in-store promotions and other promotion allowances and co-operative marketing ideas, which also
help cement good relations. As well as the maintenance or acquisition of distribution and
shelf space, other objectives are to acquire better positioning and obviously have an effect
on consumers in contexts such as supermarkets. However, much of this activity is designed
as *'push' strategy*, to get a product through the chain. Several types of retail promotions are
commonly used.

Incentives

Incentives to sales staff are popular with manufacturers but might not be with the retailer.
Such incentives would include prizes, bonuses, or simply a cash amount per sale.

Buying allowances

Buying allowances are a price reduction for a period of time where the offer is typically
'buy 100 cases and get a percentage discount'.

Advertising allowances and other co-operative promotion

The commonest form of co-operation is the advertising allowance that is money given from
the manufacturer to the retailer and is usually proportionate to orders, typically used in
a broader co-operative promotional campaign. For example a manufacturer (Heinz) may
negotiate with a retailer (Sainsbury) a 50/50 split on the costs of the retailer running press
advertising with the Heinz products being just some of lines featured. The manufacturer,
within the negotiations, will have use of trademarks, size and so on sorted out with the
retailer before the campaign begins.

Slotting allowances

Slotting allowances are buying allowances for new products, usually fee-based, and can
appear to be blackmail and discriminatory in favour of big and against small business.
There may even be a failure fee built into the deal that is a sort of fine on the manufacturer
to cover retailers' costs of handling a product that 'fails'. The problems with trade allowances are real ones with maybe only $\frac{1}{3}$ being used properly, $\frac{1}{3}$ taken by retailers and
another $\frac{1}{3}$ simply wasted. Forward buying may be practised whereby wholesalers and
retailers buy during the promotion but stock up and sell at the regular price afterwards or
they may divert stock to a different area. Companies like Procter & Gamble take measures
to try to stop such practices such as 'everyday low pricing', which cuts the price of over
60 per cent of its product line while cutting trade allowances, leaving the cost to the trade
the same but without the allowance that can be abused.

POP display material

These are many and varied and since most final purchase decisions are made in-store are
very important to the retail context. It is hard to say how effective all of this merchandising

material is. Though effective at reaching consumers, from the manufacturer's point of view, getting the retailer to agree to displays is a potential problem. The power that some retailers have ensures that they dictate the running of things.

Trade shows and exhibitions

Trade shows and exhibitions are important forums that again are a shop window where actual and potential customers can see, touch and feel products. In many contexts these are the only vehicles to display the company's wares and to interact with customers from across the management board. The total number of these vehicles is huge. The amount spent on private events and shows added together is more than advertising spend on UK national newspaper advertising. Trade shows and exhibitions are much more likely to be selling events than those vehicles mentioned above. There is, however, a strong role for public and corporate relations. Managers may view such vehicles as sales vehicles but generally, the reasons why exhibitors partake are to meet new customers, interact with current customers, introduce new products, gather intelligence and meet other channel members. Inevitably, however, they also partake to sell and this may be particularly true with smaller firms. Planning and managing shows and exhibitions is a simple yet detailed exercise, from the design and build of the stand to a record-keeping system for visitors, useful leads and contacts.

Free or subsidised training

Manufacturers, as part of the promotional effort but also of relationship-building, can offer free or subsidised training to retail and wholesale staff so that they are well informed and able to communicate the features and benefits of products to end users more effectively and efficiently. This is especially valid when the product is complicated and highly priced. Of course the manufacturer can provide brochures, manuals and advice from the sales force but training, either on the manufacturer's premises, the retailer's or wholesaler's premises or at a hotel venue, is an added extra that promotes sales.

Business-to-business (B-to-B) and industrial sales promotions

In industrial and B-to-B marketing contexts sales promotions are also used as a means of moving customers to action. Some of the above consumer and trade or retail ideas can be transferred over into the industrial and B-to-B marketing contexts but generally the choice of tools is much less. Certainly much of the trade promotion commentary applies to business-to-business marketers. However, with organisational marketing, much more emphasis is placed on brochure work that is used by sales teams and at shows and exhibitions. The Internet has had an impact in terms of, for example, web-based operations or email. Certain ideas can be transferred over from consumer sales promotions but these may have to be adapted somewhat. For example, to add value, rather than 'buy one get one free', the marketer of office computer systems might offer free training for staff or free maintenance in the first year. In this way the marketer can offer something above and beyond the normal value of the product or service so that price reductions, free products, trade-ins and promotional products as well as trade shows, training and maintenance can be used.

The Snapshot below discusses loyalty schemes and the concept of the loyalty ladder, which is to do with longer-term relationships and relationship building rather than short-term sales promotion tactics such as price reductions.

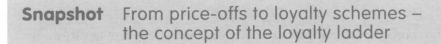

Snapshot From price-offs to loyalty schemes – the concept of the loyalty ladder

Customers respond differently to different promotional strategies. Price cutting has been and clearly still is a common and favoured form of sales promotion (Garner, 2002). Loyalty is an elusive concept, especially in consumer marketing terms, but this does not mean it cannot be achieved and the situation is different in other contexts such as business-to-business, not-for-profit or where the customer is a professional manager. Many consumers display promiscuous tendencies, i.e. they are natural switchers and this is why much promotional activity involves price (White, 2002). As with all communication a promotion has to gain attention and elicit a favourable impression where the benefits are clearly understood and that the customer clearly understands the incentive offered. The incentive itself should, in accordance with all good sales promotion practice, offer extra value.

In a study of the effects of consumer sales promotions on 427 consumers by Nagar (2009), the dilemma that sales promotions are generally seen as tools that can undermine the brand yet are a tool necessary to speed up sales in the short term was recognised. With many marketers, resorting to sales promotions to attract share from competitors is the norm. This study explored the effect of consumer sales promotions on loyal and non-loyal (switchers) consumers in fmcg contexts and found that consumer sales promotions have more influence on the latter than the former, with free gifts having more influence on switchers.

The language around customer loyalty varies considerably and words and phrases are often used interchangeably, which should not be the case. For example a customer retention programme is not the same as a customer loyalty programme. It is obvious that measuring customer satisfaction at any given time is not the same as measuring customer loyalty but it could be argued that as a process, customer satisfaction can be a starting point in the process. Clearly at a given point a customer can be satisfied with a purchase but this does not guarantee continued purchase, never mind loyalty. On the other hand a customer can remain loyal even though dissatisfied with a purchase – but this may not last forever unless this is put into the context of, for example, football supporters who are loyal to their club come hell or high water or ultimately death. In other words there are varying degrees of engagement on the part of customers, which are reflected in the 'loyalty ladder' concept. This concept suggests that at the bottom rung of the ladder there is the suspect – the potential target – who may become the target or prospect. Subsequently the prospect becomes a shopper, then a trialist customer, and then a client through repeat purchase. It is then that the marketer can persuade the customer to join the club through incentives and other devices (within IMC) that will make them want to be members and eventually advocates and even campaigners and fans in some cases. At the top of the ladder the brand is difficult to dislodge and this is a highly desirable position, especially since the old adage that it costs a lot more to get new customers than to retain existing one is also a truism.

There is clearly therefore interest in the idea that long-term relationships can be developed and that loyalty can be obtained and sustained. Dick and Basu's (1994) study considered relationships that are mediated by social norms and situational factors. This study suggests that attitudes are developed in a cognitive, affective and conative process and contribute towards loyalty along with motivational, perceptive

(Continued)

(Continued)

and behavioural consequences, and also examines what this strength of loyalty means for management wishing to engage with loyalty in order to try to gain competitive advantage. A study by Mascarenhas et al. (2006) seems to confirm the typologies that occur within a 'loyalty ladder' system as they looked at the concepts of total customer experience (TCE) and lasting customer loyalty (LCL) and suggested that if the former is strategised then the latter can be achieved. These authors maintain that TCE involves three interactive elements: physical moments; emotional involvement moments; and value chain moments.

Stop Point

Getting sales promotions right is difficult. Different kinds of sales promotions suit different occasions. Loyalty or frequent use schemes are available in many sectors with very different products or services. Undertake the following: 1. Comment on how the right kind of sales promotion can add value and help build and maintain the brand; 2. Consider the 'loyalty ladder' concept and discuss where loyalty schemes might take advantage of the varying levels within a ladder.

Assignment

Assume you are a fast-moving consumer goods (fmcg) marketer engaging with a network of wholesalers and retailers. Choose a product category within which you are intent upon building a brand franchise. You have seen the statistic that suggests that consumers make at least 70 per cent of their final decisions in-store and you firmly believe this to be the case. Your task is to design a sales promotion package that includes trade and consumer ideas within a specified time scale that is realistic within normal budgetary constraints.

Summary of Key Points

- Sales promotion's role has changed and now is a dynamic one within the integrated communications mix.
- There are advantages and disadvantages when using sales promotions. Brand damage and waste should be paid particular attention.
- Added value is key to understanding how sales promotions should work whether this be in industrial, trade or consumer promotion campaigns. Creativity is part of that added value.

- The objectives behind the use of sales promotions are very different from those associated with advertising or PR. One objective such as trial is key.

- There are various types of promotion available to marketers depending on the context that might be industrial, consumer or trade. Generally, promotion ideas cannot be transposed from consumer to industrial contexts very easily.

- Beyond the usual tactical level, strategic possibilities for the use of promotions exist and they can be part of an integrated campaign.

- Implementation of a sales promotion campaign should be executed in an efficient manner with timings and deadlines being paid particular attention.

- Evaluation of a campaign is important and constant vigilance is necessary when using techniques such as money-off coupons or competitions.

- Co-operative marketing can be part of the relationship between a manufacturer and middleman, such as a dealer or retailer, and sales promotions can be part of this.

- Promotions wars, including price wars, are to be avoided and marketers should avoid becoming involved in such situations.

Discussion Questions

1. Discuss the changing, dynamic role of sales promotion within the integrated communications mix and qualify this with the use of an example – industrial, trade or consumer – of your choice.

2. Highlight the advantages and disadvantages when using sales promotions paying particular attention to potential brand damage.

3. Added value is key to understanding how sales promotions should work. Illustrate the role of creativity in providing added value with examples from industrial and consumer promotion campaigns.

4. Discuss the objectives behind the use of sales promotions. Find examples of the objective of trial to illustrate.

5. Explain and explore the various types of promotion available to marketers, both consumer and trade. Choose one such type using at least one example to illustrate.

6. Consider sales promotions beyond the usual tactical level and discuss strategic possibilities. Discuss how this can be part of an integrated campaign.

7. Consider how sales promotions are implemented. Discuss this using a campaign of your choice.

8. Discuss evaluation of campaigns generally, explaining why it is important to be constantly vigilant when using techniques such as money-off coupons or competitions.

9. Outline the rationale behind co-operative marketing in terms of relationships between manufacturers and middlemen such as dealers and retailers. Use at least one example to illustrate.

10. Discuss the notion of price wars in relation to promotions wars. Explain how a marketer can avoid becoming involved in such situations.

Further Reading

Devlin, E., Anderson, S., Borland, R., Mackintosh, A.M. and Hastings, G. (2006) 'Development of a research tool to monitor point of sale promotions', *Social Marketing Quarterly*, 12 (1): 29–39. http://smq.sagepub.com/content/12/1//29
This article looks at tobacco sales at point of sale (POS) in the wake of the closure of other promotional avenues in the UK. The article describes the observational technique designed to monitor changes in this activity. The research suggests that tobacco marketing at POS is targeting lower socio-economic status areas.

Dick, A.S. and Basu, K. (1994) 'Customer loyalty: toward an integrated conceptual framework', *Journal of the Academy of Marketing Science*, 22 (2): 99–113. http://jam.sagepub.com/content/22/2/99
This article is about relationship marketing where relationships are mediated by social norms and situational factors. It is also about how attitudes developed in a cognitive, affective and conative process contribute towards loyalty along with motivational, perceptive and behavioural consequences, and what this means for management wishing to engage with loyalty in order to try to gain competitive advantage.

Jha-Dang, P. (2006) 'A review of psychological research on consumer promotions and a new perspective based on mental accounting', *Vision: The Journal of Business Perspective*, 10 (3): 35–43. http://vis.sagepub.com/content/10/3/35
This article reviews the theory around consumer response to promotions and suggests a change from a single product approach to evaluating consumer response to one of mental accounting theory based on a multi-product perspective. The article examines the psychological processes that lead to a cross-product impact of a promotion on the sale of regular-priced products.

Nagar, K. (2009) 'Evaluating the effects of consumer sales promotions on brand loyal and brand switching segments', *Vision: The Journal of Business Perspective*, 13 (4): 35–50. http://vis.sagepub.com/content/13/4/35
This article recognises the dilemma that sales promotions are generally seen as tools that can undermine the brand yet are necessary to speed up sales in the short term, with many marketers resorting to sales promotions to attract share from competitors. The article reports on the results of the effects of consumer sales promotions on 427 consumers. This study explores the effect of consumer sales promotions on loyal and non-loyal (switchers) consumers in fmcg contexts and finds that consumer sales promotions have more influence on the latter than the former, with free gifts having more influence on switchers.

Wansink, B. et al. (2006) 'Wine promotions in restaurants: do beverage sales contribute or cannabalize?', *Cornell Hotel and Restaurant Administration Quarterly*, 47 (4): 327–36. http://cqx.sagepub.com/content/47/4/327
This article explores the use of different types of promotions within the context of wine in restaurants. The findings suggest three key issues: that selected wine recommendations can increase sales (by as much as 12 per cent in the study); that food–wine pairing recommendations increase sales (by 7.6 per cent in the study); and that wine tastings increase sales (by 48 per cent in the study). The study suggests that most of the increase in sales of promoted wines comes from diners who would be likely to order a non-promoted wine, but that up to nearly one-third of wine sales increase comes from diners who would otherwise have ordered some other (non-wine) drink. The article provides specific implications for restaurateurs including the strong advice not to cannibalise sales by promoting a lower-margin, lower-profit wine, which is not necessary for increased sales.

REFERENCES

Admap (2010) 'Adstats, Adspend in 2010', February, pp. 46–47.

Agariya, A.K., Johari, A., Sharma, H.K., Chandraul U.N.S. and Singh, D. (2012) 'The role of packaging in brand communication', *International Journal of Scientific and Engineering Research*, 3 (2): 1–13.

BBC News Business (2012) 'Groupon given deadline to improve: voucher company Groupon has been given 3 months to improve the way it operates by UK regulator', 16 March, available at: www.bbc.co.uk/news/business-17398809

Devlin, E., Anderson, S., Borland, R., Mackintosh, A.M. and Hastings, G. (2006) 'Development of a research tool to monitor point of sale promotions', *Social Marketing Quarterly*, 12 (1): 29–39.

Dick, A.S. and Basu, K. (1994) 'Customer loyalty: toward an integrated conceptual framework', *Journal of the Academy of Marketing Science*, 22 (2): 99–113.

Elliot, S. (2006) 'Code promotions, a Madison Ave. staple, are going on line', *The New York Times*, 21 August, available at: www.nytimes.com/2006/08/21/technology/21adco.html

English Articles (2011) 'History of sales promotion', 5 July, available at: www.englisharticles.info/2011/07/05/history-of-sales-promotion/

Ganiear, D. and Martin, K. (2012) 'Kicking the sales promotion habit', *Strategy and Business*, available at: www.strategy-business.com/article/00134?pg=all

Garner, E. (2002) 'Do sales promotions really work?' *Admap*, Issue 430, July, pp. 30–32.

Jha-Dang, P. (2006) 'A review of psychological research on consumer promotions and a new perspective based on mental accounting', *Vision: The Journal of Business Perspective*, 10 (3): 35–43.

Marketing Week (2012) 'ASDA marketing strategy and marketing campaigns', 26 February, available at: www.marketingweek.co.uk/brands/asda/

Mascarenhas, O.A., Kesavan, R. and Bernacchi, M. (2006) 'Lasting customer loyalty: a total customer experience approach', *Journal of Consumer Marketing*, 23 (7): 397–405.

Nagar, K. (2009) 'Evaluating the effects of consumer sales promotions on brand loyal and brand switching segments', *Vision: The Journal of Business Perspective*, 13 (4): 35–50.

Prendergast, G. (2005) 'Behavioural response to sales promotion tools: a Hong Kong study', *International Journal of Advertising*, 24 (4): 467–86.

radioarchives.com (2013) *Little Orphan Annie*, available at: www.radioarchives.com/Little_Orphan_Annie_p/ra005.htm

Schultz, D.E. (1996) 'New Trends in Communication and Advertising', lecture to the University of Strathclyde Business School, 16 October.

Schultz, D.E., Tannenbaum S.I. and Lauterborn R.F. (1994) *Integrated Marketing Communications*. Chicago, IL: NTC Business Books.

Taylor, R. (2004) 'Driven to drink', *Promo Chief Marketer Network*, 1 January, available at: http://chiefmarketer.com/campaigns/marketing_driven_drink

Wansink, B. et al. (2006) 'Wine promotions in restaurants: do beverage sales contribute or canabalize?', *Cornell Hotel and Restaurant Administration Quarterly*, 47 (4): 327–36.

Warc (2011) 'Marketing spend falls in the UK', Warc Staff, 18 April. Available at: www.warc.com/LatestNews/News/Next.news?ID=28164

Warc (2012) 'Picture mixed for UK marketing spend', Warc Staff, 19 January. Available at: www.warc.com/LatestNews/News/Picture%20mixed%20for%20UK%20marketing%20spend.news?ID=29339

White, R. (2002) 'Sales promotion and the brand', *Admap*, Issue 430, July, pp. 12–13.

12 Direct Marketing

CHAPTER OVERVIEW

Introduction

This chapter deals with direct marketing as an interactive marketing communications tool that uses one or more communications media to achieve a measurable response. Customer databases are the result of the application of information technology in marketing and as such are very powerful tools. Database and direct marketing have developed significantly in the past few years in terms of a means to deliver a sales message to stimulate demand and supply product information. In order to take advantage of these developments, marketing managers need to understand the characteristics of direct marketing and their role in the marketing and marketing communications mix. They also need to understand creative and media opportunities and limitations. Data protection, particularly electronic data protection, is of topical interest as is marketing in the digital age. Digital media are the subject of Chapter 10 of this book.

Learning objectives

This chapter seeks to explore the nature and role of direct marketing. More specifically, on completion of this chapter, the student will be able to:

- understand the nature and role of direct marketing;
- appreciate the direct marketing process and explain this in relation to other elements of marketing communications and media;

- assess creative approaches regarding direct marketing techniques including incentives and offers and those that have gained in popularity in the digital age;
- appreciate the consumer context but also others such as business-to-business and not-for-profit;
- explain the emergence of database marketing and appreciate how it has evolved;
- understand how database marketing adds value and how it can be used to improve marketing performance;
- understand the key elements in the management of data protection and privacy issues.

DIRECT MARKETING

From B-to-B to consumer direct marketing

Direct marketing has been practised in the business-to-business (B-to-B) context for many years. There is a smaller sales universe than that of consumer marketing and targets are relatively easy to identify. Direct marketing can be very cost-effective in B-to-B contexts. However, in terms of targets, the Decision Making Unit (DMU) is an important factor when considering communications. There are usually not one but several people to consider in terms of the composite 'MAN', i.e. money, authority and need. A budget holder may have to be involved but otherwise might have no interest whatsoever in a product or service. Another person may have the need but not the money and may have to seek authorisation. It is not unusual for a presentation to be made to the whole of the Board where the cost of (say) a new computer system is high. Direct marketing can be cost effective in this role whereby regular contact can generate leads and brand awareness can be achieved through the creation of specific messages that are tailored to named persons. Sales visits can be more effective given that preparation has been undertaken to make a prospect aware of the proposition. In not-for-profit situations it is the ability to create a database within a niche or a sector and the relatively low costs that attract organisations to direct marketing. However, with the influence and impact of the Internet and online activities, as well as advances in mobile technology, has come the biggest direct marketing use by far and this is with the consumer.

Advantages and disadvantages of direct marketing

Direct marketing is in many situations a key component in the marketing communications mix when attempting to develop current customers. Direct marketing has grown with database technology and it is flexible, fast and interactive. It can be tightly targeted so that waste is reduced and is 'accountable', where responses can be observed and impact seen, and therefore it can be described as predictable. Email and telemarketing in particular are very fast means of getting a result. But this has to be paid for and direct marketing is relatively high in cost, which is why it is critical that correct targeting of the right message via a well-managed database is crucial to being cost-effective. Controlled growth is possible through the application of direct marketing whereby a build-up can be had in an almost test market fashion. In this sense direct marketing can be seen as having low investment costs.

There many problems associated with direct marketing such as the 'junk mail' image and the fact that a lot of people get annoyed about appearing on databases and their names suddenly appearing on letters. This kind of marketing has always suffered from the lack of the tactile opportunities offered by conventional retail outlets.

The direct marketing process

The process of direct marketing involves the identification and qualification of prospects, the attraction of them to the brand and the conversion and retention of these. This can be understood easily in the relationship marketing paradigm in terms of the brand develop-ment of trust, commitment and loyalty. That is not to say that direct marketing is only used with well-known brands. It is broader than mail order and has been defined by the (American) Direct Marketing Association (2012) on its website as:

> an interactive process of addressable communication that uses one or more advertising media to effect, at any location, a measurable sale, lead, retail purchase, or charitable dona-tion, with this activity analyzed on a database for the development of ongoing mutually beneficial relationships between marketers and customers, prospects, or donors.

The DMA suggest that like mass advertising direct marketing:

allows organizations to inform potential customers;
can create brand awareness;
can spur immediate purchase behaviour.

Direct marketing has the following advantages over mass advertising:

measurability;
accountability;
efficiency;
higher return on investment.

For the DMA, the power of being direct means 'relevance, responsibility, and results' (DMA, 2012).

Direct marketing is also about targeting and using lists, or more precisely databases, to be reasonably sure that those contacted are from the appropriate class, as opposed to mass marketing with its associated waste. The concept of direct marketing is simple. It allows effectiveness to be better measured and therefore to many it is a more acceptable form of communications, especially with its speed and connectivity. Instead of broadcasting a mass marketing message through television or print to a wide number of people, a customised message is instead sent on an individual basis. It is sent direct, to a much smaller number of people who are more predisposed to listening to the message and buying the product or ser-vice. There is no 'middle man' but it is interactive, two-way communications where the tar-get receives the offer in some way, whether this is through the mail or through a call centre. National television advertising is very expensive and many organisations are questioning its effectiveness. Where a direct sales force is used, it can cost £100–£200 for a face-to-face sales call (see Chapter 16 of this book) and it may take several calls to close a sale. Most would agree that direct marketing is a more cost-effective alternative for generating a sale.

History

The most common form of direct marketing is 'through-the-mail' but there are other types, for example direct-response advertising and telemarketing. Direct marketing had its first golden age in the 1950s, in the form of mail order catalogue selling, as the post-war boom drove consumer spending. However, this golden age was coming to an end in the 1960s and 1970s as the competition from television intensified. In recent years direct marketing has seen a major resurgence, with plenty of support, not unsurprisingly, from direct marketing consultants, but driven on by the less expensive alternatives to traditional channels pro-vided online and through other electronic forms. Even so, techniques such as leaflet drops have not gone away, so that leaflet distribution companies still survive. For example, Data

Discoveries Ltd, a data management company, reported on a 2012 study in New Zealand that revealed direct mail still to be a more popular option than social media interaction. With 150 hi-tech outfits questioned about database marketing techniques, social sites ranked 7th of the 12 promotional methods employed, below conventional mail and email, through which tailored messages can be sent to hand-picked targets (Data Discoveries Ltd, 2012).

According to DMG Direct Inc. (2012), direct marketing in the USA is still worth $40 billion, with a large percentage of that being spent on direct mail as 'a proven and cost effective way to reach customers'. This is because of the tried and tested benefits involving the focus, accuracy, directness and cost effectiveness to marketers that direct marketing offers. Change has come in the form of fragmented media and better ways of targeting, the increase in retailer power and own-label success at the expense of manufacturers brands (as discussed in Chapter 1 of this book) as well as the ability of retailers to build long-term relationships with customers through, for example, loyalty cards/schemes or frequent purchase rewards.

An example of the utilisation of information technology is that of K&Co (formed in 2011 by combining Great Universal with Kays and Empire Stores). The resurgence of this business was enabled by the increased productivity and processing power of information technology, which provided the maximum advantage in targeting key customers meaning that marketers were able to target minority, previously under-serviced customers. This then provided a platform for new product introduction and cross selling of other products. It also supplied a new, direct channel of distribution and the identification of prime prospects and the ability to distinguish between sales and lead generation. For marketers like K&Co, with over a 100-year history of home shopping, selling direct through its website (www.kandco.com/) would appear a natural progression.

How direct marketing works

The way direct marketing works is by utilising devices such as free-phone/toll-free telephone numbers to visit a showroom/website or join a club. The response is dependent at least in part on the way in which the offer is constructed creatively. The target should not be put on hold, there should be no rudeness nor should situations arise whereby answers to questions cannot be provided, and products should be available. This is customer need fulfilment where the product/information is put out in a convenient and timely manner so that the front end and back end are parts of the same chain. Billing and the like including the delivery company used (outsourced) become part of the organisation's organisation.

Responses in terms of interactivity can be in real time or delayed and may involve more than one medium. For example, direct response off the page or TV may direct the prospect to the telephone or Internet thus lessening the interactivity so that direct response advertising happens via a medium, mail, TV, print, radio and so on.

The idea of mediated communication in marketing has been recognised for many years. Marketers would like to treat everyone as a segment but this in most instances is hardly cost effective. However, when such contact is possible and when face-to-face personal selling takes place in real time and is company initiated, this can be highly personalised. At the other extreme, mass media advertising is mediated and non-personal and has a delayed response. Sometimes the customer or prospect will initiate the interactivity through email, telephone or fax. In these cases the company should be well placed to take advantage of this, rather than waste a valuable opportunity. However, it is recognised that personal representation, desirable as it is, may be hard to apply in the real world, not least because just what personalisation means differs for different players in the chain of events. Vesanen (2007) provides a conceptual framework for personalisation, but maintains that cooperation between actors in the value chain is hindered because of a lack of meaning and this in turn limits successful communication between the different actors.

Incentives

An incentive is usually included in a proposition made to a prospect as to what they will receive and for what in return. They are specific inducements or stimuli but vary enormously in scope from the quick response from a free gift to more complex situations including loyalty schemes. This is where the direct marketing and sales promotion interface lies and objectives tend to be sales promotion-led objectives such as trial or rewarding loyalty (see Chapter 11 of this book for a further discussion on how sales promotions work). In terms of differing targets there is a clear need to make appropriate approaches. With prospects there is a need to offer an inducement such as 'extra free', as with, for example, direct wine clubs. In this case the offer might be to 'join the club and get 15 bottles for the price of 12 on the first order'. With competition loyalists there may be a need to increase the offer in order to seduce them away, but this may not be possible and a waste. Brand switchers on the other hand are similar to prospects and, in fact, are prospects. Company loyalists have to be retained and extra sales can be had through subtler methods such as newsletters, help lines, loyalty magazines or clubs. These devices provide product involvement, status and association with others and rewards should be specifically related to loyalty schemes. There is a need to consider up-grading and up-selling, cross-selling and even cross-category possibilities such as air miles from, say, petrol purchases, as well as, for example, the use of social media.

Types of direct marketing media

Mail

Despite advances in database management the majority of through-the-mail communication is still impersonal, yet worth billions in the USA alone. Financial services and insurance are the leaders in this field, often with personalised offerings, but generally, despite software advances, it is too costly to completely personalise every 'mail shot'. The creative element of direct mail advertising is both high and low. The key to success is seen to gain involvement through keeping the brand in front of the recipient using the envelope, letter, brochure and reply card. Response rates vary and this medium would certainly lag behind telemarketing or personal selling but can be cheaper, and creativity in the promotion is the key. With the demise of the video cassette, the CD may still be included in the direct mail 'shot', but increasingly potential customers are directed to websites and video links online. Direct mail is still very important despite the 'junk mail' tag but critical to this is the quality of the list. Response rates can be enhanced by good database management, but lists have to be suitable and internal management committed to the idea of direct marketing so that the right kind of investment goes in. The use of the average response rate as a measure is dangerous, as response rates will depend upon whether the product and prospect are new or already exist and on the sector being dealt with, especially whether this is consumer or industrial. Subtler approaches can eradicate the 'intrusive' factor. Direct mail is a good medium for targeting and it can work if the creative side is right but it also offers an opportunity to provide detailed information, the reason why in the past direct marketing has been a support rather than main medium. With technological and communications changes there are now opportunities to lead with direct marketing, including direct mail.

TV and radio

The infomercial, as described earlier in Chapter 8 of this book, can be programme length. For example, advertisements usually run from 2 to 30 minutes (or even longer, up to 60 minutes) and can be inexpensive to produce because of what they are trying to achieve, which in part will be to educate the viewer. As with print, direct response advertisements are commonplace on TV and radio. Costs vary as with advertising generally. Costs can be high and this kind of direct marketing can be expensive but persuasive. All of the usual advertising pros and cons apply such as long lead times.

Print/catalogues

The equivalent to an infomercial in print is the advertorial (see Chapter 8 of this book), which is an advertisement combined with editorial material and is designed to look like editorial material but, at the same time, do the job of an advertisement by providing product, service or company information. It is usually styled to resemble the editorial of the publication that it appears in and deals with serious issues as well as promotion at one and the same time. Catalogues are one of the oldest forms of marketing with a lot of history tied to commercial development and doing business at a distance. These days direct marketing is still led by catalogue companies but catalogues are not always simply direct. IKEA, Next and Argos, for example, all have a retail presence but also a catalogue and of course catalogues have a big place in business-to-business marketing. However, the primary target for most catalogues is the consumer, usually women. More women than men use them and they can involve the telephone and the retail outlet. Electronically the catalogue is going through an interesting transition from the bulky paper-based book to the CD and now online, making it easy to keep prices, product deletions, and stock levels and so on up-to-date. Print advertising, though, still accounts for a good proportion of direct response marketing. This has both a low response rate and can be low cost. Magazines, however, can be expensive and have long lead times but are good for targeting. Inserts suffer from the usual problems of falling out of publications and causing irritation. They do get noticed but have a high cost per thousand.

Telemarketing

This might be considered as personal communication (see Chapter 16 of this book) or direct marketing. This book assumes telemarketing to fit within direct marketing rather than selling where it is considered as just one of the options in terms of personal contact. The distinction has to be made between outward (or outbound) and inward (or inbound) telemarketing. The most common understanding of the term would be the former, with the development of call centres the most prominent idea for both. Calls are taken from responses to other direct marketing such as a direct response press advertisement. Telemarketing is relatively easy to measure in terms of ROI and the cost per contact, although high, is significantly less than with face-to-face and therefore frequent contact is not such a cost issue. It should be highly targeted and messages can be tailored. It is fast but can be intrusive and aurally limiting, where the message has to be simple, and it needs managing. Outward telemarketing might be seen in the same way as junk mail and viewed with suspicion. Inward calls are positive, immediate, seen as being useful, and can create loyalty.

Internet

The digital age is now also providing companies with a new and richer source of customer information with which they can target selective audiences. Websites gather significant amounts of customer data and the company or others to whom the information is sold can use this. However, the fact that these increasingly rich sources of customer information are being collated into large customer databases is the source of much concern and debate (see the final Snapshot at the end of this chapter on privacy and security). The questions discussed later in this chapter are to do with security, limitations that should be put on the use of customer data, special rules that may be required for the Internet. At the moment the Internet is 'king of direct transactions' with low costs and increased speed of access for customers with the ease of credit card use increasing. Low cost of production and web creation and its global nature and the popularity of social media make the Internet a 'must consider' medium (see Chapter 10 of this book).

User groups/membership scheme/loyalty card

These can establish extra benefit and help move the customer towards loyalty as with, for example, air miles. A typical club to join would be the frequent flyer type as with Flying Blue, the Air France and KLM-originated club that has varying grades of membership where benefits include the cross selling of wine to members at special rates.

The Snapshot below discusses how direct marketing has grown to become a key force in consumer marketing, largely because of the impact of technology and a greater ability to achieve personalisation in communications.

Snapshot   The growth of direct marketing – how it has become a key force in consumer marketing

Growth of direct marketing is happening through increased use of the mail, telephone numbers, websites and email. It has grown and is still growing in consumer terms. From this perspective direct marketing is now very visible. Even before the turn of the millennium, writers and commentators were predicting the growth in direct marketing because of certain factors such as new ways to shop, especially from home, with the convenience that brings. This is allied to trends such as social change, for example the increased numbers of women working in many societies. Buying products and services without speaking to anyone has become the norm in many circumstances, whether this is for insurance products and services, furniture or gardening products. Many consumers around the world are used to credit and debit cards and increasingly the use of electronic transactions, especially as Internet banking grows. Direct marketing has had to become more sophisticated and more effective with, for example, the use of advances in database technology and better segmentation systems. Direct marketing does also have cost advantages.

In the USA the Direct Marketing Association (DMA) in 2011 released a report that indicated that indeed direct marketing had grown stronger. The 'Power of Direct' report suggested that direct marketing sales growth had outpaced overall economic growth with a 7.1 per cent growth rate in sales (worth nearly $2 trillion) compared with sales overall in the USA with a growth rate of 5.1 per cent in 2011. The DMA reckon that 8.7 per cent of GDP comes from direct marketing. Not surprisingly this makes direct marketing expenditure a large share of marketing communications effort ($163 billion in 2011), which equates to over 50 per cent of total advertising expenditure in the USA. In 2011 direct marketing grew at a rate of 5.6 per cent and this is a trend that is expected to continue, according to the DMA, until at least 2016. ROI for direct marketing in 2011 was projected at $12.03 of sales/$ of expenditure in comparison to $5.24 for advertising generally. According to the DMA there were, in 2011, 1.3 million direct marketing employees in the USA with support for a further

7.9 million, i.e. 9.2 million jobs. Yet despite all of these sales, the nature of direct and database marketing means that only 66,000 new jobs will be created in 2012.

Much of the growth in direct marketing is not unsurprisingly created by online media, which according to the DMA, 'continues to outpace other channels in expenditure growth'. The DMA expects digital activities to increase the share of marketing budgets in the USA, which was 19 per cent in 2011 and the DMA suggests this figure to be 21 per cent in 2012, the spend on digital marketing having grown 'by $14.5 billion since 2006'. All mobile and online advertising are set to rise further, with a 50 per cent annual growth rate for mobile, 18 per cent for search and display, and 20 per cent for things such as blogs and advergaming. While direct mail and direct response television have grown (4.6 per cent and 6.1% per cent respectively according to the DMA), direct response magazines, radio and inserts are experiencing negligible growth with direct response newspaper experiencing falling growth. Traditional media in the USA will either have very low growth or even be in 'negative territory' with the predicted slowdown of the US economy according to the DMA.

Stop Point

The growth of direct marketing has been driven in recent years by the rapid growth of digital technology applications to marketing arenas. Undertake the following: 1. Consider and comment on why this is so and in what ways a company can use direct response; 2. Consider the movements that have started and continue to develop such as Internet banking and electronic transactions and discuss the problems such movements bring in terms of security and privacy.

DATABASE MARKETING

A database is a collection of data, usually using a computer that is a useful, convenient and interactive access to information on prospective and existing targets. A database can be built up in two ways: through internal sources such as previous enquiries or current or lapsed users; and through external sources such as warranty cards, subscriptions to magazines or through the purchase or lease of lists of, for example, 4x4 car purchasers or golf enthusiasts. Database marketing is related to direct marketing, relationship marketing and customer relationship management but is not the same thing as direct marketing and the terms should not be interchanged. Database marketing is much more than 'list building' as it focuses on customers, capturing detailed data on them, not products. Database marketing is an interactive approach to marketing. Clearly it involves list compilation and individually addressable targets that are then approached with marketing materials through conventional media and channels such as the mail in the past (but this now includes email and email networks) or telephone. The task is to then manage the database in such a way that contact is made and maintained effectively and efficiently.

The development of database marketing

As suggested above, a database can be built by using both internal and external list information so that lists can be built from actual customers and prospects or they can be purchases or leased from list brokers. These allow marketers to identify their best customers, their value, needs and likely behaviours. Lists can be either or both response lists (people who have already responded to some aspect of marketing, these being expensive to lease because response rates are known to be higher) and compiled lists (collected from a variety of sources). In other words you get what you pay for since the quality of the list, rather like a sales lead, really does matter. Frequency of purchase, responsiveness to direct marketing techniques and amount spent directly are all important factors that are likely to be known from response lists. Lists can be compiled from a variety of sources such as magazine subscriptions, warranty cards and the like, where the information is bought and sold, and can be made up of conventional or email addresses. Cost of rental varies and will depend upon whether the client has access or merely provides the information/mail shot to be sent on by a broker or direct marketing company. Outsourcing is common because management of lists or better still of a database is best done by experts, although software is available for self-management. Database marketing breeds its own success.

Database marketing used to be about lists and list management was key since the right people need to be contacted. However, list building and management have moved from a state of lacking sophistication to one of finesse. In the early phase direct mail or telemarketing lists were all that were required, i.e. addresses or telephone numbers. However, the creation of the term 'junk mail' is by no means an accident. Unsolicited material or intrusive telephone calls caused many consumers to either ignore further mail shots or worse still have a very negative opinion of companies and brands, and the methods themselves. However, the route to more effective direct marketing campaigns came through better customer information to increase the relevance of the offer and better management of the communication between the company and the customer. List management capability is now huge with unlimited numbers of contacts and lists, automated list management, interaction with emails and websites, customisation and personalisation possibilities – all of which adds up to improved customer relationship management, which allows content delivery that is relevant to each prospect.

Despite the practical difficulties of building a sophisticated database operation it can be argued that the database is the greatest single application of information technology within marketing. The rapidly declining costs of hardware and software have increased the attractiveness of database marketing, resulting in a massive shift in the last decade towards its importance and use. The cost of storing and accessing a single customer name on a database has dropped dramatically over the last three decades. Nowadays companies are becoming much more precise about the type of potential customer they will mail to and the size of mail shots is reducing correspondingly, yet the effectiveness is on the increase. The cost of storage and maintenance is still relatively low with many companies offering many linked services.

The advantages and disadvantages of database marketing

The *advantages* of database marketing have been known for some time. The desire and search for one-on-one marketing may have been the 'impossible dream' for marketers seeking to personalise communications but this has given impetus to the development of database marketing. The advantages of this include the interactions that can be had between the marketer and the individual customer each time the marketer uses the database. The marketer can then look, through data analysis, for patterns in such interactions. This can then provide the marketer with ideas on how to tailor products to customer need, with adjustments to pricing and the other ways in which the marketer communicates with the customer. This analysis can provide insights into likely behaviour across a range of products and services. A key consideration is how database marketing improves marketing performance. Database techniques provide a better understanding of how many and what kind of customers an organisation has, especially in relation to marketing variables such as product or delivery types preferred. This understanding can help improve customer service in terms of transactions, complaints or problems that can be tracked. Another advantage is that a better understanding of the market can be had, especially if database information is integrated with a marketing information system that would include the results from any marketing research projects undertaken across the marketing spectrum of activities, including competitive data.

The *disadvantages* of database marketing are fewer than the advantages but they are real and have to be taken into consideration. These include the cost in terms of hard- and software requirements and skill requirements in terms of analysis and decision making. The effectiveness of database marketing is a factor of quality, not just of these skills but also of the data itself. As alluded to earlier, however, the organisation gets what it pays for and for database marketing to be cost effective it should be more than merely a tactical tool.

Measuring results

Dividing the number of responses by the number of mailed offers has been the traditional way to measure results, as a percentage response rate. Conversion rates are then derived in a similar fashion from orders received divided by responses. However, the marketer may never be sure that it was the direct marketing and not some other factor that worked. Variables working together in an integrated fashion may be the goal but this complicates measurement. However, simple techniques such as list testing via sampling techniques, offer or copy testing can be deployed, as can checks on reach and frequency as with media generally (see Chapters 9 and 17 of this book for more on traditional media and measurement respectively).

The Snapshot below discusses how database marketing has become an essential approach for charities. It suggests that it is no longer a question of using mail shots but that this has moved on to a more integrated approach to marketing communications, including digital and database-related elements.

Snapshot Database marketing for charities – an essential tool for effective targeting

Many of the actions charitable organisations take become a form of marketing. Burrows (2012) suggests some basic things that charities should be doing with marketing, including things like pinning down a USP (unique selling point or proposition), doing more with existing supporters, following up enquiries, calls or any show of interest, developing an appropriate marketing mix, engaging with segmentation and targeting and employing some form of tracking, testing and evaluation. Burrows also suggests qualifying leads, i.e. making sure that the 'sales' lead is the right type of person, the database needing to be full of people who 'qualify'.

Database marketing is an essential part of the marketing approach for charities and it is a long time since mere mail shots were undertaken as the only tool in the

(Continued)

(Continued)

toolbox. Cubit (2007) suggests that 'Ten years ago, direct marketing in the charity sector simply involved testing a mailpack or insert and subsequently rolling it out over the next couple of years. But as the market has become increasingly competitive and techniques ever more sophisticated, this is no longer enough'. Charities have to make direct marketing work harder 'thus combining various techniques and looking for more innovative routes to market'. This means moving away from just print into the digital arena, whether this is the use of text messaging and digital panels on the London Underground (Shelter), digital response television and text messaging and telephone (ActionAid), or email and newsletters (National Autistic Society). As Cubit points out 'consumers do not operate in silos so it is crucial that they are not targeted using just one channel', and not just one message so that a mix of digital media and messages can be used.

However, the issue still remains of effective databases that consist of targets that are likely to be responsive to direct marketing approaches, whatever those approaches may be in terms of message and media means to carry the message. For this to be effective the relationships that donors of one sort or another have with charities need to be understood so that preferences can be acted upon. Cubit provides the example of Cancer Research UK that uses a 'raft of traditional direct marketing techniques including cold mailings, door-drops, inserts and telemarketing, but it is also making use of more innovative strategies, including mixing and matching various activity to boost donations'. Although direct mail is still effective in stimulating the money donation process there is a clear need to look to 'other channels and the opportunities those channels can offer in terms of mixing and matching techniques if they want to ensure they secure donations from consumers across all ages and spectrums', especially since the data available are becoming more and more sophisticated and 'direct marketers can now examine an individual's lifestage, demographic and motivations, rather than simply name, address and transactional information. This means the added value and insight that can be attributed to a direct marketing campaign is enormous' (Cubit, 2007).

St Oswald's is a charity based in Gosforth, Newcastle upon Tyne, in the UK. The charity provides specialist care for local adults, young people and children and families. The service offers a day hospice, lymphoedema service, an inpatient unit, complementary therapy service, consultant outpatient clinic and an outreach service: 'Adults with life limiting conditions are referred to us for pain and symptom management and end of life care. We care for patients with cancer, as well as those with end stage neurological, cardiac and respiratory conditions' (St Oswald's, 2013). St Oswald's also have a Children's Service that offers specialist short breaks to them and their families and a service for young adults, aged 18–25.

The multi-disciplinary team at St Oswald's includes doctors, nurses, physiotherapists, occupational therapists, complementary therapists, social workers and chaplain support.

St Oswald's annual running costs exceed £10m, nearly two-thirds of which is raised through voluntary giving, and St Oswald's 'make no charge for any of our services; ensuring hospice care is available to everyone' (St Oswald's, 2013). In order to do all of this, St Oswald's has to embrace as full a range of marketing and fundraising activities and approaches as is possible, including newsletters, the St Oswald's Lottery, the St Oswald's website (www.stoswaldsuk.org/), blogs, fundraising events, the YouTube channel and other social media. Much of this activity is aided by an effective database.

Stop Point

The growth and use of database marketing can be clearly seen with many organisations and certainly the developments in this area have benefitted charities, especially those on limited budgets. Undertake the following: 1. Discuss the likely effects of adopting a database marketing approach to donations and fundraising for charities such as St Oswald's; 2. Comment on the importance of integration in the marketing communications mix, especially between the use of traditional and newer mix elements.

MANAGING PRIVACY ISSUES

Concern about misuse of information

There is concern all round over the ability these days to gather information, especially electronically. The amount of information being gathered on consumers and how this information is used are central to these concerns. Digital communications are now also providing companies with new and richer sources of customer information with which they can target selective audiences. The Internet with its many websites will gather significant amounts of customer data and personal information that can subsequently be used by companies (or others to whom the information is sold) for direct marketing. Therefore these are increasingly rich sources of customer information that are being made into large customer databases which are the source of much concern. An example in the area of mobile phone technology is that of Apple and issues around apps. According to the DMA (UK), Apple have tightened the rules over the apps for iPhone and iPad that access customers' address book data without them knowing and obviously without their permission. Social networking sites such as Facebook and Twitter collect and store information from the device. The DMA (UK) give the example of Twitter that via its 'Find Friends' feature on both iPhone and Android phones sends numbers and email addresses from the user's contact list to the company. Apple has issued a reassurance that this is against its policies and an app would require express approval to access contact data. Apple says that all apps would have to comply or be removed. Twitter have said they will change information around its import function to be more explicit while Facebook maintain they already operate on this basis (Brown, 2012).

Some questions here are:

- Are consumers sufficiently well protected from companies that can abuse information?
- What are the limits to the use of such data?
- By whom and how should the Internet be policed?

Concern is set to grow as the Internet, a huge source of data, continues to grow. For example, the small text files known as 'cookies' that contain a website name and user ID are downloaded to the hard disks of computers used by interim users, and can be used to trace a surfer's path through the Internet and pass this information back to the website owner. Cookies are seen by some as 'an evil and intrusive spying mechanism tracking your every move on the net' and by others as 'a harmless device designed to make your life easier'

(Fae, 2010). On the upside the cookie can tailor popups to the nature of the site visit, with some cookies being more sophisticated than others. For Fae (2010):

> They might record how long you spend on each page on a site, what links you click, even your preferences for page layouts and colour schemes. They can also be used to store data on what is in your shopping cart, adding items as you click. The possibilities are endless, and generally the role of cookies is beneficial, making your interaction with frequently-visited sites smoother – for no extra effort on your part. Without cookies, online shopping would be much harder.

On the down side, consumers may not want this kind of intrusion, which results in names being on lists and information being used to target individuals with direct marketing messages. Other consumers may favour control of cookies. For Fae (2010):

> The collection and storage of personal information without permission is not strictly legal in the UK. Sites that make use of cookies get around this in two ways. Firstly, if you read the small print in the Terms and Conditions, you will almost certainly find that by using a site, you are agreeing to download the site cookies. And, if that still feels a bit more invasive, almost all web browsers nowadays allow you the option to block cookies. That means you can block all cookies or, with a little more effort, you can start to pick and choose which ones to accept. It makes browsing a little clunkier – some sites do not work with the cookie-option turned off. However, if it really matters to you, then that option is always available.

Options available to deal with data privacy concerns

The EU position has been clear for some time on the protection of personal data as the growth of electronic and mobile commerce marches on. The case is seen as overwhelming in favour of a ban on unsolicited email and other personally addressed messages. However, it is perhaps the perceived lack of privacy that provides the real reason why citizens are reluctant to use new information and communications technology. The EU has stated the need for a fair balance between data user and data subject. At the centre of this are the notions of respect and transparency, especially since a person cannot opt out of something they are not aware of. A typical 'trick' would be to offer a free game on a website without the person knowing that much personal data would be collected, even down to the type of personal computer they have. EU regulators already require specific consent for marketing by fax and use of auto calling machines without human intervention. Concern is expressed about especially sensitive issues such as sexual orientation.

The DMA's (Direct Marketing Association) codes negotiated with authorities recognise the need for self-regulation and a set of ground rules. This is complex in any country around the world and therefore the DMAs have taken action. For example, the UK DMA provided a £75 easy-to-use guide to the 1998 (amended 2003) Data Protection Act (£150 non-members). This guide dealt with: increased controls over data processing; the new express provision that gives individuals a right to opt-out of receiving a company's own future direct marketing approaches; the type of information that must be provided to the data subject; what opt-outs are necessary and the wording to be used in different circumstances; the restrictions on the transfer of data to countries outside the European Economic area; the increased rights of data subjects and the notification process.

In a sense this is about 'Permission Marketing' and encouraging the data subject to opt-in. The legal obligations of any marketer that holds personal data are clear in that they must comply with the Data Protection Act (1998) Data Protection Principles: the data must be processed fairly and lawfully; the data can only be obtained for specified purposes and processed in a manner compatible with those purposes; the data must be adequate, relevant and not excessive in relation to the purposes for which they are processed; the data must be accurate and where necessary kept up-to-date; the data must not be kept longer than is necessary; the data shall only be processed in accordance with the rights of data subjects under the 1998 Act; appropriate technical and organisational measures must be taken against unauthorised or unlawful processing of personal data and against accidental loss, destruction or damage to personal data; personal data shall not be transferred outside of the European Economic Area unless there is adequate protection for the rights and freedoms of the data subject.

The overall sage advice to marketers from the DMAs is that the penalties for deliberate non-compliance are large enough that no organisation could expect to survive prosecution. Mutual benefits are to be had since respect increases trust and trust will result in better targeting and better marketing.

As long ago as 1999, *The Economist* assessed the possible options in the area of data privacy and concluded that more laws, market solutions (self regulation), infomediaries (brokers), technology (encryption allows consumers to protect information), and transparency (citizens should have access to information) would not be adequate. As the debate carries on into the second decade of the 21st century a combination of legislation and self-regulation continues. The 1995 European Union (EU) Directive on data protection obliged member states to update their data protection legislation. Under such legislation companies can use individual personal data only where the people concerned have given their consent. The exception was where legal or contractual reasons come into play: this was seen as being necessary in the area of finance, for example as with loans, but there was still the right to object to being targeted and information held on individuals. This issue then is about controlling the misuse of information and privacy protection.

As Twentyman (2012) points out, in January 2012 the European Commission proposed in a draft regulation (in force in 2014) that would force up disclosure rates of breaches in data security whereby a retailer will have 24 hours to report a security breach. Many in the industry believe the 24-hour window to be unrealistic, as it would apply to non-EU companies that serve EU customers and to data on EU customers processed outside the EU. It is the nature of the IT task that would take the time even for small breaches and small e-merchants. Clearly there are potentially much larger scenarios with multi-server situations. Another problematic aspect is how personal data are defined and the directive covers the notification of individuals if their personal data have been compromised. According to Twentyman (2012) the European Commission is 'acting by regulation, a top-down set of rules that will be imposed uniformly across its 27 member states, rather than by directive'. This means that the situation will be unlike the case with the 1995 data protection directive 'whereby nations can make their own adjustments' to the rules laid out, and the requirements of this regulation are unlikely to change.

Because of its pre-eminence within the cyber or online world, the USA is further ahead in terms of Internet usage than any other country. By the turn of the millennium there was pressure in the USA to adopt more stringent data privacy regulations for online use. Pressure to conform has grown as the trend towards privacy regulation gains momentum beyond the boundaries of the EU. Countries such as Brazil, Chile, Argentina and Canada, as well as several in Eastern Europe, are considering or have already implemented stringent, EU-style data privacy policies. US companies have been urged to go ahead and make the move to stricter privacy policies in anticipation of changes in US statutes. A 1999 Georgetown University survey examined the privacy practices at top commercial websites. The survey found that while 93 per cent of websites collect personal information about visitors, only two-thirds gave notification of how that information will be used. Worse, less than 10 per cent complied with the privacy protection standards outlined by the Federal Trade Commission (FTC). To meet the FTC standards, a site must notify users when data are being collected, give users a chance to opt out of giving information about themselves, give users access to their information so they can correct it, provide adequate security for customer databases, and provide access to a live customer contact. It may be that the more progressive organisations are addressing these issues and most might understand the problems surrounding privacy.

As Bostok (2012) points out, in Canada, the direct marketing industry is regulated by Canada's private sector privacy law – the Personal Information Protection and Electronic Documents Act (PIPEDA). First introduced in 2001, PIPEDA regulates the collection, use and disclosure of personal information in the private sector. This includes everything from name and address information to more sensitive information such as social insurance numbers, financial and health information. In the USA, the Federal Trade Commission Can-Spam Act was put in place 'in order to govern the use of unsolicited bulk email as a form of commercial advertising and prevent the abuse of email addresses by unscrupulous individuals'.

There is a cost for compliance and keeping clients' information safe, especially where keeping up with technological advancement is concerned and there is a need, at an added cost, for external verification; this clearly will affect the costs for companies, with a balance having to be made between costs and prices. Consumers may perceive that their privacy is being violated even if this is not the case, making the marketer's job more difficult – hence the need for standards and better data management in the face of 'dynamic compliance requirements', especially since data are easier to steal (Bostock, 2012).

The Snapshot below discusses technology-driven change in the context of legislation and self-regulation and what this might mean to direct marketing and marketers.

Snapshot   Technology-driven change – customer perception of security and privacy breaches and the influence on direct marketing

The safeguarding of people's personal information has to be one of the most important areas on anyone's agenda. Direct and database marketing and privacy and security go hand in hand, accentuated by the rapid development of electronic communications. It is all about someone looking into the private life of another. This may involve companies or government. The narrower but linked debate to data security and privacy regarding marketing can be more clearly understood by looking at a particular context, but some generalities can be highlighted.

The debate is about the use and potentially the abuse of personal data in a wired society where the fundamental human right to privacy and security is at stake. The problem is that whereas a few years ago the butcher used to know everything about his 100 customers, these days the butcher is Tesco or Sainsbury and now they want the same with 1 million customers. Hence the use of database marketing through sophisticated technology employing email, call centres, direct response, smart phones and the Internet, with the promise of the ultimate one-to-one, tailor-made transaction. The problems of intrusiveness (and particularly spamming on the Internet) are real. The natural reaction of consumers is to ask 'Why do you have my name and how did you get it?' This is about consent and the choice of opting in or opting out.

Over the last decade or so there have been many examples of data security and privacy breaches. For example, a district judge in the USA upheld federal regulations to prevent banks/insurance and so on from selling/renting data. Another example is that of a Swedish Data Commissioner's ruling that all travel agents have to require customers to sign privacy declarations after the American Airlines Sabine Group reservation system was found to be sending data on customers to the USA for processing. Dietary requirements that have health and religious connotations were part of the data sent. Yet another example is that of a Spanish Commissioner who fined Microsoft for sending clients' data to the USA without their knowledge.

Personal data that are identifiable information about staff, clients, suppliers and others have been regulated in Europe since the early 1980s and are still evolving. The Data Protection Act has been frequently amended, particularly in 2009 and 2010, and substantial changes will be made by 2014 that will increase the regulatory burden on European operations, increase the amount of time, money and personnel required to achieve compliance, and raise the stakes in terms of fines and brand damage arising from non-compliance (International Law Office, 2012). However, the European Commission (2012) claims that the move to a single law will 'do away with the current fragmentation and costly administrative burdens, leading to savings for businesses of around €2.3 billion a year. The initiative will help reinforce consumer confidence in online services, providing a much needed boost to growth, jobs and innovation in Europe'.

Stop Point

Put yourself in the marketer's shoes. You want information on customers and prospects and you want to use it to its fullest potential, to beat the competition. Undertake the following: 1. Consider and comment upon the consequences of non-compliance with European Commission or DMA-type codes and laws of the land on data and data protection; 2. Outline the best way forward for an organisation, a data user, to get to grips with what is expected of them when they are dealing with the rights of data subjects and what this means for direct marketing and marketers.

Assignment

Choose one of the following topics upon which to write a two-page business magazine article. Write the article in the style of a particular magazine, for example *Direct Marketing, Marketing Magazine, Marketing Week* or *Marketing Business*.

1. Targeting and direct marketing generally and more specifically geodemographics, making sure to show how the management of databases affects performance.

2. Security, on the Internet and elsewhere, within direct marketing, highlighting in particular the problems arising through the use of credit cards online or the use of personal information through smart phone apps.

3. Sensitivity and regulation addressing whether a company can be both effective and socially responsible when dealing with databases and direct marketing materials. Include an argument for the extent to which you would regulate/legislate.

Summary of Key Points

- Direct marketing is a key component of many a marketing communications mix.
- With direct marketing targeting can be tight and cost effective if well managed, despite appearing expensive.
- It has at this point almost shed the 'junk mail' image it once had but is still viewed by some as intrusive, annoying and non-tactile. It has re-emerged as a powerful marketing communications tool.
- Direct marketing works best through achieving customer need fulfilment and is growing largely because of societal changes and trends such as a lack of time because of work commitments.
- There is a key link between sales promotions and direct marketing. Incentives offered will depend on objectives and targets; for example whether they are company or competition loyalists.
- Direct marketing uses a variety of media and endeavours to be 'personal', where targeting and list creation are key.
- Databases can be made up from internal and external sources but in essence 'you pay for what you get'. Quality is key to success and resources are needed for direct marketing to breed its own success.
- Digital communications are now providing richer data but safeguarding personal data should be high on the agenda of any organisation.
- Problems still remain with intrusiveness visible. Organisations should try to persuade data subjects to 'opt-in'; otherwise this will hamper the marketing effort.

Discussion Questions

1. Explain the difference between direct and database marketing using examples to illustrate.
2. Outline the factors that have driven the resurgence of direct marketing in recent years and use examples to illustrate.
3. Explain the key role incentives play in direct response advertising and provide examples to illustrate.
4. Explain the workings of loyalty schemes using a specific example to illustrate.
5. Discuss the rationale for setting up a club such as a wine club, explaining the advantages to both club owner and consumer.
6. Outline creative approaches to direct response copy and design.
7. Outline the disadvantages and advantages of each media used with direct marketing techniques.
8. Explain how database marketing can improve marketing performance.
9. Explore the issues around Internet privacy and discuss the way that regulation is likely to develop.
10. Explain the overall ethics of direct marketing practice using examples to illustrate.

Further Reading

Bowen, D.J., Battuello, K.M. and Raats, M. (2005) 'Marketing genetic tests: empowerment or snake oil?', *Health Education Behavior*, 32 (5): 676–85. http://heb.sagepub.com/content/32/5/676

This article is concerned with the regulation and control of the promotion of genetic tests in the USA. Genetic information is complex and not easily understood by the general public and so there is concern for the emotional, psychological and social impact of such tests (currently there are more than 500 such tests that deal with genetic differences) on the general public who are being encouraged to engage with them, often through direct promotional techniques.

Cheung, M. (2008) '"Click here": the impact of new media on the encoding of persuasive messages in direct marketing', *Discourse Studies*, 10 (2): 161–89. http://dis.sagepub.com/content/10/2/161

Dealing with the encoding of persuasive messages in sales emails as direct marketing channels, the article is concerned about the use of relatively new, lower cost means of reaching potentially global audiences. In particular the content of sales letters is addressed using an analysis of discourse structures in a sample from a large database.

Lewis, M.J., Yulis, S.G., Delnevo, C. and Hrywna, M. (2004) 'Tobacco industry direct marketing after the Master Settlement Agreement', *Health Promotion Practice*, 5 (3): 75S–83S. http://hpp.sagepub.com/content/5/3_suppl/75S

This article looks at the direct marketing activities post-MSA, i.e. after the agreement in the USA to change the way tobacco products are marketed. This includes direct mail, coupons, sweepstakes, loyalty programmes, sponsorships and industry magazine activity. The empirical study is set in New Jersey, USA, with adult smokers, and looks at practices that operate currently outside of restrictions; the article seeks to redress this issue and to help limit or eliminate such practices in tobacco marketing.

Thackeray, R., Neiger, B.L., Hanson, C.L. and McKenzie, J.F. (2008) 'Enhancing promotional strategies within social marketing programs: use of Web 2.0 social media', *Health Promotion Practice*, 9 (4): 338–43. http://hpp.sagepub.com/content/9/4/338

This article is about how Web 2.0 applications can directly engage consumers in the creative process through content sharing and collaborative writing. It is concerned with social networking, bookmarking and syndication. It is essentially about how viral marketing is developing to allow health promotion practitioners more direct access to consumers and by the same token the decreased dependency on traditional channels of communication.

Wong, W.W. and Gupta, S.C. (2011) 'Plastic surgery marketing in a generation of "Tweeting"', *Aesthetic Surgery Journal*, 31 (8): 972–6. http://aes.sagepub.com/content/31/8/972

This article looks at social media and web-based technologies that are joining or replacing conventional means to promotion in the context of plastic surgery in a number of cities in the USA. The article highlights the idea of preserving professionalism regardless of what methods of communication are adopted, and is therefore concerned with ethics and web-based activities while expecting direct marketing campaign to continue to develop as plastic surgeons continue to utilise networks to enhance their practices.

REFFERENCES

Bostock, A. (2012) 'Sector report: security, privacy and compliance', *Direct Marketing*, March: 8.

Bowen, D.J., Battuello, K.M. and Raats, M. (2005) 'Marketing genetic tests: empowerment or snake oil?', *Health Education Behavior*, 32 (5): 676–85.

Brown, G. (2012) 'Apple blocks apps that infringe data privacy', 17 February, available at: www.dma.org.uk/news/apple-blocks-apps-infringe-data-privacy.

Burrows, G. (2012) 'Eight marketing essentials for your charity', ngo media, available at: www.ngomedia.org.uk/2012/04/eight-marketing-essentials-for-your-charity/2012/

Cheung, M. (2008) '"Click here": the impact of new media on the encoding of persuasive messages in direct marketing', *Discourse Studies*, 10 (2): 161–89.

Cubit, E. (2007) 'Direct marketing focus', *The Charity Times*, April–May, available at: www.charitytimes.com/pages/ct_features/apr-may07/text_features/ct_apr-may07_focusfeature_channel_surfing.htm

Data Discoveries Ltd (2012) 'Direct Mail "still a popular marketing option"', 27 March, available at: www.datadiscoveries.com/news/direct-mail-still-a-popular-marketing-option/

DMA (2003) 'A Guide to The Data Protection Act 1998', available at: www.crm-forum.com/library/dma/dma-006exe

DMA (2011) 'The Power of Direct Marketing', The Direct Marketing Association, 2 October, available at: www.the-dma.org/cgi/dispannouncements?article=1590

DMA (2012) 'What is the Direct Marketing Association?', available at: www.the-dma.org/aboutdma/whatisthedma.shtml

DMG Direct Inc. (2012) 'Why is direct marketing so popular?', available at: www.dirmarketing.com/html/why_dm_so_popular.html

The *Economist* (1999) 'The surveillance society', 29 April. Available at: www.economist.com/node/202160 (accessed 03/04/14).

European Commission (2012) 'Commission proposes comprehensive reform of data protection rules to increase users' control of their data and to cut costs for businesses', 25 January, available at: http://ec.europa.eu/justice/newsroom/data-protection/news/120125_en.htm

Fae, J. (2010) 'What are cookies?', BBC Webwise, 9 September, available at: www.bbc.co.uk/webwise/guides/about-cookies

International Law Office (2012) 'New EU data protection regulation to affect Data Protection Act', 24 April, available at: www.internationallawoffice.com/newsletters/detail.aspx?g=476507af-d583-4f10-9857-f5d82c64439a

Lewis, M.J., Yulis, S.G., Delnevo, C. and Hrywna, M. (2004) 'Tobacco industry direct marketing after the Master Settlement Agreement', *Health Promotion Practice*, 5 (3): 75S–83S.

O'Connor, J. and Galvin, E. (2001) *Marketing in the Digital Age*. Harlow: FT/Prentice Hall.

St Oswald's (2013) The St Oswald's website, available at: www.stoswaldsuk.org/

Thackeray, R., Neiger, B.L., Hanson, C.L. and McKenzie, J.F. (2008) 'Enhancing promotional strategies within social marketing programs: use of Web 2.0 social media', *Health Promotion Practice*, 9 (4): 338–43.

Twentyman, J. (2012) 'Reporting breaches: EU tightens rules', *Financial Times*, The Connected Business report on cyber security, 25 April, available at: www.ft.com/cms/s/0/4aefa602-87da-11e1-b1ea-00144feab49a.html#axzz1tLLhTMfl

Vesanen, J. (2007) 'What is personalisation? A conceptual framework', *European Journal of Marketing*, 41 (5/6): 409–18.

Wong, W.W. and Gupta, S.C. (2011) 'Plastic surgery marketing in a generation of "Tweeting"', *Aesthetic Surgery Journal*, 31 (8): 972–6.

13 Public Relations

CHAPTER OVERVIEW

Introduction

In this chapter the nature and scope of public relations (PR for short) are explored and explained. Media relations are important and knowing the media is essential. Management attitude towards and use of public relations is an important concern. The next chapter of this book deals with corporate communications and hence corporate relations, and especially corporate identity, image, personality and reputation. This chapter focuses on the product/market level, where PR might be used, for example, to support brands, assist in the launch of a new brand/product or to help throughout an event. This level has been given the name marketing public relations (MPR) as opposed to corporate public relations (CPR, Chapter 14 of this book). The same kinds of technique might be used on both levels, although ultimately the two levels should be brought together in an integrated, managed fashion. This chapter therefore discusses PR's relationship with other communications mix elements and with marketing theory. The chapter also deals with targets or 'publics', PR in practice, PR's ethical dimension, and the impact of technology on PR techniques.

Learning objectives

This chapter considers the nature and role of public relations in the context of what theory has to offer practice. More specifically, on completion of this chapter, the student will be able to:

- understand the nature and role of PR in terms of its development and characteristics;
- appreciate PR as a propagandist form of marketing communications;
- discuss PR in terms of marketing theory and relationship marketing;
- appreciate the nature of PR practice;
- relate PR to the concept of 'publics';
- understand the relationship between internal and external PR;
- appreciate the relationship between PR and legislation and control in PR practice;
- critically consider the impact of technology and the Internet on PR.

THE NATURE AND ROLE OF PR

The nature of public relations

The term 'Public Relations' is well understood these days by those in particular walks of life, for example company executives and government officials. Generally speaking the public at large, too, understand the basics of PR although perceptions have changed over time. There is still a view that PR is somehow 'sleight of hand', a con if you will, but this is perhaps less strong than in the past. Nevertheless, some may be of the view that PR is simply organised lying. More positively others might say PR is about relationships, where maintaining good relationships with various interest groups is seen as a sensible move. Of course there is a role for PR in achieving this, for example the maintenance of employee relations through internal communications, dealing with investor relations, or dealing positively with crisis management issues. The American Institute for Public Relations (IPR) lists 21 areas for research in PR. This list includes areas important to the practice of PR such as reputation and trust, ethics, new technology, change theory and diversity (IPR, 2012). There are always new challenges afoot for organisations to meet in the future, with PR becoming a strategic necessity as opposed to a tactical tool in order that organisations are able to make the most of opportunities.

The growth of PR

The growth in PR activity in recent years is undeniable. Historically PR has been used to solve problems such as announcing new products or helping prospects to find information. Latterly PR has been used more dramatically as a means of 'breaking through the clutter', to capture attention and interest. PR can be said to be versatile but its development has been hampered by its lower (than marketing) status in organisations in the past. According to White (2002) PR also lacks intellectual firepower and budgets, but with the rise in integrated communication PR has grown in terms of interest shown. For example, if the area of ethics is considered, a considerable amount of intellectual firepower is needed. Bowen (2007: 11) contends that:

> the ability to engage in ethical reasoning in public relations is growing in demand, in responsibility and in importance. Academic research, university and continuing education, and professional practice are all attending more than ever to matters of ethics. The public relations function stands at a critical and defining juncture: whether to become an ethics counsellor to top management or to remain outside the realm of the strategic decision-making core. How we choose to respond to the crisis of trust among our publics will define the public relations of the future.

The scope of PR

Dealing with ethical dilemmas and building and maintaining relationships and guiding organisational policies are said by Bowen (2007) to be the ultimate purpose of PR. The scope of PR appears infinite but at its heart there is a need for planned and purposeful communication with whoever is important at any point on a time continuum. Not surprisingly, definitions (which abound in the PR literature, as anywhere else) usually include words such as planned, sustained or mutual. Many commentators see modern PR as an essential part of any organisation's marketing mix – an essential form of communication with the organisation's market or publics. The UK Chartered Institute of Public Relations (CIPR, 2012, originally formed as the Institute of Public Relations in 1948) provide the following definition:

> Public relations is about reputation – the result of what you do, what you say and what others say about you. Public relations is the discipline which looks after reputation, with the aim of earning understanding and support and influencing opinion and behaviour. It is the planned and sustained effort to establish and maintain goodwill and mutual understanding between an organisation and its publics.

The Public Relations Society of America (PRSA, 2012b) has defined PR as:

> a strategic communication process that builds mutually beneficial relationships between organizations and their publics.

Others might simply say it is 'good will management'. PR involves not only facts and logic but also imagery and imagination designed to win 'hearts and minds' and to sustain this long term. There is a need to achieve credibility where the image matches reality. The organisation can polish the image but as some marketing commentators might put it 'you can't polish a turd', a crude but accurate 'old marketing axiom' meaning that in some circumstances there is no room for spin and nothing more can be said on the matter. Things are what they are and there is no other message that can be put out (Armstrong, 1996). However PR can reach the parts advertising cannot (see Chapter 14 of this book for a discussion on corporate image and reality).

Marketing PR (MPR)

There is a somewhat pointless debate in some texts as to whether PR is part of marketing or not, a debate that has a definite whiff of 'the Emperor's new clothes', a reference to the cautionary tale of the Emperor who, because of pride and insecurity, was very susceptible to the flattery of his subjects. He was conned into thinking he had new and wonderful clothes where in fact he had none. It took the innocence of a small child to shatter the delusion (Baker, 2000). Claiming certain things about issues, articles or objects will often produce problems in terms of what is actually delivered (Baker, 2000). It is true that historically PR and marketing came from different routes. The PRO (public relations officer) took over from the press agent. Often a PRO will report directly to the CEO and in this case will probably be dealing with corporate PR but the PR function or department will deal with MPR issues also. In this book the view taken is that MPR is part of the marketing communications mix (and for that matter CPR is viewed as part of the corporate communications mix, and part of an integrated communications whole) and is therefore part of marketing. For some organisations the functions of marketing and PR will still be distinctive departments and the best that one can hope for in this scenario is that marketing and PR are at least allies and not at loggerheads.

Marketing and Corporate PR

The relationship between marketing and public relations and the difference between marketing public relations (MPR) and corporate public relations (CPR) have been explored at length in the literature (for example Kitchen and Moss, 1995; Kitchen and Papasolomou, 1997;

Cornelissen and Harris, 2004; Balmer and Greyser, 2006; Kim and Reber, 2009; Greenberg et al., 2011). Whether or not academics argue that MPR is representative of a further attempt by marketers to 'hijack' PR seems rather irrelevant to MPR or PR practice. MPR may not represent a new marketing paradigm or even marketing or PR discipline, as predicted it would, but this does not mean that MPR is not an important element of the organisation's marketing communications mix. Philip Kotler has declared MPR to be the healthy offspring of two parents, i.e. marketing and PR. From a practitioner perspective the public relations function and public relations programmes encompass both marketing and corporate dimensions. For example the Freshwater Technology company (Freshwater Technology, 2012), a PR service company, suggest that MPR is part of the marketing communications plan and as such is part of a strategy that can influence both intermediaries and end users. CPR for this PR service provider is used to influence customer and non-customer publics (government, pressure groups, employees and other opinion formers) and they see PR as particularly relevant in marketing when such publics have to be influenced in order to gain market entry – what they call a pass strategy that focuses the attention of the public and media on an organisation's products and services and also is a response to critical issues facing society at large. Freshwater Technology suggests that examples might be 'a lobbying campaign to amend the regulatory climate or an educational programme to overcome concerns over the introduction of new technology'.

It is perhaps safe to assume, since it has been the position for some time, that MPR has a place in marketing in order to deliver a strong share of voice but also to win a share of hearts and minds. On the other hand, MPR and CPR are in a necessary strategic alliance where marketing and PR are allies not rivals. MPR can be effective in building brand awareness and knowledge (in effect 'brand seeding') in a cost effective manner compared to advertising and yet can complement advertising and break through the clutter (Kitchen and Papasolomou, 1997). It can therefore be used to launch new brands and products in a particular position in the marketplace. MPR can help reposition existing brands, create interest in a product category or help with the defence of a brand in trouble. The positive brand attitude created by MPR can positively influence customers and prospects. MPR used effectively within IMC can be part of a communications mix without the dominance of one form of communication over another. The place for MPR and CPR within the traditional marketing mix is depicted in Figure 13.1 below.

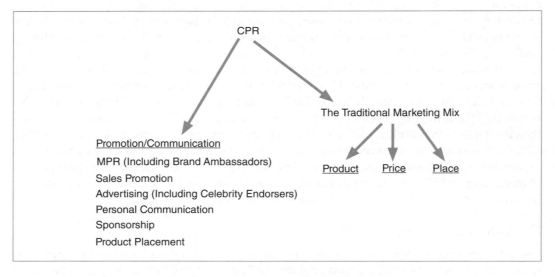

Figure 13.1   PR's place in the traditional marketing communication mix

PR in practice

PR is more about the longer-term rather than the shorter-term commercial considerations of the rest of the communications mix. It should be more than the mere ability to get around legislative restrictions on other communications tools. PR should be about, for example: newsworthy events; being objective; advice-giving; being able to reach people in a way that other forms of communication cannot; being a good citizen.

An underlying feature of PR is the lack of control the marketer has when using it since much of PR is in the hands of media editors, and in some instances the 'lap of the gods'. Lack of control can be offset against PR's cost-effectiveness, ability to create a flexible message, effective use in a crisis and perceived objectivity (i.e. not partisan).

In theory PR is about misconceptions and misunderstandings, or rather the avoidance of these. In practice it is about organisations, chief executive officers, products and policies – in fact anything that interfaces with the various publics any organisation inevitably has; for example, the general public, shareholders, politicians, pressure groups or employees. As society evolves, the practice of PR evolves too. Its documented history does not go back beyond the 20th century but its role today is seen as vital by many organisations in the avoidance of crises or having to resort to crisis management. Regardless of the type of organisational situation, specialisation is omnipresent in society. So it is not unusual to look at the PR industry and see not a holistic entity but a series of specialists engaging in PR activities. Each organisation will have its own discipline, its own way of working. This suggests that while fundamentals might remain, applications and interpretations will differ. After all, if the function of PR is to eradicate misconceptions, incomprehension and therefore avoid misunderstanding, each organisation must achieve this within its own context. All would agree, however, that it is about getting it right in the first place. PR can be the catalyst in achieving truly integrated communication.

Some of the ways PR may differ from advertising can be readily seen in terms of audience and purpose. Historically, PR can be seen as a number of associated yet separate entities that are equal partners in the integrated effort. PR's own reputation has been at times one of being manipulative or about 'fancy parties' for privileged members of certain groups. However, PR can be seen as being all the communications with all the people with whom an organisation has contact. A relationship with others exists whether an organisation wants it to or not. PR is concerned with the development and communication of competitive strategies. It is a management function that provides visibility for an organisation and this allows for it to be properly identified, positioned and understood by all of its targets. PR at the level of the product/market is a key tool in the promotional toolbox. Meeting clients, making an appointment, writing a letter or making a telephone call, the office location and decor, the efficiency of the receptionist are all examples of image forming factors. It is important to note that PR is not the 'free advertising' of some definitions. Certainly successful media relations can lead to 'free' column centimetres, but these are usually as a result of careful planning.

The role of PR

Public relations activities are many and varied but their role is a common one; to contribute to the image of an organisation using a 'soft sell' approach. PR is not advertising under another name. Many of an organisation's clients/customers may view advertising as a 'hard sell' and recognise it as having specific objectives. Public relations activities often have a greater credibility with target groups. For example an article in the business pages of a newspaper, about the impact of new legislation, will no doubt be seen in a different light because it has become editorial rather than coming from the organisation in a partisan way. The basic premise for PR's role is that a positive image is essential to retain existing customers and clients and attract new business.

The characteristics of PR

PR is characterised by its planned nature and it does not (usually) require the purchase of airtime or space in media vehicles such as television or magazines. An editor of one sort or another decides whether or not to transmit messages, not the message sponsor as with advertising, so that it is a question of degree of control. PR messages are perceived to come from the media and have a greater credibility than, say, advertising, which is perceived to come from the message sponsor and while message credibility can be high, management control on the transmission (when and what) can be low. Absolute costs are minimal, relative costs are very low (cost of reaching target audiences). The main costs are time and opportunity costs associated with things like preparing literature or press releases. PR is not always very good at reaching specific audiences, unlike advertising; therefore wastage can be quite high. In a nutshell, PR represents a very cost-effective means of carrying messages, with a high degree of credibility. However, the degree of control that management is able to exert over the transmission of messages can be limited.

An example of the characteristics of MPR in clear relief, even though not tackling brand-level problems, is the case of a material like PVC (used to make for example water pipes, cable sheathing and blood bags) being made to look aspirational in the minds of consumers. This was an exercise in repositioning products from being perceived as commodity plastics to being the material choice of the future. The versatility of PVC that provides a means to enhancing consumer lifestyles was employed by using designers and the design media to get across the concept of 'PVC for life and living'. This worked by designers challenging existing perceptions of the product and stimulated discussion about the properties of PVC. A wide range of positive coverage was achieved from national newspapers to the plastics trade press and the 'PVC for life and living' programme has re-positioned PVC as an aspirational product.

PR as propaganda

Nature and history

Propaganda is often simply described as being the dissemination of information. In a broad context this involves the whole idea of democracy and issues such as abortion rights or civil liberties. In the court of public opinion, for Center and Jackson (2003), PR practitioners are the attorneys and as such are advocates for companies, causes and issues – in short they are propagandists. For others, though, they are above all else professionals – or should be – but unfortunately as Kim and Reber (2009: 157) point out, 'many studies have found public relations suffering from low standards of professionalism'.

Propaganda is best understood when placed in a historic setting. A number of writers (for example Harrison, 2000; Fisher, 2009) refer to Hunt and Grunig's (1994) framework for the development of PR in the USA, i.e. that there are five distinct phases in this development:

- the public be fooled;
- the public be dammed;
- public information;
- propaganda and persuasion;
- public understanding.

Propaganda then is preceded by the provision of public information and succeeded by public understanding and is thus in between the beginnings of honest and truthful stories and what we see today as modern PR practice. The propaganda phase appears to stand alone in a historical continuum but the reality is somewhat different. Edward Bernays, often referred to as the father of public relations, had suggested many years ago that part of government is 'invisible' and is the true ruling power. Fisher (2009) talks of propaganda as the business of shaping perceptions and manipulating cognitions. Directing behaviour is at the heart of propaganda and PR is a legitimate activity that enhances image and perceptions.

War and peace

As Fisher (2009: 58) points out, PR has 'had a role in warfare from the beginning of recorded history'. From the Greeks to the American Revolution to the Gulf War and the war in Iraq, PR has been used in some form or another to achieve, for example, desertion on the opposing side, getting the USA into a war in the first place, as with the First World War, or the power of film during the Second World War. Rodgers (2011) explains how journalists can see through various governments' attempts to influence reporting of the 'Arab Spring' and how they can use this knowledge to improve reporting and guard against crude (or clever) attempts to influence them. War aside, the period between the First and Second World Wars saw the beginnings of propaganda being used by governments for more commercial purposes and certainly post-Second World War by commercial organisations, notably Shell and the Royal Mail in the UK. Harrison (2000) points to the Roman Catholic Church with its `Congregation of Propaganda', i.e. a committee of cardinals in charge of foreign missions to seek out unbelievers and make converts, as a case in point. Many other organisations use public relations to get a message across. For example Greenberg et al. (2011) report on corporate and NGO public relations strategies in Canada and the USA in the context of climate change.

Government

For Fisher (2009), making viewpoints known in the 'court of public opinion' is done through statements made by government leaders or information officers whose goal it is to get the official line out there through the media. The line between PR and propaganda can become thin, especially in relation to war justification. Misleading and even false information can lead to an abuse of power and cover-ups (Fisher, 2009) and certainly controversy, as with the infamous Iraqi 'weapons of mass destruction' claims of the Blair government in the UK. It has been suggested that PR today owes much of its development to Local Government, which is where the corps of PR officers was established and who formed those responsible for the setting up of the Institute of Public Relations (IPR) in the UK (L'Etang, 1998). They also contributed in an important way to PR ideology and in particular to the idea of professionalism in the articulation of their own strong public service ethos. PR's initial role was seen as being that of providing information, with intelligence seen as being a complementary service to deliver both internal and external service. The merging of intelligence with information saw local authorities attempting to share understanding with the local populace in terms of legal matters and policy. For L'Etang (1998), public authorities cannot remain mysterious, impersonal bodies that most were and many still are. Fisher (2009) suggests that in democracies the support of citizens must be won, where excellent public relations is about resolving conflict and affecting change rather than supporting the goals of war.

With local government the elected members are at the focus of communications. Local authorities usually have a PRO (public relations officer) whose job, as a local authority employee (not a political party employee), is to service the people via the elected members. In principle at least this should involve dealing with facts unfettered by distortion. There should be no political axe to grind but it is in this area where accusations of propaganda (as if a dirty word) might arise. Certainly the local authority PRO gets involved with all the useful tools of PR, from press releases to visits and visitors, for the purpose of disseminating information. Central government in peacetime operates differently from when in times of war. The acceptable face of governmental propaganda during periods of war is not necessarily acceptable at other times. This might be the 'Country Needs You' message of the First World War or the propaganda battles of the Iraq War of 2003 – where the technological communications, but especially media, comparison is stark in terms of what was available during 1914–18. If propaganda is a necessary adjunct to diplomacy (L'Etang, 1998) and as such has a part to play in democracy (rather than simply being a tool of totalitarian regimes) then it can be used by governments for educating and informing its citizens and winning their co-operation. These days, any government's Chief Information Officer necessarily involves him- or herself in communications including advertising, PR and, as some would have it, propaganda (or 'spin' as PR activities are often called in these contexts). The duty and function of his or her office are to be primarily a PR (and for some a propaganda) machine for the government. In the UK, GOV.UK (www.gov.uk/) has replaced the UK Government Information Service (formerly the sinister-sounding Ministry of Information, then the bureaucratic-sounding Central Office of Information). Directgov performed a supporting role to the Chief Information Officer and hence the ministerial departments and has now been subsumed by GOV.UK.

Looking at the way PR can work for others who should see government (both national and local) as publics, an organisation, say a local firm, can use PR to inform the local authority of its strategic intent. In other words, work with the local authority and seek to satisfy the objectives of both parties. Large organisations and trade associations should seek to influence government and the people in power in terms of, for example, the direction and strength of legislation. Select committees and the role of the 'retained' MP in recent times in the UK have been the subject of scrutiny, especially the 'cash for questions' (MPs being paid to ask questions in parliament) scandal and the more recent MPs' expenses scandal that gave rise to the debate on what is proper in Westminster parliamentary practice. For example, the 'cash for questions' saga eventually led to the defeat of former MP Neil Hamilton in the 1997 General Election. The seemingly trivial nature of the Hamilton case belies the very serious problem of business funding many things. For example the funding of academic research, such as that into the impact of wine on heart disease or garlic tablets on hardening of the arteries, will be problematic if such research is underwritten by wineries or the manufacturers of garlic tablets. Parliamentary consultants and lobbyists have a role to play and the relationships government or its ministers/officers have with the media are of course of great interest and importance within the context of PR. This should not be a question of privileged access to the media by, for example, a minister but should be a question of the importance and newsworthiness of the statement made. Lobby correspondents perform an important function, the very existence of the lobby greatly influencing communication. The nature of the prevailing party in power, and in Europe, the European Union and European Parliament, makes the entire situation more complex and interesting. The same can be said about relationships between governments and their officers and publics around the world. The 'phone hacking' Leveson Inquiry in the UK during 2012 involved the media corporation News International (and the closure of the Sunday tabloid newspaper *The News of the World*) and relationships with politicians, members of parliament and the police.

Special interest groups

This would include pressure, voluntary and charity groups. These deal with ideas and attitude change more than the usual tangible products and companies. Problems might occur for organisations because of the way a case is presented, but this might also be part of the democratic right to protest, depending upon the country's or nation state's constitution. Protesters and crusaders are not a new phenomenon. Nor are factionalisation or confrontation; these can often lead to a head-to-head with a compromise as the outcome.

Not all special interest groups are factional or sectional. Some are promotional, whereby the interests of the members of the group are promoted, as with trade unions or associations. Many, however, are sectional and some argue that the decline in voting in democratic developed societies is linked to the increase in person and group politics, especially the latter since membership of such groups has risen alongside the decline in support for traditional, established political parties. Such groups can be seen operating in the 'Arab Spring' events of 2011, the London and Manchester riots of 2011, and the student protests against the imposition of tuition fees and related issues such as youth unemployment in England in 2010. In the past there have been debates over CFCs (chlorofluorocarbons), the relationship between oil companies such as Shell and BP and global pressure groups such as Greenpeace, or the activities of Amnesty International with its ability to attract high-level celebrity support. Other organisations that lobby on behalf of members are associations such as the Automobile Association in the UK, which is frequently on television putting forward views on issues such as petrol prices, or an insider-type organisation that might lobby but also advise government, such as the BMA (the British Medical Association), which represents doctors throughout the UK.

The Snapshot below discusses the instruments of propaganda and some of the issues that surround PR and propaganda from an ethical perspective. The discussion centres on propaganda being at the heart of the problems with false or misleading claims.

Snapshot   The use of instruments of propaganda and ethical dilemmas

Many of the instruments that have been developed over the years by PR practitioners could be used for propaganda purposes. For example television has in the past been used as a prime instrument of propaganda. These days it is perhaps more problematic because much of television is entertainment and therefore not totally suitable, although nevertheless useful to some extent (in term of news programmes for example), but most of the time it is escapism. There is a modest amount of education and some public service broadcasting including public information films and, in some countries, State television adding to the possibilities. A perhaps more critical, cynical view is that in post-industrial, advanced capitalist, consumer societies the very nature of television as entertainment is an inherent part of the propaganda of those who are in control. Programme sponsorship and product placement are growing and can be viewed as a form of propaganda in the sense that they permeate in an unconscious if not subliminal way into the mind of the audience. House journals are another example that highlight how propaganda is usually mistrusted, disbelieved or derided. These days, blogs, forums and social networking sites such as Twitter can be used as instruments of propaganda. Ministers, civil servants, Members of Parliament and direct action can all be seen as instruments of propaganda, depending upon how these are used.

With the increased and increasing use of blogs for PR purposes has come the inevitable ethical dilemma. Subervi (2010), CEO of Utopia Communications Inc., an ethically focused PR agency in the USA, responded to an issue of online ethics

(Continued)

(Continued)

by suggesting the avoidance of 'ethical lapses'. In other words, no matter what the context, the PR code of ethical practice should endure. Faced with the proposition that a practitioner might be asked to visit review sites and comment as if a satisfied customer appears to be somewhat of a dilemma. However, this should not be a dilemma at all. Subervi suggests that a 'sense of discomfort is normal' around this issue. Perhaps some PR practitioners think that 'online communication is completely exempt' from the basic rules, but this is not the case, and 'they're about to find out that the FTC views the issue of transparency differently'. Subervi explains that a PR firm who sponsored freelance writers to pose as consumers and post online blog entries relating to their client and an organisation in New York, and sent out emails urging employees to spend time on and view sites pretending to be satisfied customers, in the end had to pay substantial penalties for artificially creating a buzz for products or services. Adhering to FTC guidelines avoids sloppy PR practice. Such practice goes beyond 'subjective judgment calls with the recently updated guides relating to endorsements in social media'. It is a clear guideline that employees should disclose employment relationships when promoting employers in social media and companies should understand that, in the USA at least, FTC action will follow even when they did not know, i.e. ignorance is no excuse. Penalties and potential image problems apart, it is unclear whether these kinds of tactic work anyway. For Subervi (2010) if 'the practice of phony review writing is widespread, then don't you think that savvy online shoppers are aware of it? And don't you think that they look at such over-enthusiastic endorsements with a certain amount of skepticism?'

Stop Point

There appears to be no end to the development of instruments of propaganda as technology affects types of media and their use. Undertake the following: 1. Discuss the development and use of instruments of propaganda as opposed to the same instruments being used for 'normal' PR purposes; 2. Consider and comment upon ethical dilemmas that might arise, using examples of your choice to illustrate.

PR AND MARKETING THEORY

Marketing theory and the communications interface were broadly discussed in Chapter 2 of this book. However, marketing focuses on meeting the needs of the consumer, whereas PR has a wider range of stakeholders/constituents or publics to cater for. PR can be used throughout a brand's life. Nearly two decades ago Stone (1995) identified three important issues to do with PR within product marketing:

1. Topicality (linking the product to real-time news events).
2. Credibility (the endorsement of a third party commentator who generates a degree of trust).
3. Involvement (the creation of interactive opportunities).

This suggests a role for PR across a time frame. For Millward Brown (2007) a brand's success at any point in time is dependent on many factors, PR included, which should be part of the brand's marketing mix. Moreover, Phillips (2011: 28) distinguishes between PR and advertising by suggesting that PR can be brand journalism where influence can be had 'through brand stories that are honest, transparent and built around unexpected truths; journalism not advertising'. However, Phillips warns that in the age of social media, stories decay fast and the 'story of the day is just that – daily, at best' – but authentic stories about the brand in various stages of development have, for Phillips, their place in the mix. In a similar vein, Chow (2011) discusses how Nissan made brand journalism a reality by 'telling better stories' through their media unit and recognising a number of trends: the rise of branded content, the application of social media along with upheaval of traditional media outlets, and a 'growing alignment between public relations and marketing'. For Chow (2011) this represents a move away from the traditional press release approach to PR and media relations.

Some examples of PR's involvement with marketing theory are discussed below.

The theory of the Product Life Cycle (PLC)

There is some concern in the literature about the veracity or at least usefulness of the theory of the PLC. However, it can be said with confidence that PR can be applied at any stage of a brand's or product's life. The first stage of PLC theory sees the introduction of products or brands, but before this, pre-launch or pre-introduction, PR can have a pivotal role in creating awareness of the product, informing and educating publics about the raison d'être of the product and the problems it will solve. Upon introduction, in the early days and at the growth stage, PR can continue to inform publics of the product's or brand's progress. At maturity and saturation stage, PR's role might be one of continuity. In decline, PR might be used to help phase out the product and safeguard against brand or corporate damage.

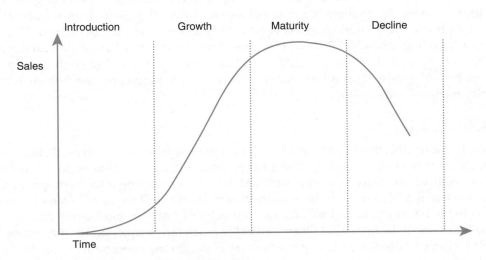

Figure 13.2 The theory of the Product Life Cycle

As discussed earlier in this book the BCG model has its origins in the analysis of the performance of Strategic Business Units (SBUs) by the US-based management consultancy. Subsequently it was used in product portfolio analysis. The BCG Matrix is repeated below.

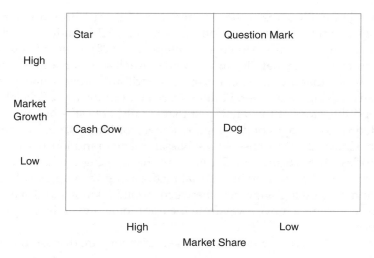

Figure 13.3   The Boston Consulting Group (BCG) matrix

Since question marks lie in the high growth/low share quadrant, they are usually at the start of the PLC so that PR's role will almost always be as discussed above in relation to the PLC, i.e. a key role, for example regarding awareness or information, especially with innovators. Stars are market leaders and generate significant funds, these being in the high growth/high share quadrant. However, there is usually a need to recover R&D costs and the marketing support that they need (especially with advertising) means that they will not generate a surplus for a while. Traditionally advertising has been the key communications tool, with PR having a minimal role to play. Cash cows have high shares of low growth markets and are usually successful stars, maintaining market leadership. They produce the cash because R&D costs have been recovered and marketing costs are less than for stars. Again there is a minimal role for PR to play. With dogs, usually at the end of their life cycle, marketing expenditure is reduced and curtailed. However, two ways of spending funds on PR should be considered. First, if any damage is sustained by the decline, PR (at both MPR and CPR levels) can help. Second, a dog might be retained as a gesture of goodwill (as a loss leader) or as part of heritage and can feature in community relations programmes.

Ansoff's Matrix

Ansoff's Product/Market Expansion Matrix is a commonly used model in marketing and in strategic management. As Hussey (1999) has pointed out, the contribution to the development of strategic managemenet of Ansoff's Matrix continued long after its original inception. This tool has been used in many contexts (see for example the application of Ansoff's Matrix in the UK vineyard sector in the case study by Richardson and Dennis, 2003)

The four cells of the matrix, as illustrated below, each throw up opportunities to use PR.

Cell 1 – Existing product/existing market may highlight the opportunity to use PR to tell existing customers of other products or services available through the company or associate organisations. A mortgage lender may wish to tell of travel insurance or other services. This might include reorganisations where products, brands or markets may be reviewed and regrouped. Various publics such as suppliers and distributors might need to know this. It might also include brand repositioning or even mere refreshment.

Cell 2 – New products/existing markets can see the use of PR to announce innovatory new developments resulting in products and brands within an existing customer base.

Core business products such as PC hardware can be supported by new multimed.
opments for example.

Cell 3 – Existing products/new markets can see the use of PR in the increasing volu.
of products sold by gaining new users. This might be done as suggested above within t.
PLC framework whereby in the new market the product or brand is a different stage of the
PLC or BLC (Brand Life Cycle).

Cell 4 – New products/new markets might see the organisation using PR in a number of
ways to help diversify with new products in new markets. PR in this instance would have
a substantive educating and informing role within the communications mix.

Relationship marketing and PR

Relationship marketing may have grown up in the business-to-business end of marketing
but the efforts on the part of bigger business with consumers as their customers testify to
the importance of relationships across the marketing board. This is competitive advantage through differentiation in a non-price area. How customers are handled or complaints
are dealt with is of the utmost importance. Getting closer to the customer and moving
from prospect to partner is achieved in a number of ways in order to create a relationship.
Informing, educating and creating understanding, often achieved through employing PR
techniques, are fundamental to building and maintaining relationships.

PR in practice

The PR Transfer Process

Expertise is required for good PR practice. Lack of expertise can lead to mistakes. The PR
Transfer Process as originally conceived by Jefkins (1995) is still a useful device in helping
to think about turning what could be negative aspects of PR practice into positive ones.
Four possible scenarios can be said to co-exist where PR has been demonstrated to have a
role to play. This conception is illustrated below:

Negative ——————————————————→ Positive

HOSTILITY is based on fear and is irrational. Hostility is often held towards products, companies or brands and can take a number of forms from country-of-origin (as for example with the
boycotting of South African produce around the world until regime change came) to the use of
certain material in products (for example fur products). In recent years much resentment has
built up against the banks – and bankers – around the world with many people blaming the
banks and their practices for a European if not world economic crisis into the second decade of
the 21st century. There are many other scenarios such as oil pollution, where hostility towards
organisations is generated. In many instances the cause of the hostility cannot (and should not)
be defended. In others, where hostility has grown out of misunderstanding, PR can be used to
set the record straight, where a good case can be presented and the situation adjusted.

PREJUDICE means that the problems are more deeply rooted but temporary and often
unjustified. The obvious forms of prejudice through, for example, people being the product of environmental conditions or the way they are brought up, are racial and sexual intol-
erance and bigotry. PR can be used to turn hatred into sympathy. There are many examples
where PR has been used to turn prejudice into acceptance, such as with solar power or
other alternative energy sources, which people may see as problematic in terms of delivery
and they may be prejudicial towards such sources. PR can help inform and educate in this
scenario and help turn prejudice towards new ideas into acceptance of such ideas, allowing other forms of communication to be used in a much more effective manner.

APATHY means that there is a certain amount of inertia on the part of people to products, services and issues. This has been evident in social marketing where advertising alone has not been able to change things. The use of PR has been crucial in moving people on issues such as alcohol and driving, wearing seat belts and crash helmets and speeding. People can become interested in such issues but in some circumstances it becomes necessary to use a combination of law, PR and advertising to get the message across.

IGNORANCE means that the publics are unaware of the company, product or brand and need to be made aware. Clearly in some cases advertising can achieve this, but in many it is sensible to use PR to inform and educate the targets before advertising and other forms of communication can be effective. By providing information and knowledge and stimulating interest that leads to understanding, the marketer can use PR to educate consumers and other targets to demolish myths, 'old wives tales' or folklore surrounding issues and problems, thus allowing other marketing communications tools to work more effectively.

The Mexican Statement and PR practitioners

A seminal moment in the international PR industry came at the International Conference of PR Societies held in Mexico City in 1978. This was expressed as:

> the art and social science of analyzing trends, predicting their consequences, counselling an organization's leadership and implementing planned programs of action which will serve both the organization's and the public's interest.

PR was thus defined in terms of practice. PR can be conducted internally or an outside consultant or company can be used. This often depends on the size of the organisation and the resources available. In smaller organisations PR may well be in the hands of an administrator or the Managing Director's secretary/PA. Opportunities exist to engage a PR consultant on a retainer basis. Larger organisations may have a dedicated PR or customer service function or indeed use a specialist company or consultant. In-company people provide expert knowledge of the organisation and its strengths and weaknesses and there should be no confidentiality worries. Unless a PR professional or set of professionals is employed there may be a lack of expertise in PR techniques and media. In smaller organisations the people or person responsible may have other duties and responsibilities. In this event, PR activity may not be done well and serious consideration should be given to retaining a PR consultant. This provides a resource but also objectivity and should be a consideration of the larger firm. Of course employing a consultant or firm of PR specialists may result in a certain lack of expertise. PR consultants can be cost effective but may not be expert in particular industries and technologies and as such there may be problems with technical aspects and market factors. There might also be problems with confidentiality and conflict of interest.

PR costs, creation and the creation of relationships

The retainer nature of PR payment has characterised the PR industry and in the past stood out in stark contrast to the billing system of the advertising industry. PR is labour intensive, the major cost being time. PR consultants are paid on a retainer basis and/or by the hour. Other costs would include costs of photography and expenses such as hospitality especially in relation to media relations and events. PR is created through building a strategy with aims and objectives in just the same way as a more general marketing communications strategy would be built and embodied in a plan (see Chapter 4 of this book). The organisation should:

- have a list of names and addresses whether conventional or email;
- cultivate relevant media contacts;
- seek out interesting people capable of being brand ambassadors who could talk positively about the organisation;
- make a list of up-and-coming stories;
- have a media contact within the organisation;
- create a general media pack;
- create templates such as that for a press release;
- be reliable, up-to-date, accurate and truthful;
- know the history of the organisation and use it;
- offer equal chances to contact so as to not offend;
- make the media feel important at events.

Costs can be reduced when relationships – partnerships or alliances – are created. This is particularly true for causes who may seek such relationships with organisations who can also benefit from such arrangements in a symbiosis kind of way. This makes PR the natural habitat of the cause-related marketing fundraiser. Money may be the ultimate objective but this relationship is also about storytelling.

In order to create relationships the organisation should:

- know who potential, lapsed and actual members of publics are;
- concentrate on a smaller number of important members of publics;
- target members of publics effectively through knowledge;
- know which contacts are one-offs and which are regular;
- develop a system of costing out in time and money the resources needed to obtain a new public member;
- seek feedback and use research tools, for example panel research, to assist in this task;
- develop, maintain and monitor a centralised database.

The concept of a 'public'

PR targets or publics

Depending upon objectives, different kinds of approaches may be used at different times with the various publics – for example, groups, stakeholders or constituents – the organisation might wish to deal with. There may be direct or indirect contact made with the various publics, the latter being made easier with the advent of online blogs, forums and other, similar tools. There may be a desire to simply tell a public about a particular issue through the transmission of information, but on other occasions the organisation may engage in a two-way communication that tries to persuade the public through effective dialogue. This may well be part of the integrated effort with other elements of the communications mix. It is important with any form of communication to know whom the organisation wants to talk to and what to say to them (or what they want to hear from the organisation). Publics are therefore carefully selected groups of people with whom the organisation communicates or wishes to communicate. Publics need to be defined at the start of the PR planning process in order to:

a) identify all groups of people relative to a PR programme;
b) establish priorities within the scope of a budget or resources;
c) select media and techniques;
d) prepare the message in acceptable and effective forms.

Publics can be from the community, potential and existing employees, suppliers, share-holders, the media, the financial community, the profession and professional associations, existing and potential clients, referral sources, local and central government. Publics can be placed in external (outward oriented) or internal (inward oriented) groupings and sub-categorised within media, financial and general public affairs.

External publics

External relations are important because these are often the channels of communication by which customers see a business. Therefore good external relations should be fostered in order to create a favourable marketing environment and should work in conjunction with internal relations. There are various external publics that the organisation needs to consider.

The media and gatekeepers

- the press (for example national, regional, daily, weekly, newspapers or magazines);
- broadcast (tv, radio, international, national and local);
- financial;
- owners, shareholders;
- suppliers, distributors;
- general public affairs;
- pressure groups, evangelists;
- educators, information-givers;
- trade unions;
- the community.

Internal publics

Internal PR should be considered as a very important part of PR generally. Internal relations and hence internal communications are all about things like staff moral and sensitivities, which are not just a question of money. The `grapevine' is pervasive where, for example, industrial disputes can arise from gossip and untruths. Employees can also feel left out if they are not included in on 'what is going on'. The internal 'feel' of the organisation should reflect and project the external image where internal activities can be made to be effective by effective internal communications. As such, internal considerations are vital to overall communications strategy. In addition, all employees of the organisation (including management/directors) are part of wider society. They are therefore influenced not only by what happens in the workplace but also by being members of the general public, members of professional bodies, members of pressure groups or societies, members of extended families, and members of local communities.

Tools to reach the publics

Information needs to be provided for the relevant, different publics. The PR tool kit to achieve this is quite extensive. Often opinion leadership and word-of-mouth are used to inform others. There is a big difference between the use of a harder, partisan celebrity endorser, as in advertising, and a softer brand ambassador, a PR device. Below are listed the PR tools commonly used to reach publics:

- FILMS/VIDEO/AUDIO-VISUAL AIDS (includes sponsored films/documentaries, PowerPoint-type presentations, photographs and working models).
- SEMINARS AND CONFERENCES are often sponsored by an organisation and connected with a specific subject or event. These may involve a number of speakers, from both within the host organisation and other guest speakers/experts.

- HOUSE JOURNALS in the form of a bulletin, newsletter or magazine/ezine can be for internal or external consumption. Useful for keeping in touch with clients, and helping to generate new enquiries by keeping them up to date on relevant matters of interest. These must be professionally produced and appear regularly for maximum effect.

- BROCHURES contain either general purpose, corporate information or can be designed to communicate information on specific topics. These can be used for clients, employees or the media. Consistency and uniformity in the integrated sense discussed in Chapter 1 of this book for the personality of organisation should be a consideration.

- EXHIBITIONS/TRADE SHOWS can be for the general public or trade or both and also part of a wider event. Permanent venues exist but mobile exhibitions are common.

- NEWS/PRESS RELEASES should have impact and be timely, relevant, topical, accurate, exclusive, and have a special angle or spin, for example human interest. These are short articles containing a newsworthy item that need to appear similar to the editorial of a particular media vehicle.

- THE FEATURE ARTICLE is more than just a long press release. It usually is an article commissioned for a particular media with specific timing rather than something destined for a more general release.

- THE MEDIA CONFERENCE. Its purpose is to give information and to receive and answer questions. It usually occurs at short notice after something newsworthy (a major event) has occurred. Often used by politicians, organisations in crisis and individuals appealing for help (e.g. police). Media kits with detailed information including a background to the story should always be available.

- THE MEDIA RECEPTION. This is more planned and less formal than a media conference that will include a presentation and refreshments. This can be used for example with new product launches or special announcements.

- THE OPEN DAY. A media trip to new premises is an example of an event that usually involves for example organising transport and hospitality. The media should perceive this as having something worthwhile and newsworthy involved.

- THE MEDIA LUNCH. This is usually organised for the media to meet key personnel in an organisation and to informally brief on topics of interest. This should be somewhat intimate as opposed to a large party. There well may be further contacts as a result of this, as with for example an invitation to write an article.

- CLIENT ENTERTAINING. This will have similar objectives to the lunch above, but will involve the entertainment of key clients or potential clients and opinion leaders for the purposes of goodwill and information. Other opportunities may arise but this is not the primary concern.

- EVENTS can be product related such as book signings in stores. They can be involved with open days or factory visits and also cause-related marketing activities.

- LOBBYING is the representation of an organisation or industry group within local and national government. Lobbyists provide a flow of information to policy makers and attempt to represent the views of their client/s in shaping policy and legislation.

- WEB NEWS PAGE AND E-MAIL. The use of websites, web pages, email, blogs and forums decreases the importance of the traditional gatekeeper, and offers opportunities to profile employees, outline business philosophy and provide information on investments to name but a few activities.

- ANNUAL REPORT offers a vehicle for PR activities such as the Chairman's Statement, fund-raising and charitable activities. The annual report could well be web-based.

The news or media/press release

The commonest form of PR expression is perhaps the news or media/press release. With the news release, language is important and must be appropriate. Photography is usually welcome. The story should be clear and succinct. The opening paragraph should tell the whole story in one. This allows the recipient to tell at a glance if the story has some value. Of importance are what the story is about, the organisation itself, where the story unfolds, what the advantages are (what is new or special in a factual way), who benefits, how these benefits can be enjoyed, and who to contact for more information. News releases can be background, intended to be a briefing, or part of a speech. They can also be in report form, a picture caption or an announcement. In effect we can think of this in the 'six serving men' sense of Kipling (the *Just So* stories – 'The Elephant's Child'): the what, where, who, why, when and how in every story.

There are many tips from a variety of sources as to how to create the news release:

- keep the main paragraph short;
- write stories;
- match the story to the publication/programme and audience by knowing audiences' interests;
- write tight copy in a concise journalistic style;
- keep to short sentences;
- avoid superlatives;
- substantiate claims;
- quote from reliable sources;
- draft and redraft, edit and polish;
- get rid of irrelevancies;
- do not use jargon;
- be accurate and factual;
- never exaggerate or create a misleading impression.

The video news release

In addition, with video news releases:

- make sure the story has a strong visual impact;
- make sure of clarity;
- provide a new perspective on the angle/issue;
- make it possible to be used as background footage while news copy is read;
- make it unique and not available elsewhere.

The feature article

This is similar to the news release but usually an expert or specialist is commissioned by the editor to write it. Alternatively it may be written by a columnist (such as a wine writer) and actually signed, becoming a signed feature article. It is generally bigger than the result of a news release, it possibly being several pages long. The process may involve a proposal to an editor including number of words, illustrations and date for publication. Alternatively a list of general feature articles could be prepared to present in an informative and authoritative way matters of interest to a particular target market. There are many opportunities to take items of topical interest and turn them into articles.

Feature articles should contain:

- an opening paragraph;
- the problem or opportunity;
- the solution to the problem or benefits of the opportunity;
- the results achieved;
- a closing paragraph;
- sources of information.

Documentary video

Although important, the above two tools are not always the most appropriate. With employee relations, fears may have to be allayed and support won. This is not going to happen at a time of speculation, insecurity or criticism that the company's technology is out of date. News releases, articles and a letter by the chairman can have the opposite effect to that intended. This can be read as under-managed communication that lacks objectivity. Allied to the video news release is the technique known as the documentary video that has a professional, independent narrator. The video will typically address problems in an acquired company starting with interviews with a range of employees at differing levels, allowing them to tell of concerns and doubts. This is meant to be frank, open and honest without gloss or platitudes. Executives might be put on the spot or contented employees from previous acquisitions interviewed. The logic is that it is one thing to hear executives say things, and quite another to have others such as employees, customers or an external analyst say it. The video will also deal with plans for change with a commitment to keep staff informed about the unknown as it becomes known. Although change can be a difficult thing, far better to be open about it to prevent cynicism and rumour.

Other techniques

Other, allied, techniques such as team briefings and brochures can provide extensive questions and answers and stated, known plans. Local and financial press and media can be important within this process since employees will seek out information in the local media and not the financial pages of the broadsheets. The acquirer can use this to advantage by influencing local opinion formers or shapers such as councillors or MPs. Brochures can be sent and meetings arranged. Sincerity is the watchword, as it is with any financial communications. Dealings here can be tricky, and preparation is key. The acquirer should be able to answer questions clearly and honestly, with facts at hand, about the acquisition and the fallout that follows. The media usually want to know how the deal is being funded, what the strategic logic is, and a sensible rationale for the announced purchase price and information on earnings. Advances in technology have fundamentally changed the way information is put out and this is discussed in the next section of this chapter.

The Snapshot below discusses how PR, or more specifically crisis avoidance or management, can be used when things begin to go wrong and how social media are now a necessary part of such an approach.

Snapshot   In times of crisis the need for PR is clear – how Wall Street, the banks and the *New York Times* avoided a crisis

Good internal communication is fundamental to good management, but the kind of management is important. Management style clearly has an enormous influence on internal communications. Formal (rather than informal) situations dictate relationships and the tools used to communicate with the various publics. For example, in order to restore investor faith in Wall Street after the Internet stock crash of 1999, a new image was needed after confidence was shattered, especially since in 2001 Wall Street's image was further tarnished by alleged rigged prices and large, hidden fees that cost shareholders billions of dollars. Investors apparently wanted the money back.

(Continued)

(Continued)

Two main accusations were made. The first was that banks doled out wads of under-priced shares to institutional investors that were almost guaranteed to rise once trading started. The institutions then gave the banks a huge commission per share and it was alleged that such payments were not properly disclosed. The second, linked, accusation was that the technique of 'laddering' (artificially inflating prices) causes ordinary retail investors to have to pay more for shares. When the 'ladderers' pull out the prices tumble and the retailers lose out. At first Wall Street responded with apparent unconcern. Press releases insisted that the firms had followed accepted industry practices but the finance industry more generally, apparently, had a different view, with predictions of settlements (worth billions of dollars) but also the illumination of additional sordid behaviour.

Ethically Wall Street has been likened to the tobacco industry in terms of damages. By 2003 it was claimed that Wall Street had begun to realise that it is hard to win back public confidence after a series of scandals. However, leading US banks did attempt to restore investor faith despite an uphill struggle against the image of the corrupt investment bank worker. What was needed from a PR perspective was for Wall Street as a whole to articulate a clear programme from top management as to how it is going to do business against the fear of the appearance of lip-service being paid to serious problems. As the housing bubble burst and economic recession followed around the world but especially in the USA in the late noughties, the banks were in the spotlight again but this time not just with investors. The general public (and all 'publics' generally) became aware of the role of the banks in sub-prime lending and other activities that led not just to economic problems but also to social and other problems.

In the above context, as things unfolded, the need for PR has never been clearer in an era that has been likened to the Great Depression of some 80 years ago. As Fathi (2013) points out, the use of social media for 'releasing corporate news, managing customer service issues, and interacting with key audiences and stakeholders' now has to be acknowledged. Fathi uses the example of the *New York Times* whereby the 'website and app outages highlighted one of the more practical and necessary reasons for maintaining a social presence'. The *New York Times* crisis involved speculation from other media that this problem was a hacker attack but the newspaper was able to harness the power of social media 'to stay ahead of the story and communicate with its customers, proving that social media can be a company's best resource for doing so – even if the company is one of the largest publishers in the world'. Through the use of Facebook, Twitter and other social media the *New York Times* was able to stay ahead of the game and keep the picture clear. The incident, says Fathi, 'helps confirm the importance of social media in crisis communications' and this leads to the conclusion that as an essential part of PR strategy all 'companies should have a social media strategy built into their crisis communications plan'.

Stop Point

It is easy to see how important that aspect of PR – or more specifically crisis avoidance or management – is for any organisation large or small. Undertake the following: 1. Comment on the notion that it is better to avoid a crisis than to have to manage one; 2. Outline the differences in approach to a crisis between the Wall Street/banking sector response and that of the *New York Times*.

TECHNOLOGY, REGULATION AND CONTROL IN PR

PR Practice

Policy to deal with PR projects within a code of professional conduct is essential, especially in terms of today's turbulent environment where technology and communications are in a state of constant flux.

Regulation and control in PR

In terms of human behaviour and social conduct both laws and codes have been developed to regulate and control many things, including the PR activities of companies and other organisations. Public opinion and what is acceptable behaviour are important. The phrase 'the court of public opinion' underlines this but in any event actual law may override this, i.e. just what is permissible and what is prohibited by the law of the land. This will vary from country to country as will social mores – what is moral and what is not, often having a religious base. Codes of practice encapsulate the ethical standards set by professions, organisations and the self, based, in theory at least, on conscience, i.e. what is right, fair or just to oneself and to others. This is a general condition but one that applies within the context of PR.

Entities such as companies, unlike most people, do not have a conscience as such and therefore need a code of conduct based on ethical principles that are inevitably influenced by the personal values and ethics of key players in the organisation. Some form of group consensus as to what is acceptable behaviour may have a powerful influence. The various professional bodies provide a code of ethics that organisations can adopt and endeavour to educate such organisations through their membership. It is then up to the organisation itself, in turn, to educate its employees on ethical behaviour and practices. Done correctly this would get over the age-old problem of prescription (of ethical standards) for others while not practising such standards themselves.

Codes of ethical practice have emerged across the globe and are maturing, perhaps more slowly than some would like. It has been nearly a century since the four watchwords of 'legal, decent, honest and truthful' were first used in relation to commercial enterprise by the International Chamber of Commerce, established in 1919. The ICC code was firmly established by 1937. The PR profession is no exception to having codes of conduct. For example the Public Relations Society of America's (PRSA) 'Ethical Guidance for Public Relations Practitioners' (2012a) suggests that the practice of public relations 'can present unique and challenging ethical issues' while 'At the same time, protecting integrity and the public trust are fundamental to the profession's role and reputation'. For the PRSA, successful public relations hinges on the ethical stance of practitioners and so this body has developed and maintained its code of practice in order to help its members, who 'pledge to core values, principles and practice guidelines that define their professionalism and advance their success'. The PRSA Code was created and is maintained by the PRSA Board of Ethics and Professional Standards (BEPS) and has the core values of advocacy, honesty, loyalty, professional development and objectivity. The Code advises professionals to:

- protect and advance the free flow of accurate and truthful information;
- foster informed decision making through open communication;
- protect confidential and private information;
- promote healthy and fair competition among professionals;
- avoid conflicts of interest;
- work to strengthen the public's trust in the profession.

In terms of values and principles the PRSA advocate that professionals should:

- be honest and accurate in all communications;
- reveal sponsors for represented causes and interests;
- act in the best interest of clients or employers;
- disclose financial interests in a client's organisation;
- safeguard the confidences and privacy rights of clients and employees;
- follow ethical hiring practices to respect free and open competition;
- avoid conflicts between personal and professional interests;
- decline representation of clients requiring actions contrary to the code;
- accurately define what public relations activities can accomplish;
- report all ethical violations to the appropriate authority.

The PRSA suggests that 'all public relations professionals should look to it as a model of professional behavior' and that the Code is a 'model for other professions, organizations and professionals' (PRSA, 2012b).

Technology, the Internet and PR

The rapid advances in technology have created their own range of opportunities and problems. The integration of traditional and online communication methods has provided the key to successful Internet marketing for many commentators over the last few years (for example Ashcroft and Hoey, 2001; Garau, 2008; Jensen, 2008). Growth in Internet use has been phenomenal in the last two decades. The size of the Internet doubles every year in the UK and worldwide this figure is even more impressive. Chapter 10 of this book deals with these issues in more detail but here the concern is specifically for PR. When things really got going with the Internet, circa 1995, the main PR tool appeared to be the bulletin board. This was seen as being analogous with the notice board, the electronic equivalent of a communal place where notices could be placed for anyone to read and be informed. In practice this evolved into a place for group communication and interaction. Online, there are no real time and place restrictions. There are therefore opportunities for enhancing or changing brand and company/organisation images, how the organisation is perceived and how status can be maintained or enhanced. Both internal and external relations have been established by some organisations using web-based tools that are extensions of conventional PR tools such as the news release. News release pages are available on many websites or emailed to target public members. For example, a new service can be announced from a website, combined with email and the more conventional tools into an integrated whole.

The Snapshot below illustrates how the Internet is being used by PR practitioners, as the move from mere information documents being available online to the use of, for example, reviews, forums, blogs and social media content has occurred at a pace. It discusses some of the opportunities and problems that rapid advances in technology have brought to the PR practitioner's table.

Snapshot   Internet adoption by PR professionals – the possibilities of truly integrated marketing communication

At the turn of the millennium, according to Hurme (2001), PR practitioners who did not use Internet communications potentially caused damage to their clients or employers. The move towards dialogue and away from monologue is as visible with PR as it is with advertising – perhaps even more so. Interactive communication generally has gained so much ground but the use of the Internet has a number of problems. The Internet and online activity have moved on at a pace. The old online, static, brochure work of 20 years ago has long been superseded and so this is no longer a problem because of the increased intelligent use of the medium. However, since much material that goes onto the Internet no longer passes through traditional gatekeepers such as editors, policing is another kind of (ethical) problem. With the advancements in mobile technology such problems are magnified.

For IMC that includes online being truly interactive and integrated this has to include online PR activities such as blogs and forums. Research into the use of PR on the Internet started some years ago. In the biotechnology sector Ranchhod et al. (2002) revealed that biotechnology companies attempt to use the Internet as a comprehensive PR medium to explain complex issues. This is an attempt to turn apathy and ignorance into sympathy and understanding. Diagrammatic information, interactivity through discussion forum and hyperlinks to scientific databases are effective tools for the likes of Monsanto who can forge these into an integrated, online communications strategy. Some companies may not be investing as well as they might, which has resulted in mere transference of documents. Hyperlinks and video have been used to great effect for companies involved with a complex, controversial and risk-inherent industry such as biotechnology. Key to the effective use of PR on the Internet is targeting of the various publics. In this example that would be targets such as science and technology journalists, purchasers, suppliers and employees.

For interactivity to work dialogue is all-important and part of dialogue online, from a PR viewpoint, is the use of blogs and forums. Porter et al. (2009) suggest that blogging and placing stories in blogs are having a substantial impact on the PR industry. The personal blog has increased with perhaps the professional blog lagging behind in development, but it is developing. These researchers are interested in the impact of roles and gender but maintain that PR practitioners have waited for developments with the general population before fully embracing the blog as a PR tool, which follows the development of the World Wide Web generally.

As PR activity on the Internet continues to evolve it can be said to have grown up in Western countries. However, PR professionals from other countries are now active and research has begun to filter through. For example Al-Shohaib et al. (2009) present the case of Internet adoption by Saudi PR professionals. These researchers highlight the role culture plays in PR practice. Whereas Western companies are driven by a business orientation, in Arab firms organisational structure plays a more defining role and politics and religion influence decisions that are made out of different cultural values. The Internet is a primary medium for communication with the public and PR practices will have to conform to certain cultural values.

(Continued)

(Continued)

Similarly, Kirat (2007) looked at the use of the Internet by PR departments in the United Arab Emirates (UAE). The growth of PR and the promotion and development of relations with news media are, for Kirat, happening because Internet and online offer a better performance and more effective PR. However, the adoption of online PR activities will depend on how they are conceived and practised 'in real life', which requires PR practitioners to adopt transparency, democracy and symmetric two-way communications.

Stop Point

Consider how important it is to invest in PR generally and online PR in particular. The mere transference of documents onto a website is not the only way to use PR online, although information provision may still be part of an organisation's PR activities. Consider the tools available to PR practitioners that are or should be part of an ideal integrated communications approach to strategy. Undertake the following: 1. Discuss the use of online activities such as reviews, forums, social media and blogs – their usefulness and associated problems in terms of misuse, reputation, editorial decision making and the penalties that might have to be paid; 2. Outline the many opportunities for genuine communication and the notion of relationship building and trust through the use of effective online PR.

Assignment

You are part of a team of PR consultants for a range of clients in different industries. Illustrate the kinds of work you would typically become involved with by choosing one from the list below. Provide an outline report on the topical issues you would expect to be dealing with.

- A regional theatre's new production.
- A children's charity special appeal for nursery equipment.
- A pop music video to be used to launch a new single.
- An industrial hose manufacturer's use of innovative material for fire fighting.
- A technical service provider's establishment of a new team of specialists.
- A financial service provider's new range of loan products.
- An international healthcare company's newly established division for 'Respiratory Therapy and Care'.
- The introduction of an innovative 'Rough Terrain Materials Handler' for use in construction, civil engineering, farming and military contexts.

Summary of Key Points

- PR is about relationships with various interest groups.
- Marketing PR (as opposed to Corporate PR) has emerged as the commercial brand/ product level function responsible for a set of activities that deal with shorter-term issues.
- Key to any PR is the notion that it fundamentally functions as a creator of a favourable marketing environment.
- PR is characterised by a lack of control and has very different qualities from those of other communications tools.
- PR uses a 'soft sell' approach rather than the 'harder' approaches of other elements of the communications mix.
- PR uses objectivity and can be seen as non-partisan.
- PR can be viewed as propaganda with many media forms culpable, i.e. house journals and newsletters are propaganda tools.
- With marketing the focus is on meeting the needs of customers. PR has a wider range of stakeholders/constituents.
- The use of PR can be explained in conjunction with parts of marketing theory such as the PLC, the BCG Matrix and Ansoff's Matrix
- The concept of a 'public' is well established and can be broadly split into internal and external publics who can be reached directly and indirectly.
- There is a raft of tools to reach publics, the most-well known of which is the news release.
- Codes of ethics in PR practice have been developed and are available. Such codes have links with other ethically charged areas such as advertising.
- The key to new PR techniques is interactivity. Good PR practice should strive to create an integrative whole.

Discussion Questions

1. Distinguish between marketing PR and corporate PR. Explain, using examples, why the techniques used at both levels might be similar if not the same.
2. Explain what the word propaganda means and why it is such a `dirty' word. Give your considered view on the opportunities and problems propaganda may provide for PR practitioners, illustrating with examples.
3. Distinguish between advertising and PR in terms of control. Discuss, using examples, the very different qualities PR has to those found in other communications tools.
4. Comment on the notion that the internal feel of an organization will reflect its external reality. Provide practical examples of instances where this is the case.

(Continued)

(Continued)

5. Explain where PR fits in the marketing communications' scheme of things. Provide in your answer at least two examples of the interface between PR and other elements of the communications' mix.

6. Explain why the relationship between PR and marketing theory is best illustrated by use of the marketing theory such as that of the Product Life Cycle or Innovation Theory.

7. 'The PR Transfer Process is a simple but effective guideline for use by the PR practitioner when critically assessing PR problems'. Discuss and illustrate.

8. Explain the concept of a 'public'. Choose an internal and external public and illustrate, using actual examples, how each could be reached directly and indirectly.

9. Discuss codes of ethics in PR practice using examples to illustrate key points. Explain why there are obvious and clear links to other areas of business.

10. Explain how PR tools can be used on the Internet. Illustrate this with actual instances you are aware of, including those involving social media.

Further Reading

Curtin, P. A. (2012) 'Public relations and philosophy: paring paradigms', *Public Relations Inquiry*, 1 (1): 31–47. http://pri.sagepub.com/content/1/1/31
This is a philosophical article on how PR researchers have dealt with the idea of paradigms and inevitably the work of Thomas Kuhn. The author looks at PR not as a single entity but one that is a 'four-paradigm schematic' for the PR field. The author urges PR researchers to accept a diversity of perspectives that come with concomitant research values.

Fawkes, J. (2012) 'Interpreting ethics: public relations and strong hermeneutics', *Public Relations Inquiry*, 1 (2): 117–40. http://pri.sagepub.com/content/1/2/117
This article suggests that PR inadequately engages with the complexities of ethical theory, and this contributes toward the public's loss of trust in PR activities. The author argues that communicators could take more responsibility for professional ethics and considers that concepts of professionalism shift and buckle under global economic and social pressures, making the time right to reconsider PR's ethical outlook.

Ihlen, O. (2011) 'On barnyard scrambles: towards a rhetoric of PR', *Management Communication Quarterly*, 25 (3): 455–73. http://mcq.sagepub.com/content/25/3/455
The author looks to gain a better understanding of PR rhetoric and how organisational rhetoric can help make society a good place. The author expresses the need to go beyond the usual literature on crisis communication and apologia to utilise discourse to help analyse other subfields and types of PR. The article is about how a rhetorical situation can help guide this quest in providing a critical discussion around whether organisational rhetoric helps to improve society.

Radford, G.P. (2012) 'Public relations in a postmodern world', *Public Relations Inquiry*, 1 (1): 49–67. http://pri.sagepub.com/content/1/1/49
This article discusses the notion that PR is a modernist conception while the idea of the public is postmodern, and that there are implications that stem from this dichotomy

for the ways in which PR practice and scholarship are spoken and understood. The author argues that postmodernism can be used to foreground the ways in which PR is talked about.

Roper, J. (2012) 'Environmental risk, sustainability discourse and public relations', *Public Relations Inquiry*, 1 (1): 69–87. http://pri.sagepub.com/content/1/1/69
This article is about modern societies and the impact of environmental costs and industrialisation, with the traditional voice of economic growth being met by those of ascendant discourses of sustainability. This is about environmental policy in New Zealand and the role of PR professionals in discursive struggle – and the implications for PR and organisations in the longer term.

REFERENCES

Al-Shohaib, K., Ali, A.J., Al-Kandari, M. and Abdulrahim, A. (2009) 'Internet adoption by Saudi public relations professionals', *Journal of Communications Management*, 13 (1): 21–36.

Armstrong, S. (1996) 'So much at steak', *The Guardian*, 25 March: 12.

Ashcroft, L. and Hoey, C. (2001) 'PR, marketing and the internet: implications for information professionals', *Library Management*, 22 (1/2): 68–74.

Baker, P. (2000) 'Schizophrenia and the Emperor's (not so) new clothes', *Asylum – The Magazine for Democratic Psychiatry*, 12, 1. Available at: www.critpsynet.freeuk.com/Baker.htm

Balmer, J.M.T. and Greser, S.A. (2006) 'Corporate marketing: integrating corporate identity, corporate branding, corporate communications, corporate image and corporate reputation', *European Journal of Marketing*, 40 (7): 730–41.

Barrett, C. (2008) 'The changing face of public relations', *Music Week*, 29 November.

Bowen, S.A. (2007) 'Ethics and public relations', The Institute for Public Relations, 30 October, available at: www.instituteforpr.org/topics/ethics-and-public-relations/

Center, A.H. and Jackson, P. (2003) *Public Relations Practices*, 6th edn. Upper Saddle River New Jersey, USA: Prentice Hall.

Chow, L.L. (2011) 'Kotozukuri: how Nissan made "brand journalism" a reality', *Event Reports*, ThinkTank Live, November, available through warc.com

CIPR (2012) Definition of PR, the CIPR, available at: www.cipr.co.uk/content/careers-cpd/careers-pr/what-pr

Cornelissen, J.P. and Harris, P. (2004) 'Interdependencies between marketing and public relations disciplines as correlates of communication organisation', *Journal of Marketing Management*, 20 (1–2): 237–64.

Curtin, P. A. (2012) 'Public relations and philosophy: paring paradigms', *Public Relations Inquiry*, 1 (1): 31–47.

Fathi, S. (2013) 'Public Relations – New York Times outage reinforces need for a social presence in a crisis', *Marketing Profs*, 12 September, available at: www.marketingprofs.com/articles/2013/11621/new-york-times-outage-reinforces-need-for-a-social-presence-in-a-crisis

Fawkes, J. (2012) 'Interpreting ethics: public relations and strong hermeneutics', *Public Relations Inquiry*, 1 (2): 117–40.

Fisher, J.R. (2009) 'Public relations and war: socially responsible or unethical', *International Academy of Business Disciplines and Frostburg State University*, November, 4 (1): 54–67.

Freshwater Technology (2012) 'Public Relations Forum, Freshwater Technology Ltd', available at: www.freshwatertechnology.com/mainpages/forum_prf.html

Garau, C. (2008) 'Integrated online marketing communication: implementation and management', *Journal of Communication Management*, 12 (2): 169–84.

Greenberg, J., Knight, G. and Westersund, E. (2011) 'Spinning climate change: corporate and NGO public relations strategies in Canada and the United States', *International Communications Gazette*, 73 (1–2): 65–82.

Harrison, S. (2000) *PR – An Introduction*, 2nd edn. London: Routledge.

Hunt, T. and Grunig, J.E. (1994) *Public Relations Techniques*. Fort Worth, TX: Holt, Reinhart & Winston.

Hurme, P. (2001) 'Online PR: emerging organisational practice', *Corporate Communications – An International Journal*, 6 (2): 71–5.

Hussey, D. (1999) 'Igor Ansoff's continuing contribution to strategic management', *Strategic Change*, 8 (7): 375–392.

Ihlen, O. (2011) 'On barnyard scrambles: towards a rhetoric of PR', *Management Communication Quarterly*, 25 (3): 455–73.

IPR (2012) 'Research topics', the Institute for Public Relations (IPR), available at: www.institute forpr.org/research/topics/.

Jefkins, F. (1995) *Modern Marketing Communications*. London: Blackie Academic and Professional.

Jensen, M.B. (2008) 'Online marketing communications potential: priorities in Danish firms and advertising agencies', *European Journal of Marketing*, 42 (3): 502–25.

Kim S.-Y. and Reber, B.H. (2009) 'How public relations professionalism influences corporate social responsibility: a survey of practitioners', *Journalism & Mass Communication Quarterly*, 86 (1): 157–74.

Kirat, M. (2007) 'Promoting online media relations: public relations departments' use of Internet in the UAE', *Public Relations Review*, 33 (2): 166–74.

Kitchen, P.J. and Moss, D. (1995) 'Marketing and public relations: an exploratory study', The World Association of Research Professionals, Amsterdam, The Netherlands.

Kitchen, P.J. and Papasolomou, I.C. (1997) 'Marketing public relations: conceptual legitimacy or window dressing?', *Marketing Intelligence and Planning*, 15 (2): 71–84.

L'Etang, J. (1998) 'State Propaganda and bureaucratic intelligence: the creation of PR in twentieth century Britain', *PR Review*, Winter, 24 (4): 413.

Macalister, T. (2010) 'UK/Canada: Tar sands crude is reaching British petrol stations, Greenpeace say', *The Guardian* (UK), 9 May, on CorpWatch, available at: www.corpwatch.org/article.php?id=15579

Millward Brown (2007) 'How can PR affect my brand?', Millward Brown Knowledge Point, available through warc.com.

PRSA (2012a) 'Ethics – Ethical guidance for the public relations practitioners', the PRSA, available at: www.prsa.org/aboutprsa/ethics/

PRSA (2012b) 'Public relations defined: a modern definition for the new era of public relations', PRSA staff, 11 April, available at: http://prdefinition.prsa.org/index.php/2012/04/11/the-modern-definition-of-public-relations/

Phillips, G. (2011) 'Storytelling: brand journalism', *Admap*, October: 28–30.

Porter, L., Sweetser, K. and Chung, D. (2009) 'The blogosphere and public relations: investigating practitioner's roles and blog use', *Journal of Communications Management*, 13 (3): 250–67.

Radford, G.P. (2012) 'Public relations in a postmodern world', *Public Relations Inquiry*, 1 (1): 49–67.

Ranchhod, A., Gurau, C. and Lace, J. (2002) 'On-line messages: developing an integrated communications model for biotech companies', *Quarterly Marketing Review – An International Journal*, 5 (1): 6–18.

Richardson, O. and Dennis, C. (2003) 'UK vineyards sector case study: analysis of retail activities using exemplar strategic tools', *British Food Journal*, 105 (9): 634–52.

Roper, J. (2012) 'Environmental risk, sustainability discourse and public relations', *Public Relations Inquiry*, 1 (1): 69–87.

Rodgers, J. (2011) 'Piercing the fog of propaganda', *British Journalism Review*, 22 (4): 79–84.

Smith, B.G. (2008) 'Representing PR in the marketing mix – a study on public relations variables in marketing mix modelling', The Institute for Public Relations, 28 September, available at: www.instituteforpr.org/wp-content/uploads/BG_SmithKetchum1.pdf

Smith, B.G. (2010) 'Whither the public relations role? Exploring the influence of integrated communication on public relations', The Institute for Public Relations, 28 September, available at: www.instituteforpr.org/wp-content/uploads/PublicRelationsIntegration_Smith.pdf

Subervi, A. (2010) 'Avoiding ethical lapses online', *Public Relations Tactics*, 17 (1): 6.

Stone, N. (1995) *The Management and Practice of PR*. Basingstoke: Palgrave Macmillan.

White, R. (2002) 'Public relations in the marketing mix', the World Advertising Research Centre Quick Briefs, available at: www.warc.com/fulltext/Bestpractice/72468.htm

 Corporate Communications

CHAPTER OVERVIEW

Introduction

In this chapter the nature of corporate communication is explored and relationships developed with the marketing mix and marketing communications mix. Corporate communications are placed within an integrated communications context for the organisation as a whole. Organisations can be seen to use three forms of communication – management communication that is used by senior managers to approach both internal and external targets, marketing communications (as defined and discussed in Chapter 1 of this book), and organisational communications (traditionally corporate public relations and advertising and latterly corporate affairs, with the usual target groups of, for example the media, shareholders or the community). Broadly, corporate communications should be seen as an aid to solving problems or addressing issues as part of corporate strategy. Corporate communications should be seen as a process not an end in itself. This chapter is also about relations as well as communications so that things other than corporate advertising impact upon performance. Corporate identity is defined in relation to corporate image. This involves a critical analysis of behaviour, symbolism and communication that leads to corporate personality. Consistency and transparency in corporate behaviour and communications are clearly important.

Learning objectives

This chapter explores how the organisation can initiate, develop and maintain an effective corporate communications programme. More specifically, on completion of this chapter, the student will be able to:

- explore the concepts that underpin corporate communications and its functions;
- outline the relationship between corporate communications and its functions;
- explore the future of corporate communications in terms of integration, social responsibility and account-ability, behaviour and symbolism;
- outline major corporate communications tools that are at the disposal of the organisation within the framework of an identity and image plan.

BACKGROUND TO CORPORATE COMMUNICATIONS

Objectives of corporate communications

Corporate communications involve changing attitudes and perceptions that impact upon beliefs about an organisation and therefore about keeping management informed about how the various audiences might react. Ultimately they are about improving the economic performance of the organisation through the creation of awareness, understanding, appreciation, agreement, consensus and resolving conflicts.

The principles of corporate communications include the analysis of corporate image and corporate identity. This area of study provides techniques to improve the effectiveness of corporate communication programmes via a planning approach. The focus of many campaigns is the immediate relations between corporate strategy, corporate identity and corporate image. There is much more to communications than this and, as discussed in Chapter 1 of this book, many things communicate and potentially become part of the vastness and totality of the communications domain, as illustrated below in Figure 14.1.

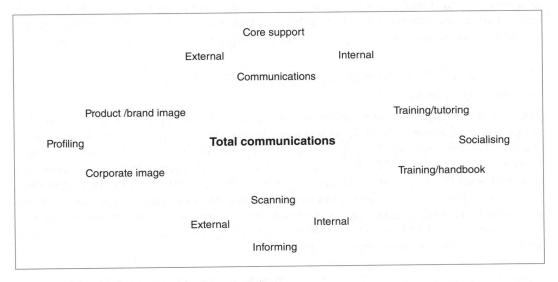

Figure 14.1   The total communications domain

Corporate communications defined

Corporate communications can be defined as:

> an all-embracing framework coordinating marketing, organisational and management communications that integrates the total organisational message.

More narrowly it can be seen as achieving organisational goals with a key tool to be used to develop relationships and understanding. The orchestration of this in terms of organisational corporate communications is often in the hands of a communications specialist. Mistakes can be made if communication is not integrated, timely and well managed. For example, if a manufacturer of fork lift trucks, dump trucks and other construction, plant and equipment announces, through the PR agency employed, that a large order has been obtained and this is picked up by the online and offline media – television, radio, local and national press – the agency is doing what it should and this could be seen as a success. If, however, the order is an old one and the company is in fact in trouble and having to rationalise its workforce through shop-floor redundancies and rumours of this also appear in the same media, then in this scenario it would be a corporate PR disaster. It is quite obvious that corporate level communications should be part of an integrative approach with the marketing communications mix. For a fully integrated approach, the application of communication elements should extend to the other functions of the enterprise, where communication must be coordinated across enterprise functions and target groups. Contradiction, which could harm the corporate image, should therefore be avoided. In this sense this is not so much a model of IMC but one of Integrated Corporate and Marketing Communications (ICMC).

A key player in the success of integrated communications activities is the CEO, so that the importance of the symbolic role of the CEO cannot be underestimated. Key components of corporate communication are both internal, between individuals and/ or divisions or departments, usually in terms of day-to-day shorter-term activities, and external, which includes corporate (or public) affairs and policy, investor relations and financial performance and value. Also included are recruitment communication, which provides an opportunity to put the corporate identity and image on display, and corporate advertising, which again is an opportunity to deal with image and identity.

The role of the corporate communication executive and key components

The role of the corporate communications executive is unique and is a key role in understanding the organisation's environment and being able to act upon this in an appropriate manner. The role involves 'looking out for stormy weather' but is one that provides objective and detailed analytical thinking regarding the impact that forces from the environment might have on the organisation. The executive has to be seen to be making the best of what is available. This list clearly incorporates those elements of PR that are operational at the corporate level, such as lobbying local or national government, media relations and customer relations so that, for example, the image of the organisation rather than the brand as such is part of the vision or corporate future.

Audiences for corporate communications

Corporate communication is a significant management discipline. The audiences that receive such communication are variously called stakeholders, publics (UK) or constituents

(USA). There are both internal and external audiences. The audience list may be the same as or very similar to that of the 'publics' of Marketing Public Relations as discussed in the previous chapter of this book, but objectives and messages may differ substantially. Internal communications and relations, often seen as a Cinderella subject by some, can have a big impact on external communications and relations in terms of the internal feel of an organisation. Senior management should nurture enthusiasm, acceptance and respect for the organisation itself, for new ideas or products, in order to achieve commitment and loyalty.

People project values, they being in effect ambassadors for the organisation. Staff morale is crucial in this sense to competitive advantage. Success with external communications and relations requires an ever-widening knowledge of socio-economic and cultural concerns. The stakeholders involved will depend upon the size of the organisation, whether it is local, international or global in its scope. The list would include the media, opinion leaders and formers, shareholders and politicians, with regard to issues such as take-overs and acquisitions, privatisation, new directions or positioning for the organisation, and of course perceptions of the organisation.

The Snapshot below looks at the programme developed by Cummins, the global diesel-engine manufacturer, who facilitated the unleashing of creativity of employees to help establish a new dynamic in a rapidly changing business environment.

Snapshot Cummins' VISION programme – culture, employees and the encouragement of innovation while unleashing creativity

Forward-thinking organisations encourage innovation and help unleash creativity in employees by promoting a particular culture. The culture of an organisation can be changed so that strengths are kept and a shared vision can help re-energise the whole organisation. One such organisation is Cummins – www.cummins.com/cmi/ – the manufacturer of high-performance, low-emission diesel engines and power generation systems and a component technology and power leader globally. Part of Cummins' mission has been to 'improve the lives of people' in helping customers to succeed, improving local communities and generating new solutions to reduce emissions and benefit the wider environment. Cummins has been involved not only in increased geographical diversification, but also in product diversification, moving beyond its traditional diesel engine business into other technologies.

A particular aspect of the Cummins' effort was the VISION programme, the subject of a Times 100 case study (*The Times*, 2012). The major purpose of this programme was to introduce people to a new way of working whereby their ideas are valued and they are encouraged to contribute rather than simply listen or be told. The special events put on by Cummins were very lively and showed how the company wanted to create a culture that encouraged the unleashing of new ideas, so that everyone could make a creative input into what is a dynamic business. Cummins strove for a business culture that nurtured the innovative ideas generated by employees at all levels of the company. The resource available to the company was recognised as the creative

(Continued)

(Continued)

energy of its own people that encouraged an atmosphere of thinking 'outside-the-box'. The VISION programme helped place the emphasis on informality and enjoyment with high energy, use of music, fun activities, much audience participation and creative-thinking group sessions with feedback being used. Unlike the usual training and development activities, events did not generate notes to take away, because the principal purpose behind them was motivational and inspirational. This was a programme to win the hearts and minds of participants – but with a fun aspect. It was coupled with a serious underlying theme, i.e. that of moving the company forward, so that it became 'more flexible, fast-acting, creative, efficient and ultimately more profitable'. Cummins developed a shared vision where employees were asked to 'act like owners working together'.

The culture, or 'the way we do things around here' of the organisation, refers to shared beliefs, policies and procedures. A starting point in understanding an organisation's culture can be observation of employees but by talking to those employees greater depth can be had. Some organisations appear dynamic where risk-taking and innovation are apparent. Others organisations are more cautious or administratively oriented where risk-taking is less likely to be encouraged or even tolerated. This latter type could well be unable to cope with change, without which the organisation might well founder. At Cummins change was embraced and in preparing for it the company used focus workshops across the board, which were 'inclusive' of every type of employee worldwide. Thus aspects of working life thought worth retaining, referred to as the organisation's 'sacred bundles' such as 'a sense of community' and 'respect for others', were highlighted. This enabled the organisation to build on existing values and practice while moving forward. The focus groups revealed a high degree of pride in the ability of the company, its products and its employees. The strap-line 'Making People's Lives Better by Unleashing the Power of Cummins' came from this. The 'Unleashing the Power of Cummins' was achieved by: motivating people to act like owners working together; exceeding customer expectations by always being first to market with the best products; partnering with their customers to make sure they succeed; demanding that everything Cummins did would lead to a cleaner, healthier, safer environment that created wealth for all stakeholders.

Stop Point

Cummins successfully re-energised its existing culture by encouraging people to say what they valued about the existing culture and by creating a more innovative company that was better placed to deal with a changing and competitive global business environment. The key to success lay in encouraging everybody to become involved and to contribute their own ideas and thinking in a way that modelled an inclusive and innovative company. Undertake the following: 1. Discuss organisational culture and the importance to any organisation of being innovative and participatory; 2. Comment on the importance of the generation of new ideas within the organisation, and the approach to change adopted by Cummins and how this could be adopted by other organisations.

CORPORATE IDENTITY, PERSONALITY AND IMAGE

Corporate Identity

There is a clear distinction between corporate image and corporate identity. The latter is the way in which the organisation presents itself to target groups. The former is the perception of the organisation by target groups and other stakeholders. Corporate identity has to be created, through the use of some form of signs and symbols to capture the essence of the organisation, and then experienced through everything the organisation says, does or makes, and then has to be managed. The corporate identity is revealed through communications policies. The corporate identity mix consists of symbols, communications, and organisational behaviour. Corporate personality can be defined as the manifestation of the organisation's self-perception including intent, i.e. the cultural glue for often-disparate parts of the organisation that binds.

Corporate identity should be strategically planned and measured. It should also be based on company philosophy, long-term company goals, and a particular desired image. In effect it is the sum of all methods of portrayal, visual and non-visual, that the company uses to present itself to relevant targets. It is a reflection of the distinctive capabilities and the recognisable individual characteristics of the company. It can also be said to be the tangible manifestation of the company and a reflection and projection of the real personality of the company meant to be experienced, and is therefore an aesthetic, formal expression and behaviour. As van Raay and Korzilius (2008) suggest, both public and business organisations understand the importance of corporate image and how stakeholders see the organisation and it has been the view of many writers in this area for a long time (for example van Riel, 1995) that corporate identity should, if it is worth anything, be an enhancer of performance and efficiency, a coordinator of values and information, and an integrator of the organisation's communications.

Many writers over the decades have distinguished between corporate identity and image (for example Markwick and Fill, 1997; Baskin, 1998; Dolphin, 1999; Kim and Hatcher, 2009). Markwick and Fill (1997) argue that there are linkages between corporate identity and image, personality and reputation. There is a need to understand stakeholder images and this understanding can provide a means to developing sustainable competitive advantage through a corporate identity management process. Dolphin (1999) has placed identity within the mission statement, the first formal act of the organisation's identity that defines the corporation and its goals and principles. Identity is also embodied in a sense of self in terms of history, beliefs and philosophy. Corporate identity change is therefore not a 'face lift'. There should be a concrete, and not a cosmetic, link between identity, communications and image. For Baskin (1998) it is also about leadership and vision since 'identity can focus managers' attention specifically on what they need to do to keep their organisation

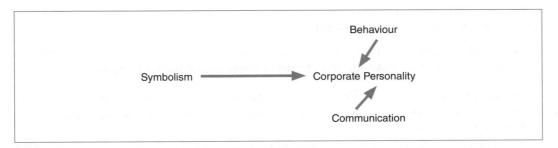

Figure 14.2 Corporate personality as a manifestation of the organisation's self-perception

competitive'. Kim and Hatcher (2009) suggest that corporate identities should be monitored and regulated in order to have effective performance measurement as part of corporate identity management. As with organisations such as IBM or British Airways, in the past and in the present, all organisations should endeavour to manage the corporate identity, image, personality and reputation. Managing corporate vision/culture is a leadership responsibility and change can be a deliberate management act brought about through positioning or repositioning activities that result in, for example, being seen as a global rather than national corporation. This has classically been the case with British Airways and more latterly with Facebook.

Identity is made up of signs and symbols such as name, logo, colours, icons, heraldry, flags, marks, uniforms and even the corporate HQ. Other communication, whether verbal or non-verbal, is important too, as is action or behaviour. For example, signs and symbols bring with them associations. On its own a new logo will not work beyond the cognitive. Other forms of communication and the ways in which an organisation behaves can produce something quite different. There may be a new house style but couple this with a collegiate feeling, a sense of belonging and of recognition, and the style becomes something else such as the impression of high esteem, quality and performance.

Hill (2002) provides a summary of Grayson and Hodges's (2002) seven-step model aimed at helping managers marry corporate identity with responsibility. The seven 'win-win' steps are:

- Step 1 is a trigger for action: it suggests 13 common triggers. This may be an externally generated event; for example, a media exposé of conditions in the company's Third World factories or the threat of a campaign against the business. The trick, however, is to get ahead of the wave – and generate your own trigger for action.
- Step 2 then involves articulating a compelling business case for action appropriate to the specific business.
- Step 3 suggests a business needs to scope the critical emerging management issues it faces. Tools include stakeholder dialogue, benchmarking, assessing business impacts and using scenarios.
- Step 4 is about committing to action, which may involve changes to a company's vision and mission, new governance arrangements, and perhaps making a public commitment through signing up for something like the global compact or joining a business coalition promoting socially responsible business.
- Step 5 suggests a business needs to integrate strategies, both by stretching existing policies and processes, or, for example, where there is a strong risk management culture or a commitment to total quality management, and these can be extended to incorporate the emerging management issues. Almost certainly, however, there will also need to be some new strategies developed.
- Step 6 is about implementation and engaging with stakeholders, for example, incorporating these issues into job specifications, appraisals, management training and rewards systems, and addressing community needs.
- Step 7 suggests measuring and reporting on impacts that the business has, and using these as a trigger to start the process again.

Measurement of corporate identity

An accepted categorisation of types of corporate identity to explain the possibilities of different depictions of the organisation in terms of style, policy and strategy is:

- Monolithic Identity – where the whole organisation uses one visual style (for example Shell, Philips, BMW).
- Endorsed Identity – where subsidiaries have their own style but where the parent is recognisable (for example GM, L'Oreal).
- Branded Identity – where subsidiaries have their own style but the parent is not recognisable (for example Diageo, P&G).

It should be noted that a combination of these could be used and that other language might be adopted to describe the same thing, such as 'umbrella' and 'endorsed'. The visibility of the parent is pivotal and this, of course, is to do with degree of control and of 'content guiding' whereby the parent might have high/low visibility and strict/no content guiding, or some degree of each.

Methods of analysis of corporate identity

There have been a number of methods developed to analyse corporate identity. As van Raay and Korzilius (2008) point out, corporate identity is not a static phenomenon as it is constantly changing. This is to be expected and therefore analysis and measurement of the corporate identity need to be a practical affair in order to assess the corporate identity quickly. The methods that have been developed focus on the management of the organisation who wish to present an unambiguous view to the outside world, bearing in mind that employees may be inside the organisation but are also important stakeholders. Two of the most commonly used methods that use management thoughts and ideas are the 'cobweb' and the 'star':

- Bernstein's *cobweb* method is useful for putting managers' ideas into a more explicit form. In this sense the method is about building a management consensus about a company's desired identity (van Riel and Fombrun, 2007). It facilitates an effective means (Quinton and Harridge-March, 2006, for example) to arrive at areas of conflict within the management team and expose them. This brings out in the open the terms in which the managers are thinking so that they can arrive at an unambiguous statement of the corporate identity desired by the management. This method measures in the first instance the view that they may have of their company, which is not necessarily the same as the view of the company held by other observers. This is the weakness of the method since it does not actually measure existing identity of the company and should perhaps mainly be considered a method for initiating a discussion on the goals of the organisation. The eight attributes of quality, integrity, value for money, imagination, reliability, service, social responsibility and technical innovation are then mapped on a scaled graph and the collective view of participants and their estimation of the public view can then be compared.

- Lux's *star* method is similar to Bernstein's cobweb. The value of this is also limited to the stimulation of a discussion among senior management along the lines that corporate identity should be following. This is still a useful and practical tool. With the Lux method the distinguishing attributes of the company are predetermined, i.e. that there are seven dimensions that always underlie the personality of a company – needs, interests, attitudes, temperament, competencies, origin and constitution (this after Guilford's 1954 study that established such characterising dimensions).

Corporate identity and personality

As suggested above, linkages between corporate identity, image personality and reputation have been identified (Markwick and Fill, 1997). Indeed there have been many calls for integration of these entities, for example Balmer and Geyser (2006) who suggest this should all be under the umbrella of 'corporate marketing' within a 6C framework. The nature of corporate personality has been expressed through the notion of 'who the organisation is' (Olins, 1989). Symbols, other communication and behaviour add up to corporate identity. This is a story that can be told. Communication can, for example, say 'we are innovative'. Behaviour of the organisation can back this up. A logo can be an instantly recognisable sign. The culmination of these leads to corporate personality. Corporate personality emerges from the concrete triangle of symbolism, communication and behaviour and therefore corporate image consists of all forms of expression by which the organisation reveals its personality and thus the uniqueness of the organisation. This is displayed in Figure 14.3 overleaf.

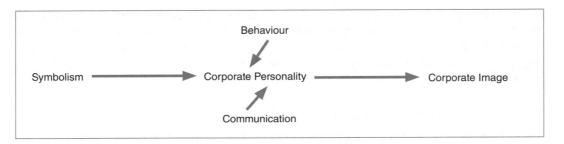

Figure 14.3 Factors that determine corporate image

The relevance of corporate identity has been summed up in four ways by van Riel (1995):

1. Rising moderation among employees that is an internal effect of corporate identity in the feeling that allows employees to identify with the organisation. This is an internal feel that increases commitment to the organisation and has an external projection. This is a better use of human capital.

2. Inspiring confidence among external target groups since consistent signals help such targets to develop a clear picture that reduces the risk of inconsistency.

3. Acknowledging the vital role of customers to help build customer confidence and relationships for the longer term.

4. Acknowledging the vital role of financial target groups, which inspires confidence in the company especially since they are dealing with financial risk.

Of course the notion of the desired identity leading to desired image is different from the notion of the actual identity leading to actual image. At least in part, self-preservation of the company lies in the corporate identity, in the manifestation of a bundle of characteristics (or distinguishing features) that form around the organisation, displaying its personality. Corporate identity can be seen as existing in cues offered about itself by the organisation in its self-presentation via behaviour, communication and symbolism, which are forms of expression. The persona therefore reflects the reality of the organisation and on this basis the observer can judge an organisation and its people.

Corporate image and reputation

The corporate identity should mirror or match corporate image. If corporate identity combines symbolism, communications and behaviour to form corporate personality, corporate image is determined not by the organisation, but by the perceptions of the target group (and others), and can be good, bad, indifferent, bland or confusing.

Corporate image can be described as a set of meanings by which a corporation is known that can be used by the observer to describe, remember and relate to it via the interaction of beliefs, feelings, perceptions and impressions. Corporate image is seen by some (for example Dolphin, 1999) in the same way that a photographic image can be seen by an observer. By the same token the organisation can view itself, but there is a danger here of distortion. A receiver will decode an encoded message and even if nothing has been deliberately encoded and apparently does nothing consciously, there will still be an image. The organisation must therefore realise that it has to manage the expectations of its potential publics, especially with regard to corporate reputation. A stable and consistent reputation can only be viewed as the overall estimation of the organisation by its stakeholders. It must also try to view itself in an objective manner in the context of trying to maintain a recognisable image and a favourable reputation (Gray and Balmer, 1998). Nguyen and Lablanc's (2001) study suggested that a degree of customer loyalty appeared higher when corporate image and reputation were perceived to be strongly favourable. A favourable corporate reputation is therefore a tool that can be used to positive effect. It is created by other tools and is necessary for competitive advantage.

The importance of a favourable image, a favourable representation in the mind, is unquestionable. Corporate image should be a strategic instrument of top management, an incentive for sales, an aid to recruiting employees, partners, investors, analysts and customers, a generator of faith among internal and external groups, a provider of authority, a creator of emotional added value, a provider of a means to competitive advantage, a changer of attitudes and potentially behaviour, a decider for consumers when the situation is too complex, when information is sparse or too wide-ranging, or when obstructions such as time constraints affect buyer behaviour (van Riel, 1995). Herbig and Milewicz (1995) highlight the relationship between reputation and credibility as key for competitive advantage where 'credibility transactions' (negative or positive) can impact upon an organisation and competitors. They argue that it takes many transactions to get back to a position after some fall from grace has taken place or where an organisation has not lived up to its claims. From the point of view that positive actions can enhance the corporate image and reputation of the organisation, Varadarajan et al. (2006) suggest that effective brand deletions, which free up resources that can be used for the benefit of the rest of the portfolio, represent such an action when recognised as good corporate decision making.

Symbolism as an agent in binding corporate identity and image

Symbolism as a binding agent is not new. Names, symbols, traditions or rites of passage all need to be invented or reinvented; for example, a sense of grandeur though a palatial corporate HQ or a house style that promotes unity and recognition. This is the establishment and maintenance of corporate identity. Done successfully and, for example, company pride among employees can produce a readiness to co-operate. There are basically two forms: indicative (pragmatic, that which is recognisable, the symbol) and thematic (dogmatic, an expression of the strategic principles of the organisation that transmits values). Thus name choice can be allied to flags, ceremonies or rituals, as with HSBC's long-running communications campaign where the corporation became 'the world's local bank', just as before it British Airways was 'the world's favourite airline'. Visual devices such as logos have to be designed to work on a number of levels. They have to be recognisable, distinctive, easily remembered, reducible and flexible in order to work in different media contexts such as magazines and television. The Internet in particular has had a big influence on the simplification of visual devices that will work in that medium. Mostly, however, they have to symbolise something and therefore metaphors, metonyms, allegories and the like are used to achieve this. For example, the organisation can humanise itself to communicate that it is about people, as with the Peugeot lion to suggest strength.

By the early 1980s David Bernstein had suggested that image, identity, personality, character, impression, representation and presentation are fundamental words to use in relation to an organisation wishing to be aware of how it is seen in reality (Bernstein, 1984). Musing on the large company's state of being Bernstein suggests that the company should question whether it has an image problem or that identity might be out of line with product performance, whether a consistent personality is expressed, whether all communications convey the character of the corporation, and whether what is said conveys the desired impression. Bernstein was concerned about what are actuality and perception, where any mismatch is the perception itself in the mind of the transmitter. This makes a lot of sense in the real world of everyday experience. The experience may be the observation that a relatively small travel company calls itself something like Target Travel. It calls itself that because it sees itself getting people to their destination like a dart or an arrow. They then choose a target, as in archery, because a target looks like an attractive logo. The problem is that there is no real link, just a perceived link in the mind of the transmitter.

The company should be concerned about being perceived at all and if so how signals are being received and how the company is perceived in relation to its self-image. This is a continual struggle, not something that a company can sort out once and for all. Unfortunately people find most change uncomfortable. This is unfortunate because management is about change. We cling to a set of values and conditions that we recognise and are undemanding of our own commitment and effort. Sir John Harvey-Jones, the late British businessman and consultant, in his book *Making it Happen* (1988), underlined the importance of the ability to create and manage the future in the way we wish. This is what differentiates the good manager from the bad and appears in its starkest form in this (20th) century of industrial change.

The Snapshot below reflects on the last three decades or so of the role of symbolism in corporate identity, image and personality construction.

Snapshot Corporate image levels – Bernstein's Detachable Entities, van Riel's Strategic Instrument, and Balmer's 6Ss of Corporate Marketing

Bernstein's (1984) notion of *detachable entities* – what a company does and how it is perceived – is a useful construct. There is a potential mismatch between what it would like to be and what actually appears to be the reality, the danger being distorted perception on the part of the transmitter. Companies therefore seek to have image(s) for the company itself and/or its brands and these are usually strong rather than weak, open rather than devious, warm rather than cold, and flexible rather than rigid. For the receiver the perception of the reality is the everyday reality where the reaction is not to an abstract reality but to the perception of this reality. It is this perception that is reality. In other words consumers are highly likely to accept a degree of illusion and choose a particular brand to join a club. In this sense, products (or for that matter politicians) are not packaged as is normally assumed but are given more than this – they are given a personality. Bernstein's analogy of a baby's clothes equating to packaging of the brand/politician in terms of growing and developing personalities is useful in understanding personality. With corporate advertising the image is adjusted. With product advertising the image is built into a product offering, usually a brand that becomes the embodiment of the person – the organisation or corporation such as VW or Guinness. The difficulty lies in the problem of reality shifting and therefore is one of control. The Corporate Communications Manager (if not the CEO) is the guardian of the corporate image and the product/brand manager is the product/brand guardian. Image is therefore 'a fabrication' and an impression that appeals to the audience rather than a reality. This, for Bernstein, implies a degree of falseness whereby the reality rarely matches up to the image of a product or a politician. The failure to project an effective image will produce distortion. Obviously, without distortion a clearer image or picture will appear. Bernstein (1984) sees image as one would a photographic image that develops in the mind of the viewer. The true image is therefore the viewer's perception and not that of management.

If management want to look into the mirror and see something target groups do not then they do so at their peril. As van Riel (1995) has it, an image is therefore a *strategic instrument* and has been defined in a number of ways; image is subjective knowledge and a representation or imprint of reality, the sum of 'functional qualities' and 'psychological attributes' in the consumer's mind, the result of the way the object is assessed (tangibility, relevance and degree of correspondence with self image). Expressed another way this becomes the 'sum of impressions and expectations'. Image is built from product aspects (such as brand names or advertising symbols) combined with a 'hierarchical meaning structure' that consists of 'means-ends value chains'. Image can also be viewed as 'holistic' and a 'vivid impression' that is then held as a result of information processing on the receiver's part. Some of this is transmitted by the organisation as part of marketing and corporate communications. Van Riel recognises three areas of opinion on how image works – social critics, analytic writers and utility writers. The first group are interested in learning as the way of viewing organisations. The second are interested in cognition and elaboration. The third, utility, consists of both academics and practitioners and is by far the commonest approach taken by the industry in terms of image creation. This approach, which for van Riel was the key to corporate communications, is illustrated below in Figure 14.4.

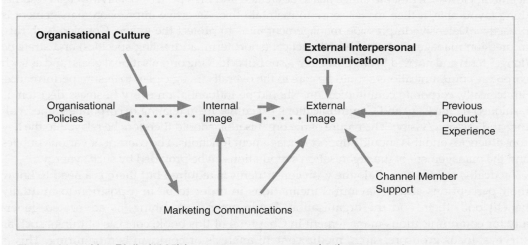

Figure 14.4 Van Riel's (1995) key to corporate communications concept

More recently *corporate marketing* (Balmer and Geyser, 2006; Balmer, 2009) has been described as a marketing and management paradigm that 'synthesises practical and theoretical insights from corporate image and reputation, corporate identity, corporate communications and corporate branding among other corporate-level constructs' (Balmer, 2009: 544). This leads to the 6Cs of the corporate marketing mix (Balmer and Geyser, 2006) that are Character (including assets, activities, philosophy and history), Culture (including the collective feelings of employees that are derived from values and beliefs about the organisation), Communication (outbound and inbound), Conceptualisations (perceptions held of the corporate brand by customers and other key stakeholders), Constituencies (external and internal groups) and Covenant (an informal contract that binds stakeholders to the corporate brand). This is an organisation-wide philosophy and should permeate throughout the organisation, influencing how people think and behave on behalf of that organisation.

Stop Point

Organisations are said to have cultures that can be positive or negative and problematic. Corporate image is manageable but this can be helped by the use of frameworks, models or conceptualisations. Undertake the following: 1. Discuss the 6Cs model and contrast it with conceptualisations such as Detachable Entities or Strategic Instrument; 2. Explain how an organisation can work on its internal feel so that this can be used in turn to help build a positive corporate image.

IMPRESSION MANAGEMENT AND CORPORATE IMAGE

Objectives, strategy and tactics

As with any managed programme, clear objectives, strategy and tactics have to be stated. One organisation may wish to move to a radically new position because of some major upheaval in its environment. Another may have a more incremental, subtle approach to impression management. However, first the image has to be created and then protected. Having created something favourable, it then makes sense to maintain this. Assertive impression management is proactive. Defensive impression management aims to protect the image. Coupled with this, impression management can be both tactical (short term, addressing specifics) and strategic (longer term and not tied to one particular issue but achieving organisational goals) and as such corporate communications should be core to the overall strategic plan to ensure performance. Strategically, corporate communications should be influential on every business decision as fashioned by the CEO and Communications Executive Team relating to corporate values, culture and mission/vision. The nature of the organisation should therefore be relayed to the key constituencies and this should support management functions. The consent of various publics and the management of the organisation's reputation can be provided by such synergy.

Tactically, an effective dialogue with constituents is required but there is a need to know their perceptions and behavioural inclinations in order to be in a position to mutually benefit both them and the organisation. Environmental scanning, as advocated generally for communications management in Chapter 4 of this book, consists of things such as surveys, focus group research, media content analysis or complaints monitoring. This is exchange of knowledge in order to learn more about significant constituents in the pursuit of competitive advantage. The corporate communication tools of, for example, lobbying and advocation, can then be utilised more effectively. In terms of both corporate identity and impression management, models have been developed to aid practitioners. These are very much akin to the general decision sequence model found in Chapter 4 of this book that follows the APIC system that is a step or stage model that moves from situation or context analysis through to evaluation and control.

Crisis management and avoidance

In a similar vein to the APIC model discussed in Chapter 4 of this book, crises have to be managed (or preferably avoided). This was discussed fully in the previous chapter in general public relations terms but becomes part of corporate relations and affairs when the crisis is at corporate level and corporate communication is a requisite part of problem solving. Crises at the corporate level can include political or social controversy, financial problems, or something also associated with the brand level such as product defects. The solutions to the highlighted problems can be followed through using a decision sequence framework. The nature of the problem will simply be at the corporate rather than the product level. The sage advice in the literature on corporate image or reputation is an advocation not only of defending a reputation but also of pre-empting crises (for example Davies et al., 2003). Once in place corporate reputations are constantly in danger of being eroded or damaged – perhaps even destroyed. Foreseeing a disaster is a great skill at any level.

Understanding of the customer/consumer corporate brand relationship

Chapter 7 of this book discussed how the customer/consumer knows to trust a brand. At the corporate level this comes about through confidence, integrity, consistency, competency, honesty, responsibility, helpfulness and benevolence – perceived or otherwise. This is a build-up, over time, of communications, performance, and functional and representational values. There has to be a mechanism whereby trust can be aroused and sustained. The role of communications is to take the aspect(s) of the corporate brand that matter and seal it, remembering that fundamentals like product defects will kill the effort even when the communication, say, the strapline, does the job. Communications are there to reinforce the idea that, for example, 'Tesco will look after me' and 'If they say so it must be true'. For Morgan and Hunt (1994) relationships characterised by trust are highly valued and within these benefits termination costs and shared values directly influence the trust-commitment-loyalty process, but that communications and opportunistic behaviour also have a role.

The Snapshot below looks at the ways in which organisations might control and improve impression management and the enhancement of image and reputation. In particular it highlights The Blue Angel as a 'seal of approval' and an 'ecological beacon'.

Snapshot   Corporate Impression Management – tools, techniques, pitfalls and seal of approval

On a personal level, impression management is the way that a person influences how others view them. The same arguments can be applied to how corporations try to manage the impression that various stakeholders hold. With the person this is done through grooming, through the clothes worn or through various types of behaviour. Similarly there are a number of tools and techniques that are available to organisations at the corporate level. These are part of the established external PR armoury such as press releases and receptions, facility visits, the annual report or corporate social responsibility activities such as the sponsoring of charities or eco-friendly activities.

Internally the organisation can also choose from a range of activities in order to communicate with its internal publics such as employees. This includes newsletters, email and actual meetings.

The organisation is multi-faceted and potentially has a number of personas that it may or may not wish to have in the eyes of both external and internal publics. By having open management the organisation can strive for authenticity or, because of its practices, it may present an idealised persona – an ideal type – that accentuates the positives and down-plays any negatives. The danger is that management might take this too far. In terms of impression and reputation enhancement or damage, the organisation

(Continued)

(Continued)

can walk a fine line. For example, by making claims to be eco-friendly through waste reduction or less packaging, the organisation can claim to be 'green' or at least 'greener' than it once was or than the competition, making the claim into a form of competitive advantage. This could be well worth the investment if the corporate image and reputation are truly enhanced. However, if the action does not have any significant impact on relevant publics or if in fact a claim rebounds on the organisation and causes corporate and brand level damage, then clearly this is not good news. The organisation might be seen as one that uses devious tactics to curry favour with its various publics and the negative publicity that ensues could be much more than the organisation bargained for if those publics see the real persona of the organisation as being manipulative, devious and untrustworthy, a position that could take a long time and much resources to rectify.

Something that can guide organisations on the path to being good corporate citizens is an official 'seal of approval' that acts as a stamp of authority. For example, the oldest such seal of approval in the area of eco-friendliness is Der Blauer Engel (The Blue Angel), the first environment-related label for products and services in the world. This seal was first set up in 1978 and according to its website (The Blue Angel, 2013) it has 'set the standard for eco-friendly products and services selected by an independent jury in line with defined criteria'. The Blue Angel eco-label has 'guided consumers in choosing environmentally friendly products for 35 years'. This seal of approval is 'only awarded to products and services which – from a holistic point of view – are of considerable benefit to the environment and, at the same time, meet high standards of serviceability, health, and occupational protection'. The Blue Angel sees itself as a 'market-conform instrument of environmental policy designed to distinguish the positive environmental features of products and services on a voluntary basis ... an ecological beacon showing the consumer the way to the ecologically superior product and promotes environmentally conscious consumption'.

Stop Point

Organisations can use such seals of approval in a professional way in promoting the organisation itself and/or brands, making this a win-win situation. Undertake the following: 1. Comment on the idea that there is never a good day to bury bad news; 2. Discuss The Blue Angel as an example of an official 'seal of approval' in terms of the benefits to organisations and society.

Assignment

Select a corporate identity and explain its composition in terms of shape, colour, form or any other structures and comment on what it symbolises. Explore other forms of communication and behaviours currently engaged in by the same organisation and explain its corporate personality. Comment on the likely corporate image and reputation this organisation will have with its various constituents.

Summary of Key Points

- Corporate communications are ultimately about improving performance and gaining competitive advantage.
- Corporate communications' role is that of the integration of functions to project the total business message.
- Corporate communications management should know that there is no external communication that does not impact internally and this can affect staff morale, adding or subtracting to competitive advantage.
- There is a clear distinction between corporate identity and image involving corporate personality and reputation. Identity is the way in which an organisation presents itself; image is the way it is perceived by various constituents.
- A combination of signs and symbols make up the corporate identity. This symbolism along with other communication and behaviour of the organisation add up to corporate personality. This projection becomes the corporate image as perceived by target groups over time. Corporate reputation then ensues, it being a collective representation of an organisation's past action and results.
- The link between branding, brand strategy and corporate identity and image is crucial. Other factors such as behaviour help take the new logo beyond a mere cognitive impulse.
- There is an intimate relationship between corporate identity, personality, image and reputation. Presentation, perception, representation and reality are important considerations in impression management.
- Impression management involves strategic and tactical activity that is part of the strategic corporate plan.
- To get to the true meaning of corporate identity and imagery, more than traditional/conventional research is required. It is easy and tempting to survey and gather information on recall/recognition. It is much more difficult to get to the true meaning, but qualitative techniques have emerged as an aid to this end.

Discussion Questions

1. Explain why organisations need to develop a culture that is innovative and participatory. Include in your answer consideration of the generation of new ideas within the organisation.
2. In terms of the employees of an organisation, discuss why it is important to make people feel that their ideas and opinions count, and why passion about the job and the organisation and an opportunity to work as a member of a team matter.

(Continued)

(Continued)

3. 'The IMC concept is misleading when consideration of the corporate level is made. The acronym IMCC is more appropriate in today's competitive world'. Discuss this statement in relation to the idea of 'total corporate communications'.

4. With reference to a particular example, explain how an organisation might seek to communicate its corporate brand identity.

5. Explain why an organisation might use the colours red, blue or green in its identity. Bring into your discussion consideration of shape and form and any other devices that are used for identity development, using examples to illustrate.

6. Discuss how the creation of a new brand identity might help an organisation to steer its way through difficult as well as easy times. Explain the relationship between identity, communications and behaviour.

7. Examine the relationship between corporate personality and corporate image. Explain where the notion of reality comes into the picture.

8. Corporate reputation is said to be the result of past and present actions and results. Discuss corporate reputation in the context of an organisation of your choice.

9. Impression management involves strategic and tactical activity. Discuss in detail one of the tools of impression management at an organisation's disposal.

10. Outline the kinds of issues an organisation might wish to research in order to monitor true levels of corporate image and reputation.

Further Reading

Argenti, P.A. (2006) 'How technology has influenced the field of corporate communication', *Journal of Business and Technical Communication*, 20 (3): 357–70. http://jbt.sagepub.com/content/20/3/357.full.pdf+html
This article discusses the particular effects that technology has had on corporate communications, both as a business function and as a discipline. It explores both changes and opportunities the new technologies have brought, with implications for teaching and research.

Caruana, R. and Crane, A. (2008) 'Constructing consumer responsibility: exploring the role of corporate communications', *Organization Studies*, 29 (12): 1495–519. http://oss.sagepub.com/content/29/12/1495.full.pdf+html
This article looks at the role of corporations in constructing the nature, meaning and implications of consumer responsibility. It employs a theoretical framework to discuss objects, subjects and concepts that are configured in organisational discourse, and uses critical discourse analysis to look at consumer responsibility that is organised into meaningful cultural knowledge through corporate communications. This relies on strategic juxtapositions that offer a morally non-conflicting concept of consumer responsibility that is facilitative of market choice.

Christensen, L.T. and Cornelissen, J. (2010) 'Bridging corporate and organisational communication: review, development and a look to the future', *Management Communication Quarterly*, 25 (3): 383–414. http://mcq.sagepub.com/content/25/3/383.full.pdf+html

This article discusses the wholeness and consistency of corporate messages that increasingly influence the domain of contemporary organisational communications. It provides a formative and critical review of research on corporate communications as a platform for highlighting the crucial intersections of differing research traditions.

Llewellyn, N. and Harrison, A. (2006) 'Resisting corporate communications insights into folk linguistics', *Human Relations*,59 (4): 567–96. http://hum.sagepub.com/content/59/4/567. full.pdf+html

This article examines how employees read corporate communications. Through the employment of focus groups this research produces empirical research that exposes an anti-managerial stance and cynicism toward corporate communications on the part of 'shopfloor' employees. The research employs discourse analysis to explore how text is analysed and how discursive controversies are identified vis-à-vis management practice.

Varadarajan, R., DeFanti, M.P. and Busch, P.S. (2006) 'Brand portfolio, corporate image and reputation: managing brand deletions', *Journal of the Academy of Marketing Science*, 34 (2): 195–205. http://jam.sagepub.com/content/34/2/195.full.pdf+html

This article is about, as the title suggests, brand deletions within portfolio management and the propensity of management to free up resources to support other brands in the portfolio. This can have an effect on corporate image and reputation. The authors discuss the organisational and environmental drivers of brand deletion propensity and provide a conceptual model of this process.

REFERENCES

Argent, P.A. (2006) 'How technology has influenced the field of corporate communication', *Journal of Business and Technical Communication*, 20 (3): 357–70.

Balmer, J.M.T. (2009) 'Corporate marketing: apocalypse, advent and epiphany', *Management Decision*, 47 (4): 544–72.

Balmer, J.M.T. and Geyser, S.A. (2006) 'Corporate marketing: integrating corporate identity, corporate branding, corporate communications, corporate image and corporate reputation', *European Journal of Marketing*, 40 (7/8): 730–41.

Baskin, K. (1998) *Corporate DNA – Learning From Life*. Oxford: Butterworth-Heinemann.

Bernstein, D. (1984) *Company Image and Reality*. London: Holt, Reinhart and Winston.

The Blue Angel (2013) 'The Blue Angel – Active in Climate Protection', available at: www. blauer-engel.de/en/index.php

Caruana, R. and Crane, A. (2008) 'Constructing consumer responsibility: exploring the role of corporate communications', *Organization Studies*, 29 (12): 1495–519.

Christensen, L.T. and Cornelissen, J. (2010) 'Bridging corporate and organisational communication: review, development and a look to the future', *Management Communication Quarterly*, 25 (3): 383–414.

Davies, G., Chun, R., da Silva, R. and Roper, S. (2003) *Corporate Reputation and Competitiveness*. London: Routledge.

Dolphin, R. (1999) *The Fundamentals of Corporate Relations*. Oxford: Butterworth-Heinemann.

Gray, E.R. and Balmer, J.M.T. (1998) 'Managing corporate image and corporate reputation', *Long Range Planning*, 31 (5): 695–702.

Grayson, D. and Hodges, A. (2002) *Everybody's Business: Managing Risks and Opportunities in Today's Global Society*. New York: DK Publishing.

Harvey-Jones, J. (1988) *Making it Happen: Reflections on Leadership*. London: HarperCollins Business.

Herbig, P. and Milewicz, J. (1995) 'To be or not to be … credible that is: a model of reputation and credibility among competing firms', *Market Intelligence and Planning*, 13 (6): 24–33.

Hill, N. (2002) 'Corporate identity: a seven step model', *Society Guardian*, 26 March, available at: http://society.guardian.co.uk/conferences/story/0,9744,672417,00.hml

Kim, J. and Hatcher, C. (2009) 'Measuring and regulating corporate identities using the balanced scorecard', *Journal of Communications Management*, 13 (2): 116–35.

Llewellyn, N. and Harrison, A. (2006) 'Resisting corporate communications insights into folk linguistics', *Human Relations*, 59 (4): 567–96.

Markwick, N. and Fill, C. (1997) 'Towards a framework for managing corporate identity', *European Journal of Marketing*, 31 (5/6): 396–409.

Morgan, R.M. and Hunt, S.D. (1994) 'The commitment-trust theory of relationship marketing', *Journal of Marketing*, July, 58 (3): 20–38.

Nguyen, N. and Lablanc, G. (2001) 'Corporate image and corporate reputation in customer's retention decisions in services', *Journal of Retailing and Consumer Services*, 8 (4): 227–36.

Olins, W. (1989) *Corporate identity: Making Business Strategy Visible Through Design*. London: Thames and Hudson.

Oswald, L.R. (2007) 'Semiotics and Strategic Brand Management, Marketing Semiotics Inc., and the University of Illinois', available at: www.marketingsemiotics.com/pdf/semiotic_brand.pdf

Quinton, S. and Harridge-March, S. (2006) 'Why keep a cobweb in your cellar?: a diagnostic tool to evaluate the use of e-commerce and technology in wine marketing', 3rd International Wine Business Research Conference, Montpellier, 6–8 July.

The *Times* (2012) The Times 100 Business Case Studies, Powered Forward With a New Vision – A Cummins Case Study, available at: http://businesscasestudies.co.uk/cummins/powering-forward-with-a-new-vision/rolling-out-the-vision-programme.html

van Raay, L. and Korzilius, H. (2008) 'Identity and culture under one roof – the development of assessment instruments for strategic communications in housing associations', in R. Crijns and J. Thalheim (eds), *Kooperation Und Effizientz In Der Unternehmenskommunikation*, 1: 49–66. New York: Springer Publishing Company.

van Riel, C.B.M. (1995) *Principles of Corporate Communications*. London: Prentice Hall.

van Riel, C.B.M. and Fombrum, C.J. (2007) *Essentials of Corporate Communications: Implementing Practices for Effective Reputation Management*. Oxford: Routledge.

Varadarajan, R., DeFanti, M.P. and Busch, P.S. (2006) 'Brand portfolio, corporate image and reputation: managing brand deletions', *Journal of the Academy of Marketing Science*, 34 (2): 195–205.

15 Sponsorship

CHAPTER OVERVIEW

Introduction

In this chapter the nature of sponsorship is explored and relationships developed with the marketing communications mix. Sponsorship is placed within an integrated and strategic context. Sponsorship involves an exchange whereby one party permits another an opportunity to exploit an association with an activity, for commercial advantage, in return for funds, services or resources. This is often seen in relation to sports, particularly when televised, which can extend audience coverage. This is part of event-related marketing and the sponsorship of events of all sorts from especially sports but also causes and the arts. Venues can also be used as a focus for corporate entertaining, as with football boxes or racecourse marquees. Cause-related marketing includes the sponsorship of causes, most often charities. Sponsorship of television programmes is now commonplace. Ambush marketing and product placement are included as an allied but somewhat different marketing communications optional tool. This chapter explores these areas and makes a case for sponsorship's elevation to a strategic rather than simply philanthropic status.

Learning objectives

The chapter seeks to explore the nature and role of sponsorship in the context of what theory has to offer sponsorship practice. More specifically, after reading this chapter, the student will be able to:

- understand the nature and role of sponsorship;
- appreciate sponsorship in relation to other marketing communications tools;
- discuss sponsorship in terms of marketing theory and relationship marketing;
- assess the various types of sponsorship in the three domains of causes, sports and the arts;
- assess other sponsorships, particularly those associated with TV programming;
- appreciate the nature of sponsorship practice in relation to strategy;
- situate the tools of ambush marketing and product placement in relation to sponsorship.

THE NATURE AND ROLE OF SPONSORSHIP

The nature of sponsorship

There are many reasons why an organisation may wish to sponsor. For example, government policies on tobacco or alcohol advertising may see companies switching to sponsorship (which is increasingly problematic) or for the soft brand association that can be achieved through the use of sponsorship. Former Coca-Cola Chief Marketing Officer Sergio Zyman, in his book *The End of Advertising As We Know It*, says the term sponsorship should be dropped, because it is patronising, and that it should be replaced with 'marketing property utilisation' (Admap, 2002). Sponsorship is about someone paying to be part of something else – a project or an activity – or it is about someone entering into an agreement on behalf of another. Or it may be about someone who makes himself responsible for certain things (Sleight, 1989). However, this view, for Sleight, may be rather erroneous. As early as 1989, Sleight chose to define sponsorship in terms of relationships, a sentiment upon which many writers on sponsorship would agree since it involves more than lending a name or hosting an event. The sponsor is the provider of funds, resources or services to an individual, an event or organisation, offered in return for rights of association, usually to be used for commercial advantage. The sponsee (or property) is the receiver of the funds, resources or services and the giver of the rights of association.

It is no longer simply the chairman's wife who gets to choose a charity to support, although it is clear that this kind of activity is still part of sponsorship. Lamont and Dowell (2008: 253) remind us that local sponsorship involving SMEs is still extant and 'small scale sports tourism events have been adopted by regional communities as an economic diversification strategy in response to global pressures such as industrialisation and urbanisation'. Sponsorship in this sense is often used to occur at the marketing operational level in the form of philanthropy, so that it is not just about sports but also causes and the arts and other aspects of the community. Increasingly, and over the last few decades, certain partnerships emerged that were much more strategic in nature, reflecting the changing nature of this particular tool which has become much more associated with branding and the marketing of brands. Sponsorship is not at all new and can be traced back to, for example, Roman times where sponsorship of the arts was common. Sponsorship has been and still is in many instances about altruism, philanthropy and making people aware of a company's involvement in a particular project to create a positive feel for the company. In this sense it is still about PR with less control than is to be had with many other forms of communication.

Reference to sponsorship in the marketing communications literature is often found under either cause-related marketing or event-related marketing. With the former in particular there has been an increase in in-kind sponsorship at the expense of cash. There is also a worthwhile distinction that can be made between corporate philanthropy and commercial sponsorship where respectively one is pure giving and the other is giving but seeking reward (Bennett, 1998). The latter appears to be the stronger trend with in-kind sponsorship having a number of additional benefits including community involvement and staff training and development. Event-related sponsorship has, for example, included the name of the cigarette brand Marlboro, which has been associated with Formula 1 and other racing for many years, but this has been severely curtailed by health/anti-tobacco legislation, especially in Europe but also in many other countries. Critics point to the move from advertising to sponsorship and then to more subliminal attempts with, for example, the logo – if not on the car itself then on drivers' gear. Likewise, the Benson & Hedges brand of cigarettes was for many years synonymous with both cricket and golf, this being replaced with, for example, Brit Insurance for the England cricket team and the likes of HSBC and Cadillac for the golf World PGA tour.

Sponsorship, therefore, has a long history of involvement with athletes/sportsmen and women, the arts, media programming and causes/philanthropy. The term 'soap opera' has become part of the English language and is used now in a wider context than its origins – the sponsorship of drama by 'soap' companies. Apart from the now obvious and some might say distasteful sponsoring of (usually sporting) events by tobacco companies in order to avoid advertising restrictions, in recent times there have been two identifiable occurrences. First, the highly publicised 'marriage' between brand names and non-profit-making organisations, such as charities like Save the Children being associated with Cadbury or the Barcelona/UNICEF partnership, is established practice. Second, television programmes have been sponsored by brands, again such as Cadbury for a time sponsoring *Coronation Street*, the UK's premier television soap opera. Other, past, examples of such sponsorship in the UK are Pepsi and the *Pepsi Chart Show*, HSBC and ITV Drama, and Diageo brands and Film on Four (i.e. Channel 4). Diageo brands such as Bell's Whisky and Bailey's Irish Cream are a good example of targeting, Diageo having the ability to change the brand depending upon the film and particular audiences. Cause-related examples are Marks & Spencer (Age Concern and Mencap), Unilever's Flora margarine brand (the London Marathon until 2009, which is now the Virgin London Marathon), and the private medical brand BUPA's sponsorship of the BUPA Great North Run.

There are different types of brand sponsorship. Brand sponsorship is a tool now thought to be an essential part of the programme of communications, in part due to the decline in traditional advertising effectiveness, which has been evident now for more than a decade (Stewart and Short, 1997; Erdogan and Kitchen, 1998). Industry opinion suggests that online advertising and in particular that associated with social media have been changing and will continue to change the media landscape (see Chapters 9 and 10 of this book). In the USA interactive media spend was estimated to be $55 billion in 2014, representing 21 per cent of all marketing spend. This includes search, display, email, social and mobile. The reason for this is simple. Traditional media will continue to decline in favour of less expensive yet more effective interactive tools and services (Solis, 2011). Consumers are more sophisticated, experienced and respond less to traditional forms of advertising, thus making it less cost effective. This means reduced margins for companies and generally a rise in the cost of marketing unless there is a switch to interactive. Marketers and agencies have had to deal with such trends by changing the communications mix and this has included a changed role for sponsorship.

Allowing the brand name to be associated with causes/charities, sports, the arts and aspects of the media, particularly television programmes, is thought to make the communication more direct and as such more effective. It has been known for some time that brands work by having a positive effect on consumer decision making or choice process (for example Doyle, 1990). This implies that, if brands are positively associated with organisations in these domains, then this will help to limit the need for choice. Whatever the type of sponsorship it can be said that the parties involved gain some degree of mutual satisfaction. Beyond the marriage analogy there is a suggestion of an emergence of symbiotic alliances between sponsors and causes and between the causes themselves (Copley, 1999). The sponsee gains valuable financial help and the organisation or brand benefits by public association where such publicity will enhance image, enlist consumer loyalty, and even increase sales (Savage, 1996). Brand image encompasses the total set of brand-related activities engaged in by the brand/manufacturer. Obviously such sponsorship will form part of that total set of activities and thus affect the consumer's understanding of the brand.

Targets

The targets for sponsorship will depend upon the context in which the sponsorship takes place. Targets might be at a corporate or marketing level, for example the media or a particular section of the general public. Clearly the target might be younger people (sponsorship of a music event), older people (sponsorship of a relevant health or age concern event), or more specific – say golf, or an arts venue or event. Usually there is more than one target, which could include employees (internal marketing) as well as customers and consumers as part of a planned marketing communications effort by the sponsor.

Objectives of sponsorship

The sponsor is generally looking to achieve a positive association, i.e. a positive image transfer from sponsee to sponsor, this being a relationship that has to be appropriate. Corporate and marketing objectives have been seen as primary, for example awareness and image (Witcher et al., 1991), or secondary, for example to support channel members, staff morale building, or influence other stakeholders such as shareholders. This becomes more important as management attitudes change and sponsorship becomes a more strategic tool (Dolphin, 2003). The degree of involvement is also important. The sponsor may simply donate money or become involved in reshaping an organisation, perhaps sending out a specialist member of staff (on secondment), rather like a footballer (on loan but no fee), to a sponsee such as a charity. The distinction between the objective of achieving the status of the corporate good citizen and that of achieving brand or market-led media coverage through sponsorship is clearly an important one. The organisation has to decide if it wants to reinforce brand values or use sponsorship in a secondary role, for example as a source of information.

Large companies are much more likely to want sponsorship by results whereas smaller companies are more likely to be philanthropists (Copley, 1999). Lamont and Dowell (2008) found that motives for sponsoring events in a regional context are still commonly philanthropic with small firms, contra to some in the literature who have heralded the extinction of philanthropy, which is clearly not the case as can be seen in many studies involving small firms (for example Copley et al., 2012). Positive image associations are achievable because sponsorship has been seen as being less commercially biased (than advertising) and has helped sports to develop, the sports people to develop and, of course, causes and the arts to develop. However, Bennett (1998) suggests a sponsor might be concerned about being viewed as exploitative and with negative connotations.

Generally the effects of sponsorship are expected to be long-term rather than immediate direct sales, the brand being linked to an event and/or an organisation or person over a period of time. For example, Guinness has sponsored the arts in order to build image and corporate goodwill. Perhaps the key objective is to gain media coverage. That is why, for example, Formula One sponsorship is such an important issue, especially as it is televised and broadcast around the world. In situations like this, without media coverage the sponsorship deal will collapse. If television coverage were sought, there would be little point in companies, such as brewers, sponsoring football if they can no longer have their brand logo on players' chests in markets where this is banned from television. This is a fluid, dynamic situation. The Thai beer brand Chang, for example, has been on English Premiership club Everton's players' chests since 2004 but this partnership might change, not least because of the nature of the product (alcohol) and relations with television coverage or other societal concerns, despite this being a good targeting opportunity for Chang. Everton, of course, through this partnership, has a big opportunity to develop its fan base in Asia. The Chang/Everton example typifies the complex range of sponsorships and mix of sponsors at any given time. With Chang the main sponsor, other sponsors include Nike, Kitbag, Thomas Cook, Crabbies, Paddypower, EA Sports and Britannia.

The role of sponsorship

Spend on sponsorship globally

A lot of money is now dedicated to sponsorship activities around the world. Admap in 2010, using industry source Group M figures, provided global sponsorship spend figures that predicted a 2 per cent fall in 2010, which would be a reversal of the 'double-digit' annual increases during 2006–8. Admap provide the following key points:

- Asia Pacific still expanding its sponsorship spend while this has contracted slightly in Europe. In 2010, 36% of sponsorship spend calculated to originate in North America with Europe at 26% and Asia Pacific 25%.
- Figures suggest that in the USA (the world's largest sponsorship market) sport will dominate with more than two thirds of sponsorship dollars spent in 2010.
- Generally sponsorship deals are long term with the objective of increasing brand loyalty – important for 70% of sponsors – and stimulating sales – the objective for 38% of sponsors.
- Half of sponsors' ROI has increased in recent years while just 3% have seen a decline.

Admap (2010) provide more, such as a breakdown of sponsorship spend by type in the USA which is: sports (68%); entertainment tours and attractions (10%); causes (9%); arts (5%); festivals, fairs and annual events (5%); associations and membership organisations (3%). Another part of the detail is a list of the top ten sponsors by dollars in the USA for 2008 headed by Pepsi Co at $362.5m and followed by Coca-Cola at £262.5m.

The IEG Sponsorship Report of 4 January 2011 suggested that the industry rebounded quickly from the historic low point of 2009. IEG suggested that globally sponsorship grew in 2010 by 5.2 per cent to a value of $46.3 billion and in North America the comparable figures were 3.9 per cent to $17.2 billion. Based on conversations with significant sponsors and properties (sponsees) IEG suggested increased spend in 2011 of 5.9 per cent to $18.2 billion in North America and globally 5.2 per cent to $48.7 billion. Sponsorship growth remains ahead of both advertising and sales promotion. Media spend in North America rose 2 per cent in 2010 with an increase of 3.9 per cent in 2011.

The Snapshot below illustrates the kinds of sponsorship partnerships and opportunities that involve global corporations and brands as sponsors and entities that are property (or, when the deal is done, sponsees). As such these deals become part of the sponsor's corporate and marketing communications mix, for a time at least. The challenge lies in making sponsorships work effectively alongside advertising, public relations, branding, design and other communications.

Snapshot   Global Sponsorships: Why Sports?

The ways in which global sponsorship has developed in the last few decades seem to major in sports sponsorship deals. As the 2012 London Olympics approached, most marketers were thinking in some way about sponsorship. There were, as usual, an array of sponsors; Coca-Cola, Acer and Samsung being three of the main sponsors. Although the value of contracts is not usually released (until after the event and sometimes not at all) they were estimated to sell on average for $100 million (around £65 million) for the main sponsors but some would pay more and get more out of the deal. One of the parameters was the length of time involved. For example, Procter & Gamble (with brands such as Pampers, Pringles, Gillette and Ariel) signed a 10-year agreement with the IOC (International Olympics Committee). The IOC was hoping the revenue from sponsorship would top the $1 billion mark. However, not all are the size of P&G, there being some 750 firms being sought who would pay around £10,000 and SMEs would have a chance with the 'support the team' fund worth around £25 million. According to the BBC (2010), P&G also had a deal with the US Olympic team, which P&G reckoned helped boost market share and generated an additional $100 million in sales. Dahlen, Lange and Smith (2010) discuss sponsorship in relation to the Beijing Olympics and how Samsung used this global event in order to enhance global sales but also image. Dahlen, Lange and Smith (2010) break down events on the scale of the Olympics to four areas: television; event ticketing; corporate sponsorship; and licensing. They highlight different levels of sponsorship with the top 12 sponsors, for example Coca-Cola paying $72m, but with lots of lower levels of local sponsors and suppliers who were able to buy-in to the Olympic images and logos.

MasterCard have many marketing activities and sponsorship is a big part of that, including music and fashion around the world as well as sports – but sports are important to MasterCard. International football (not American football but what the USA call soccer) is high on the agenda. MasterCard was an official sponsor of the UEFA European Championships (Euro 2008) and the UEFA Champions League. In Latin America, through alliances, it sponsors the Copa America and the South American Qualifiers. In golf it is the Official Payment System and sponsor of the PGA tour. MasterCard is the preferred method of payment in tour shops and Tournament Players Clubs. They have both Tom Watson and Natalie Gulbis as global spokespersons and sponsor a number of tournaments such as the Senior Open Championship, Royal Troon, Scotland, the MasterCard Championship at Kona, Hawaii, the MasterCard Classic at Mexico City, and the Arnold Palmer Invitation at Orlando. Baseball's Major League has MasterCard as an official sponsor, is the preferred method of payment and also sponsors the Major League Baseball website, MLB.com. At club level MasterCard has exclusive sponsorship alliances with 15 MLB clubs, including the Boston Red Sox and the New York Yankees. MasterCard is the Official Payment System of the New Zealand Rugby Union. MasterCard claims it is able to create business–building opportunities for the financial institutions (customers) and offer value and priceless experiences to card holders around the world. Visit www.mastercard.com/us/company/en/whatwedo/current_sponsorships.html.

Surprising news in May 2011 was that FC Barcelona, who in December 2010 signed a 30 million Euro per season deal to 2016 with the Qatar Foundation, which promotes education and research in the Middle East, had a new sponsorship deal with UNICEF (their former sponsors). This would mean the Qatar Foundation logo on the front of the jersey and the UNICEF logo on the back, under the player's number. The UNICEF deal was due to end in 2011. Barcelona now has Qatar Airways on the front of their shirt.

Stop Point

Think about these examples of sponsorship partnering and the global potential for each. Undertake the following: 1. Consider and expand upon the possibilities for smaller firms with the Olympics and the prestige that could bring. Explore also the possibilities for big players like P&G and MasterCard and the various levels and types of sponsorship within the Olympics event; 2. Consider other opportunities such as the UEFA Champions League or golf's PGA tour for global players like MasterCard. Discuss the benefits that the likes of FC Barcelona have had from its Foundation's partnership with UNICEF and what the club might have gained from its deal with the Qatar Foundation and Qatar Airways.

HOW SPONSORSHIP WORKS

Problems with awareness, attitudes and behaviour

Sponsorship can have an effect within each of the established stages of the hierarchy of effects model – i.e. cognitive, affective and behavioural (see Chapter 3 of this book) – but such a model should be used with caution (Hansen and Scotwin, 1995). Clearly marketers should be interested in exposure effects where one-off sponsorship exposure differs considerably from continuous exposure, the sponsor preference generally being for long-term, continuous sponsorship. The concern is whether one-off exposure can manage to achieve any of the sponsor's objectives, for example to become part of the target's evoked set (see Chapter 3 of this book). If sponsorship is congruent with expectations then it will work better and longer-term sponsorships help with congruency. Additionally, longer exposure may increase involvement. If the event or sponsee is liked then the sponsoring brand is more likely to be liked. The expectation or assumption that if there is a positive mood or atmosphere then this will pass on to the brand is a prevalent, cognitively driven one. On the other hand, behaviourists argue that operant conditioning is at play where reinforcement and vicarious learning are important in terms of how a product can be used. For example the credibility of the athlete (positive in many cases but negative in other cases where credibility is lost) will either positively reinforce brand image or, conversely, damage it. Apart from the obvious (for example athletes taking illegal drugs, sex scandals or embezzlement of a charitable cause's funds) and the inevitable (increased costs, 'ambush marketing' – see later in this chapter), there is clearly a need to understand the sponsorship-brand association (Scherer, 2007) and memory decay effects (Crimmins and Horn, 1996). Much has been written in the area of awareness, usually through some form of recall testing.

Association

Association between sponsor and sponsee can be important but emotional involvement (attitude strength, actual purchase, and positive word-of-mouth) is crucial in terms of recall because of the way attitudes towards the brand are shaped within an environment (Hansen and Scotwin, 1995). A strong emotional response and positive moods add up to increased value attached to the brand. The source of the message in terms of the usual parameters such as trust or perceived expertise might be important. There is evidence to suggest, for example, that the sponsee can be seen as being more neutral than the sponsor (Quester and Farrelly, 1998). These researchers have focused on awareness and recall but admit that emotion is missing from the equation. Bal (2009: 2) suggests that emotion is ignored by sponsors, the preference being for 'visibility, mediatisation and PR potential'. If researchers merely ask for recall of events and the brand associated with it then this would tell of the association but little else. Consumers may know that the English (football) Premier League is sponsored by Barclays (bank) but this kind of research would say nothing about how they really feel about Barclays as an organisation or the League itself. For Gwinner (1997) repeated exposure is key, while for Quester and Farrelly (1998) long-term impact is important whereby spontaneous awareness may be initially low but long term the message might sink in. Previous exposure to the brand is important to recall but length of association and local familiarity are important for both recall and preference. Where sponsorship is used to gain wider coverage, for example by appearing on national television, the importance of the local parameter is lessened. High/low recall is associated with high/low expressed preference (Nicholls et al., 1999).

Familiarity

At a fundamental level people develop a preference for things because they are familiar with them. This is often called the familiarity principle. Bennett (1999) looked at recall in terms of Zajonc's (1968) 'mere exposure' hypothesis and the 'false consensus' theorem of Ross (1977) in terms of football match spectators and posters around the perimeter of the pitch, whereby fans purchase the brands sponsored at the event and so too do the general public who are not attendees but become familiar by other means, usually via television coverage. This is also found in occasional attendees, suggesting the importance of sponsorship in strengthening brand image. Even if the brand is not the main sponsor, the greater the frequency of exposure the higher the level of recall, i.e. it is more likely that research informants will name perimeter advertising of specific brands as examples of product categories. Bennett suggests that studies show that percentage recall increases as aiding or prompting is increased but that this is still relatively low. When dealing with the official team sponsor, however, recall is dramatically increased. Bennett highlights a number of other issues such as length of association and social cohesion of attendees that have an influence, particularly on message decay. After 20–30 minutes recall can be down by as much as one quarter and after 24 hours by as much as one half. Even after prompting using product categories as a stimulus, recall can fall back substantially so that the 'emotional environment' affects recall in terms of involvement. This might be especially so where a team sponsor's message might be more than 'mere exposure' but may have a positive effect in terms of attributes that are attractive in some way to the recipient of the message. Wakefield et al. (2007) tested four key factors in sponsorship recall: sponsor relatedness to the event; sponsor prominence in the marketplace; corporate exposure; and individual exposure/identification with the team. Prominence and relatedness were the two key factors individuals relied on when identifying sponsors for an event. This research also discovered that free, direct recall is generally more accurate than cued recall, i.e. recall that relies on reconstructive processes.

Differentiation

In terms of sponsorship achieving more than awareness, the sponsorship of the British and Irish Lions by HSBC in South Africa is a case in point. HSBC did not need awareness as an objective, but it did need further differentiation from other high street banks and had, of course, already developed its 'The world's local bank' idea. Sponsorship indents were developed to help achieve the objectives of awareness of HSBC as a sponsor, of providing meaning to the association and, longer term, to reinforce HSBC's 'The world's local bank' as both a brand idea and a commercial driver (Cannes Creative Lions, 2011). The diversity and worldliness of both organisations were clear to see and this sponsorship partnering high-lighted the local element in the South African environment of wild animals in the savannah. The results from this campaign confirm the achievement of the three objectives set.

Branding and sponsorship

Involvement

Bal's (2009: 5) research suggests that there is a fundamental affective relationship 'between consumer and sponsored property – and exerting an emotive, rather than cognitive, influence on consumer behaviour'. Bal urges practitioners to think again about the use of emotions in sport-related property sponsorship. Involvement appears to be the key. With sports sponsorship the affinity between viewer and sport appears to get stronger with, for example, the opportunity for displays of great skills (say football) or to see danger (say motor racing). If there is excessive involvement in an event this can be detrimental to recall, i.e. there is a threshold of involvement whereby more sponsorship beyond a point would be a waste (Quester and Farrelly, 1998). Involvement with the event is not, of course, the same as involvement with the brand unless the event and brand are inextricably linked. There is often the assumption that the sheer volume of the exposure will result in penetration with desirable results. This argument has, of course, been used before in terms of advertising and other communication tools. Ultimately the question within the hierarchy is whether or not increased exposure and familiarity lead to increased preference and positive behaviour towards a brand. In a study by Copley and Hudson (2000) there was no evidence that strength of attitude will depend upon variables such as length of time in front of a message, but the research did suggest a relationship between intensity and strength of involvement with brands and activities. There was also an apparent link between recalled brand and preferences found in this study, suggesting that when recall is high brand preference will be high, and where recall is low preference will be low. The evidence also supported the notion that brands can have positive mental characteristics and where this is the case strong attitudes are developed towards chosen brands. The study supported the idea that the greater the involvement with the activity the greater the chance the sponsorship message would work, thus agreeing with Nicholls et al. (1999).

Innovation

Sponsorship can be a way of reminding the consumer of the brand but it is more likely to be used as a way of associating the sponsor with another organisation for positive gain. Consumers are more discerning than ever before and their higher level of understanding demands that amusement and innovation are a necessary part of communications. New approaches to accessing the consumer's mind are thus being sought. Innovation in communication media as well as communication message has been at the forefront of (necessary) change. This change encompasses the further development of brand sponsorship. As the stakes rise, with the ever-growing 'own label', so manufacturers seek new ways to differentiate and build their brands. Brands are now recognised as valuable assets that appear on a firm's balance sheet. Brand equity may be difficult to measure but this must somehow be done for the sake of the development of effective brand strategies (de Chernatony, 1998).

High-fit

Brands that create strong attitudinal bonds with the consumer through investing in rational, emotional and saliency-based advantages are likely to be worth more to their owners in the future than brands that are bought on availability or pricing (Farr, 1998). Historically advertising was thought to be sufficient, then in the late 1980s and early 1990s quality and service were deemed the best way of creating brands (Doyle, 1990). Sponsorship offers ways of reaching targets or extending brands because of its unique properties. Becker-Olsen and Hill (2006) suggest that high-fit sponsorships with non-profit service providers positively influence brand identity through broad association and brand meaning, response and relationships through specific associations (the opposite being the case for low-fit sponsorships). This obviously means seeking high-fit if sponsor brand equity is to be enhanced rather than impaired, and that both partners should think strategically about sponsorship for long-term objectives' achievement.

The Snapshot below discusses the notion of 'fit' between sponsor and sponsee and challenges the notion that 'fit' will always be an obvious choice for pairings of the parties.

Snapshot   Sponsorship 'fit': Self-evident or in need of Deeper Scrutiny?

'Much of the sponsorship reportage concerns its role in developing brand awareness for the sponsor and the reciprocal flow of funds for the sport' (Smith, 1999). The long-term strategic role of sponsorship, for Smith at that time, had been neglected in terms of building brand values or a brand personality as part of strategy. However, it is now known that consumers are even more sophisticated when it comes not only to understanding marketing communications, and advertising in particular, but also what sponsorship means. Certainly there has been the realisation that 'fit' is needed between sponsor and sponsee (or property), which involves 'sincerity, longevity and a sizeable commitment to achieving strong positive transfers from the sport to the sponsoring brand'. Sponsorships have to appropriate and 'match their actual or desired target customer profile' (Smith, 1999).

It is often thought that a good 'fit' between sponsor – for example a sportswear manufacturer – and sponsee – for example a sporting event – will produce a strong impact. This resultant strong impact may very well be the case. For example, the high-quality sporting apparel brand Under Armour renewed their presenting sponsorship in the USA with the NFL for the 2010 NFL Scouting Combine. According to Scibetti (2010) this was 'one partnership that really offers an excellent and natural fit between the property and the sponsor'. Under Armour has apparently built the brand around the idea of 'high-quality apparel for peak athletic performance', a concept that has been 'consistent throughout all of their various marketing platforms' where there is a focus on 'the imagery of intense workouts and competition'. Scibetti maintains that the sponsorship offers 'coverage of athlete workouts whereby the brand will feature on every potential draft pick that participates in combine drills, and with the increased coverage of the event on NFL Network and NFL.com, the exposure level and overall media value should be even greater than last year'.

Under Armour combined this with local events and Scibetti maintains that a sponsorship deal with another area of activity such as a food chain or financial firm or 'some other disconnected industry segment' would be 'more challenging to build a successful campaign around the event'.

However, academics, quite naturally, take a more analytical view of such pairings. For example Cornwell et al. (2006) suggest that not all brands 'fit' in a self-evident way. These researchers are aware of brand awareness and image in such cases but are interested in getting at the effectiveness of the pairing. The study concludes that while congruent sponsors have a natural memory advantage, articulation can help memory improvements in incongruent sponsor-event pairings, making such pairings possibilities in terms of being effective pairings. In another study Gwinner and Bennett (2008) investigated the influences of brand cohesiveness and sport identification on 'fit' perceptions. These researchers found that 'fit' does impact attitude towards the sponsor, which has a positive influence on the purchase intentions of consumers, but these researchers maintain that rather than focusing on the outcomes of 'fit' there is a need to look at variables that influence 'fit'.

Although it might seem that there are obvious couplings between sponsor and sponsee, there is clearly a need for a greater understanding of the concept of 'fit' since opportunities may be lost by discounting a less than traditional and obvious pairing.

Stop Point

Sponsorship has changed over the last few decades having become more strategic in nature and employed to achieve different objectives than in earlier times. Undertake the following: 1. Discuss whether or not sponsorship deals that involve multiple brands such as those of the various partners of a FA Premiership club like Everton FC might lead to confusion and more cynicism from spectators, viewers and fans. Include in your discussion consideration as to whether the main shirt sponsor gets most benefit while others are potentially viewed as secondary and inferior; 2. Comment on the effectiveness of sponsorship where the 'fit' is deliberately distant to facilitate a radical repositioning of a brand rather than a more conventional 'fit' such as that of Under Armour/NFL Scouting Combine.

SPONSORSHIP IN PRACTICE

Measurement considerations

The broad range of sponsorships available means that the world of sponsorship is increasingly complex and 'big business' (globally worth $4.6 billion in 2010 according to industry sources as used by Meenaghan, 2011) and with large budgets involved inevitably the effectiveness of sponsorship has come into play. Sponsorship 'needs a broad range of metrics that form comprehensive effectiveness measurement' in order to justify sponsorship's place 'in marketing budgets' (Meenaghan, 2011: 2). With a global financial crisis affecting many things, added pressure is on companies to justify the use of things like the corporate hospitality that is often integral to a sponsorship. As mentioned above it is often measures like brand awareness, exposure and sometimes attempts to link to sales figures that are used. Increasingly, however, new and different approaches are needed to measure against objectives that are to do not only with involvement but also engagement (Meenaghan, 2011).

Meenaghan (2011) suggests that most sponsors do not measure effectiveness but advocates that they should for a number of reasons, not least accountability. Numbers can be physically counted at an event and TV audiences measured, therefore reach and frequency can be ascertained. The communication effects can be measured (as with Quester and Farrelly, 1998), usually in the area of awareness and interest rather than behaviour as mentioned above. Bennett et al. (2006) claim that their research at a particular professional tennis tournament measured the effect of sponsorship on spectators' attitudes towards the sponsor (how these were shaped) and also their purchase decision on sponsors' goods and services, with over half apparently suggesting an influence. Focus has been placed on sponsor confusion or whether there is a clear link between brand and event. A number of sources use 'PIE', the Persuasive Impact Equation (for example Crimmins and Horn, 1996), which suggests that persuasive impact is a product of the strength of the link, duration and gratitude felt due to the link plus perceptual change due to the link. This would mean that the more the target is aware of the link, the longer it is in front of them and the more positive the perceptual change is about image, then the more impact the sponsorship will have.

Effectiveness measurement has to be more than mere 'opportunity to see'-type measures, which are relatively easy to achieve in terms of reach and frequency, as suggested immediately above. This is a quantitative measure but there is clearly a realisation that both quantitative and qualitative audience research can be used. The quality of audience delivery is important as is the impact on brand perceptions. Millward Brown's 'Sponsorship Insight' tool was designed to combine detailed audience profiling with a comprehensive understanding of the relevance of the partnership (Thomson and Vickers, 2002). Ventura and Cardani (2010) introduce the event and sponsorship 'valuator' that helps companies make decisions on buying-in to events and sponsorship based on research and market data by calculating the media equivalent value in terms of visibility and added value in terms of consumer engagement and brand values, suggesting this is more than mere media equivalence. Kraak and Oliver (1997), interested in the consumer response to sponsorship exposure, concluded, among other things, that sponsorship exposure can be as effective as television advertising in terms of brand name recall but challenge the industry Sponsorship Exposure Value norm that uses a down-weighting factor to measure effectiveness. Fast (2011) advocates a three-point approach to sponsorship measurement: first, understand the audience by going beyond the standard demographic information and seek insight on audience engagement (as Meenaghan, 2011) with a basic argument that to build a brand relationship you have to first understand it; second, lay the groundwork by partners understanding each other better to achieve synergy; and third, provide valuable data, from pre, during and post stages of a campaign through the use of the usual survey questionnaires, focus groups and so on in the various media, including social media. A more specific example of the measurement of the effects of sponsorship is the work of Herrmann et al. (2011), who are particularly interested in the memorisation effects of sponsorship through looking at consumer consideration of sponsor brands they do not remember. These researchers found that sponsorship increases the chances of a sponsored brand being part of a spectator's consideration (or evoked) set, even among those not conscious of the sponsorship. They also found that sponsorships can decrease the implicit perceptual memory for competitor brands.

Choice considerations – types of sponsorship

As already indicated in this chapter, the money spent varies enormously across the varying types of sponsorship, especially if money for supporting communications is included. Broadly it can be said that sponsors are involved in one or more of four types of sponsorship; causes, sports, the arts and media. Appropriation runs from millions (for example Coca-Cola and the Olympics) to very little (for example a smaller firm engaging with minority sports). The type of sponsorship chosen will depend to a large extent on top-level management involvement and whether the investment required is put in at the corporate or marketing level or both. It can be argued that generally speaking, sports sponsorship is more akin to advertising at the marketing level but cause-related sponsorship is more akin to corporate PR. This has led to change regarding sponsorship and the goals behind investing in it. Global projects like yacht races are more relational than the many more tactical events that could be chosen. Most are long-term associations and so ride the storm of recession and budget cutting so that sponsorship becomes a means of defending a market and providing triggers for recall and recognition.

Most sponsorship deals can be put into these boxes but sponsorships exist across a wide variety of projects and there is probably room for a miscellaneous box. Sponsorship is not, therefore, strictly cause-related, arts, sports or media. It may be the environment with which the sponsor has a vested interest such as car manufacturer sponsoring motoring or aspects of the community that are not causes as such but which free up money to be spent on other things. A local firm looking after the maintenance of a landscaped area such as a park or roundabout will mean that a local council can spend money on other things such as community services. This is an interesting twist in social marketing campaigns. Another example is where a sponsor provides for an advertising slot with a social message, as for example a car company sponsoring an anti-speed campaign.

Cause-related sponsorship

With cause-related sponsorship there are two basic outcomes for the sponsoring organisation; increased visibility of brand or organisation, and image building or enhancement in terms of being seen as being socially responsible (Bennett, 1998), this kind of arrangement being a 'win-win', symbiotic alliance (Copley, 1999; Copley et al., 2012). Sponsorship 'fit' is of course important but from the cause or not-for-profit organisation side, even if the 'fit' is low, the organisation can use supportive communications to counter risk in such a strategic alliance (Becker-Olsen and Hill, 2006). The same could be said for the sponsoring firm. Increased sophistication in the manner that consumers perceive things and behave and government pressure on companies to help with community needs are two of the drivers for such alliances to happen. Motives of the sponsor almost certainly vary between the various forms of sponsorship. Organisations that become involved with charities want primarily to enhance their reputation but also to increase sales. A large percentage of the population in most countries are more likely to buy from a company that supports the community (Bennett, 1998).

Cause-related sponsorship may have a positive effect with people willing to pay more or brand switch but as much evidence exists to the contrary as it does to support this proposition. Sponsorship of causes needs to be understood in terms of both sponsor and sponsee practitioner perspectives. It is also important to understand the effects of sponsorship on the sponsor's customers and consumers generally; donor motivations and other processes that lead to corporate donations and possibly partnerships or strategic alliances and 'lateral partnerships' (between causes which may or may not be in competition), and where 'strategic fit' is seen as pre-eminent. Research by Copley (1999) enabled the construction of a 'strategic and lateral partnership/alliance' conceptual model. This attempts to explain how symbiosis is increasingly becoming important to the success of such activities and how changes from within the causes themselves are driving them towards alliances in a more positive way.

Sports sponsorship

Sports sponsorship is probably the most researched and written about form of the marketing tool. It is a massive part of the industry and worth billions of dollars globally as figures for the 2012 London Olympics alone bear out. The problem for sponsors is that sports sponsorship is attractive, usually because of high media coverage and large audiences, it facilitates targeting with large targets of shared characteristics and events are visible, there are a lot to choose from, especially for big corporations like Coca-Cola. As already alluded to earlier in the chapter, golf has been used to promote many things, for example products and brands like whisky (Johnny Walker and the Wentworth World Matchplay Championship), by car manufacturers like Toyota who used local golf involvement to build dealerships, or Guinness who sponsored the Rugby World Cup. Coca-Cola have exploited sponsorship of football (soccer) by the choice of sport but also the use of all forms of media PR, sales promotions and internal communication. There are many more examples and the list is seemingly endless. From small firms sponsoring regional sport tourism (Lamont and Dowell, 2008) to large corporations such as Adidas sponsoring rugby and in the process having created an online rugby game featuring the New Zealand All Blacks (Scherer, 2007). As Whannel (2009: 205) points out the days of shared domestic leisure where this involved viewing the major channels are almost gone in the face of fragmentation and the growth of online services, yet 'sport provides the exception, an instance when around the world millions share a live and unpredictable viewing experience'.

Arts sponsorship

Business is now, and has been for a long time, a key funder of the arts. It may have begun as philanthropy, but it has mutated into activities such as corporate hospitality, making appeals to particular targets. Arts sponsorship is less expensive than sports sponsorship generally speaking and it involves many things from art galleries to music festivals to ballet. Much sponsorship of the arts is to do with image building by association. Mobile phone manufacturers and brewers have used sponsorship to target a younger audience and this has included rock festivals and events like Glastonbury. In-kind sponsorship by supporting local artists with materials or photocopying services still exists but is less common than it used to be. Given the risks involved in sponsoring sports or sports people as alluded to earlier, arts sponsorship as a safer alternative can be an attractive proposition. Brand sponsorship at dance music events is another example of sponsorships worth millions of dollars globally. Corporations with brands such as Rizla, Durex, Carling and Smirnoff are examples of brand sponsorship of such events. This is not only logical but also allows the brand owner to communicate its proposition, develop style and tone, to sample and even sell, with opportunities to promote the brand to a wider audience outside the event. Brewer Miller's Yacht Party in Ibiza was typical of this kind of sponsorship, offering clubbers a ticket to a one-off exclusive party on a privately chartered schooner (Bagnall, 2002).

Research into more conventional arts sponsorship by Quester and Thompson (2002) revealed that, unlike advertising that is viewed as self-serving, arts sponsorship is perceived as facilitating the staging of performances that could be viewed and enjoyed for what they are. Before and after tests revealed a significant attitude shift, although Quester and Thompson concede that their research is general and 'many questions remain unanswered' such as whether particular demographic groups are more sensitive than others to sponsorship. Saha (2007) warns that commercial sponsorship can be problematic when corporate intervention in culturally diverse arts situations occurs. The very reason why the artistic endeavour exists could be threatened as in the case of telecommunications company 02's sponsorship of the photographic exhibition 'Changing Faces', a collection of images of British Asian youth that challenged the stereotypical representations of Asian youth culture. Here, the counter-hegemonic potential of the exhibition was seen as being undermined by such a sponsorship (Saha, 2007). This can be contrasted with the sponsorship of the Royal Swedish Opera. As Lund (2009) contends, arts sponsorship is moving from a passive donor position to mutually beneficial alliances, similar to the symbiosis found with cause-related alliances by Copley (1999), and as such all parties can gain from knowledge sharing within an alliance or partnership.

Media-related sponsorship

The motive for organisations employing television programme sponsorship is increased brand awareness and sales. These organisations seek to communicate with the consumer through the programmes or films that they like to watch. Brands are provided with 'stature and legitimacy' through broadcast association, a 'marketing platform in its own right' (Peters, 2010). By using these immediately pre- and post-programme and commercial break slots the marketer has a greater opportunity to catch the consumer's attention before they switch channel to see what else is being shown. In a sense television programme sponsorship is relatively new (as it has developed more slowly in some markets, often because of legislation) yet at the same time it is an old concept, especially in the USA where the 'soap opera' was born and well established by the 1980s. However, it is relatively recent to Europe but is growing. It might well be the case that public-owned TV will allow sponsorship of programming if not commercial advertising, in many markets where presently it does not. Certainly this can be problematic, where conflicts of interest have been detected, as with for example the BBC, where conflict arose over on-air sponsorships such as Sports Personality of the Year, also involving commercial inputs such as from Robinsons, the drinks company (Sweney, 2008). Programme sponsorship is now valued at billions of dollars globally.

A fundamental point to make is the critical relationship between programming and the very nature of television. Links between programmes and brands at times may be difficult to make. Others are more than obvious. Fizzy drink brands such as Tango have sponsored youth-oriented programming, with a clear synergy for the particular target concerned. Others are not so easy to understand, such as an assurance company's sponsorship of a film channel, where there is no obvious connection. This can be compared with the much clearer feel for Stella Artois, the Belgian beer brand, or Diageo brands such as Bell's Whisky, sponsoring the same kind of programming. Also sponsorship-type deals are more cost effective and some allow more control. For example, in the UK, *The Network Chart Show*, a rival pop music chart show to the BBC's Top 40 show on Sunday radio and a run-up to the new number one single for each week, was originally sponsored by Nescafé. Pepsi took over as sponsor in 1993 and the Pepsi Chart Show was actually produced in Capitol Radio studios in London. This lasted until 2002 and in 2003 it became *Hit 40 UK*, then *The Big Top 40 Show*, powered by iTunes, and is now the *Vodafone Big Top 40 Show*. This kind of programming allows the sponsor total control over the image and therefore enables them to remain consistent with all other forms of communication taking place (Mazur, 1998).Online activity is now an integral part of sponsorship. Engagement is through, for example, online games such as Adidas's 'Beat Rugby' free, downloadable game, whereby the Adidas brand was projected as 'globally cool' (Scherer, 2007: 475). Online donation facilitation is now commonplace. One of the growth areas in recent times is in the area of sponsored links (Lin and Hung, 2009). The likes of Google, Yahoo and more recently Bing from Microsoft are firmly established players in the 'key words' search engine area of marketing activity. Most writers would classify 'sponsored links' as a form of online advertising rather than sponsorship, for example Lin and Hung (2009) and Chen et al. (2009).

It has been suggested for some time that programme sponsorship can only really work through association, and should not try to be another way of advertising. For example a client may want association with a sport where some of the glamour rubs off on the sponsor's brand (Bryant, 1992). The sponsor's brand, if targeting is done well, will be clearly identifiable with the programme's audience and can be more focused than advertising since the sponsor's message is there right at the start and restart of the programme as well as the end. Clearly the audience profile has to match as closely as possible the brand target characteristics. The creation, maintenance and awareness of the brand and brand's presence on television are an accepted outcome of sponsorship but it was the appropriateness links and image transference that made sponsorship more than spot advertising (Millman, 2000). In recent times, however, concern has been raised that sponsorship is now so influential that, like its communications cousin, advertising, in the past, it can affect the nature of television programming so that programmes have to fit in with the needs of the sponsor and 'be like the brand'. McAllister (2010: 1476), discussing hypercommercialism and televisuality in relation to television (college) sports sponsorship, reports on a significant decrease in advertising-free broadcast time, because of the increased use of on-screen graphics with 'commercial iconography', but also the style of the broadcast now being characterised 'by integrated marketing techniques that blur distinctions between content categories'. More generally, McAllister (2010: 1487) expresses concern over 'Digital manipulation of corporate symbols' and an array of issues such as effects on ticket prices, the ever-present concern over motives behind alcohol/beer brand sponsorship, and other ethical concerns (see Chapter 6 of this book for a broader look at such concerns in marketing communications).

Product placement

There is no doubting the value and realism product placement brings to entertainment and why producers are attracted to it. The Snapshot in Chapter 1 of this book on product placement highlighted recent changes to product placement on television in the European context (Hauck, 2011; Robinson, 2010) and there is clearly a need for regulatory frameworks. There are differing layers of concern over public safety, ethics and the use of product placement as 'covert advertising', and the powerful effects this can have on consumers, particularly young consumers and the promotion of unhealthy lifestyles. The fear is that 'nutrient-poor, calorie-dense foods' will dominate television product placements in particular as evidenced in the USA, as the Yale University study mentioned in Chapter 1 of this book suggests (Naish, 2011). Certainly the regulatory frameworks try to deal with issues such as high in salt, fat and sugar products and product categories such alcohol, gambling and escort agencies (Robinson, 2010). Television and film have been used for a very long time for placing products in a particular context. The IKEA couch in a television programme, James Bond using a BMW Z3 or a Lotus Esprit in a Bond film, or Ray-Ban Aviator glasses as worn by Tom Cruise in the film *Top Gun*, are examples of product (or brand) placements. The consumer is not necessarily aware that this is a deliberate act, product placement often being referred to as embedded marketing. Indeed this is one of the technique's strengths, where it can be more potent than advertising with more people noticing the product or brand without knowing it. This has also been called 'subliminal product placement'.

Research indicates that brand recall is stronger with product placement than with advertising but that a combination of both can potentially almost double the effect. This fits with the idea that traditional media have become less important with consumers becoming tired of being told what to do and marketers seeking engagement. However, more research is needed in this area of marketing activity. The assumption that positive associations are stored in the memory when a brand is noticed as a result of unconscious exposure may be erroneous. Memory may not be involved and may not affect behaviour and attitudes towards the brand and the influence of context (the programme, film and so on) needs to be understood (Percy, 2006). This will also depend upon product categories within which brands need to be managed and controlled, and this requires research. Kydd's (2009) example of Tom Cruise's Lexus having a central role in the film *Minority Report*, yet scoring relatively low recognition as opposed to the relative success of the Audi RSQ as driven by Will Smith in the film *I Robot*, suggests more research for reasons why recognition levels are higher in some contexts than others would be beneficial, as would research into cultural differences and ethical considerations. Certainly, as with celebrity endorsers, product placement has to fit well into the context, otherwise there will be reduced, a lack of or even negative impact (Homer, 2009) and research suggests that brand memory will be increased positively where the placement is seen in a non-commercial way (van Reijmersdal et al., 2009); this fits with the idea of branding having an emotional basis and where a brand–consumer relationship needs to be created, nurtured and protected.

Television programming product placement is said to be worth 5 per cent of television advertising revenue in the USA, making it potentially worth £150m on current figures in the UK for example (Sweney, 2011). A brand can be incorporated into any script. In a film, a protagonist may smoke a cigarette but not just any cigarette; or drink a whisky but not just any old whisky, depending upon any sponsorship deal that has been cut. In a similar vein, in magazines a piece of fashion photography might be accompanied by a particular car marque or models who wear particular clothes. This is a form of merchandising where the product or more accurately the brand is placed within a set.

Most product placement is thought of in terms of feature films and television programmes. The objective behind product placement is usually to build national recognition but it may also be used to enhance brand image and bring excitement to the brand, especially where there is implied celebrity endorsement, in an (often) uncluttered environment. Product placement can be used for market testing before launch to get consumers to try the brand. For this privilege companies have to pay and pay handsomely. The Bond cars are a particularly good example of the history of the development of product placement as a marketing tool. At first the makers of the films were told by manufacturers that they would have to pay for the cars they needed as part of the film script. It took a little while for this particular tail to stop wagging the dog, but eventually it did and the value of placing a product or a brand was realised.

With basic product placement, the product will be placed in an incidental or casual way so that integration and control are both low but this will be a relatively inexpensive placement, such as a video game billboard on a race circuit. This still needs to be relevant and have a connection. This is akin to use of props that predate legalised product placement in many countries such as the UK. If control is enhanced but integration is still low then this means that product (brand) features are in the plot and this increases control. If the product is integrated but control is low, this means that there is heightened integration. The product (brand) will feature highly in the plot – typically this describes product placements in the Bond films or the Wilson brand in the Tom Hanks film *Castaway*. If both integration and control are high, this means that the product (brand) is fundamental to the plot, at the centre, such as *Adidas Power Soccer* or the *Pepsi Chart Show*.

Event-related sponsorship

Sports, the arts and entertainment sponsorship more often than not involve an event of some sort. Event-related marketing is often to do with excellence, success and winning, as well as extra media exposure. Quester and Farrelly (1998), with a four-year longitudinal study of the Australian Formula One Grand Prix, show this to be the case whereby uppermost in the sponsors' minds is (the strength of) the association between the event and the sponsors' brands. This includes any kind of sponsored event but is usually either sport-related or arts-related, this latter category including rock/pop music events. Events can be sponsored in cash or in kind. Most of the money in sponsorship is spent on sports, followed by the arts and causes, but in some countries TV programming has caught up with or exceeded cause-related sponsorship. Compared with advertising, event sponsorship is very cost-effective in terms of reaching a target. From opera to sports, events' targets can be reached in order to meet several kinds of objectives. There is much activity in the event sponsorship area. For example, Chan (2010) provides an account of the ways in which value was added to brands through the sponsorship of the Shanghai Expo. Local brands gained the most at this long event but gains were also made by the likes of Coca-Cola. Another example is provided by Perkins (2010) who takes the reader through the success of the O2 Arena in London – from failed Millennium Dome, a national embarrassment, to a source of national pride and the world's most successful entertainment venue. This is a story of sponsorship and branding but also strategy and measurement, and not least the 'four principles of success', i.e. putting the customer first, being integral to the business, breathing rather than simply badging, and demonstrating accountability (Perkins, 2010: 22). There are, however, a number of downsides. For example, spending lots of money on deals that cannot be justified or the event alienating some customers and potential customers by having a particular sponsor rather than a rival, can cause problems.

Ambush Marketing

Ambush (sometimes called guerrilla, sometimes parasitic) marketing is the association of an organisation, usually with an event, especially the big events such as the Football World Cup or the Olympics, without being an official sponsor. Through the use of the media, the organisation can appear to be a big sponsor, or by sponsoring one team or one player or by overstating involvement, the organisation achieves a similar effect to the official sponsor, usually at a lot less cost. This verges on the illegal and is viewed by many as theft. There are many examples to draw on, for example, Sony sponsored ITV coverage of the Rugby World Cup and managed to get first mention on the programming even though Sony was not a sponsor of the event itself. Corporations like Adidas will try to stop Nike from ambushing them and vice versa. During the 2010 Football World Cup, the game between Denmark and Holland was attended by 36 women wearing bright-orange mini-dresses. They were advertising a Dutch brewery (Bavaria) and were ejected by stewards at half time, but had a worldwide television audience, including Holland, as well as the stadium crowd, a lot of whom would have been Dutch. Budweiser, the official sponsor of the event and the only brand allowed to advertise inside, would not have liked the stunt, which was followed by media coverage of it, adding to the success of the ambush. This activity is seen as a real threat to co-branding and to strategic objectives of partnering organisations, especially those sought from the relationship (Farrelly et al., 2005). However, these researchers make the point that ambushes can be countered and used to advantage by using issues of legitimacy and enhancing corporate and brand authenticity through an appeal to consumers' dislike of disingenuous brands.

The Snapshot below discusses the notion of symbiosis in sponsorship whereby the various parties gain in a win-win scenario. The Great North Run is used as an example to illustrate.

Snapshot Symbiosis in sponsorship – The Great North Run: Probably the Best Half Marathon in the World

It appears that people can be made sensitive to both emotional and rational appeals and both negative and positive messages (Belhout and Copley, 1997). With corporate giving, enhancing the corporate image appears to be the overriding concern (Savage, 1996)

but with movement toward more tangible goals in evidence (Sargeant and Stephenson, 1997). Aurora et al. (2005) distinguish between commercial and philanthropic sponsorship. Commercial sponsorship attempts to get direct benefits for the sponsor such as awareness increase or direct sales. With philanthropy, in general, society should benefit and more specifically the cause, but not the sponsor or donor, apart from the expected good will, social recognition, and the improvement to corporate image. There can be ideological or attitudinal barriers toward being involved with commercial sponsorship posed by a cause's management that affects performance (Balabanis et al., 1997). However, many partnerships and alliances are mutually beneficial and successful, especially where symbiosis is achieved (Copley, 1999; Copley et al., 2012). There have been difficulties, such as when a large corporation sponsors a cause, sports or some aspect of art that appears to be sponsor driven where the sponsee is almost an incidental part (Mawdsley, 1998). There should be a strategic fit but also with any partnering there should also be benefits for both parties, derived from symbiosis, and not a one-sided affair where the benefits are greater for the sponsor than the sponsee, making the activity much less of a partnership. The role of brokers in this can be crucial. As Farquarson (1998) points out, 'dating agencies' may be resented by fund-raisers but until now such agencies have been seen as being crucial to success. Successful matching, then, is central to the success of the particular activity and beyond.

One of the best examples of symbiosis has to be the Great North Run. With 52,000 runners taking part in 2011 and 56,000 in 2013 (including Olympian Mo Farah who narrowly came second), it is the world's most popular half marathon, with most if not all of the runners doing it for charity. This is the iconic BUPA-sponsored Great North Run from the centre of the Town Moor in Newcastle to South Shields on the coast, just south of the Tyne. This event is involved with most types of sponsorship. It involves running, of course, and there are serious distance runners in what is, after all, a race event. It is televised and like the London and other marathons it is watched by millions. It is about entertainment, for the fun runners themselves and those who follow them at the event or on television. But above all this event is about support for causes and all-in-all the race raises millions. The electrifying atmosphere on the day is something people say can only be appreciated by being there and taking part. Celebrity runners are there next to fun runners and professional athletes. There is corporate activity as well as individual efforts. There is terrific support all the way along the rather interesting route, some of it along the south bank of the Tyne, some of it along the North Sea front, but many people say that the best bit is getting to the iconic Tyne Bridge, usually still at a walking pace for most because of the sheer number of bodies involved. Support comes in the form of what the organisers provide, such as drinking water, but it is the crowd all along the way with whistles, cheering sticks, horns, loudhailers and a lot of other noises from well-wishers, family and friends that boost the runners. Many causes gain income from people who are themselves sponsored to run. The causes include Cancer Research UK, Marie Curie Cancer Care, Macmillan Cancer Support, and Children with Cancer UK.

Visit www.greatrun.org/events/Event.aspx?id=1 for a history, images of the event, past winners with times, The Great North Run Hall of Fame, which now has many famous names from around the world including Benson Masya, Kevin Keegan, Sir Christopher Chataway and the Red Arrows, and a list of charities and associated Great Runs and events.

Stop Point

With an event like the Great North Run, many elements of sponsorship can be seen and understood. This kind of event is one of the most visibly sponsored events, much of it not contrived but organic and natural. The Great North Run is such a rich event in terms of emotion yet there is a rational perspective to it. Undertake the following: 1. Consider what the Great North Run is about and discuss what you feel BUPA get out of being the main sponsor; 2. Comment on what the many causes might get from being a part of this great event and also what the people who take part get out of this great day out.

Assignment

Choose a car manufacturing company that you feel would benefit from a sponsorship deal. In report format, map out the communications objectives behind the sponsorship programme and the reasons why the type(s) of sponsorship would be a better choice in achieving these than advertising. Describe the targets for the sponsorship and the nature of the activities that potentially would be undertaken. Highlight key advantages and disadvantages to such a deal and how its effectiveness might be monitored.

Summary of Key Points

- Marketing and corporate sponsorships are about relationships with various interest groups.
- Marketing sponsorship (as opposed to corporate sponsorship) has emerged as the commercial brand/product level function responsible for a set of activities that form the basis of a relationship between a sponsor and a sponsee.
- Sponsorship follows communication theory and can fit in with the integrated communications mix.
- Sponsorship is constantly changing and evolving. One constant is the need to evaluate its effectiveness.
- Objectives may vary with different forms of sponsorship. There are basically two broad objectives. On the one hand to raise awareness and on the other to enhance image. A number of sub-objectives co-exist with these.
- There are fundamental differences behind the use of different forms of sponsorship within the four broad categories of sports, the arts, causes and media programming.
- Event sponsorship is concerned with sports, the arts and causes, or a combination of these.
- Sponsorship has a relationship with both product placement and ambush marketing.

Discussion Questions

1. Distinguish between marketing sponsorship and corporate sponsorship. Explain, using examples, why the techniques used at both levels might be similar if not the same.
2. Explain what the word sponsorship means. Distinguish between this and other forms of communication such as advertising or PR.
3. Discuss how sponsorship works in theory, using examples to illustrate.
4. Comment on the notion that sponsorship is changing and evolving using examples of instances where this is the case to illustrate.
5. Discuss how different types of sponsorship can be used to reach different target audiences and achieve different objectives. Provide in your answer at least two examples of targets and objectives such as those behind sponsoring a sporting event or the arts.
6. Sponsorship comes in a number of forms. Explain the interface between sponsorship and other elements of the communications mix, using examples to illustrate.
7. Cause-related sponsorship can be used to achieve very different objectives from those of sports or media-related sponsorship. Discuss this notion and illustrate with examples.
8. Explain the concept of television programming sponsorship. Choose an example of such sponsorship to illustrate why an organisation might engage with this form of communications.
9. Discuss sponsorship practice in terms of the dangers of ambush marketing.
10. Explain how the effectiveness of sponsorship can be evaluated. Illustrate your answer with actual instances you are aware of.

Further Reading

Lamont, M. and Dowell, R. (2008) 'A process model of small and medium enterprise sponsorship of regional sport tourism events', *Journal of Vacation Marketing*, 14 (3): 253–66. http://jvm.sagepub.com/content/14/3/253
The idea that small firms only sponsor for philanthropic and non-strategic reasons is dispelled in this article. According to the authors, small-scale sports tourism events have been adopted by regional communities as part of an economic diversification strategy in response to industrialisation and urbanisation whereby sponsorship is often the only means available for financial support. The paper offers a conceptual model of the processes and interactions in sponsorship agreements that are intended to serve as a platform for further research.

McAllister, M.P. (2010) 'Hypercommercialism, televisuality, and the changing nature of college sports sponsorship', *American Behavioral Scientist*, 53 (10): 1476–491. http://abs.sagepub.com/content/53/10/1476

(Continued)

(Continued)

This article looks at commercial intrusion in the US national college football champion television broadcasts. It concludes that there has been an increase in advertising-free broadcast time directly as a result of the increased use of screen graphics with commercial iconography, and that there are implications for the use of hypercommercialism of sports and broadcasting as opposed to other areas such as fine arts or politics.

Saha, A. (2007) 'Changing ambivalences: exploring corporate sponsorship in the new culturally diverse artistic practices', *Journal of Creative Communications*, 2 (1&2): 23–41. http://crc.sagepub.com/content/2/1-2/23

This article looks at the commodification of difference in the context of corporate sponsorship of the particular photography exhibition 'Changing Faces', a collection of images of British Asian youth that challenged stereotypical representations of Asian youth cultures. According to the author the counter-hegemonic potential was undermined by the sponsorship (O2). This article adopts a cultural economy approach and suggests elaborate and entangled relations through which culture is mediated.

Scherer, J. (2007) 'Globalisation, promotional culture and the production/consumption of online games: engaging Adidas's "Beat Rugby" campaign', *New Media Society*, 9 (3): 475–96. http://nms.sagepub.com/content/9/3/475

The author is interested in the little-explored context of the production and consumption of online games. The study looks at a free downloadable rugby game and a parallel website for Adidas's sponsorship of the New Zealand All Blacks (Beat Rugby). This was meant to articulate the brand as globally cool with the company-wide target known as Jeeks (male, sports-loving, computer-literate 12 to 20-year-olds). The game and the electronic community facilitated a range of consumption and communication experiences for a transnational audience in a branded environment.

Steiner, T.J. (2008) 'Ethical issues arising from commercial sponsorship and from relationships with the pharmaceutical industry – report and recommendations of the ethics subcommittee of the International Headache Society', *Cephalalgia*, 28 (1): 1–25. http://cep.sagepub.com/content/28/3_suppl/1

This is an authoritative report for the ethics subcommittee of the International Headache Society on ethical issues in relation to commercial sponsorship within the pharmaceutical industry. The report makes two recommendations: 1. That sponsors' behaviour, which is controlled elsewhere, should be set within standards in relationships with sponsors that the International Headache Society should expect of its members. 2. That IHS members do not give support or legitimacy to any marketing activities of companies that do not conform to the Society's objectives that lead to meeting patients' needs.

REFERENCES

Admap (2002) 'Sponsorship', 432, p. 15, October, available at: www.warc.com/Content/ContentViewer.aspx?ID=881e449d-e8b1-4351-826c-9d112bae474d&CID=A76939&PUB=ADMAP&MasterContentRef=881e449d-e8b1-4351-826c-9d112bae474d

Admap (2010) 'Adstats: global sponsorship', May, pp. 46–7, available at: www.warc.com/Content/ContentViewer.aspx?ID=e67c20a4-9151-4595-971e-94ef77e7e-2df&q=sponsorship+evaluation&CID=A91828&PUB=ADMAP&MasterContentRef=e67c20a4-9151-4595-971e-94ef77e7e2df

Aurora, C.M., Mas-Ruiz, F.J. and Nicolau-Gonzalbez, J.L. (2005) 'Commercial and philanthropic sponsorship: direct and interaction effects on company performance', *International Journal of Market Research*, 47 (1): 75–99.

Bagnall, M. (2002) 'Event sponsorship: is the worst yet to come?', *Admap*, Issue 427, April. Available at: www.warc.com/Content/ContentViewer.aspx?ID=961f56a6-b21a-4e58-ac78-2a39fabfb177&CID=A72525&PUB=ADMAP&MasterContentRef=961f56a6-b21a-4e58-ac78-2a39fabfb177

Bal, C. (2009) 'Understanding sport-related emotions in sponsorship', *Admap*, November: 1–7.

Balabanis, G., Stables, R.E. and Phillips, H.C. (1997) 'Market orientation in the top 200 British charity organisations and its impact on their performance', *European Journal of Marketing*, 31 (8): 583–603.

BBC (2010) 'Procter and Gamble in London 2012 Olympics sponsor deal', *BBC News* – Business, 28 July.

Becker-Olsen, K. and Hill, R.P. (2006) 'The impact of sponsor fit on brand equity', *Journal of Service Research*, 9 (1): 73–83.

Belhout, L. and Copley, P. (1997) 'Message strategies for promoting humanitarian causes in the United Kingdom', in Proceedings of the 1st Academy of Marketing Conference, Manchester, Manchester Metropolitan University, pp. 1245–9.

Bennett, R. (1998) 'Corporate philanthropy in France, Germany and the UK', *International Marketing Review*, 15 (6): 458–75.

Bennett, R. (1999) 'Sports sponsorship, spectator recall and false consensus', *European Journal of Marketing*, 33 (3/4): 291–313.

Bennett, G., Cunningham, G. and Dees, W. (2006) 'Measuring the marketing communication activations of a professional tennis tournament', *Sport Marketing Quarterly*, 15 (2): 91–101.

Brennan, D. (2011) 'A review of existing research into how broadcast sponsorship works', Thinkbox, available at: www.thinkbox.tv/server/show/nav.949

Bryant, N. (1992) 'Breaking down the barriers', *Admap*, July. Available at: www.warc.com/Content/ContentViewer.aspx?ID=389d35c5-533c-40f3-ab68-c0c7e37bc7d3&CID=A490&PUB=ADMAP&MasterContentRef=389d35c5-533c-40f3-ab68-c0c7 e37bc7d3

Cannes Creative Lions (2011) 'HSBC British and Irish Lions Sponsorship: Lions, lions, lions – a story of rugby, wild animals and creativity', Creative Effectiveness Awards, available at: www.warc.com/Content/ContentViewer.aspx?ID=95dde75e-e441-4afb-b96d-79b81e96d2aa&CID=A94435&PUB=CANNES&MasterContentRef=95dde75e-e441-4afb-b96d-79b81e96d2aa

Chan, A. (2010) 'Shanghai Expo sponsorship delivers for brands', Warc Excusive, Starcom Mediavest, pp.1–9, available at: www.warc.com/Content/ContentViewer.aspx?ID=a3f249ed-c372-46b4-af78-cfc8a47c7435&CID=A93031&PUB=WARC-EXCLUSIVE&MasterContentRef=a3f249ed-c372-46b4-af78-cfc8a47c7435

Chen, J., Liu, D. and Whinston, A.B. (2009) 'Auctioning keywords in online search', *Journal of Marketing*, July, 73: 125–41.

Copley, P. (1999) 'Street walking with the Saatchis? Symbiosis through sponsorship in strategic alliances – a conceptual model from the humanitarian cause-related marketing field', in the McAuley and Sparks edited proceedings of the Academy of Marketing's annual conference, July, Stirling: University of Stirling.

Copley, P. and Hudson, J. (2000) 'Consumer perception of the brand/sponsorship relationship', in R. Mayer, S. Carter, L. Marshall and N. Ellis (eds), *Proceedings of the Academy of Marketing Conference*, Bridging the Divide, July, Derby: Derby University.

Copley, P., McLean, A. and Baker, J. (2012) 'A CSR-driven strategic alliance case study of the launch of the small business children's clothing brand Baggers and Tyne Gateway, a local North East England children's charity', *Proceedings of the Institute for Small Business and Entrepreneurship (ISBE) Conference*, November, Dublin: ISBE.

Cornwell, T.B., Humphreys, M.S., Maguire, A.M., Weeks, C.S. and Tellegen, C.L. (2006) 'Sponsorship-linked marketing: the role of articulation in memory', *Journal of Consumer Research*, December, 33: 312–21.

Crimmins, J. and Horn, M. (1996) 'Sponsorship: from management ego trip to marketing success', *Journal of Advertising Research*, 36 (4): 11–21.

Dahlen, M., Lange, F. and Smith, T. (2010) *Marketing Communications – A Brand Narrative Approach*. Chichester: Wiley.

de Chernatony, L. (1998) 'Dynamic brands need dynamic methods of measurement', *Researchplus*, January: 4.

Dolphin, R.R. (2003) 'Sponsorship: perspectives on its strategic role', *Corporate Communications, an International Journal*, 8 (3): 173–86.

Doyle, P. (1990) 'Building successful brands: the strategic options', *Journal of Consumer Marketing*, 7 (2): 5–20.

Erdogan, B.Z. and Kitchen, P. (1998) 'Managerial mindsets and the symbiotic relationship between sponsorship and advertising', *Market Intelligence and Planning*, 16 (6): 369–74.

Farquarson, A. (1998) 'Two causes, a single choice: which one gets your cash?', *The Guardian*, 25 November, pp. 9–10.

Farr, A. (1998) 'How brand values sort the strong from the vulnerable', *Researchplus*, January: 12–13.

Farrelly, F., Quester, P. and Greyser, S. (2005) 'Defending the co-branding benefits of sponsorship B2B partnerships: the case of ambush marketing', *Journal of Advertising Research*, 45 (3): 339–48.

Fast, J. (2011) 'Measuring the effects of sponsorship', The Marketing Donut/Slingshot Sponsorship, available at: www.marketingdonut.co.uk/marketing/advertising/sponsorship/measuring-the-effects-of-sponsorship

Gwinner, K. (1997) 'A model of image creation and image transfer in event sponsorship', *International Marketing Review*, 14 (3): 145–58.

Gwinner, K. and Bennett, G. (2008) 'The impact of brand cohesiveness and sport identification on brand fit in a sponsorship context', *Journal of Sport Management*, 22 (4): 410–26.

Hansen, F. and Scotwin, L. (1995) 'An experimental inquiry into sponsoring: what effects can be measured?', *Marketing and Research Today*, August, pp. 173–81.

Hauck, B. (2011) 'Will product placement change TV?', *BBC News*, available at: www.bbc.co.uk/news/magazine-12449502

Herrmann, J., Walliser, B. and Kacha, M. (2011) 'Consumer consideration of sponsor brands they do not remember: taking a wider look at the memorisation effects of sponsorship', *International Journal of Advertising*, 30 (2): 259–81.

Homer, P.M. (2009) 'Product placements – the impact of placement type and repetition on attitude', *Journal of Advertising*, Fall, 38 (3): 21–31.

Hoult, N. (2010) 'Npower may withdraw England Test sponsorship', *The Telegraph*, 18 March, available at: www.telegraph.co.uk/sport/cricket/international/england/7474978/Npower-may-withdraw-England-Test-sponsorship.html

IEG (2011) 'Sponsorship spending: 2010 proves better than expected; bigger gains set for 2011', IEG Sponsorship Report, 4 January.

Kraack, M. and Oliver, A. (1997) 'Sponsorship effectiveness: what is driving consumer response?' Proceedings of the ESOMAR Conference on Advertising, Sponsorships and Promotions, New Ways of Optimising Integrated Communication, April, Paris.

Kydd, J.M. (2009) 'Product placement's rise can be good for brand and viewer', *Admap*, 504, April, available at: www.warc.com/Content/ContentViewer.aspx?ID=6798b4a3-3e67-4e32-aa4c-32f9f2eb6a01&q=AID%3a89241&CID=A89241&PUB=ADMAP&MasterContentRef=6798b4a3-3e67-4e32-aa4c-32f9f2eb6a01

Lamont, M. and Dowell, R. (2008) 'A process model of small and medium enterprise sponsorship of regional sport tourism events', *Journal of Vacation Marketing*, 14 (3): 253–66.

Lin, F. and Hung, Y. (2009) 'The value of and attitude toward sponsored links for Internet information searchers', *Journal of Electronic Commerce Research*, 10 (4): 235–51.

Lund, R. (2009) 'Inter-organisational dynamics in sponsorship alliances – the case of the Royal Swedish Opera', Stockholm University School of Business Internal Paper, 18 May.

McAllister, M.P. (2010) 'Hypercommercialism, televisuality and the changing nature of college sports sponsorship', *American Behavioral Scientist*, 53 (10): 1476–1491.

Mawdsley, C. (1998) 'Measuring the effects of integrated campaigns', in *Proceedings of the Advertising and Academia Seminar*, September, London: IPA.

Mazur, L. (1998) 'Getting the most bang for your media buck these days calls for a much smarter, more lateral approach – something too many marketers have yet to master', *Marketing Business*, July/August, p. 24.

Meenaghan, T. (2011) 'Mind the gap in sponsorship measurement', *Admap*, February: 1–6.

Millman, I. (2000) 'Broadcast sponsorship works', Admap, April. Available at: www.warc.com/Content/ContentViewer.aspx?ID=d8245bfa-8d7c-4713-a497-d68820e569e9&-q=events+and+sponsorship&CID=A13717&PUB=ADMAP&MasterContentRef=d8245bfa-8d7c-4713-a497-d68820e569e9

Naish, J. (2011) 'Not now Mum, we're watching junk food TV', *The Times*, 8 February, pp. 48–9.

Nicholls, J.A.F., Roslow, S. and Dublish, S. (1999) 'Brand recall and brand preference at sponsored golf and tennis tournaments', *European Journal of Marketing*, 33 (3/4): 365–87.

Percy, L. (2006) 'Are product placements effective?', *International Journal of Advertising*, 25 (1): 112–14.

Perkins, A. (2010) 'The O2: a new blueprint for sponsorship', Institute of Practitioners in Advertising, Gold, Best media, IPA Effectiveness Awards: 1–23.

Peters, D. (2010) 'Sponsorship: TV imbues brand with validity and fame', *Admap*, April: 1–6.

Quester, P. and Farrelly, F. (1998) 'Brand association and memory decay effects of sponsorship: the case of the Australian Formula One Grand Prix', *Journal of Product and Brand Management*, 7 (6): 539–56.

Quester, P. and Thomson, B. (2001) 'Advertising and promotion leverage on arts sponsorship effectiveness', *Journal of Advertising Research*, January/February, 41 (1): 33–47.

Robinson, J. (2010) 'Ofcom confirms product placement on UK TV', available at: www.guardian.co.uk/media/2010/dec/20/ofcom-product-placement-uk-tv

Ross, L. (1977) 'The intuitive psychologist and his shortcomings: Distortions in the attribution process' in L. Berkowitz (ed.), *Advances in Experimental Social Psychology*, 10, pp. 173–220. New York: Academic Press.

Saha, A. (2007) 'Changing ambivalences: exploring corporate sponsorship in the new culturally diverse artistic practices', *Journal of Creative Communications*, 2 (1 & 2): 23–41.

Sargeant, A. and Stephenson, H. (1997) 'Banishing the battleship ladies – the emergence of a new paradigm of corporate giving', in *Proceedings of the 1st Academy of Marketing Conference*. Manchester: Manchester Metropolitan University: 903–16.

Savage, M. (1996) 'Rich and needy in perfect partnership', *Research*, August: 20.

Scherer, J. (2007) 'Globalisation, promotional culture and the production/ consumption of online games: engaging Adidas's "Beat Rugby" campaign', *New Media Society*, 9 (3): 475–96.

Scibetti, R. (2010) 'A presenting sponsorship that fits', *The Business of Sports*, 4 February, available at: www.thebusinessofsports.com/2010/02/04/a-presenting-sponsorship-that-fits/

Sleight, S. (1989) *Sponsorship*. London: McGraw Hill.

Smith, G. (1999) 'Sponsor "fit" with brand is new debate', *Marketing Week*, 22 April, available at: www.marketingweek.co.uk/sponsor-fit-with-brand-is-new-debate/2021411.article

Solis, B. (2011) 'The decline of traditional advertising and the rise of social media', CIPR, available at: http://conversation.cipr.co.uk/posts/brian.solis/the-decline-of-traditional-advertising-and-the-rise-of-social-media.

Stewart. D. and Short, S. (1997) 'Sponsorship: a facilitator of commercial communication', *Proceedings of the 1st Academy of Marketing Conference*. Manchester: Manchester Metropolitan University. pp. 1501–4.

Sweney, M. (2008) 'No more sponsorship of BBC-run events after damming report', *The Guardian*, 21 July, available at: www.guardian.co.uk/media/2008/jul/21/bbc.television3

Sweney, M. (2009) 'Internet overtakes television to become biggest advertising sector in the UK', *The Guardian*, 30 September, available at: www.guardian.co.uk/media/2009/sep/30/internet-biggest-uk-advertising-sector

Sweney, M. (2011) 'What future for product placement?', *The Guardian*, 28 February, available at: www.theguardian.com/media/2011/feb/28/product-placement-british-television

Thompson, I. and Vickers, S. (2002) 'Sponsorship: the real deal', *Admap*, 432, October: 19–22.

Van Reijmersdal, E., Neijens, P. and Smit, E.G. (2009) 'A new branch of advertising: reviewing factors that influence reactions to product placements', *Journal of Advertising Research*, December, 49 (4): 429–49.

Ventura, C. and Cardani, M. (2010) 'Event and sponsorship valuator: a smart approach to evaluate the sponsorship', ESOMAR, WM3, Berlin, October.

Wakefield, K.L., Becker-Olsen, K. and Cornwall, T.B. (2006) 'I spy a sponsor: the effects of sponsorship level, prominence, relatedness and cueing on recall accuracy', *Journal of Advertising*, 36 (4): 61–74.

Whannel, G. (2009) 'Television and the transformation of sport', *Annals of the American Academy of Political and Social Science*, 625 (September): 205–18.

Witcher, B.J., Craigen, G., Culligan, D. and Harvey, A. (1991) 'The links between objectives and function in organisational sponsorship', *International Journal of Advertising*, 10 (1): 13–21.

Zajonc, R.B. (1968) 'Attitudinal effects of mere exposure', *Journal of Personality and Social Psychology Mongraph Supplement*, 9 (2, pt. 2): pp.1–27.

16 Personal Selling

CHAPTER OVERVIEW

Introduction

This chapter deals with personal selling's role in the marketing and marketing communications mix. This book acknowledges the traditional marketing concept-type view of selling (satisfaction of customer needs) and the relationship selling approach but also recognises the more aggressive variants of selling that exist that could be considered selling orientation rather than marketing or relationship marketing orientation. The approach taken in this book is to treat personal selling as part of the marketing communications mix. The differences between personal selling and representation are made. Personal selling is put into the context of the selling/buying process. The nature and role of personal selling are obviously changing over time to reflect changes in the communications mix as well as society. Technological advances that threatened to mean less jobs in terms of what were conventional sales forces may now play a more supportive role to the salesperson/representative who can concentrate more on interpersonal skills. Selling is portrayed here in terms of ideas around motivation, objectives and the role of sales training rather than other related topics such as sales force management that are left to more general marketing or sales management texts.

Learning objectives

The chapter seeks to explore and explain the nature of personal selling and its role within the marketing and communications mix. More specifically, after reading this chapter the student will be able to:

- explore the nature and role of personal selling within integrated marketing communications;
- consider different types of selling and the role of representation in differing contexts;
- outline the advantages and disadvantages of personal selling in contrast to those of other parts of the marketing communications mix;
- investigate selling as a process that informs personal selling in practice;
- assess approaches to sales training and development;
- understand and appreciate selling performance and effectiveness.

THE NATURE AND TYPES OF PERSONAL SELLING

The nature of personal selling

In terms of other forms of communication, personal communication is relatively expensive. A face-to-face sales meeting may be up to ten times the cost of a telephone call. Costs can vary quite substantially depending upon the context. Generally the cost per face-to-face contact that includes salaries and expenses has been estimated to exceed £100 (about $150) and some observers might suggest this figure to be much higher. Christie (2013) calculates the cost of a sales call on this kind of basis and suggests a figure of up to $250 (about £170) as a general average. However, Mack (2008) suggests a cost of between $201 and $500 (about £130–£330) for a pharmaceutical industry call. Another example comes from Minster (2012) who calculates the average cost per call at $336 (about £220 per call). The message is that face-to-face personal selling costs vary but are never inexpensive.

Personal selling is often called dyadic communication because it involves more than one person, but this is somewhat of a misnomer since it suggests a dyad, i.e. two. Personal selling very often involves more than two players. It is inevitably constantly in competition with other forms of communication, especially with digital forms. However, advances in technology should make life easier and more effective for those involved with personal selling, although advances in interactivity (see Chapter 10 of this book) appear to threaten the one-to-one hold that personal selling has had over other elements of the communications mix.

Selling and sales are, of course, part of the marketing communications mix and there is clearly a marketing–sales interface that Hughes et al. (2012) suggest is often sub-optimal and therefore can act as an inhibitor to success and the ability of the firm to create lasting customer value. Not only should marketing as a whole be integrated but so too should marketing communications, as discussed in Chapter 1 of this book and where selling interfaces and (hopefully) integrates with other communication elements. The effects of increasing or decreasing spending on one element as opposed to another are of interest to Smith et al. (2006) who highlight the importance of timing and sequential marketing communications on the effectiveness of multimedia spending in terms of generating sales leads, securing appointments with customers and closing sales. As with any other form of communication, the basic model of the communication process is a useful starting point in understanding the nature of personal selling. The sender–receiver, basic communication model outlined in Chapter 2 of this book again applies, but here of course the person doing the selling becomes the source of the message, usually for and on behalf of an organisation. The receiver may be a channel member customer, a direct customer or the consumer depending upon the selling context. As discussed later in this chapter, the selling process is basically different from other forms of communication in terms of message, noise and feedback, but the general model still applies.

Personal communication

Personal selling is a form of personal communication – or forms, since personal selling varies a lot in its style. It is sometimes described as the 'hard sell' that is epitomised by the 'foot in the door' sales type, characterised by unscrupulous timeshare operators or the archetypal secondhand car salesman. Clearly this is not the case for the most part. Selling activities take many forms in the buying/selling process depending upon the context in which selling takes place. Sometimes the sales people are information providers and representatives of the organisation, sometimes order takers, and other times order makers. The main difference between personal selling and the other types of marketing communication is that this form of communication is two-way, enabling immediate feedback and an evaluation of transmitted messages. Personal selling messages can be tailored to the consumer's individual needs. A key part of personal selling is that objections can be overcome by quickly providing an explanation and if needs be information. As will be discussed later in this chapter another important part that personal selling has to play is the encouragement of the placing of orders and closing the sale. This is not something that can be done with much of the rest of the communications mix, but it is set against a backdrop of relatively recently introduced consumer protection in, for example, the UK by way of devices such as cooling-off periods. As the environment has changed so too have selling styles.

The old, ethical, position that once dominated and that followed the marketing concept of meeting customer need was superseded by a much more aggressive approach during the 1980s and beyond. Since the 1990s links have been made with the relationship marketing and indeed the customer relationship management (CRM) paradigms. Here relationship marketing and selling involves consideration of long-term cost effectiveness that is linked with mutual benefit as opposed to what can be termed transactional marketing and selling. Such relationships are seen as an important resource in developing a sustainable competitive advantage for sellers and buyers (Abed and Haghighi, 2009). Research conducted by Boorom et al. (1998) on relational communication traits suggests that salespeople with lower levels of communication apprehension are more highly involved with communication interactions, which facilitates increased adaptiveness and sales performance. This has meaning for those concerned with sales performance and its relationship with improved salesperson communication skills and consequently training to acquire such improvements. Communication apprehension has been shown to have small but significant affects on salesperson performance (Pitt et al., 1999). In the hotel services context Lee et al. (2005) found that a salesperson's experience, willingness and power have an effect on the life-expectancy of the relationship between meeting planners and hotel salespersons, with trust and satisfaction with the latter on the part of the former being central to such a relationship.

Personal selling activities have changed although the nature of personal selling in essence has not, apart from the move toward relationships as suggested above. What have also changed are the methods of contact with the advent of email, video conferencing, Skype, (having replaced the retired Windows Messenger in 2013) and online team meetings. Other changes include PowerPoint-type presentations and the ubiquitous cell phone (often referred to as mobile or smart phones depending upon their capabilities), tablets and other similar devices. Sales people are involved still with, as expected, actual selling, working with channel members, route planning and guiding (servicing products and accounts), surveying (collecting and feeding back information), training and recruitment, entertaining, travelling, conferences and seminars. Key account management is not new but has gained a certain prominence in recent times whereby a kind of 80/20 rule of thumb Pareto-type Principle applies to the selling situation, i.e. that 80 per cent of the organisation's effort goes into the 20 per cent of its client base that are key accounts. Some see a danger in this in that too much of the company resources might go to too small a number of clients. Others see the benefits and have set up key account divisions or teams.

Advantages and disadvantages of personal selling

The advantages of using personal communication are that it is at least two-way interaction and instant feedback can be had. There is much less noise in the system compared with other communication tools. With personal selling, participation in the decision process is greater on the part of the seller. Messages can be tailored, particularly in response to feedback that should be actively sought by the seller, which becomes part of the organisation's marketing information system. The net result is that the selling process, if handled and managed well, has a huge potential to solve customer and consumer problems. Targeting, negotiation and flexibility help make personal selling efficient and this function can genuinely break through the clutter and engender behaviour change. The disadvantages are the aforementioned high cost per contact, low reach, frequency and control over the message in terms of being told by the organisation what to say and not say. There are some situations therefore that arise whereby the reason for using the personal approach in the first place is defeated. Some of these problems, such as motivation, can be solved through training and development as discussed later in this chapter.

The future of selling

Personal communications generally and selling in particular are changing radically. In particular the integrating of direct (especially tele) marketing in field sales operations has already happened for cost reasons if nothing else. Screening leads and credit ratings are all possible thanks to technology and better, faster communications. The net result is cost reduction and higher rates of closure. This will become even more potent should organisations improve their relations with audiences through public relations activities and improved aftercare. Worries over technology wiping out the selling function that surfaced around the beginning of the new millennium appear to be unfounded. However, more than a decade later and in the middle of a prolonged recessionary period around the world but around Europe in particular, there is evidence of high street retailing (and hence retail selling jobs) coming under threat at least in part from the success of the Internet and e-commerce. For example Reilly (2013), using information from the UK Centre for Retail Research, suggests that Internet sales 'will close 5000 High Street stores and cost 50,000 jobs' in the UK alone. This is said to reflect a 20 per cent increase in online shopping fuelled by increased use of smart phones and tablets. According to Reilly 'Britons spent 14 million hours trawling websites paying around 113 million visits to online retailers' on Boxing Day 2012. Apparently, online sales for the John Lewis organisation are growing at 40 per cent per year.

Types of selling

In terms of dealing with the various players in the chain, including customers and suppliers, salespeople will have to acquire new skills. They will have to become more opportunistic but also better market analysts and researchers and much more team oriented, contributing more towards things like new product development. In other words, the salesperson's role is constantly changing. Salespeople can be many things. They can be viewed in quite a narrow way such as:

- persuaders;
- prospectors;
- sellers of goods and services;
- procreators or order getters;
- problem solvers;
- order takers or collectors;
- order supporters and providers of information and advice;
- demonstrators;
- representatives of the brand or company.

There is, however, a broader view. Personal selling can be viewed as part of personal communication and as such as a discipline that is multi-functional, including relationship building and the maintenance and servicing of accounts. There is also a need to clarify the context in which selling is to be applied since the nature and role of the function will vary enormously depending upon the context.

Customer types

A broad way of seeing the various types of buyer is to create a divide on the basis of the consumer, customer and client with whom selling activities will be of a differing nature. In many situations these types or labels can be used interchangeably. For example with hotel services the terms customer, client, patron or guest might equally apply.

- *Consumer* is the term used for the user or consumer of the product or service. In this instance the consumer acquires goods or services for personal use or ownership, i.e. is not a reseller.
- *Customer* is the term used for the purchaser of the product or service, where the type of selling often requires contact with the retail trade (the seller's customer within channels of distribution) and/or the consumer direct. A customer in this instance may be referred to as a shopper if the purchaser is dealing with a retailer. Alternatively the customer may be industrial or organisational within B-to-B markets and where, for example, components will be sold to manufacturers to be incorporated into a finished product.
- *Client* is the term used for the user of a professional product or service where the type of selling may require specifications and the offering is often tailored to client needs. In some cases a client will be a reseller after, for example, a product is modified and sold on by the client to another user.

Selling activity can also be classified according to customer buying behaviour and, consequently, the type of approach needed:

- Creative selling occurs in 'first buy' situations where analysis and assessment, preparation and presentation, are required for a successful sale.
- Order taking is routine and either a straight or modified re-buy.
- Missionary selling does not involve persuasion or taking orders but is more of a supportive function, where influence is key to a successful sale.
- Retail selling should involve sound product knowledge in many situations since customers need advice and assistance in order to make buying decisions (but sadly this is not always the case in reality).

The Snapshot below discusses the nature of sales representation and then offers two contrasting scenarios (retail generally and medical/healthcare) in which the role of the 'sales rep' is very different and requires consideration of different functions.

Snapshot   Different kinds of sales representation: on being in retail or being a medical sales representative

In many industries and sectors the representative must have specialist, requisite product, company and industry or at least sector knowledge and knowledge of the self and customers (whether actual or potential). In pharmaceutical contexts for example, sales representatives are highly trained and often drug specialists with perhaps a degree or even a PhD in chemistry or a related science such as biology. At the very least the representative would have to understand scientific and medical terms. In many other industries and sectors this is not the case, for example if the sales representative is dealing with domestic furniture. Nevertheless, in such cases knowledge of different sorts is still key. The role may or may not involve travel just as there may or may not be a degree of 'cold calling'. Representation may only occur if there are substantive sales leads where a high level of interest in products or services has been shown. There may even be a prescribed way of selling within a company in which the representative is trained. There is variability in terms of, for example, the representative's ability to offer discounts or price reductions or on remuneration and other forms of payment, for example whether commission only is paid or whether there is a basic salary with bonuses.

The retail context

Depending upon the requirements of management the retail sales representative may have to deal with a range of functions including:

- Conducting basic marketing research by engaging with customers and asking them about issues such as level of service or store layout.
- Dealing with complaints and handling returns and exchanges or, if appropriate, suggesting alternatives.
- Merchandising.
- Stocking, re-stocking and general inventory control.
- Actually taking and closing the sale or passing the customer on to someone else in the chain.
- Dealing with store opening and closing and generally store hygiene.

The medical context

The rep will specialise within a particular area of medicine or health care and consequently be responsible for particular products or product ranges. For example the rep may be involved with respiratory care and therefore with nurses and consultants but also physiotherapists, all of who can influence sales of oxygen masks, breathing tubes and other apparatus relating to pre- and post-operative situations where aids to respiration are crucial to patient care. Typically the rep will be involved with:

- Identifying the various types of customer needs and feeding back information on, for example, competitor activity and on competitive products, to the sales manager/director.

- Making presentations to the various influencers involved with various situations. This might be to hospital doctors and nurses and consultants or to general practitioners (GPs) and other staff in general practice surgeries. Alternatively this may involve physiotherapists, pharmacists or other practitioners.
- Attending sales meetings often organised around the ideas of the 'journey cycle' every three months with an annual meeting once per year.
- Actual selling through persuasion, closing the sale and engaging with support activities post purchase but also building and maintaining relationships and achieving sales targets.
- Organising conferences/events and attending such events, managing display stands and associated activities, and managing the budgets for such activities.
- Developing and maintaining knowledge of clinical data and other aspects of products and medical techniques and procedures relevant to the particular area of medicine or healthcare. Attend training courses and seminars/conferences to help facilitate this.
- The usual daily tasks of keeping records, contact development, planning work schedules with others in the team and the team or area manager, arranging appointments, and where appropriate engaging with 'cold calling'.

Stop Point

Consider the role of the sales representative generally and also in terms of a retail and a medical/healthcare-type context. Undertake the following: 1. Think about the differences between consumer and organisational marketing and selling. Examine the similarities and differences that exist within these two distinct contexts; 2. Think also about the level of training required generally for these two contexts. Draw up a list of typical sales training activities for each.

PERSONAL SELLING AS PART OF THE COMMUNICATIONS MIX

Personal selling, as alluded to above, is the most expensive part of the communications mix when analysed on a cost per contact basis. Personal selling is generally most effective in the latter stages of the hierarchy of effects model (see Chapter 3 of this book) and is more closely associated with action and decision making than building awareness. This is important when considering the integrated marketing communications mix. Each tool should be used when it is most appropriate within the marketing communications plan.

When to use selling in the marketing and communications mix

The marketing mix

When the product or service is a complex one or the purchase decision is a major one the features of the product will have to be shown and this may require demonstration and/or trial. This would be typical of any B-to-B situation. Where channel members are involved, product/service training can be needed. Price, especially the final price, may be subject to negotiation. With the larger manufacturers large margins are usually available to support the selling operation.

The communications mix

There are clearly key areas for consideration within the interfaces between selling and other marketing communications elements. Below are some of these more specific interfaces that have associated qualities.

Personal selling and advertising

Advertising may not be an appropriate tool when information needed by the buyer is too complex or detailed to convey. This may be linked to the complexity of a product's context and the buying situation (see Chapter 3 of this book on buyer behaviour, decision making and information search) where personal selling allows unmediated communication that can work well in conjunction with mediated communication, such as advertising in terms of achieving different objectives with different communication forms. The message may be too specific for the more general media and targets dispersed, meaning that the advertising does not reach the target market effectively. Therefore both media and effectiveness of message issues arise. The relative importance of the mix functions was discussed earlier in this book in relation to, for example, stages of the product life cycle where advertising may be relatively important in the early stages to create awareness but selling is more important as explanation is needed. The size of the target is important, as is information need, the value of the purchase, the resources available, product complexity, and post-purchase requirements in terms of assurance and support. Much of this could be resolved by injecting money but doing so could prove wasteful. Advertising can be used before the salesperson makes contact. In industrial selling certainly advertising can be used to provide information, especially facts, before contact is made, making the communication process more efficient by saving on personal contact time. Personal selling improves reach and can increase profit or have the opposite effect if done badly, i.e. increase costs and harm profit. Advertising can be an aid to selling when it:

- saves time;
- provides useful information before contact;
- can be used as a visual aid in follow-up;
- is an ego booster;
- is a refresher;
- helps build brands;
- gets the customer involved.

Personal selling and PR

Similar logic can be applied to PR (see Chapter 13 of this book) where the situation is much the same as with advertising with regard to the complexity of the context, but with PR communications objectives are different where generally there is an emphasis on the 'feel good factors' associated with PR. It has long been argued that the raison d'être for PR is to provide a better marketing environment in which to sell. Salespeople are bound to feel better if they are operating against a backdrop of good publicity, a strong corporate image and/or brand image. Of course the opposite will be the case if negative PR ensues.

Personal selling and direct marketing

This includes the obvious link to data base marketing and telemarketing as discussed in Chapter 12 of this book. Direct marketing support leads to, for example, better closing, more time selling and more information disseminated.

Personal selling and sales promotions

This link has always existed in terms of incentives and other promotions and the selling function. The usual rationale for sales promotions is discussed in Chapter 11 of this book. At the selling/sales promotions interface free merchandise, offers and other sales promotion techniques can add excitement to the selling situation, giving it that extra buzz and a real lift, if handled with care.

Personal selling, relational marketing and networking

Networking is particularly relevant to organisational and SME marketing whereby it has been increasingly understood that information exchange and collaborative relationships are a requirement. This would include relationships with customers but also distributors, suppliers, and even symbiotic relationships with competitors. For example, a number of competing SMEs can get together in order to provide enough clout to be able to tender for a contract that on their own would not be possible. Personal representation in such a networking situation would be essential.

THE SELLING PROCESS

The elements of the selling process

Before a salesperson can begin to sell to customers she/he must research and plan. The selling process therefore contains the following (see Figure 16.1).

Salesperson ⟶ Research ⟶ Plan ⟶ Sell ⟶ Customer

Figure 16.1 Elements of the selling process

This fits within the overall framework of the sales process that begins with a search for (potential) customers and moves through a sequence of events to closing the sale and aftercare. In terms of the AIDA model (as discussed in Chapter 3 of this book), selling involves:

Attention
(Attract)
Interest
(Rouse)
Desire
(Develop)
Action
(Close)

The hierarchy of effects is therefore revisited in terms of personal communication. The message is not a monologue but part of a dialogue (the dyadic communication mentioned in Chapter 1 of this book) and as such the sender/messenger is in a much better position to explain, discuss, or meet objections.

Other schema can be used to explain the selling process, for example the stimulus-response S-R behaviourist model, which includes mediated feedback and a problem-solving (cognitive) model that suggests a problem-solution-purchase sequence having the brand as the solution that leads to satisfaction (see Chapter 3 of this book).

The selling process is a combination of:

- preparing – prospecting, qualifying targets, developing relationships;
- presenting – presenting sales materials, meeting objections, closing;
- after sales support – further developing relationships, maintaining trust and commitment.

There is first Preparation and then Presentation to consider in developing the selling process (see Table 16.1).

Table 16.1   Preparation and presentation in developing the selling process

Preparation	Needs	Pre-call planning	Approach
Analysis to build profiles and lists, qualified into types	Knowledge of products, company objectives and channels, DMUs, history	Developing a rapport Using telephone, email for advance appointments Avoid mistakes and assumptions	What are the needs, wants, desires, features and benefits sought?

Presentation	Objections	Closing	Follow-Up
Of features and benefits Tailored or 'canned'/pre-done presentation?	Make clear what the objection is Agree and counter Compensate the objection with a benefit Boomerang the objection Probe/feel if the objection is emotional Deny/contradict	Look for buying signals – gestures, nodding, comments, questions Assumed close (assume deal is done) Either/or close (give reasons) Social Validation close (what others do) Impending Event close (tie in to event) No Closing close (leave to trust)	Check on satisfaction Check even when nothing bought Trust may be highest with no close

Care should be taken, especially with the type of closing technique chosen. There is evidence in the literature that the act of closing when deliberately choosing a closing technique may reduce the amount of trust a prospect has in the seller and have a potentially negative effect on the buyer–seller relationship (for example, Hawes et al., 1996).

Once the sale is complete the next step is After Sales Support. It has long been recognised that there is a need for an after sales support function and strategy (for example Armistead and Clark, 1991; Clark and Armistead, 1991). After sales support is a set of activities provided to cater for eventualities once a good or service has been sold. Most sets would include guarantees/warranties, depending upon the type of product upgrades, and a repair service. Many instances include strong relationships between manufacturer and customer that go beyond often shorter periods of time attached to warranties or guarantees typically seen on consumer products. After sales support is crucial for long-term brand development whereby the customer can be helped to use the brand in the way it was intended to be used. Trust, commitment, and possibly some degree of brand loyalty (perhaps, at least, repeat business) can be helped along by after sales support that can help achieve customer satisfaction with the brand.

After sales support, depending upon the context, can also involve:

- Maintenance.
- Servicing involving parts and/or labour.
- Technical support, often via a help desk or telephone helpline or one that is Internet/online-based and often operating on a 24/7/365 basis: this can include the kind of support that is proactive and which provides preventative measures as well as solutions to problems.

A professional approach to after sales support will help sell products but also assist with customer retention and satisfaction. For example, as research in the automotive industry by Ahmad and Butt (2011) suggests, after sales service is a related, if separate and unique, dimension of consumer-based brand equity.

Things that make a sales person an effective communicator

A good number of things help to make this happen:

1. Apprehension can affect the salesperson's performance. Pitt et al. (1999) discuss the effects of communication apprehension on a number of variables including performance variables of the salesperson where this research found a small but significant effect on such performance. Similarly Boorom et al. (1998) found that sales people with lower levels of communication apprehension are likely to be highly involved with communication interactions which lead to increased sales performance.

2. The level of flexibility exercised by the salesperson should be as high as possible since the freedom to adapt messages is a positive thing if the salesperson can be trusted to use this facility well. If training is of high quality there should be no need to exercise control. One of the advantages and strengths of personal communication, and hence personal selling, as discussed earlier in this chapter, is the ability to create a dialogue and dyadic communication.

3. Building customer relationships, remembering that depending upon the selling context, relationships can be very simple or very complex. They may or may not have a pivotal role to play in the success of a deal. The fast moving consumer good (fmcg) context may see a relatively simple relationship with channel members compared to, for example, a business-to-business situation where a £2m deal on dump and fork lift trucks with training, maintenance and other issues as part of a long-term contract. With the latter, personal selling, representation, customer care and support, after sale support and relationship development become much more relevant than other elements of the communications mix such as PR or advertising. For example advertising would normally be highly relevant to and a key element of an fmcg campaign, whereas it would feature less prominently in an organisational marketing setting. Personal selling has long been seen as the marketing function that increases in importance over other forms of communication as it moves along the spectrum of companies from fmcg towards heavy industry. Alongside this is the relationship with behaviour models with the emphasis on search and risk as discussed in more depth in Chapter 3 of this book.

Other factors such as timeliness become more important in organisational/industrial markets. Of course it is recognised that consumer behaviour will start to look something like organisational buyer behaviour as one moves from fmcg to consumer durables, but the same logic applies since consumers will behave in many instances in a much more rational (as opposed to an emotional or impulsive) way. The traits for effective salespeople have been identified by James (2012) as:

- *Assertiveness.* This is neither passive nor aggressive but allows the sale to move forward without the customer being offended or frustrated and where the close can be achieved 'without forcing the customer's pace'.
- *Self-Awareness.* This is essential for the building of stronger customer relationships though controlling emotions and expanding positive ones.

- *Empathy.* This may require adaptation of behaviour to the moods and emotions of the customer. This requires listening and observing in order to read and get to know what the customer is feeling and guage how to empathise.

- *Problem Solving.* This leads to 'new ways to satisfy the customer's needs' whether these are financial or emotional. This is a process that guides the customer through the decision-making process and is the opposite of simply making a sales pitch.

- *Optimism.* Here a sense of balance is needed. If a sales call goes badly the view on it should be that the next one will be better.

Other writers might use different words to mean the same thing or add new ones such as strong self-esteem, having a sense of getting things done, being a risk-taker, being competitive, being sociable or being sceptical, but this does depend on selling style (see below).

- The old argument that sales people should have knowledge and empathy with the prospect and for example be punctual, organised, energetic, enthusiastic and honest still holds when dealing with personalities and what is required to do the job well. The opposite, of course, of the effective sales person is one who is unprepared, a problem avoider, is not dependable, is presumptuous, or is late for appointments.

- Source considerations were deemed important generally in the discussion in Chapter 2 of this book on source characteristics. Since personal selling is based to a large extent on the relationship between seller and buyer, source characteristics become personal characteristics, and these are clearly very important to achieving effective communication. Likeability and credibility are crucial if the communication is to be effective. First impressions are important and can impact on whether a customer likes or dislikes the sales person. Dress code and personal hygiene therefore matter. Relationships are important and familiarity is useful in terms of liking, but it can breed contempt. Rewarding the customer engenders likeability where the reward may be material and/or psychological and empathy is a positive thing. Similarity of the salesperson to the customer can engender likeability. Credibility will make the salesperson more persuasive and therefore being trustworthy, honest, and expert in the field is useful.

- Message considerations include appeals to interests and/or immediate concerns and needs. Having empathy with a customer's predisposition and allowing the customer to participate are important. Benefits not features should be transmitted and the USP considered. A unique or unusual sales presentation can work but can also backfire and simple messages might work best of all. There is a case for both one-sided and two-sided messages (in a similar fashion to those used in advertising as discussed in Chapter 8 of this book), depending upon the education platform of the prospect. The interest shown by the prospect is important in terms of where the key benefit is used. If interest is low then key benefits should be expressed quickly. If interest is high then a build-up should be considered with key benefits being used near the end of the sales interview. This, again, is the equivalent of primacy and recency being used to deliver advertising messages as discussed in Chapter 8 of this book. Relative advantage(s) of new products over old should be expressed in terms of benefits.

- Noise considerations include the atmosphere in which the sales meeting takes place, the attitude of other players such as secretaries, the receptionist and other gatekeepers, and the knowledge levels of the salesperson. Many things can constitute noise, or barriers to communication (see Chapter 2 of this book).

- Feedback considerations can be formal or informal perceptions of the salesperson and the extent to which that salesperson is receptive to signals and other cues. The extent to which salespeople are willing to disclose information along with feedback determines the size of the information base that is public (see Chapter 2 of this book).

The Snapshot below illustrates some of the dilemmas facing charities and other causes when contemplating adopting and adapting business and commercial tools like those of marketing and selling.

Snapshot   Why charities should sell like
a business – or not!

The Scottish Social Enterprise Academy (2012) describes a retail selling situation as follows:

> Half hidden up a side street in Inverness lies Ness Soap, a shop like few others. The products are delightful, all locally produced and of the highest quality. They are made by people with a range of barriers to employment; disability, learning difficulties and the like. The benefit to the trainees is obvious, a real job in a safe and supportive working environment.

The Academy suggests that this kind of approach to raising money for causes is attracting attention. Put simply Ness Soap trades like a business and sells to consumers (shoppers) and to hotels and restaurants 'across the Highlands, trading like a business, or a more accurately a social enterprise'. The Academy attributes the success of the cause's marketing strategy to Director and Academy tutor Lindsey Kelly who is a specialist in marketing for non-profit distributing organisations and is experienced in work with charities and community organisations 'who are also beginning to sell goods and services rather than shake tins for their income'. According to the Academy Programme Manager David Bryan, social enterprise 'is beginning to take hold across the Highlands as an alternative to the public sector delivering key services'. Bryan believes that:

> The challenge comes with the detail: Can the social benefit be sold to the customer at the same time as the product? How does earned income sit with charitable status? How can a charity be taken seriously by big private sector corporations?

These are some of the key questions in this area of social and commercial activity based on activities happening in the Scottish Highlands. Across in New York, Dan Pallotta (2012), writing in the *Wall Street Journal*, asks 'Why can't we sell charity like we sell perfume?' and 'What if we let philanthropies operate like businesses?' This could mean that charities should 'pay for talent, advertise aggressively to build market share even build a stock market for charity', or it could mean that charities and causes simply take advantage of some of the tools that are available from the business world, tools such as effective sales techniques.

Pallotta mentions this in the context of the early Puritan settlers and points out the dilemma of being 'pulled in opposite directions by competing value systems. They were extremely aggressive capitalists, but they were also strict Calvinists, taught that self-interest was a sure path to eternal damnation' and asks 'How could they negotiate this psychological tension?', suggesting that 'Charity became a big part of the answer – an economic sanctuary in which they could do penance for their profit-making tendencies, at five cents on the dollar'.

Another key question is one of wages, salaries or other payments and rewards within charitable organisations and how much especially the top people are paid for their services. Pallotta asks 'Want to pay someone a half-million dollars to try to find a

(Continued)

(Continued)

cure for pediatric leukemia?', suggesting that, if so, they may be 'considered a parasite'. As Pallotta points out, the USA is a philanthropic nation and compares this with the UK, suggesting that Americans give twice as much to causes of one type or another and yet 'we cling to a puritan approach to how those donations are spent: self-deprivation is our strategy for social change'. Pallotta sees this as dysfunctional and makes a case for getting rid of the 'narrow, negative label' that is 'not-for-profit', suggesting that it is 'time to change how society thinks about charity and social reform'.

Stop Point

Consider the role that business and commercial tools and activities like sales and other marketing techniques might have. Undertake the following: 1. Consider the suggestion that there is a dilemma or series of dilemmas that face charitable organisations and other causes when it comes to the adoption and adaption of such techniques. Develop a discussion around the suggestion that charities and other causes should employ the best sales and marketing professionals who are then paid for their successes for and on behalf of such organisations; 2. Think also about the idea that labelling organisations as not-for-profit is narrow and dysfunctional. Make a case for either keeping the label 'not-for-profit' or for giving charities and other causes different, more commercial and business-like names.

MAKING PERSONAL COMMUNICATION WORK FOR SELLING

Planning and managing the selling process

There is a need to plan and manage personal communication, especially the selling process. This is not sales management, which is concerned with issues such as territory design which clearly are important but are part of the broader sales management textbooks. The concern here is with the management of a form of communication that includes prospecting and identifying potential need and sufficient resources for acquiring products/services. This requires pre-call planning, finding sales leads, qualifying prospects, or preparing for initial contact through training and establishing which style may be appropriate to follow. The impact of the technological and communications revolution on personal communication and the selling function is clearly important.

Prospecting and making appointments

Prospecting includes identifying someone who has a potential need and sufficient resources for acquiring products/services. The process begins with pre-call planning – finding sales leads, qualifying prospects, and preparing for initial contact. Prospecting also includes the activities in the establishing and the analysis part of the persuading styles discussed earlier. Prospecting therefore deals with:

- identifying the market geographically;
- researching and identifying market potential;
- instigating the approach and checking on buying days;

- confirming appointments;
- gaining an understanding of consumer tastes, needs, other brands and competitors;
- the preparation of things such as testimonial material, advertising copy, coupon information, samples or market surveys;
- recognition of buyer authority and location in the organisation;
- finding ways of getting to the decision maker.

Barriers to communication

Some of the barriers to communication are a lack of knowledge, ways of greeting, indifference, personal appearance, distractions, emotion, and competitive offering. Good sales practice includes consideration of sales training and presentation; for example techniques for closure, meeting objections, and helping develop selling styles for particular situations utilising interpersonal awareness. The salesperson needs to research in order to obtain knowledge, integrity and trustworthiness. Sellers must have these to match the buyer/customer desire for them to have knowledge of problems, keep their needs in mind and have the ability to show they are trustworthy. Overcoming these and other barriers can be achieved by good sales training and preparation. Consider the following:

- enthusiasm – act on it;
- self organisation;
- silence – listen and observe, show interest and seek agreement;
- use questions to find out wants;
- be sincere, show confidence and attention;
- knowledge – know the key issue(s);
- honesty and praise where due;
- remember names and faces;
- do not forget a customer;
- close the sale in a final action.

The seller should therefore remember that:

- the customer is important regarding needs;
- identification and analysis of needs to explain behaviour are required;
- benefits, not features, should be sold;
- demonstration as to how needs can be satisfied should be shown.

There are four basic areas of knowledge that a salesperson should be concerned with:

- themselves;
- the company;
- the product(s);
- the customer(s).

Sales training

There are many sales training packages available. Most follow the basic idea that there is a need to train to prepare and a need to train to present, including closing. There is greater recognition now that salespeople need to be aware of relationships and the importance of after sale care and support and the further development and maintenance of the relationship. This of course assumes that relationships are indeed important, which they may not be in some contexts. The following is a typical example of scenario training.

Preparing for the sales interview

- Research the customer (find out who it really is).
- Research the product (be trained in it, carry literature and/or online links).
- Research relationships (between the organisation and the customer).
- Objectives (number of calls required).
- Objectives (regarding other products for the same customer).
- Objectives (regarding other customers for the same product).
- Ask questions (to gain information about client needs).
- Ask questions (to obtain leads).
- Ask questions (to keep control of the interview)

Questions to ask about preparing for the interview

- WHAT should a salesperson do to determine prospects?
- WHAT information should be kept on customers or potential customers?
- HOW can a sales appointment be arranged?
- SHOULD all calls be by appointment?
- WHAT system should a salesperson develop to know on whom to call – and when?
- HOW should sales literature and/or online material be used at a meeting?
- HOW should any products/samples be used?
- WHAT techniques can be used to keep control of a sales interview?
- WHAT should a salesperson know?
- HOW would you find leads for cold calls?

The sales presentation

- Explain the benefits, not the features, and talk in terms of customer need.
- Meet objections and probe to make any objection specific. Put any objection into perspective.
- Close the sale by looking for buying signals, seal the deal, and then keep quiet.

Questions to ask about the presentation

- WHAT techniques can salespeople use to close the sale?
- HOW can a price objection be handled? How can objections be overcome?
- WHAT are the differences between features and benefits?
- HOW should a salesperson conclude an interview that has not resulted in a sale?
- WHAT should salespeople avoid doing in handling objections?
- WHEN offering alternatives to close the sale, how should this alternative package be structured?
- HOW should a salesperson use customer needs – identified by questions – to help close?

Motivation

How best to motivate is a key area in terms of positive versus negative treatment, where a reward and punishment approach may not work on its own. A more 'cultivate rather than threaten' approach to the salesperson's needs can motivate, and keep motivated, people in what can be a very difficult job where they can feel autonomy and good about themselves. Positive reinforcement can enhance job satisfaction rather than merely telling people within a sales force what to do. Role models are very appropriate whereby leading by example can be the appropriate behaviour to build trust and have a positive effect on overall performance. This can be facilitated by the following:

Regular meetings

- Clear definitions of roles, providing freedom from emotional exhaustion.
- Remuneration, guidance and incentives all help to avoid emotional burnout in what can be a lonely job and can bolster commitment and loyalty.

It should be noted that the remuneration debate over what is the best balance between commission-only, fixed salary or a combination of both is recognised but not developed here as it is more of a sales management issue. The pros and cons to this can be found in most standard marketing and sales management texts.

Selling styles

Competencies

Training courses address issues surrounding the use of technology such as the Internet, connectivity devices and electronic record keeping, but the core of many sales training programmes remains prospecting, presenting, closing and 'keeping the doors open'. In the 'situational selling' approach there is an emphasis on adapting styles to meet the needs of customers. Changing styles requires the ability to use a variety of different behaviours depending on the situation. Selling style is the salesperson's pattern of behaviour as perceived by customers and it is the way the salesperson comes across to customers which influences them. The customer's interpretation can be quite different from what the seller intended. In a behavioural selling approach, Hersey (1988) has suggested four areas of competency that are necessary in selling that affect selling styles:

1. *Establishing competency* deals with the product, company and sales person. This is necessary when the prospect is uninformed and uncommitted in order to provide information about the salesperson, product and company. The purpose of the call should be stated and questions regarding the sale asked that are carefully designed to have a positive consequence that is either a direct sale or helps build rapport.

2. *Persuading competency* clearly deals with persuasion. This is appropriate when the prospect is uninformed but interested. Questioning should be designed to gain insights into the prospect's needs and problems. The salesperson should be encouraging and guiding, showing the prospect that they are interested, and probing to find important information. They should also be advocating by matching features of the product to the prospect's expressed needs. Features that fulfil needs become benefits and acceptance of benefits is a critical bridge.

3. *Committing competency* where prospects are knowledgeable but encouragement and problem solving are required since interest brings apprehension. The salesperson can enhance the situation by summarising acknowledged needs and capitalising on buying signals. The order should be asked for and buying signals followed. A trial close of sale can follow while responding to any objections that may reflect scepticism misunderstanding, drawbacks and any attempt to postpone, i.e. achieve customer commitment.

4. *Fulfilling competency* where there should be continued follow-up to ensure a long-term relationship based on customer satisfaction is achieved. This involves maintenance and monitoring of the account, expanding business inside (new products) and outside (referrals) the customer's organisation, and responding to complaints. The salesperson should listen, understand and reflect back to the customer. Acknowledging problems helps to maintain rapport.

A salesperson should have a wide range of flexibility and be able to use all four (or a combination of the four) competencies in order to address differing situations.

Style adaptability

Diagnostic skills are the key to adaptability since these provide indications of what style(s) to use and when to use it/them. Selling personality differs from selling style in that it combines the salesperson's self-perception with the perceptions of others. A useful framework for describing selling personality and helping increase interpersonal awareness is the Johari Window (Luft and Ingham, 1955). Joe Luft and Harry Ingham (hence Jo+hari = Johari) were two US psychologists interested in personal and group development and self-awareness in terms of the self in relation to others and disclosure and feedback of information. The Johari Window model was devised from studies of group dynamics as a tool of assessment that can help understand and improve such relationships. The model is still seen today as relevant to soft skills development where empathy, cooperation, or interpersonal development is important to communication and team development.

The Johari Window model is used generally in a self-development context and of particular interest here in sales training to depict the relationship between a salesperson's self-perception of selling behaviour and the perception of others (usually customers). The Johari Window has four cells or areas/regions, usually displayed in a grid as shown in Figure 16.2.

	(known/unknown to salesperson about self)	
	KNOWN	UNKNOWN
(known/unknown to customer about salesperson)		
KNOWN	Public	Blind
UNKNOWN	Private	Unknown

Figure 16.2   The Johari Window

- The *public area* is known to both salesperson and customer by others and the self where there is knowledge about feelings, attitudes, perceptions, experience and skills/competencies. The public area is where cooperation and effective communication rather than conflict and confusion/misunderstanding can occur. It is desirable to develop this area from the company sales function perspective but it is inevitable that established salespeople will have larger public areas than new salespeople of whom less is known

- The *blind area* is unknown to the salesperson but known to the customer either because of lack of feedback (customer says nothing) or because the salesperson has been inattentive to verbal and non-verbal customer communication.

- The *private area* is known to the salesperson but unknown to the customer and is private because the salesperson has not disclosed information to customers (or customers have not received and understood any communication). This describes the hidden self of the salesperson.

- The *unknown area* is often referred to as the subconscious of the salesperson but also involves activities unknown to others, here especially customers but also other players such as distributors or suppliers. The aim is to reduce this as far as possible.

The size and shape of the areas are important. Feedback and disclosure can affect these. Feedback is the extent to which customers are willing to share their perceptions with the salesperson and the extent to which the salesperson is receptive to customer communication. Disclosure is the extent to which salespeople are willing to share information with customers and the extent to which customers are interested in and receptive to other salesperson communication. Feedback and disclosure determine the size of the public area since information can evolve that was previously unknown to both parties.

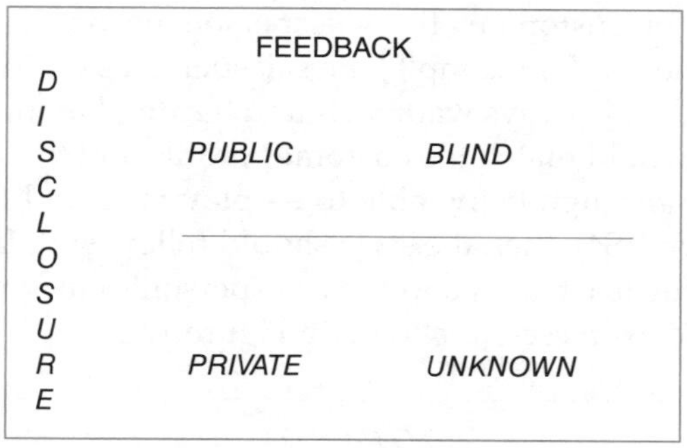

```
                        FEEDBACK
    D
    I
    S       PUBLIC          BLIND
    C
    L       _____
    O
    S
    U
    R       PRIVATE         UNKNOWN
    E
```

Figure 16.3   Feedback and disclosure effects

The Johari Window model is related to other behavioural models that are used extensively in team and self-development training where the goal is to look at the performance of people and teams and the effort required to deal with internal workings and external outputs. For example, Tuckman's Forming, Storming, Norming and Performing model is used in team development and the Hersey-Blanchard Situational Leadership model is used in team development and the development of management styles. There are links also to emotional intelligence theory (the awareness and development of emotional intelligence) and to Transactional Analysis (understanding the unknown cell in particular). This can also be linked to Maslow's self-actualisation element of the Hierarchy of Needs model as discussed in Chapter 3 of this book.

Sales types

Successful salespeople constantly monitor their relationships with the customers they contact. If things are going well then the seller must try to determine the reasons why. If they are not going well they must then try to determine what to do for success next time. There are various ways of getting the information on the customer they need in order to build up customer profiles but these are often built up over the experience of a long relationship. Below (see Figure 16.4) is a commonly used example of selling styles or types.

- S_1 is formal, controlled, disciplined, head-oriented, organised and appears reserved, withholds feelings, is task-oriented, cool and distant.
- S_2 is aggressive, pushy, communicates readily, appears confident, authoritative, someone who takes charge, assertive, overbearing, direct and active.
- S_3 is passive, gentle, hesitant, quiet, difficult, submissive, accepting, shy, thoughtful and subtle.
- S_4 is informal, responsive, spontaneous, gut-oriented, apparently disorganised, impulsive, someone who expresses feelings, warm, close and relationship-oriented.

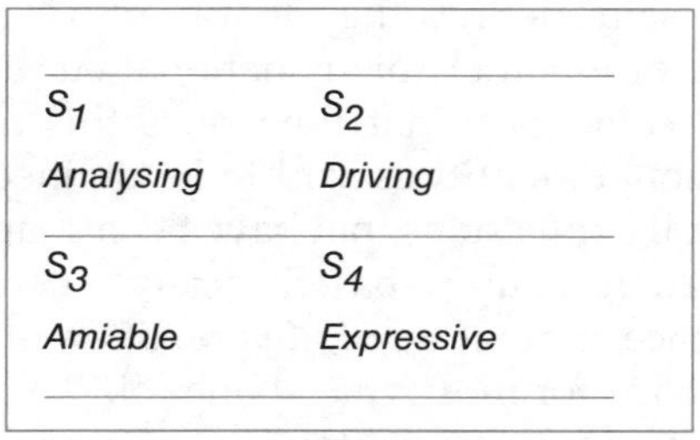

S_1	S_2
Analysing	*Driving*
S_3	S_4
Amiable	*Expressive*

Figure 16.4   Selling styles or types

With different types of customers the salesperson needs to adjust their behaviour accordingly (change style). If, for example, the salesperson's customers are all of one type (Analysing, S1) and they will always want facts and figures, having little time for chit-chat, then an analysing style would match the customer profile and the salesperson would need to control the interview through being able to employ facts and figures. If, however, the customers are Expressives (S4), then the style should follow suit. In reality these scenarios would be very rare if they exist at all and the salesperson's customer base is likely to be a mix of types. This can be expressed as shown in Figure 16.5.

```
                            C O N T R O L

              (Self-controlled)              (Dominant/Assertive)
                 ANALYSING                        DRIVING
      ASK                                                          TELL
                  AMIABLE                        EXPRESSIVE
                 (Easy going)              (Spontaneous/emotive)

                             E M O T E
```

Figure 16.5   A salesperson's requirements in order to adjust behaviour

Any organisation that takes selling seriously will invest in sales training but will also wish to know how well the function is working. Performance evaluation relies on both quantitative and qualitative measures. Quantitative measures are things such as call reports, number of calls, which customers or prospects, what was disclosed, and the outcomes of sales meetings in terms of volume and value. Qualitative measures are much more subjective and deal with things like attitude and commitment, product knowledge and appearance. In short the latter is more to do with behaviour and how to control salespeople rather than more concrete, tangible outcomes. Research and evaluation in personal selling are considered in more depth in Chapter 17 of this book.

The Snapshot below discusses what coffee means as a cultural artefact and symbol in Thailand, or more specifically Bangkok, and asks the reader to consider cultural change and its effect on sales and the selling process in the context of the various forms of coffee available.

Snapshot   Selling coffee in Thailand – why cultural framing matters

Cultural analysis is, as Sunderland and Denny 2007: 57) point out, 'inherently multimodal' and is about 'listening as well as observing … about actions as well as artefacts'. Culture, it is often said, defines the identity of a nation. However, the more searching question is one of whether this is national culture, regional culture, subculture or multi-cultural contexts. What then does this mean for retail selling in Thailand? Thailand's national identity is said to be defined by the gentleness of its language and other cultural expressions that have been shaped by its history and traditions; these stem from an agriculture-based society whereby most people still live in rural areas where the pace and nature of life are different from those of New York, Paris or London, and perhaps for most Thais Bangkok, Thailand's capital, where the population is clearly urban and cosmopolitan in common with most capital cities.

Selling coffee in Bangkok is, however, for the likes of Starbucks, a different challenge from that in London, Paris or New York. According to anthropologists and marketing researchers Sunderland and Denny (2007), what Parisians see when they imagine coffee is 'imagery of smoky cafés and brasseries, metallic espresso machines encased by small cups, saucers, spoons, sugar cubes, and the (recently added) chocolate morsel, a comptoir and tiny tables crowded and bound through intense conversation'. However, in the USA 'images of a cardboard cup-carrying workforce' or perhaps 'bookstores, laidback social settings' might be created in the minds of those who are asked about what they see. In Bangkok the reality of coffee consumption on the go is 'coffee poured over ice in plastic bags' with 'condensed and evaporated milk' in 'bags tied for easy carrying and punctured with a straw' according to Sunderland and Denny (2007). These researchers suggest that 'the meaning of coffee, indeed the meaning of most things, is located in a tangled web of our own creation'.

The answer to the question of how we see things like coffee 'is discerned through a decoding of the signs and symbols we might observe in the consumption of coffee – whether in Paris or Bangkok, in the selling of coffee (advertisements or retail environments) and implicit in the talk about coffee'. Sunderland and Denny's (2002) study suggested that in Bangkok 'Coffee is not black and is not hot' and 'Coffee's presence is indexically marked by the evaporated milk cans, often Carnation ... That is to say, if one sees Carnation, coffee is likely nearby, just as smoke is a semiotic index of fire.' It also suggested that 'Coffee does not have a place' like it does in Parisian cafés or US coffee houses. Rather it is routinely sold on the street by street vendors as well as in 'Old storefronts in Chinatown'. It is of course sold in Starbucks which in Bangkok, according to Sunderland and Denny, is 'truly a place for coffee ... inhabited by young, cell phone carrying professionals. Starbucks is about fashion and social currency. Coffee more generally, is not ... when served, is not "refined" through a mechanical process' and there is 'no homage to bean grinding machinery or dripping process; there is an absence of mechanical spectacle'.

However, while the influence of the likes of Starbucks cannot be denied, in recent times Bangkok has seen many cafes and coffee shops opening with changing consumption habits that mean changes to what is being offered for sale. There is competition with coffee offerings in the form of energy drinks that contain caffeine and are a substitute for people seeking caffeine hits, but coffee too has moved on as independent establishments seek to reposition coffee offerings upmarket in line with coffee consumption worldwide. This means a move away from instant coffee towards the sourcing of a higher quality coffee bean and different methods of brewing coffee where the goal is flavour rather than a quick cold drink.

Stop Point

In order for a company like Starbucks to achieve successful sales in a market like Thailand, or more specifically Bangkok, it needs to know that market, just as it would any other. Think about what coffee means in a cultural sense in Bangkok. Undertake the following: 1. Discuss what you would recommend to a company interested in investing in coffee houses or cafes about how to sell its coffee offerings in Bangkok. Include in your discuss consideration of the importance of the local or insider point of view and also the importance of local culture in terms of how this frames the way coffee products are sold and what kind of coffee product is sold; 2. Examine the importance of the symbolic nature of the various forms of coffee in terms of coffee consumption in Bangkok, whether this is the traditional Thai street vendor coffee,

(Continued)

(Continued)

Starbucks, or coffee offered by an independent coffee house. Comment on cultural change in terms of the move from instant coffee as a symbol of Western modernity to more upmarket coffee offerings being symbolic of Thai (or at least Bangkok) modernity and the influence of this on the selling process in the Bangkok context.

Profiling Exercise	
S_1	S_2
Analysing	*Driving*
S_3	S_4
Amiable	*Expressive*

Figure 16.6   Selling styles

Assignment

- S_1 is formal, controlled, disciplined, head-oriented, organised and appears reserved, withholds feelings, is task-oriented, cool and distant.
- S_2 is aggressive, pushy, communicates readily, appears confident, authoritative, someone who takes charge, assertive, overbearing, direct and active.
- S_3 is passive, gentle, hesitant, quiet, difficult, submissive, accepting, shy, thoughtful and subtle.
- S_4 is informal, responsive, spontaneous, gut-oriented, apparently disorganised, impulsive, someone who expresses feelings, warm, close and relationship-oriented.

Use the grid to describe the kinds of customer profile each of the other four selling styles would match.

Consider the following.

Think about yourself in relation to others and other people in relation to others, how they perceive themselves and how others perceive them in order to help develop selling styles. Someone who knows you well and likes you has been asked to give a brief description of your general behaviour or character style.

How do you imagine their description read? How would someone who doesn't like you alter the description?

Summary of Key Points

- Personal selling is a form of personal communication that lies within the integrated marketing communications mix.
- Communicating personally has advantages and disadvantages and this is the case also for personal selling.

- There are different types of selling that operate in differing contexts. The sales-person may be out to get a sale or to represent the organisation in a missionary or ambassadorial way.
- Personal communication is a process that informs the personal selling process. This is usually denoted as a sequential set of events or stages.
- Approaches to sales training and development have become more sophisticated in the last decade or so. Stereotyping still exists and can be problematic and a hindrance to successful selling.
- Selling performance and effectiveness should and can be measured.
- The emergence of the Internet and other technology has impacted upon the selling function. As technology evolves this impact will be even greater.

Discussion Questions

1. Discuss the difference in meaning between the terms personal communications and personal selling.
2. Examine how personal selling can best be incorporated into the IMC mix.
3. Discuss the recent changes that have taken place in the personal selling function and the impact of relational ideas on such changes.
4. Outline the personal selling process, highlighting, with examples, the fundamental importance of interactivity.
5. Discuss the importance of closing the sale, illustrating this with at least one closing method.
6. Write a brief account of emerging roles within the selling function taking account of the impact of new technology.
7. Examine the relationship between frequency and cost per contact.
8. Discuss the balance that can be achieved between fixed salary, bonuses and incentives, and the link with motivation of salespeople.
9. Account for the interfaces between selling and other marketing communications mix elements, detailing one such interface with examples.
10. Discuss the importance of measuring sales performance. Include in your discussion examples of both qualitative and quantitative measures.

Further Reading

Amir, I. and Qureshi, K. (2007) 'SBE (Pvt.) Ltd: the focussed selling approach', *Asian Journal of Management Cases*, 4 (2): 143–59. http://ajc.sagepub.com/content/4/2/117.2 The case study at the centre of this article is Unilever Pakistan Limited (UPL) and a Lahore distributor – SBE (Pvt.) Limited. UPL wanted better sales growth and in order to achieve this the multinational launched Project Ferrari in July 2002. The authors provide the reader

(Continued)

(Continued)

with an account of UPL's efforts to achieve double-digit distribution growth and SBE's concerns about the efficacy of Project Ferrari.

Faulkner, S., Leaver, A., Vis, F. and Williams, K. (2008) 'Art for art's sake or selling up', *European Journal of Communication*, 23 (3): 295–317. http://ejc.sagepub.com/content/23/3/295
This article is both theoretical and empirical in its intent. It is based on the discrepancy between the pursuit of art and the realities of the marketplace set in the television production context. At the theoretical level it deals with the idea of creative liberation, yet on the empirical level it deals with the pragmatic nature of the market including slow growth, regulatory changes, external financial backers, and the acquisition of small firms by what the authors call 'acquisitive super-indies'. Ultimately this article is about creative people 'selling up', i.e. selling their assets for the 'right' price, and therefore it is about exposing the tension between creativity and money-making.

Kara, A., Andaleeb, S.S., Turan, M. and Cabuk, S. (2013) 'An examination of the effects of adaptive selling behaviour and customer orientation on performance of pharmaceutical salespeople in an emerging market', *Journal of Medical marketing: Device, Diagnostic and Pharmaceutical Marketing*, 13 (2): 102–14. http://mmj.sagepub.com/content/13/2/102
This article is about customer orientation and adaptive selling behaviour and the effects on sales performance. This topic has been researched in developed markets but less so in emerging markets. This article is about Turkish pharmaceutical sales people and sales performance in relation to both customer orientation and satisfaction, where it was found that customer orientation is a significant factor in terms of performance, satisfaction and adaptive selling but that adaptive selling behaviour, while significantly related to sales performance and customer orientation, is not so crucial to satisfaction.

Lee, S., Su, H-J. and Dubinsky, A.J. (2005) 'Relationship selling in the meeting planner/ hotel salesperson dyad', *Journal of Hospitality & Tourism Research*, 29 (4): 427–47. http:// jht.sagepub.com/content/29/4/427
The authors claim that meeting planners can be a substantial source of revenue and yet hotels and their salespeople are under-researched when it comes to this potentially key area of hotels' business. The article distinguishes between transactional and relationship marketing and selling and puts forward a case for trust and satisfaction being achieved by the latter.

Mai, R. and Hoffmann, S. (2011) 'Four positive effects of a salesperson's regional dialect in services selling', *Journal of Service Research*, 14 (4): 460–74. http://jsr.sagepub.com/ content/14/4/460
This article provides an account of how buyers react to salespeople with dialects. The results of the study show that buyers do not devalue salespersons with a dialect, which may be contrary to popular belief. Rather, the quality of speech and associations with the regional dialect can improve satisfaction with the salesperson and the selling organisation and foster purchase intention. This is linked to expectations on the part of the buyer with respect to the quality of speech. The authors suggest that companies should consider training in speech quality rather than salespeople concealing regional dialects.

REFERENCES

Abed, G.M. and Haghighi, M. (2009) 'The effect of selling strategies on sales performance', *Business Strategy Series*, 10 (5): 266–82.

Ahmad, S. and Butt, I.P. (2011) 'Can after sales service generate brand equity?', *Marketing Intelligence and Planning*, 30 (3): 307–23.

Amir, I. and Qureshi, K. (2007) 'SBE (Pvt.) Ltd: The focussed selling approach', *Asian Journal of Management Cases*, 4 (2): 143–59.

Armistead, C. and Clark, G. (1991) 'A framework for formulating after sales support strategy', *International Journal of Operations and Production Management*, 2 (3): 111–24.

Boorom, M.L., Goolsby, J.R. and Ramsey, R.P. (1998) 'Relational communication traits and their effects on adaptiveness and sales performance', *Journal of the Academy of Marketing Science*, 26 (16): 16–30.

Christie, M. (2013) 'Calculating the cost of a sales call', SalesForce Training and Consulting, 5 March, available at: www.salesforcetraining.com/sales-training-blog/sales-management-training/calculating-the-cost-of-a-sales-call/

Clark, G. and Armistead, C. (1991) 'After sales support strategy: a research agenda', Operations Management Group, Cranfield School of Management, Cranfield Institute of Technology.

Denny, R.M. and Sunderland, P.L. (2002) 'What is Coffee in Bangkok?', *Research*, November, Chicago: Practica Group, available at: http://www.practicagroup.com/pdfs/Denny_and_Sunderland_What_is_Coffee.pdf

Faulkner, S., Leaver, A., Vis, F. and Williams, K. (2008) 'Art for art's sake or selling up', *European Journal of Communication*, 23 (3): 295–317.

Hawes, J.M., Strong, J.T. and Winick, B.S. (1996) 'Do closing techniques diminish prospect trust?', *Industrial Marketing Management*, 25 (5): 349–60.

Hersey, P. (1988) *Selling – A Behavioural Science Approach*, London: Prentice Hall.

Hughes, D.E., Le Bon, J. and Malshe, A. (2012) 'The marketing-sales interface at the interface: creating market-based capabilities through organisational synergy', *Journal of Personal Selling and Sales Management*, winter, 32 (1): 57–72.

James, G. (2012) '5 traits of highly successful salesmen', *Inc. Magazine*, 27 January, available at: www.inc.com/geoffrey-james/5-traits-of-highly-successful-salesmen.html

Kara, A., Andaleeb, S.S., Turan, M. and Cabuk, S. (2013) 'An examination of the effects of adaptive selling behaviour and customer orientation on performance of pharmaceutical salespeople in an emerging market', *Journal of Medical marketing: Device, Diagnostic and Pharmaceutical Marketing*, 13 (2): 102–14.

Lee, S., Su, H.-J. and Dubinsky, A.J. (2005) 'Relationship selling in the meeting planner/hotel salesperson dyad', *Journal of Hospitality & Tourism Research*, 29 (4): 427–47.

Luft, J. and Ingham, H.V. (1955) 'The Johari window – a graphic model of interpersonal awareness', Proceedings of the Western Training Laboratory in Group Development, Los Angeles: UCLA Extension Office.

Mack, J. (2008) 'Fewer sales reps leads to higher costs', Pharma Marketing Blog, available at: http://pharmamkting.blogspot.co.uk/2008/11/less-sales-reps-lead-to-higher-costs.html

Mai, R. and Hoffmann, S. (2011) 'Four positive effects of a salesperson's regional dialect in services selling', *Journal of Service Research*, 14 (4): 460–74.

Minster, A. (2012) 'How much does a sales call cost?', Experts 4 Entrepreneurs Blog, 17 December, available at: www.e4ecommunity.com/_blog/Blog/post/How_Much_Does_a_Sales_Call_Really_Cost.

Pallotta, D. (2012) 'Why can't we sell charity like we sell perfume? The Saturday Essay', *Wall Street Journal*, 14 September, available at: http://online.wsj.com/article/SB10000872396390444017504577647502309260064.html

Pitt, L.F., Berthon, P.R. and Robson, M.J. (1999) 'Communication apprehension and perceptions of salesperson performance: a multinational perspective', *Journal of Managerial Psychology*, 15 (1): 68–86.

Reilly, J. (2013) 'Booming internet sales will close 5000 High Street stores and cost 50,000 jobs', *MailOnline*, 2 January, available at: www.dailymail.co.uk/news/article-2255677/

The Scottish Social Enterprise Academy (2012) 'How can a charity sell like a business?', 12 June, available at: www.theacademy-ssea.org/latest/news/735_how_can_a_charity_sell_like_a_business

Smith, T.M., Gopalakrishna, S. and Chatterjee, R. (2006) 'Integrating marketing communications at the marketing-sales interface', The Marketing Science Institute, Cambridge MA: MSI Reports.

Sunderland, P.L. and Denny, R.M. (2007) 'Framing cultural questions: what is coffee in Benton Harbour and Bangkok?', in P.L. Sunderland and R.M. Denny (eds), *Doing Anthropology in Consumer Research*. California: Left Coast Press Inc., pp. 57–78.

17 Marketing Research and Evaluation

CHAPTER OVERVIEW

Introduction

This chapter deals with research in and evaluation of marketing communications. The notion that each element of the communications mix needs to be part of a carefully planned, integrated strategy in order to maximise effectiveness, to obtain a 'unified message', was put forward at the beginning of this book in Chapter 1. In Chapter 4 of this book a decision sequence model/framework was described as a framework for the development of this integrated strategy, the key stages being some form of situation analysis followed by decisions on targeting, objectives and positioning, then strategies, budgets and implementation, and finally evaluation and control. In other words, the final stage of the model attempts to answer the question 'Did we get there?' in a post-mortem kind of way. However, it is crucial that a campaign be monitored and evaluation and control be concurrent with an 'Are we getting there?' approach to marketing communications management, so that evaluation and control are exercised before, during and after a campaign. This chapter uses the APIC decision sequence model as discussed in Chapter 4 of this book and maps out where research has a part to play in what is essentially a risk-reduction set of exercises designed to enhance and facilitate decision making. As such this is the marketing research–marketing communications interface. The nature of research at the pre, during and post stages of campaigns is considered in terms of message creation and achievement of objectives and marketing research is applied to the elements of the marketing communications mix.

Learning objectives

This chapter seeks to explore the nature of research and evaluation in terms of marketing communication as part of the overall marketing effort. More specifically after reading this chapter the student will be able to:

- understand the nature and role of research and evaluation in relation to marketing communications and define the role of integration in this process;
- outline research issues at the varying stages of a marketing communications plan;
- explain the types of research and data collection (including online) methods that are appropriate and available at each stage;
- understand how a research and evaluation attitude adds value and how it can be used to improve marketing performance;
- become familiar with research techniques including those of a digital nature that have gained in popularity in recent times;
- become familiar with the use of continuous research in marketing communications;
- explain how marketing research can be applied to the elements of the marketing communications mix.

RESEARCH AND EVALUATION WITHIN A DECISION SEQUENCE FRAMEWORK

The question of when to apply research and evaluation can be answered simply by considering the decision sequence framework or model as advocated in Chapter 4 of this book. Research and evaluation can be appropriate in one form or another at each stage but in broader terms takes place before, during and after a campaign in terms of pre, concurrent and post testing:

- Pre testing is carried out before a campaign is launched.
- After implementation monitoring and evaluation research comes in the guise of concurrent (or during) testing.
- Post testing occurs after the target has been exposed to the whole of the communication campaign and is a kind of 'post-mortem'.

For example, attitudes may be tracked via tracking studies over a long period with regular testing at intervals to measure the effects of a particular communication so that the communication itself, a brand and purchase intentions may be involved.

Evaluation of the marketing communications effort can involve the obvious; sales increases for example. It is desirable to be 100 per cent sure but this is not possible. This kind of evaluation is very tempting, especially in today's climate of pressurised performance, but cause and effect, especially with advertising, is not as concrete as it is with, for example, sales promotion coupon redemptions. Research is fundamental to marketing communications management because it aids decision making and provides direction. Research should be used frequently throughout a campaign, from before the campaign starts, throughout its various stages as well as in a post-campaign way. As mentioned in Chapter 4, the research and evaluation process can be linked with the marketing communications decision sequence model in the following ways.

Analysis

- Situation analysis and targeting – consumer research, competitive research and product research.

Planning

- Targets, objectives and positioning – internal and feasibility research.
- Strategy development – developmental pre-test of concepts.

Implementation

- Budget – final pre-test and execution of production.
- Implementation – test marketing and internal feasibility research.

Control

- Evaluation – post-test against objectives.
- New situation analysis research – cycle begins again.

Research can either be conducted in situ, i.e. in the field, or artificially in the 'laboratory'. With the latter, respondents are exposed to a variety of devices such as concept boards or animatics/photomatics (see below) and asked to discuss various aspects or answer questions regarding certain issues. This is controlled by the researcher but lacks the realism of actual situations where marketing communications has to operate. A discussion around a coffee table about certain concepts, however, is not meant to be a substitute for a piece of 'real life' communication that is absorbed with distractions or noise of one sort or another. Research conducted 'in the field' sees communication being examined under more natural settings but leads to different kinds of issues being tested, such as competitive activity or media content. Marketing research reaches out to people to find out who they are, what they prefer, what attitudes they have, what appeals to them most, what they respond to, how they react and ultimately who buys. In other words who does the target audience consists of what do they want, when do they need it, where does it sell best, how does it reach them, and why do they buy it.

Advertising (and to an extent other forms of communication) effectiveness testing can be divided into the two components of communication and behaviour. This can then be combined with a consideration of the three stages of pre, during and post campaign research testing (see Table 17.1).

Clearly this incorporates the 'hierarchy of effects' models where communications move consumers through a series of stages from source to the purchase, as discussed in Chapter 3 of this book (the usual unawareness, awareness, knowledge, liking, preference, conviction and purchase) and considers the type of testing appropriate at each stage. As can be seen, pre, during and post testing are considered under communication factors where source variables factors include attitude change, trust or credibility, likeability and, on the negative side, the possibility that the source might dominate the message at the expense of the brand/product/service. The message and the means by which it is communicated (delivery, usually a medium of one sort or another) are bases for evaluation. The message is usually tested to see if intended meaning has been communicated to the receiver, and this might include the effectiveness of individual message elements; for example copy, straplines and headlines. Media decisions need to be made based on research so that the marketer is better able to decide on the media class (broadcast or print) and sub-class (newspapers or magazines), or specific vehicles (one magazine rather than another). Placement within vehicles can also be the subject of research as can number of insertions, length of a television commercial and best means of scheduling, possibly using bought-in audience research such as data from the National Readership Survey (NRS) or the Broadcasters Audience Research Board (BARB) (see Chapters 9 and 10 of this book).

Table 17.1   The three stages of campaign research testing

	COMMUNICATION		BEHAVIOUR
	Source, Message, Media		Pseudo-purchase, Purchase
PRE-TESTS	Focus groups	Physiological	Test marketing
	Checklists	Direct mail	Single-source
	Split-run	Theatre	
	Readability	On-the-air	
CONCURRENT	Recall		Single-source
	Attitude		Diaries
	Tracking		Store cupboard checks
	Coincidental		
POST-TESTS	Readership	Attitude	Single-source
	Recall	Association	Split-cable
	Awareness	Audience	Enquiry
		assessment	Sales counts

Behavioural factors include intent to buy, trial and purchase and brand loyalty. The actual practice of consumers can be very different from the theoretical stance of the hierarchy of effects and therefore action measures, which allude to an intention to purchase rather than actual behaviour and include brand choice, calls or written contact and/or store visits. Such measures are important in the early stages of the PLC where one objective will almost certainly be awareness. Clearly the objectives of the communication need to be stated at the outset and measured accordingly. When there is high involvement there is a great likelihood that intention to purchase will become an actual purchase, as with luxury goods such as fashion items.

Before the marketing communications effort (pre-testing)

Unfinished communication

This largely relates to communications materials, marketing or corporate, for example visuals, copy, mock ups, roughs or animatics/photomatics. Pre-testing the ideas contained within this decreases risk but costs money. This might be viewed as a waste or it may be done as a matter of course, in conjunction with testing of the broader marketing mix as with new product development. Whether or not these devices represent the real thing is questionable but both qualitative and quantitative testing can be conducted. Concept testing is used to weed through, for example, creative ideas and ideas on positioning. Roughs are used, i.e. early artwork, storyboards or some other form of expression, to get across the gist of the concept to participants who are usually part of a focus group. This is the commonest form of qualitative research where a small number of people will freely discuss meanings or other aspects of, for example, mock advertisements or roughs. The direction of the discussion will depend upon the brief and the objectives of the research. For example the group may discuss alternative ideas, be expected to suggest other directions or choose between competing concepts. Participants might be observed through the use of recordings, digital cameras 'live' or 'live' through one-way mirrors. Participants' reactions to images, advertisements/roughs and the like can therefore be observed. The consumer jury is a more formal (quantitative) evaluation tool where juries are made up of representatives of a target group. The jury is asked to rank concepts on rating scales and this again can be facilitated by the employment of tools like roughs.

It is argued that this form of testing is too artificial and that the measure of persuasion shift is too simple and unrealistic. Furthermore, some believe that many respondents know what is happening and make changes because it is expected of them in the role of respondent (a form of respondent bias).

Finished communication

Finished communication can be tested by dummy vehicles (allied to the folder or portfolio tests), designed to expose a group of participants to advertisements, being mainly used with press advertising, mostly magazines, but also employed in packaging research. An advertisement being tested is inserted into a dummy magazine. The context is artificial, the tests usually taking place in a theatre, lab or some other form of meeting place. This problem can be reduced by the use of a more natural environment such as the participants' homes or workplaces. Both editorial and advertising can be the subject of the readers' attention in order to make the whole process more normal where participants are asked to consume the magazine in the normal way. Later on they are asked questions about the entire magazine – editorial and advertisements. This type of testing has increased realism since it approximates to real conditions rather than participants looking at advertising in isolation.

Readability tests were developed by Rudolf Flesch (and then with Peter Kinkaid) in the 1970s (Flesch-Kinkaid). This is a formula to assess the ease with which print copy could be read. It involves, for example, determining the average number of syllables per 100 words of copy, the average length of sentence, and the percentage of personal words and sentences. The educational level of the target audience has to be taken into consideration for comparison purposes and this works best with short sentences, concrete words, and where there is frequent use of personal references. This is useful for printed advertising, especially outdoor. Advertising generally should have shorter sentences, and a small number of words and words that are concrete rather than abstract.

Theatre tests are mainly used to test finished broadcast advertising. Participants (whose details are known as part of the selection process) are invited to a theatre (or hall, the origin of 'hall tests') where advertising in particular is previewed. The material is then analysed in either a simple or more complex fashion using both qualitative and quantitative techniques, whereby change in the participants' position is sought in terms of attitudinal and other change.

There may be pressure or even a requirement to be 'accountable', which might drive the use of more quantitative techniques. Physiological measures involve involuntary physical responses leading to the use of a variety of devices. Examples are as follows.

The Pupilometer, whereby pupil dilation is measured in reaction to a stimulus. A constricted pupil is equated with low levels of interest and the opposite suggesting arousal. This test is used for packaging design and determining interest in particular advertisements but has high cost and is used infrequently.

The Eye Camera, whereby cameras track the movement of the eye as it scans an advertisement or packs on a mocked-up shelf. Straplines, headlines, pictures, illustrations and other such devices can be tested in this way but the interpretation of results is a critical factor. For example, Ipsos Australia offers biometrics and eye tracking on the basis that 'people are not good at verbalising their feelings and responses. Our new biometrics analysis helps us tap into these emotional responses' in order to 'understand consumers' non-conscious reactions and emotions'. The Ipsos ASI Biometrics Kiosk utilises a 'pop-up' facility in 'an offline central location' where responses can be measured among samples of target audiences: 'These are then combined to produce your Biometric Trace and help you understand whether and how your ad is generating emotional engagement' (Ipsos, 2013).

The Psychogalvanometer tests galvanic skin response and measures amount of sweat produced by looking at advertisements and other images. This is the same principle as a lie detector and the Pupilometer in that if an informant is aroused or interested they are more likely to sweat. One problem with the Psychogalvanometer is that although no doubt some form of emotional arousal is detected the research does not reveal whether this is positive or negative.

The Tachistoscope measures the ability of an advertisement or packaging to attract attention. The time of exposure is varied from very short exposure to light in a blacked-out field to relatively much longer. The range may be something like 1/1000th of a second to two seconds. This is useful to identify those elements that are perceived first, often in a subliminal manner, so that shape is perceived before the colour of a logo on a piece of packaging.

The EEG (electroencephalograph) measures brain activity. Its use in marketing is very questionable, although claims are made that it essentially performs the same function as some of the above, i.e. the measurement of arousal and interest.

Voice recognition or more accurately pitch analysis determines when a voice is raised. If this occurs and positive comments are recorded then this is seen as a positive reaction to the stimulus.

Unfortunately the use of strange equipment and the fact that participants are aware that testing is occurring make the use of these tools problematic for marketers. They are also costly and can really only achieve small-scale studies, but used intelligently can be invaluable and yield insightful data available for use.

During and after marketing communications effort – concurrent and post testing

This is a large and important area of marketing research and certainly the largest area of communications research in terms of spend. Research for management decisions in communications therefore tends to be concentrated in this area. Much of the research in advertising deals with the ability to get through the clutter to consumers using devices such as pictorial value or empathy.

There are important but differing questions relating to research and evaluation. 'Are we getting there?' reflects the concurrent (during) nature of a campaign and its objectives. 'Did we get there?' reflects the post-campaign nature of communications objectives, which is effectively a post-mortem. The option to leave things with pre-testing is there but this might only save a small sum and leave the organisation with little or no information and knowledge on how things are working or have worked in practice. The advantage of doing research during and/or after the campaign rather than simply using pre-testing is that the communication is being tested in situ, in the real world. Most concurrent and post-tests concentrate on awareness of the communication, sales data, and market share data. Some of the tests are:

1. *Inquiry tests.* These are quantitative approaches such as coupon counting and are real-to-life, i.e. they measure the numbers of inquiries or direct responses stimulated by communication, as with telephone numbers used in the commercial. Latterly clicks online can be measured per day or by tracking analytics across different media. They can be used on a single piece of communication or on an entire campaign and often employ some form of split-run testing involving more than one

communication in, for example, the same issue of a magazine. Clearly this is quantitative informa-tion, but data gathered are merely inquiries, not sales, and the reasons why consumers did not respond may never be known.

2. *Recall tests.* Concurrent and post testing involves recall (aided and unaided) and recognition tests. Here the concern is to draw the threads of research together and show how different research techniques can be applied to the totality of marketing communications. Recall tests are designed to assess the impression the communication has on the memory of the target market. Typically, inform-ants are asked what programmes they remember watching on TV and what advertisements they recall seeing. If unaided then there is no prompt used to aid recall but if a prompt is used then this is aided recall, and both are usually DAR (day after recall). The degree to which things change as a result of exposure is therefore measured in a quantitative fashion. This can measure the effectiveness of advertisements in terms of exposure but the reasons as to why are left unknown. The reliability of such tests is high since these can be repeated without great difficulty. Though used a lot, validity is low since there is no known relationship between recall and sales and they are expensive, making their use more difficult to justify.

In a study of Polish consumers it was found that in positive and negative newspaper advertising con-texts the positive context led to more positive attitudes and better content recall and that rational mes-sages resulted in more positive attitudes, higher purchase intent and better content recall. However, attitudes towards emotional content and content recall were significantly more positive in the positive context. For rational advertising, purchase intent and content recall were higher in the negative context (De Pelsmaker et al., 2002). A study in the USA on children's programming supports the notion that the outcomes of this kind of research will be dependent on numerous variables, in this case the nature of the target (children) and children's television programming. This research suggests that health and nutrition claims are 'understood by food marketers to not be salient concerns among children and as such are not selling points to children'. The emotional appeals that appear to work on children are 'fun, happiness and play followed by fantasy/imagination, social enhancement/peer acceptance and cool-ness/hipness' (Page and Brewster, 2007: 323).

3. Recognition tests require participants to look at a media vehicle and then to look at particular features, articles or actual advertisements. They are then asked about particular aspects of what they are seeing and what they thought about particular aspects. The number of participants who remember seeing the piece of communication, how much and what they remember seeing, and how many recognising a particular aspect of the communication such as the actual brand are recorded. Here, like recall tests, reliability is high, but unlike recall, validity is high also but this does not get over the problem of participants falsifying things. Costs are lower and it easy to put into place the required simple questioning procedure. Recognition testing stems from the Starch Tests, which were a classic series of tests pioneered during the 1920s by Daniel Starch (a psychologist who like many other psychologists went into advertising, specialising in advertising research). The tests measured audience recognition, particularly in newspapers and magazine advertising, originally named 'recognition research'. These tests were widely accepted and used to compare the effectiveness of adverts in relation to others in the same issue of the same publication. This is an aid to improving the way advertising improves the ability to grab attention but not a measure of how good the advertising is at selling things. A proprietary form of Starch recognition research is part of the GfK MRI Starch Ad Readership Studies.

4. Market-based tests can be difficult to use since they are historical and expensive and it is difficult to identify the direct link between one form of communication and sales because so many other variables may also be factors. The use of the test market, the mini test market and single source data using controlled exposure to advertising correlated to sales is an option but an expensive one.

The Snapshot below discusses two contrasting case studies from Qualtrics (Qualtrics, 2013). Both of the companies concerned, CafeMom and eHarmony, employed the Qualtrics Research Suite, which provided them with real-time research insights to help solve their marketing and marketing communications' problems.

Snapshot Qualtrics offer fast results to companies like CafeMom and eHarmony

According to Qualtrics (2013) they are the 'world's leading provider of enterprise data collection and analysis software' products for market research. They are involved with the 'voice of customer', 'employee performance' and 'academic research'. The company claims that 'Through an intuitive, easy-to-use interface and award-winning services and support, Qualtrics products enable both professional and DIY researchers to conduct quantitative research at a lower cost and in less time than competing alternatives'.

Qualtrics was founded in 2002, and claim to have more than 5,000 clients worldwide, 'including half of the Fortune 100, over 1,300 colleges and universities, and 95 of the top 100 business schools'. Qualtrics claim that the results provided for clients mean improved research turnaround time from weeks to days, tripling of efficiency by more in-house research and to be able to provide the kind of data for decision-making, yet at the same time providing 'Significantly reduced outsourced research costs' to provide 'a data-driven CEO the necessary facts for decision-making' and 'Improved research capabilities to match and even exceed the research quality of large advertising research firms'. Qualtrics help gather real-time customer insights for better informed decision making.

CafeMom claims to be the leading media company for mothers (moms) with an audience of more than 20 million across its various entities of CafeMom.com, MamasLatinas.com, CafeMom Studios, and the CafeMom Plus Network. It is the 'premier strategic marketing partner to brands that want to reach moms in a rapidly changing digital environment'. Steven Armour, Vice President of Research CafeMom, says that 'Our clients are top Fortune 50 brands with exceptionally high standards. To get the right insights from our large population of digital moms, we had to become a powerful research company, as well as a media company. Our clients count on us to provide the real-time research that drives their product and advertising strategies.' However, they appeared to be lacking in the survey platform department and needed a sophisticated yet simple solution to this problem and found it in the Qualtrics Research Suite, which is used to 'Conduct in-house ad effectiveness studies, allowing for closer collaboration with clients, and cutting down on the time and expense of outsourcing research'. There is the creation of 'appealing surveys for digital moms, such as the annual MomIndex to track moms' overall quality of life and outlook on their families, health, communities, and more'. There is research conducted 'with industry-leading brands, such as Chase Blueprint for a survey on moms' financial attitudes, to gain actionable insights on topics of greatest concern to moms', and also the harmonisation of surveys 'across departments to ask questions in the same way, and leverage insights and best practices across the organization'.

eHarmony Inc. is the Santa Monica-based company founded in 2000 that is seen as a pioneer in using relationship science to match singles seeking long-term relationships. Its service 'presents users with compatible matches based on key dimensions of personality that are scientifically proven to predict highly successful long-term relationships'. eHarmony claims that 'On average, 542 people marry every day in the US as a result of being matched on eHarmony, nearly 5% of new marriages'. eHarmony operates online in the USA, Canada, UK, Australia and Brazil. It is also affiliated with eDarling in 16 countries throughout continental

(Continued)

(Continued)

Europe. Qualtrics has a role in this business, announcing in February 2013 that it has a 'collaboration with eHarmony'. The US dating services industry is worth $2b per annum and eHarmony is the market leader. It has successfully used Qualtrics Research Suite in order to gain real-time customer insight. This has provided the platform for to help tailor its sophisticated website that needs to cater for matching requirements of clients. eHarmony was able to 'capture the voice of the customer' but also 'conduct important concept testing and competitive brand analysis' through the employment of the Qualtrics Research Suite, which helped with the setting up of 'accounts on a mobile device … restructured its mobile application based on specific customer suggestions and increased the number of new customers signing up via mobile devices by 40 percent'. eHarmony also provided a 'What If?' feature in its mobile application – giving users the option to expand matching requirements, such as age and distance, to view a greater number of profiles.

Stop Point

Consider what the Qualtrics Research Suite offers these two contrasting organisations. Clearly a key advantage of employing the Qualtrics Research Suite system is the speed at which information for decision making is gathered, analysed and becomes ready for use. Undertake the following: 1. What are the benefits of gaining real-time customer insight? 2. What are the likely limitations on the nature of marketing research in real time for certain types of decision making?

APPLICATION OF RESEARCH AND EVALUATION TO THE MARKETING COMMUNICATIONS MIX

Advertising

Many of the above tests have been developed in the advertising area. Evaluation has to be conducted on the basis of what it is trying to achieve. If the objective is awareness then this is what should be tested for and not something else. For this reason guidelines or checklists have been developed to help marketers choose appropriate tests. In following the decision sequence model approach it is then possible to identify communications objectives and use AIDA-type model approaches in a systematic way. One such system developed within advertising is PACT, a set of guidelines developed primarily to assist in the research for television advertising, but also can be applied to advertising in other media. PACT stands for Positioning Advertising Copy Testing, and was developed in 1982 by 21 of the largest US advertising agencies to improve research used in testing advertising and thereby provide a better, creative product for clients and control the costs of, especially, TV advertising. The nine principles of PACT are illustrated below:

1. Provide measurements that are relevant to the objectives of the advertising.
2. Require agreement about how the results will be used in advance of each specific test.
3. Provide multiple measurements because single measurements are not adequate to assess advertising performance.

4. Be based on a model of human response to communications – the reception of a stimulus, the comprehension of the stimulus and the response to the stimulus.

5. Allow for consideration of whether the advertising stimulus should be exposed more than once.

6. Require that the more finished a piece of copy is the more soundly it can be evaluated and as a minimum that alternative executions be tested in the same degree of finish.

7. Provide controls to avoid the biasing effects of the exposure context.

8. Take into account the basic considerations of sample definition.

9. Demonstrate reliability and validity.

Most communication and research companies would agree with this, and commercial products are born because of such a rationale. For example Link™ is a tool from Millward Brown that helps predict and optimise the impact of advertising. According to this research-based consultancy, this is the 'world's leading copy testing solution'. This company claims that 'Between your creative, our experts and our database of more than 84,000 ads, you can't be more confident you've got a winning campaign'. Link is a tool for creative development and evaluation that identifies what is working and what is not within advertising; how an advert might be further developed or fine tuned: 'Over 40 percent of the ads in our database have been tested in unfinished formats – a testament to the value marketers find in the insights uncovered by Link' as a 'valuable as part of a continuous cycle of creative development, evaluation, and optimization' (Millward Brown, 2013).

Every part of the communications process, as explained in Chapter 2 of this book, can potentially be tested and evaluated, and this is particularly true for advertising. For example, the source of the message – say, a celebrity – can be evaluated in terms of audience response to any trust, liking or respect that is generated. It may be that the goal is to have an effective spokesperson for the organisation. A corporate or brand image can also be part of the source and be tested in some way. The signal, message or channel can be tested in terms of effective delivery and whether the message is working using the research tools outlined above. In short the communication should be achieving the objectives set and hopefully decoded by the recipient in the way the sender intended.

The Snapshot below discusses the use of marketing research to look at the group viewing behaviours of event television shows such as *The X Factor* and what this might mean for advertisers. It also discusses how such viewers are more likely now to share information via Twitter than in a face-to-face way.

Snapshot   Passion and motivation towards Event TV – the role of research in gaining a deeper understanding of group viewing habits, and the importance of Twitter rather than the water cooler

Event television shows like *The X Factor* can be very important to capturing audiences, especially during prime-time viewing. In 2008 ITV (Independent Television) in the UK published the findings of a report based on a major study of group television viewing and the benefits it offered to advertisers interested in event television.

(Continued)

(Continued)

ITV commissioned the research from the marketing research agency Other Lines of Enquiry, for themselves and in order to share information with their clients (advertisers likely to buy time from ITV). The 'detailed ethnographic study of 16 viewing groups and a quantitative study of 5,000 people' were set up 'to learn more about group viewing behaviour and establish what unique benefits group viewing of particular content offers advertisers, starting with the hypothesis that not all TV viewing is equal'. A key finding was the identification of 'true fans' of Event TV who have the strongest relationship with television. The study also established a firm definition of Event TV as being 'high-interest content delivered at the right time and place to its true fans'. According to ITV, 'Event TV works hardest among "true fans" and creates unique qualities, including being highly anticipated, time-sensitive and an experience shared up and down the country, making it the UK's most talked-about and enjoyed TV'. ITV now have a 'deeper understanding of group viewing habits and the level of passion and motivation that true fans show towards Event TV'. The study showed that a 'significant proportion' of ITV's mass audience were 'more engaged with Event TV and view in group situations'. This means that 'brands advertising around Event TV are more likely to be discussed, considered and purchased by viewers'. For advertisers this means that Event TV delivers 'significant increases across key advertiser metrics, including recommendation and brand perceptions'. ITV noted that:

- Viewers have a higher level of awareness of ads.
- Ad breaks are more likely to be watched and group viewing stimulates discussion of ads.
- Commercial breaks on ITV are also recognised by viewers as being of higher quality.
- Event TV unifies families and friends (group viewing) across the week, particularly at weekends.
- Event TV viewers are more passionate about television than other viewers – to the extent that they are willing to build their social lives around key televised events.

Mangan (2012) notes that Twitter, apparently, saved Event TV: 'We used to gather round the office water cooler to discuss the previous night's telly. Now, tweeting offers the most immediate means of sharing our excitement'. This means of exchanging real-time responses to events, situations and many other things through the use of tweets and television viewing is no exception. Marketing research associated with social media generally and Twitter in particular is not new but, of course, not yet that old. According to Mangan, social media are:

> restoring a sense of excitement to television … Event TV was thought to be dying as channels proliferated, people timeshifted their viewing and audiences fragmented in a way that made the viewing figures of yesteryear (21.6 million to find out who shot JR, 28 million every time Eric and Ernie popped their Christmas hats on, 32.3 million for the 1966 World Cup) seem like the fevered dream of an overstrained ITV exec.

Mangan argues that our interaction and ability to comment on such things as television programmes make reality TV at least more interesting and popular than it would be otherwise but that with quality TV programming this is not the case where 'people will still pay undivided attention if the material is worthy of it'. In the meantime Twitter actively encourages TV producers to use the medium.

Stop Point

The impact of social media globally is huge and has many contexts. Event television viewing and the interaction during and after shows such as *The X Factor* via social media such as Twitter are one such context. Undertake the following: 1. Discuss the difference between group television viewing and individual television viewing; 2. Comment on the likely interaction, including the use of social media, between viewers and its effect on the way event television is viewed.

Other communications mix tools

The rest of the communications mix can be, to a lesser extent, subjected to testing. For example, POS material, packaging, sales promotions, coupons, competitions or special offers can all be tested at each of the pre-, concurrent and post-testing stages. Most communications research has been in the area of advertising because of advertising's pre-eminence in the communications mix, with much of the allocation assigned to it. The changes that have occurred in the media, lifestyles, technology and the environment generally, have meant that sales promotion, public relations, direct marketing, selling, and more latterly sponsorship and product placement have become significant enough to warrant testing and evaluation. After all, the goal should be to communicate effectively with the target market in an integrated manner. Each of the broad elements of the communications mix is briefly assessed below.

Sales promotion

Whereas advertising tends to be longer term and deals with objectives such as awareness, sales promotion devices are shorter term and attempt to change behaviour, and research and evaluation have for this reason tended to be more quantitative than qualitative. However, this is not to say that sales promotion research and evaluation are simplistic. Usually the use of sales promotion is to increase sales in some way and therefore sales-based measurement techniques, often customised, are used. There is some diversity of sales promotion objectives that might involve, for example, enhancing product value and brand equity or reacting to the competition. Sales promotions' evaluations have the appearance of speed, ease and precision but there is still an element of uncontrollable variables in the equation, even though compared with advertising this is much smaller. Technology plays a major role in effective promotions and can help marketers target spend at certain periods when consumers are known to be most responsive.

Pre-testing will invariably involve perceptions of value of the offer and of risk, especially if the brand is unknown or untested in a particular sector, on the part of the customer who will necessarily weigh up the consequences of being seduced by the offer. Pre-testing can be used to assess this through the use of, for example, focus groups, consumer juries or consumer panels. Portfolio tests that expose the customer to a range of ideas can be used as can trial purchases. These latter tests tend to increase the cost of the exercise as is the use of experimentation that uses variations on the brand in different store locations. Behaviourally the test market or mini test market is a much-used pre-test of sales promotion in situ.

During and post campaign scanning and tracking devices can be used as well as actual figures generated, observation and survey methods. As might be expected piloting is a choice to help identify problems and simple measures such as the counting of redeemed coupons offer reliable sales measurement. Concurrent (during) testing allows for any adjustments if thought to be needed. For example, if the promotion is a contest the number of entries received can be monitored and an extension to the contest deadline made if necessary. Post-testing is carried out after the promotion period is over. Effects on sales or entries to a competition are obvious quantitative measurements but may not be the full story. The employment of qualitative research is needed to understand the reasons why a sales promotion has been success or not.

There is a need also to evaluate the likely responses of resellers to a particular customer or consumer sales promotion idea before implementation and the promotion could very well be a joint promotion between manufacturer and reseller. Even if the promotion is strictly manufacturer to consumer it is necessary to get the reseller on board, especially if retail auditing is to be used. In the case of sales promotion being used by a reseller like a supermarket chain, stock movement can be measured when promotions are implemented. Some companies will also attempt to measure the effect of sales force incentives as a form of sales promotion or tie in image tracking studies with any of the above measures.

Public Relations

PR is probably the most difficult element of the communications mix to evaluate because it is often used in conjunction with other elements. Much of PR activity deals with opinions and therefore is not easily observable. Corporate PR (Chapter 14 of this book) deals with corporate identity and image, and crisis management. Many image studies are ongoing and are tracking studies that measure, for example, interest, attitudes and goodwill. Work can be done with stakeholders to determine important attributes that can then be measured against standards and the competition. Employees should be seen as a stakeholder group and surveyed regularly in some way. Crisis management as discussed in Chapter 13 of this book should have research and evaluation built into any decision sequence model used, with an in-built pre, during and post attitude toward, for example, image.

Often feedback is received through a 'cuttings' or 'clipping' service. These at least identify any media coverage, i.e. the types of media, journalists and audience. Here the quantitative measure of column inches is used and often the erroneous comparison made with the same coverage using advertising, with the huge savings that go with this. Content analysis should be applied to such coverage to establish quality, but the mere opportunity to see argument is equally as valid here as it is with advertising. Press releases can be pre-coded with the technology in place to measure effects on sales and sales leads and improved analysis. Survey methods can be used to monitor change.

Personal selling

Personal selling requires a different approach to evaluation from the rest of the communications mix. Continuous improvement in sales and selling is often the mantra of the selling organisation (see Chapter 16 of this book). There are numerous obvious quantitative measures that have been applied to personal selling contexts over the years – such as number of calls made or number of sales interviews attended – all of which can be measured against an existing company benchmark. It is no surprise to see a company wishing to measure how much something costs against how much money an activity generates and the selling/salesperson situation is no different. Quite naturally there is interest in the notion of contribution toward profits, and this has a different set of inputs and expectations. Therefore cost per call, cost per sales area or territory, and ultimately the cost of the salesperson, are measured against income and comparisons made against others. Simple ratios can be used to manage such quantitative measures.

More latterly, interest in qualitative measures has been shown such as skills and knowledge levels. At the sales-force level this kind of work can be applied in an aggregate fashion but change occurs that has to be managed such as the move towards a relationship marketing and selling paradigm, so that managing customer relationships has led to a move away from short-term orientation regarding selling. Added to this is the multi-channel reality of selling these days that has a profit rather than cost perspective. At the individual level there are many salesperson activities that are impossible to quantify but can be qualified. It is recognised, however, that some things cannot be evaluated, even subjectively. If the selling role is one of representation rather than, for example, an order-taker, performance in terms of, say, good-will creation and maintenance is much more difficult to measure. There are a wide variety of variables to consider in the sales environment so that it becomes difficult if not impossible to make comparisons or even measure activities against company benchmarks. The time taken for example to develop some accounts against others may be a factor, or it may be that some situations are reliant on more than one person's effort, making it difficult to assess individual performance and reward in an appropriate manner.

Other marketing communications tools

Sponsorship these days needs to be separated out from the rest of the mix and evaluated (see Chapter 15 of this book). One problem is the temptation to use audience size as a measure, but since the event or other sponsorship activities is the reason why the audience wants to view the spectacle this is the reason for being involved, not the sponsor, when they watch motor racing or football. In many cases it may only be an opportunity to see a sponsor's logo. Research in the sponsorship area has been conducted by using varying tools in both quantitative and qualitative studies; for example, quantitative surveys using a structured questionnaire through to the use of interviewing and focus groups in qualitative research.

Product placement research and evaluation are relatively recent but have accelerated because of the emergence of product placement as an important marketing issue, princi-pally because of its success as a marketing tool. It has become a common occurrence to see products (or more likely brands) placed in mainstream media outlets such as film, television broadcast and cable television programming, computer and video games, music videos/ DVDs, magazines and even books, comics, staged musicals and plays, on radio, online in for example blogs, and mobile phones (see Chapter 15 of this book for a little more consid-eration of the nature of product placement). The impact and effectiveness of product place-ment are of course crucial to the success of the brand. One of the main reasons why product placement has replaced some of the advertising that would have been created is because of the ways in which advertising is now being perceived by consumers who are able and want to zip past advertising but who cannot do this if the brand is placed within (say) a game or a film. Williams et al. (2011: 19) suggest that although 'some preliminary conclusions with regard to product placements have been reached, the industry is far from a comprehensive analysis and testing of all the antecedents and consequences of product placement'. The key to the success of product placement appears to lie in the subtlety of how it works in an integration-like way where the integration between, say, a television drama's storyline and the brand is remembered. Research tools that can be used in the product placement area are similar to those in sponsorship and advertising research as mentioned above.

Direct marketing was discussed and explained in Chapter 12 of this book. Direct market-ing can be monitored by actually recording activities like telemarketing and managing and controlling databases. As with other forms of marketing communication, direct marketing research employs many of the tools and techniques used in advertising research, such as quantitative surveys using structured questionnaires or qualitative research using focus groups to pre-test a particular approach to, for example, through-the-mail letter-writing.

Online research includes much of what can be done within the broad elements of the marketing communications mix as discuss immediately above. Of growing importance is desk or secondary research online. There are many resources on the Internet that can be found using search engines but often there will be a designated web address of companies or other organisations such as industry or professional bodies, e.g. the UK Advertising Association (www.adassoc.org.uk/Home or www.aaaindia.org/) and the Institute of Practitioners in Advertising (www.ipa.co.uk/) with sites developed to provide information. There are news and discussion groups, forums and blogs that can be useful sources of information which of course should be used with care because much of the information provided is unverifiable. Online primary research can be commissioned using professional-body guidelines such as with the UK Market Research Society (MRS, 2012) whose guidelines for client organisations to follow include:

1. Provide the research organisation with a detailed brief for the usual reason of both parties understanding what is to be achieved and to avoid confusion.
2. Decide what is important and consider whether it is speed or depth that is required.
3. Make sure there are enough resources to achieve the desired results.
4. Make sure that the higher level risk of deception that exists online is minimised.
5. Pre-screened access panels, which greatly reduce this risk and allow agencies fast access to a representative audience if that is desirable.

Many of the advantages and disadvantages of using online primary research have now been known for some time. Advantages include speed, global reach, relative low cost (but this is changing), data quality, flexibility and interactivity. The disadvantages include over-mechanistic tools, an over-populated and congested universe, rising costs and the stateless nature of the Internet. The usual tools of research are developing online, including surveys with tools such as SurveyMonkey readily available. Surveys have the advantage speed and cost but suffer from boredom setting in and 'drop out'. Online focus groups are possible and offer speed and cost reduction but this tool suffers from problems such as a lack of sensory effects and representativeness. Live, depth or personal interviews have been developed but these might in fact be online discussions rather than interviews. They offer speed and cost but with this tool sampling and bias remains a problem.

Social media marketing research is growing with organisations now employing people solely to monitor what is being said on the likes of Facebook and Twitter. This includes text, photographs, videos, social bookmarks, blogs and micro blogs. There has been a realisation that this kind of content is extremely useful in gaining insights into, for example, segmentation, needs analysis and customer profiling (Tuten and Solomon, 2013). Social media research can be qualitative and quantitative but is mostly the former. It can also be secondary as well as primary. With the former, Tuten and Solomon (2013) suggest that, for example, there is residual evidence of activities and opinions, which is, in effect, a social footprint and part of quantitative secondary or desk research. There is quantitative research in the form of frequency counts and descriptive statistics. For example, monitoring and tracking require software that will search for and find key words or phrases by crawling or scraping the web. With primary social media research many of the conventional primary marketing research tools have been adopted and adapted for use with social media so that diaries, interviews, focus groups and surveys all take place on social media using, for example, Facebook Groups for focus groups or a proprietary online community blog 'to engage participants in a multiday forum' (Tuten and Solomon, 2013: 197). In addition to the speed and cost of obtaining results is the advantage that getting participants to open up is lessened because of the nature of social media use and users and also the relative ease of reaching niche groups.

Mobile marketing research is now well underway. From a mobile research platform companies can conduct both quantitative and qualitative marketing research. One of the key advantages to the use of this technology is the speed of data collection. Another is the ability to reach participants who are 'on the go' against the backdrop of problems with access to participants because of increasingly hectic lifestyles and their unwillingness or inability to partake in marketing research activities. Since mobile and smart phones are now an indispensable part of many people's lives and with a high incidence of ownership and use in most countries, mobile devices, especially among younger demographics, are the obvious contact method for many studiers and applications. An example of an agency offering mobile marketing research is Research Now (Research Now, 2013) with its Research Now Mobile offering. Its mobile research platform offers clients both quantitative (for example shopper experience, media habits and purchase intent) and qualitative (for example ad copy testing, concept testing and mystery shopping).

Continuous and *ad hoc* research is widely available for marketing but also marketing communications support. Whereas continuous research is often a survey conducted regularly and either frequently or at intervals over a longer period, ad hoc research is carried out at a specific time. Ad hoc marketing research is usually commissioned as and when needed through a specific marketing research brief, although there may be certain amount of leeway and improvisation. For example the essence of the brief may be to determine the current level of corporate image, to determine consumer reaction to a particular advertising campaign, or it may involve customer satisfaction levels. Online panels and opinion polls have proven to be successful and are now part of continuous research services. There are also other sources that are external to the company but can be bought in, including Target Group Index (TGI), an international tool, offered in the UK by the British Market Research Bureau (BMRB). TGI has a 24,000-strong sample of adult informants who are willing, for a small incentive, to self-complete a very large questionnaire. This seeks to gather data on a wide range of products and product usage, as well as brands and extent of use. This information is cross-tabulated with a range of things from demographics, psychographics, and media consumption. Buying in to TGI provides the marketer with an aid not only to targeting but also to message construction and media selection. Audits more generally are an aid to monitoring and these days can be had in an online format.

Some continuous research tools useful to marketing communications management are: EPOS (electronic point-of-sale) and other electronic auditing such as loyalty/bonus cards; geodemographic systems that offer links between geography and demography, allowing for targeted campaigns and research; and psychographic systems such as those that have evolved from the original VALS (Values Attitudes and Life Styles) as developed in the USA by Maslow and Rockeach in 1975 and which modelled American society in terms of AOI (attitudes, opinions and interests). Such systems allow the marketing communicator to fire messages at a much better known target, domestically and internationally; syndicated research such as that offered by Mintel and Keynote; the Omnibus Survey that covers particular industries, sectors or special interest groups and allows participants to, for example, measure awareness; media research can also be bought in a non-ad hoc manner, so that the marketing communicator can, for example, buy in to the National Readership Survey (NRS) in the UK; tracking studies (or tracking research) deal with both new and established products/brands on a continuous or periodic basis. The research tracks product use or usage, image and other marketing variables, through various media.

The Snapshot below discusses two different examples of the use of viral marketing in the context of word-of-mouth communication and the measurement of its effectiveness in terms of making things sharable, i.e. worth sharing. The challenge is to get viral marketing achieving objectives other than awareness as it has in the cases of the Stolichnaya and V05 brands.

Snapshot   Q. What have Stolichnaya and VO5 got in common? A. Viral (Social) Marketing and EWOM

Going viral now means using some form of marketing communications that can be shared with others in a compelling way but through social networks. As with older concepts such as opinion leadership and word-of-mouth there is a social element, what Rodic and Koivisto (2012) call the 'social object' – a compelling message that is relevant, entertaining, positive, and attracts the interaction of the target audience which is at the least a 'conversation starter' and might involve 'advergames and social advergames'. Rodic and Koivisto (2012) use the example of 'a Facebook version of a common children's game with a prize to be won and easy-to-share features'. All three – interactivity, entertainment and positive, inspiring messages – might be included. This needs the 'viral mechanics' that carry the message, i.e. 'make it as sharable as possible', and social media like Facebook do this via a brand's social media page, website, blogs, and other digital platforms. In marketing research terms the tracking of viral mechanisms allows for tracking of the spread of a message and the dissemination rate, but as Rodic and Koivisto (2012) point out this is 'quantitative data which also restricts viral marketing's role within the integrated marketing communications context'.

This means that viral marketing has in the past been restricted to the objective of achieving awareness and marketing research to the quantitative measurement of awareness. Now the challenge is to make viral marketing work for other objectives such as brand trust or more effective integration with other communications tools. Marketing research would then be tasked to measure different things, both quantitative and qualitative.

Stolichnaya vodka

According to econsultancy.com (2004), in 2004 Stolichnaya Russian vodka was launched and for the first time online viral marketing was used. The agency, Revolver Communications with the help of Skive Creative, built brand identity by suggesting the brand was made by Russians in Russia for Russians, yet it was the best-selling vodka worldwide. The campaign, which ran for two months and hosted at www.stolibrides.com, represents a relatively early attempt to 'go viral' with a spoof of the dating game that allows the target (men aged 25–34) to fill out a form with favourite characteristics to determine a perfect match with a Stoli bride. This was billed as 'for research purposes only' but designed to garner curiosity. The target is prompted to fill out favourite attributes and hobbies and is then shown the ideal match which is of course a joke match. The target is then prompted to send this on. There is a sales promotion thrown in – a chance to win a free case of the famous vodka, the authentic vodka brand that is made by Russians, in Russia, for Russians. This move into viral content went beyond the hitherto use of devices like banners, allowing the brand to become more interactive.

VO5 Extreme Style hair products

This campaign used YouTube with comments and a clever set of ideas to engage the viewer such as the sell-out nature of a pageant and the humorous style of a video, which 'leans more towards Borat than a cute local pageant'. The viewer is eventually led to the Pliktisijiteur Village website 'where the homepage video is the true advertisement for V05', and the product placement is left 'until the very end of the video rather than jumping straight in there. Cleverly, they've realised that their audience are no strangers to the wonders of the internet, and giving them something to explore is better than laying it out on a plate for them' (Wordpress.com, 2011). The aim, of course, was to promote discussion on the brand's Facebook page and YouTube channel. The year after, as reported by *The Drum* magazine, 'the first ever iAd to use Twitter and its camera function, ahead of the launch of a new ad on 1 May' was launched to the 14–24-year-old target audience which 'builds on previous Pliktisijiteur Village Pageant activity, by inviting people to "village your hair" by manipulating a photo with various styles'. The rebellious nature of the advertising (and hence the brand) is of course designed to appeal to the 14 to 24-year-old target. On Twitter they can tweet pictures of their hairstyles and Vicky Metcalfe, marketing director for V05, is quoted in *The Drum* article as being 'very pleased with the iAd which builds on the great "Pageant" work for V05 Extreme Style and is set to generate further traction amongst our 14–24 year old target that love to discover and share new content'.

Stop Point

The creative side of both of these cases cannot be denied. The challenge is to put forward means to measure critical success factors and to understand why particular campaigns are successful or not. Undertake the following: 1. Propose a means to evaluating the success of video use on social media; 2. Suggest uses for social media tracking studies that go beyond the measurement of brand awareness.

Assignment

According to Poynter (2013), 'research communities are being adopted in Japan, China, India, Singapore and Vietnam'. Poynter's research 'explores the implications of cultural differences and different technologies (especially in terms of internet and mobile) in setting up Asia-Pacific communities'.

Conduct your own research into the current status of research communities globally in order to do the following:

- Define international research communities.
- Provide a global overview of research communities.
- Make suggestions about where research communities are going next.
- Select a particular country and outline its specific status in terms of research communities and what this means for marketing communications research.

Summary of Key Points

- There are clear benefits to evaluating marketing communications campaigns.
- There are clear difficulties in measurement because of the lagged and cumulative effects of different stimuli and individual differences.
- Briefing and proposal writing are an integral part of developing research.
- Pre, during and post testing is commonplace in marketing communications practice.
- Secondary research (often termed 'desk' research) is research that examines both external published data (for example government statistics) and internal published data (for example sales records) and bought-in published data (for example Mintel), and it should be relevant (current, up-to-date), accurate and impartial.
- Both quantitative and qualitative research have a role to play in communications research.
- Both quantitative and qualitative research can be conducted online but so far for practical reasons online quantitative research has been developed further than online qualitative research.
- Online research has seen rapid development where both primary and secondary research are now conducted online and involve data from search engines, websites, news and discussion groups, forums and blogs, but also primary sources such as survey research (for example SurveyMonkey) and focus groups.
- More recently social media research has also developed.
- Continuous research is usually bought by subscription, data being based on audits, panels and also surveys. It is sometimes syndicated and is usually a survey conducted both regularly and frequently. Continuous research is undertaken repeatedly and continually as opposed to ad hoc research, which is carried out at specific times.
- During a campaign it is common to use DAR, unaided or aided tests. Recognition testing can be used to establish the elements of a piece of communication.
- Post campaign is dominated by quantitative sales effect-type research.
- Most of the research and evaluation methods and tools have been developed in advertising and packaging research, but other communication elements are being evaluated as their use increases.

Discussion Questions

1. Explain what is meant by the term 'research and evaluation' in marketing communications terms.
2. Write a typical research brief for an fmcg brand and explain what a research company would have to put in a proposal to have a chance of getting the account.
3. Explain the difference between primary and secondary research in marketing communications, using examples to illustrate.

4. Explain the difference between quantitative and qualitative (both on and offline) research in marketing communications, using examples to illustrate.

5. Discuss the kinds of 'off the peg' research a marketer can buy-in to that are useful in marketing communications' terms.

6. Outline media (including social media) research issues that are relevant for today's marketing communicator.

7. Outline the kinds of research typical to sales promotion campaigns.

8. Discuss PR in relation to research, and in particular image studies, using examples to illustrate.

9. Distinguish between qualitative and quantitative research that might be used in sales-person and sales force research.

10. Discuss other elements of the communications mix, such as sponsorship, in relation the kinds of research that might be advocated in order to assess effectiveness, using examples to illustrate.

Further Reading

Cornwell, T.B., Humphreys, M.S., Quinn, E.A. and McAlister, A.R. (2012) 'Memory of sponsorship-linked marketing communications: the effect of competitor mentions', *Sage Open*, 2 (4): 1–14. http://sgo.sagepub.com/content/2/4/2158244012468139

This article brings into question the value of corporate sponsorship because of confusion over who are the true sponsors. It points to the importance of understanding memory-based characteristics of measurement and memory-supported decision-making tasks that are potentially influenced by the sponsorship. This study showed good memory for sponsors and that the mention of direct competition can help facilitate recall of true sponsors and events.

Freeman, L. and Spanjaard, D. (2012) 'Bridging the gap: the case for expanding ethnographic techniques in the marketing research curriculum', *Journal of Marketing Education*, 34 (3): 238–50. http://jmd.sagepub.com/content/34/3/238

This article is about the marketing research curriculum and the place for ethnography and ethnographic techniques in such a curriculum. The authors discuss the dangers of limiting the range of qualitative research to focus groups and interviewing and the benefits of including ethnography as a viable alternative method.

Khang, H., Ki, E.-J. and Ye, L. (2012) 'Social media research in advertising, communication, marketing and public relations', *Journalism & Mass Communication Quarterly*, 89 (2): 279–98. http://jmq.sagepub.com/content/89/2/279

The article draws on the phenomenon that is social media, taking an historical perspective on the rapid development of what was until recently a new set of media driven by user-generated content. The authors suggest that social media be broadly defined to include discussion boards, messaging and home pages as well as the likes of YouTube, and look at the present and future use of such media across a range of marketing areas.

Leonard, K.M., Van Scotter, J.R., Pakdil, F., Chamseddine, N.J., Esatoglu, E., Gumus, M., Koyuncu, M., Wu, L.L. , Mochaitis, A.I., Salciuviene, L., Oktem, M.K., Surkiene, G. and

(Continued)

(Continued)

Tsai, F-S. (2011) 'Examining media effectiveness across cultures and national borders: a review and multi-level framework', *International Journal of Cross Cultural Management*, 11 (1): 83–103. http://ccm.sagepub.com/content/11/1/83

This large group of authors explore how perceptions of media effectiveness are affected by differing cultural impacts, both societal and organisational as well as individual characteristics and technology acceptance, especially in this globalised world. As this is central to the communications process, the authors look at shared values, rules and experiences that affect the way meaning is understood or misunderstood with particular media types, and develop a framework that highlights the intersection of salient variables.

Park, Y.A and Gretzel, U. (2007) 'Success factors for destination marketing web sites: a qualitative meta-analysis', *Journal of Travel Research*, 46 (1): 46–63. http://jtr.sagepub.com/content/46/1/46

Website effectiveness and ROI are the focus of this study in destination marketing. The study uses qualitative meta-analysis methodology to build a framework of nine website success factors with additional factors added based on particular dimensions of web communication.

REFERENCES

Cornwell, T.B., Humphreys, M.S., Quinn, E.A. and McAlister, A.R. (2012) 'Memory of sponsorship-linked marketing communications: the effect of competitor mentions', *Sage Open*, 2 (4): 1–14.

De Pelsmacker, P., Maison, D. and Geuens, M. (2002) 'Emotional and rational advertising messages in positive and negative Polish media contexts', *Advances in International Marketing*, 12: 121–35.

The Drum (2012) 'VO5 breaks the mould with Euro-RSCG London with iAd for latest Pliktisijiteur village pageant burst', *The Drum* magazine, 18 April, available at: www.thedrum.com/news/2012/04/18/vo5-breaks-mould-euro-rscg-london-iad-latest-pliktisijiteur-village-pageant-burst

econsultancy.com (2004) 'Stolichnaya launches viral campaign', available at: http://econsultancy.com/uk/press-releases/296-stolichnaya-launches-viral-campaign

Freeman, L. and Spanjaard, D. (2012) 'Bridging the gap: the case for expanding ethnographic techniques in the marketing research curriculum', *Journal of Marketing Education*, 34 (3): 238–50.

Ipsos (2013) 'Biometrics & eye tracking', IPSOS Australia, available at: http://ipsos.com.au/ipsos-asi/biometrics-eye-tracking/

ITV (2008) 'Event TV – meet the true fans', available at: www.itvmedia.co.uk/202041/research/event-tv

Khang, H., Ki, E.-J. and Ye, L. (2012) 'Social media research in advertising, communication, marketing and public relations', *Journalism & Mass Communication Quarterly*, 89 (2): 279–98.

Leonard, K.M., Van Scotter, J.R., Pakdil, F. Chamseddine, N.J., Esatoglu, E., Gumus, M., Koyuncu, M., Wu, L.L., Mochaitis, A.I., Salciuviene, L., Oktem, M.K., Surkiene, G. and Tsai, F.-S. (2011) 'Examining media effectiveness across cultures and national borders: a review and multi-level framework', *International Journal of Cross Cultural Management*, 11 (1): 83–103.

Mangan, L. (2012) 'How Twitter saved Event TV', *The Guardian*, 18 January, available at: www.guardian.co.uk/technology/2012/jan/18/how-twitter-saved-event-tv

Market Research Society (2012) 'MRS guidelines for online research', January, available at: www.mrs.org.uk/pdf/2012-02-16%20Online%20Research%20Guidelines.pdf

Millward Brown (2013) 'Predict and optimize the impact of your advertising', available at: www.millwardbrown.com/Solutions/Creative_Development/link.aspx

Page, R.M. and Brewster, A. (2007) 'Emotional and rational product appeals in televised food advertisements for children: analysis of commercials shown on US broadcast networks', *Journal of Child Health Care*, 11 (4): 323–40.

Park, Y.A and Gretzel, U. (2007) 'Success factors for destination marketing web sites: a qualitative meta-analysis', *Journal of Travel Research*, 46 (1): 46–63.

Poynter, R. (2013) 'Research communities in Asia Pacific: A review of similarities and contrasts', April, ESOMAR, Asia Pacific, Ho Chi Minh City.

Qualtrics (2013) 'Sophisticated research made simple', available at: www.qualtrics.com

Research Now (2013) 'Catch the wave and capture the moment with Research Now Mobile', available at: www.researchnow.com/en-GB/Services/Research_Now_Mobile.aspx

Rodic, N. and Koivisto, E. (2012) 'Best practices in viral marketing', Media+Mark, Aalto University School of Business, Department of Economics, Helsinki, Finland.

Tuten, T.L. and Solomon, M.R. (2013) *Social Media Marketing*. New Jersey: Pearson Education Inc.

Williams, K., Petrosky, A., Hernandez, E. and Page, R. (2011) 'Product placement effectiveness: revisited and renewed', *Journal of Management and Marketing Research*, April, 7: 1–24.

Wordpress.com (2011) 'Ellie on ads, Pliktisijiteur Village Pageant – V05's viral campaign', Wordpress.com, available at: http://ellieonads.wordpress.com/2011/10/11/pliktisijiteur-pageant-v05-viral-campaign/

International Marketing
Communications

CHAPTER OVERVIEW

Introduction

This chapter raises some of the key communications issues that affect the existing international marketer or the marketer who has decided that it is time to 'go international'. It may very well be the case that for all but the very local micro business, going international is no longer an option but is an inevitable consequence of being. The last few decades have seen tremendous growth in world trade and this growth has been accompanied by a very large growth in communications and not least, of course, the Internet and e-commerce. Having a global or international presence throws up even more barriers to communication for organisations that struggle in the first place to communicate effectively in the domestic market. For example, different cultural elements, a different media landscape and different legal requirements impact in different ways in different markets. The continuous struggle is not just to do with what is different but is also to do with what is (or can be) the same, with an inevitable drive toward standardised marketing. Other drivers are, for example, achieving economies of scale, using up excess capacity or down time. There are benefits to diversification and not having all of one's eggs in a particular market basket but the difficulties and consequences of trading in different markets should never be underestimated. The literature is littered with examples of blunders perpetrated by the most unlikely of large corporations, not least of all in the communications arena.

Learning objectives

This chapter seeks to provide a final platform upon which the reader can contemplate further study in a number of international directions. More specifically, after reading this chapter the student will be able to:

- explore international communications and underscore the parameters that make it different from the communications outlined in Chapter 1 of this book;
- examine the communications process in the international context and highlight any differences to the process outlined in Chapter 2 of this book;
- examine the idea of achieving uniformity of marketing and marketing communications effort in terms of the adaptation/standardisation debate;
- outline environmental patterns around the world and explore some of the consequences of going or being international;
- outline the APIC managerial framework espoused in Chapter 4 of this book in the context of managing international communications campaigns.

THE NATURE OF INTERNATIONAL COMMUNICATIONS

A brief historical note on international communication

The term advertising comes from the French 'avertir' – variously translated as to warn, to inform, to tell or to give public notice – but there are many interpretations of the word, for example that it is most probably 15th century and was defined in 1694 as being 'a crime committed with many witnesses' (de Mooij, 1994). Since that time it has evolved as information and this can be observed by looking at early copies of *The Times* newspaper. This demonstrates that advertising was a continual repetition of information. Artwork costs were more expensive due to letterpress print technology. Advertisers learnt to promote products effectively, sometimes through, for example, glamour, sex, or humour in order to make them more effective, grabbing attention more readily. The development of communication worldwide (which follows that of marketing and business generally) is in itself fascinating. Advertising grew quickly between 1850 and 1900 and developed with the change to lithographic printing techniques. The emergence of TV in the 1950s and radio between the first and second World Wars also influenced development. In socialist states such as the USSR and China, advertising emerged as an instrument of propaganda, whereas in free market economies such as the USA, processed foods, tobacco and drugs were the order of the day. After Stalin's death socialist countries recognised that advertising encouraged sales and therefore was a necessary evil. In China however, during the time of Mao (after 1949), commercial advertising was denounced. Not all countries therefore believed advertising to be a good thing. However, since the 1960s advertising has become established in many countries including many of the Third World. International advertising has grown particularly, with companies having offices in many countries.

For some time now the advertising industry has had many agencies that are international, the USA, UK, France and Japan having been important base countries. Agencies such as those of the WPP Group (for example J Walter Thompson, or now JWT and rivals Ogilvy and Mather or O&M), Grey Group and Lowe all have a presence now in, for example, China (Beijing and/or Shanghai). Most are privately owned and have for some time now considered themselves to be communications agencies (IPA, 1999), reflecting not only the growth of sales promotions, public relations, and direct marketing techniques, but also the move toward IMC as addressed in Chapter 1 of this book.

Latterly, the impact of the Internet, and the rapid growth of e-commerce and social media, as discussed in Chapter 10 of this book, have forced the industry and clients to move with the times, or at least try to. In today's increasingly wireless and socially networked world marketing is constantly changing, albeit not in a fundamental philosophical way but in the way it is practised.

'Clients have moved to social. Companies like 360i, which specializes in social (but is growing into new platforms) have grown on the massive rise in the demand for social media and SEO by clients', according to Goodson (2012). Other factors that have influenced growth include the growing world markets for consumer goods, local agencies needing modern techniques to promote products, and reduced tax costs in some countries on foreign advertising. Consumerism emerged in the 1960s and endeavoured to redress the balance of power in an imperfect market and protect individual consumers in the process. Consumerists exist either as organisations or loose groups of individuals with similar minds. Consumerism is stronger in developed countries. In the Third World the consumer movement has little power but this is changing. As Alozie (2011: 35) suggests, with developing and emerging countries, 'the debate about the role of advertising in socioeconomic and cultural development of developing nations' continues.

International communication defined

Communication involves the skilful use of all the capacities of language organised into a system of tools, techniques and transmission devices. For example, if the idea of advertising is to create, in the customer's mind, utility and value this means that the marketer has to position the product in a way that makes it desirable to the customer, enabling transference of a basic need into a want. This was discussed in relation to Abraham Maslow's 'hierarchy of needs' used extensively throughout marketing in the last five decades or so (see Chapter 3 of this book). International integrated communication involves the formulation of vision that results in strategy and implementation of an integrated communications plan in more than one country in various parts of the world, as opposed to the entire world, which would then make it global.

The international communications process

The communications process generally was dealt with earlier in Chapter 2 of this book. Both the international marketing and marketing communications literature deal with this by adding some international elements to the basic process. The task that the sender has is to use socio-cultural cues and symbols familiar to the receiver and to select media that are socio-culturally and legally appropriate (if available). The increased difficulties are underscored by the idea of both the sender's and the receiver's 'realm of understanding' and 'field of experience'. Clearly, factors affecting communication in the international context are such things as language (for example brand names), perception (for example colour), values and beliefs (for example veneration of the elderly), or local advertising regulations (for example comparative advertising). This is depicted opposite in Figure 18.1.

The complexity of the situation is clear to see. The difficulties of getting the message across the sender–receiver divide were explained in Chapter 2 of this book. These difficulties are exacerbated in the international setting and key factors are discussed in more depth in the rest of this chapter.

The Snapshot below provides an illustration of some of the difficulties international companies encounter when 'going international' with brand names and straplines, but that such difficulties are not just caused through translations. They are also a result of 'silo thinking'.

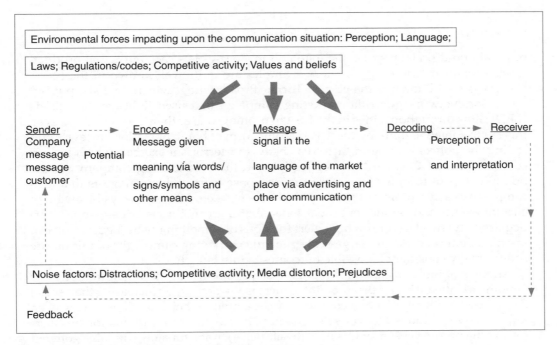

Figure 18.1   The international communications process

Snapshot   Going international and getting lost in translation or some other faux pas?

Kirpich (2013) comments that it may actually be good marketing rather than a mistake on the part of Abercrombie & Fitch when it was announced that A&F did not wish to sell clothes to fat people. Apparently the A&F CEO said as much and on the surface this might appear to be an own goal. However, as Kirpich points out, this may be another way of expressing a marketing fundamental principle – segment the market and market to targets or a target market since A&F wish to market their products to 'cool kids' and no one else and this is good market 'positioning' and 'a solid marketing strategy' and so perhaps not a faux pas (a well-used term in marketing for a mistake, or social blunder) – although a point made in Kirpich's article is very relevant, i.e. making a good marketing move is one thing but 'crowing about it' publically might be the actual faux pas.

Sibley (2012) lists what she considers to be major examples of the making of a marketing faux pas that really cost the company concerned. Sibley, like many of us, appears genuinely shocked that such large, experienced companies and corporations manage to make such howlers, although to be fair there are many things that can go wrong in marketing and marketing communications in particular. Sibley's list includes Gap and Coca-Cola, both of whom appeared to miss the idea that their original brand and identity were worth quite a lot when they changed part of the

(Continued)

(Continued)

original brand (in Gap's case the logo and in Coca-Cola's case the actual product) in an attempt to 'modernise'. These examples are quite well known in the literature. Less well known is the case of Turner Broadcasting, which, in 2007, put out a Cartoon Network guerrilla marketing campaign that used light-emitting diode (LED) signs throughout cities in the USA to promote one of their cartoons. However. this led to someone thinking these were some form of bomb or explosive device and calling the police, leading in turn to a costly anti-terrorism exercise which in turn cost 'the head of Cartoon Network his job and the broadcasting company $2 million in compensation for the emergency response team'. Sibley suggests that 'this campaign is a symptom of thinking in a silo – marketers must always be aware of current events and public sentiment when crafting campaigns. Most people, particularly city dwellers, are on high alert for signs of something fishy. I guess you can say hindsight is 20/20, but large-scale guerrilla marketing campaigns of this nature should really consider all possible outcomes before launch'.

Another of Sibley's examples that is less well known in the literature is that of Timothy's Coffee, a brand that thought to increase awareness by increasing their social media reach with an offer of a coupon or free sample for being a follower. However, rather like the famous Hoover sales promotion example of air flights for products (where the product cost a lot less than the air ticket) 'unfortunately, Timothy's offered more than they could deliver, depleting their supply of free K-cup packs after only three days. Two weeks later, they sent out a message saying it was "first come, first serve". Talk about too little too late. Despite an apology video and the potential for receiving a free coupon in the mail, Timothy's is still trying to recover from the fan backlash on social media'. Sibley rightly urges caution with such promotions that, if they work, might easily harm the brand if the marketer cannot meet the commitments that come with successful marketing communications.

Stop Point

There are many examples of losing something in translation and more besides, especially when it means that the marketer does not understanding the meaning and essence of the brand. Undertake the following: 1. Examine the kinds of messages that can get 'lost in translation' from a marketing perspective and suggest ways in which marketers can avoid such mistakes; 2. Discuss the kinds of issues that arise out of 'silo thinking' and suggest ways in which the temptation to take this route can be avoided.

UNIFORMITY OR NOT – THE STANDARDISATION/ADAPTATION DEBATE

The theme of standardisation/adaptation runs across the subject of international business, marketing and communications. It is associated with economies of scale generally but more specifically here with creative production and number of personnel involved. At the level of the organisation there are a number of ways that can be employed to operate marketing internationally. For example the marketer might opt for central control where the marketing and communication effort is directed from the centre. Another way is to have the HQ act as a resource centre where local managers are free to develop within central directives on agencies and media buying. Another is to have autonomy for each business in each marketplace where minimal or no justification of actions is required. It is unlikely that the business would have complete autonomy, with some sort of approval system in place. Generally speaking the notion of products being culture-bound is well known and used in the literature and could affect this kind of decision, depending upon the nature of the product or service offered.

An alternative strategy in terms of just what might be the same and just what might have to be adjusted, even if only slightly, in different parts of the world has to be a consideration. This applies in the communication arena probably more so than any other type of parameter.

Standardised brand/product and standardised communication are possible but there are other choices, such as:

- standardised brand/product and locally adapted communications;
- locally adapted product/brand and standardised communications;
- locally adapted brand/product and locally adapted communications.

The organisation may or may not have to adapt or customise or modify promotional strategy because of local differences brought about socio-culturally, economically, legally or by the availability – or not – of particular media and media vehicles. With this in mind communications strategy has to be developed and implemented. The usual kind of decision sequence model as propagated in Chapter 4 of this book is also appropriate here and this is dealt with in the last section of this chapter. The central debate remains that of degree of uniformity. The issues (both positive and negative) are rather obvious and include on the plus side economies of scale, consistent message across markets and centralised control, and on the minus side different market characteristics, media availability and costs and government regulations. The stronger argument appears to be that different strategy appears to work in different situations, rather than a totally standardised campaign. Once these geographical issues are decided upon then the scope of the campaign, objectives and elements of strategy can be worked on.

Whether the organisation develops a message for one market and then transposes this intact into others or if it develops a message with a number of markets in mind from the start, it may be centrally conceived in both cases. This is popular because of coordination and control providing the benefit of speed of roll-out. With easier production and fewer staff involved the cost benefits are easy to see. The danger is that factors such as the need for voice-overs/dubbing may not be adequate or may even be disastrous. However, the search for universal symbols and meaning transference in many markets with the same message is an attractive proposition. There are three ways to choose:

- Adoption, where the whole thing is exported, language and all. This can work, for example, with a brand of French perfume.
- Prototype, where concepts and central ideas remain intact but where local input is made use of. The control of this remains in the hands of the company but depends on the quality of the local input.
- Concept cooperation or guideline, where a certain amount of control is kept with the brand and company facets intact, for example company colours, or straplines. This raises the dangers of a lack of control but also the imposition of facets that are wrong for particular markets.

Four creative impediments to centralisation might exist: locals wishing to take control and prove themselves, cost reduction through adapting campaigns that pays less to the agencies than creating a new campaign, local managers do not wish to see their authority decline, and the 'not invented here' syndrome (de Mooij, 1994). The last impediment still persists as an issue for international business theorists. For example Schweizer (2010), commenting on MNCs in India, suggests that there is still a global integration-local responsiveness dilemma because the former is the desired coordination of activities across countries and the latter is the need to respond to specific local need. The local company's identification with the parent can reduce 'not invented here' syndrome issues and problems.

Many authors cover the standardisation/adaptation debate as it applies to branding and communication because it is so fundamental. Standardisation is possible where audiences are similar (for example lifestyles and values), where the same images can be used and where the nature and use of the product is the same or similar, for example involving innovation/innovators and a common technical language of 'high tech' products and where products have a nationalistic flavour (for example country of origin can be important and work). Adaptation is necessary where concentration on the differences is seen as important/necessary to tackle problems encountered by a standardised approach across the marketing environment (from technological to political to social/cultural to media infrastructure). Mueller (1996) adds that where internal differences such as stage in the product/brand life cycle need to be catered for, adaptation will be necessary. Adaptation or customisation will be necessary when market behaviour and in particular consumer behaviour, tastes or habits are different and might even be culture bound. Failure to know about or to recognise differences and be able to meet local needs by adjusting what is being offered can lead to the loss of market opportunities, a waste of resources, and brand or company damage. An example of a company running into trouble was Parker Pen who before the takeover by Gillette in the early 1990s had a decentralised structure and 500 products in its portfolio that were not being managed, there being no economies of scale and no unified driving strategy (Jain et al., 2011).

There is also recognition that the adaptation approach does not necessarily mean changing fundamentals such as core values of the brand. In communication terms the actors in a commercial may be changed (as with Coca-Cola using different national sports and therefore players) at a surface level.

KEY FACTORS AFFECTING INTERNATIONAL MARKETING COMMUNICATIONS

There are myriad factors that potentially affect the international marketing communications process. Key factors have been placed into the three broad groups of (1) constraints/restraints, (2) culture, creativity and branding; and (3) media and production.

Constraints and restraints on communication around the world
Self-regulation

Ethical and regulatory considerations were discussed in Chapter 6 of this book but here the concern is for the international context. Marketing communicators need to be aware of regulations, codes and any other restrictions on any part of the communications process in a country market. They should also endeavour to monitor any changes that may occur. Many in the marketing communications industry believe they should support regulation but at the same time be pro self-regulation. In particular advertising and sales promotion regulations are developed to a reasonable extent in only a relatively small number of countries. The European Advertising Standards Alliance (EASA) suggest that all EU member states have mature self-regulatory codes of advertising practice through self-regulatory organisations (SROs) at national level, all of which are affiliated to the EASA. The EASA has links with 13 industry federations. Many other countries such as the USA, Canada, Australia and South Africa all have mature codes for advertising and sales promotion and there are a sizable number of other countries, more than 50, which at least have some regulation. This is less so for other forms of communication. There are so many situations worldwide regarding different types of products such as alcohol and different types of audience such as children. The whole issue is compounded by the nature of integrated campaigns, i.e. the marketer is not usually dealing with advertising in isolation but with PR, sponsorship or direct marketing and much has changed because of the impact of digital (see Chapter 10 of this book). Self-regulation has three objectives. The first is to protect consumers against false or misleading adverts, against adverts that intrude on privacy, or adverts that are of an offensive nature. The second is to protect legitimate advertisers against false or misleading adverting by the competition. The third is to promote the public acceptance of advertising so that it can remain effective. The marketing communications industry established its own codes of practice to prevent the interference of governments in its affairs. More broadly in terms of consumer protection, self-regulation is promoted by business for business but this has its critics, especially pressure groups such as Consumers International (2013), 'the global campaigning voice for consumers' that was established in 1960 as the world federation of consumer rights groups 'with over 240 member organisations spanning 120 countries'.

The communications environment

Standardisation/adaptation has to be seen in terms of the context of communicating with members of the 'Global Village', a term coined by Marshall McLuhan in the 1960s and a reference now not just to the media and advertising in particular (as McLuhan intended) but also to the entire business world and beyond. 'New World Order' is a term used to describe the economic power shifts occurring continually and has its origins in the study of the development of the world economy. In other words, there is a need to deal with the communication process as a whole and including all of the environmental factors as an integral part of the communications model. The world appears to be rapidly converging in terms of activities, interests, preferences and demographic characteristics leading to readily accessible, homogeneous market groupings. This has a fundamental effect in terms of the communication (and of course the marketing) process. The marketer, in short, has had to question the idea of stereotyping across cultures that might be possible but not desirable or even necessary. The marketer needs to be aware of differences in many things including regulation, laws and unwritten customs and practice. STEP/PEST-type models as discussed in Chapter 4 of this book contain factors that are used to look at situations from a strategic marketing viewpoint are of course relevant to international communication. It is these that underpin activities across markets around the globe. Of course, it may be the case that because of the differences that exist in environmental factors in different countries, certain elements of the communications mix (say certain types of advertising) may not be possible in some markets. Or it may be that for some sector situations (say machine tools), advertising will take a lesser role. The major communication tool might be personal communication of some sort but this mix element can be very different in application in one market rather than in another. The scope of communication will depend on the type of society. For example, in Saudi society much of what goes on in marketing communication terms is a function of religion and hence the law; in the UK marketing communications (and in particular advertising) excesses are restrained by a different code and a different ethic.

International rules, regulations and codes

Regulations made by a country depend on the cultural and otherwise make-up of that country as to whether advertising is seen as being a negative or positive force. The notion that marketing (and advertising in particular) is intrinsically good/bad is important with respect to different countries' and governments' attitude toward it. The role and nature of transnational agencies are an important area in terms of this issue since advertising in particular has had effects, especially in the Third World where there are negative issues such as raising expectations, causing agitation, exercising cultural imperialism and changing the nature of the media. More positively, issues such as the provision of money to develop local advertising and media industries and hence aid development exist.

There are different types of regulatory controls. These include national governments able to control the operations of multinational enterprises through their own law. They can decide which companies can promote which products and how. This means a multinational company needs to seek advice about what it may do in each country. This will vary because of the different origins of laws in different countries, for example whether driven by socialism or Islam. In market economies regulation is usually used only to enable fair competition and to protect the consumer. In the Third World the needs of the economy to develop are important. If the statistics on advertising expenditure and GDP (Gross Domestic Product) are scrutinised the inference is often drawn that there is a positive correlation between advertising expenditure and stage of economic development. The types of media availability vary enormously around the globe and this is not just a function of economic status. It could be easy to draw wildly inaccurate conclusions in this area. Typical measures in the past have been a good correlation for example between economic status and the number of television sets per capita (Toyne and Walters, 1993). More recently van der Wurff and Bakker (2008: 28), exploring the relationships between economic growth and advertising expenditures in various media in 21 industrialised countries, suggested that newspaper advertising expenditures depend more strongly on economic development, more so than advertising spent in other media. Where GDP is higher, newspapers are an important advertising medium and 'a larger proportion of GDP is spent on advertising' and 'Intermedia competition has little impact' but 'generally speaking, economic growth goes hand in hand with rising advertising expenditures', therefore 'advertising expenditures are a measure for aggregate advertising demand'. The debate as to the future of printed newspapers in the context of rising digital formats and access was addressed in Chapter 10 of this book.

It is usually argued in the literature that ethical and regulatory questions have to be addressed since the social benefits of advertising – or the reverse – are particularly sharpened in the international context. The issues include economic value, competitive practices and consumer protection. Economic groupings like the EU offer an interesting insight into the legalistic wrangles. There are a number of issues that are important such as subsidiarity, product issues (usually tobacco, pharmaceuticals, alcohol and financial services), allowance of comparative advertising and sensitive issues such as contraception. Most people believe it is wrong to misrepresent a product. For example, by 1893 the English had a Sale of Goods Act and the situation that sees a fairly mature legal system where advertisers are not allowed to misrepresent facts or breach confidence. In the USA the Federal Trade Commission Act of 1938 set restrictions on the advertising of food, drugs and cosmetics.

The International Chamber of Commerce

As long ago as 1925 The International Chamber of Commerce (ICC), founded in 1919, was shaping things to come and in 1937 established a Code of Standards in Advertising Practice (International Chamber of Commerce, 2013a). The ICC Commission on Marketing and Advertising (International Chamber of Commerce, 2013b) provides 'insightful guidance on marketing and advertising around the globe'. The ICC has thousands of business members globally and is a 'key player in the ever-changing landscape of modern marketing and advertising' that promotes effective self-regulation and best practice. The ICC belief is that effective self-regulation 'builds trust with consumers by ensuring advertising that is honest, legal, decent and truthful' and provides 'quick and easy redress when transgressions occur'. There are now 35 countries on six continents operating under ICC self-regulatory systems with six more countries under development, including China. For example, in April 2011 the ICC code 'served as the foundation of the China Responsible Marketing Code endorsed by the Chinese advertising industry' (International Chamber of Commerce, 2013c).

Regional bodies

Country groupings are an important consideration for the international marketer. Regionally, non-profit making SROs have been formed. For example in Europe the European Advertising Standards Alliance (EASA, formed in 1992) had an average of 53,116 complaints per annum during 2006 to 2010, which the ICC suggests is 'far larger than is likely to realistically be addressed in one year through the official legal system'. About one third of such complaints were upheld while less than half were not upheld (International Chamber of Commerce, 2013c).

A fundamental proposition is that either the business community is capable of self-regulation or, left to their own devices, some firms would break the rules. After all, business exists to make money not moral or ethical judgements. On the other hand intervention is justified for consumer protection. Consider the following contrasting examples of self-regulation versus imposed regulation:

> Within the European Union (EU) European Commission (EC) directives have increasingly become important in all member states. The Directive on Misleading and Comparative Advertising (EC, 2013) has the purpose of protecting 'traders against misleading advertising and its consequences' and it also 'aims to lay down the conditions under which comparative advertising is permitted'. The Directive therefore 'harmonises the rules of the EU countries on comparative advertising' and interfaces with other directives such as the Directive on Unfair Commercial Practices and while it deals with traders at the same time 'Its provisions on comparative advertising also apply in the context of advertising directed at consumers'. Misleading advertising in this context is 'any advertising which, in any way, including in its presentation, is capable of: deceiving the persons to whom it is addressed; distorting their economic behaviour; or as a consequence, harming the interests of competitors'. This is dependent on factors such as the characteristics of the goods or services concerned; the price; the conditions of delivery of the goods or provision of the services involved; the nature, attributes and rights of the advertiser. Comparative advertising within the Directive 'requires traders to make sure that their advertisements: are not misleading; compare "like with like" – goods and services meeting same needs or intended for the same purpose; objectively compare important features of the products or services concerned; do not discredit other companies trademarks; do not create confusion among traders'. The expectation is that each member state will competently enforce the Directive by setting up appropriate and adequate mechanisms that allows and enables 'persons and organisations having a legitimate interest to bring an action to the competent courts or administrative authorities for the cessation and/or the prohibition of misleading or unlawful comparative advertising'. (EU, 2013)

The Gulf Co-operation Council (GCC) consists of Saudi Arabia, Qatar, Kuwait, Oman, UAE and Bahrain. The GCC is a regional organisation that was set up in 1981, its objectives being to 'enhance coordination, integration and inter-connection among its members' (EU, 2013). The GCC members are members of the Arab League and four (Qatar, Saudi Arabia, Kuwait and the UAE) are prominent members of OPEC (the Organisation of Petroleum Exporting Countries): 'The EU established bilateral relations with the GCC countries through the 1988 Cooperation Agreement, intended to: strengthen stability in a region of strategic importance; facilitate political and economic relations; broaden economic and technical cooperation; broaden cooperation on energy, industry, trade and services, agriculture, fisheries, investment, science, technology and environment' (EU, 2013). According to the EU 'The GCC is the EU's fifth largest export market (€75 bns worth of exports in 2011), and the EU is the grouping's biggest trading partner, with trade flows totalling €130 billion, or 13.5% of the GCC's global trade'. The 1988 Agreement is one of a commitment to enter into negotiations on a free trade agreement and although started the negotiations have been suspended several times since, the last suspension being by the GCC in 2010, but informal contacts remain.

In terms of business control within the GCC, regulatory regimes of each of the GCC countries have developed over time where 'market practice has emerged, partly based on legislation, and partly resulting from the idiosyncrasies of each jurisdictions' regulatory bodies' (Ahmedani and Azzam, 2012). According to these authors, in terms of the marketing of securities and financial services, 'recent measures by many of the GCC countries to monitor and restrict marketing activities more closely represent a departure from prior practice and can be seen as a local effort to correspond to the more publicized and burdensome legislation enacted in the US and across the EU'. Within the GCC framework there are still independent regulatory regimes, 'which, in most cases, restrict marketing to local investors without approval from the relevant regulatory bodies' and in recent times 'mainly as a result of the global financial crisis, regulators in some GCC countries have recently taken measures to ratchet up enforcement of laws addressing marketing of foreign securities and financial services, laws developed to protect the local investors from predatory marketing activity. In so doing, they have replicated, to a large extent, the more restrictive rules in Saudi Arabia, where marketing onshore is permitted solely by coordinating with the Saudi Arabian Capital Markets Authority and through locally licensed persons authorized to carry out such activities' (Ahmedani and Azzam, 2012). In marketing communications terms, an example is the idea of 'cold calling' being avoided as is 'negotiating with potential or existing investors while inside or outside the country' whereby local agents become an important ingredient in doing business. Ahmedani and Azzam (2012) suggest that these 'themes are found, to varying degrees, in all GCC countries'. Another example is in Bahrain where 'public presentations or road shows' should be avoided. In this sense there are considerable differences between the EU and the GCC. In terms of marketing activity, the GCC is much more of an umbrella advisory organisation to its member states than the EC's 'directives' orientation.

Examples of other groupings with regulations and codes of conduct that have influence on companies and marketing activities within member states are ASEAN (Association of Southeast Asian Nations) or NAFTA (North American Free Trade Agreement).

Country bodies

Restraint is still very much domestically driven. Local law, culture and technology are all being taken into consideration. A consensus is achieved through consultation with industry and other experts. The voluntary rules and standards of practice go beyond legal obligations and are 'policed' by self-regulatory organisations (SROs): 'They offer consumers increased protection and a cost-effective, accessible and responsive alternative to legal avenues' (International Chamber of Commerce, 2013c).

An ICC example from South America is Consejo de Autorregulación Publicitaria (CONARP), the Argentinian non-profit association whereby most of the complaints received over the last four years have dealt 'with the issue of social sensitivities and truthfulness' and television advertising 'consistently ranks as the leading cause for complaints filed'.

An ICC example from the USA, The Children's Advertising Review Unit (CARU) is a division of the National Advertising Review Council (NARC), the children's arm of the US advertising industry's self-regulation programme that 'evaluates child-directed advertising and promotional material in all media to advance truthfulness, accuracy and consistency through compliance with its Self-Regulatory Guidelines for Children's Advertising and relevant laws'. This suggests that children and more youthful audiences need special consideration and therefore 'CARU performs a high level of monitoring, including the scrutinizing of over ten thousand television commercials, and the review of advertisements in print, radio and online media'. CARU's guidelines address issues including age restrictions on certain types of advertising and data collection, enhanced privacy protection, the need for parental approval, blurring of ads and programme content, avoidance of sales pressure, and ensuring safe, age-appropriate products and messages. According to the ICC, CARU also 'takes an active role in initiating its own reviews. Each year since 2008, the number of advertisements that CARU identified as problematic has dramatically decreased, indicating that advertisers are taking self-regulation seriously and are using CARU's guidance to avoid issues' (International Chamber of Commerce, 2013c).

The United Nations

Some international regulation takes place through the auspices of a small number of international bodies. The regulations regarding advertising and sales promotions are many and varied. The host countries are important and usually are the principal regulators because international law allows for national state sovereignty over their people and resources when at home. The United Nations (UN), however, acts as an international regulator and has a restricted role through the General Assembly's adopted 1985 guidelines on consumer protection, especially in the Third World. The guidelines have been expanded and upgraded, for example in 1999. More latterly there have been calls to upgrade to incorporate digital issues (Consumers International, 2013).

The World Health Organisation

Some international organisations check on specific matters, for example the World Health Organisation (WHO). Boseley (2013) reports that the WHO, the 'public health arm of the UN' has accused companies of deliberately 'finding ways to bypass the rules on advertising unhealthy products to children and fuelling the obesity epidemic'. The WHO's concern is that regulations (and presumably self-regulation also) in Britain on marketing to children are not enough. The issue seems to be one of programming since 'There are tough rules on advertising during children's TV programmes but not on shows such as ITV1's Britain's Got Talent and The X Factor, which research shows are widely watched by younger viewers'. Boseley adds that 'Increasingly, food companies are also targeting children through computer games, mobile phones and social networks such as Facebook' and the WHO report calls for tighter regulation across the whole of Europe 'of the marketing to children of foods high in fat, salt and sugar', with the regional director for Europe suggesting that 'Millions of children across the region are being subjected to unacceptable marketing practices … Policy simply must catch up and address the reality of an obese childhood in the 21st century' (Boseley, 2013).

Product perspectives

Commercial advertising is not allowed in some countries for certain products. Time of day and programming restrictions exist in many countries. The importance of product categories in this area cannot be underestimated. Specific laws and regulations exist with those products associated with health and safety. The main areas for concern in terms of products appear to be the most obvious. Some examples are tobacco, alcohol, pharmaceuticals, financial services, children's products (especially toys but increasingly food and drink), baby food, and cosmetics. For example with tobacco, much is debated here but basically there are two viewpoints. First, a ban on advertising will cut cigarette consumption. Second, advertising only affects brand differentiation, not the number of smokers. The UK has gone for a ban while Germany, the Netherlands, Denmark and Greece still oppose a total ban. With France, references to social and financial success are not permitted adding to an already severely restrictive situation for alcohol marketers that have a requirement to include health warnings. Another example is concern about food products with high salt, fat and sugar content and the advertising and other marketing communication that surround them. This is especially the case where children are involved, as reflected in the WHO report mentioned earlier. There is concern, for example, by Ofcom, the UK broadcasting regulator, about children's exposure to advertising, when children are viewing and the viewing of family rather than children's television. Other concerns are in the areas of the Internet, mobile phones, social media, within gaming, other ambient media, and not least sponsorship by the likes of Kellogg's, McDonald's and Coca-Cola. These multinationals of course defend their positions. Boseley (2013) reports that in the case of Kellogg's, 'The Company says that its partnership with the Amateur Swimming Association is one involving the corporate brand, Kellogg's, and there is no branding for products such as Coco Pops'. McDonald's and Coca-Cola suggest that Olympic sponsorships encourage sport, fitness and people's wellbeing.

Creative content perspectives

Creative content is of particular concern for marketers, especially those who use advertising, sales promotions and direct marketing tools. For example, some countries have laws as to whether foreign language can be used in the adverting. In Germany comparative advertising was been banned in 1909 but the EC appears to like comparative advertising since it apparently assists consumers (when it is not misleading) and this has been relaxed across the EU. Further afield than the EU and EC Directives, the world picture is rather diffused in terms of what restrictions there are on creative content. In the Arab world for example, Islam plays a huge part, it being a fusion of culture/religion and law and not least of importance here is the role and representation of women. In many countries there is concern for dishonesty in advertising. Of interest in Saudi Arabia in particular are products such as alcohol and activities such as gambling. Real rather than perceived benefits are valued otherwise fraud is seen as being committed. In Saudi Arabia the government controls television programming and advertising. Traditionally there has been concern for the prevention of sins and order of good deeds. Kettman-Kervinen (2013) suggests that in Saudi Arabia changes are being made and fresh ideas being brought in. For example there is recognition of the 'younger demographics of the country' and this means the marketing communications (particularly advertising) industry 'want to see more of this local talent working with them. And as it all evolves boutique consultancies and ad agencies are setting up shops and seeing more clients walk in. Now the clients of the ad agencies more than ever before are ready to take risks and use gimmicks.' It also means that the media has changed to incorporate smart phones, social media and other online engagement 'which represents an incredible potential for the ad industry'. On top of this 'More and more non-Arabic speakers (non-Saudis) are leading marketing teams, bringing in their own accent. Women are finally adding a much needed "feminine' touch"'. Kettman-Kervinen admits there are still cultural taboos and the 'strict laws that seem to be the main braking element in the process of modernization', but adds that 'Sometimes strict regulations can become a motivating factor to bend the simple creativity and go even beyond it. If you still have doubts, just check out some visuals originated in Saudi Arabia and evaluates their creativity for yourself'. One example is the way the launch of the Change Lingerie brand in Saudi Arabia was handled by utilising the concept behind censorship.

Social responsibility and ethics

Chapter 6 of this book discussed aspects of social responsibility, ethics and regulation generally. The area of social responsibility and ethics internationally encompasses many things. International marketers should be aware that the Consumer Movement is generally in favour of legislation to provide consumers with information (data, especially comparative), education and knowledge of, for example, how to deal with companies, protection against deception and health and safety. Basically and generally speaking, self-regulation is not trusted. Advertising in particular is seen by supporters as being a positive force serving to educate, inform, to provide lower prices and improve quality, to stimulate the local economy and provide jobs, and can generally be used for the social good as within social marketing campaigns such as for the promotion of condom use in anti-Aids campaigns. Alternatively, detractors see it as a negative force that engenders cultural imperialism, raises expectations and causes agitation, and mitigates against consumer protection. International business is seen by some to hit local competition hard especially where status is attached to having the big brands, and responsible for exaggerated claims and even deceit (deception is considered a crime in most countries). There is a distinction between hard and soft advertising issues of sex, decency, tastelessness, sexist, racist, demeaning through stereotyping, violence against and the objectification of women (where there is no relevance) and obscenity. In most cases, however, it is down to interpretation but there may be rules to prevent the promotion of many Western goods that may be viewed as too tempting. Some countries will only allow home-produced goods in order to encourage local demand. Religious principles may prevent certain products from being advertised. General laws tend to exist to ensure that advertising content is not false, misleading or unfair. These may be adopted and become mandatory in a particular market so that marketers need to be aware of change, including restrictions on the media. There is much interest in Corporate Social Responsibility (CSR) as a useful tool in enhancing corporate image.

The Snapshot below highlights the tensions created between multinational corporations and the consumer movement in the developing world by the activities of both 'sides'. The discussion focuses on Unilever and Corporate Watch and hints at some of the reasons why tensions exist and why it is essential that clear communication of objectives relating to projects such as clean water or sanitation is a necessity. It also discusses the unlikely alliance between McDonald's and Greenpeace.

Snapshot   Saving or using the developing world?
Unilever versus Corporate Watch:
McDonald's versus Greenpeace?

Global companies and brands such as Unilever, Procter and Gamble, Microsoft, Google, Apple or McDonald's influence many people throughout the world, including those poorer countries classified as developing countries that have the lowest incomes. The success of the multinational company and brands will still depend,

(Continued)

(Continued)

however, on the customer's willingness and ability to buy. How much change occurs from advertising and communications and how much from the product and brands is debatable. However, brand consumption can lead to a change in behaviour but certain behaviour is seen as correct in different societies and situations. If the company get this wrong in any part of the development process, for example within advertising and communications, then a project can easily fail as when the wrong message is sent because of lack of understanding of customs and practices. One reason that global communication is so difficult to achieve is because our individual understanding of it is different due to differences in values and beliefs and hence customs and practices. Multinational corporations such as Unilever work in developing countries on projects such as 'World Toilet Day' (Unilever, 2012). For example, the project in Vietnam is based on 'Toilets for Health'; a white paper by the London School of Hygiene and Tropical Medicine and the Unilever brand Domestos, 'gives new insights in the sanitation crisis. In Ho Chi Minh City the first Domestos Toilet Academy was opened and in London an interactive statue "The Public Toilet" was revealed. The United Nations has declared access to sanitation a basic human right, yet almost a third of the world's population suffer from a lack of access to improved sanitation. Unilever, under its Sustainable Living Plan, has committed to helping more than one billion people take action to improve their health and well-being' (Unilever, 2012).

Such projects are not without their critics and nor are the multinationals themselves. For example Corporate Watch (2013) provide a list of Unilever's 'Corporate Crimes', including 'promoting consumerism'. Corporate Watch suggest that 'Unilever spends a lot of energy and money on marketing and commercialisation of consumer products all over the world'. Corporate Watch provide a number of Unilever brand examples which they say are part of the crime of 'promoting consumerism'. For example the 'Paint the World Yellow' Lipton tea brand marketing campaign 'which provide everything with the Lipton Logo, from surfboards to Chevrolets – was a tremendous success, according to Unilever. It created a much bigger Lipton Logo awareness amongst consumers'. However, Corporate Watch suggest that this is just part of an expansion move into the southern hemisphere because the 'Northern consumer market is saturated'. While Unilever's aim is to maximise the processing of food by 'adding value to "improve" products and then charge more for these products', according to Corporate Watch 'Unilever changes the product only slightly (e.g. strawberry toothpaste), or just changes the visual language in order to sell exactly the same product'. The accusation is that such 'new improved' products are of little or no value and demand is created by the manufactures using tools such as advertising but also brand image to seduce people into wanting products 'because of their supposed "high quality" and because they can be associated with luxurious, western lifestyles'.

There are clearly tensions between multinational corporations and consumer and environmental organisations, especially in the developing world where international business is under particular scrutiny. There are signs, however, that the two 'sides' can actually work together. For example Sauven (2006) explains how Greenpeace worked with McDonald's to change the food industry's attitude towards Amazon soya production that is damaging the rainforest. As Sauven points out 'Business journalists have often been quick to accuse groups like Greenpeace of nurturing a knee-jerk hostility to global corporations. Well, yes, we do hold the view that multinationals are responsible for much of the environmental degradation blighting our planet'. However, alliances are not impossible, Sauven adding that 'I cannot say it came naturally to Greenpeace to jump into bed with the world's largest fast food company! But it is a fact that, in this instance, the company immediately recognised the nature of the problem'.

Stop Point

The multinationals fulfil a vital role in the developing resources but at the same time are held to account by shareholders. Consumer and environmental organisations exist to, for example, fight the excesses of such organisations. Undertake the following: 1. Comment on the extent to which multinationals are likely to use southern hemisphere contexts in order to develop business that has reached its limits in the northern hemisphere; 2. Explain why, after years of attrition, Greenpeace and McDonald's in 2006 became bedfellows in order to tackle the food industry's attitude toward Amazon soya and the degradation of the environment.

CULTURE, CREATIVITY, BRANDING AND MEDIA

Culturally plausible international communication

A popular strategic position for international organisations to adopt is one of 'plan global, act local'. In communication terms there may be a great temptation to engage in stereotyping in terms of nationalities but generally this should be avoided, whether in the context of selling into a particular country or in terms of using 'country of origin effect', except in certain specific cases where it has been shown to work. Using stereotypes can lead to huge and inaccurate generalisations. Examples of this are where 'the Germans' are seen as being rational, descriptive and informative, 'the British' as subtle, understated, ironic and humorous, 'the French' as innovative, modern and attention getting, and 'the Americans' as emotional, lifestyle-obsessed and glamorous. This is not really at all helpful unless based on a firm foundation of sound research. The relationship between culture and behaviour is important. Culture has many definitions as discussed in Chapter 3 of this book. As a reminder, Hofstede (1980: 43) for example defines culture as 'the collective mental programming of the people in an environment' where culture is not a characteristic of individuals but rather it 'encompasses a number of people who were conditioned by the same education and life experience'. Culture is important in marketing because it differs between societies. What may be very acceptable in one country might not be in another. This is because culture is learnt. Culture has also been defined as 'the sum total of learned beliefs, values and customs that serve to direct the consumer behaviour of members of a particular society' (Schiffman et al., 2008: 368).

Levels of culture

There are a number of different aspects of culture important to the international organisation. This includes things like national culture and this is often used in a humorous way but there is a danger of stereotyping, as mentioned above. Consider for example eating habits, dress habits at work, Sunday dress habits, gender roles, or social class as discussed in Chapter 3 of this book. All of these are cultural artefacts and can have a profound effect on the ability of the international organisation to have a standardised approach to its communications as well as other things. In order to gain a better understanding at the international level a number of tools have been developed over the last few decades, as follows.

Expressions of culture can be better understood by using Hofstede's 'onion model' as discussed in Chapter 3 of this book, i.e. symbolic, heroes, rituals, values and beliefs and customs and practices with the resultant expressions of culture. Symbols carry meaning that is interpreted differently according to culture. These symbols include objects, pictures, gestures and words. Words of course are obvious; the language is not just the words and their individual meanings in different countries but the jargon specific to that part of a region of a country. Gestures are important. The Japanese for example smile a lot when they do not understand. Some people nod their head up and down when they mean no, others from side-to-side. The Eskimos have many words for snow. The Hopi (a tribe of Native American people) deal in facts not present/past. The word 'coke' has lots of meanings in the West and this is increasing elsewhere. There are lots of faux pas around, as mentioned in Chapter 17 of this book, because of poor translation, from the Nova (a 'won't go' car in Spanish) to the lack of understanding of the symbolic importance to the meaning of colour (white or black can mean mourning, yellow death). A hero that might be of use in the international context would have to have the same meaning and be valued in the same way in many societies otherwise the communication would fail because of lost or distorted meaning. In order to get it right a brand like Coca-Cola might use sport as a platform but change the sport and hence change the sporting hero who, as a celebrity, is used to endorse the brand and is better at communicating attributes of the brand. Rituals are considered essential within society until they are eroded. Nationalism and pride can be tied up with rituals, for example, consider the London 2012 Olympics. It is often not possible for an observer to understand the reasoning behind the ritual, but get it wrong in an advert and the product may be doomed. Certain values are held by some cultures to be more important than others. For example a car advert in the UK had a storyline whereby a woman celebrated her divorce. This would not be seen as an appropriate storyline in a country where the divorce rate is very low and ending a marriage is frowned upon. Beliefs are feelings people have about things, often expressed through non-verbal communication or verbal statements. Values are more important than beliefs because many in a society see them as a guide to what is appropriate. These mental images affect how a person will respond to an advert and whether the effect will be desirable. Globalisation and increased world business and communication may have led to the creation of global cultures around companies and brands. There exists some global advertising and communication, for example Pepsi, Coca-Cola, McDonald's or Marlboro. The corporate cultures of multinational companies tend to reflect the cultures of the companies involved. Undeniably, advertising in particular can have influence on people in countries as diverse as the USA, Estonia, Tanzania, Jordan or Australia.

Hofstede's 6 Dimensions model, as discussed in Chapter 3 of this book, originally had four dimensions and then five when long-term orientation was added, then six when indulgence versus restraint was added. Clearly in the international setting there are certain additional constraints on the creation and execution of communication. Hofstede's 6 Dimensions model is a useful tool to break down the amorphous mass that culture can be and as such is used extensively in the literature, not least by de Mooij and/or Hofstede himself (see for example de Mooij and Hofstede, 2010; de Mooij and Goodrich, 2011; or de Mooij and Hofstede, 2011), but also in practice by agencies/consultancies.

The context of culture has been used extensively in the literature and is based on the work by anthropologist Edward T. Hall (Hall, 1976). The Maximum/Minimum Continuum, as presented by Mueller (1996) is one of compared cultures and a useful construct for the manager wishing to understand cultural differences and similarities. One example at the maximum end of the sociocultural continuum is the apparent difference between what is Western and what is Asian. The argument is that if one takes a deeper look into this divide it might be found that in some respects a farmer in China has more in common with a farmer in the USA than the latter does with a Wall Street executive. Maximum sociocultural differences are said to exist in divides such as gender or geographical location (urban/rural).

Culture has a powerful effect on communication where context means that which surrounds and is the background to all things including communication and other related happenings or events. High context cultures include most of the Middle East, Asia, Africa, and South America. Peoples within these areas are said to be relational and collectivist (showing the clear link with Hofstede's Dimensions Model). They are also said to be intuitive (rather than reasoned) and contemplative, and therefore interpersonal relationships are emphasised with a preference for the harmony of the group and consensus rather than confrontation or the individual's achievement. In communication terms words are less important than tone of voice or non-verbal communication such as facial gestures or posture so that communication in high context is formal and language more fluid and expansive. Humility is a key factor and apology common. Low context cultures include the USA, Canada and much of Western Europe. Peoples within these areas are more individualistic and action-oriented (which tallies with the VALS-type system as discussed in Chapter 3 of this book). Logic is valued as are facts and directness whereby problem solving tends to be much more linear in terms of evaluation. Communication therefore has a tendency to be direct and concise and this is seen as being efficient with few but precise words. Actions are concluded and deals signed off, something that can be a stark contrast to high context 'word is my bond' scenarios.

Many writers and researchers have used and developed Hall's theory of context, for example Mueller's (1987) whose research distinguishes between high and low context culture citing Japan as collectivist and the USA as individualist, illustrating the importance to marketers the difference when they are dealing with Japanese or US culture. This begs the question as to how context can help explain miscommunication between Americans and Japanese and the need for international organisations to become better international communicators. Marketers have to consider how useful the concept of context is when looking at different cultures, especially from an international marketing and communications management viewpoint, since the kinds of differences there might be between Japanese and US culture, and what similarities might exist, will have an impact on message construction or brand image. This may mean the difference high-low-medium product involvement makes the marketing process and why it is more important in some contexts than in others. Appeals and associations might therefore work differently in different cultures. De Mooij (2010) using the example of individualism, looks deeper into the US and Japanese context and concludes that individualism exists in both cultures but these are very different. From a management perspective this means that individualism can be used creatively in both but obviously with different treatments with plenty of scope to take advantage of similarities and differences, especially in the knowledge that a 'picture says a thousand words' (see also de Mooij and Hofstede, 2010).

Culture, consumer behaviour and creative strategy

Here we look at how advertising and other aspects of marketing communications may work creatively but in the international setting. Prescriptions from admen, theories from academics or social commentary from journalists – it seems that most people are fascinated by advertising in particular and how it works. However, the approach taken in the international context will very much depend on the company and its understanding of international marketing. International communication may be seen as being designed to help market the same product in different countries and cultures. However, this implies that the communication can be standardised; many authors agree that this is not the case with even companies such as IKEA, 'often cited as an example of a "global" retailer which pursues a similar "standardized" approach in every market' opting to adapt (Burt et al., 2008). These authors look at 'four commonly identified retail marketing mix activities – merchandise, location and store format, the selling and service environment, and market communication' in three countries (Sweden, the

UK and China) and conclude that 'whilst IKEA operates a standardized concept, degrees of adaptation can be observed in customer facing elements, and in the supporting "back office" processes which support these elements'. They suggest that the 'adaptations arise from differences in consumer cultures and the length of time and subsequent exposure to and experience of the market', and suggest that it may be that 'replicating the concept, rather than replicating the activities' is what is required.

Creative themes and concepts, discussed in Chapter 8 of this book, can be viewed as 'how it is said' rather than what, and involves copy and dialogue (verbal) and visuals and illustrations (non-verbal) communications. The two broad kinds of appeal are on the one hand rational and the other emotional. This is often referred to as hard and soft sell respectively. For example the French are said to like humour and sex appeals while the British display a great fondness for class division, eccentric behaviour and puns. The reality of situations is more complex than this rather simple distinction, these kind of statements being as they are very much generalisations. With verbal communication (copy and dialogue) things like brand names come to the fore but it is much more than this. Linguistic and managerial guidelines in this area in the international context have been covered in the literature for some time, although this is an important area of study that is fluid in terms of research. For example Hornikx et al. (2010) look at whether English or a local language should be used for advertising slogans in the Netherlands. This research found that easy to understand English slogans, were preferred to harder to understand English slogans, but also that when slogans were easy to understand in both English and Dutch, English was preferred. When slogans were difficult to understand in both languages, English was appreciated as much as Dutch. The authors suggest that within this particular context a standardised approach was appropriate. However, with non-verbal communication (visuals and illustrations), the usual claim is that less confusion will be the outcome because of the lack of translation difficulties. Settings and backdrops have different meanings for different people of different cultures (Mueller, 1996). These hinder standardised campaigns in the same vein it is dangerous to ignore symbolism. For example in a Nigerian study of the use of different types of symbols and language, Alozie (2011) looked at the relationship between advertising and culture through the use of semiotic analysis. It was found that common symbols were of human bodies and products and not Nigerian ethnic or national symbols. Rather, African and Western symbols were found to be used, but there was a lack of the use of Nigerian languages, including Pidgin English that is widely used in Nigerian society and other African countries.

Universal or culture-bound themes and concepts do exist but the assumption that there are universal themes and concepts available is not always a good one. The pursuit of universals can stifle creativity. De Mooij (1994) makes the distinction between the appeal and the execution whereby the strategy may be universal but the execution may well be localised. For example the family appeal of McDonald's is universal but, within Spain, or rather Catalonia, the execution is Catalan and is different to other parts of Spain. Ideas generated centrally might remain while surface-level treatments differ. Below is a closer look at both the universal and the culture-bound themes and concepts.

Universal – de Mooij (for example 1994) suggests that such themes and concepts could be applied everywhere and are capable of offering solutions to problems in any landscape or environment. This can achieve improved quality or productivity. Basic everyday themes (for example motherhood or jealousy), new products (novel features or new concerns such as environmentalism), service (particularly in industrial marketing) or special expertise (particularly technology or engineering) all can be employed. There are many more; for example the 'made in' concept (country of origin effect, appealing to national pride or particular expertise), demonstration, universal images (such as the Red Cross), media-driven concepts (such has the youthfulness of MTV), lifestyle concepts (but where adaptation of execution may be necessary), and heroes (possible but with adaptation of execution). From a practical viewpoint agency IM! (2013) acknowledge that 'We are all different' but that 'we have more in common than differences'. IM! use University of Michigan social psychology research on human universals to illustrate the many universals there are and that can be harnessed for use in international communication, including gift-giving and healing the sick. IM! also acknowledge, however, that 'Naturally, these common "hot buttons" must be shaped into a universal form and convey symbolism that can be understood and assimilated by everyone. To this end, campaign execution is critical'. The agency uses the phrase 'deep encoding generators' since if used effectively such themes can achieve 'deep memory encoding' and suggest that 'It's all about associating a brand or product with a stable, long-lasting recollection. The memory trace is stronger, as is the potential for dynamic behavioural effects.'

Culture-bound – Many writers, such as Mueller (2011), also cover the (almost) opposite of universals, i.e. culture-bound themes and concepts. This includes things that are personal ideas and opinions (for example the notion of slimness being attractive is not universally held), customs and moral values (for example nudity in France is not such a big a hang-up as it seems to be in the UK), humour (does not travel well), motivation (can be seen in examples of household products that are convenient, i.e. there is an incentive so that time can be freed up), individuality and the role of women (involving clothing and sexual overtones), and comparative advertising (the differences between markets, for example Japan and the USA, where losing face is looked on very differently in these two cultures). De Mooij (2010) emphasises that like language, visuals are strongly culture-bound. If this is so then translation would be a requirement in order to enhance meaning. Much of this is debatable, however, and in need of qualification. For example, with humour, there is little doubt that what makes the French laugh might fall flat elsewhere outside of France but the use of incongruity, i.e. contrast highlighted by that which is expected and unexpected, the use of a certain type of clown or an actual type of humour such as 'slapstick' comedy (of the Charlie Chaplin kind), might be considered universals.

The importance of branding internationally

Chapter 7 of this book dealt with branding and advertising. The relationship between brands and communication (particularly advertising) at the international level is crucial. International communication of one form or another is therefore placed within the management of the organisation and a link between the philosophy of the organisation, say, Coca-Cola, and its advertising, say, a global message of one world harmony whereby its mission involves refreshing the world, to inspire moments of optimism and happiness and to create value and make a difference. The standardisation/adaptation debate is inescapable. The importance of corporate mission and vision that deal with 'what you are doing' and 'where and what you want to be doing', at some time in the future, cannot be overlooked. Mission should be viewed as a strategic discipline, part of the intellect of the organisation, the cultural glue that binds the organisation's often-disparate elements – in essence the soul of the organisation and the reason for being.

Branding as competitive strategy and comparative advantage can be achieved through the product trade cycle (Product Life Cycle, trade and investment) where notions of 'trickle down' as opposed to 'waterfall' effects should be considered. The latter represents the rapid diffusion of brands internationally, the former the slower diffusion of brands in marketplaces. The configuration and coordination of the business and marketing effort and the ease or difficulty of implementing a standardised strategy are determined by culture, infrastructure, economic and technological effects but driven by such things as economies of scale and global corporate/brand image. Branding and advertising have their place in emerging homogeneous, single markets where successful brand names and personalities are themselves determined by linguistics, distinctiveness, adaptability, international applicability, logos and graphics, national characteristics of brand attributes, and culturally plausible advertising platforms.

International and global branding and communication therefore involves the encouragement of competition, economies of scale, product development, stimulation of economic growth, improved products due to competition amongst brands, lower prices, and greater variety. These are seen to be the case irrespective of whether the economy is centrally planned or market-oriented. Conventional wisdom seems to say that no amount of advertising, however good, will enable a poor product to succeed. It is clear, however, that communication plays a vital role in getting across the benefits and availability of a product and also can explain how a product may be used to best advantage.

The media and production across borders

Chapter 9 dealt with the traditional media and media planning generally and Chapter 10 with the newer, digital media forms. Both chapters make some allusion toward the international context. Put in this context the various media can be severely limiting for certain product types. For example there is a complex situation with regard to alcohol in France where largely marketing communications are not allowed. Despite being one of the world's most important wine producers the Evin Law of 1991 almost entirely banned the advertising of alcohol and tobacco across France in order to combat, in the case of wine, alcoholism. The law dealt with issues such as drinks over 1.2 per cent alcohol by volume, the targeting of young people, a ban on advertising on television and in cinemas, and sponsorship of cultural or sports events. There are proposals to go further during 2013–17 with further bans on the Internet and social media including wine promotion. Although wine producers' websites would be exempt, blogging would not and this would counter the modification of the law in 2009 whereby 'many online sites have been allowed to relax their strict anti-alcohol rules'. However, there are other moves to distinguish between wine and other alcohol given that 'wine remains the major source of direct and indirect jobs, and the second largest income earner for the government at export' (Anson, 2013). There are many other examples of disparities between different countries and market situations around the availability and access to the various media, such as that of TV and radio advertising, that has only relatively recently been allowed in Saudi Arabia (1992), but as Kalliny et al. (2008) suggest television advertising in the Arab world has enormous potential because of the proliferation of satellite television across the region and there are some similarities with television advertising in the USA.

With advertising in multi-country settings the restrictions on the use of materials and content are magnified beyond those of the domestic context. Some of these issues may have a profound effect on the organisation's ability to produce standardised communication. There is a vast array of issues to deal with. For example the use of foreign words in communications in some countries is not allowed and there may even be restrictions on the use of foreigners. Music may have to be prepared locally with local actors (including for voice-overs) and crews. There are varying rules for the use of children as actors (child actors) that may be linked to the film and television programme industry generally. The use of actual professional practitioners such as doctors and dentists varies around the world. Government attitudes towards public ownership, especially of the broadcast media, are important here. An obvious example is the nature and future of the BBC (British Broadcasting Corporation) where there is no broadcast advertising as such in the UK, but this is much more complex across the BBC's worldwide activities and across different media. The BBC's own website in this matter proclaims that 'advertising on BBC Worldwide commercial TV channels, platforms and properties and on BBC World News connects brands to influential, affluent and engaged audiences, and aligns them with the creative thinking and campaign expertise of BBC Advertising. Work with BBC Advertising to find the best opportunities for advertising, sponsorship and branded partnerships for your client or your brand' (BBC, 2013). With television and radio broadcasting alone, many other countries have a mix of commercial and state-run television and radio broadcasting from Greece to Nigeria, China to Russia, in a highly complex worldwide marketing communications context.

The media briefing should include giving those involved clear ideas of media objectives, targets, balance and placement. For example Four Communications were involved with the Jumeirah Golf Estates (JGE), part of Leisurecorp, formed by Dubai World. This client's golf development was due to be the host of the Dubai World Classic Golf Tournament and the objective of the campaign to which Four Communications were appointed was to 'promote internationally the Phase One developments which were targeted to be fully sold by the end of 2007'. In order to achieve this, targets were identified in the UK, Europe, Russia and India and 'Print and online media were the key drivers of the campaign. A mixture of indigenous and international publications was identified from within property, lifestyle magazines, business and the lifestyle supplement market in order to talk to target audiences in a multitude of environments and mind sets.' In addition 'A full 3 day exclusive sponsorship of the European tour website was negotiated to coincide with the announcement of The Race to Dubai'. The result was that the Phase One developments 'were fully sold by the beginning of December' and Four Communications still works closely with JGE (Four Communications, 2013). Another example is that of Danone, the French food product multinational. Macleod (2013) comments that Danone has 'plans of consolidating its arrangements' and is 'looking to consolidate its media arrangements into either a single network or a network for each of Europe, North America and Asia'. In this case a full briefing would be expected.

The Snapshot below illustrates the temptation to use stereotypes in marketing communication, particularly in advertising, at any level. Whether the business is a small firm or a multinational corporation the argument against is the same; the superficial use of stereotypes will harm the business and/or brand and the message is an old one – strive to understand the target customer.

Snapshot Stereotyping gender and national culture – pink or blue or red, white and blue?

Ringer (2013) of the advertising agency Anthem contends that for gender stereotyping 'anything goes' these days and the temptation to 'play to safe gender stereotypes' should be ditched since times have changed: 'Women are increasingly taking on traditional male roles on building sites, banks and at the helm of Fortune 500 companies. Meanwhile an increasing number of their gender opposites are taking on typically female roles; the rise of the stay-at-home Dad has been well documented'. Ringer is of course referring to particular societies and not all societies when it comes to issues of gender. In his example of children's toys, girls are typically pink and the focus is on kitchen equipment and infant care, 'However, thanks to the growing shift in gender roles, traditional colour, design, merchandising and advertising in the toy industry is now finally starting to look past simple pink and blue branding'. Ringer makes reference to toy maker Hasbro and its move away from purple (apparently a 'traditionally feminine colour') to black and silver for a

(Continued)

(Continued)

toy oven that will be launched as a gender-neutral product, as the purple version Hasbro created was 'reinforcing the stereotype that the kitchen is a place for girls only'. Ringer urges Hasbro to 're-evaluate its entire product portfolio' since it 'could be a fresh platform that breaks convention' and suggests that 'consumer restlessness against demographic stereotypes' is growing and 'widening the demand for gender-neutral toys' but also suggests that this is 'less about gender and more about attitudes, aptitudes and mindsets'.

Wolfe (2013) argues that customers are individuals with feelings and should not be pegged 'into mass impersonal groups based on stereotypes', and urges the reader not to make assumptions such as 'all retirees are interested in gardening, all women are interested in buying shoes, or all men are sports-crazy' since this can 'lead to disastrous results in advertising and marketing' while recognising that many 'corporations still try to capitalize on stereotypes'. Highlighting stereotype myths, Wolfe illustrates with a number of examples including stereotyping video games as only being for kids whereas 'Nearly a quarter of all video games are purchased by consumers aged 40 and older, and 38% of all video game sales are made by women'. Another example is the stereotyping of 'men's' products 'including sports items and expensive cars' although women spend more than men on these products and 'Senior citizens have become the fastest-growing population in the United States', yet according to Wolfe, mass marketing to seniors has remained somewhat elusive. Several pioneers in the senior marketing industry note that age alone has little to do with the interests of senior consumers.' Lumping people together in this stereotyping way has led to failure 'and miserably so'. Wolfe argues 'It pays to see your customers as individuals, with common needs, but not as groups who, because of stereotype images, have lemming-like behaviors when it comes to making purchases'.

Stop Point

It may appear the obvious thing for a marketer and advertiser to do but the use of stereotypes can be a dangerous move for any business large and small. It may be that there is a use for stereotyping in certain situations. Undertake the following: 1. Discuss the notion that gender roles have changed in some societies but perhaps not in others and there is therefore a need for marketers to be constantly vigilant with regard to the messages they send and avoid the use of stereotypes; 2. Discuss the use of national stereotypes and the use of symbols such as national flags in international marketing communication campaigns.

Assignment

You are required to write a consultative report for an organisation of your choice. The report should include an outline communications plan that follows the steps of the APIC decision sequence model advocated in Chapter 4 of this book and reflect ideas at the international level discussed in this chapter. In effect you are designing a case study. Your case should deal with all aspects of international communications for the chosen organisation. The case should have specific, international communication 'problems' or issues as its focus.

The quality and relevance of the communications problems posed are important. You may choose a situation that involves an existing company or brand or choose something hypothetical such as the launch of an international brand or brand extension. The focus might be the launch of a new product into a marketplace where the company is unknown or already known, and it could suggest the addition of a new brand to an existing range applied to a country or countries of your choice.

Summary of Key Points

- There is a history to international integrated marketing and corporate communications.
- International communications is well defined and understood in the literature.
- There has been, over the last few decades, major growth in e-commerce and digital technologies, including social media, which have impacted upon international commerce.
- Problems within the communications process are exacerbated in the international context.
- The standardisation/adaptation debate is very important in international communications.
- There are strategic choices to be made but many would agree that it is best to 'think global, act local' or go 'glocal'.
- The three broad areas that have the biggest impact on international marketing communications are restrictions and codes of conduct, culture and branding, and media and production.
- There are difficulties with international marketing research in terms of achieving equivalence across markets.
- There is an international dimension to the elements of the environment in which communication has to work.
- The full range of the marketing communications mix elements can be used with adjustments at the international level.
- Implementation of international marketing communications campaigns is fraught with difficulties within multilocal contexts.
- The APIC decision sequence model is equally apt in the international marketing communications context.

Discussion Questions

1. Define international communications. Examine how a historical perspective can give an insight into current-day change for marketers using marketing communications.
2. Highlight what is likely to be different about the communications process in the international context as opposed to the domestic situation.

(Continued)

(Continued)

3. Briefly explain the standardisation/adaptation debate as applied to marketing communications. Explain, in broad terms, the strategic options available to marketers.

4. Broadly distinguish between laws and self-regulatory codes that affect company communications. Use examples to illustrate this difference in the international context.

5. Explain the relationship between branding and communication at the international level using examples to illustrate.

6. Explain why you agree or disagree that national stereotyping is a dangerous thing to do in international marketing communications campaigns.

7. Discuss the importance for managers of having some form of target market classification system rather than relying on aspects of culture approach within particular markets.

8. Given the advent of the Internet and other digital media forms and the fragmentation that has taken place in recent years, examine the current trends in media worldwide using examples of your choice to illustrate.

9. Outline the key sources of information for effective international media selection using examples to illustrate.

10. Explain the use of the APIC decision sequence model as an aid to international integrated marketing communications.

Further Reading

Al-Areefi, M.A., Hassali, M.A. and Ibrahim, M.I.B.M. (2013) 'A qualitative study exploring medical representatives' views on current drug promotion techniques in Yemen', *Journal of Medical Marketing*, 12 (3): 143–9. http://mmj.sagepub.com/content/12/3/143
The authors are concerned about the use of free medical samples, bonuses and commissions paid, when promoting pharmaceutical products using representatives who are a key part of marketing strategy for the big pharmaceutical companies around the world. This study is set in Yemen and as such represents an in-depth look at drug promotion in a particular market context. The findings suggest that like in many other contexts, medical representatives in Yemen are concerned about patients and unethical practices and the need to have professional ethics, law enactment and policies for drug promotion.

Alozie, E.C. (2010) 'Advertising and culture: semiotic analysis and dominant symbols found in Nigerian mass media advertising', *Journal of Creative Communications*, 5 (1): 1–22. http://crc.sagepub.com/content/5/1/1
This article looks at culture and cultural values through the use of semiotic analysis of Nigerian advertisements. The author found that the common symbols found were of human bodies and products and not Nigerian ethnic or national symbols, while African and Western symbols were found to be used. The study also found a lack of the use of Nigerian languages, including Pidgin English that is widely used in Nigerian society and other African countries.

Hornikx, J., van Meurs, F. and de Boer, A. (2010) 'English or a local language?: the appreciation of easy and difficult English slogans in the Netherlands', *Journal of Business Communication*, 47 (2):169–88. http://job.sagepub.com/content/47/2/169

This Dutch study looks at the use of English versus local language in advertising. The authors used car advertising with both easy and more difficult to understand slogans in an empirical study on preference. Easy to understand English slogans were found in the study to be preferred to harder to understand English slogans but also that when slogans were easy to understand in both English and Dutch, English was preferred. When slogans were difficult to understand in both languages, English was appreciated as much as Dutch. The authors make comments on the practical implications for issues such as standardisation and adaptation, the study results supporting the former rather than the latter.

Hou, Z., Zhu, Y. and Bromley, M. (2013) 'Understanding public relations in China: multiple logics and identities', *Journal of Business and Technical Communication*, 27 (3): 308–28. http://jbt.sagepub.com/content/27/3/308

The authors provide a contribution to critical public relations (PR) in terms of the social construction of PR by various actors in Chinese cultural contexts. The authors found multiple competing logics among PR industry practitioners within these contexts that serve as a repertoire from which stakeholders can draw 'institutional logics' and 'legitimise' their PR practice interpretations.

Jackson, S. (2013) 'Reflections on communications and sport: on advertising and promotion culture', *Communication & Sport*, 1 (1–2): 100–12. http://com.sagepub.com/content/1/1-2/100

The author describes this piece as an essay on communication and advertising relationships that exist and offers an insight into sport, globalisation and corporate nationalism in relation to promotional culture. The author points towards issues such as the increased consolidation of global media, the media's capacity to communicate messages across a wide spectrum of contemporary social life, and the rapid changes in the technological landscape that are affecting media and promotional culture within the notion of the commodification and commercialisation of 'everything'.

REFERENCES

Ahmedani, Z.A. and Azzam, S. (2012) 'Regulatory developments in the marketing of securities and financial services within Bahrain, Kuwait and the UAE', Corporate Livewire, Wired, 9 February. Available at: http://www.corporatelivewire.com/top-story.html?id=regulatory-developments-in-the-marketing-of-securities-and-financial-services-within-bahrain-kuwait-and-the-uae

Al-Areefi, M.A., Hassali, M.A. and Ibrahim, M.I.B.M. (2013) 'A qualitative study exploring medical representatives' views on current drug promotion techniques in Yemen', *Journal of Medical Marketing*, 12 (3): 143–9.

Alozie, E.C. (2011) 'Advertising and globalisation: the transmission of culture in Nigerian print advertising', in E.C. Alozie (ed.), *Advertising in Developing and Emerging Countries*. Surrey: Gower Publishing.

Anson, J. (2013) 'Total crackdown on online alcohol promotion in France, health lobby report will recommend', *Decanter Magazine*, 12 June, available at: www.decanter.com/news/wine-news/583988/total-crackdown-on-online-alcohol-promotion-in-france-health-lobby-report-will-recommend

BBC (2013) 'Welcome to BBC Advertising', BBC Advertising, available at: http://advertising.bbcworldwide.com/

Boseley, S. (2013) 'Junk food still marketed to children as companies bypass rules: clampdown on marketing to British children through TV advertising is not enough to protect them, says WHO report', *The Guardian*, 18 June, available at: www.theguardian.com/lifeandstyle/2013/jun/18/junk-food-children-marketing-who-tv

Burt, S., Johansson, U. and Thelander, A. (2008) 'Standardised marketing strategies in retailing? IKEA's marketing strategies in Sweden, the UK and China', Paper accepted for presentation at the 1st Nordic Retail and Wholesale Conference in Stockholm (Norrtälje), 6–7 November.

Consumers International (2013) 'Updating the UN Guidelines for Consumer Protection for the Digital Age', Consumers International, Kuala Lumpur, available at: www.consumersinternational. org/media/1353300/updating-ungcp.pdf

Corporate Watch (2013) 'Unilever: Corporate Crimes, Corporate Watch', available at: www. corporatewatch.org.uk/?lid=260.

de Mooij, M. (1994) *Advertising Worldwide*, 2nd edn. London: Prentice Hall.

de Mooij, M. (1998) *Global Marketing and Advertising – Understanding Cultural Paradoxes*. Thousand Oaks, CA: Sage Publishing Inc.

de Mooij, M. (2010) *Global Marketing and Advertising – Understanding Cultural Paradoxes*, 3rd edn. Thousand Oaks, CA: Sage Publishing Inc.

de Mooij, M. and Hofstede, G. (2010) 'The Hofstede model – applications to global branding and advertising strategy and research', *International Journal of Advertising*, 29 (1): 85–110.

de Mooij, M. and Hofstede, G. (2011) 'Cross-cultural consumer behaviour: a review of research findings', *Journal of International Consumer Marketing*, 23: 181–92.

EC (2013) 'Misleading advertising: Directive on Misleading and Comparative Advertising', European Commission, Justice, available at: http://ec.europa.eu/justice/consumer-marketing/ unfair-trade/false-advertising/

EU (2013) 'EU Relations with the Gulf Cooperation Council', EU External, available at http:// eeas.europa.eu/gulf_cooperation/index_en.htm

Four Communications (2013) 'Jumeirah Golf Estates case study', Four Communications, available at: www.fourcommunications.com/media/property-media/case-studies/jumeirah-golf-estates/

Goodrich, K. and de Mooij, M. (2011) 'New technology mirrors old habits: online buying mirrors cross-national variance of conventional buying', *Journal of International Consumer Marketing*, 23(3-4): 26–259.

Goodson, S. (2012) 'Top 100 global ad agencies that know social media and Google', *Forbes Magazine*, August, available at: www.forbes.com/sites/marketshare/2012/08/22/7637/

Hall, E.T. (1976) *Beyond Culture*. New York: Anchor Press.

Hofstede, G. (1980) 'Motivation, leadership and organisation: do American theories apply abroad?', *Organisational Dynamics*, Summer: 42–63.

Hornikx, J., van Meurs, F. and de Boer, A. (2010) 'English or a local language?: the appreciation of easy and difficult English slogans in the Netherlands', *Journal of Business Communication*, 47 (2): 169–88.

Hou, Z., Zhu, Y. and Bromley, M. (2013) 'Understanding public relations in China: multiple logics and identities', *Journal of Business and Technical Communication*, 27 (3): 308–28.

IM! (2013) 'International Reach: Universal Behaviour', Impact mémoire, available at: www.i-memoire.com/Universal-behaviour

International Chamber of Commerce (2013a), 'History of ICC, The Merchants of Peace', available at: www.iccwbo.org/about-icc/history/

International Chamber of Commerce (2013b) 'ICC Commission on Marketing and Advertising', available at: www.iccwbo.org/advocacy-codes-and-rules/areas-of-work/marketing-and-advertising/

International Chamber of Commerce (2013c), 'An efficient, cost-effective approach to ethical marketing and advertising communications practices', available at: www.iccwbo.org/advocacy-codes-and-rules/areas-of-work/marketing-and-advertising/

IPA (1999) 'Global Advertising', Proceedings of the 4th Annual Marketing Educators' Advertising and Academia Forum. London: IPA.

Jackson, S. (2013) 'Reflections on communications and sport: on advertising and promotion culture', *Communication & Sport*, 1 (1–2): 100–12.

Jain, A., V, H., Sinha, N. and Sharma, A. (2011) 'Parker: penning global strategy', Chennai, India: Great Lakes Institute of Management, 18 November.

Kalliny, M., Dagher, G., Minor, M.S. and de los Santos, G. (2008) 'Television advertising in the Arab world: a status report', *Journal of Advertising Research*, 48 (2): 215–23.

Kettman-Kervinen, L. (2013) 'Surprising Advertising Trends in Saudi Arabia', *Brand Republic*, 3April, available at: http://globalvoices.brandrepublic.com/2013/04/03/surprising-advertising-trends-in-saudi-arabia/

Kirpich, Judy (2013) 'Abercrombie & Fitch: solid marketing or marketing faux pas?', *Business of Design Branding*, 4, 13 May. Available at: http://www.grafik.com/2013/05/ (accessed on 03/04/14).

Macleod, I. (2013) 'Danone puts global media planning and buying business to pitch', *The Drum*, 26 April, available at: www.thedrum.com/news/2013/04/26/danone-puts-global-media-planning-and-buying-business-pitch

Mueller, B. (1987) 'Reflections of culture: an analysis of Japanese and American advertising appeals', *Journal of Advertising Research*, June/July, 27 (3): 51–9.

Mueller, B. (1992) 'Standardisation versus specialisation: an investigation of Westernization in Japanese advertising', *Journal of Advertising Research*, January/February, 32 (1): 15–24.

Mueller, B. (1996) *International Advertising – Communicating Across Borders*. Belmont, CA: Wadsworth Publishing Company.

Mueller, B. (2011) *Dynamics of International Advertising: Theoretical and Practical Perspectives*, 2nd edn. New York: Peter Lang Publishing.

Ringer, M. (2013) 'Gender, Stereotypes: Pink or blue?', *The Marketer*, 30 July. Available at: www.themarketer.co.uk/opinion/pink-or-blue/

Sauven, J. (2006) 'The odd couple: how Greenpeace and McDonald's are working together', Greenpeace, 2 August, available at: www.greenpeace.org.uk/blog/forests/the-odd-couple.

Schiffman, L. Hansen, H. and Kanuk, L.L. (2008) *Consumer Behaviour: A European Outlook*. Harlow, UK: Pearson Education.

Schweizer, R. (2010) 'Headquarters-subsidiary relationships during dramatic strategic changes – the local implementation of a global merger between MNCs in India', *Review of Market Integration*, 2 (1): 101–34.

Sibley, A. (2012) '8 of the biggest marketing faux pas of all time', Hubspot, 17 July, available at: http://blog.hubspot.com/blog/tabid/6307/bid/33396/8-of-the-Biggest-Marketing-Faux-Pas-of-All-Time.aspx

Toyne, B. and Walters, P.G.P. (1993) *Global Marketing Management: A Strategic Perspective*, 2nd edn. Boston, MA: Allyn and Bacon.

Unilever (2012) 'World Toilet Day 2012', Unilever, available at: www.unilever.com/mediacentre/pressreleases/2012/Unilevers-brand-domestos-to-break-taboo-of-the-loo.aspx

van der Wurff, R. and Bakker, P. (2008) 'Economic growth and advertising expenditures in different media in different countries', *Journal of Media Economics*, 21(1): 28–52.

Wolfe, L. (2013) 'Dangers of using stereotypes in advertising and marketing', *Marketing Psychology*, About.com, available at: http://womeninbusiness.about.com/od/marketing psychology/a/markstereotypes.htm

GLOSSARY

4Ps A traditional expression of the marketing elements of product, place price and promotion which are combined to form a mix of activities and tools that can be used to achieve organisational objectives.

Advertising Advertising at the basic level is any paid-for communication designed to inform and/or persuade. Advertising is also the word for a profession or industry that is involved with the planning and designing of advertisements.

Ambush marketing Ambush marketing is the well-established practice of a company or brand being associated with, for example, an event or a team such as the Olympics without paying for the right to do so whereas a competitor who is an official sponsor has done so, often at great expense. Ambush marketing is often associated with the terms guerrilla or parasitic marketing. Ambush marketing is carried out often as a result of a major competitor becoming an official sponsor of an event whereby the company attempts to usurp this position, usually for a lot less money than the actual cost of the sponsorship. This kind of marketing is mostly restricted to events where large amounts of money are involved.

Animatics Animatics in marketing communications and in particular the advertising industry are used to test television commercials before they go into full-up production. Several ideas for campaigns are developed, usually in storyboard form, and once approved can be developed further into an animated form and tested before proceeding.

Appropriation Appropriation in marketing communications terms is the total amount of money allocated to marketing communications over a specified time period. Appropriation is then split up into individual budgets which then fund the various elements of the marketing communications mix such as the advertising budget. Depending upon the organisation the term advertising appropriation may be used to refer to the total amount of money allocated to advertising which is then split up into budgets to fund different media types such as the television advertising budget.

Association Association in marketing research terms is often used as spontaneous word association 'off the top of the head'. This employs hot, cold and neutral words to overcome defensive tactics. Participants are asked to give the first word that comes to mind immediately after being shown or told a word. This reveals attitudes toward the subject being researched.

Attitude tests Attitude tests involve scale measurement to assess a person's (strength of) feelings about the self, an event or object. In marketing the test is likely to involve a brand or marketing communication elements.

Brand ambassador Brand ambassador is a term used to describe a person employed to promote an organisation and/or its products and services whereby the ambassador becomes the embodiment of and spokesperson for the brand but in a PR way as opposed to using a celebrity endorser in advertising.

Brand attributes   Brand attributes consist of core, tangible and intangible aspects of a brand expressed in words and symbols in relation to brand essence or promise which position the brand in the marketplace in the minds of the target audience.

Brand equity   Brand equity is a measure of a brand's worth to its owner and to customers who purchase it. Brand equity has both tangible and intangible values. Brand equity is the commercial value that can be derived by a customer from the brand and its name as perceived by the customer of a product or service rather than the product or service itself. Brand equity is a difficult concept but one which has become part of valuations of companies since a brand is often viewed as one of a company's most enduring and valuable assets.

Brand Image   Brand Image is almost the opposite of the USP (as coined by Rosser Reaves of the Ted Bates agency in the 1960s) and appears to work in many product/service categories where competing brands are very similar and the USP may not exist, or at least it may be difficult to implement. Brand image was championed by David Ogilvy, founder of Ogilvy, Benson and Mather. Ogilvy advocated that advertising's task was to develop a strong, memorable identity for a brand through 'image advertising' where an image is developed that will appeal to product users. Thus Ogilvy, contra Reeves, comes down largely on the side of emotion rather than reason, but not exclusively so.

Brand loyalty   There are many ways that brand loyalty has been defined. These usually involve a customer's continuing, repeat purchase of the same brand in a product category but this can be described as mere repeat purchase. A strong and unyielding trust in and commitment to the brand whereby the customer is truly attached to it suggest a stronger relationship between a customer and a particular brand.

Brand seeding   Brand seeding is the start of the process of brand-building by using a variety of communication techniques including those from advertising and PR. The process is analogous to planting a seed and nurturing it until it grows. For example brand seeding might use viral advertising or blogging online which can induce users to warm to the brand through conversation and word-of-mouth rather than overtly promoting the brand.

Brand values   Brand values consist of a unique set of characteristics that position a brand in a marketplace.

Burst   A burst at the start of a campaign's media schedule means there is a requirement to achieve high reach/high impact, making as many of the target as is possible aware of the brand. Depending upon the number of ratings bought i.e. weight of advertising, the frequency in particular media has to be determined and as a campaign progresses less reach but increased frequency may be required, whereby a much more continuous, regular drip or continuity campaign (see drip and continuity).

Cause-related marketing   Cause-related marketing (CRM) is a symbiotic collaboration between a corporation and a not-for-profit organisation, usually a charity, which combine to create mutual benefits from strategic alliances or partnerships.

Cause-related sponsorship   Cause-related sponsorship occurs when a sponsor aligns itself with a not-for-profit organisation, usually a charity, by providing funds, goods/services or other resources such as an expert or a manager in exchange for rights of association with a property such as a charity. This might come in the form of a percentage of the sales price of a brand going to the cause.

Celebrity endorsement   Celebrity endorsement is usually associated with branding and advertising involving a well-known person who can trade their fame for payment by becoming the spokesperson for the brand and in many cases its embodiment. Perfumes, all manner of clothing, cars, food and in fact most products and services are or can be represented in this way. The now classic use of celebrity endorsement techniques involves television and other media advertising, launch and other events and appearances such as at a charity fundraiser in the marketing of goods and services.

Client   A client is the user of a professional product or service where the type of selling may require specifications and the offering is often tailored to client needs. In some cases a client will be a reseller after, for example, a product is modified and sold on by the client to another user.

Commission system   The commission system is traditionally based on an advertising agency placing an advertisement for a client with the media owner paying commission to the agency usually at a 15% rate. The marketer pays the money to the agency and keeps 15% and the remaining 85% goes to the media owner. The commission that the agency receives pays for the services it provides to the marketer. Traditionally a mark-up to 17.65% will be made on the commission for physically producing advertisements in a form that is acceptable to the media.

Concurrent testing   Concurrent testing in marketing communications is used pervasively in the development of a campaign or programme in order to detect any problems in the system and to keep the campaign on course, picking up on any unexpected interference among concurrent tasks.

Consumer Movement   The Consumer Movement is a major social force that questions the true nature of modernist marketing's 'sovereign consumer' where the growth of public interest and pressure or accountability groups have formed to combat exploitation in many consumer markets.

Consumer sales promotion   This is usually a short-term incentive directed at consumers who buy things for personal consumption.

Contingency reserve   A contingency reserve is a reserve fund that enables the marketer to respond to situations, such as market changes or crises, quickly and to finance actions where necessary. As such it helps to deal with contingency measures in contingency plans. Sudden drops in sales or competitive activity are two of the commonest causes of the need for a contingency reserve.

Corporate communications   Corporate communications is a term that refers to a mix of activities and tools used to manage internal and external communication with targeted customers and other stakeholders in order to create a favourable marketing environment within which marketing communications can operate more effectively in order to achieve organisational objectives. Corporate communications has been described as an all-embracing framework for co-ordinating marketing, organisational and management communications that integrates the total business message.

Corporate image   Corporate image refers to how an organisation (corporation) is perceived, what it represents and the position it holds from the viewpoint of society. This includes the organisation's practices such as advertising, sponsorships, its stance on issues and other elements that affect appearance in the mind of the public. Corporate image is therefore the perception of the organisation by target groups and other stakeholders. The corporate image is influenced through an organisation's communications strategy, tactics and policies. It is a continuously changing impression influenced by circumstance as well as media coverage, advertising and other deliberate communication activities.

Corporate lobbying Corporate lobbying is activity that organisations, especially corporations, carry out in order to try to influence government and other stakeholders in some way to gain attention and interest in an issue or issues that are of topical import to that organisation or corporation.

Corporate personality Corporate personality can be defined as the manifestation of the organisation's self-perception including intent, i.e. the cultural glue for often disparate parts of the organisation that binds. Symbols, other communication and behaviour add up to corporate identity. Communication can, for example, say 'we are innovative'. Behaviour of the organisation can back this up. A logo can be an instantly recognisable sign.

Corporate reputation Corporate reputation, if favourable, is a tool that can be used to positive effect where the relationship between reputation and credibility are key for competitive advantage and where credibility transactions (negative or positive) can impact upon an organisation and competitors. An organisation's reputation and subsequent credibility are a result of the continuous process of credibility transactions. It takes many transactions to get back to a position after some fall from grace has taken place or where an organisation has not lived up to its claims.

Corporate Social Responsibility (CSR) CSR is a strand of the sustainable development concept which is a stakeholder approach that requires the company to meet its responsibilities as a member of society. It is therefore a social strand that is affected by the external (or macro) elements of the marketing environment.

Court of public opinion The court of public opinion is an expression that refers to the use of news media or other means to send a message into the public domain and allow the public to be the judge of the content of the message. This would typically be an organisation's reputation being judged.

Creative appeal A creative appeal is a label for the way in which an advertising message is formulated in order to achieve a desired response from a receiver of the message. Creative appeals are broadly split into two types; rational and emotional. Some writers might describe this split as product-orientated or consumer-orientated appeals. A typical emotional appeal is humour and a typical rational appeal is performance.

Creative boutique A creative boutique is an agency that specialises in the creative aspects of advertising. Boutique agencies offer services that have to do with the creation of advertisements. There is usually a small but highly creative staff base and services are bought on a fee basis per job. Freelancers are often associated with boutique agencies.

Creative brief The creative brief is a system or framework that aids the development of marketing communications materials for use in a marketing communications campaign. The creative brief is, therefore, a planning tool that is widely used, especially by advertising agencies and their clients. It is meant to be a tool that can facilitate cooperation on the part of all involved with a particular project. It allows thinking and analysis around the best ways to achieve objectives and it can also reduce time and costs if used properly since a more efficient approach to marketing communications problems will ensue, where all the key participants can agree on important factors at the beginning of a campaign.

Creative strategy   Creative strategy is a key stage in the communications planning process, and should determine what action is required from the audience, what the messages should say or communicate, and what the 'big idea' is.

Customer Relationship Management (CRM)   CRM is the function that facilitates the management of the interaction that an organisation has with its customers. CRM is involved with the management of information and as such builds and uses databases about its customers in order to better develop products that match customer needs and requirements.

Database marketing   Database marketing is related to direct marketing, relationship marketing and customer relationship management. Database marketing is much more than 'list building' as it focuses on customers, capturing detailed data on them that can then be used with them. Clearly it involves list compilation and individually addressable targets that are then approached with marketing materials through conventional and electronic media such as the mail, email or telephone. The task is to then manage the database in such a way that contact is made and maintained effectively and efficiently.

Direct Marketing   Direct marketing is in many situations a key component in the marketing communications mix when attempting to communicate directly with customers. Direct marketing is an interactive marketing approach that has grown with database technology and which uses one or more advertising media to affect a measurable, often immediate response and/or transaction at any location.

Direct response advertising   This form of marketing communications seeks to stimulate immediate action from the target audience via television and other media channels.

Drip   Drip refers to a much lighter weight of advertising over a longer time than burst. This is a kind of flighting that can be used when a 'slow burner' campaign is required and again there is a relationship between reach, frequency and weight (see burst).

Dyadic communication   Dyadic communication is a term used to refer to communication between two entities. Dyadic communication can be formal (for example between seller and buyer) or informal (for example a chat between a father and daughter).

Ecommerce   Ecommerce refers to commerce that is conducted on the internet or other electronic networks. The term ecommerce has its origins in the late 1940s in the context of document exchange during the Berlin blockade and airlift and developed into the electronic data interchange (EDI) standard. Ecommerce now encompasses a much wider set of activities and is generally considered to be electronic sales activity.

Emotional appeals   Emotional appeals used in advertising include many techniques such as fear, humour, sex, music, fantasy and surrealism. These can be used to play on personal states such as safety and love or on social states such as status or rejection. Marketers use emotional appeals to produce positive feelings that cause a favourable evaluation of the brand in the mind of the audience.

Environmental (green) marketing   Environmental marketing, often referred to as green marketing, has developed into an attitude and performance commitment that places corporate environmental stewardship fully in perspective. It is a response to the relatively recent rise of environmentalism and 'green' issues highlighted by the growing number of pressure and accountability groups around the world.

Event sponsorship   Event sponsorship occurs when a sponsor aligns itself to an actual event that might involve sports, the arts, causes or some other sponsored entity by providing funds, goods/services or other resources such as training equipment or facilities in exchange for rights of association with a property such as a football stadium or an entertainment arena.

Exchange   Refers to the situation where something of value is traded for something else of value, such a customer's money for a branded product or service. Exchange, whether market (as with money for a brand) or relational (a more collaborative, longer term arrangement), is a core concept of marketing since it is the marketing function that facilitates people and/or organisations coming together to engage in the exchange something of perceived value for something else of perceived value.

Exhibition   The exhibition is an important forum, a means for organisations in a specific industry or a context to showcase and demonstrate their new products and services. Exhibitions can involve both consumer and trade, but often they are exclusively trade and are not open to the public, typically being attended by organisational representatives and journalists in a reporting role. Exhibitions might include the offering of franchising and other business opportunities. They are typically held in large and accessible venues such as arenas or purpose-built centres. Hotels may be used, especially for smaller, local exhibitions.

Fair trade   Fair trade is about trading partnerships that include empowerment and sustainable development for farmers and other artisans formerly excluded, marginalised and disadvantaged. The objective is better trading conditions. It is about economics but also social and environmental issues such as a living wage and health and safety. Fair trade is not, therefore, merely about fair prices for commodities or products.

Features and benefits   The features and benefits approach has long distinguished feature from benefits. A product, service or brand feature is a physical or technical property or function that is inherent in the design of the product or service. A photocopier might have a technologically advanced lens that is cutting edge. The benefit that is sold to the customer however might be superbly clean photocopies. In all cases the benefit results from the feature and the customer needs to know what the feature means in terms of benefit.

Flighting   Flighting may be chosen when the marketer wants to use resources over a longer period but not all of the time. Flighting may be erratic, regular or used in a burst-like way for the start of a campaign. Flighting is a flexible way of dealing with seasonality and other such issues and may be regular, irregular or blocked. Flighting offers the opportunity to concentrate on the best purchasing cycle period.

FMCG (Fast Moving Consumer Good)   FMCG is a common abbreviation for the term fast moving consumer good, often used to describe a consumer non-durable, packaged product that is sold often, usually at a relatively low price, such as the many products that are classified as groceries or toiletries items. FMCGs can be perishable, such as fruit and vegetables, or those with longer lives but still a relatively high turnover in contrast to consumer durables such as washing machines which have much longer life expectancies.

Focus groups　Focus groups are used in marketing research to test ideas for new products, to uncover attitudes or to understand needs, and are a straightforward way to qualitative research and data collection. Focus groups are a data collection method and research technique for engaging a group of usually 6-10 people with, for example, questions about products, brands or ideas. Bringing together a group provides a relatively natural setting than (more so than one-to-one depth interviews) that allows participants to share stories and ideas through interactive discussion that yields rich data.

Fragmentation (in marketing)　Refers to the increased number of choices people have in terms of media consumption, with their choices spread over a greater selection of general and special interest viewing, listening and reading media types and vehicles.

Full-service agency　A full service advertising agency offers a wide range of marketing services across the marketing and corporate communications mix, marketing research and services like new product development, so that for example design, sales promotion, PR, exhibition and trade show work are all handled under one roof.

Guerrilla marketing　Guerrilla marketing is so called because of its non-conventional marketing nature. The conventional marketing objectives of sales turnover, profit or growth remain but it is the means to achieving the objectives that are different. Rather than simply spending money, guerrilla marketing involves the investment of time and imagination to create marketing that is relatively much less costly than conventional marketing activities, making it very attractive to smaller firms and other organisations on tight budgets.

Hearts and minds　Hearts and minds is a phrase that is usually used in conjunction with winning. To win hearts and minds in PR terms is to win over the public or particular publics through a PR campaign that appeals to both emotion and reason or intellect.

In-kind sponsorship　In-kind sponsorship is a deal whereby the sponsor, usually in return for rights of association with a property, does not pay money but instead offers goods and services or some other resource such as an on-loan expert or member of staff in lieu of cash payment.

Inquiry tests　Inquiry tests are quantitative approaches such as coupon counting and are real-to-life i.e. they measure the numbers of inquiries or direct responses stimulated by communication, as with telephone numbers used in the commercial. Latterly clicks online can be measured per day or by tracking analytics across different media.

Integrated Marketing Communication (IMC)　Is the cohesive, integrated mix of marketing communications activities, tools and techniques that deliver a coordinated and consistent message to target customers and consumers synergistically in order to achieve organisational goals.

Key Account Management　Key Account Management is a term used for the system of organising and managing a small number of the most important customers. Within this function the coordination of marketing tasks takes place in order to service selected customers who are of great significance to the organisation.

Levels of culture (Hofstede)　'Levels of culture' is a term used by Hofstede to explain layers of culture that exist around a core of culture which has cultural values that are relatively stable. Rituals are contained in the first layer and are things like personal hygiene. The next layer contains heroes such as film stars or footballers. The final outer layer contains symbols such as flags or national brands. Customs and practices cut across the layers or levels of culture.

Lifestyle marketing   Lifestyle marketing *is* a 1970s phenomenon that is based on psychographics and based upon studies into activities, interests and opinions (AIO) whereby the marketer is not reliant solely upon demographics or the old ABC1C2DE (UK) socio-economic classification system.

Loyalty schemes   Many organisations now have a loyalty scheme of one sort or another. Most involve some sort of point system and the ability then to trade points for merchandise. The apparent objective is to create and sustain loyalty, so that it is about relationship and database marketing. However, the 'loyalty scheme' is somewhat of a misnomer and they should perhaps be called 'frequent purchaser scheme' as with the airline industry favourite 'frequent flyer'.

Market segmentation base   For consumer marketing many bases have been developed that are either descriptive, including demographics, psychographics, and geographical or behavioural bases such as benefit segmentation. For organisational markets bases such as customer size, location, industry classification, usage rate and nature of operations are commonly used.

Marketing collateral   Marketing collateral is the mix of tools used to support the sales of a product or service and to enhance the brand's presence in the market place. Web content, presentations and brochures are examples of marketing collateral.

Marketing communications   Generally acknowledged as a mix or combination of elements, techniques or activities, such as advertising, sales promotions, selling, sponsorships, public relations or product placements, that an organisation employs to connect with, influence and persuade its target markets to take a particular action or response such as brand purchase or some form of further interaction.

Marketing communications management   This is a process that utilises different models/theories to inform its various stages. It involves a series of individual but fully integrated communications elements that form the marketing communications mix that is part of a carefully planned marketing management effort in order to achieve objectives and maximise the effectiveness of campaigns.

Marketing concept   The marketing concept is a managerial philosophy that holds that the marketer should begin with identifying customer needs and wants or requirements and then, through a series of coordinated activities, should satisfy such requirements more effectively than the competition while achieving organisational goals.

Marketing research process   This process is an organised sequence of steps involves in the systematic collection, analysis and presentation of marketing data and depicts how a marketing investigation is designed and implemented.

Media Buyer   Media buyer is a function that negotiates special deals with the media owners, and buying the best parcels of `slots' to achieve the best cost (normally measured in terms of the cost per thousand viewers, or per thousand household `impressions', or per thousand impressions on the target audience. The 'best cost' can also be measured by the cost per lead, in the case of direct response marketing. The growth of the very large, international, agencies has been partly justified by their increased buying power over the media owners.

Media planning   Media planning can be undertaken by the marketer but usually an agency is employed to find and plan out the details of the most appropriate media class, types and vehicles on behalf of the marketer or client. This requires skills and expertise if the best media mix is to be achieved in order to achieve marketing communications objectives and therefore the planner is involved with the reach, frequency, weight, scheduling and costs of advertising in order to deliver the optimum media plan for the client.

Media scheduling   Media scheduling refers to the pattern of advertising involving the selection of spots over time. Advertising has to be scheduled so that communication can work at optimum and favourable times and lengths of exposures, for example in relation to particular selling periods such as Christmas or Valentine's Day. The classic scheduling models are continuity, flighting and pulsing (including burst and drip) and variations and combinations of these.

Media selection   Media selection usually refers to advertising media and is the process of choosing the most cost-effective media for an advertising campaign. Within media planning, media selection will need to achieve the required coverage and number of OTSs or exposures in a particular audience.

Media-related sponsorship   Media-related sponsorship occurs when a sponsor aligns itself to a television programme, most commonly a soap opera, or some other media form such as radio or increasingly online, by providing funds, goods/services or other resources such as actual branded goods or services and equipment in exchange for rights of association with a property such a weather report or film programming.

Message   The communication of meaning through words, visuals, symbols, metaphors and other devices designed to influence a receiver after decoding.

Mission statement   A mission statement explains the purpose the organization and its raison d'être or reason for being. The statement is a document that is a guide to the organisation's decision making and actions which will achieve its overall aim and take it on its desired course.

Multilocal   Multilocal is an expression used to explain the strategic approach that removes cultural, geographic and trade barriers by dealing with the needs of multiple markets individually, usually through autonomous subsidiaries.

Negotiated commission   Negotiated commission is a compensation method used by advertising agencies and clients that moves away from the traditional 15% commission structure. The system means that there is a negotiated, reduced or variable commission percentage.

One-sided and two-sided message   One-sided and two-sided message are terms that refer to persuasive communication. The former presents only one point of view or appeal that is in frequent use in advertising communications where audiences are less well educated and may be favourably disposed toward the view or a product, service, brand or organisation. The two-sided message presents both points of view but then puts forward arguments for the chosen view and which counter the opposing view. The two-sided message is used in advertising where audiences are better educated and would not wish to be patronised by a singular view. This is prevalent in many selling situations and especially in meeting objections.

Percentage of sales method   The percentage of sales method is a simple method for setting a budget as a percentage of past sales and can be simply set by choosing a percentage or set either through advertising industry sources or by the norm for the sector in which the organisation is based.

PEST   PEST is an acronym that stands for Political, Economic, Social and Technological. This is a commonly-used framework for investigating the macro environment (business or marketing). PEST has been extended into other acronyms for the same kind of analysis that accounts for forces that impact on the planning process such as PESTEL (Political, Economic, Social, Technological, Environmental and Legal).

Positioning   Positioning is the process of choosing attributes of an organisation or a brand in order to differentiate the organisation or brand from the competition and to occupy a unique position in the market place. The rational and/or emotional approaches form a creative strategy to communicate with the target audience. Positioning in advertising was championed by Reis and Trout in the 1970s who saw it as the basis of creative development where communications activity is used to 'position' the product or service in a particular place in consumers' minds.

Post-testing   Posttesting is applied after the marketing communications (or more specifically an element such as advertising) campaign has ended to find out the extent to which it has been successful and is in effect a post-mortem that might involve, for example, attitude change.

PR Transfer Process   The PR transfer process is a framework conceived originally by Frank Jefkins that helps the management/practitioner to move from a negative to a positive position. Jefkins categorised negative images into four distinct areas; hostility, prejudice, apathy and ignorance, the idea being for management to transfer issues from the negative categories to their opposites of sympathy, acceptance, interest and knowledge.

Premium   A premium is an extra item offered at a low price or free. Premiums can be effective at increasing sales but can also be a distraction from the brand properties. Premiums can attract brand switchers and be used with current users to increase repeat purchases. A premium can be free or have some cost to the consumer.

Pre-testing   Pre-testing in marketing communications exists is to help marketers identify successful communication. There is a large range of pre-test measures that can be applied in order to enhance and support decision making including copy testing or the use of animatics.

Product differentiation   Product differentiation should be based on customer perceptions where differentiation is based on tangible and intangible features and characteristics of a product or service that distinguishes it from the competition, often through branding.

Product placement   Product placement is sometimes called embedded marketing. This technique places a product (or more likely a brand) in use (or is clearly visible) in a film, television programme or some other situation where the opportunity exists to place a product such as in gaming, a book or magazine, or an event where products are place, as with refreshments at a tennis match. The marketer pays a fee and/or provides free products/props for this privilege.

Profiling (of target markets)   Profiling refers to the characteristics of customers/consumers/households that are based on demographic, geographic, psychographic and behavioural bases and refers to the likely buying behaviour and habits of targets.

Prospecting   Prospecting in sales and selling terms is a key, critical skill needed to develop sales performance and to increase long term sales performance and success. As such it is seen as an integral part of sales and selling.

Publicity   Publicity is the deliberate and sustained attempt to manage the public perception of a subject such as a company, a brand or a politician. Publicity is part of Public Relations which in turn is seen as a key element of the marketing communications mix of any organisation.

Reach   Reach is a quantitative measure of how many people a particular advertisement reaches. This involves the notion of opportunity to see (OTS), sometimes referred to as exposures or impressions, and this helps advertisers to measure how many people have an OTS the advertisement but does not indicate how they react to it. Reach is measured by media specialists who use sampling and tools such as the People Meter for television audience research.

Readability test   Readability tests are tools used in advertising and marketing communications to measure the ease at which advertising copy can be read. A prime example in advertising is the Flesch Reading Ease Score where the higher the score means that more people could easily read and understand the advertising copy.

Reference group   A reference group is a group of people who appear to have lifestyles that are an influence on other and to which others aspire. A reference group contains people whose attitudes, beliefs, opinions and behaviour are used by an individual as the basis for aspirations and judgement. A person can be influenced by such a group even if the person is not a member or does not aspire to be so.

Relationship selling   Relationship selling is part of the relationship marketing paradigm and is about building a relational approach to selling to existing customers and prospects and includes some form of needs analysis by listening to them. With existing customers this is about keeping them; with prospects it is about converting them into customers. This is achieved by exhibiting care and gaining trust.

Research brief   The research brief is a verbal or written instruction outlining the problems as perceived by the marketer.

Research proposal   The research proposal is a remedy to fulfil the research brief, but it also has to sell the agency or research/communications company who will wish to 'pitch' for the work based not just on the proposal content but with a Curriculum Vitae which would include relevant experience and evidence of reputation.

Return on brand investment (ROBI)   ROBI is return on investment (ROI) that comes from the investment made in a brand. There are many ways to measure ROBI, some of which are qualitative while others are quantitative. Examples are awareness, recognition, positioning, the number of customers found or lost, market share, purchase patterns or customer satisfaction. As many as 20 such measures might be applied to give a clear picture of before and after the investment. ROBI is therefore a measure of a brand's performance in terms of changes in customer preferences or any other movements such as shifts in loyalty that need to be tackled in the light of insights into brand performance.

Return on customer investment (ROCI)   ROCI latterly has been seen as a more important measure than communications effects on behaviour. While communication effects on, for example, awareness or attitudes are of course important, the efficiency in the way money spent works is of prime importance. Of course the more efficient and effective communication effects are, the more this will enhance ROCI. ROCI is essentially a return on investment (ROI) system within the marketing arena that attempts to quantify the return on money spent on, especially, marketing communications, rather than simply communication effects such as levels of awareness. This is linked to activity-based costing (ABC) and economic value assessment (EVA).

Sampling   Sampling is use to achieve the objective of trial and is a key tool in inducing trial and breaking old loyalties. Sampling is associated with products of low unit value and can only be used if the product is divisible and brand features and benefits can be adequately demonstrated. Sampling therefore is much used by FMCG packaged goods manufacturers. With technology moving forward and the Internet's pace of development more and more opportunities for creative sampling distribution are being found.

Search engine marketing (SEM) and Search engine marketing and optimisation (SEO)   Search engine marketing (SEM) is a paid-for marketing tool that helps to build website traffic and visibility from search engines in their results pages (SERPs). As such it involves buying traffic through paid search listings. In contrast search engine optimisation (SEO) is about obtaining traffic through unpaid for, free listings. SEO involves re-writing of website content to achieve a higher ranking in SERPs.

Segmentation (market segmentation)   Segmentation is at the heart of modern marketing which suggests that markets can be broken up into segments, populated by homogenous groups whose needs should be met. A segment has its own requirements that should be met by its own marketing programme.

Semiotics   Semiotics is the application of the 'science' of semiology (of signs and symbols). Semiotics is best known in marketing for its study of visual phenomena such as logos and signs in advertising and packaging that make up aspects of brand image and identity and therefore personality. However, semiotics can be about much more than this since a sign can take the form of many things in terms of words, images, sounds, gestures or objects within an active system of signs in which meanings are constructed.

Social media marketing research   Social media marketing research has grown through the sharing across differing forms of social media, text, photographs, videos, social bookmarks, blogs and micro blogs. The analysis and use of this kind of content is seen as being extremely useful in gaining insights into marketing phenomena such as segmentation, needs analysis and customer profiling. Social media marketing research can be qualitative and quantitative but is mostly the former. It can also be secondary as well as primary.

Source of the message   The source of the message might be the organisation itself, a spokesperson, the CEO, or a celebrity. The key to source credibility is trust and the audience must believe the source and their motives. The key components to developing credibility/ trust are expertise, knowledge, motives, likeability and similarity to consumer. Often corporate or brand names carry a good reputation so these are included as part of the source. The medium and media vehicles used also have characteristics that can be seen as part of the source of the message.

Special Interest Group   A Special Interest Group (SIG) is a community, often a community of practice (CoP) whose purpose is to advance things like knowledge of the particular area of interest. The characteristics of a SIG include being an advocate or lobbyist on issues within the area of interest and as such may become a form of advocacy or pressure group.

Sponsorship   Sponsorship is the practice whereby an organisation pays in some way to be a sponsor of something or somebody else i.e. that which becomes sponsored or the sponsee (sometimes referred to as the property). This allows the sponsor to advertise and promote itself (or its brand) in association with the sponsee, either solely or in conjunction with others, depending upon sponsorship arrangements.

Spread   Spread refers to spread of frequencies whereby parts of the audience have more OTSs than others. Average frequency is used in calculations but the reality is that there is an uneven spread of exposure to the message within an audience reached. Those who receive fewer are potentially insufficiently motivated, and extra advertising is wasted on those who receive more. Ideally all members of the audience should receive the same but it is, of course, impossible to achieve this ideal. The pattern is usually weighted towards a smaller number of heavy viewers, for example, who receive significantly more OTS, and away from the difficult last few per cent. However, a good media buyer manages the resulting spread of frequencies to weigh it close to the average, with as few audience members as possible below the average.

Star method   Lux's star method is similar to Bernstein's cobweb and it too has value that is limited to the stimulation of discussion among senior management along the lines that corporate identity should be following. This is a practical tool where the distinguishing attributes of the company are predetermined i.e. that there are seven dimensions that always underlie personality of a company - needs, interests, attitudes, temperament, competencies, origin and constitution.

Stealth marketing   Stealth marketing is often seen as a subset of guerrilla marketing and is a potentially dangerous way to practise marketing. Stealth marketing practices are often called 'undercover' marketing or 'buzz' marketing, because consumers often do not know they are being targeted. A person might be paid to use a brand in a social setting, exposing other people within that context to the brand.

Subliminal advertising   Subliminal advertising involves subliminal messaging through advertising media. Sensory stimuli that are below the threshold of conscious perception are used in the creation of a message by the marketer. Subliminal perception refers to the perception of things below the conscious level.

Sustainable development   Sustainable development is about how the company operates in terms of how it consumes, directly or indirectly, natural resources. It is about how the company can be profitable while not compromising the needs of future generations at the same time as building a long term future. It is based on the belief in give and take, in a commitment to protecting the environment, reducing the company's carbon (ecological) footprint, and gaining acceptance of its corporate behaviour by society.

Symbiotic relationship   A symbiotic relationship in general terms is one in which two organisms equally benefit from each other. In marketing and selling such a relationship is often one between seller and buyer, but could exist between other players in the chain such as between seller and supplier.

Telemarketing   Telemarketing is either outward (or outbound) and inward (or inbound). The most common understanding of the term would be the former, with the development of call centres the most prominent idea for both. Calls are taken from responses to other direct marketing such as a direct response press advertisement. Outward telemarketing might be seen in the same way as junk mail and viewed with suspicion. Inward calls are positive, immediate, seen as being useful and can create loyalty.

Television ratings (TVRs)   Audience delivery is measured in TVRs. A TVR, like a GRP, is a product of reach and time spent viewing through frequency of OTSs. A single TVR represents 1% of viewers of a particular type, for example 18 to 34 year olds or adults, rather than all viewers who had an OTS an advertisement. The cost varies depending upon the target audience and is reflected in its weight of viewing. Ten adult TVRs means 10% of all adults had an OTS the commercial. Each spot therefore has a value depending on the size of the audience and the demographic bought. For example, a spot in a break around a programme delivering 20 adult TVRs is worth 10 times as much as a slot in a break that delivers just two adult TVRs.

The communications process   The communications process is the process by which oral, written, visual or sensory information is sent from sender to receiver with the objective of sharing meaning between sender and receiver.

The Mexican Statement   PR was defined in terms of practice at the 1978 Mexico City international PR conference as 'the art and social science of analysing trends, predicting their consequences, counselling an organization's leadership and implementing planned programs of action which will serve both the organization's and the public's interest'.

Trade fair/show   Trade fairs and export promotion are intimately linked and usually involve a regular trade event at which manufacturers from a particular industry present their products and show their capabilities to distributors, wholesalers, retailers, and even end-users. Such fairs (like the many in Hanover) attract participants and visitors from all over the world. Trade shows and exhibitions are important forums that are a shop window where actual and potential customers can see, touch and feel products. In many contexts these are the only vehicles to display the company's wares and to interact with customers from across the management board. The total number of these vehicles is huge.

Transactional marketing and selling   Transactional marketing is a form of marketing that is seen as being in opposition to the relationship marketing paradigm. Transactional selling is part of the transactional marketing paradigm that uses strategy to target customers to make a one-off sale in order to maximise volume at a point in time rather than developing on-going customer relationships.

Unique selling proposition (USP)   The USP is a concept developed by Rosser Reeves (1961) of the Ted Bates agency. Reeves suggested that there are three characteristics of a USP – that each advertisement make a unique proposition, provide a tangible benefit to the consumer, be one that the competition either cannot or does not offer, and be strong enough to move people and pull over new customers to the brand, either through taking market share from competitors or expanding the size of the market or both.

Universal theme A universal theme as used in marketing communication and in particular advertising is one which can be applied everywhere and are capable of offering solutions to communications problems in any landscape or environment. This includes things such as motherhood, jealousy, new or novel features or concerns, service or special expertise and demonstration.

Unmediated communication Unmediated communication is direct communication that has no intervening persons, agents or channels involved between the sender and audience or receiver of a message as opposed to mediated communication that uses channels or intermediaries to impart a signal or message to an audience or receiver.

Viral marketing Viral marketing can see any marketing message passed on over the internet. Users pass messages on to other users, creating a huge potential growth in the number of people exposed to the message.

Word-of-mouth (WOM) communication WOM is informal communication, usually about a marketer's product or service, between one person and another, originally and usually in a personal network of family, friends, workplaces and other contextualised associates. WOM is usually referred to as e-WOM but also as word-of-mouse or viral marketing if in the context of online marketing.

INDEX

02, 348
4Ps, 2. *See also* marketing mix
72andSunny (agency), 116–117

ABC (activity-based costing), 159
ABC (Audit Bureau of Circulations), 200–201
Abercrombie & Fitch, 411
account directors, 109
account executives (account managers, account
    representatives), 109
account planners, 109
Acer, 340
ACORN (A Classification of Residential
    Neighbourhoods), 257
ActionAid, 278
ad hoc marketing research, 401
adaptation/standardisation debate, 9–10, 412–414
Ad:Check, 138
Adidas, 348, 349, 352
Admap, 339
admass, 39, 42
adoption, 413
advertising
    brand image and, 158
    history of, 409–410
    impact on society of, 127
    introduction to, 151–152
    objectives of, 158–160
    origin of term, 409
    personal selling and, 368
    positioning and, 165–166
    vs. public relations, 4–5
    research and evaluation of, 394–397
    tasks of, 8
    theory of, 152–157
    unique selling propositions and, 164–165
advertising agencies, 108–109
advertising allowances, 261
Advertising Association, 400
advertising managers, 119
Advertising Standards Authority (ASA), 137, 138,
    143, 163, 181–182, 258
advertising value equivalence (AVE), 5
advertorials, 184–185, 273
Agariya, A.K., 260
Age UK, 72
agencies
    client–agency relationship and, 119–121
    evaluation of performance in, 113
    remuneration of, 2, 110–113
    roles and structures in, 107–117
Ahmad, S., 371
AIDA model, 154, 209–210, 254, 369
Air France, 259, 274
Al-Shohaib, K., 309
alcohol, 420, 428

Alibaba, 243
Alleyne, R., 135
Alozie, E.C., 410, 426
ambush marketing (guerrilla marketing), 9, 139–140, 352
American Airlines, 283
American Behaviourism, 250
American Idol (TV show), 6
Amnesty International, 295
Anabtawi, S., 72
analogue television, 222
analysers, 83
Anderson, J., 22
Andjelic, A., 107–108
animation, 178, 180, 232
annual reports, 303
Ansoff's Matrix, 298–299
Anthem (agency), 429
APIC (Analysis, Planning, Implementation, Control)
    system
    case study, 95–97
    critique of, 91–92
    introduction to, 79
    overview, 84–91, *84–87, 91*
    for research and evaluation, 387–388
    summary of, *92–95*
Apple, 158, 160, 175, 176
appropriation, 90, 209
Argos, 224, 273
Armour, S., 393
art directors, 108
arts sponsorship, 348
artworkers, 109
ASDA, 249
assertiveness, 371
Association of National Advertisers (ANA), 113
ATR (awareness, trial, and reinforcement) model, 67
attitudes, 68–69
Audi, 350
audio-visual aids, 302
Augugliaro, M., 238
Aurora, C.M., 353
automated answering systems, 223
Automobile Association (AA), 36, 295
awareness, interest, desire and action (AIDA) model,
    154, 209–210, 254, 369
Axe (Lynx), 163–164

B&Q, 184
Baack, D., 65, 67
Baggers Originals, 132–134
Baidu, 243
Baker, C., 105
Bakker, P., 416
Bal, C., 341–342, 343
Balboni, B., 15
Balmer, J.M.T., 323

banner advertisements, 224, 229–230
Barclays, 342
Barnardo's, 130
Bartle, Bogle and Hegarty (agency), 21, 165
baseball, 340
Baskin, K., 321
Baskin, M., 105
Baskind, C., 144
Basu, K., 263–264
Bavaria, 352
BBC (British Broadcasting Corporation), 340, 349,
    428–429
BBC News, 238
Becker-Olsen, K., 344
Beckham, D., 36
Beckham, V., 36
behavioural learning, 66
behavioural theory. *See* buyer behaviour
behavioural variables, 82
Beijing Olympics (2008), 340
Belch, G., 62–63, 66, 67, 68–69
Belch, M., 62–63, 66, 67, 68–69
beliefs, 52, 424
Benady, A., 120
Benady, D., 72
benefit, 82
Benetton, 116–117
Bennett, G., 345, 346
Bennett, R., 338, 342
Benson & Hedges, 180, 337
Bernstein, D., 157, 323, 325–326
Bhat, S., 161
billboards, 230
Binet, L., 103
Bing, 349
Der Blauer Engel (The Blue Angel), 330
blind testing, 157
Blodgett, J.G., 51
blogs, 239
Bloomberg Businessweek (magazine), 44
BMW, 61–62, 175, 350
Board of Ethics and Professional Standards (BEPS),
    307–308
The Body Shop, 133
Bold, B., 180
bonus packs, 258–259
Boorom, M.L., 363, 371
Boseley, S., 419
Bostock, A., 282
Boston Consulting Group (BCG) matrix,
    297–298, *298*
Bowen, S.A., 288
brand ambassadors, 39
brand extensions, 158
brand image
    advertising and, 158
    creative strategy and, 175
    overview, 157, 165
    sales promotions and, 249
    trust and, 43–44, 160–162
brand loyalty, 43–44, 229
brand managers, 118
brand personality, 260

brand recall, 350
brand strategy, 158
brand symbols, 52
brand systems, 162
brand values, 260
branded identity, 322–323
branding
    brand systems and, 162
    definition of, 157–158, *158*
    international brands and, 162
    international marketing communications and,
        427–428
    Internet and, 229
    introduction to, 151–152
    product differentiation and, 81
    rebranding and, 166–168
    sponsorship and, 343–345
Branson, R., 37, 40
Brewer Miller, 348
Brit Insurance, 337
British Airways, 322, 325
British Audience Research Board (BARB), 200
British Heart Foundation, 6
British Market Research Bureau (BMRB), 401
British Medical Association (BMA), 295
British Telecom (BT), 178
Broadband TV News, 226–227
broadcast advertising, 390
broadcast media, 222. *See also* radio; television
brochures, 303, 305
Brown, S., 7, 79, 92
Brownlie, D., 7
Bryan,D., 373
Buck, L., 215
budgets, 90, 209–210
Budweiser, 352
BUPA, 337, 353
Burrows, G., 277–278
burst, 204–205, *205*
Burton, N., 139–140
business-to-business (B-to-B), 262, 269
Butt, I.P., 371
Buttle, F.A., 32
buttons, 230
buy one get one free (BOGOF), 259
buyer behaviour
    culture and, 53–58
    introduction to, 50–51
    sales promotions and, 250–251
buyer learning theory
    attitudes and, 68–69
    cognition and, 63
    consumer learning process and, 65–67
    evoked set and, 67–68
    hierarchy of effects models and, 69–70, **70**
    information processing model and, 63–64
    introduction to, 50–51
    involvement and, 58–59, 61–62
    motivation and, 59–61
    perception and, 62–63
    simulated consumer decision-making process
        models and, 64–65
    types of customers and, 71–73

buyer readiness, 82
buying allowances, 261

Cadbury, 36, 175, 337
Cadillac, 337
CafeMom, 392–394
call centres, 223
Cancer Research UK, 278
Canning, L., 40
Carbolic Smoke Ball Company, 142
Cardani, M., 346
Carling, 348
Carlsberg, 137
cash-backs, 258
Cassidy, A., 117
Castaway (film), 351
catalogues, 270, 273
category managers, 118
Catling, T., 175
cause-related marketing (CRM), 129–131
cause-related sponsorship, 347
CD-ROMs, 194, 222, 272
celebrity endorsement, 6, 36–37, 39–41
Center, A.H., 292
Centre for Retail Research, 364
Chadwick, S., 104, 139–140
Chan, A., 352
Chang, 339
Change Lingerie, 420–421
Chapman, M., 167
charities and charitable causes
    database marketing and, 277–279
    digital media and, 214–215
    personal selling and, 372–374
    symbiosis and, 132–134
    word-of-mouth communication and, 44–45
Chartered Institute of Public Relations (CIPR), 289
Chattopadhyay, S.P., 139
Chen, J., 349
chief executive officers (CEOs)
    corporate communications and, 328
    endorsement and, 37, 255–256
    public relations officers and, 289
    role of, 318
children
    regulations and, 134, 138, 419, 420
    sales promotions and, 127–128
    targeting and, 137–138
Children's Advertising Review Unit (CARU, US),
        138, 419
Child's i Foundation, 215
Chow, L.L., 297
Christie, M., 362
Chruszcz, K., 6
cinema, 196
classical conditioning, 66, 250
Clay, R.A., 137–138
Clearcast, 163–164
Clews, M.-L., 181–182
client entertaining, 303
client organisations
    client–agency relationship and, 119–121
    roles and structures in, 118–120

clients, 365
Clover, J., 226
Clow, K.E., 65, 67
Club 18–30, 137
co-branding, 158, 162
cobweb method, 323
Coca-Cola
    brand image and, 160
    international marketing communications and, 427
    marketing communications process and, 411
    product placement and, 6
    sponsorship and, 340, 348, 420
Code of Advertising Practice (CAP), 258
codes of practice, 142–144, 258, 307, 415
cognition, 63
cognitive learning theory, 66–67
cognitive maps, 65
commercial sponsorship, 353
commission fees, 112
commitment, 43–44, 161
communication appeals, 177–182
communication theory, 29–35, 29, 33
communications executive teams, 328
communications networks, 226
comparative advertising, 420
competencies, 377
competitions (contests), 231, 258
competitive parity, 211
compliance, 35, 36–37
computer telephony integration (CTI), 223
concept cooperation, 413
concept fees, 112
conferences, 302
Consejo de Autorregulación Publicitaria (CONARP,
        Argentina), 418
consultancy fees, 112
consumer movement, 134, 142
consumer sales promotions, 257–261
consumerism, 142–145
consumers, 365
Consumers International, 415
content analysis, 398
content communities, 240–241
contests (competitions), 231, 258
contingency reserve, 214
continuous research, 401
control
    evaluation and, 90, 386–387, 394–403
    overview, 90–91
    See also marketing research
cookies, 138–139, 229, 279–280
Copley, P., 130, 343, 347, 348
copywriters, 109
Cornelissen, J., 13
Cornwell, T.B., 344–345
Coronation Street (soap opera), 337
Corporate Accountability International, 144–145
corporate branding, 162
corporate communications
    audiences for, 319–320
    definition of, 317–318, 318
    introduction to, 316–317
    objectives of, 317

corporate identity, 321–328, *321*
corporate image, 321, 324–330, *324, 327*
corporate impression management, 328–330
corporate marketing, 327
corporate personality, 323–324
corporate public relations (CPR), 3, 289–290, 398
corporate social responsibility (CSR), 96, 129, 421
Corporate Watch, 422
Cosmopolitan (magazine), 204
Costill, A., 237–238
costs, 205–206
coupons, 231, 248, 253, 257–258
court of public opinion, 293, 307
Cracker Jack, 253
Crane, A., 130
creative designers, 108
creative planning, 164, 174
creative selling, 365
creativity and creative strategy
    agencies and, 107–108
    communication appeals and, 177–182
    culture and, 425–427
    development of, 175–177
    introduction to, 173
    marketing communications and, 174–177
    message strategy design considerations and,
        182–186
    overview, 87–88
    positioning and, 165
crisis management, 328–329, 398
Crosier, K., 154
Cubit, E., 278
culture
    buyer behaviour and, 53–58
    context of, 56, 424–425
    creative strategy and, 425–427
    definition of, 51
    dimensions of, 56–58, 424
    expressions of, 51–53, *52*, 423–424
    levels of, 51, *52*, 423–425
    personal selling and, 380–381
Cummins, 319–320
customer relationship management (CRM), 363
customers, 71–73, 365

DAGMAR model (designing advertising goals for
    measured advertising results), 85, 159
Dahlen, M., 32, 340
Danone, 429
D'Arcy, Masius Benton and Bowles (agency), 166
Dare, 186
Data Discoveries Ltd, 270–271
data protection, 268, 280–281, 283
Data Protection Act (UK, 1998), 280–281, 283
database marketing, 268–269, 275–279
Davidson, M., 157, 167
Davies, M., 175
de Mooij, M., 51, 56–58, 425, 426, 427
De Pelsmaker, P., 202, 214
decision-making units (DMUs), 41, 269
decision sequence model (DSM), 79, 80–84, 328,
    387–394, 413
defenders, 83

demographic environment, 19
demographic variables, 82
Denny, R.M., 380–381
descriptive variables, 82
detachable entities, 326
Diageo, 337, 349
Dichter, E., 60
Dick, A.S., 263–264
differentiation, 342–343
Diffin, E., 231–232
digital agencies, 115
digital media, 104, 214–215, 220–221.
    See also Internet
digital news, 197–198
digital television, 222
direct mail marketing, 270–271, 272
direct marketing
    advantages and disadvantages of, 269
    business-to-business and, 269
    coupons and, 258
    growth of, 274–275
    history of, 270–271
    impact on society of, 128
    incentives and, 272
    Internet and, 222, 231, 273–274, 275,
        279–280, 281
    introduction to, 268–269
    overview, 195
    personal selling and, 368
    privacy and, 279–283
    process of, 269–270
    research and evaluation of, 399
    types of media and, 272–275
    See also database marketing
Direct Marketing Association (DMA, UK), 114, 279,
    280–281
Direct Marketing Association (DMA, US), 114, 270,
    274–275
direct marketing companies, 113–114
DirectGov, 294
directors of photography, 109
Disney, 179
display advertising, 229
DMG Direct Inc., 271
documentary video, 304–305
Dolphin, R., 321
Domino's, 183
Dorsey, J., 239
Dowell, R., 336, 338
drip, 204–205, *205*
drivers, 104
The Drum (magazine), 403
dual branding, 162
Duncan, T., 103, 160
Durex, 348
DVDs, 194, 222
dyadic communication, 362
Dyson, 162

e-mail
    direct marketing and, 222, 232, 269
    public relations and, 303
early adopters, 42

early majorities, 42
Ebrahimi, H., 182
economic environment, 19
The Economist (newspaper), 242–243, 281
econsultancy.com, 402
EEG (electroencephalograph), 391
effective reach, 201–202, *201–202*
effectiveness culture, 104–105
eHarmony, 392–394
Ehrenberg, A., 67
elaboration likelihood model (ELM), 64
electronic-word-of-mouth (EWOM) communication, 45, 231
Elliot, S., 248, 255–256
embedded marketing, 350
emotional appeals, 179, 180
empathy, 372
enablers, 104
The End of Advertising as we Know it (Zyman), 336
endorsed identity, 322–323
environmental marketing (green marketing), 132
environmental scanning, 328
environmentalism, 132
Esure, 228
ethical environment, 19
ethics and ethical considerations
    impact of marketing communications elements on society and, 127–128
    international marketing communications and, 421–423
    introduction to, 126–127
    product placement and, 6
    public relations and, 295–296
    social responsibility and, 128–134
    unethical practice and, 134–141
European Advertising Standards Alliance (EASA), 143, 414, 417
European Commission, 281, 283
European Union (EU), 138–139, 280, 281
EVA (economic value assessment), 159
evaluation, 90
event sponsorship, 351–352
Event TV, 395–396
events, 303
Everett, S.E., 103
Everton, 339
Evin Law (France, 1991), 428
evoked set, 67–68, 341
exchange, 7–10
exhibitions, 4, 259–260, 262, 303
external publics, 302
eye camera, 390–391

Fabrica (agency), 116–117
Facebook, 236–237, 322
facsimile machine (fax machine), 194, 222
Fae, J., 280
fair trade, 131
Fairtrade Foundation, 131
familiarity principle, 342
Farrelly, F., 342, 351
Fast Forward Now Ltd., 133
Fast, J., 346

fast-moving consumer goods (FMCGs), 249, 257
Fathi, S., 306
fax machine (facsimile machine), 194, 222
FC Barcelona, 340
feature articles, 303, 304
Federal Trade Commission (FTC), 281–282
Federal Trade Commission Act (USA, 1938), 416
Federal Trade Commission CAN-SPAM Act (US), 282
fees, 2, 111–112
Fernandez, J., 181
Fill, C., 9, 211, 321
Film on Four, 337
films, 302
Financial and Strategic Integration, 11
Fionda, A.M., 40
Fiore, Q., 193
Fisher, J.R., 293
Fletcher, J., 29
FlexMR, 242
Flickr, 241
Flying Blue, 259, 274
Foodstuffs, 40
Foot, Cone and Belding (agency), 70
Formula One, 338–339, 351
Foster's, 183
Four Communications, 429
Fraj-Andres, E., 129
Fraj, E., 56
frame of reference, 32
Freeland, C., 110
frequency, 202–203, *203*
Freshwater Technology, 290
Freud, S., 60–61
full service agencies, 110
funding, 89

Gabrielli, V., 15
Galvin, E., 225
Gambling Act (2005), 258
Ganiear, D., 252
Gap, 238, 411
gatekeepers, 302
Gates, B., 37
gender stereotyping, 136
Generation Y, 56
geo-demographic environment, 19
geodemographic systems, 82, 401
geographic variables, 82
Geordie Shore (TV show), 89
gestures, 424
Geyser, S.A., 323
Gheorghe, P., 15–16
Gillette, 414
Gillin, P., 197–198
Glasspoole, K., 207–208
Glenday, J., 229
Global Village, 415
global warming, 132
globalisation, 9–10, 53
Golding, K.M., 131–132
golf, 340, 348
Good Housekeeping (magazine), 206
Goodhart, G., 67

Goodson, S., 410
Google, 349
Google AdWords, 234
Google Analytics, 242
government regulation, 142
governments, 293–294
graphic designers, 108
Grayson, D., 322
Great North Run, 352–354
Green Giant, 178
green marketing (environmental marketing), 132
Greenberg, J., 293
Greenpeace, 295, 422–423
gross rating points, 204
Groupon, 231, 256
Grunig, J.E., 292
The Guardian (newspaper), 130
guerrilla marketing (ambush marketing), 9, 139–140, 352
Guinness, 179, 338, 348
Gulbis, N., 340
Gulf Co-operation Council (GCC), 417–418
Gupta, A., 236, 241
Gwinner, K., 342, 345

Haagen Dazs, 39, 165, 179
Haggerty, A., 230
Hainmueller, J., 131
Hall, E.T., 424–425
hall tests, 390
Hallward, J., 175
Hamilton, N., 294
Handyside, M., 105
Harley Davidson, 72–73
Harrison, S., 293
Harrods, 155–157
Harvey-Jones, J., 326
Hasbro, 429–430
Hatcher, C., 321–322
Head and Shoulders, 178
hedonic experiential model (HEM), 64–65
Hegarty, J., 21, 165
Heinz, 178
Henry, J., 61
Henry, T., 60
Herbig, P., 325
heroes, 52, 424
Herrmann, J., 346
Hersey, P., 377
Hetzel, P., 33
Heussner, K.M., 237
hierarchy of effects models
    advertising and, 153–155
    overview, 69–70, **70**
    personal selling and, 367
    for research and evaluation, 388
    sponsorship and, 341
high-fit sponsorship, 343–345
Hill, N., 322
Hill. R.P., 344
Hills, J., 15
Hodges, A., 322
Hofstede, G., 51, *52*, 56–58, 423–425
Holm, O., 10

Honey Creative, 155–157
Hoover, 412
Hornikx, J., 426
house branding, 162
house journals, 303
Howard, J.A., 67
HSBC, 325, 337, 342–343
Hudson, J., 343
The Huffington Post (newspaper), 116
Hughes, D.E., 362
Hughes, G., 9
Hung, Y., 349
Hunt, J.B., 51
Hunt, S.D., 43, 160, 329
Hunt, T., 292
Hurme, P., 309
Hussey, D., 298
hypertext mark-up language (HTML), 224

I Robot (film), 350
IBISWorld, 107
identification, 35
IEG Sponsorship Report, 339
Iglo, 180–182
IKEA, 224, 273, 350, 425–426
illustrators, 108
IM! (agency), 427
implementation, 89–90
impression management, 328–330
in-house communications function, 115–116
in-kind sponsorship, 348
incentives
    direct marketing and, 272
    sales promotions and, 249, 261, 272
individualism/collectivism dimension, 57
indulgence/restraint dimension, 57
industrial sales promotions, 262
infomercials, 185, 272–273
Information Commissioner's Office (ICO), 139
information processing model, 63–64
innovation, 343
innovation theory, 41–42, *41–42*
innovators, 42
inquiry tests, 391–392
instant coupons, 258
Institute for Public Relations
        (IPR, US), 288
Institute for Public Relations (now Chartered
        Institute of Public Relations, UK), 293
Institute of Direct Marketing, 114
Institute of Practitioners in Advertising (IPA),
        110–111, 112, 249–250, 400
instrumental conditioning, 66
Integrated Corporate and Marketing
        Communications (ICMC), 318
integrated marketing communications (IMC)
    background, 10–11
    barriers to, 12–14
    benefits of, 12
    drivers of, 11
    quest for, 103
    small firms and, 14–16
Intel, 175

interactive agencies, 115
interactive voice response (IVR), 223
interactivity, 223–224, 228, 271, 309
internal publics, 302
internalisation, 35
international brands, 162
International Chamber of Commerce (ICC), 143, 307, 416–417, 418
international marketing communications
  branding and, 427–428
  constraints in, 414–423
  creative strategy and, 425–427
  definition of, 410
  history of, 409–410
  introduction to, 408–409
  media and, 428–429
  process of, 410–412, *411*
  standardisation/adaptation debate and, 9–10, 412–414
  stereotypes and, 429–430
International Olympics Committee (IOC), 340
Internet
  direct marketing and, 222, 231, 273–274, 275, 279–280, 281
  growth of, 221
  IMC and, 11
  impact on marketing communications of, 3
  online design and management issues, 227–235
  overview, 224–225
  privacy and, 279–280, 281
  public relations and, 303, 308–310
  sales promotions and, 255–256, 262
  See also social media; social networking
Internet Advertising Bureau (IAB), 9
Internet radio, 221, 222
interstitials, 230
interventionism, 9
Intranets, 226
involvement
  hierarchy of effects models and, 70
  opinion leaders and, 39
  overview, 58–59, 61–62
  sponsorship and, 343
Ipsos Australia, 390–391
Ipsos MORI, 54, 207
iTunes, 349
ITV (Independent Television), 5–6, 337, 395–396

Jack Daniel's, 39
Jackson, P., 292
James, G., 371–372
Jarvis, M., 117
J.C. Penney, 252
Jefkins, F., 299
Jensen, M.B., 3, 106
Jersey Shore (TV show), 89
Jeurissen, R.J.M., 130
jingles, 184
Johari Window, 378–379, *378–379*
Jones, J.-P., 203
Jumeirah Golf Estates (JGE), 429
JustGiving, 215, 232

K&Co, 271
Kalliny, M., 428
Kellogg's, 178, 180, 420
Kelly, L., 373
Kelman, H., 35–37, *35*, 154, 155
Kemp, E., 180
Kent, R.A., 2
Kettman-Kervinen, L., 420
key account management, 363–364
key performance indicators (KPIs), 112
Keynote, 401
Kiam, V., 37
Kim, J., 321–322
Kim S.-Y., 292
Kirat, M., 310
Kirpich, J., 411
Kitchen, P.J.
  on creativity, 174
  on IMC, 10, 11, 14
  on ROCI, 91, 92, 159
Kliatchto, J., 11, 13–14
KLM, 259, 274
Kodak, 158
Koivisto, E., 402
Kolk, A., 130
Korzilius, H., 323
Kotler, P., 7, 17, 290
Kraack, M., 346
Krugman, H.E., 202
Kydd, J.M., 350

Lablanc, G., 324–325
laggards, 42
Lamont, M., 336, 338
language, 424
Lasswell, H., 30
lasting customer loyalty (LCL), 264
late majorities, 42
Lawes, R., 34
Lawson, A., 167
leaflet distribution companies, 270–271
learning and learning theories, 65–67, 250–251
Lee, D., 236–237
Lee, K., 234–235
Lee, S., 363
legal environment, 19
Leggatt, H., 113
Leveson Inquiry, 294
Levi Strauss & Co., 21–22
Levinson, J.C., 139
Lewis, M., 140–141
Lexus, 350
licensing, 162
licensing fees, 112
lifestyle systems, 83
lifestyles, 55–56
Lin, F., 349
LinkedIn, 238–239
Linton, I., 12
Little Orphan Annie (radio show), 248, 253
Liu, J., 119–120
lobbying, 303
Logman, M., 65

London Olympics (2012), 340, 347
long term orientation (LTO) dimension, 57
L'Oreal, 36
Lotus, 350
LoveFilm, 225
Lovemarks, 162
loyalty
   direct marketing and, 272
   trust and, 43–44
loyalty ladder, 262–264
loyalty schemes
   direct marketing and, 274
   overview, 252, 259, 262–264
   research and evaluation of, 401
   technology and, 222
Lozano, J.M., 129
Lufthansa Cargo, 40
Lund, R., 348
Lux, P.G.C., 323
Lynx (Axe), 163–164

Mack, J., 362
Macleod, I., 238–239, 429
macro environment (MAE), 17, *18*, 19, 22–23, 85
magazines, 195–198, 204, 221, 222
Magners, 207–208
Magnini, V.P., 40
mail order catalogue selling, 270, 273
Making it Happen (Harvey-Jones), 326
Mangan, L., 396
Marafiote, F., 183
marginal analysis, 212
Marie-Claire (magazine), 204
Marion, G ., 33
Mark, R., 36
market-based tests, 392
market exchange, 7–8
Market Research Society, 400
marketing
   definition of, 7
   exchange and, 7–10
marketing communications
   change and, 9–10
   costs of elements in, 213–214
   creativity and, 174–177
   decision sequence model and, 80–84, 328, 387–394, 413
   evaluation of, 90, 386–387, 394–403
   impact on society of, 127–128
   introduction to, 1–2
   public relations and, 290, *290*
   strategic marketing and, 2–5, *3*, *4*
   tasks of, 8–9
marketing communications environment, 16–23, *18*
marketing communications industry
   client needs and, 102–107
   introduction to, 101–102
   See also agencies
marketing communications management
   APIC system, 79, 84–97, *84–87*, *91*
   decision sequence model and, 79, 80–84, 328, 387–394, 413
   introduction to, 79–80

marketing communications managers, 119
marketing communications mix
   personal selling and, 368
   public relations and, 290, *290*
   research and evaluation of, 394–403
marketing communications process
   advertising and, 154
   communication theory and, *33*
   international marketing and, 410–412
marketing concept, 2, 7, 363
marketing mix, 2, 367
marketing public relations (MPR), 287, 289–290, 292
marketing research
   agencies and, 110
   APIC and, 91, *91*
   decision sequence framework for, 387–394, **389**
   introduction to, 386–387
   marketing communications mix and, 394–403
marketing services managers, 119
marketing theory
   communication theory and, 29–35, *29*
   innovation theory and, 41–42, *41–42*
   introduction to, 28–29
   public relations and, 296–307
   relational exchange and, 42–45
   Source Characteristics Model (Kelman) and, 35–37, *35*
   step flow or personal influence models and, 37–41, *38*
Marketing Week (magazine), 178
Marks & Spencer, 43, 161, 337
Markwick, N., 321
Marlboro, 259
Martin, K., 252
Martinez, E., 56
Mascarenhas, O. A., 264
masculinity/femininity dimension, 57
Maslow, A.H., 59–60, 401
mass communication, 2–3, 29–31
mass marketing, 80
MasterCard, 340
McAllister, M.P., 350
McDonald, G.W., 44, 160
McDonald's, 127–128, 259, 420, 422–423
McKee, S., 175
McKenzie, H., 243
McLean, A., 133
McLuhan, M., 9, 53, 193, 224, 415
media
   international marketing communications and, 428–429
   public relations and, 302
   See also digital media; traditional media
media buyers, 109, 199–200
media conferences, 303
media lunches, 303
media planners, 109, 198–199
media planning, 88–89, 198–208, *200–203*, *205*
media receptions, 303
media-related sponsorship, 349–350
media scheduling, 204–205
media strategy, 88–89
Meenaghan, T., 345

membership schemes, 274
Merritt, J., 140
message involvement, 39
Metcalfe, V., 403
Mexican Statement, 300
micro blogs, 239
micro environment (MIE), 17–18, *18*, 85
Microsoft, 283
Miles, R.E., 83
Milewicz, J., 325
Millward Brown, 297, 346, 395
Minitel, 222
Minkov, M., 57
Minority Report (film), 350
Minster, A., 362
Mintel, 401
mission, 162
missionary selling, 365
MMS (multimedia message service), 233
mobile marketing, 233, 401
Mobile Marketing Association (MMA), 233
mobile phones, 233
modified re-buy, 365
Mohamed, S., 207–208
Mokhov, O., 229
money-off coupons, 231, 248, 253, 257–258
money refunds, 258
monitoring, 90–91
monolithic identity, 322–323
Moore, C.M., 40
Morgan, R.M., 43, 160, 329
Morley, K., 12
Mosaic, 257
Moss, K., 36
motivation, 59–61, 376–377
Mr Muscle, 178
MTV, 89, 199
Mueller, B., 56, 414, 424–425, 427
Murillo, D., 129
Myspace, 237–238

Nader, R., 142
Nagar, K., 263
Naish, J., 6
Naples, M.J., 202
narrowcasting, 3, 89, 193
National Autistic Society, 278
National Endowment for Science, Technology and
    the Arts (NESTA), 130
National Readership Survey (NRS), 54, 401
National Society for the Prevention of Cruelty to
    Children (NSPCC), 134
natural environment, 20
Nescafé, 178, 349
Ness Soap, 373–374
Netflix, 225
networking, 369
New World Order, 415
The New York Times (newspaper), 306–307
Newell, S.J., 37
News International, 294
The News of the World (newspaper), 294
news releases, 303–304

newspapers, 195, 197–198, 221, 222
Newsweek (magazine), 197–198
Next, 273
Nguyen, N., 324–325
niche marketing, 80
Nicholls, J.A.F., 343
Nielsen, 200
Nielsen, A.E., 129
Nijhof, A.H.J., 130
Nike, 175, 352
Nissan, 297
non-linear communications, 43
not-for-profit organisations
    direct marketing and, 269
    word-of-mouth communication and, 44–45
NS-SEC (National Statistics Socio-Economic
    Classification), 54, 82

O2 Arena, 352
occasions, 82
O'Connor, J., 225
Ofcom, 5, 143–144, 420
off-the-shelf rate fees (output fees), 112
OFT (Office of Fair Trading), 256
Ogilvy Centre for Research & Development, 70
Ogilvy, D., 165, 179
Oliver, A., 346
Oliver, J., 36, 40
Omnibus Survey, 401
one-sided messages, 183
online research, 399–400
OPEC (Organisation of Petroleum Exporting
    Countries), 417
open days, 303
operant conditioning, 66, 250
opinion leaders, formers and followers, 37, 38–39, 42
opportunity to see (OTS), 201–202
opt-in emails, 232
optimism, 372
order taking, 365
O'Reilly, L., 186
Other Lines of Enquiry (agency), 395–396
out-of-home media, 196
outdoor displays, 222
output fees (off-the-shelf rate fees), 112
outsourcing, 102–103
Ovaltine, 248, 252–254
Owen, A., 72

packaging, 128, 231, 260–261
Packard, V.O., 152
PACT (Positioning Advertising Copy Testing),
    394–395
Pallotta, D., 373–374
Pang, L., 34
Parekh, R., 117
Pareto Principle (80/20 law), 82, 160, 213
Parker Pen, 414
Pati, A., 215
Pavlov, I., 66, 250
payday loan companies, 140–141
payment by results (PBR) schemes, 111, 112–113
Pepsi, 253, 337, 349

percentage of sales method, 210–211, 214
perception, 62–63
perceptual maps, 86–87, *86–87*
Perkins, A., 352
permission marketing, 9
Perry, K., 239
personal communication
    vs. advertising, 153
    costs of, 213
    overview, 3
    personal selling and, 363–364, 374–382, *378–380*
    telemarketing and, 273
personal influence models, 37–41, *38*
Personal Information Protection and Electronic
    Documents Act (PIPEDA 2001, Canada), 282
personal selling
    advantages and disadvantages of, 364
    charities and, 372–374
    future of, 364
    introduction to, 361–362
    nature of, 362–364, 366–367
    as part of the communications mix, 4, 367–369
    personal communication and, 363–364, 374–382,
        378–380
    research and evaluation of, 398–399
    selling process and, 369–374, *369*, **370**
    types of, 364–365
personality, 82
PEST (Political, Economic, Social and Technological)
    analysis, 16, 85, 415
Peterson, T., 237
philanthropy, 336, 348, 353
Philip Morris, 259
Phillips, G., 297
phishing, 232
Pickton, D., 11
PIE (Persuasive Impact Equation), 346
Pinder, L., 163
pitch analysis, 391
Pitt, L.F., 371
Plummer, J.T., 55–56, 83
political environment, 19
POP display material, 261–262
pop-ups, 230
Porter, L., 309
positioning
    advertising and, 165–166
    APIC and, 86–87
    creative strategy and, 175
Positioning (Ries and Trout), 166
post-testing, 391–392, 398
power, 36–37
power distance (PD) dimension, 57
Powers, T.L., 56
PR transfer process, 299–300
practices, 52–53
pre-testing, 389–391, 397–398
Precourt, G., 21
premiums, 248, 258–259
press releases, 303–304
Prestel system, 222
price-offs, 258–259
primacy effect, 183

print media, 195–198, 204, 221, 222
privacy
    direct marketing and, 279–283
    Internet and, 237, 241–242, 279–280, 281
problem solving, 372
Procter and Gamble (P&G), 118, 209, 253, 261, 340
producers, 108
product differentiation, 81
product involvement, 39
Product Life Cycle (PLC), 90, 297–298, *297*
product placement
    overview, 350–351
    regulations and, 5–6
    research and evaluation of, 399
    subliminal messages and, 6, 135–136, 350
project fees, 111
promotion, 3. *See also* marketing communications
promotions managers, 119
propaganda, 292–296, 409
prospecting, 374–375
prospectors, 83
prototypes, 413
psychogalvanometer, 391
psychographic systems, 401
psychographic variables, 83
public relations (PR)
    vs. advertising, 4–5
    characteristics of, 292
    corporate public relations, 3, 289–290, 398
    costs of, 213, 300–301
    growth of, 288
    impact on society of, 128
    Internet and, 231
    introduction to, 287–288
    marketing communications mix and, 290, *290*
    marketing public relations, 287, 289–290, 292
    marketing theory and, 296–307, *297–298*
    nature of, 288
    as part of the communications mix, 4
    personal selling and, 368
    in practice, 291
    as propaganda, 292–296
    publics and, 301–302
    relationship marketing and, 299
    research and evaluation of, 398
    role of, 291–292
    scope of, 288–289
    tasks of, 8
    technology, regulation and control in, 307–310
    tools for, 302–305
Public Relations Consultants Association (PRCA), 120
public relations firms, 114–115
public relations officers (PROs), 119, 289, 293–294
Public Relations Society of America (PRSA),
    289, 307
Publicis, 166
publicity, 152–153
publics (stakeholders), 301–305, 319
pupilometer, 390
Pychyl, T.A., 61

Qatar Foundation, 340
Quaker Oats Company, 180

Qualtrics, 392–394
Quester, P., 342, 348, 351

radio and radio advertising
   direct marketing and, 272–273
   evolution of, 194
   revival of, 221
   sales promotions and, 248, 253
Ranchhod, A., 309
Range Rover, 158
rational appeals, 179–180
Ray-Ban, 350
reach, 201–202, *201–202*
reactors, 83
readability tests, 390
rebates, 258
Reber, B.H., 292
rebranding, 166–168
recall tests, 392
recency effect, 183
Reckitt Benckiser, 238
recognition tests, 392
Reddy, K., 161
Reeves, R., 164–165
reference groups, 54–55
refunds, 258
regulations and regulatory bodies
   children and, 134, 138, 419, 420
   consumerism and, 142–145
   international marketing communications and,
      415–423
   product placement and, 5–6
   public relations and, 307–308
   sales promotions and, 258
Reilly, J., 364
reinforcement, 66
relational exchange, 7–8, 42–45
relational marketing, 369
relationship marketing, 299
Renren, 237
reputation, 324–325
Research Now, 401
retail selling, 365
retailer sales promotions, 261–262
retainer fees, 111
return on brand investment (ROBI), 11, 91, 159–160
return on customer investment (ROCI), 11, 91, 92, 159
Revolver Communications, 402
Ries, A., 165–166
Ringer, M., 429–430
rituals, 52, 424
Rizla, 348
Robinsons, 349
Rockeach, M., 401
Roddick, A., 133
Rodgers, J., 293
Rodic, N., 402
Rogers, E.M., 41–42
Roman Catholic Church, 293
Roosebooom, M., 105
Ross, L., 342
Rothschild, M.L., 159
Roy, A., 139

Royal Swedish Opera, 348
rugby, 348

S-R (stimulus-response) Psychology, 250
Saha, A., 348
Sainsbury's, 36, 40
Sale and Supply of Goods Act (1994), 258
Sale of Goods Act (1893), 416
sales presentations, 376
sales promotion agencies, 114
sales promotions
   advantages and disadvantages of, 252
   business-to-business and, 262
   buyer behaviour theory and, 250–251
   costs of, 213
   growth of, 251–252
   impact on society of, 127–128
   indutrial markets and, 262
   Internet and, 230–231, 255–256
   introduction to, 248–249
   nature of, 249–250
   objectives of, 254–255
   origins of, 252–254
   personal selling and, 369
   research and evaluation of, 397–398
   targeting and, 254
   types of, 256–262
sales response curves, 212, *212–213*
sales training, 375–376
sales types, 379–382, *379*
sampling, 231, 257
Samsung, 340
satellite radio, 221
Saunders, J., 104
Sauven, J., 422
Save the Children, 337
scale fees, 111–112
Schiffman, L., 51
Schonfeld & Associates, 210
Schramm W., 30
Schultz, D.E.
   on creativity, 174
   on IMC, 10, 11, 14
   on ROCI, 91, 92, 159
   on sales promotions, 251
Schultz, E., 116
Schultz, H.F., 14
Schweizer, R., 414
Scibetti, R., 344
Scottish Social Enterprise Academy, 373–374
search engine marketing (SEM), 234–235
Search Engine Marketing Professionals' Organisation
   (SEMPO), 234
search engine optimisation (SEO), 234–235
search engines, 224
segmentation (market segmentation), 80, 81–84
Seiko, 137
Seitanidi, M.M., 130
self-actualisation, 59
self-awareness, 371
self-involvement, 39
self-regulation, 142–144, 280, 414–415
seminars, 302

semiotic analysis, 426
semiotics, 33–35
Shannon, C., 30
share of market (SOM), 211–212, *212*
share of voice (SOV), 211–212, *212*
Shelter, 278
Shemwell, D.J., 37
Sheth, J.N., 67
Shimamura, A.P., 176
Short Term Ad Strength (STAS) scan data approach, 203
Sibley, A., 411–412
silverhairs.com, 72
Simpson, C., 232
simulated consumer decision-making process
        models, 64–65
simulation, 232
Sina Weibo, 240
situational selling, 377
Skinner, F., 66, 250–251
Skive Creative, 402
Skype, 222–223
skyscrapers, 230
Slater, S.F., 83–84
Sleight, S., 336
Slideshare, 241
slotting allowances, 261
SMART objectives, 85
smart television, 225–227
Smirnoff, 348
Smith, G., 344
Smith, P.R., 10
Smith, T.M., 362
SMS (short message service) advertising, 233
Snow, C.C., 83
soap operas, 337
soccer, 340, 348
social class, 54, 82
social grades, 54
social media, 42–43, 236–243, 305–307, 400
social networking, 42–43, 236–239
socio-cultural environment, 20
Solomon, M.R., 400
Sommers, M., 102
songs, 184
Sony, 352
Source Characteristics Model (Kelman), 35–37, *35*,
        154, 155
spam, 232
spamming, 138
special interest groups (SIGs), 222, 294–295
specialist agencies (specialist communication
        companies), 113–115
Specific Media, 238
spend issues, 89–90, 208–215, *212–213*
sponsorship
    advertising and, 153
    ambush marketing and, 140
    functioning of, 341–345
    Internet and, 231–232
    introduction to, 335–336
    as marketing communications element, 3
    measurement and, 345–346
    nature of, 336–339

sponsorship *cont.*
    regulations and, 420
    research and evaluation of, 399
    role of, 339–341
    symbiosis in, 352–354
    targets and objectives of, 338–339
    types of, 346–354
Sponsorship Exposure Value, 346
sports sponsorship, 347–348
St. Elmo Lewis, E., 70
St Oswald's, 278
stakeholders (publics), 301–305, 319
standardisation/adaptation debate, 9–10, 412–414
star method, 323
Starch, D., 392
stealth marketing, 139
Stella Artois, 349
step flow models, 37–41, *38*
stereotypes, 136, 429–430
Stolichnaya vodka, 402
Stone, B., 239
Stone, N., 296
straight re-buy, 365
strategy, 87–89
Strong, E.K. Jr., 70
sub-cultures, 53–54
Subervi, A., 295–296
subliminal advertising, 135
subliminal perception, 63
subliminal product placement, 6, 135–136, 350
Sugar Puffs, 180
Sunderland, P.L., 380–381
superstitials, 230
sustainable development, 128–129, 132. *See also*
        corporate social responsibility (CSR)
Swain, W.N., 14, 106
sweepstakes, 258
Sweney, M., 9
symbols, 52, 325, 423–424
Szulc, J.C., 21

tablets, 233
tachistoscope, 391
Tadajewski, M., 7
Tan, V., 240
Tango, 349
Target Group Index (TGI), 401
target rating points (TRPs), 204
targeting
    direct marketing and, 269, 271
    interactivity and, 223–224
    radio advertising and, 221
    rationale for, 80–81
    sales promotions and, 254
    sensitive and vulnerable groups and, 137–138
    traditional media and, 194
Tata, R., 37
Tata Group, 68, 180
Taylor, R., 253
Taylor Nelson Sofres (TNS), 200
The Teachers Corner, 240
team briefings, 305
technological environment, 19

technology
    communication and, 221–227
    public relations and, 308–310
    See also Internet
The Telegraph (newspaper), 239
telemarketing, 269, 273
telephone, 222–223
Teletext, 194
television and television advertising
    direct marketing and, 272–273
    evolution of, 152, 194, 221
    Internet and, 228, 231
    product placement and, 5–6
    sales promotions and, 248
    smart television, 225–227
    technology and, 222
television programme sponsorship, 349
television ratings (TVRs), 203, *203*
Tencent, 242–243
Tesco
    branding and, 157, 161
    Internet and, 224
    rebranding and, 166–168
    sales promotions and, 259
    trust and, 43
Tetley, 180, 185–186
Texas Rangers TV shows, 248, 253
TGI (Target Group Index), 200
Tham K.M., 117
Third Sector (magazine), 214
Thompson, S., 104–105
Thomsen, C., 129
Thomson, B., 348
Thorndyke, E., 250
Timberlake, J., 238
Time (magazine), 198
Timothy's Coffee, 412
tobacco, 136, 420, 428
Toshiba, 162
total customer experience (TCE), 264
Toyota, 348
tracking studies (tracking research), 401
trade sales promotions, 261–262
trade shows, 4, 262, 303
traditional media
    characteristics of, 193–198
    introduction to, 191–192
    media planning and, 198–208,
        200–203, 205
    spend issues and, 208–215, *212–213*
training, 262
Trout, J., 165–166
trust
    brand image and, 43–44, 160–162
    direct marketing and, 269–270
Turner Broadcasting, 412
Tuten, T.L., 400
Tutssel, M., 176–177
Tuttle, B., 178
Twentyman, J., 281
Twitter, 239, 396
two-sided messages, 183
Tyne Gateway, 132–134

umbrella branding, 162
uncertainty avoidance dimension, 57
Under Armour, 344
unethical practice, 134–141
UNICEF, 340
Unilever
    branding and, 163
    Corporate Watch and, 421–422
    creative strategy and, 185–186
    sponsorship and, 337
    stereotyping and, 136
unique selling propositions (USPs), 164–165, 175
United Nations (UN), 419, 422
universal themes, 426–427
Unsafe at Any Speed (Nader), 142
USA Today (newspaper), 197
usage, 82
user groups, 274
user status, 82
Utopia Communications Inc., 295–296

Valentine, D.B., 56
value-based remuneration, 113
values, 52, 55–56, 424
Values, Attitudes and Lifestyles (VALS) model, 83, 401
van der Wurff, R., 416
Van Raay, L., 323
van Riel, C.B.M., 324, 327, *327*
van Tunder, R., 130
Varadarajan, R., 325
variable fees, 111
Vaughn, R., 70
Vegas, J., 186
Ventura, C., 346
Vesanen, J., 271
Vicary, J., 135
video clips, 230
video conferencing, 222–223
video news releases, 302, 304
Vijayenthiran, V., 62
viral marketing, 231, 401–403
Virgin, 40, 67–68, 161
virtual game worlds, 241
virtual reality, 232
virtual social worlds, 241
vision, 162
VISION programme, 319–320
VO5 Extreme Style, 402–403
Vodafone, 349
Voice of the Listener and Viewer (pressure group), 6
voice recognition, 391
Volvo, 165

Wakefield, K.L., 342
Wal-Mart, 175
Wall Street, 305–307
Wallop, H., 166–167
wallpapers, 230
WAP (Wireless Application Protocol) technology, 233
war, 293, 294
Warc, 249–250
Watchdog (BBC program), 142
Watson, J., 250, 251

Watson, T., 340
Weaver, W., 30
web news pages, 303
webmasters (web developers), 227
The Week, 225
Weibo, 240
weight, 203
Welby, J., 140–141
West, D., 40
Whannel, G., 348
Which? (magazine), 142
Whiting, D., 13
Wikipedia, 240
Williams, K., 399
Wilson, 351
Windows Server System, 40
Wolfe, L., 430

Wonga, 140–141
Woods, T., 36
Woodward, S., 225
word-of-mouth (WOM) communication, 42–43, 44–45
World Health Organization (WHO), 419

X Factor (TV show), 395–397
Xiaonei, 237

Yahoo, 349
YouTube, 240–241

Zajonc, R.B., 342
Zaltman, G., 7
Zetsche, D., 255–256
Zuckerberg, M., 236
Zyman, S., 336